W9-BYA-125

Police Administration

Larry K. Gaines
California State University

John L. Worrall
California State University

Mittie D. Southerland
Murray State University

John E. Angell
University of Alaska

Second Edition

Boston   Burr Ridge, IL   Dubuque, IA   Madison, WI   New York
San Francisco   St. Louis   Bangkok   Bogotá   Caracas   Kuala Lumpur
Lisbon   London   Madrid   Mexico City   Milan   Montreal   New Delhi
Santiago   Seoul   Singapore   Sydney   Taipei   Toronto

McGraw-Hill

*A Division of The **McGraw·Hill** Companies*

POLICE ADMINISTRATION
Published by McGraw-Hill, a business unit of The McGraw-Hill Companies, Inc., 1221 Avenue of the Americas, New York, NY, 10020. Copyright © 2003, 1991 by The McGraw-Hill Companies, Inc. All rights reserved. No part of this publication may be reproduced or distributed in any form or by any means, or stored in a database or retrieval system, without the prior written consent of The McGraw-Hill Companies, Inc., including, but not limited to, in any network or other electronic storage or transmission, or broadcast for distance learning.

Some ancillaries, including electronic and print components, may not be available to customers outside the United States.

This book is printed on acid-free paper.

3 4 5 6 7 8 9 0 FGR/FGR 0 9 8 7 6 5

ISBN 0-07-022809-4

Publisher: *Phillip A. Butcher*
Senior sponsoring editor: *Carolyn Henderson Meier*
Senior marketing manager: *Daniel M. Loch*
Media producer: *Shannon Rider*
Project manager: *Diane M. Folliard*
Lead production supervisor: *Lori Koetters*
Coordinator of freelance design: *Mary E. Kazak*
Supplement associate: *Kate Boylan*
Photo research coordinator: *Nora Agbayani*
Cover design: *Amy Stirnkorb*
Cover photo: *© Richard B. Levine*
Typeface: *10/12 Palatino*
Compositor: *Electronic Publishing Services, Inc., TN*
Printer: *Quebecor World Fairfield, Inc.*

Library of Congress Cataloging-in-Publication Data

Police administration / Larry Gaines ... [et al.].—2nd ed.
   p. cm.
Rev. ed. of: Police administration / Larry K. Gaines, Mittie D. Southerland, John E. Angell. 1991.
Includes index.
ISBN 0-07-022809-4 (hc. : alk. paper)
   1. Police administration—United States. I. Gaines, Larry K. II. Gains, Larry K. Police administration.
HV8141 .P54 2003
363.2'068—dc21

                                                                                2002070981

www.mhhe.com

To my loving family, Jean, Ashley, Courtney, and Cody,
who tolerated me through this endeavor and the many
other endeavors over the years.

LKG

To Larry Steele and everyone at A. R.
Thanks for 10 educational years.

JLW

To my good-natured husband, Joel, who has been extremely
supportive of all my professional endeavors. To my daughters,
who gave me their support even though it took time from them.
To my parents, Woodrow and Mary Davis, who inspired my
interest in administration and management.

MDS

To those who have supported me the most,
my mother Phelma, my wife Jan, and my children,
Lisa, Candi, Louanne, and Eric.

JEA

About the Authors

Larry K. Gaines is professor and chair of the Department of Criminal Justice at California State University, San Bernardino. He earned his Ph.D. for Sam Houston State University in 1975. His academic interests are in the area of racial profiling, police operations, and police administration. He is the former Executive Director of the Kentucky Association of Chiefs of Police and is a Past President of the Academy of Criminal Justice Sciences.

John L. Worrall is an assistant professor in the Department of Criminal Justice at California State University, San Bernardino. He received his Ph.D. in Political Science from Washington State University in 1999. His primary areas of interest are legal and organizational issues in policing, longitudinal analysis of crime control policies, and quantitative methods as applied to macro-level criminological problems. He is the author of recent articles on litigation against criminal justice officials (*Crime and Delinquency*) and asset forfeiture in the war on drugs (*Journal of Criminal Justice*). He is also the author of *Civil Lawsuits, Citizen Complaints, and Policing Innovations* (LFB Scholarly: 2001).

Mittie D. Southerland is professor and director of Criminal Justice at Murray State University. She earned an M.S. in criminal justice at Eastern Kentucky University in 1973 and a Ph.D. in social and philosophical studies in higher education at the University of Kentucky in 1984. Dr. Southerland recently served for two years as public safety director at her university and has previous experience as a criminal justice planner and juvenile counselor. Dr. Southerland's expertise is in the areas of administration, management, and supervision, with particular emphasis on organizational environments and change in the police setting. Dr. Southerland has served as a consultant to a number of police agencies and has conducted field research and evaluation of community policing. She is Immediate Past President of the Academy of Criminal Justice Sciences

(ACJS) and has served two previous terms as a Trustee on the Academy of Criminal Justice Sciences Executive Board. Dr. Southerland chaired the ACJS Committee on Minimum Standards for Criminal Justice Education and later chaired the ACJS Academic Review Committee. She is a past president of the Southern Criminal Justice Association. In 1997, Dr. Southerland received the Educator of the Year Award from the Southern Criminal Justice Association and the Outstanding Faculty Member award from the Murray State University Center for Continuing Education and Academic Outreach. Dr. Southerland is also recognized as an expert on criminal justice education.

John E. Angell is Professer Emeritus at the University of Alaska, Anchorage. He earned his Ph.D. from Michigan State University. His major emphasis throughout his career has been on organizational design, theory, and research. He has served in Zenia, Ohio; Dayton, Ohio; and Multnomah County, Oregon, police agencies.

Preface

Although there are several police administration textbooks on the market, we have been frustrated in our attempt to find a book that blends theory, research, results, and practical examples at a level that students can understand, even as they are challenged to learn the various significant topics that are important to police administration and management today. *Police Administration* is our attempt to fill that gap in the current police management texts.

We wrote this book to meet the special needs of those interested not only in the theory of administration and management, but also the practical applications of the concepts to policing. It is not a "how-to" text, but it does provide examples so that the student can see the concepts in context. The text is written for those who have little or no police experience, but it should be equally helpful to those who have lengthy experience at the line, supervisory, or administrative level. It approaches the topic of police administration from an overview perspective and is ideal for use in the first police administration and management course in the college curriculum or in a training curriculum for those preparing for careers in police administration and management.

We do not assume that everyone who reads this text is currently or will become a police administrator or manager. We expect that most who study this text will become neither, but will more likely enter the police organization as officers and have careers that ultimately involve supervision, management, or administration. This book will be useful in helping them to adjust to the environment of the department and to respond appropriately to it with reasonable expectations of their role in the organization. The study of administration and management should also help them to appreciate the unique demands on and concerns of administrators and managers and thereby to better understand the decisions made in the organization. This appreciation and understanding should enable these officers to be better organizational citizens and to be more productive in their department.

Police Administration takes a particular stance regarding police administration. It assumes that there is no one "best" way to administer or manage all police agencies, but there is a best way for a particular department, at a particular time, given the department's circumstances and human resources. This text assumes contingency, or situational, management and administration will help the administrator to determine the best way to approach the problem at hand. Therefore, there are many tools presented in this book. All of them may be useful during the career of an administrator. The "trick of the trade" is to know when to select a particular tool and how to use it effectively in a given situation. This text will provide the tools. With proper study of the practical information, students can develop some knowledge about the appropriate selection of tools. The effective use of the tools must be developed through practice in a training or real-world setting. That is not, and cannot be, a function of this text. It is much like a book on painting. The student with artistic ability can read a book on painting, which gives theory, research, and practical examples, yet the book cannot be a painting skill development text. Skills must be developed through demonstration, practice, and evaluation, which are beyond the scope of this text.

We eagerly await your critiques of our effort. Your suggestions are welcomed. We consider this book to be a text in transition. It must be updated regularly to remain useful to the student who needs an up-to-date source for theory, research, and practice in police administration.

SECOND EDITION

The second edition of *Police Administration* represents a major revision of the text. There have been substantial changes in police administration since the first edition. The institutionalization of community policing perhaps has had the most profound effect. Community policing is now implemented in the majority of police departments in the United States, and its presence has made new demands on policing and administration. Since community policing is so important today, we have added a chapter devoted to it, and we have integrated it to some extent throughout the text. This is not a text on community policing, but it describes how community policing affects police administration and management.

There has been a considerable amount of police research and theory development since the first edition. We have labored to include as much of this new material as possible. We see this book as a mode of technology and information transfer; to be effective, it must be comprehensive and up-to-date. We hope that we have achieved this goal. Specifically, the following changes appear in this edition:

- A section on diversity and racial profiling was added.
- A new chapter, Chapter 3, is devoted entirely to administration and community policing.
- In Chapter 5, several new theories were added, including Mintzberg's Five Organizational Forms and Total Quality Management.

- In Chapter 6, a number of new theories relating to leadership were added, including transformational leadership, which is a key leadership form necessary to implement community policing.
- Chapter 7 was substantially expanded. In addition to addressing motivation in the police organization, a section on the police work culture was introduced.
- Chapter 8, Communications, Negotiations, and Conflict Resolution, has an expanded section on conflict resolution.
- Chapter 9, on stress, has been updated, and a new section addressing administrator stress has been included.
- The human resources chapter, Chapter 10, was substantially updated and new sections on sexual harassment and the Americans with Disabilities Act were added.
- The chapter on planning, programming, and budgeting was expanded and updated. Specifically, the budget section includes a number of new budget documents that assist the reader in better understanding the budget process.
- The control and productivity chapter, Chapter 12, was substantially enhanced. More contemporary measures, such as citizen satisfaction with the police, were elaborated and discussed.
- Chapter 14, Accountability, was substantially expanded. The section on police discipline now includes information on citizen review boards and other contemporary disciplinary issues. The police bill of rights was included and discussed. Finally, the discussion of tort law relative to police discipline and civil liability was expanded.
- Chapter 15 is devoted to change in the police organization. Since community policing is the dominant police organizational arrangement, a large part of the chapter was devoted to changing the traditional police department and implementing community policing.

ORGANIZATION

Like the previous edition, *Police Administration* consists of four parts. Part I, The Nature and Setting of Police Organizations, consists of three chapters. This part of the text is devoted to providing a foundation for the study of police administration. The first chapter focuses on some of the terminology that will be used throughout the text. It also provides an description of the structure of police departments. The second chapter examines the environment. Police departments are a part of society and as such, society has a substantial impact on their mission and operation. The final chapter in Part I is devoted to community policing. Community policing is an integral part of police department and requires substantial coverage in a police administration text.

Part II is Organizational Perspectives. It consists of two chapters. The first chapter, Foundations of Police Organization, describes in detail traditional police administration, especially in terms of classical organizational theory. Although police administration is constantly changing and evolving, classical theory remains the foundation for most American police departments. Chapter 5 examines contemporary management practices. It overviews a number of organizational and managerial changes that have taken place in police administration. It provides an array of tools or possibilities when redesigning the police organization.

Part III, People in the Police Organization, addresses a number of managerial processes that are important in the police department. A variety of topics are included in this section: leadership, motivation, communication, stress, and human resource management. Essentially, this part of the book is devoted to "getting things done through people." The most important resource for any police department is its officers and civilian support personnel. Police administrators, managers, and supervisors must have the skills and abilities to lead people toward the accomplishment of departmental goals and objectives.

Part IV, Control Processes in Police Management, consists of information that assists the police manager in keeping the department on track. Chapter 12 examines control and productivity in the police department. It examines how the administrator can evaluate officers and units in the department, and how he or she might ensure that units meet departmental expectations. There is a substantial chapter on planning. This chapter addresses how the department implements new programs and, more important, the budgetary processes that are used to fund them. Chapter 14 examines accountability. Here, police disciplinary procedures and police civil liability are examined. Finally, change is examined in Chapter 15. Change is an important managerial process. Since the environment is constantly changing, so too must the police department. It must remain abreast of community expectations, new laws, and technology.

PEDAGOGICAL AIDS

Several pedagogical aids have been added to the text:

- First, we provide a chapter outline and learning objectives at the beginning of each chapter as a "road map" for the chapter, previewing for the reader how chapter material will unfold.
- Second, "On the Job" boxes in many chapters are written by police chiefs from around the country and not only bring a practical, real-world slant to the material being studied, but also assist the reader in understanding the complexity of police administration.
- Third, important vocabulary terms are highlighted in the text and accompanied by clear, succinct definitions that enable the reader to master the text's most critical concepts.
- Fourth, a summary at the end of every chapter provides an invaluable review tool, and end-of-chapter study questions help provoke analysis and contemplation about the chapter material and how it may be applied.
- Finally, the "Net Resources" section at the end of every chapter lists websites the reader can explore for additional information about the chapter's key topics.

SUPPLEMENTS PACKAGE

As a full-service publisher of quality educational products, McGraw-Hill does much more than just sell textbooks. The company creates and publishes an extensvie array of print, video, and digital supplements for students and instructors. This edition of *Police Administration* is accompanied by the following supplement:

- Instructor's Manual/Testbank—chapter outlines, key terms, overviews, lecture notes, discussion questions, and a complete testbank.

ACKNOWLEDGMENTS

Writing a textbook is a taxing endeavor. It has perhaps been as taxing to those around us as it has been to us. There are many persons who played a part in the completion of this project, particularly our colleagues and the reviewers who all provided us with comments and suggestions:

Terry L. Campbell, *Western Illinois University*
David Carter, *Michigan State University*
Alejandro del Carmen, *University of Texas at Arlington*
Carolyn Dennis, *Fayetteville Technical Community College*
Donna Hale, *Shippensburg University*
Brian Johnson, *Grand Valley State University*
Daniel Kearney, *Henry Ford Community College*
Walter Ruger, *Nassau Community College*
Calvin Swank, *Youngstown State University*
James J. Vardalis, *Florida International University*

In addition, there were a number of police departments and police executives who provided information, exhibits, and feedback. The many people who assisted us facilitated the new edition's integration of police practice and theory and we greatly appreciate their assistance and tolerance.

Contents

2 The Environment of Administration 36

3 Community Policing 74

PART II
Organizational Perspectives   103

4   Foundations of Police Organization   104

5   Contemporary Organizational Theories and Management Systems   142

8   Communication, Negotiation, and Conflict Resolution   252

9 Managing and Responding to Stress   296

10 Police Human Resources Management   340

11   Labor Relations   398

PART IV
Control Processes in Police Management 433

12 Control and Productivity in the Police Setting 436

13 Planning Programming and Budgeting 480

14 Accountability   530

15 Change   572

Part I

The Nature and Setting of Police Administration

When we think of police organizations, the first images that come to mind often are lights, sirens, and badges. Yet policing means much more. It means concern for the needs and welfare of the community, protecting the weak and helpless, dedication to the police code of ethics, and safeguarding the Constitution and the laws of the land. Police administration is providing the proper structure, direction, and atmosphere for effective policing to occur. Part I, The Nature and Setting of Police Administration, consists of three chapters that form a framework for understanding the nature of police organizations and the environment in which they operate. This is the foundation for the study of police administration.

Chapter 1 is an overview of police administration. Police organizations are presented as unique institutions with a variety of problems and difficulties. Here the department is examined as an organization. The administrator's role and functions are presented. The levels of management and the various perspectives of managers at different levels of the department are portrayed. An abridged history is presented to provide additional perspective. This history assists the reader in understanding why police departments operate as they do today. The first chapter also focuses on some of the terminology that will be used throughout the text.

The second chapter examines the environment. Police departments are a part of society and society has a substantial impact on their mission and operation. It is not sufficient to recognize that society exerts this influence; the nature and the types of influences must be explored. Chapter 2 provides a foundation for understanding the social, economic, and political forces that shape the law enforcement mission. The section on racial profiling included here explores what is perhaps the most potent issue facing American policing today. To add further context, open-systems theory is explored. Open-systems theory requires that police departments recognize social forces and account for them. The final sections of the chapter detail further the idea of community and environment. Several barriers to good police–community relations are examined, and, finally, specific citizen attitudes toward the police are considered.

Chapter 3, Community Policing, examines community policing from an administrative standpoint. Today, community policing is the dominant mode by which police departments provide services to communities. Thus the police administrator must develop a comprehensive, working knowledge of it. Community policing is examined in terms of how it is translated into action throughout the department. If community policing is to be implemented effectively, it cannot be piecemeal. It must be ingrained throughout management and operations. It should be recognized that there are a number of barriers to the effective implementation of community policing. They are discussed here. Finally, the evaluation process, determining if a department has effectively implemented community policing, is examined.

Part I provides the basis for understanding police administration. It provides perspective. The reader will be armed with an understanding of the nature and setting of police organizations and will be ready to examine the tools that police administrators and managers use in running their departments and units. The final chapter in Part I is devoted to community policing, an integral part of police work that receives substantial coverage throughout this book.

1

Introduction to Police Administration

Michael Newman/PhotoEdit

Chapter Outline

Introduction

The Police Department as an Organization

The Role of the Administrator
Organization
Management
Management Levels

How Police Departments Differ from Other Organizations

The Role of Police: A Search for Goals

The Police Mission: A Historical Perspective
The Political Era
The Police Enter the Progressive Reform Era
The Professional Police Era
The Community Relations Era
Return to Law and Order
Community Policing

Summary

Learning Objectives

After reading this chapter, you should be able to

1. Understand the importance that administration plays in the operation of the police organization.
2. Develop a familiarity with the roles of management and organization in police administration.
3. Discuss the role of supervisors, commanders, and administrators in the police organization.
4. Know the different goals of police organizations and how police departments attempt to fulfill goals and objectives.
5. Understand the different historical eras of policing and how the police functioned within each of these eras.

T he Charlotte-Mecklenberg Police Department (CMPD) has approximately 1,300 officers and serves a population of about 475,000. It is one of the few police departments in the United States where the city and county organizations were merged into one agency. The CMPD, like several other departments, implemented community policing a number of years ago. Recently, one of the community police officers identified a problem in the Remount Road and West Boulevard area. Citizen complaints had been filed as a result of speeding, traffic accidents, and fatality accidents. Also, residents complained of high volumes of crime, disorder, and neighborhood deterioration. Administrators in the department decided to use a comprehensive approach to solve the problem, ultimately enlisting several different units and organizations.

The primary tactic used was saturation patrols, where police units attempted to increase the amount of enforcement in the area. The Highway Interdiction and Traffic Safety (HITS) unit intensified traffic enforcement. The CMPD Street Crimes Unit increased enforcement of misdemeanor offenses in the area. The Alcohol Law Enforcement Division of the North Carolina Department of Alcohol and Public Safety began performing more tavern checks as well as checking for sales to minors in liquor stores. The Mecklenburg County Sheriff's Department also increased the number of deputies patrolling the area. The CMPD's Strategic Planning and Crime Analysis Unit collected data about the crime problem and surveyed citizens about their perceptions of problems and how the police should respond (Priest and Carter, 2001).

This one incident demonstrates how complicated the police response to a problem area can be. Ultimately, three different agencies and five different units were involved in the police operations. First, administrators had to analyze the problem to identify the types of response needed, thus establishing goals. Second, unit assignments were made. Finally, administrators had to coordinate the efforts of the several units to ensure that they were not counterproductive. This example is police administration in action.

INTRODUCTION

Police administrators' primary responsibilities are to provide leadership and structure to the police organization so that the agency can effectively meet the needs of citizens for an orderly and safe environment in which to live and work. Historically, all societies have recognized the need to control the degree to which members of society violate norms or laws. They have used some form of police to provide protection from personal and property crimes. From kin police, to the Praetorian Guard, the "tything" system, Peel's London Metropolitan Police, and current organizations, the police have been responsible for guarding society's norms and preventing lawlessness. The nature of policing as an institution of social control and service presents both challenges and opportunities to police administrators.

The institution of police, in American society, is unique in three ways. First, police *work* is unique; employees handle a wide range of roles and tasks. The diversity of roles and tasks is illustrated by the service role of responding to barking dog complaints and the contrasting law enforcement role of solving murders. Although the police are typically evaluated on their response to crime through the law enforcement role of investigation and arrest, the police are also expected to provide a wide range of services such as assisting citizens and providing information. These services often seem of little importance to the police officer, who may refer to them as nuisance calls, while the citizen may view them as quite important. This sets the stage for conflict and for conflicting expectations for police performance. The police administrator must provide leadership and structure to minimize such conflict and to ensure that officers understand and willingly perform all their roles and tasks. Perhaps there is no other institution in our society that is charged with so many tasks and responsibilities, making the police administrator's job complicated and sometimes difficult.

Second, police *authority* is unique; sworn officers have the authority to arrest and use deadly force when necessary in the enforcement of the criminal law. We, as citizens, have given up our right to forcefully resolve criminal conflicts and have delegated this right and the resultant authority to the police and the criminal justice system. In return, we expect our police to apply this authority in a consistent and fair manner. Police authority, although an essential tool for accomplishing the police job, continues to be a source of conflict and complaint. Often the complaint is merely the result of misunderstanding or misperception and can be easily resolved. This might be the case when individuals believe they should not be arrested or should not have to adhere to an order by an officer. Complaints can also arise when individuals want an officer to make an arrest or issue an order and it is not forthcoming. The most problematic type of complaint results from the intentional misuse or abuse of force or authority by a police officer. Guarding against and resolving such issues is one of the most important undertakings of police administration.

Third, police *availability* is unique; police agencies, in many communities, are among the very few public institutions expected to operate 24 hours a day, seven days a week, every day of the year. Before the introduction of other service delivery institutions, the police were the institution called on to provide all citizen services. Even with the large number of service delivery agencies currently available in most communities, the police (particularly in smaller communities) remain the only on-duty agency at night and on weekends and holidays. The advent of the 911 emergency telephone number made the police more accessible, and citizens routinely call the police rather than attempting to contact a more appropriate social service agency. The ready availability of police results in a significant increase in calls and workload, especially for problems that historically fell outside the purview of the police. The public and their elected representatives expect the police to handle all calls for service in an efficient, effective, and professional manner. Although some problems might be more appropriately and better served by other agencies, the police are responsible for making the initial assessment and appropriate referrals. Police administrators must ensure that officers are properly prepared to provide information, make referrals, and handle calls for service.

Policing has unique features, yet many of the problems and concerns that confront police managers and administrators are the same ones that face managers and administrators in other lines of work in both public agencies and private businesses. For example, employees in every line of work must be recruited, selected, trained, supervised, evaluated, and promoted, and provisions must be made for their retirement. Budgets must be prepared and executed, services must be rendered, and accountability must be ensured by the agency head. How managers and administrators respond to problems, concerns, and difficulties determines whether their organization is successful, their people are motivated and productive, and the climate (internal environment) of their organization is challenging and rewarding.

Organizations become more difficult to administer as their activities and responsibilities increase in number and complexity. This is true even for the very small department. The chief of a department with 10 officers is faced with the same problems and expectations as the big-city police chief. The difference between managing large and small departments is a matter of scale. Chiefs of large departments are faced with a larger volume of many of the same problems chiefs of small departments face. Yet the chief of a small department not only must deal with all these managerial concerns but, in many cases, also performs the duties of a working officer. Police administrators, in large or small agencies, are faced with intricate, complicated responsibilities, and they must have the necessary management skills, abilities, and knowledge to meet these responsibilities.

THE POLICE DEPARTMENT AS AN ORGANIZATION

Robbins defined an organization as "a consciously coordinated social entity, with a relatively identifiable boundary, that functions on a relatively continuous basis to achieve a common goal or set of goals" (1990:4). The term *consciously coordinated* implies management. *Social entity* refers to the fact that organizations are composed of people who interact with each other and with people and other organizations within the organization's environment (external to the organization but affecting it in some way). *Relatively identifiable boundary* pertains to the department's jurisdiction or service population.

An organization, therefore, is a group of people working together to accomplish a desired goal. It is this goal or group of goals that legitimizes the very existence of the organization. Organizations are not formed merely to provide employment or to occupy their workers; organizations must serve a useful role in society if they are to survive. Any organization's survival is dependent on the successful, or at least partial, accomplishment of its goals. Police organizations are responsible for accomplishing a number of tasks—arresting lawbreakers, controlling traffic, maintaining order, preventing crime, and providing services to citizens such as aiding stranded motorists or assisting lost children. A police department must do all these activities well.

To consciously coordinate a police department is to manage it. A police agency is organized into a number of units such as patrol, traffic, criminal investigation, planning, and records. The administrator must ensure that these various units work with each other as opposed to operating independently. If individuals or units concentrate on their own objectives without considering the department's overall goals, other units' activities may be adversely affected. This process is referred to as *suboptimization*. This situation leads to conflict, competition, and a lack of cooperation. Classic examples of this problem are the rivalry between patrol officers and detectives and the precinct station's emphasis on its individual needs over the department's goals and directives.

A police department is a social entity composed of people and organizational units. In every organization people are charged with performing tasks or activities. Since organizations are created to accomplish specific goals; people within organizations must ultimately be involved in work-related activities that are directed toward goal accomplishment. Within most large organizations, three distinct categories of activity are performed by people: (1) task performance, (2) facilitating or helping those who perform the tasks, and (3) supervising task performance. Those personnel who perform fundamental police activities or supervise them are referred to as *line personnel*; personnel who help line personnel by providing support and assistance are referred to as *staff personnel*. For example, officers assigned to the planning unit assist patrol efforts by identifying crime trends; planning is a staff function. On the other hand, patrol officers will use the information to attempt to solve a particular crime problem and as such are involved in doing the actual work of the department; patrol is a line function.

As an organization becomes larger, it is necessary for people to work cooperatively to achieve organizational goals. A cooperative work setting requires that people working in the organization understand their individual and collective duties and responsibilities as well as the relationships between and among individuals and work groups within the organization. Such relationships are the essence of an organization. Patterns of interaction and work activities do not randomly emerge, but are designed through the administrative process of assigning work and responsibilities, that is, establishing work boundaries for people and units.

Police departments have relatively identifiable boundaries. *Boundaries* refer to the department's goals and the people it serves. The term "relatively identifiable" implies that a department's goals to some extent constantly change because it is extremely difficult to determine the exact nature of a community's needs at any given time. Although a police department has several goals that never change, such as serving the public and arresting criminals, a department must be adaptive in nature and continually alter its direction as new problems are encountered by the community and new expectations are levied on the police. This adaptive behavior leads to increased effectiveness relative to the department's overall performance.

THE ROLE OF THE ADMINISTRATOR

Administration refers to the general managing and organizing that occurs at the highest levels of an organization. It entails the establishment of the department's overall purposes or mission as well as the establishment of policies and procedures which serve as guideposts for the department to achieve its overall purposes. Administrators must develop ways of controlling the department to ensure that personnel and units follow the guideposts that are in place. Additionally, administrators must ensure that there is adequate funding for the programs that are implemented. Administration of a police department is a complicated task, especially as the department becomes larger. Administrators

On the Job

SEATTLE, WASHINGTON POLICE DEPARTMENT
By Chief Gil Kerlikowske

Courtesy of Chief Kerlikowske

The role of a police chief in today's society is one of the most complicated and complex among executive positions. At one level, the chief is accountable to elected and appointed officials, on the other, the chief must be responsive to citizens and constituent groups of the community. The chief is the principal point of contact between the police department and the citizens it serves.

Making the task even more complicated is the wide array of tasks a modern police force is called on to perform. These services include working with schools, assisting the homeless, managing intervention programs for children at risk, educating people about domestic violence, providing crime prevention services and much more. These services are generally directed through the community political process, with different groups having different ideas about what

and how services should be delivered. In every case, the police department must make it work for the community.

In Seattle, I work with a variety of people inside and outside the formal government. Seattleites have two great addictions—coffee, and process. Each group I meet with has its own ideas about needs and solutions. Those needs differ from neighborhood to neighborhood—and the ideas often differ within each neighborhood. Our challenge as a department is to be responsive to the different needs and requests, and to work within the process to develop solutions that impact the community.

The Seattle Police Department has 1,300 officers and 700 support personnel, and is divided into nine bureaus. Within those bureaus are divisions that provide enforcement, crime prevention, service, information technology, and many other diverse functions. It is an enormous challenge to manage those divisions and personnel while meeting the needs of the community.

As chief of police, my responsibilities can be divided into three areas: organizing the department, managing the department, and supporting community outreach and engagement. To organize the department, I must develop the units within the department and assign personnel to them so they can be responsive to the community. For example, the implementation of community policing has resulted in a number of new activities and the

Continued

alteration of units within the department. My role is to ensure that all units cooperate and communicate with each other to accomplish the department's mission.

The management function includes monitoring and evaluating the department to ensure that goals are being met. I must review and evaluate the selection, training and promotion system so that highly qualified individuals are selected, trained and promoted. I also must manage disciplinary and accountability systems, which are critical to the department's relationship of trust and confidence with the community.

Last, community outreach and engagement are important so that citizens are informed and involved in the workings of their police department. Through this outreach, citizens are fully part of the process, and understand their role in democratic policing.

As the city continues to grow, the department must also adapt and change to meet new challenges. We constantly review and adjust policies and procedures to meet community needs. Today's urban police department is evolving, and requires personnel who understand the importance of organizational change while continuing to provide a high level of service and open communication with the people it serves.

must exert substantial effort to ensure that the department remains on track and citizens receive the best possible protection and service.

The best way to understand administration and what administrators do is to identify the activities associated with administration. Gulick (1937), an early administrative theorist, outlined administrative responsibilities using the acronym *POSDCORB*. This classic description of administration is still accepted today as one of the most appropriate for identifying administrative functions:

1. *Planning* is the determination of what is to be accomplished (goals) and how it is to be accomplished.
2. *Organizing* is the application of organizational principles in determining the department's formal organization, including the chain of command, job specialization, and how various units are coordinated.
3. *Staffing* is the personnel function, particularly focusing on the recruitment, training, placement, and promotion of competent, qualified applicants.
4. *Directing* is where managers provide direction to employees in terms of policies and orders.
5. *Coordinating* is the task of interrelating the numerous component units within the organization to ensure goal accomplishment.
6. *Reporting* is the task of keeping everyone informed regarding operations through verbal and written directives, records, and inspection.
7. *Budgeting* is the task of fiscal planning, accounting, and control to ensure that the department has the resources necessary to pursue goals and objectives.

All too often, people not in administrative positions have simplistic impressions of what administrators do. Many view administrators as "paper shufflers" while others see administrators as people who impede achievement through constant memoranda and rules and regulations. As noted above, the administrator has many responsibilities. To be successful, an administrator must be diligent, competent, and dedicated to the department and the community. Administrative activities consist of two components, organization and management.

Organization

Organization, the first component within administration, refers to structuring and staffing, or the placing of people in the department. Organization should be accomplished in a manner that facilitates the working relationships of personnel and goal attainment. Organization corresponds to the bones that structure or give form to the body. The placement of bones and the manner in which they are put together determines the effectiveness of the body's performance. Imagine, for instance, that the fingers were a single mass of bone rather than four separate fingers and a thumb made up of bones joined by cartilage so that they are flexible. The design of the fingers determines their usefulness or effectiveness in performing various tasks. The mass of bones could not, because of its structure, play musical instruments, hold a pencil, or grip a baseball bat. A police department's organization is analogous. It must be structured properly if it is to be effective in fulfilling its many, diverse goals.

Organization may not be important in a township police department consisting of three officers, but it is extremely important in cities such as New York City, which has more than 39,100 full-time sworn officers (Hickman and Reaves, 2001). When administrators make decisions relative to organization, they consider how many and what types of units should exist within the department and how they should be staffed. For example, if a department consists of 100 police officers, the chief could structure or create a variety of units, assign personnel to those units, and assign responsibilities to the units. This process of organizing the department will affect how the department operates. Public and governmental expectations of the police must be carefully considered when organizing a police department so that maximum effectiveness is achieved.

Even though there is almost an infinite number of ways to organize a department, if it is done without careful consideration, the department will not be able to efficiently respond to public safety needs. For example, the implementation of too many specialized units such as community relations, media relations, or crime analysis may obligate too many personnel to these functions and render patrol ineffective due to a personnel shortage in other areas. Today, approximately 56 to 90 percent of sworn officers are assigned to patrol (Hickman and Reaves, 2001). Smaller departments are at the high end of this range, while larger departments have more specialized units and have a lower percentage of their officers assigned to patrol. If a smaller percentage of officers is assigned to patrol, the back of the primary line unit is broken and specialization

Officers discuss tactical operations in mobile command center.
Dwayne Newton/PhotoEdit

flourishes at the expense of the delivery of fundamental police services. A police department's structure and staffing should be determined by the available resources and mission.

Management

Management, the second component within administration, refers to the processes administrators use to give an organization direction and to influence people to work toward organizational goals. It is the actions taken by administrators to implement decisions and policies. Organization and management are related in that a department's organization directly affects the management style used by commanders and supervisors. A manager—in making decisions, leading, or commanding—is restricted by the structure of the department in terms of the number of subordinates, amount of authority, and type and degree of responsibility. At the same time, a manager's philosophy about how the department should be operated will affect how the manager organizes the department.

Management consists of those activities which are designed to induce cooperation and facilitate work. Managers are involved in activities such as decision making, planning, providing direction, leading, communicating, and motivating. Since managers can perform these activities in a number of ways, it is important to examine the various ways one might manage. It is also important to determine which managerial methods are most successful in gaining subordinates' cooperative compliance and ultimately in reaching departmental goals.

Figure 1–1
Factors affecting management processes.

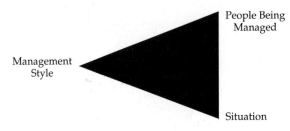

People Being
Managed

Management
Style

Situation

A police manager is confronted with numerous situations and conditions necessitating a variety of management techniques. For example, the management style used by a commander facing a barricaded person would be different from the style used by a supervisor who manages a burglary investigation unit. Situational necessity often determines what tools a manager will use and how they will be used. Also, a manager will use different styles to direct subordinates based on the ability and motivational level of the subordinates. In general, an inexperienced employee will require more direction than an experienced employee. A stressed or burned-out employee will require more attention and support than one who is not experiencing such problems. Thus management is conditional and the good manager must possess a variety of knowledge, skills, and abilities. Management style is always contingent on the situation and people being managed. Figure 1–1 depicts the relationship as a triangle where each side affects the others, and the three parts must match or be integrated for the department to be successful.

Management Levels

Management occurs throughout the police organization. The typical police organization resembles a military structure, with management levels that include administrators (chief, assistant chiefs, and majors), commanders or midlevel managers (captains and lieutenants), and supervisors (sergeants). These titles and duties may change depending on the size of the department; for example, a lieutenant in a medium-sized department may have the same duties as a captain or major in a larger one. Figure 1–2 shows the hierarchy of managers within a typical police organization.

The roles of managers are changing in modern organizations. They are no longer mere "taskmasters," concerned solely with work. The manager has taken on a mission of assisting the employee by providing the equipment and technical support necessary for the employee to function effectively. Managers also clarify tasks and guide the employee to become more effective. This is accomplished through direction, the issuance of policies, procedures and orders, and employee development (i.e., ongoing training and placement of employees in the organization). The supervisor is responsible for an individual

Figure 1–2
Hierarchy of managers within the typical police organization.

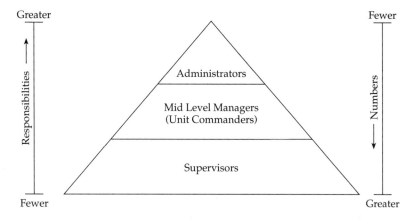

Table 1–1

Specifics of Managerial Orientation

People and Task Orientation	Mission and Goal Orientation
Narrow view of the organization	Broad view of the organization
Unit approach	Organizational approach
Emphasis on task accomplishment through:	Emphasis on mission accomplishment through:
Directing	Planning
Controlling	Evaluating
Supervising	Budgeting
Leading individuals	Organizational leadership
Activity-oriented:	Vision-oriented:
Carries out assigned tasks	Formulates/originates mission, role, and goals
Uses existing structures	Creates, changes, and eliminates structure
Emphasizes technical knowledge	Emphasizes understanding

unit while the administrator is responsible for larger organizational areas. Both apply management processes to their part of the department.

Another way to conceptualize the differences between administrators, managers, and supervisors is to look at their organizational perspectives. In Table 1–1, the management perspective is separated into two parts: (1) a people and task orientation and (2) a mission and goal orientation. It is apparent from examining this table that supervisors, managers, and administrators are each involved in both managerial perspectives. The depth of their involvement is what gives each a somewhat distinct orientation. Supervisors are much more involved in people and task activities while administrators concern themselves more with a mission and goal orientation. Figure 1–3 sets forth the specifics of

Figure 1–3
Overview of management perspectives.

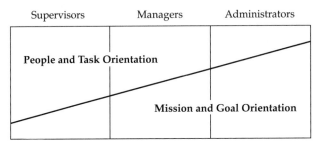

each managerial orientation. Operationally, the manner in which these specifics are combined will differ with the level of management and the situation faced, as well as the size of the department.

Police departments are always changing and, as such, the administrator is concerned with two general management aspects: organizational maintenance and adaptation. *Organizational maintenance* refers to those administrative activities that maintain the department's ability to respond to public needs. Organizational maintenance includes activities such as staffing, training, and organizational development. These activities enable the department to be in a better position to respond to any need, situation, or crisis. *Adaptation* refers to the fact that public expectations and needs are constantly changing, requiring the department to change or adapt to these changes. If a community is confronted with an increase in gang violence, the department must be able to react to this new threat. The effective administrator is an understanding visionary who is able to realize community needs and steer the department toward those identified ends. Simultaneously, the effective police administrator manages the department so that it accomplishes goals and provides employees with a fulfilling work environment. The police administrator is constantly balancing these two management responsibilities. This dual responsibility is a difficult task for the police administrator.

HOW POLICE DEPARTMENTS DIFFER FROM OTHER ORGANIZATIONS

Police departments differ from all other organizations because only the police possess legitimate arrest power and authority within our society. This responsibility results in police officers performing a variety of tasks and meeting the need for services continuously, as discussed previously. Police departments are also distinctive because they are government organizations. Rainey (1991) identified six areas where government organizations differ from private organizations. First, public organizations exist within a political environment. Individual citizens, groups of citizens, and political organizations can exert significant influence on government and the police department through the political process. Private businesses are largely immune from such intervention. Second, governmental agencies do not have a profit motive. This sometimes makes it more difficult to identify goals and evaluate their effectiveness. Third, government is involved in the provision of services as opposed to goods. This also tends to muddle the dynamics of goal setting and evaluation. Fourth, the existence of bureaucratic governmental rules and regulations stymie creativity and flexibility. Oftentimes, how governmental agencies respond to situations is dictated by law or regulation, and there always exists a conflict between control of government and efficiency. Fifth, government has limited, inflexible resources. Public organizations must live within their budgets regardless of crisis or need. Businesses most always have the ability to raise capital when contingencies or opportunities avail themselves. Finally, a business or company must answer to its stockholders, whereas a government must answer to its many and diverse citizens.

Another way to examine the differences between government and the private sector is their service orientation. Many private companies provide services in today's economy, but most, if not all, governmental agencies are service-oriented. Although the governmental aspect limits the activities of public agencies, their service orientation provides a better understanding of the nature of public service as it relates to management. Along these lines, Hodge and his colleagues (1996) identified five problems facing the service industry that are virtually nonexistent in the manufacturing sector. First, service providers deliver an intangible product. The Toyota Camry plant in Georgetown, Kentucky, provides a finite product, a quality automobile. Police departments, on the other hand, are required to provide a wide variety of services. The police product has a large measure of uncertainty associated with it. Second, service providers must have built-in flexibility for responding to differing service needs. The Camry plant's operations are fairly standardized. Indeed, every activity is mechanized as much as possible. In contrast, police officers have a great deal of discretion and may be required to respond differently to each call. There is substantial variability in what police officers do and how they do it. Third, service organizations have a higher degree of customer participation. Toyota makes a car and then markets or convinces customers they should buy it. An individual customer alone can do very little to cause a new product to be delivered. Everything that service organizations do is dictated by customers. The driving force behind police activity is individual citizens calling the police and requesting service. Fourth, timing distinguishes service organizations from manufacturing organizations. Manufacturing organizations can manufacture ample reserve products for deviations in demand. Service organizations must respond immediately to every request for service. Finally, service organizations are labor-intensive, whereas manufacturing uses robots and other types of automation. When an organization such as a police department provides a service, it requires someone to personally provide the service. Labor-intensive organizations require a higher degree of accountability and a management system that facilitates work through people.

The very nature of police organizations necessitates a distinctive management style and organizational structure. The Toyota manufacturing plant may be a model in terms of its organization, management, and product, but its nature is distinctly different from law enforcement, and it would be fruitless to assume that a police department could be managed like Toyota. In the end, police departments must develop management systems that are effective within the political and environmental constraints confronting them. Although we can learn about management practices from Fortune 500 companies, such practices do not necessarily have absolute application in law enforcement.

THE ROLE OF POLICE: A SEARCH FOR GOALS

The environment exerts numerous, diverse pressures on the police organization to deliver a myriad of services. As people and institutions request new police services or demand higher levels of current services, the police administrator and the governing body are responsible for determining whether the police organization is the appropriate agency for providing the service and, if so, for determining whether the organization has the resources to provide the service. If it is decided that the police agency is the appropriate service provider and the resources are available to provide the service, the police administrator is then responsible for translating and incorporating the requested service into the department's mission, roles, and goal statements.

A *mission statement* is used to enumerate the department's purpose. Greene, Bergman, and McLaughlin (1994) discuss three purposes served by a mission statement. First, it serves to notify and educate officers and citizens alike about the department's values. The mission statement establishes, without a question, that which is important. Second, the mission statement provides a yardstick by which to measure the department's successes and failures. How well is the department performing relative to its intentions? Third, a mission statement can serve as a guide to establishing training and other socialization programs which change the informal organization's culture and values. Police departments must implement mechanisms which ensure that their employees' values, aspirations, and way of doing things are consistent with the department's mission. The Denton, Texas, police department's mission statement meets these criteria:

> The mission of the Denton Police Department is to positively impact the quality of life throughout the community. To achieve these ends, the department is committed to forming practical partnerships with the citizenry, which includes a mutual goal-setting process aimed at resolving problems, reducing fear, preserving the peace, and enforcing the law; thereby providing a safe environment for all citizens.

Moore and Stephens (1991) caution that a mission statement should not be static or unchanging, but it should change in accordance with fluctuations and alterations in the environment. Executives should be imaginative, considering every alternative when developing their department's mission statement. The mission statement should represent the best match of the department's strategic response to the environment's needs.

The *role* of the police can be defined as any proper or customary function performed by the police. The police agency's role in a given situation is the part that it plays in the drama of the community. Three primary police roles have been identified: order maintenance, public service, and law enforcement (Wilson, 1968). Within each of these roles is a range of activities that might be performed by the police. These roles prescribe a course of action for police officers and for the leadership in the police department. Police agencies usually assume all three roles, and each is emphasized or given higher priority at different points in time and under different circumstances. Since each department serves a different population of citizens, faces different problems, and is governed differently, the relative combination of the roles of one police department most likely will differ from that of another. For instance, when a community experiences a period of high property or violent crime, it is appropriate for the department to emphasize the law enforcement role; when the community experiences a period of social disorder, it is appropriate for the department to emphasize the order maintenance role; when the community experiences relative tranquility in terms of order and crime, it is appropriate for the department to emphasize the public service role.

Goals are the specific results or achievements toward which the police organization directs its efforts. They are specific conditions or benchmarks the organization desires to achieve or the state of affairs the organization strives to realize. Etzioni (1964) notes that the raison d'être for every organization is the service of goals. Goals are directly tied to the mission and roles of the organization. Within the framework of the mission and roles, each police department identifies goals and subsequently prioritizes them based on the needs and demands of the community. Police goals may include statements about the level of crime or the level of service provided to the community.

Once goals are identified, the department's staff will develop specific programs to achieve them. For example, a department that has the mission "to protect citizens from criminal activities" and emphasizes the role of "law enforcement" might pursue the goal of "crime reduction" by establishing a program of intensive enforcement and directed patrol when faced with a high level of property crime in a specific locale. An agency that has the same mission but that emphasizes the role of "public service" might pursue the goal of "crime reduction" by establishing a public education program to make the targets of the property crime more secure and by organizing neighborhood groups to watch for strangers in the community or youth activities leagues to keep juveniles in the community busy since unoccupied youth are often involved in the commission of property crimes. These are only a few examples of the manner in which the same mission can be translated into diverse roles, goals, and programs.

The previous sections defined police administration and discussed how management differed from organization. We also described police departments as goal-seeking organizations. The following section examines the police mission and the various roles assumed by the police historically. There have been substantial changes in the police mission as police departments attempt to respond to their environment, and one way to better understand today's police mission and operation is to examine how they developed historically.

THE POLICE MISSION: A HISTORICAL PERSPECTIVE

The mission of the police in America has changed, as has the way that police organizations are managed. Six general eras or historical periods are discussed: the political, progressive reform, professional police, community relations, return to "law and order," and community policing. It is important to study the police organization in a historical context since such a study provides a better understanding of current operations and how those operations were derived.

The Political Era

Police administration, especially in the larger cities, during the early twentieth century could be characterized as political, decentralized arms of the local politicians. In the large cities, police precinct stations were run not by the police chief, but by police captains who generally reported directly to political party chairmen. Politicians dictated what laws were enforced, who was arrested, who was hired, and who was promoted within the precinct. Most actions taken by the police were in the furtherance of the political party in power. As Fogelson (1977) notes, police chiefs of the period were more or less figureheads.

Historically, the primary roles of police were order maintenance and provision of services to the community. Indeed, some effectively argue that the police were created not to control crime, but to curb lawlessness and disorder (Monkkonen, 1992). The police assumed these roles primarily because local governments were responsible for providing social services. The federal government and state governments did not have any welfare machinery to assist the disabled, unemployed, or homeless. Furthermore, politicians controlling government and the police realized that few votes were gained by arresting people, but many votes could be garnered by helping people.

For example, Lane (1967) points out that in the 1834 cholera epidemic, the Boston police visited every house to check for cholera, and police stations served as temporary hospital facilities. The police removed 1,500 loads of dirt and emptied 3,120 privies during this period. In 1860, the Boston police provided lodging for 17,352 non-arrestees. Similarly, in New York from 1861 to 1869 police furnished lodging for 880,161 persons while arrests accounted for a similar number, 898,489. The police were providing lodging for almost as many people as they were arresting (Whitehouse, 1973). Douthit (1975) points out that the Oakland, California, chief of police suggested in 1915 that the police participate in the parole system and help the poor by enforcing tenement laws. In 1919, August Vollmer presented a paper to the International Association of Chiefs of Police (IACP) titled "The Policeman as a Social Worker." In 1916, the New York police entertained over 40,000 children for Christmas, and in 1917, police officers were assigned to serve as juvenile delinquency prevention officers (Fosdick, 1969). The provision of community service dominated American law enforcement through the first quarter of the twentieth century.

In terms of police organization, Fosdick's (1969) examination of departments of the political era determined that they were disorganized and bore little relationship to the community they served. Daily police activities were more a matter of tradition and undirected evolution. Officers frequently did not know their responsibilities and waited for direction to come from superiors. When there was no direction, activities were haphazard and seldom constituted activities that might be considered police work as we know it today.

The Police Enter the Progressive Reform Era

During the decades of the 1920s and 1930s, the police moved toward what may be characterized as an era of progressive reform. This reform was the result of police administrators attempting to improve the police, while many outside of policing recognized the same need. The passage of prohibition along with the Great Depression created an enormous underclass and criminal element in the United States.

The progressive reform era was punctuated by a shift from order maintenance and provision of services to that of law enforcement or crime fighting. This shift was largely due to the Volstead Act and the Great Depression and the subsequent rising crime rate (Douthit, 1975: Moore, 1978). On January 16, 1920, the Volstead Act was passed. It prohibited the manufacture, sale, and transportation of all intoxicating beverages. At no time in history had the police been called on to enforce anything as unpopular as the total prohibition of alcoholic beverages, and there had never been any enforcement problem of the magnitude of prohibition enforcement.

The ultimate effects of prohibition on the police and society were profound. It led to the evolution of small, scattered gangs who were engaged in bootlegging, gambling, prostitution, and other vice and criminal activities at a local level. These local gangs eventually evolved into nationally operated criminal enterprises. The police did not have the experience or capacity to effectively deal with the problems resulting from prohibition. They had to choose between becoming corrupt or making a nuisance of themselves by enforcing the unpopular laws.

During the Great Depression of the 1930s, many people lost their jobs and became homeless as a result of the banks foreclosing on their homes and farms. People would work for as little as 50 cents a day in order to have income, and in many cases, people worked for food. Public attention was drawn to the escapades of infamous criminals like John Dillinger, Baby Face Nelson, Machine Gun Kelly, and Bonnie Parker and Clyde Barrow. These criminals and their gangs more or less ravaged the countryside at will. Many citizens came to view them as heroes, because they robbed the rich bankers and businessmen who had taken their homes and forced them out into the streets. They were also viewed as heroes because the local police could do little to stop them. Local police were so disorganized, ill-trained and unequipped, and unprepared that they posed little threat to the marauding criminal gangs.

The Wickersham Commission

Because of the increased crime rates and the inability of the police to cope with the problem, in 1929, President Herbert Hoover convened the National Commission on Law Observance and Law Enforcement (better known as the Wickersham

Commission). In 1931, the commission delivered its report to President Hoover. The commission identified the lack of police effectiveness as a primary cause of rising crime rates:

> The general failure of the police to detect and arrest criminals guilty of the many murders, spectacular bank, payroll and other holdups, sensational robberies with guns, frequently resulting in the death of the robbed victim, has caused a loss of public confidence in the police of our country. (National Commission on Law Observance and Enforcement, 1931:1)

Essentially, the Wickersham Commission advocated redefinition of the police role from order maintenance of law enforcement. Wilson (1968) summarized the impact of the Wickersham Commission on American policing:

1. The law enforcement function became uppermost in the minds of the police and the public.
2. The police were given sole responsibility for the reduction of crime.
3. The police used unethical means to meet the public's expectations of crime reduction—the manipulation of crime statistics.
4. The peacekeeping (community service) functions (soup kitchens, providing lodging, referral agents, etc.) became looked upon as not "real police work."
5. The policeman, in effect, took on an adversarial relationship with the public.
6. The number of arrests by a police officer became the criterion for promotion.
7. The public looked upon the policeman as mainly involved in fighting crime and doing very little in the way of peacekeeping (order maintenance or community service) (pp. 133–134).

Federal Law Enforcement

As a result of prohibition and increased crime, federal law enforcement agencies were given the responsibility to intervene in many of the criminal problems of the time. Most notably the Treasury Department and the Federal Bureau of Investigation (FBI) became active participants in the war against crime. In a very short time, they became the role models to which local and state law enforcement agencies aspired.

Federal Treasury agents were given the responsibility of enforcing prohibition. They undertook investigations and conducted highly publicized raids. Their enforcement efforts covered most of the United States as they attempted to prevent the smuggling of alcoholic beverages into the country and to prevent citizens from distilling and selling alcohol. Their actions revealed how professionals should go about enforcing the law.

About the same time, J. Edgar Hoover was transforming the old Bureau of Investigation from a corrupt, inept federal law enforcement agency into an FBI that came to be recognized as the preeminent law enforcement agency of the time. Hoover's agents pursued high-profile criminals all over the United States. These pursuits resulted in highly publicized arrests and sometimes shootouts between the agents and the criminals they sought.

Agents of the Treasury and the Federal Bureau of Investigation had a professional appearance and were dedicated solely to law enforcement. They were an elite corps of well-trained agents who were capable of dealing with the law enforcement problems of the time. Their demeanor and qualifications gave them high status in the public's eyes. Consequently, local police became interested in attaining a similar status.

Police administrators and citizens, as a result of the crime problem, the depression, and the federal law enforcement model, began to wrest control of their departments from the politicians. Fogelson (1977) notes that the times resulted in a number of changes in police administration. First, police chiefs began to create staff and middle-management positions in their departments. In earlier times, a department had a chief and precinct captains. Assistant chiefs, majors, and other middle-management ranks were added. These new ranks were responsible for assisting the chief in exerting better control over the department. Second, specialized units such as criminal investigation and anti-crime units were created and worked out of a central headquarters. This gave police executives direct control of an operational force that could be assigned to precincts when the precinct commanders and officers were not doing their jobs. Finally, police administrators began to implement selection and training standards. Selection procedures were implemented to improve the quality of personnel and to thwart politicians from appointing unqualified persons to their departments. Administrators developed training programs to provide officers with the knowledge and skills to be effective police officers and to instill an esprit de corps and commitment to policing. Professional police administration originated in the problems of the time.

The Professional Police Era

During the decades of the 1940s and 1950s, the role of the police as law enforcers or "crook catchers" crystallized. Police officers came to see themselves as professional law enforcers. They felt that activities outside the realm of law enforcement were chores that should be relegated to other agencies. Administrators strove for professional status along the lines of the federal model, which they equated with efficient crime fighting. The service role was deemphasized in many departments and lost altogether in others. Administrators attacked the longtime problem of police corruption by segregating the police from the public, which also contributed to the reduction in services provided by the police.

Large numbers of men returned from World War II and were exposed to a new systematic approach to training police officers. These men brought with them a discipline and respect for the military organizational structure that became ingrained in policing. Their prior military experience coincided with the police's movement toward the law enforcement role. As those with military experience moved into police leadership positions, police departments were organized in a quasi-military fashion with the purpose of making them more efficient in fighting crime. Some police departments became extremely bureaucratic.

Technological innovations supplemented the police and their fight against crime. Police radios replaced call boxes. Increasingly, officers walking beats were replaced with vehicular patrols, which provided the police with the mobility to respond to "trouble" calls and crimes in progress. Radios and patrol cars afforded administrators greater control over their officers. The radios and patrol cars helped to further segregate the police from citizens. Advancements made in scientific criminal investigation greatly enhanced police capabilities in evidence collection and fingerprint and laboratory technology.

During this period, police professionalism substantially increased, as did public expectations for the police to be more proficient in their primary task—fighting crime. Police chiefs across the country encouraged the public's acceptance of the law enforcement role. They eliminated many services such as providing security to hospitals and other public facilities and providing ambulance services. Other chiefs reduced their department's role in regulating traffic and in other support services that had been performed previously for the convenience of the community. Departments attempted to reduce their involvement in social service roles, believing that such activities detracted from their ability to fight crime. Whether they were any more effective in reducing crime during this period relative to earlier times is questionable. What was certain, however, is that there was a greater "appearance" of combating crime.

The Community Relations Era

During the decades of the 1960s and 1970s, America witnessed unprecedented strife, violence, public disorder, and crime related to the Vietnam War and the civil rights movement. The police and criminal justice system were unprepared for the onslaught of problems. The police in their pursuit of administrative efficiency and crime-fighting capacity essentially had isolated themselves from the public; in many cases they were incapable of responding to the nation's crime and disorder problems. Social scientists and police officials alike began to realize that assuming the crime-fighting role exclusively would not effectively deal with the many diverse problems confronting our police.

During this period, overall crime increased by approximately 176 percent according to the FBI's *Uniform Crime Reports* (1970). Crimes against persons increased 156.5 percent while crimes against property increased 179.7 percent. The greatest increases were in larceny, which increased 244.9 percent, and robbery, which increased 224.4 percent. During the same period, the population of the United States increased approximately 15 percent. The percentage increase in the crime rate was approximately 11 times more than the percentage growth in population.

Although increases in crime rates were significant and caused a great deal of concern on the part of public officials and citizens, the police's inability to effectively deal with collective violence and assassinations had an even more powerful influence on federal and state governments. In 1962, Medgar Evers, a field representative for the National Association for the Advancement of Colored

People (NAACP), was gunned down in Jackson, Mississippi. The following year President John F. Kennedy was assassinated in Dallas, Texas. The assassination of Senator Robert F. Kennedy in Los Angeles and Martin Luther King Jr. in Memphis also shocked the nation and made the public more aware of the problems of violence in American society.

Civil unrest and riots swept the college campuses and large cities of America. The President's Commission on Law Enforcement and Administration of Justice was established by President Lyndon Johnson to study the tragic situation and to recommend strategies to improve the criminal justice system. The President's Commission (1967) hypothesized that it may have been society's blind reaction to inhumane living conditions that precipitated a great deal of the urban crime, and that the ghetto riots of the 1960s were symptoms of the problem. The 1965 riot in the Watts section of Los Angeles left 34 dead, 1,032 injured, 3,952 arrested, and $40 million in property damage. A riot in Detroit the following year left another 43 persons dead. Major riots also took place in Tampa, Cincinnati, Atlanta, and Newark. The National Advisory Commission on Civil Disorders (1968) identified the basic causes of the riots as pervasive discrimination and segregation. The commission also noted that most of the major riots were touched off by police arresting African-Americans for minor offenses. Essentially, the police were caught in the middle of a social problem of the greatest magnitude.

> The policeman in the ghetto is a symbol of increasingly bitter social debate over law enforcement. One side, disturbed and perplexed by sharp increases in crime and urban violence, exerts extreme pressure on police for tougher law enforcement. Another group, inflamed against police as agents of repression, tends toward defiance of what it regards as order maintained at the expense of justice. (National Advisory Commission on Civil Disorders, 1968)

The police response to the increased violence was to further entrench themselves in the role of crime fighters. Emphasis was placed on making arrests, writing citations, and restoring order through force. The police were given an impossible mandate without the tools to carry out their mission. Subsequently, the police felt pressured into violating the law for the sake of order. The police came to depend on confessions as the primary method of clearing criminal cases. In many cases, the police beat suspects until they confessed. The coerced confession basically supplanted the collection of evidence and solid criminal investigating.

Police actions increasingly were questioned in the courts, and subsequently the 1960s brought a "due process revolution" in the United States. Earl Warren as Chief Justice led a Supreme Court that included a majority of liberal-minded associate justices. The Court rendered decision after decision restricting the activities of the police when investigating criminal activities. These restrictive decisions brought charges from police officials that the Court was "handcuffing" the police. The result of the due process revolution of the 1960s was that the Court struck down a number of police procedures that had been sacred to police investigators for decades.

The collective impact of increased crime, riots, and other violence and the Court's attack on traditional police procedures was the realization that police and the criminal justice machinery in general were not adequately prepared to confront America's social ills. In 1968, Congress passed the Omnibus Crime Control and Safe Streets Act, which created the Law Enforcement Assistance Administration (LEAA). The thrust of LEAA was to improve law enforcement at the local level. Subsequently, millions of dollars were pumped into local criminal justice programs, with the majority of the funding going into policing. The police were able to develop programs and purchase equipment never before available because of the lack of funds. The LEAA also funded a tremendous amount of research focusing on police and their role in our society.

One conclusion with which there was almost unanimous agreement was that the police had isolated themselves from the community as a result of their law enforcement role. This isolation created two distinct but related problems. First, large segments of the minority population distrusted the police and were uncooperative when confronted by the police. This relationship heightened the tension between the police and minorities, especially in those situations where the police were called on to intervene in and quell conflicts. Second, crime is usually highest in minority communities. When the police attempted to investigate crimes and other problems, they were met with distrust and uncooperativeness. This only helped to widen the chasm between the police and the public.

The lack of positive police–community relations resulted in a renewed interest in the police as providers of services. Citizens increasingly questioned the quantity and quality of services they received when they "called a cop" and began to demand better services. Consequently, police administrators developed a wide range of programs for the purpose of improving the levels of service provided by the police and, concomitantly, to improve their departments' images. A realization that police cannot have an effect on crime rates without citizen cooperation and assistance also developed and became a cornerstone for new programs.

Although police departments had police–community relations units as early as 1957, when St. Louis developed one, there was no widespread national interest until the late 1960s and early 1970s. Spurred by negative community sentiment and federal funding, police departments created units and implemented programs. These programs took two distinct directions: public relations and community relations. *Public relations programs* focused on improving the police department's image through public education. Departments used public displays, demonstrations, lectures, and television and radio to inform and educate the public about police operations and problems, crime, and crime prevention. The thrust of this programming was to "sell" the police to the public. Police administrators believed that when citizens understood the police and their problems, the public would better accept and cooperate with the police.

Community relations programs, on the other hand, represented police intervention into community problems. Police administrators came to understand that public acceptance, especially in minority neighborhoods, would be achieved only if the police were genuinely interested in and helped to solve community problems. Departments operated programs to provide recreational opportunities for disadvantaged youth, set up neighborhood centers to provide assistance and refer citizens to social service agencies, and established neighborhood watch and other programs actively involving citizens in crime prevention. The community relations programs had a greater impact than public relations programs because they required closer working relationships between the police and the public.

Return to Law and Order

The 1980s saw yet another shift in police philosophy. In 1982, Ronald Reagan's election was the beginning of 12 years of conservative "law-and-order" government. Columbian drug cartels were exporting massive amounts of cocaine into the United States. Drugs and drug-related crime became the country's most significant law enforcement issue. Drug-related homicides increased dramatically and steadily, as did the number of arrests of drug dealers and the amount of drugs confiscated by the police. Politicians continually highlighted drugs and crime, making them campaign issues. Fear of crime increased, which resulted in additional pressures on the police.

The federal government made large amounts of money available to the states and local police departments in the form of block grants and funded programs. Federal law enforcement agencies, particularly the FBI, the Drug Enforcement Agency (DEA), and the Bureau of Alcohol, Tobacco, and Firearms (ATF), began to cooperate and work with state and local departments by implementing multi-jurisdictional drug enforcement programs. They also implemented larger numbers of enforcement programs that increased the number of drug-related arrests. Simultaneously, local and state police agencies added and increased the number of personnel assigned to drug enforcement. All of this activity resulted in increased arrests, but the drug problem continued to worsen.

The community relations programs of the 1960s and 1970s evolved into crime prevention programs. Crime prevention programs were particularly appealing to the police because they were seen as a way of coping with crime and they targeted the business community and middle-class Americans who were the political elite within many communities. Police administrators recognized a need to obtain these citizens' support and to enlist them in the war against crime.

No matter how much money was thrown into the drug and crime wars, the problems persisted. There was a slow realization in some law enforcement circles that law enforcement measures alone would not ameliorate the problems. Some in policing began to recognize that law enforcement, in conjunction with attacking other social problems in neighborhoods, was more effective as a police strategy. For example, Weisel (1990) examined ways the police could incorporate community-building projects with law enforcement to have more success in public housing, while Block and Block (1993) suggested a similar strategy to deal with gangs. Others suggested that the police have a vested interest in the social condition of neighborhoods and should be directly involved in community building and the elimination of neighborhood disorder (Skogan and Maxfield, 1981; Wilson and Kelling, 1982).

Community Policing

Community policing as a philosophy and operational strategy essentially is the culmination of a number of experiments and other strategies that have been employed over the past 30 years. First, it is rooted in team policing, which was implemented in a number of jurisdictions in the 1970s (Walker, 1993). Team policing used participatory management, geographic stability of assignment, and community involvement, three hallmarks of today's community policing. It also has roots in the foot patrol studies conducted in Flint, Michigan (Trojanowicz, 1982), and Newark, New Jersey (Police Foundation, 1981). These studies found that foot patrols resulted in closer, more productive relationships between the police and citizens. These relationships in turn caused citizens to fear crime less. Finally, community policing is founded on the realization that social disorder and community deterioration lead to increased crime, and perhaps the police's primary role in a community is to stop or reduce social disorder (Katz, Webb, and Schaefer, 2001; Skogan and Maxfield, 1981; Wilson and Kelling, 1982).

Community policing has been embraced by politicians and police executives throughout the country. It has been advocated by Presidents George Bush and Bill Clinton as an effective way of dealing with a variety of community problems. At the local level, mayors and city managers have encouraged police executives to adopt community policing. A majority of American police departments have implemented community policing for a variety of reasons. For example, Weisel and Eck examined community policing in six different cities and found a variety of reasons for its implementation:

> The perceived stimulus or precipitating event for implementation ranged from new leadership and adapting an agency for organizational efficiency to advancement of a philosophical commitment to the approach as an effective system for delivery of services to an effort to resolve potential or existing racial conflict with the community. (1994:63)

There is no single form of community policing. In some cases, departments have added special units to conduct community policing, while others have attempted to get large numbers of patrol, traffic, and investigative officers involved in community policing programs. Indeed, the police are engaged in a number of diverse programs and tactics with the explicit objective of developing a partnership with the citizenry to solve crime and disorder problems. For example, in a study of eight cities funded by the Bureau of Justice Administration, Sadd and Grinc (1994) found departments used tactics such as ombudsmen, coordinating councils, neighborhood police stations, enforcement crackdowns, advertising campaigns, problem solving, and foot patrols. The diversity of programming in community policing led Bayley to observe:

Despite the benefits claimed for community policing, programmatic implementation of it has been very uneven. Although widely, almost universally, said to be important, it means different things to different people . . . Community policing on the ground often seems less a program than a set of aspirations wrapped in a slogan. (1998:225)

Community policing, appears to be a compilation of traditional police methods applied differently. Goldstein (1993) identified five areas where policing must change if it is to effectively apply community policing. First, the police must refine the police function and public expectations. Traditionally, the police have seen themselves primarily as crime fighters. However, it must be realized that crime fighting constitutes only a small portion of a police officer's activity and time. Order maintenance activities, on the other hand, require larger portions of officers' time, and this function touches a larger number of citizens. Citizens must also learn that the police cannot contend with the many problems facing a community without citizen involvement and support. Community justice must be seen as a partnership between the police and the public.

Second, the police must get involved in the substance of policing. Traditionally, the police have come to see themselves as call-takers: they respond to a call, take some action, and then respond to another call. Their default objective has been short-term satisfaction rather than long-term solutions. The police must begin to delve into problems and search for resolutions. Such a strategy reduces calls for service and crime, and it instills public faith in the police.

Third, the relationship between the police and the criminal justice system should be reconsidered. Arrest and other traditional police responses have limited utility in solving problems. The police simply cannot limit their responses to problems exclusively using the criminal justice system. The resources and support of citizens, social agencies, and other private agencies should be considered and used.

Fourth, the police must more effectively search for alternatives when dealing with problems, and responses should not be limited to one tactic or method of intervention. Many times, such as when dealing with neighborhood drug problems, enforcement in conjunction with other social programs is the most effective response (Block and Block, 1993).

Fifth, police administrators must change the department's working environment to facilitate community policing. Management systems must be flexible and open, allowing officers to experiment with problem solving. Management must recognize that police officers, in order to be effective, must be given latitude in how they respond to neighborhood problems. This is accomplished when departments move from bureaucratic models to open, participative management structures.

Goldstein effectively outlines how departments can move toward community policing. From an operational perspective, departments are approaching community policing differently, but each of Goldstein's five areas must be addressed if a department is to successfully implement community policing. That is, community policing must be a priority at all levels in a department.

By examining the police across history, one can obtain a better understanding of today's police organization. It is important to note that the phases or eras of policing have coincided with the structure of society. Table 1–2 summarizes of the eras of policing.

Table 1–2

The Police Role and Activities by Eras

Era	Police Role	Departmental Structure
Political	Providing services, especially to the disadvantaged. Occasionally performing law enforcement duties.	Decentralized, controlled by community politicians. Few standards with most decisions political in nature.
Progressive reform	Providing services to larger segments of the community. Law enforcement gaining prominence.	Introduction of selection standards. Central authority beginning to wrest control of departments from local politicians.
Professional	Law enforcement and crime fighting. Little attention given to soft crime issues such as service and order maintenance.	Highly centralized authority using military model with officers segregated from community. Emphasis on selection, promotion, and training standards.
Community relations	Renewed emphasis on service and order maintenance. Realization that police cannot fight crime without citizen help and support.	Participative management enters law enforcement. Limited emphasis on group decision making and job restructuring.
Return to "law and order"	Emphasis on crime prevention and law enforcement functions. Belief that arrests and crime suppression activities were the most effective in solving community problems.	Return to a traditional police organization with a strict chain of command. The creation and expansion of drug enforcement units.
Community policing	Emphasis on active participation by citizens in law enforcement issues. Police are seen as community change and social agents.	Contingency planning where police response is molded by need and problems. Police develop partnerships with other public and private agencies to manage problems.

Summary

This chapter provides a foundation for understanding police administration. The terms administration, management, and organization often are used interchangeably, but they represent distinct behaviors and activities. To a great extent, management is the act of leading and organization is determining how the department should be arranged. The police administrator must give both management and organization adequate attention if the department is to function effectively. Here, the police administrator must determine the number and kinds of specialized units that are created and their command structure.

Police departments are very different from other organizations and institutions. They provide a vast array of services to the community and frequently are held accountable for their successes and failures. As such, their mission and goals are constantly evolving. Police departments are open systems that constantly strive to meet the needs of the community. By examining the police from a historical perspective we can gain a better understanding of why they currently operate the way they do. Historically, the police have progressed through the political, professional, and community relations eras. Today, most police departments are using a community policing model, which is an attempt to better respond to crime and disorder and to create better relations with the community, especially disenfranchised groups. Community policing from an administrative perspective is addressed in more detail in Chapter 3.

Study Questions

1. How are service organizations such as police departments different from manufacturing organizations?

2. Discuss three ways in which the institution of police is unique in American society.

3. What is the distinction between line and staff personnel?

4. Identify the various administrative functions or responsibilities in Gulick's acronym.

5. What are the differences between administration, management, and organization?

6. Describe the two managerial orientations as they apply to administrators, managers, and supervisors.

7. What are the differences between the terms mission, role, and goal? What are the mission, roles, and goals of policing?

8. What are the historical phases through which police have progressed since the turn of the twentieth century?

9. What purposes do goals serve for organizations?

Net Resources

http://www.lib.jjay.cuny.edu/len/ Homepage for *Law Enforcement News,* a popular law enforcement periodical.

http://www.fbi.gov/publications/leb/leb.htm Homepage for *Law Enforcement Bulletin,* a law enforcement newsletter published by the FBI.

http://www.theiacp.org/ Homepage for International Association of Chiefs of Police, the largest police executive's association in the U.S.

References

Bayley, D. H. (1988). Community policing: A report from the devil's advocate. In J. Greene and S. Mastrofski (eds.), *Community Policing: Rhetoric or Reality.* New York: Praeger.

Bittner, E. (1970). *The Functions of the Police in a Modern Society.* Washington: National Institute of Mental Health.

Block, C., and Block, R. (1993). *Street Gang Crime in Chicago.* Research in Brief. Washington National Institute of Justice.

Cordner, G. (1980). Police patrol research and its utilization. *Police Studies* 2(4):12–21.

Daft, R. (1986). *Organization Theory and Design.* St. Paul: West Publishing.

Douthit, N. (1975). Enforcement and nonenforcement roles in policing: A historical inquiry. *Journal of Police Science and Administration* 3(3):336–345.

Downs, A. (1967). *Inside Bureaucracy.* Boston: Little, Brown.

Etzioni, A. (1964). *Modern Organizations.* Englewood Cliffs, NJ: Prentice-Hall.

Federal Bureau of Investigation (1971). *Uniform Crime Reports.* Washington: Government Printing Office.

Fogelson, R. (1977). *Big City Police.* Cambridge, MA: Harvard University Press.

Fosdick, R. B. (1969). *American Police Systems,* reprint ed. Montclair, NJ: Patterson Smith.

Goldstein, H. (1977). *Policing a Free Society.* Cambridge, MA: Ballinger.

Goldstein, H. (1993). *The New Policing: Confronting Complexity.* Research in Brief. Washington National Institute of Justice.

Greene, J. R., Bergman, W. T., and McLaughlin, E. J. (1994). Implementing community policing: Cultural and structural change in police organizations. In D. Rosenbaum (ed.), *The Challenge of Community Policing: Testing the Promises.* Thousand Oaks, CA: Sage.

Gulick, L. (1937). Notes on the theory of organization. In L. Gulick and L . Urwick (eds.), *Papers on the Science of Administration.* New York: Macmillan.

Hickman, M. J., and Reaves, B. A. (2001). *Local Police Departments.* Washington: Bureau of Justice Statistics.

Hodge, B. J., Anthony, W. P., and Gales, L. M. (1996). *Organization Theory: A Strategic Approach.* Upper Saddle River, NJ: Prentice Hall.

Hoover, L. T. (1992). Police mission: An era of debate. In L. Hoover (ed.), *Police Management: Issues and Perspectives.* Washington Police Executive Research Forum.

Katz, C. M., Webb, V. J., and Schaefer, D. R. (2001). An assessment of the impact of quality-of-life policing on crime and disorder. *Justice Quarterly* 18(4):825–876.

Lane, R. (1967). *Policing the City: Boston, 1822–1885.* Cambridge, MA: Harvard University Press.

Manning, P. K. (1988). Community policing as drama control. In J. Greene and S. Mastrofski (eds.), *Community Policing: Rhetoric or Reality?* New York: Praeger.

Massie, J. L., and Douglas, J. (1981). Managing: A Contemporary Introduction. Englewood Cliffs, NJ: Prentice Hall.

Merton, R. K. (1957). *Social Theory and Social Structure.* New York: Free Press.

Monkkonen, E. H. (1992). History of urban police. In M. Tonry and N. Morris (eds.), *Modern Policing.* Chicago: University of Chicago Press.

Moore, M. (1978). The police: In search of direction. In L. K. Gaines and T. Ricks (eds.), *Managing the Police Organization.* St. Paul: West Publishing.

Moore, M. H., and Stephens, D. W. (1991). *Beyond Command and Control: The Strategic Management of Police Departments.* Washington: Police Executive Research Forum.

National Advisory Commission on Civil Disorders (1968). *Report of the National Advisory Commission on Civil Disorders.* New York: Bantam Books.

National Commission on Law Observance and Enforcement (1931). *Report on the Police.* Washington: NCLOE.

Pate, T., Bowers, R.A., and Parks, R. (1976). *Three Approaches to Criminal Apprehension in Kansas City: An Evaluation Report.* Washington: Police Foundation.

Police Foundation (1981). *The Newark Foot Patrol Experiment.* Washington, DC: Author.

President's Commission on Law Enforcement and Administration of Justice (1967). *Task Force Report: Police.* Washington: Government Printing Office.

Priest, T. B., and Carter, D. B. (2001). Community-oriented policing: Assessing a police saturation operation. In D. Stevens (ed.), *Policing and Community Partnerships.* Upper Saddle River, NJ: Prentice Hall, pp. 111–124.

Rainey, H. G. (1991). *Understanding and Managing Public Organizations.* San Francisco: Jossey-Bass.

Reiss, A. J. (1971). *The Police and the Public.* New Haven: Yale University Press.

Richardson, J. (1974). *Urban Police in the United States.* Port Washington, NY: Kennikat Press.

Robbins, S. P. (1990). *Organization Theory: Structure, Design, and Applications.* Englewood Cliffs, NJ: Prentice Hall.

Sadd, S., and Grinc, R. (1994). Innovative neighborhood oriented policing: An evaluation of community policing programs in eight cities. In D. Rosenbaum (ed.), *The Challenge of Community Policing: Testing the Promises.* Thousand Oaks, CA: Sage.

Skogan, W., and Maxfield, M. (1981). *Coping with Crime: Individual and Neighborhood Reactions.* Beverly Hills, CA: Sage.

Skolnick, J. (1966). *Justice without Trial: Law Enforcement in Democratic Society.* New York: Wiley.

Thompson, V. A. (1961). *Modern Organization.* New York: Knopf.

Trojanowicz, R. (1982). *An Evaluation of the Neighborhood Foot Patrol Program in Flint, Michigan.* East Lansing: Michigan State University.

Walker, S. (1993). Does anyone remember team policing? Lessons of the team policing experience for community policing. *American Journal of Police* 12(1):57–74.

Weisel, D. L. (1990). *Tackling Drug Problems in Public Housing: A Guide for Police.* Washington Police Executive Research Forum.

Weisel, D. L., and Eck, J. E. (1994). Toward a practical approach to organizational change: Community policing initiatives in six cities. In D. Rosenbaum (ed.), *The Challenge of Community Policing: Testing the Promises.* Thousand Oaks, CA: Sage.

Westley, W. A. (1970). *Violence and the Police: A Sociological Study of Law, Custom, and Morality.* Cambridge, MA: MIT Press.

Whitehouse, J. E. (1973). Historical perspectives on the police community service function. *Journal of Police Science and Administration* 1(1):336–345.

Wilson, J. Q. (1968). *Varieties of Police Behavior: The Management of Law and Order in Eight Communities.* New York: Atheneum.

Wilson, J. Q., and Kelling, G. (1982). Making neighborhoods safe. *Atlantic Monthly* 29 (March):29–38.

2

The Environment of Administration

Andrew Lichtenstein/The Image Works

Chapter Outline

Learning Objectives

After reading this chapter, you should be able to

1. Understand the meaning and implication of cultural diversity within the context of policing.
2. Know what racial profiling is and its implications for policing.
3. Distinguish why a police department must be an open system and respond to its environment.

4. Understand the nature of politics and how politics affects the police organization.

5. Identify a community's power structure and its implications for the police manager.

6. Evaluate the relationship between the police and community, and understand the barriers to developing better relationships.

7. Discuss the attitudes that different groups have toward the police and how those attitudes are shaped.

8. Discuss the role of the media in police administration and how the police executive can develop better relations with the media.

The Louisville, Kentucky, Police Department has approximately 700 police officers and serves a population of approximately 400,000. As with many large departments, the police operate out of five different district stations. Each of the district stations is commanded by a captain, a rank protected by civil service. A former chief in that city once commented that he had considered making the district station commanders majors. When asked why, he replied that it would reduce the number of problems he had with the district commanders. He noted that the department had a limited number of captain's positions and therefore transfer was not an option when the captains did not perform well. If the district commanders were majors, he could reduce their rank and would have more control over their behavior. His most significant problem was the district captains going to their council members and complaining about the administration of the department.

The former chief noted that several captains had the same philosophy: "Nothing good can happen to me until something bad happens to you." This essentially meant that some of the captains believed that their opportunities for advancement were enhanced when there was a new chief. They were essentially correct because in many departments, a new chief usually appoints a new command staff (assistant chiefs and majors). Thus, in Louisville, the chief was constantly fighting fires—some started by captains.

This example shows how internal politics can become a reality for the police chief. There are all sorts of environmental factors that a chief must consider, and politics, internal and external, are just one of those factors. This example provides some insights into this process. The environment of police administration is addressed in this chapter.

INTRODUCTION

A police organization does not exist in a vacuum. It is an interdependent institution of society, which affects and is affected by other institutions within the social, political, and economic environment. For our purposes, the *environment* of police administration is the group of social, cultural, and physical conditions that surround and affect the nature of the police agency. The pressures produced by the environment dictate most of the activities performed by the police organization, and to some extent, as police officers carry out their police responsibilities, they change or have an impact on the environment. This chapter examines the environment of police administration for the purpose of assisting administrators to effectively cope with the environment in which they must work.

ORGANIZATIONAL ENVIRONMENTS

The police organization exists—as all organizations do—in a complex environment that encompasses a number of dimensions. Specific characteristics or conditions within an environment vary from one locale to another, and each condition has consequences for overall governmental administration as well as for police administration.

The Environment of Government

Rainey (1991) identified seven environmental conditions that affect the structure and nature of government: technological, legal, political, economic, demographic, ecological, and cultural. We will consider each in this section.

Technological Conditions

A jurisdiction's technological complexity influences citizen's quality of life and, subsequently, the expectations and demands placed on law enforcement. More advanced societies generally make greater demands and tend to hold their police accountable for what they are able to accomplish. Technology contributes to the economy and citizens' standard of living. American society continues to become more technical in nature.

Some cities are more technologically advanced than others. For example, cities in California's "silicon valley" have a large number of computer-related industries. These technical firms have a substantial impact on the community and the police. First, the high employment and highly paid jobs result in a substantial tax base, and cities generally are able to fund many more services relative to other cities that do not have an equivalent tax base. More money in a community also results in more order and less crime. Second, these types of firms attract a large number of highly educated employees, who come to have greater and different expectations of their police.

Legal Conditions

Legal conditions refer to the attitudes of the legislature, courts, and local governing bodies with respect to how the police enforce the law. There is substantial variability in legal limitations and expectations across jurisdictions. Some communities have laws and ordinances that provide for more control over citizen behavior. For example, fire codes, building codes, and zoning serve to structure a community. A well-thought-out system of codes and ordinances often results in more order in a community. It also allows the police to use civil codes to deal with some crime problems. For example, the police in Oakland, California, attacked drug houses by enforcing building codes (Greene, 1996).

Political Conditions

Politics exist in every police jurisdiction. The nature of these politics influences the police department. The degree of liberalism or conservatism, degree of community homogeneity, political stability, and overall government effectiveness interact with and affect how well the police provide law enforcement services. Some cities are governed by city councils that are very political. That is, council members are more easily influenced by citizens and community groups relative to other jurisdictions. When this occurs, politicians and citizens are able to influence when and how the police enforce the law or how they provide services. When this occurs the common good is subjugated by the interests of a few. A community's political structure should strive to provide equitable services to all citizens regardless of race, sex, ethnicity, religion, sexual orientation, or financial status.

Economic Conditions

A number of factors determine a community's economy, but generally the nature and structure of business and industry in the community or near-by communities are the primary determining factors. A community's economic viability largely determines its police department's available resources. Departments in communities with a strong economic base usually have better equipment and salaries than departments with weaker economies. They have more resources to implement more programs and confront a variety of problems that may occur.

Demographic Conditions

The age, race, sex, and religious characteristics for a community substantially influence law enforcement. Various population groups make different demands on the police, and the police must be organized to satisfy these differential requests and expectations. The aftermath of the destruction of the World Trade Center in New York City on September 11, 2001, is perhaps the best example of the implications of demographics on the police. Many communities with large Arab or Muslim populations saw a drastic increase in tension as a result of the disaster. In some cases, the Federal Bureau of Investigation asked local law enforcement to assist in profiling and interrogating Arab and Muslim suspects. This exacerbated the situation. Moreover, hate crimes committed against a variety of groups occur rather frequently in this country. Approximately 50,000 hate crimes are committed in the United States each year (Southern Poverty Law Center, 2001).

Ecological Conditions

Ecological conditions relate to a jurisdiction's location, natural resources, climate, and other geographical characteristics. Ecological conditions have a direct impact on a jurisdiction's technological and economic conditions. Ecological conditions affect tourism. Cities with warmer climates and beaches have large tourism industries that seasonally affect the demand for police services. Some communities are restricted geographically by rivers, mountains, or other physical barriers that result in a denser population for the community. Communities with dense populations often have increased problems with crime and disorder. Finally, large bodies of water such as rivers, lakes, and oceans facilitate the transportation of goods, which affect the community's economy.

Cultural Conditions

Values, beliefs, and social customs influence an individual's propensity to commit crime, support the police, and contribute to the development of a productive society. For example, many southern communities have very different expectations of their police than citizens in midwestern or northeastern cities. Some communities are less tolerant of vice activities, which often results in pressure on the police to more actively enforce vice laws.

As cultural diversity increases, the task of law enforcement becomes more complex. One cultural group may be tolerant of certain behaviors, while another group finds the same behavior to be morally wrong. This often leads to conflict and disorder in the community. In many cases, the police must mediate the differences among various cultural groups.

Reactions to the Environment

Two theories attempt to explain how organizations react to their environment or mediate the foregoing conditions. The first is the *theory of uncertainty and dependence* (Stoner and Freeman, 1992). Organizations face the problem of *uncertainty* when they lack information about the environment. The seven environmental conditions mentioned above are always changing, which forces the organization to continually react in an attempt to maintain a balance between organizational outcomes and environmental expectations. As uncertainty increases, the alignment between the organization and the environment becomes more tenuous. *Dependence*, on the other hand, refers to organizations' dependence on the environment for resources, information, and support. Citizens support their police when they are satisfied with a police department's performance. Support generally equates to greater resources through the political process. Uncertainty and dependence tie a police department to its community and force it to deal with various environmental conditions.

Aldrich and Mindlin (1978) note that organizations react to their environments through a process of natural selection. This *theory of natural selection* is rooted in biology and basically states that organizations react to their environments, some more efficiently than others. Those that do a poor job of meeting the environment's demands ultimately are eliminated or forced to change. For example, businesses that make bad decisions sustain losses; if the number of bad decisions and losses is substantial, the business fails. If a police administrator makes enough bad decisions, the department loses support and the chief is likely to be replaced. Most police chiefs are very familiar with the idea of natural selection, and they labor to maintain solid relations with as many elements in the community as they possibly can.

On the Job

GALLATIN, TENNESSEE POLICE DEPARTMENT
By Chief Walter Tangel

Courtesy of Chief Tangel

The Gallatin Police Department is a small department consisting of 70 sworn and civilian employees serving a population of about 25,000. As chief, I face many of the same difficulties in working with the community as chiefs in larger cities; yet, there are two primary differences. Large-agency chiefs have staffs to assist them in working with the community, while as a small-town chief many duties fall directly on my shoulders. Second, problems involving police in smaller communities tend to resonate more, and have a greater impact on citizens' attitudes toward the police. I am always scrutinized by large numbers of citizens in the city. Thus, I must be ever mindful about what is going on in the community. I must diligently manage the department's relations with the community.

In the "information age," I have found that the most important point of contact with the community is the media. In a city such as Gallatin, we interact primarily with local and regional media outlets; however on occasion, local stories are picked up by national outlets. The local media includes a newspaper and a radio station. They cover many issues and events not of primary interest to the regional media. The regional media include television stations and newspapers from Nashville. I have managed media relations by being honest and forthright. These efforts result in a greater level of trust and, in the end, the department is treated more positively and is able to deliver its message. Frequently, I give interviews about cases and new programs in the department which are of particular interest locally. I also have a monthly radio show that deals with traffic safety and justice issues. A number of citizens listen to the show and respond to it positively.

I work hard to develop and maintain good relationships with the myriad of organizations that reflect the diverse nature of the Gallatin community. I recently ended a three-year term on the Board of Directors for the Gallatin Chamber of Commerce. I am active in Scouting, serving as the District Committee finance chairman and as a Boy Scout Troop assistant scoutmaster. The Gallatin Police Department sponsors an Explorer Post. Additionally, I serve as

Continued

the vice president of the Gallatin Rotary club. My wife and children are also active in a variety of community organizations. Being active in these organizations gives me the opportunity to meet and talk with people in the community, which provides valuable insight about citizen issues and problems. These activities build the community support necessary to leverage appropriate resources for police mission and goal accomplishment.

Minority relations are an issue in every community, and Gallatin is no different. The department has made a concerted effort to ensure we respond to the minority community's needs. In our hiring process, we investigate and question candidates about their ability to work in a diverse environment. We continually work toward building a department that is reflective of this diversity. We instituted a policy that prohibits racial profiling and we monitor arrest and citation statistics to ensure fairness in delivering police service. The agency maintains an ongoing dialogue with the local chapter of the NAACP. The police department supports a faith-based group sponsored by local ministers called the Shalom Zone, which works toward bringing peace and justice specifically to the black community and the city of Gallatin. These relationships provide positive communication links that permit all parties to discuss and work out issues and concerns before they become crises.

A challenging part of my job is working with the mayor and city council. Police departments are often the largest and most visible department in city governments. Generally, elected officials have specific ideas about how a police department should operate. They are sincere and really want to add to the quality of life in the community; however, sometimes they are not familiar with legal restrictions placed on police by state and federal statutes. This necessitates that I work closely with the mayor and council so they are fully aware of what the department is doing and its legal and ethical obligations.

In summary, being a small city chief is a challenge and an adventure that entails a lot of work. I spend a great deal of time working with the community, and it has its rewards. It is indeed a positive experience to be a police chief in a community where you have good relations with its citizenry.

These theories demonstrate that a police department is unquestionably linked to its environment. The variety and constant change of conditions force the department to adjust in an effort to maintain some level of equilibrium with the environment. If equilibrium is maintained, the department should be in a better strategic position to thrive as an organization and to meet its environmental challenges. In a broad sense, cultural diversity is the overarching factor that determines a substantial amount of police activities. Cultural diversity is also important from the perspective that the police must understand it and be able to mediate problems as a result of it.

CULTURAL DIVERSITY:
UNDERSTANDING THE ENVIRONMENT

Perhaps the most important condition influencing a police organization as it interacts with its environment is cultural diversity. *Cultural diversity* refers to the number and population of various cultural and ethnic groups which reside in a community. Although our society consists of diverse cultures, every culture shares or has overlapping values and beliefs with other cultures and larger society. Some of the general cultures within the United States are Native American, European, Asian, Hispanic, and African-American. There are even distinct subcultures within the general categories. For example, Chinese, Koreans, Laotians, and Thais are all Asian, but they often maintain their own cultural distinctiveness.

Cultures exist throughout the United States. They have their roots in a number of variables; including race, religion, ethnicity, region of state and country where an individual might reside, and nationality. The majority subculture in the United States is West European, but other cultural groups are growing at a much faster rate. It is predicted that, midway through the 21st century, white Americans will no longer be the majority in the United States. Indeed, in California white Americans now constitute less than 50 percent of the state's population. For the past 200 years, the United States has been the great melting pot, with immigrants from every other country in the world. Even though most people subscribe to an "American way of life," there remain numerous differences, and sometimes the American way of life is not easy to define.

It would be incorrect to say that every culture has been totally integrated into our society. Indeed, there remain vast social, political, and economic differences among many of the subcultures that exist in our society. Even though we do not have a caste system to determine standing in our society, our society is highly stratified. Cultural groups have had varying experiences in integrating into mainstream society and participating in our economic system. Consequently, some cultures are more represented in the higher strata of the economic system, while others have greater representation in the lower strata. These substantial differences have created conflict and competition among various cultures. When competition and conflict heighten, the police are met with a number of problems. Since the police are the primary form of social control in our society, disadvantaged cultures often view the police as an arm of the dominant class with the primary function of repressing the disadvantaged culture.

Historically, the police have been highly resistant to the idea of cultural diversity. There are several reasons for this resistance (Gould, 1997). First, the police view themselves and are viewed by the larger public as guardians of the status quo, or dominant culture. When cultural groups challenge the norms of the dominant class, they come into conflict with larger society and quite possibly the police. Second, the police by their nature are conservative and do not always view cultural diversity issues as problems or impediments to justice. Finally, the professionalization of the police has led the police to adhere to a legalistic philosophy or mode of operation. Here officers see the violation of law as the only determinant to take action. Mitigating circumstances are often disregarded. "Soft" issues such as cultural diversity do not fit within the average police officer's equation of how law enforcement works.

Police departments today are attempting to resolve conflicts with cultures through community policing. *Community policing* is a philosophical and organizational effort on the part of police departments to provide productive police services to every segment of a community. It recognizes that differences do exist across neighborhoods and communities and that these differences should be discerned and addressed. Such efforts are best reflected in police value statements which many police departments are adopting as guideposts for police behavior and departmental achievement. Carter and Radelet (1999:50) have identified value statements that are common to many departments. The following apply to dealing with cultural diversity:

1. Protecting constitutional rights and democratic values.
2. Engaging a wide range of police resources to further the ends of crime reduction.
3. Engaging in crime prevention.
4. Developing an understanding of neighborhood crime problems and the corresponding concerns of citizens.
5. Conducting themselves with integrity and honesty.
6. Soliciting citizen input into the police enterprise.
7. Encouraging and developing community partnerships for improving the community.

Such values are relatively easily implemented when viewed as applicable only to the "majority" community. The difficulty comes when the jurisdiction has multiple and diverse communities. The department must ensure that *all* departmental personnel understand that they are responsible for and will be held accountable for applying these values throughout the jurisdiction in every decision made and action taken.

Before the implementation of community policing, most police agencies viewed the handling of crime and disorder as their primary objective. There was little recognition that problems and needs varied from one neighborhood to another. The police tended to develop one strategy and apply it across every neighborhood and community in the jurisdiction. As a result, many cultural areas received inadequate service. This has been particularly true in many lower-class neighborhoods, where the primary criticism of the police is inadequate enforcement of the law (Gaines, Kappeler, and Vaughn, 1999; Jaccob, 1971; Walker, 1992). The preceeding value statements imply that the police have a responsibility to every cultural group and neighborhood within their jurisdiction. The police must attempt to discover problems and implement solutions. Police actions in a neighborhood should be contingent on needs. This micro approach to providing police services ensures that the police are able to deal with individual neighborhoods. When every community receives an adequate level of service, the department is better able to maintain equilibrium with the community.

RACIAL PROFILING OR BIASED POLICING

Perhaps the most controversial issue facing police administrators in the area of cultural diversity and citizen satisfaction with the police is the charge that many police departments are engaging in racial profiling. *Racial profiling* is "any police-initiated action that relies on the race, ethnicity, or national origin rather than the behavior of an individual or information that leads police to a particular individual who has been identified as being, or having been, engaged in criminal behavior" (Ramirez, McDevitt, and Farrell, 2000). Many minority drivers believe that when the police stop and search their vehicles at a rate that surpasses reasonable expectations, their rights to privacy have been invaded. Minorities appear to be targeted at a higher rate by some police departments, as evidenced by the disproportionate number of traffic citations issued to them. The issue has received substantial media coverage and is the source of increasing litigation. Many civil rights and minority groups have been protesting police racial profiling practices.

The United States Supreme Court in *Whren* v. *United States* (1996) upheld the police use of *pretextual* traffic stops. A pretextual traffic stop occurs when an officer uses the pretext of a minor traffic violation to stop and possibly search a vehicle. Conducting a pretextual traffic stop based solely on a driver's race is not legally permissible. However, if a traffic offense occurs, no matter how minor, then an officer can make a pretextual stop. The police use these stops to search for drugs, weapons, and other contraband. Since minorities are over-represented in pretextual traffic stops, many charge that race often is the sole criterion being used by officers.

It appears that police departments are using pretextual stops to accomplish two goals. First, a number of departments are using them to interdict drugs and to increase revenues as the result of asset forfeiture. Such stops are generally conducted along interstate highways by state police officers and sheriff's deputies. Over the past several years, police departments have come to see asset forfeiture as a significant source of income (Worrall, 2001), and some departments have substantially increased the number of traffic stops for this purpose. In many cases, it is unclear if the department's motive is the war on drugs or a quest for discretionary funding.

The second motivation behind pretextual traffic stops is to conduct directed patrols in high-crime areas. Aggressive, directed patrols are seen as the most promising method of combating crime in crime hot spots or high-crime areas (Sherman et al., 1997). Here, the motivation seems to be the interdiction of drugs, gangs, and firearms. Police officers stop suspicious persons in an effort to make arrests, deter criminal activities, or confiscate contraband such as drugs or weapons. Since high-crime areas often include a disproportionately high number of minorities, minorities are frequently targeted for these pretextual stops. Research indicates that these aggressive, directed patrols have mixed results in deterring crime (McGarrell et al., 2001).

A number of departments have conducted studies examining charges of racial profiling. These include San Jose, San Diego, North Carolina, and New Jersey, but perhaps the most comprehensive study was conducted by the New

Jersey Office of the Attorney General examining the New Jersey State Police (Verniero and Zoubek, 1999). The study found that African-Americans and Hispanics were the subject of a disproportionately higher rate of vehicle searches. Approximately 60 percent of all stops involved white motorists, but African-Americans were the subject of 53.1 percent of the searches and Hispanics were the subject of 24.1 percent of the searches. Of the 2,871 arrests made, 32.5 percent were for whites, 61.7 percent were for African-Americans, and 5.8 percent involved persons of other races. Similarly, a 1992 examination of police stops in Florida revealed that African-Americans and Hispanics represented only 5 percent of drivers on Florida interstate highways, yet they constituted 70 percent of the drivers stopped and 80 percent of those who were searched (Roberts, 1999). These data seem to indicate that not only are minorities stopped and searched more frequently, but they are also at greater risk of facing arrest, especially for minor violations. Skolnick and Caplovitz (2001) note that the police often overidentify people of color as "symbolic assailants" because their actions or dress is nonconforming or they fit officers' perceptions of what criminals look like.

Administrators must take action to control traffic stops and ensure that racial biases are not driving such stops. If administrators do not react to racial profiling, they in essence condone these behaviors and contribute to an eroding public confidence in the police. The New Jersey State Police, as a result of charges of racial profiling, took a number of steps to prevent the problem:

1. Issuing a policy prohibiting racial profiling.
2. Providing officers with in-service training about racial profiling.
3. Issuing training bulletins discussing the issue.
4. Requiring officers to have a reasonable suspicion before asking permission to search, a requirement that exceeds the requirements of state and federal case law.
5. Prohibiting troopers from spotlighting occupants of vehicles at night before deciding whether to stop the vehicle.

Unfortunately, these procedures failed to eliminate the problem. The New Jersey State Police's efforts demonstrate that departments must not only issue policies, but they must also constantly monitor vehicle stops to ensure that racial biases are not exhibited. Administrators must change the culture of the department.

Police discretion lies at the "heart and soul" of this issue. Since the beginning of policing, officers have observed people, places, and activities and investigated those that appeared suspicious. Indeed, such activities are the nexus of police investigative efforts, and no one can question their importance. However, a variety of cues trigger police officers' suspicions. It becomes problematic if the police use race alone or use race as the overriding criterion to determine suspiciousness. Police policies must endeavor to educate police officers to concentrate on other cues, those cues that most likely are more informative about a citizen's character and intentions.

INTERACTION BETWEEN ENVIRONMENT AND ORGANIZATION

Systems theory provides a good understanding of the interaction between the environment and an organization. According to Donnelly, Gibson, and Ivancevich (1995: 529), a *system* is a "collection of objects united by some form of regular interaction and interdependence." System theory defines two categories of system, closed systems and open systems. Each can serve as a philosophical basis for understanding how administration relates to the environment. Table 2–1 compares the characteristics of open and closed systems.

Closed Systems

The term *closed system* connotes a managerial philosophy whereby planning, decision making, and day-to-day operations are conducted without regard to the environment. The values, priorities, and opinions held by people within the organization, and too often by only those at the top, provide the guidance for administration when a closed-system philosophy predominates. The professional model of policing that prevailed in the 1950s supported the adoption of a closed-system perspective to isolate police organizations and officers from political influence and corruption. This approach is believed to have played a major role in setting the scene for conflicts between police and citizens that became conspicuous in the 1960s and 1970s.

Munro (1971) identified two major problems with using a closed-systems model in criminal justice management. First, closed-system managers tend to consider information and input from nonpolice sources to be *at best* useless or inconsequential and at worst dysfunctional. When citizens or other criminal justice, governmental, or social organizations make requests or demands, the closed-system police manager may resist such demands as being out of the domain or not the responsibility of the police department. Such requests are viewed as infringing on the police administrator's "managerial prerogatives." That is, the police believe that a department's agenda should be set by its own administrators, who know what should be done. This perspective results in isolationism, ineffectiveness, and in some cases failure on the part of police departments.

Second, the closed system limits the administrator's ability by focusing on how things have always been done. In the closed-system organization, only current problems, issues, and needs are addressed in planning and decision making. This perspective reduces the police agency's ability to cope with changes in the community. A closed-system approach causes a manager to neglect the desired *end* product and emphasize the *means* of production in a manner that eventually results in organizational stagnation (i.e., the organization loses its ability to be creative, innovate, make changes, or effectively perform its function in society).

There are numerous examples of how a closed system affects policing. A narcotics unit targeting only large drug dealers rather than drug trafficking in

Table 2–1

The Characteristics of a Closed System Compared to Those of an Open System

The Closed Model of Police Organization	The Open Model of Police Organization
1. Centralized decision making providing strict controls against unauthorized use of discretion	1. Decentralized decision making—decisions made at the lowest possible level of the organization
2. Authority based on rank	2. Authority based on position and knowledge rather than rank
3. Accountability achieved through the chain of command	3. Accountability not only through superiors (hierarchically) but through peers (horizontally)
4. Organizational members isolated from society	4. Organizational members and the organization perceived as part of society
5. Coercive compliance systems demanding loyalty and obedience to superiors and the organization	5. Loyalty and responsibility belonging to the organization as a whole
6. Hierarchical structure of organization shaped like a pyramid	6. The organization perceived as a fluidic network structure with permeable walls
7. Labor divided into functional specialties	7. Specialized knowledge possessed by one member of the organization applied to a variety of tasks undertaken by various other members of the organization—tasks are performed by generalists with assistance, if needed, from persons with special expertise in the area of need
8. Standard operating procedures determining proper conduct of activities	8. Policies utilized merely to guide job accomplishment
9. Career routes clearly established with a common entry point and promotion based on impersonal evaluations by superiors	9. Career routes not clearly established: entry point is flexible and promotion is based on ability to perform in the sought position
10. Status among employees directly related to positions (jobs) and ranks	10. "Externalized" prestige—personal status in the organization is determined largely by professional ability and reputation
11. Unity of command—one and only one person in control of a given person or situation—strictly followed	11. Interaction directed toward accomplishment of mission—advice rather than command characterizes superior–subordinate relationships
12. A firmly established impersonal system in which most employees and clients are powerless to initiate changes or stop the system's motion	12. All employees and the public contribute to resolving problems and changing the organization
13. One-way downward communications in the form of orders	13. Horizontal as well as vertical interaction between people within the organization (Cordner, 1978:13).

neighborhoods, or a traffic unit writing traffic citations only where they are easy to write rather than where accidents occur or where there are numerous citizen complaints are prime examples. A closed system does not allow the department to target problems identified by citizens.

Contemporary administrative authorities have come to view the closed-system perspective as inappropriate for the management of police departments. A closed-system philosophy leads to the creation of system boundaries that eliminate the influences from and interaction with the environment. These boundaries place the police agency in a position that is *apart from,* rather than *a part of* its community. Community policing dictates that a police department adopt an open-systems perspective.

Open Systems

Managers adhering to the *open-system* philosophy, on the other hand, view the organization as being involved in dynamic interaction with the environment. This philosophy is based on the perspective that the environment affects the organization; the action of one institution in the environment will, to some degree, affect the actions of other institutions in the environment. Open-systems managers react to changes in the environment and balance the actions of the organization with the environmental situation.

The characteristics of open and closed systems (see Katz and Kahn, 1966; Munro, 1971), which were presented in Table 2–1, are applied to a police organization in Figures 2–1 and 2–2. These figures illustrate the dramatic differences between closed and open models. The closed police organization is "boxed in," as indicated by the solid line surrounding the organization, with no influence directed inward from external sources. It is apparent that all decision making is made on an internal basis and the police organization acts on the community with no sharing of influence between the community and the police organization.

The open police organization differs from the closed organization on several levels. First, the open system provides for *continuous exchanges* between the police agency and its environment. It creates a dynamic situation where actions

Figure 2–1

Closed police organization (arrows indicate the direction of influence).

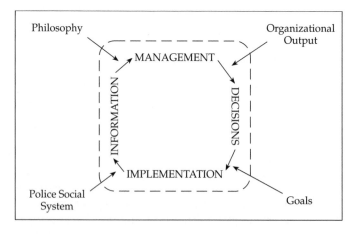

Figure 2–2
Open police organization.

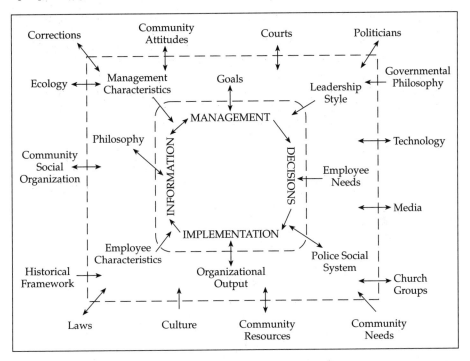

external to the organization influence the police, and, simultaneously, the police recognize how their programs and actions affect the environment. Klinger (1997) discusses the importance of the environment as a determinant of police behavior. The environment influences not only the organization, but individual members as well. Second, the open system recognizes that *energy is imported* into the department from the community and surrounding environment. This imported energy consists of financial resources, public support, and information from a variety of sources including governmental, political, and social agencies as well as individuals being served within the environment. There are numerous types of energy, all of which are necessary to successful policing. Third, this energy is *consumed by the organization and converted into output*. Output includes services provided, arrests of offenders, regulation of traffic, and other such services.

The *conversion process* through which energy is converted to outputs includes planning, decision making, and the implementation of plans and decisions. The result of the conversion process is determined by summing the effects of management and organization within the police department. Fourth, open systems attempt to maintain a *dynamic homeostasis*, or equilibrium with the environment. To do this, the organization must remain abreast of environmental conditions and adapt to them. Finally, as open systems become larger, they must *specialize*. Specialization is the division of tasks among various work groups in a department for the purpose of improving organizational efficiency.

In summary, an open-systems-oriented police department is integrally tied to the community and environment. It attempts to tailor its operations and services to community conditions and needs. A number of agencies are currently adopting community policing. Community policing is excellent example of open-systems policing in that it emphasizes involving the community in solving community problems.

POLICE AND POLITICAL/GOVERNMENTAL INTERACTION

The key to understanding how the American government affects police administration is understanding the constitutional principles of separation of powers and federalism. *Separation of powers* refers to the fact that in our form of government the act of governing is divided into three constitutionally defined branches: legislative, executive, and judicial. The police belong to the executive branch, which is responsible for carrying out or enforcing legislation enacted by the legislative branch of government. The judicial branch scrutinizes the policies, procedures, and actions of the executive branch and the laws enacted by the legislative branch. The judicial branch is responsible for interpreting the Constitution.

Federalism is the division of political power among the federal, state, and local governments. The Tenth Amendment to the Constitution established the principle of federalism by enumerating the powers of the federal government and stating that all *remaining* powers are reserved for the states. The states through state constitutions and laws in turn reserved certain powers for local units of government. This three-tiered form of government provides checks and balances whereby the needs of municipal, county, state, and federal governments are constantly weighed and remain in balance. Therefore, checks and balances occur horizontally between the branches of each government at each of the levels of government. The implication for a police administrator can be overwhelming. A municipal police department must follow the laws and mandates of three legislative bodies—the city council, the state legislature, and the United States Congress, the executive mandates or policies that are promulgated at all three levels, and judicial decisions at all three levels.

Most police agencies—approximately 18,500—are at the local level (Reaves, 1998). A serious threat to the longevity of the police administrator comes into play when the administrator fails to understand the political realities of the functioning of government within his or her governmental sphere.

There is much diversity in the manner in which these forms of city government are carried out in reality. One of the most important jobs police administrators can undertake is to carefully observe the manner in which their government functions and to develop strategies for meeting community needs while playing within the rules of power and authority that operate within the jurisdiction. When there are multiple executives in municipal government—a mayor, city manager, and police commissioner, for example—the relationships can be complex. It may be difficult to determine to whom the chief of police "really" reports. Communication is the critical factor in establishing clear guidelines for performance and accountability. The better the chief's relationship with each of these players, the more likely the chief is to understand his or her position relative to these executives and to have a longer tenure as chief.

The government is the direct link between the citizenry and the police and frequently serves as a conduit for sending information, requests, and feedback to the police from the public. The municipal police administrator is directly responsible to the mayor, city manager, and/or council, since they determine the police department's budget and can mandate changes through the budgetary process and through political persuasion. The mayor and council are held accountable by the public through the election process for their actions, as well as the actions of the city manager and personnel in the various governmental units, including the police. Elected officials often intervene in police affairs as part of their accountability to the public. Police chiefs often resent these intrusions; however, they must expect and accept such intrusions as a political reality of life.

O'Brien (1978) identified three types of municipal executives who, through intrusion or lack of direction, create problems for the police administrator: misfeasors, nonfeasors, and malfeasors. The *misfeasor* exerts a great deal of effort to become involved and get things going. Frequently these executives are fearful of being accused of not doing anything, and to compensate for these misgivings they become overly involved and frequently usurp the chief's authority. The second type, *nonfeasor,* is almost the opposite of the misfeasor. These executives frequently abdicate their authority, choosing to do little or nothing to avoid upsetting community leaders. They provide little guidance or support to the police manager, and when there is guidance it often conflicts with other policies or is incoherent with regard to other policies. Finally, the *malfeasor* promotes corrupt practices or allows them to exist within government. Examples vary from selection and promotion of officers based on political patronage to pressure on the police regarding whom to arrest and whom not to arrest. The actions of this municipal executive can injure all aspects of police management. When the malfeasor controls government, the chief is placed in a tenuous position.

Not all municipal executives fit one of the three types. Most police managers are able to work cooperatively with their municipal executives. Nevertheless, the task of interacting with government is not an easy one even when the municipal executive is very cooperative, because the police managers' task is complicated by the size and complexity of government. Officials who have a direct influence on the police executive include the mayor, the city manager, city council members, officials from various administrative offices in city government such as human resources or finance, and potentially the representatives from a civil service commission. The larger the city, the more decentralized power and authority tend to be, thereby increasing the number of participants in the decision-making process. This complicates the police manager's task by making cooperation and coordination more difficult and necessitating the development of coalitions.

Along these lines, Mastrofski (1988) studied the relationship between police executives and municipal executives. He found that three distinct relationships existed. First, there was the *team approach*, where the police executive and government executive form an active partnership and collaborate in much of the police decision and policy making. Second, the *professional autonomy approach*, where the police executive has virtual autonomy over police policy formulation. Budget issues tend to be the only issues where police and government executives negotiate. Finally, in the *political activist approach*, governmental executives tend to perceive themselves as the primary law enforcement executive and generally dictate policy to the police chief. In these departments, the police chief serves more as an administrative assistant than an actual chief executive. This approach is most prevalent in smaller agencies, whereas police executives in larger agencies tend to have more autonomy.

The Police Executive and the Political Environment

The problems police executives experience with the political process are evidenced by their attrition rate. The average police chief has held the position for approximately 5.5 years (Enter, 1986; Tunnell and Gaines, 1996; Witham, 1985). Tunnell and Gaines investigated the reasons police chiefs left their departments. The reasons and frequency of occurrence are found in Table 2–2. Retirement after successful service as chief accounted for only 17.7 percent of the chiefs' attrition. A substantial number of the chiefs left or were forced to leave their positions as a result of political intrusion or pressures.

Tunnell and Gaines (1996) further investigated the sources and types of political pressures brought to bear on police executives, as summarized in Table 2–3. Mayors and city council members exerted about the same levels of pressure across the board. The greatest pressures came in the areas of arresting offenders and enforcing specific laws (e.g., responding to a specific traffic problem or arresting an

Table 2–2

Reasons Given for Predecessor Chiefs' Departure from the Department

Reason	Number	Person
Personal reasons	30	26.5
Retired after successful service	20	17.7
Terminated by the government	20	17.7
Resigned due to political pressure	19	16.8
Retired due to political pressure	11	9.7
Demoted within the department	10	8.8
Died	3	2.7

Table 2–3

Police Chief Self-Reporting on Type and Location of Political Pressure (Percent)

Source	Personnel Decisions	Promotion Decisions	Personnel Assignments	Arrest and Enforcement	Special Services
Mayor	21.0	15.8	23.0	28.0	27.0
City council	21.6	16.5	17.1	29.0	29.1
Business leaders	10.0	0	6.3	6.3	12.6

individual from an influential family causing a problem) and providing special services (e.g., traffic control at a construction site or special event). In most cases, political officials have a legitimate interest in these types of decisions as long as they are not acts of malfeasance. However, intervention into selection, promotion, and personnel assignment decisions infringe on the chief's discretion and should be outside the purview of politicians (Andrews, 1985; Murphy, 1985).

It should be recognized that government officials will always oversee, to some degree, what the police will do. Many political candidates have gained office by promising the public that crime or traffic congestion will be reduced. These politicians, once elected, have an obligation to fulfill their promises and, in so doing, make great demands on the police. Attempting to satisfy these demands is a police responsibility that must be recognized by the police administrator. If the demands are not satisfied, there may be dire consequences for the administrator and the police department in the form of personnel actions or adverse budget recommendations. Governmental executives have a limited right to formulate police goals, but the police administrator must maintain control over how to best achieve those goals.

There are also instances where personnel within the department may attempt to push their own programs or obtain resources, personnel, or promotions by communicating directly with city officials, thereby circumventing the administrator's authority. For example, commanders of particular units may attempt to influence political and government officials to have additional personnel assigned to their units or to give them additional powers and authority within the department. Police union officials frequently attempt to affect policy by working around the chief and communicating with governmental executives. Once an administrator's authority has been circumvented, it is extremely difficult to regain control of the organization.

The position of the police chief is rather tenuous due to the unsure and ever-changing relationship with city hall. Patrick Murphy (1985), a past president of the Police Foundation and commissioner of the New York City Police Department, suggests that chiefs should negotiate the extent of their authority and responsibilities with government heads. Murphy notes that areas such as personnel matters are nonnegotiable and should be controlled by the chief. Other matters such as media relations and police priorities are negotiable since city administrators have an interest in their effective performance. It is vital that the relationship between the police chief and city administrators be clear. The stability and success of the government and the police organization are threatened by the extent to which the chief's relationship with city administration is unclear. As Andrews notes, "Without clear bounds of legally established authority, clear day-to-day relationships cannot be established, and consequently much personal and organizational energy must be expended on each issue or event as it develops to define power and the working relationships" (1985:7).

The police executive can develop and nurture good working relationships with government executives through cooperativeness and open communications. The police chief must meet frequently with city officials to keep them abreast of current police activities and to learn about their concerns regarding police operations. With close communications and working relationships, police administrators may be able to forestall unreasonable demands by city officials and be in a better position to negotiate on behalf of the police agency.

It is evident the police chief's role includes "political" activities. The chief must constantly attempt to gain the support of the mayor, city council, and community groups so that resources may be obtained for the department and its programs. These efforts are political in the sense that they involve the use of a variety of methods, maneuvers, or strategies designed to enhance trust relationships and achieve power or control. To carry out such political efforts, the chief must be a diplomat who is articulate, skilled in interpersonal relations, competent, and has foresight and unselfish devotion to the interests of the department and the community. Such political activities must be nonpartisan in nature. In fact, the police chief must make every attempt to isolate the department and its personnel from partisan politics. The use of the department and its personnel for a political party or an individual's gain ultimately will completely undermine the department's operating effectiveness.

The Community Power Structure and the Police

The community exerts a variety of influences on its police department. To a large extent the community decides police goals via the political process. A police executive must thoroughly understand the community, its problems, and its needs, and must respond appropriately to them if the department is to be effective. If the citizens of a jurisdiction come to believe that their police department is ineffective or that it does not respond to community needs, they may exert political pressure to bring about desired changes. The police executive and the department must remain abreast of community concerns and problems.

There are a number of sources of influence on the police in every community. *Community power* is defined as the politics, decision making, and other processes that determine community direction. A community's power structure is dependent on a number of variables: industrial makeup, age, national region, growth characteristics, size, density, temporal dimensions, and government structure. These variables interact and contribute to a community's power structure. In an attempt to explain the interactions and contributions of the variables to the community's power structure, Gilbert (1967:373–374) identified four types of power within a given community:

1. The *party organization* involves political party structures, councils, departments, elected and appointed officials, government employees, and experts.
2. *Parapolitical organizations* include businesses, newspapers, and religious, educational, voluntary and formal organizations, and all of their leaders.
3. *Informal organizations* include ad hoc groups formed around particular issues, and their leaders.
4. The *population of the city* in terms of masses, minorities, economic classes, publics, and voters.

Each of these sources of community power has a direct impact on the police. The party organization was discussed in the previous section on police and political/governmental interaction. The remaining dimensions of community power represent forces that are constantly competing for control of the party organization. Leaders of parapolitical organizations, or ruling elites, are the primary power merchants in a city. Business leaders frequently exert pressure to increase the police role in protecting their businesses from street crime. Certain religious groups frequently call for police crackdowns on prostitution, pornography, and other vice activities. Special interest and informal organizations such as civil rights and neighborhood groups united by a common cause periodically pressure the party organization and police. The final dimension, the population, comes to expect certain services from the party organization and the police. The nature of these pressures depends on the demographic, sociological, and economic makeup of the population. Cities develop over time and in doing so, develop particular perspectives regarding government and the police.

A number of factors affect the degree of influence individuals and groups have in a political entity. One factor is size of the community. Mayhew (1973) points out that as jurisdictions become larger, the relative power of members from the ruling elite decreases. The power of an individual or group external to the party organization is obscured due to the number of people in the community. As jurisdictions and governments become larger, they become less responsive to the needs of interest groups and, possibly, the people. This is because there are so many demands placed on government. This is also true for police departments. In researching the effects of police agency size on services, Ostrom, Parks, and Whitaker (1978) found that smaller police departments appeared to be less bureaucratic and more responsive to the public compared to larger departments.

In some cases, governments take a more pluralistic view as the community becomes larger. *Pluralism* involves taking more than one idea, concept, principle, or element into account. Since power is widespread, decision makers often attempt to satisfy the greatest number of power holders within the power structure. When this occurs, it becomes increasingly difficult to respond to a small group without alienating large blocks of voters. The pluralist-oriented government places greater demands on the police in terms of the number and variety of services the department is expected to provide. There are pressures for particular police performance in every community. The specific direction of these pressures depends on the configuration of the community's political environment.

In examining the relationship between the police and their environment, Wilson (1972) found police departments were "keenly sensitive" to their political environment, although they generally were not governed by the political environment. That is, the police paid attention to particular elements within the community when formulating policy, but they did not allow the political process to control the policy formulation. The police allowed the political process to only partially alter policy.

BARRIERS TO A POLICE–COMMUNITY PARTNERSHIP

The police in order to be effective must forge a partnership with the community. As previously noted, this partnership results in numerous benefits to both the police and the public. Since the police are charged with serving and protecting the public, working closely with citizens is important for the police. Sometimes a police department cannot easily develop an alliance with its citizens. Historically, police departments have had poor relations with minority segments of communities. In other examples, departments have been alienated from a majority of their citizens. For a department to have negative relations with large segments of its community, a significant event must have occurred such as the Rodney King incident in Los Angeles, or the department must have failed to respond to citizen needs and tended to treat citizens negatively for long periods of time. Carter and Radelet (1999) identified five departmental behaviors that contribute to police problems in the community: excessive force, corruption, rudeness, authoritarianism, and politics. Police administrators must recognize these issues and make efforts to ensure that they are absent from the department.

Excessive Force

Perhaps the best-known example of police use of excessive force was the Rodney King incident. A civilian videocamera captured a number of police officers repeatedly beating Mr. King. The incident resulted in a major riot in Los Angeles and highly publicized civil and criminal trials. The incident touched off a furor that shook the foundation of American society. The media meticulously reported the incident, and the majority of people observing the many televised accounts of the incident immediately started questioning the propriety of their own officers' behavior. Essentially, the event had a ripple effect throughout America.

More important, the event had a profound impact on the Los Angeles Police Department (LAPD). Prior to the incident, the LAPD was recognized as one of the more professional departments in the United States. Its chief, Darryl Gates, had been credited with starting the Drug Abuse Resistance Education (DARE) program that had been implemented in many of the nation's schools.

Presidents Reagan and Bush had recognized the department for its efforts to deal with the drug problem. Many innovative programs in the area of police training, tactics, and community relations had started in the LAPD. In the end, however, Chief Gates was forced to retire, and the department was disgraced.

Although the LAPD was outwardly professional, it was later determined that the department suffered a number of problems relating to brutality and racism. The Christopher Commission was appointed to study the department in the aftermath of the riots. The commission examined the department's mobile data terminal system (MDTS) and found numerous incidents of police officers using racial slurs and comments about how they routinely used excessive force when dealing with citizens. The commission determined that the problem was fairly widespread throughout the department. The commission also found that LAPD administrators essentially refused to deal with the problems.

Charges of excessive force for most departments are not commonplace, but nonetheless, in the aggregate, there are substantial numbers of cases of police use of excessive force. Not all cases are of the magnitude of the King case, but each has the potential of significantly stigmatizing police officers and police departments. Police–community relations can be severely damaged with only one brutality incident. Minor cases of excessive force by police officers can become major public relations problems.

Police Corruption

There are numerous forms of police corruption. They range from taking small gifts or payments from business people to the protection and involvement in criminal activities. America's drug problem has contributed notably to the corruption problem. The illegal drug industry is so widespread and embodies such vast amounts of money that police are afforded numerous opportunities to engage in corrupt activities. Drugs have been related to a precipitous increase in police corruption. (Kappeler, Sluder, and Alpert, 1994).

Two important dimensions associated with corruption must be mentioned. First, corruption that is uncovered in one city will affect citizens' attitudes in other cities. People tend to generalize about the police and evaluate them based on information that is usually provided by the popular media. Second, the severity of the corruption case has little bearing on the magnitude of the public relations backlash. Corruption, regardless of magnitude, is a violation of trust that cuts to the heart of public morale and feelings of safety and security.

Police scandals undermine the public's confidence in the police. For example, in 2000, the Rampart Division scandal in Los Angeles caused citizens and the courts to question the work of all Los Angeles police officers, and other communities pondered whether their officers were also engaged in planting evidence and lying in court. If the police are dishonest, who will protect the citizens? Our democratic form of government dictates that the citizens abdicate sole responsibility for enforcing the law and dealing with criminals to the police, and when the trust is abridged, citizens feel powerless and alienated from government and the police.

Rudeness

Perhaps rudeness is the most frequently lodged complaint against the police. It is also the most frequent topic of conversation when citizens complain about the police. Rudeness seems to surface when officers are writing citations or making arrests, interviewing suspects and witnesses, and even during on-the-street encounters when citizens request assistance or directions. Rude behavior can occur in any police–citizen interaction. Persistent rudeness tends to undermine public confidence in the police.

This is not to say that all police officers are rude, or that police officers who tend to be rude are always rude. It is important to understand that rudeness is a matter of perception. Each officer must actively guard against the perception of rudeness. Rudeness has several sources. First, police officers traditionally have been taught to assume a businesslike demeanor when interacting with citizens. Some officers take an extreme approach and as a result are rude or appear to be rude. Although a professional, businesslike demeanor should never result in rudeness, it does have the potential to be misinterpreted as rudeness. Second, rudeness can result when the vast majority of contacts officers have with citizens are negative. Repeated negative contacts with citizens ultimately will take their toll even on well-intentioned officers. Community policing, with its emphasis on positive community contacts, may help ameliorate this problem. Finally, rudeness can be a symptom of stress (either job-related or within the officer's personal life). Police officers are placed in a variety of stressful situations. Ultimately stress will affect the attitude and demeanor of officers if there is no attempt to provide alternative methods to cope with stress. Police management is responsible for ensuring that police treat all citizens with respect.

Authoritarianism

Essentially, police authority, when reduced to an act, is used when police officers take command and control of situations or people by issuing orders or directives. Authoritarianism is an attitude or approach used when exercising authority and is typically seen as negative. According to Kappeler, Sluder, and Alpert (1994), authoritarianism consists of cynicism, aggression, and rigid behavior. Barker and Carter (1991) found that authoritarianism is a dominant trait among police officers. Since police officers tend to become more authoritarian over time, management must attempt to reduce it and its behavioral consequences. Community policing, through more positive police–community contacts, may help reduce the degree of authoritarianism that develops in officers. Authoritarianism and community policing are incompatible. Police authority must be applied assertively within the context of the department's values and goals.

A large measure of the police officer's job is to get people to act in certain ways. For example, officers attempt to control others' behavior when they make an arrest or issue a traffic citation. Even when the citizen contact is positive, the police officer is generally attempting to change the citizen's behavior, as in the case of a crime prevention program or DARE program. Police work is about getting others to do what police officers want them to do. Use of authority is a core component of the police job; however, the attitude with which authority is used must coincide with the rule of law and the service role of policing.

Politics

Politics have long been a part of law enforcement, as noted in Chapter 1. From the earliest times, politicians have attempted to use the police to serve their ends. Internally, political influence has been exerted to control who was hired, promoted, or placed in specialized units such as criminal investigation or narcotics. Externally, politics were used to influence who was arrested or cited and which vice activities were allowed to continue without police interference. Partisan politics almost always leads to some miscreants receiving preferential treatment.

Americans, for the most part, cling to the ideas of equality, justice, and democracy. When citizens observe others receiving differential treatment, especially from their police, they immediately have disdain for the police. When the police allow some citizens to get away with violations while citing others, or when the police provide services to some while refusing others, most people's sense of justice is violated. Furthermore, the injustice as a result of the act is diffused across the spectrum of police activity. People tend to distrust the police in every respect.

It is important for the police administrator to take measures to control each of these five problem areas. The police cannot successfully serve their constituents without trust and cooperation. When the police use excessive force, routinely or occasionally, engage in corruption, are rude, are authoritarian, or allow politics to influence enforcement decisions, citizens will very quickly lose faith in their police. The police always remain in the public eye, and they must measure up to citizens' expectations. The following section provides perspective on this issue by examining citizen perceptions of the police.

PUBLIC ATTITUDES TOWARD THE POLICE

There has been substantial study of citizens' attitudes about the police and their performance over the past quarter century. This research has found that citizens, for the most part, support their police. Even though citizens support the police generally, this support is not uniform across all groups of people. Perhaps the best way to study and understand citizen support for the police is to study the levels of support across individual variables. Researchers find that individual variables serve to mold and describe the types and levels of support that exist in a community (Decker, 1981; Worrall, 1999). Individual variables include factors such as sex, race, and personal experience with the police. On the other hand, community variables include factors such as socioeconomic status, likelihood of victimization, general community attitudes toward the police, and crime rates. These factors are explored in the following sections.

Age

The consensus among researchers is that older persons tend to view the police more positively than do younger citizens (e.g., see Hadar and Snortum, 1975; Smith and Hawkins, 1973). Campbell and Schuman (1973) found that after negative contacts with the police, younger persons were more prone to view the police less positively than older persons. Walker and colleagues (1973) found that young persons gave the police the lowest ratings for competence on the job and impartiality. Persons under the age of 30 were especially critical of the police.

A number of reasons explain why younger persons do not view the police as positively as their older counterparts. First, younger persons are resistant to and less respectful of authority figures. Younger persons tend to value their freedom and tend to resent control. When police officers inquire into their activities or stop them for traffic violations, many young people see this as an infringement on their freedom. Second, younger persons tend to have a greater number of negative contacts with the police (Smith and Hawkins, 1973). This is especially true with regard to traffic violations and other minor offenses. Some youths come to believe that the police tend to focus or "pick on" young people because of the increased attention. A third explanation is that older people are more vulnerable to crime and victimization, which engenders more positive feelings for the police. Older persons, especially senior citizens, exhibit higher levels of fear and come to view the police as their allies regardless of the quality of service provided by the police, but when the police provide the elderly with crime prevention and community relations programs, ratings of the police are extremely high (Zevitz and Rettammel, 1990).

Race

There is a consensus in the research that white citizens tend to view the police more positively than do minority citizens. Hahn (1971) found that African American urban residents had poor perceptions of the police, and in a similar study by Jaccob (1971), African Americans tended to believe that the police were more corrupt, more unfair, harsher, tougher, less friendly, and crueler than did whites. Jaccob also found that African Americans generally were more dissatisfied with police services in comparison to the white population. Bordua and Tift (1971) had findings similar to those of Jaccob. They found that African Americans were more angry, unhappy, and upset about encounters with the police. Moreover, middle-class African Americans were more critical of the police than those from the lower socioeconomic stratum (Weitzer and Tuch, 1999). Weitzer (2000) found that these differences of opinion were due to perceptions that the police treated minorities differently from whites. Complaints of racial profiling are a good example of this problem.

Carter (1983, 1985) assessed the attitudes of Hispanics toward the police. His findings coincided with the research on African American attitudes toward the police. Overall he found that Hispanics (1) feel less safe concerning crime in comparison to the general population, (2) do not feel that the police are capable of reducing the incidence of crime, (3) feel that they receive less than adequate protection from the police, and (4) generally evaluate the police lower relative to the general population. More specifically, Carter found that Hispanics believed the police did a poor job. Police officers were believed to have a bad attitude, needed to do a better job of investigating crimes, needed to decrease response times, and in general needed to reduce the level of discrimination against Hispanics. However, Cheurprakobkit (2000) found that Hispanics did have a more positive view of the police than did African Americans. Along these same lines, Cheurprakobkit and Bartsch (1999) found that Spanish-speaking Hispanics were more cooperative and viewed the police more positively than did English-speaking Hispanics.

Again, there appear to be a multitude of explanations for these attitudes. First, minorities have a higher number of negative contacts with the police relative to nonminorities. Minorities tend to have a higher representation in arrest statistics. Second, minorities tend to be victimized at higher rates than to nonminorities. Victimization tends to adversely affect one's view of the police, especially when the police fail to apprehend the perpetrator or provide what is perceived as poor service. Finally, as the research suggests, it may be that generally police officers do in fact treat minority citizens differently from white citizens. Police officers, especially white officers, typically do not comprehend or understand other cultures, which may cause them to treat minorities differently, and, unfortunately, some officers are biased against minorities, which often affects how they treat minority suspects or victims.

Gender

Although it is commonly thought that females view police more positively than their male counterparts, the research does not support this hypothesis. In their studies of attitudes toward the police, Campbell and Schuman (1973) and Smith and Hawkins (1973) found that gender accounted for little of the variance in citizen attitudes toward the police. It seems that males and females have no differences of opinion when it comes to the police.

Police Performance and Citizen Attitudes toward the Police

How the police perform or treat people when they come into contact with citizens has a great deal of bearing on citizen attitudes toward the police. Hadar and Snortum (1975) found that persons who had been victims of crimes and had an unsatisfactory experience with the police had negative attitudes toward the police. Other researchers have found that persons may be fearful of being victimized, yet they do not view the police unfavorably (Zamble and Annesley, 1987). Priest and Carter (1999) found that police demeanor when responding to calls for service weighed heavily in African-Americans' attitudes toward the police. Perceptions of a lack of safety, poor service by officers, and a slow police response time negatively affect attitudes. Thus the important factor in attitude formulation is the interaction between the police officer and citizens—how well citizens are treated when they call the police.

Neighborhood and Socioeconomic Factors

Social class and residence have an impact on how the police are viewed. Kusow, Wilson, and Martin (1997) found that African Americans and whites living in the suburbs tended to view the police more positively than did residents of urban areas. Suburban African Americans even viewed the police more positively than did urban whites. Their findings were supported by Reisig and Parks (2000), who found that African Americans living in better neighborhoods tended to view the police more positively. Thus social class seems to play a key role in forming citizens' perceptions of the police.

Public support for the police is critical to effective law enforcement. The police depend on citizens to provide them information and support when investigating crimes and other problems. The research indicates that there is substantial variation among various groups of citizens in terms of their support for the police. The police administrator must recognize these differences and develop initiatives that improve relations with all neighborhoods and community groups. Moreover, no group or groups can be neglected. Every group of citizens or neighborhood has a role to play in providing a safer community.

THE MEDIA: THE POLICE DEPARTMENT'S WINDOW TO THE WORLD

Average citizens have little understanding about the operation of a police department. What little understanding they do have comes largely from the news and entertainment media. The entertainment media through numerous television programs and movies depict the police in a variety of ways. Sometimes the police are shown to be industrious, competent investigators who protect citizens from ever-present criminals. They are also shown to be bumbling incompetents who would never catch a criminal without assistance from civilian sleuths. On other occasions they are characterized as authoritarian bigots or, worse still, corrupt cops who add to the increasing criminal problem. Even when police officers are depicted positively by the entertainment industry, they are often characterized as heroes working outside the bounds of a corrupt or incompetent police department and criminal justice system (Bailey, 1993). The average citizen can differentiate television and movie fiction from real life, but these characterizations very likely have some influence on how the police are perceived and community expectations for the police.

Members of the news media, on the other hand, consider themselves to be the fourth branch of government; news reporters and pundits see themselves as the dispensers of truth, responsible for holding government accountable to the people. In essence, they see their primary responsibility as "reporting the news." However, the news media routinely go beyond merely reporting, and

Police hold news conference to update citizens on a recent police operation.
Bob Daemmrich/Stock Boston

reporters often attempt to construct a "social reality" of crime and government (Barak, 1994; Surette, 1992). History shows us that different spins or interpretations can be added to any event to give the event new meaning. When engaging in this type of reporting, the news media attempt either to shape public policy or to capitalize on public fears and attitudes. The primary vehicle used in this process is the sensationalism of some event, which is designed to create more interest and lead to higher ratings and sales. The primary job of the news media is not the reporting of the news but the selling of news, which entails packaging news so that sales are maximized. This packaging can lead to public misunderstanding, distrust, and apathy toward the police.

The police and the media, to a great extent, depend on each other. Police activities consume a large percentage of news reporting. Gleick (1991) found that, on any given day, 30 percent of the typical local news television time contained law enforcement news. Guyot (1991) notes that crime news is some of the easiest news to write or broadcast, enhancing its likelihood of being covered. Along these lines, Wilson and McLaren (1977) identified three areas which are of interest to the media:

1. Stories about criminal activity, especially those of a sensational nature or those involving local residents.
2. Feature stories about police officers and programs.
3. Stories about police corruption or improper behavior such as police brutality or illegal arrests.

The news media are interested in crime stories. Such stories have high public appeal because of their sensational nature. This is why a brutal murder in one city will receive media attention throughout the United States. These stories are highly emotional and result in substantial public interest. The police are also interested in broadcasting information about crime, since it may have a crime prevention effect by educating the public about current crime problems. For example, if there is a series of residential burglaries, news coverage may encourage citizens to take more and better precautions to prevent burglaries. Crime reporting also builds support for the police by providing the public with information about the difficult task confronting the police.

Real-time televised police dramas such as *COPS* may be seen by the police as having substantial benefits for police. Hallett and Powell (1995) found that officers involved in filming *COPS* episodes felt that the program helps the public to better understand the nature and stresses of police work, even though the portrayal of policework on *COPS* was seen as unrealistic by these same officers. In a separate study, Chermak (1995) documents the symbiotic nature of the media–police relationship as well as the manner and degree to which police departments influence news selection and production decisions of the media. Since the late 1960s, much attention has been devoted to the importance of police understanding the media and attempting to manage the manner in which crime and the police department are covered. The skill of the police in dealing with the media seems to be improving.

The police and media sometimes face conflict as a result of crime reporting. Reporters may push the police to reveal names of witnesses and victims and to release information about the evidence in criminal cases. In these instances, the police believe the reporter has no regard for the potential negative impact of such disclosures on the successful prosecution of the case. Following clear media policies and procedures will help the police ensure that their cases are not jeopardized while the legitimate right of the public for information is achieved. Police administrators should strive to understand the media role and educate the media to the role and needs of the police. A police attitude of openness, cooperation, and assistance limited only by reasonable policy and procedural guidelines will reduce the degree of conflict with the media.

Feature stories about police officers and police activities are sometimes used to garner support for the police. These stories generally center on officers, their families, or some new program implemented by the department. For example, a television news program may feature a story about the rigor and difficulties facing officers as they go through the training academy or how the police department selects and trains its canines. Human interest stories involving the police are of great interest to the public. Citizens routinely see police officers only in their official capacity, and human interest stories reassure citizens that the police are no different from other citizens. Police officials see feature stories as helping to build public support for the department and police programs.

Finally, the news media view stories about police corruption and wrongdoing as an important part of news reporting. Such stories are highly sensational and demand substantial public attention. The media typically devote maximum attention to such stories. The police, on the other hand, often believe that corruption and wrongdoing are best handled internally and resent public intrusion into an otherwise administrative problem. The police often feel that reporters twist the facts in an effort to obtain maximum effect. Reporters see the police as failing to cooperate in these matters. Too often, police administrators fail to be forthright, or they hold back critical facts. This can ultimately result in charges of coverup by the media. The administrator should be as honest as possible without jeopardizing any pending criminal or disciplinary action.

Guffey (1992:40) examined the relationship between the police and media and identified several complaints often voiced by the media:

1. The police are seldom forthcoming with information.
2. The police fail to accept legitimate criticism from the media.
3. The police sometimes withhold critical information from the media.
4. The police too frequently hide behind the Sixth Amendment when refusing to disclose information.
5. The police are often uncooperative, especially when dealing with important cases.
6. The police refuse to accept the media as an integral part of the process to hold the police accountable.

Along these same lines, Guffey identified several complaints often voiced by the police. They include:

1. The media interfere with ongoing investigations.
2. The media refuse to respect victims' privacy rights.
3. The media refuse to recognize that their reporting has a number of negative effects on the police.
4. The media practice sensationalism with little regard for accuracy.

Managing the Police–Media Relationship

It is critical that the police department be prepared to deal with the media. Guffey (1992) identified several steps that administrators can take to ensure that the department effectively deals with the media. First, a public information officer should be assigned to deal with the media. The public information officer should be someone who is educated, articulate, and fully capable of dealing with people in stressful situations. The pubic information officer should handle media relations for all major events and should respond to special requests by reporters. Second, reporters should be encouraged to participate in police ride-alongs. This will allow the reporters to better understand and, it is hoped, empathize with police officers and their jobs. Third, police officers at all levels should be trained in media relations. Not only should officers be trained on departmental media policy; they should also be taught how to make media presentations. Sooner or later, many officers are required to respond to a reporter's questions or to appear on television. They should be provided with the skills to do so proficiently.

Fourth, reporters should have free access to all departmental records that are legally available to them. Other records and information should be made available if they do not interfere with an open case or the operation of the department. Along these same lines, reporters should be allowed to talk with officers who are working on cases or participating in programs. Fifth, the public information officer and chief should conduct regular meetings with the media to ensure that lines of communication remain open. Sixth, departmental officials should participate in talk shows and other broadcasts to open communications with the public. Seventh, departments should issue press credentials to ensure that only legitimate reporters are given access to information. Finally, the public information officer should receive training in conflict management. Such training provides the officer with a wider range of skills for dealing with the media.

Police departments should have media procedures that include most of these steps. Additionally, the media policy should specify what information is accessible to the press and what is not accessible. Most states forbid the release of information about juvenile offenders or arrestees. These laws also prohibit taking their pictures. Departments should adopt a policy of not releasing the names of sexual assault victims. Policy should enumerate which departmental records and information can and cannot be released. Obviously, any information relative to an ongoing case should be closely scrutinized before it is released to the media. Standard procedures should be established in policy so that officers will easily be able to determine the propriety of responding to any request for information.

The news media represent a significant challenge for the police administrator. On one hand, the relationship is adversarial when reporters doggedly pursue information that might embarrass the police or result in community or legal problems upon its release. On the other hand, the media represent an important resource that can be used in crime prevention and public information programs. The police administrator must learn to use this resource, balancing the media's unquenchable thirst for news with the department's need to protect and inform.

Summary

The police are an integral part of the community in that the community affects how the police operate, and the police have an impact on the daily affairs of any community. It is important for the police to understand this relationship. To do so means that administrators must adopt an open-systems perspective and make every effort to ensure that the department's operations maintain an equilibrium with the community. When a police department fails to meet the needs of the community or segments within the community, the department has failed to live up to the community's expectations.

Further, it is important for administrators to understand that each community consists of a number of elements. For example, a variety of cultures can be found within most communities. A vast array of socioeconomic and political variables contribute to differences in groups of citizens within a given community. Finally, a community's geographical location and its natural resources affect the social fiber of the community. All of these factors interplay with government and police services, making it critical for the police to understand and respond to the environment.

Study Questions

1. Identify and discuss the seven environmental conditions affecting the structure and nature of government.

2. Discuss the differences between open and closed systems of police organizations.

3. Why is cultural diversity an important issue for understanding the environment of policing? How should the administrator go about ensuring that the department adapts to its environment?

4. How do the separation of powers and federalism affect local police management?

5. Describe the primary types of municipal government structure. Discuss the potential benefits and constraints of working as a police chief under each of the forms of government.

6. Describe the community power structure and how it affects the administration of a police department.

7. Identify and discuss each of the barriers to a good police–community relationship. How would you avoid them if you were a police administrator? How would they differ if you were head of a federal agency, state agency, sheriff's office, and a municipal agency?

8. Discuss the key complaints police and media representatives have regarding each other. Why is a good media relationship important for successful police administration? What strategy would you use to develop a good relationship with local media?

Net Resources

http://www.findlaw.com Website for statutes and caselaw related to law enforcement and other criminal justice issues.

http://www.policeforum.org/racial.html Racial profiling report from Police Executive Research Forum (PERF) the leading organization for research on police administration.

http://www.law.nyu.edu/mirskyc/uspohtml/index.htm Report on Police Brutality and Accountability in the United States.

References

Aldrich, H. E., and Mindlin, S. (1978). Uncertainty and dependence: Two perspectives on environment. In L. Karpk (ed.), *Organization and Environment*. Beverly Hills, CA: Sage, pp. 149–170.

Andrews, A. (1985). Political independence of the police chief. In W. Geller (ed.), *Police Leadership in America*. New York: Praeger.

Bailey, F. (1993). Real life vigilantism and vigilantism in popular films. *Justice Professional* 8(1):33–52.

Barak, G. (1994). *Media, Process, and the Social Construction of Crime*. New York: Garland Press.

Barker, T., and Carter, D. (1991). *Police Deviance*, 2nd ed. Cincinnati: Anderson Publishing.

Bordua, D. J., and Tift, L. L. (1971). Citizen interviews, organizational feedback, and police community relations decisions. *Law and Society Review* (6):155–182.

Campbell, A., and Schuman, H. (1973). A comparison of black and white attitudes and experiences in the city. In C. M. Haar (ed.), *The End of Innocence: A Suburban Reader*. Glenview, IL: Scott Foresman.

Carter, D. (1983). Hispanic interaction with the criminal justice system in Texas: Experiences, attitudes, and perceptions. *Journal of Criminal Justice* (11):213–227.

Carter, D. (1985). Hispanic perception of police performance: An empirical assessment. *Journal of Criminal Justice* (13):487–500.

Carter, D., and Radelet, L. (1999). *The Police and the Community*, 6th ed. Upper Saddle River, NJ: Prentice Hall.

Chermak, S. (1995). Image control: How police affect the presentation of crime news. *American Journal of Police* 14(2):21–43.

Cheurprakobkit, S. (2000). Police–citizen contact and police performance: Attitudinal differences between Hispanics and non-Hispanics. *Journal of Criminal Justice* 28(4):325–336.

Cheurprakobkit, S., and Bartsch, R. A. (1999). Assessing attitudes of city officials, Spanish-speaking Hispanics, and their English-speaking counterparts. *Journal of Criminal Justice* 27(2):87–100.

Decker, S. (1981). Citizen attitudes toward the police: A review of past findings and suggestions for future policy. *Journal of Police Science and Administration* 9:80–87.

Donnelly, J. H., Gibson, J. L., and Ivancevich, J. M. (1995). *Fundamentals of Management*, 9th ed. Chicago: Irwin.

Enter, J. (1986). The rise to the top: An analysis of police chief career patterns. *Journal of Police Science and Administration* 14(4):334–346.

Gaines, L. K., Kappeler, V., and Vaughn, J. (1999). *Policing in America*, 2nd ed. Cincinnati: Anderson Publishing.

Gilbert, C. W. (1967). Some trends in community politics: A secondary analysis of power structure data from 166 communities. *Social Science Quarterly* 48:373–381.

Gleick, R. H. (1991). Public information officers: Trained to deal with the media. *Law and Order*, May, p. 98.

Gould, L. A. (1997). Can an old dog be taught new tricks? Teaching cultural diversity to police officers. *Policing: An International Journal of Police Strategies and Management* 20(2):339–356.

Greene, L. (1996). *Policing Places with Drug Problems.* Thousand Oaks, CA: Sage.

Guffey, J. E. (1992). The police and the media: Proposal for managing conflict productively. *American Journal of Police* 11(1):33–51.

Guyot, D. (1991). *Policing as though Other People Matter.* Philadelphia: Temple University Press.

Hadar, I., and Snortum, J. R. (1975). The eye of the beholder: Differential perceptions of police and the public. *Criminal Justice and Behavior* 2:37–54.

Hahn, H. (1971). Ghetto assessments of police protection and authority. *Law and Society Review* 6:183–194.

Hallett, M., and Powell, D. (1995). Backstage with "COPS": The dramaturgical reification of police subculture in American crime "info-tainment." *American Journal of Police* 14(1):101–129.

Jaccob, H. (1971). Black and white perceptions of justice in the city. *Law and Society Review* 5:69–89.

Kappeler, V. E., Sluder, R. D., and Alpert, G. P. (1994). *Forces of Deviance: Understanding the Dark Side of Policing.* Prospect Heights, IL: Waveland.

Katz, D., and Kahn, R. L. (1996). *The Special Psychology of Organizations.* New York: Wiley.

Klinger, D. (1997). Negotiating order in patrol work: An ecological theory of police response to deviance. *Criminology* 35(2):277–306.

Kusow, A. M., Wilson, L. C., and Martin, D. E. (1997). Determinants of citizen satisfaction with the police: The effects of residential location. *Policing: An International Journal of Police Strategy and Management* 20(4):655–664.

Mastrofski, S. (1988). Varieties of police governance in metropolitan America. *Politics and Policy* 8:12–31.

Mayhew, B. H. (1973). System size and ruling elites. *American Sociological Review* 38:468–475.

McGarrell, E. F., Chermak, S., Weiss, A., and Wilson, J. (2001). Reducing firearms violence through directed police patrol. *Criminology and Public Policy* 1(1):119–148.

Munro, J. (1971). Towards a theory of criminal justice administration: A general systems perspective. *Public Administration Review* 31(6):621–631.

Murphy, P. (1985). The prospective chief's negotiation of authority with the mayor. In W. Geller (ed.), *Police Leadership in America.* New York: Praeger.

O'Brien, J. T. (1978). The chief and the executive: Direction or political interference? *Journal of Police Science and Administration* 6(4):394–401.

Ostrom, E., Parks, R., and Whitaker, G. (1978). Police agency size: Some evidence on its effects. *Police Studies,* March, pp. 34–46.

Priest, T. B., and Carter, D. B. (1999). Evaluations of police performance in an African-American sample. *Journal of Criminal Justice* 27(5):457–465.

Rainey, H. G. (1991). *Understanding and Managing Public Organizations.* San Francisco: Jossey-Bass.

Ramirez, D., McDevitt, J., and Farrell, A. (2000). *A Resource Guide on Racial Profiling Data Collection Systems*. Washington: U.S. Department of Justice.

Reisig, M. D., and Parks, R. B. (2000). Experience, quality of life, and neighborhood context: A hierarchical analysis of satisfaction with police. *Justice Quarterly* 17(3):607–630.

Reaves, B. A. (1998). *Census of State and Local Law Enforcement Agencies, 1996*. Washington: U.S. Department of Justice.

Roberts, D. E. (1999). Race, vagueness, and the social meaning of order-maintenance policing. *Journal of Criminal Law and Criminology* 89(3):775–836.

Sherman, L. W., Gottfredson, D., MacKenzie, D., Eck, J., Reuter, P., and Bushway, S. (1997). *Preventing Crime: What Works, What Doesn't, What's Promising*. Washington: Office of Justice Programs.

Skolnick, J. H., and Caplovitz, A. (2001). Guns, drugs, and profiling: Ways to target guns and minimize racial profiling. *Arizona Law Review* 43:413–437.

Smith, P. E., and Hawkins, R.O. (1973). Victimization, types of citizen contacts, and attitudes toward the police. *Law and Society Review* (8):135–152.

Southern Poverty Law Center (2001). Discounting hate. *Intelligence Report*, Winter, pp. 7–11.

Stoner, J. A., and Freeman, R. E. (1992). *Management*, 5th ed. Englewood Cliffs, NJ: Prentice Hall.

Surette, R. (1992). *Media, Crime and Criminal Justice*. Pacific Grove, CA: Brooks/Cole.

Tunnell, K., and Gaines, L. K. (1996). Political pressures and influences on police executives: A descriptive analysis. In G. Cordner and D. Kenney (eds.), *Managing Police Organizations*. Cincinnati: Anderson Publishing, pp. 5–18.

Verniero, P., and Zoubek, P. (1999). *Interim Report of the State Police Review Team Regarding Allegations of Racial Profiling*. Trenton, NJ: Office of the Attorney General.

Walker, D., Richardson, R. J., Williams, O., Denyer, T., and McGaughey, S. (1973). Contact and support: An empirical assessment of public attitudes toward the police and the courts. *North Carolina Law Review* 51:43–79.

Walker, S. (1992). *The Police in America*, 2nd ed. New York: McGraw-Hill.

Weitzer, R. (2000). Racialized policing: Residents' perceptions in three neighborhoods. *Law and Society Review* 34(1):129–156.

Weitzer, R., and Tuch, S. A. (1999). Race, class, and perceptions of discrimination by the police. *Crime and Delinquency* 45(4):494–507.

Whren v. United States, 517 U.S. 806, 116 S.Ct. 1769 (1996).

Wilson, J. Q. (1972). *Varieties of Police Behavior: Management of Law Enforcement in Eight Communities*. New York: Atheneum.

Wilson, W. J. (1987). *The Truly Disadvantaged: The Inner City, the Underclass, and Public Policy*. Chicago: University of Chicago Press.

Witham, D. C. (1985). *The American Law Enforcement Chief Executive: A Management Profile*. Washington: Police Executive Research Forum.

Worrall, J. (1999). Public perceptions of police efficacy and image: The "fuzziness" of support for the police. *American Journal of Criminal Justice* 24(1):47–66.

Worrall, J. (2001). Addicted to the drug war: The role of civil asset forfeiture as a budgetary necessity in contemporary law enforcement. *Journal of Criminal Justice* 29:171–187.

Zamble, E., and Annesley, P. (1987). Some determinants of public attitudes toward the police. *Journal of Police Science and Administration* 15(4):285–290.

Zevitz, R. G., and Rettammel, R. J. (1990). Elderly attitudes about police service. *American Journal of Police* 9(2):25–39.

3

Community Policing

Bob Daemmrich/Stock Boston

Introduction

What Is Community Policing?

A Comprehensive View of Community Policing
The Philosophical Dimension
The Strategic Dimension
The Programmatic Dimension

Administrative Issues in Implementing Community Policing
Absence of Police Planning for Community Policing
Resistance to Change
Officer Difficulties in Accepting Community Policing
Requirement of Additional Resources
Difficulties in Getting the Community Involved

Evaluating a Department's Community Policing Efforts
Departmental Structure
Community Involvement
Quality of Police Services in a Community
Measuring Community Satisfaction with the Police
Employee Understanding and Acceptance of Community Policing

Summary

Learning Objectives

After reading this chapter, you should be able to

1. Understand the difference between community policing and the traditional or professional model of policing.
2. Articulate the philosophical, strategic, and programmatic dimensions of community policing as a model.
3. Understand the intricacies of implementing community policing and some of the problems that an administrator may incur.
4. Understand how to evaluate a department's community policing efforts.
5. Understand the benefits of community policing relative to past practices.

In the summer of 1998, the St. Petersburg, Florida, Police Department held a retreat. The purpose of the retreat was to examine how community policing could be fully implemented in the department. The department had already implemented a variety of programs, but community policing had not been integrated fully in the department. The agenda for the retreat included supervision, accountability, staffing, partnerships, departmental morale, and training. After the retreat, Chief Davis created a number of committees and subcommittees within the department to assist with implementation. Members from across the department were assigned to every committee. The committees then developed action plans that were later implemented. These action plans were then used to reorganize the department so that it would be more effective in providing community policing services (Stevens, 2001). This retreat exemplifies the comprehensive nature of community policing and the attention required by police administrators to implement it.

INTRODUCTION

This chapter examines community policing from an administrative perspective. It addresses what community policing is and how it should be integrated throughout the department. It addresses some of the problems encountered when it is implemented. Benchmarks for success are discussed to equip the administrator with information about how to determine whether the department's efforts are working.

Community policing represents a new policing philosophy and mode of operation for American policing. It is a drastic departure from the professional model of policing that dominated American law enforcement from the 1950s through the 1970s. The professional model developed from the work of Wilson, superintendent of the Chicago Police Department, and Parker, chief of Los Angeles. The professional model evolved in a response to the political era of policing when the police were very corrupt (Fogelson, 1977). Professional policing was seen a way of fighting corruption and the corrupt politicians who dominated the scene at the time.

The professional model of policing was very similar to the military or bureaucratic model of management. Police departments established police officer selection criteria, rigid training programs, and a chain of command that attempted to control police discretion from the top through close supervision. The professional police administrators reasoned that if you could control what officers did on the street, you could eliminate outside unwholesome influences and corruption. Officers were discouraged from "getting close" to citizens for fear that personal contact with citizens could lead to corruption. The professional model of policing essentially built a wall between the police and the public they served.

Community policing evolved from the police–community relations programs of the 1950s and 1960s, team policing strategies of the 1970s, and the increase in citizen fear of crime and drugs that began to dominate public policy formulation in the 1980s (Greene, 1987; Walker, 1993a). The basis of community policing was first articulated with Goldstein's (1979) article on *problem-oriented policing* and Wilson and Kelling's (1982) article on "broken windows," which discussed the causes of community disorder and crime. Goldstein noted that the police were, more or less, treating symptoms of problems—responding to calls and taking superficial action—rather than treating problems themselves. The police would never be successful until actual problems were confronted and resolved. He also criticized the police for placing too much emphasis on rapid response to calls for service and doing too little once they arrived at a call. Goldstein believed that police responses failed to deal with the real issue—solving community problems.

Wilson and Kelling, on the other hand, viewed *community disorder* as the precursor to crime. The deterioration of the quality of life in neighborhoods is an evolutionary process that begins with minor neglect and disorder problems. If these problems go unchecked over time, they continue to worsen until drastic measures are required by residents or government to reclaim the neighborhood. Therefore, the best way to attack crime and disorder is to deal with minor problems such as panhandling, unrepaired homes and businesses, unmowed lots and yards, junk cars in yards, and minor crimes, before they foster larger ones.

These two concepts, broken windows and problem solving, spawned a rethinking of American police. Policing began to move from a reactive, law enforcement mode to a proactive, community-building mode whereby the police and the community functioned cooperatively to deal with crime, disorder, and social problems. The primary police function shifted from law enforcement and returned to service and order maintenance.

Explorations regarding the distinctions between urban policing and policing in small towns and rural environments have concluded that rural police are more attuned to and have a longstanding acceptance of the basic tenets of community policing (Crank, 1990; McDonald, 1996; Weisheit, Falcone, and Wells, 1996). Weisheit et al. (1996) identified three broad themes of community policing:

1. The police should be *accountable* to the community.
2. They should be *connected* and integrated into the community on a personal level.
3. They should be oriented to *solving general problems* instead of focusing on incidents.

They found these themes to have a stronger presence in rural policing than in urban policing. Cain found that rural police were "capable of learning the norms of the community they policed and interested in conforming to them. Neither of these essential ingredients of peace-keeping by consensus was present in the city" (1971:77). Indeed, a publication of the International Association of Chiefs of Police (IACP) noted, "Urban police tend to be efficient; rural police tend to be effective" (1990:8). The IACP attributed the effectiveness of rural policing to the closeness of police to the community, that is, "being a part of the local culture" rather than apart from it. The importance of the community for rural police may, in part, be the result of a different approach to accountability. "The urban officer answers to the police department. The rural or small town officer is held accountable for his actions by the community" (IACP, 1990:9). Community policing attempts to insert this sense of "community" in large urban departments.

On the Job

REDLANDS, CALIFORNIA, POLICE DEPARTMENT
By Chief Jim Bueermann

Courtesy of Chief Bueermann

In Redlands, community policing has served as a vehicle for the department to provide its citizens with a wider array of services and to provide those services more effectively. Although most police departments adhere to the community policing model, most have implemented it by developing a variety of programs to meet specific needs. Redlands has taken a different approach. We recognize that in order for community policing to provide the best results, it must be applied throughout the department, in an orderly fashion. It must not only have an impact on police services, but it must also change the way the department as a whole conducts business. As such, we began the process with a strategic plan and have been working to fully implement it for a number of years. Our community policing philosophy and strategies are

constantly changing to reflect changes in the community.

One of the first things we did was reorganize and reorient our department. The essence of community policing is the development of better relations with citizens, community partnerships, and community oriented services. To accomplish this, we made major structural changes in our organization. We created a captain's position in the department, whose sole responsibility is to oversee and coordinate our community policing efforts. A number of social services were moved from city government and placed within the police department. These services include: recreation, senior citizen services, community centers, housing programs, and cultural arts. Housing these services in the police department allows the department to work more closely with citizens and citizen groups. It also enhances our crime prevention mission in two ways. First, it allows us to build crime prevention programming into some of these functions. Second, it allows officers to work closely with a variety of citizens who come to know and trust their police. These types of relations often lead to a better flow of communication, especially information about crime problems.

Another program that has been developed is Risk Focused Policing. The department currently is working with the Police Foundation on a project that maps and assesses social problems

Continued

and youths-at-risk in the community. As a result of this work, we have identified several areas in the City where there is a concentration of youths-at-risk, and there are few services to assist them in avoiding delinquency. Our Risk Focused Policing entails that once problems are identified, we use community policing to provide specific recreational, educational, and social programs in an effort to provide opportunities for a more fruitful life. Here, the police work with a variety of community groups to ensure that the most comprehensive services are provided.

We have also partnered with a variety of city departments to deal with problem neighborhoods, and we have taken the "broken windows" approach when dealing with marginal neighborhoods. The department's MET Unit was designed to attack our gang and street crimes problems. Crime analysis and mapping allows us to focus on hot spots or concentrated problems. We have instituted the Neighborhood Improvement Team consisting of community policing officers, fire inspectors, code enforcement, building and safety inspectors, the city attorney's office, and housing specialists. This group meets monthly to review statistics, crime maps, and crime analyst information. They then identify problems that are tackled by the police and other city agencies. For example, here the police might work with code enforcement in an effort to reverse neighborhood blight. The department also has a landlord program, which assists in the eviction of drug dealers and emphasizes the maintenance of a crime-free environment.

As I noted, our community policing programming constantly is evolving. We continually communicate with our citizens to identify their needs and respond to them. We totally adhere to the idea that our citizens who are customers deserve the best possible service from their police. We continually assess our efforts and add new programs as needs arise. We are committed to maintaining the quality of life in Redlands and see the police as a key element in accomplishing this goal.

WHAT IS COMMUNITY POLICING?

As noted, community policing is a departure from the professional model. It has been adopted by a large number of departments. In a recent study, Reaves and Goldberg (1997) found that about 90 percent of all departments serving cities with a population of 10,000 or larger have adopted a community policing policy. It has taken a number of directions (Rosenbaum, 1994) and in some sense has come to mean different things to different people. Bayley summarized this perspective:

> Some departments have seen it as a vehicle to develop better relations with the community, while others have emphasized more law enforcement. Community policing, as operationalized, is a flexible format allowing departments to address a variety of community needs. It also allows departments to change direction as new needs are identified.

Table 3–1

Examples of Community Policing Programs or Initiatives

Enhanced Patrols	Crime Prevention	Disorder Abatement	Community Relations/ Communications
Police substations	DARE	Curfew enforcement	Citizen academies
Neighborhood watches	GREAT	Renter eviction programs	Neighborhood newsletters
Horse patrols	Security surveys	Code enforcement teams	Spouse academies
Bike patrols	Operation ID	Underage drinking enforcement	Police athletic leagues
Aggressive patrols	School resource officers		Neighborhood councils and meetings
	Crimestoppers		

Although community policing has taken a number of directions, there does seem to be a common overarching structure to it. It consists of two primary components: community partnerships and problem solving. *Community partnerships* refers to efforts by the police to work with the community to solve common problems. The police cannot effectively deal with many of today's problems without these kinds of partnerships. *Problem solving* is the act of identifying problems that are issues with the police and public and attempting to solve them, rather than merely responding to them. Community policing, then, is a cooperative effort to substantively solve crime and disorder problems. Table 3–1 provides examples of some of the programs that departments have implemented under community policing.

The following discussion emphasizes a systems approach to implementation of community policing. We provide this discussion for three reasons. First, community policing has been adopted by the vast majority of larger departments in the country. Second, our discussion elaborates how community policing affects the total department. A police administrator cannot successfully implement community policing by implementing a few programs. It must be implemented from the top to the bottom of the department. Finally, community policing is the most effective mode of operation when serving the needs of a community. It is a critical part of policing and police administration.

A COMPREHENSIVE VIEW OF COMMUNITY POLICING

When implementing community policing, the administrator must consider how it is to affect each unit in the department. Numerous departments have envisioned community policing as a hodgepodge of programs. These departments implement programs that address specific problems. When this occurs,

Figure 3–1
How community policing is applied to a department.

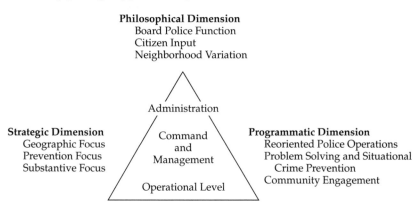

Philosophical Dimension
Board Police Function
Citizen Input
Neighborhood Variation

Administration

Strategic Dimension
Geographic Focus
Prevention Focus
Substantive Focus

Command
and
Management

Operational Level

Programmatic Dimension
Reoriented Police Operations
Problem Solving and Situational
Crime Prevention
Community Engagement

there generally are holes in the coverage. Moreover, when community policing is implemented piecemeal, resentment and strain often develop between the community policing units and other operational units.

Cordner (1999) identified a comprehensive system by which to implement community policing. He notes that there are three major dimensions encompassed within community policing: (1) the philosophical dimension, (2) the strategic dimension, and (3) the programmatic dimension. All three dimensions must exist if a department is indeed implementing community policing. This paradigm is presented in Figure 3–1.

The Philosophical Dimension

Historically, even though American law enforcement has experienced sporadic variations in theme, substantively it has remained a legal-bureaucratic organization focusing on professional law enforcement. Outputs such as numbers of arrests, changes in crime rates, volume of recovered property, numbers of citations issued, and a rapid response to calls have been more important than solving problems. This philosophy translated into a reactive police force focusing on "bean counting" (Spellman, 1988) but doing little to tangibly deal with problems.

Cordner notes that, philosophically, community policing consists of a number of community-based elements that differentiate it from the traditional professional model. Three of community policing's core ideas are (1) broad police function, (2) citizen input, and (3) neighborhood variation.

Broad Police Function

Community policing dictates that police departments move from law enforcement or crime fighting as the primary function (Goldstein, 1979). The police should have a broader function that incorporates fear reduction and order maintenance. Indeed, fear reduction and order maintenance become the primary goals for the department, supplanting crime reduction (Trojanowicz, Kappeler, and Gaines, 2002). This change in police philosophy emanates from two general directions. First, research examining police operations and crime statistics tends to point out that police have not been totally effective in combating crime. Crime is a product of social conditions and therefore cannot be controlled solely through crime-fighting measures. Crime is best influenced by controlling or attacking the social conditions that contribute to crime. The police can, at best, only manage and document most crime. Furthermore, order maintenance is a legitimate police goal in itself. Social control and domestic tranquility contribute to the quality of life, and order-maintenance activities help reduce crime in a community (Mastrofski, 1988).

Second, fear has a far greater debilitating effect on a community or individuals than do crime rates. The fear of crime results in persons becoming virtual prisoners in their own homes; it inhibits commerce; and it poses a subtle psychological cost to everyone. Research shows that oftentimes the degree to which an individual fears crime bears no relationship to the actual amount of crime or victimization. Police-sponsored fear-reduction programs have the potential to yield positive results in a number of areas: citizen participation in crime prevention programs, citizen crime reporting, positive relations with citizens, and a reduction in crime rates. A number of such programs have been implemented and have been shown to be successful (Trojanowicz, Kappeler, and Gaines, 2002).

Citizen Input

The police traditionally have implemented programs that involved citizens. For the most part, however, these programs bordered on public relations schemes with little consideration given to community or citizen needs. Some of the police–community relations programs of earlier years seriously involved and considered citizens, but for the most part, the police were concerned with educating the public about police needs rather than listening to the public about citizen problems. The police were interested in changing the public, rather than changing themselves to meet citizen needs.

Community policing employs methods that cause the police to work more closely with citizens. To develop a better relationship, police departments collect information about citizen attitudes toward crime problems and the effectiveness of the police. For example, the police in Baltimore County, Reno, Atlanta, Newport News, St. Louis, and other cities have used citizen surveys to collect information about citizen concerns. Other departments collected information by holding town or neighborhood meetings or by meeting with minority and business groups. Gathering information from citizens allows the police to accomplish several tasks. Survey information can be used to evaluate the effectiveness of police programs in terms of fear reduction or attitudes toward the police. They also gauge citizen behavior such as victimization or crime prevention efforts. They can also be used to collect data to assist the police in establishing goals and priorities (Peak and Glensor, 1999). Community policing attempts to encourage citizen involvement by fostering two-way communications.

Collecting information from the community about police priorities is no easy task. Murphy (1988) performed a community survey of a random sample of 1,400 adults living in Toronto and was unable to discern a consensus about community problems. Webb and Graham (1994) in a similar study found substantial variation. Only enforcement of drug laws and gang activities received a high level of consensus. Webb and Katz (1997) examined citizen perceptions in Omaha. They found police enforcement activities to be more important to the public than "preventive" activities that usually have an indirect impact on crime. Citizen input seems to suggest that citizens are more interested in the police providing traditional law activities than community policing. This very likely is the result of citizens not understanding what community policing is (Sadd and Grinc, 1994). Grinc (1994) also notes that citizens are reluctant to become involved in community policing for several reasons: (1) fear of retaliation, (2) historically poor relationship between the police and community, and (3) general apathy. It seems that if citizen involvement is to be achieved, the police must educate citizens as to their roles and need for involvement in community safety.

Neighborhood Variation

Traditional, professional policing mandated that police officers disavow the existence of police discretion; rather, the same methods were used to police every situation and neighborhood. The police were expected to exert full and uniform enforcement of the law. Community policing, on the other hand, recognizes that a political jurisdiction is composed of a number of communities or neighborhoods, each with its own set of problems and expectations. Stable neighborhoods have relative homogeneity of activity, people, and values. As neighborhoods are defined by ethnic, religious, and other socioeconomic factors, differential expectations within neighborhoods evolve. Particular neighborhoods develop expectations not only about what the police should do, but also about what types of behavior are acceptable or unacceptable by residents and nonresidents.

The most problematic communities or neighborhoods for the police are those that are poor or impoverished. They typically have the highest levels of crime, especially violent crime (Bursik and Grasmick, 1993; Wilson, 1987). Conditions in poorer neighborhoods seem to encourage criminal behavior. Such neighborhoods tend to be socially disorganized with few, if any, social control mechanisms such as churches, recreational facilities, or schools that reach out into the community. The prevalence of crime provides residents with ample role models for the young to follow into a career of crime. Unemployment is usually very high in these neighborhoods, so many residents have the time and opportunity to "wander" into criminal activities. These neighborhoods provide the greatest challenge to police administrators when attempting to "serve the needs" of the community.

Community policing dictates that the police follow the "will of the community" when dealing with situations and enforcing the law. There is little variation in how the police react to serious crimes or felonies. However, the police must be cognizant of community standards in policing minor infractions of the law and dealing with activities that may be acceptable in one neighborhood but not another. For example, a citizen working on his car while it is parked on the street would not be acceptable in most upper- and middle-class neighborhoods, but such informality is a way of life for many people residing in poor neighborhoods. Police officers must rely on community or neighborhood standards when they encounter such situations. The police must maintain a balance between neighborhood values and overall police goals and objectives.

The Strategic Dimension

The police must develop strategies by which to implement the philosophy of community policing. Strategic plans provide guidelines for the development of specific programs. Cordner (1999) has identified reoriented operations, geographical focus, prevention focus, and substantive focus as parameters that should guide planning in implementing community policing.

Reoriented Operations Focus

Traditional law enforcement focuses on time and function as opposed to locations or areas within a jurisdiction. In terms of time, police departments revolve around shift work. Patrol officers, detectives, and other officers are assigned to shifts. Police effectiveness is measured by activities across time; that is, what occurred on a particular shift. In terms of function, police departments are highly specialized with a number of different units (e.g., patrol, criminal investigation, traffic, community relations) that are responsible for their own unique tasks. Officers assigned to one functional area seldom have the time or inclination to work or worry about activities that fall into another functional area. In fact, typically only the chief in small and medium departments and precinct commanders in large departments have full responsibility for a given geographical area. Specialization by time and task inhibits the evaluation or even articulation of policing at the citizen or neighborhood level. The police should abandon such bureaucratic inhibitions and focus on working with people to solve problems.

Geographical Focus

Geographical focus refers to assigning officers to a geographical area (beat or district) on a permanent basis so that they become familiar with residents, activities, and social problems. Police officers are permanently assigned to an area in hopes that they will come to develop a territorial imperative (Wilson and McLaren, 1977). *Territorial imperative* is identification with the area, which will lead the officer to take greater care in safeguarding it and working to solve its problems. This territorial imperative does not end with police officers. Command staff must also come to identify with and take responsibility for specific geographical areas. Once there is a level of geographical accountability within police departments, officers and units will respond more effectively to citizen and neighborhood needs and demands.

Prevention Focus

As previously alluded to, community policing dictates that the police be proactive rather than react to problems and situations. A central part of proaction is prevention. In dealing with crime and disorder, prevention is a much more attractive alternative than enforcement because it potentially reduces the level of victimization in a community. Operationally, *prevention* refers to ferreting out the problems and conditions that cause crime and disorder and taking some action to reduce the probability that future crime and disorder will occur. In essence, the police must examine the conditions surrounding crime and disorder "hot spots" in an effort to develop effective measures of eliminating them. Patrol, criminal investigation, and other operational units must become actively involved in prevention and problem solving.

Second, crime prevention units in police departments must become more active and broaden their range of activities. Historically, crime prevention has centered around a few activities such as home and business surveys, but crime prevention units must become more active. In addition to their regular target-hardening activities such as recommending security devices to citizens and businesses, officers should assist operational units by serving as a resource when dealing with specific crime problems or hot spots, and they should work closely with crime analysis and operational units to identify crime and disorder problems and solutions. In essence, crime prevention should have a neighborhood focus.

Finally, a part of a police department's crime prevention responsibility includes attacking the problems and conditions that contribute to or result in crime. Police departments must take the lead in implementing programs that attack causes of crime. Here, the police can assume a number of social welfare roles. Police departments now have programs to assist and refer people to appropriate social welfare agencies; they have initiated educational programs such as after-school tutoring programs and recreational programs such as police athletic leagues (PALs) aimed at providing wholesome life skills experiences for underprivileged youth; and in some cases, police departments have begun to provide direct services to the needy. Crime prevention also means helping people at risk attain a minimum standard of living.

Substantive Focus

Community policing means more than responding to calls or generating activity such as arrests and citations. As Goldstein (1979) has discussed, it means that the police must engage in complex activities that address problems as well as their accompanying symptoms. The police must go beyond "answering calls for service." It also means that police departments must broaden the range of problems they address, because there are a number of social problems that result in or are intertwined with crime and disorder. Finally, a substantive focus requires that the police not act alone. They must actively solicit the support and assistance of other governmental and private agencies as well as the community in dealing with problems. The police must engage in community partnerships.

The Programmatic Dimension

The philosophy and strategies just discussed must be implemented through specific tactics or programs. For the most part, community policing is implemented through (1) reoriented police operations, (2) problem solving and situational crime prevention, and (3) community engagement.

Reoriented Police Operations

The traditional police response to crime and disorder primarily consisted of random, routine patrols. It was believed that random patrols would deter crime through a consistent unpredictable police presence. If patrols were unable to prevent crime, then officers as a result of their distribution across beats would be in a good position to observe the criminal activity and apprehend criminals. Finally, if this failed, detectives and other police specialists would be dispatched to intervene in the problem.

Community policing means going beyond this reactive strategy. It means not waiting to be called, but identifying and targeting problems and hot spots and implementing solutions. Police operational units must use foot patrols, directed patrols, citizen surveys, and other alternatives to random patrol to target crime and disorder problems. The police must ensure that they have an intensified police presence through larger numbers of positive and negative citizen contacts. The police must not only focus on serious crime, but also attend to minor offenses, disorder, and incivilities that lead to increased levels of crime. Order maintenance and the provision of service become more important.

Problem Solving and Situational Crime Prevention

Two primary tactics in community policing are problem solving (Eck and Spellman, 1987) and situational crime prevention (Clarke, 1992). *Problem solving* consists of the following four-step process:

1. Specific identification of the problem.
2. Careful analysis of the problem and its attributes.
3. Identification of possible solutions.
4. Implementation of a solution and a subsequent evaluation to measure the effectiveness of the solution.

When attempting to solve problems, officers should ask themselves simple questions such as, What is the problem? What is causing the problem? And what can I do to resolve it? Effective solutions require comprehensive responses. For

Officers patrolling in nation's capitol.
Judy Gelles/Stock Boston

effective problem solving to occur, solutions must go beyond traditional police responses. Possible solutions include encouraging the city to demolish an abandoned building being used as a crack house; tighter enforcement of alcohol and disorder laws in and around bars and taverns that experience high levels of disorder; and encouraging citizens to construct fences around residential areas to prevent transients from entering the neighborhood and committing property crimes.

Situational crime prevention, a form of problem solving, consists of reducing criminal opportunities (1) directed at specific forms of crime; (2) that involve the management or manipulation of the environment; and (3) so as to increase the amount of effort the criminal must exert, increase the risk of apprehension, and reduce the rewards as perceived by potential offenders (Clarke, 1992). Adherents of situational crime prevention believe that crime is a product of "rational choices," where criminals weigh the likelihood of being discovered and punished against the potential benefits of the act (Cornish and Clarke, 1987). Increases in difficulty of committing crime or increasing the likelihood of apprehension results in reduced levels of crime. Therefore, crime prevention plays a key role in reducing crime.

Community Engagement

Community policing dictates that the community become involved in protecting itself. People must realize that crime and disorder are not the exclusive domain of the police and government. People have a responsibility to assist the police, especially in their own neighborhoods. At the operational level, citizens can become involved in a variety of ways. They can form neighborhood watches or citizen patrols, report criminal or suspicious activities, become involved in sports or educational activities for disadvantaged youth, assist non-governmental agencies in providing social services to the disadvantaged, or volunteer services to the police. The police must encourage, motivate, or otherwise induce citizens to become involved. This is best accomplished by planning for and providing opportunities for their involvement.

The police must also become involved in community building and empowerment. As discussed above, a neighborhood or community can be so disorganized that it does not have the resources to become involved in helping itself (Bursik and Grasmick, 1993). Thus the police must engage the community, identify leaders, and begin building the community—by no means an easy task. The police must work with religious and civic leaders to increase the level of neighborhood governance, and they must work to improve governance even when a neighborhood has a strong infrastructure. The reduction in crime and disorder should be concomitant with increases in self-governance. In essence, the police must assist in building a neighborhood's ability to ward off crime.

The preceeding sections provide a theoretical foundation for community policing. Community policing, as a model, is very complex; it entails implementation throughout a police department, not just by selected units or officers. It is complex also because it requires that the police department, at every level, be in synchronization with the community it serves. Finally, it is complex because it not only requires police agencies to do different things—meet with the community, allow citizen input into police operations, or emphasize order maintenance over law enforcement—but also means that police departments perform many of their old tasks differently.

Police organizations across America have implemented community policing in one form or another. Due to the complexity of the model and the diverse activities community policing might encompass, no single model has been developed to gauge how consistently community policing has been implemented. Regardless, community policing is the most effective mode of providing police services. Police administrators must embrace it and ensure that it is effectively implemented.

ADMINISTRATIVE ISSUES IN IMPLEMENTING COMMUNITY POLICING

Community policing, like any other program and strategy, is not easily implemented. Organization change, which is discussed in Chapter 15, is an intricate process that requires substantial effort and, sometimes, costs. As noted in the previous section, community policing affects the whole police organization, and to ensure that it is properly implemented throughout the department is quite laborious. Therefore, it is important to recognize some of the issues that may become problematic when a chief attempts to implement community policing.

Absence of Police Planning for Community Policing

We have noted how some police administrators have come to define community policing as a set of programs. Further, the previous section provides a comprehensive outline of how community policing is integrated into the police organization. When a police department is properly committed to community policing, the strategy affects each and every division, unit, and officer in the department. It is not just a set of independent programs that are implemented to give the appearance of community policing. The only way community policing can be properly implemented is through comprehensive planning (planning is discussed in more detail in Chapter 13). This plan should include:

1. What the department intends to accomplish.
2. How tasks will be divided across units within the department.
3. How old working conditions will change.
4. Who is responsible for specific activities.
5. Assignment of new tasks and responsibilities through direction and training.
6. Monitoring activities to ensure that community policing functions as it should, and that it results in the desired outcomes.

Resistance to Change

Perhaps the most formidable obstacle to implementing community policing is a department's resistance to change. Organizations, like people, are resistant to change. (This is why we devote a full chapter on the change process.) People get into routines, and in time these routines become comfortable. Moreover, these routines are constantly reinforced through supervision, policies, and training. It is extremely difficult to change this imprint on employees and the organization itself. Moreover, as the department implements community policing through the change process, it is likely to find that the change has unintended consequences in other areas. Obviously, community policing is considerably more complex than any other program or strategy that a department may have attempted to implement previously. Community policing touches all facets of the police organization, and when implemented, it intrudes on everyone's way of doing things. Typically, people resist this, which often results in poor performance. Administrators must constantly monitor all facets of the department to ensure that implementation is progressing as it should.

Officer Difficulties in Accepting Community Policing

Considerable research shows that officers are resistant to community policing. Lord (1996) examined officers in the Charlotte-Mecklenburg County Police Department and found that community policing contributed to substantial officer stress. Along these same lines, Yates and Pillai (1996) found that the implementation of community policing resulted in officer strain and frustration. Zhao, He, and Lovrich (1999) examined community policing in a medium-sized police department and found that its implementation led to a change in police values, but the changes were inconsistent with community policing. When community policing was implemented in Philadelphia, the union opposed it (Greene, Bergman, and McLaughlin, 1994). Hoover assessed community policing in Houston as follows:

> At least 80 percent of the patrol officers involved remain strong skeptics. Most are outright critics. Command staff indicate that at best 20 percent of the officers who have been involved in the neighborhood-oriented patrol effort are supporters. Indeed, skeptical managers point out that the 20 percent support may well represent individuals who have decided that the politically correct way to get ahead in the organization is to support the initiatives of central administration. Keep in mind that these are not patrol officers who have merely received a one-hour orientation to community policing. They have had a great deal of training, have been in numerous discussion sessions on neighborhood-oriented patrol, and have been assigned to neighborhood-oriented patrol areas for a number of years. (1992:23–24)

Administrators must recognize that such resistance exists. If officers do not accept community policing, it will not function properly. Administrators must take action to overcome these officer problems. It seems that much of this resistance is rooted in job satisfaction and role confusion. Officers become less satisfied with their jobs when community policing is implemented. This must be considered when implementing it.

Requirement of Additional Resources

The implementation of community policing is costly. Although proponents of community policing discuss reorienting police services to emphasize order maintenance and the provision of services to the community over law enforcement, police departments must continue to perform law enforcement activities. Some of a department's resources and personnel may be reallocated to community policing, but a need for additional personnel, equipment, and facilities is very likely. For example, if a department as part of its community policing initiative decides to open community policing centers in disadvantaged neighborhoods, a strategy used by many community policing departments, facilities will have to be secured and staffed. Along the same lines, if the department begins offering a citizen academy, it will require substantial training resources. Many departments do not have the resources to fully implement community policing.

Difficulties in Getting the Community Involved

As noted above, community partnerships are one of the two primary principles underlying community policing. To understand how the community is involved in community policing, we must first define what a community is. Trojanowicz, Kappeler, and Gaines (2002) have identified eight attributes of a community:

1. It has a particular geographic area or location.
2. It is a recognized legal entity.

Police officer talks to preschool class about home safety in Port Angeles, Washington.
Paul Conklin/PhotoEdit

3. Social interactions within it include a division of labor and a sense of interdependence.
4. It is composed of citizens with a shared culture, interest, outlook, or perspective.
5. It possesses a moral dimension where values are transmitted.
6. Social interactions within it collectively shape its character.
7. It is defined by processes of inclusion and exclusion.
8. Its citizens possess a shared sentiment, a sense of belonging and interdependence.

These attributes show that a community is more than a neighborhood that is defined by artificial geographical boundaries. It is a place where residents interact socially and develop a sense of shared responsibility.

Unfortunately, many communities or neighborhoods suffer from social disorganization or transition to the point that they do not meet the eight attributes. Generally, such communities are exemplified by a significant amount of poverty, low-cost rental property with a continuous turnover of occupants, lack of a sense of community, and high levels of disorder and crime. These are the communities or neighborhoods that pose the greatest challenges to the police, and they are the neighborhoods where the police must exert the greatest efforts. Essentially, they lack a "sense of community" and the police must help organize the neighborhoods to combat crime and disorder. These communities will never be turned around with a partnership between the police and the citizens. Some see community building in such neighborhoods as an impossible task; however, for the police to make any headway, they need the assistance of the neighborhood residents.

EVALUATING A DEPARTMENT'S COMMUNITY POLICING EFFORTS

We have discussed how community policing should be implemented in the police agency and some of the pitfalls and problems when implementing it. Clearly, a department should ensure that it is implemented properly and that it results in the desired outcomes. Activating a series of programs or initiatives is not enough; a department should develop evaluation criteria that can be used to monitor the efforts and determine if it functions according to expectations. Watson, Stone, and DeLuca (1998) identified five areas that must be evaluated and monitored: departmental structure, community involvement, quality of service, citizen satisfaction, and employee satisfaction. Table 3–2 outlines the areas that must be addressed.

Table 3–2

Areas for Evaluating Community Policing

Departmental Structure

How are police services delivered?
Is there a proper allocation of human resources?
Do officers have the discretion to engage in community policing?
Do managers and supervisors understand their roles in community policing?
Is there adequate coordination among police units?

Community Involvement

Is there community policing in all aspects of the department?
Are all communities represented in the department?
Have the police built adequate community partnerships?

Quality of Police Services in a Community

Does the department have a shared sense of mission?
Does the department have a customer orientation?

Measuring Community Satisfaction with the Police

Is there evidence of citizen satisfaction?
How do citizens in disenfranchised neighborhoods feel about the police?
Do the community and police have a mutual understanding of community policing?

Employee Understanding and Acceptance of Community Policing

Have officers been properly trained in community policing?
Are officers committed to community policing?
Do officers have proper support?

Departmental Structure

In implementing community policing, administrators tailor the department's structure and management practices to ensure effective operation. This may include creating new special units, assigning new tasks to units, and monitoring units' activities to ensure that the community policing program is effective. Police administrators when implementing community policing tend to focus on changing officers rather than the organization (Gianakis and Davis, 1998). Equal attention must be given to officers and the departmental structure. The following are some of the structural areas that the administrator should consider.

How Are Police Services Delivered?

Community policing requires that operational personnel, especially uniformed officers, be heavily involved in the delivery of police services. Many police departments assign large numbers of officers to desk jobs, where they never come into contact with citizens. Administrators must ask, Are as many of our officers as possible assigned to the street, working with people? Have we increased the interaction between the police and the public to foster better relations and assist in developing a cooperative relationship? Parks and his colleagues (1999) found that when officers are meeting with and engaging citizens they tend to spend a majority of their time with citizens they know or citizens who have no problems with the police. Administrators and supervisors must take action to ensure that officers spend an increasing amount of time with disenfranchised citizens and communities.

Is There a Proper Allocation of Human Resources?

Patrol has always been the backbone of the police department. Patrol is responsible for answering calls for service and preventing crime. Now, many police departments expect their patrol officers to be involved in community policing. Patrol officers are required to meet with citizens to discuss their concerns and problems. Since patrol officers are on the front lines, administrators desire that they assist the department in identifying problems that should be addressed. They are often expected to deliver the services that are required to alleviate identified problems.

However, to fulfill these expectations, patrol officers must have the time to work with the community. Many departments have such a high volume of calls for service that officers spend the majority of their time responding to calls. Do officers have the time to engage in community policing activities? Community policing is doomed to failure if officers cannot participate in community policing activities. As noted above, community policing is expensive in that it entails a wide range of new activities and responsibilities. Administrators must ensure that operational units such as patrol have enough personnel to perform community policing activities. This may require assigning additional officers to patrol or reducing their workload by having some tasks assigned to another unit.

Do Officers Have the Discretion to Engage in Community Policing?

Traditionally, police officers have had a tremendous amount of discretion in dealing with the public (Walker, 1993b). The professional model of policing attempted to limit discretion to reduce police corruption and officer misbehavior. Police departments limited discretion by implementing restrictive policies and providing officers with close supervision. How officers responded to calls for service and crime was fairly well restricted. Community policing, on the other hand, assumes that officers have substantial discretion. Under the community policing paradigm, officers are expected to work with citizens and other agencies to devise the best possible response to a situation or problem. For example, officers need the discretion to call on the sanitation department to assist in cleaning up a neighborhood, or to call on the recreation department to assist in offering after-school recreation programs in a disadvantaged neighborhood that has a large number of youth who are beginning to be involved in crime and disorder activities. Community policing requires that officers have maximum discretion. Do police officers engaging in community policing have the discretion to do their jobs properly?

Do Managers and Supervisors Understand Their Roles in Community Policing?

Police managers and supervisors are at the heart of community policing. They are responsible for ensuring that it is properly implemented. Thus, managers must guarantee that line units have the personnel to perform community policing tasks. They must also delegate authority and decision-making responsibilities to line officers and units. Here, do managers and supervisors take on a facilitative role rather than a supervisory role? Do they assist and guide officers in problem solving and building community relationships? Have bureaucratic impediments such as excessive paperwork, restrictive policies, or assignments that do not contribute to the police mission been reduced?

Is There Adequate Coordination among Police Units?

Patrol is not the only unit involved in community policing. The planning unit should develop plans that facilitate its implementation. The community relations unit should develop programs such as police athletic leagues, community crime prevention, neighborhood watches, and after-school tutoring programs. Police officials need to organize and attend neighborhood meetings. Administrators must develop cooperative relations with other governmental and private agencies to provide needed services. All of these programs are needed to implement community policing. Are all units engaged in community policing properly coordinated? This is accomplished through the development of new policies and meetings to constantly monitor activities and make adjustments when necessary.

Community Involvement

As noted earlier in this chapter, community partnerships are one of the primary ingredients in community policing. There are several areas that should be monitored to ensure that the department is connecting with the community.

Is There Community Policing in All Aspects of the Department?

Community partnerships do not mean just working with a patrol or a specialized unit devoted to community policing. It means that the community has feedback into all aspects of a department's operations. Patrol should be targeting problems that are identified as high priorities by the community. The department's disciplinary and complaint investigations should respond to problems in the department that affect the community. Criminal investigators need to focus on victims' needs rather than concentrating on processing cases. Traffic officers should enforce traffic laws where there is a history of citizen complaints as opposed to writing tickets where offenses are easily observed. Do all units operate within the philosophy of community policing?

Are All Communities Represented in the Department?

Every city or jurisdiction is composed of several different communities or neighborhoods. They range across a wide spectrum of social class, economic viability, and racial and ethnic composition. Each of these communities has its own unique needs, and the police must ensure that those needs are served. In most jurisdictions, the police have the greatest concentration of officers or resources in the high-crime areas, which generally are low socioeconomic neighborhoods. Even if these areas receive a disproportionate level of services, they may not be adequately served. Do the police go beyond answering calls for service and engage in problem solving to reduce the problems in every neighborhood that contribute to crime and disorder?

On the other hand, numerous neighborhoods have low levels of calls for services. The police tend to be driven by the number of calls for service they receive, and therefore they sometimes neglect or disregard these areas. The police must remember that these neighborhoods also have needs and concerns. The police, therefore, periodically should take a close look at what is happening in these neighborhoods and respond to any needs. Are the needs of these neighborhoods being addressed?

Have the Police Built Adequate Community Partnerships?

There are two kinds of partnerships the police must be concerned with. First, the police must partner with people in neighborhoods and community organizations such as churches and neighborhood associations. These types of partnerships will facilitate getting people involved in combating crime and disorder. Here, are the people involved in attacking crime and disorder problems?

The second kind of partnership consists of relationships with other governmental, social, and private agencies. These agencies can provide a vast array of services to a community or neighborhood. For example, the police in some cities work with social service agencies to host job fairs in disadvantaged communities in an effort to relieve unemployment. The police can work with schools to develop after-school tutoring programs or with school officials to offer classes in anger management for youths who are having problems in school. Is the department maximizing its relations with other agencies and organizations to facilitate community policing?

Quality of Police Services in a Community

Police administrators often concentrate on outputs, or the number and types of services provided to the community. Police administrators must also consider the quality of services. That is, do the services accomplish a goal that fits within the police mission? There are several measures that the administrator can consider when attempting to evaluate whether the department is providing quality services.

Does the Department Have a Shared Sense of Mission?

A police department's values should reflect the needs of its community. This ensures that the department is interconnected to the community and is providing the best possible police services. The department's mission and value statements should reflect an understanding of each neighborhood or community's needs. Does everyone in the department have a shared understanding of the department's community policing mission?

Does the Department Have a Customer Orientation?

The police department is a governmental agency whose purpose is to serve the public. Are citizens satisfied with the service they receive? Are they satisfied with how they are treated by the police? Do the police do everything in every case to provide the utmost service to their constituency, the citizens? These are questions that departments, as well as each officer, should constantly ask. The police should never lose sight of their purpose.

Measuring Community Satisfaction with the Police

Thus far in this section, we have discussed how the police should respond to the public. It is important for the police to obtain feedback on how the department is serving community needs. The following are several questions that should be addressed when attempting to determine if the police have been successful in meeting community needs.

Is There Evidence of Citizen Satisfaction?

Does the police department receive feedback from citizens substantiating that the department is doing a good job? This evidence may be in the form of letters to the editor and stories in the newspaper, comments to the chief when he or she attends various community functions, or information gained from surveys mailed to the public. A lack of information of this sort likely reflects major problems between the police and the community.

How Do Citizens in Disenfranchised Neighborhoods Feel about the Police?

The police in an effort to solve crime problems in high-crime areas have been using aggressive patrolling. This results in a number of negative contacts with many law-abiding citizens that are expressed in complaints of racial profiling, excessive police force, or bias-based policing. Have there been efforts to mediate the effects of aggressive policing on the ill feelings that they cause? Has the department addressed the problems of racial profiling that often result from aggressive policing?

Do the Community and Police Have a Mutual Understanding of Community Policing?

Since its inception, politicians have advocated community policing as the panacea to end all problems. Police administrators engaged in it understand that community policing will help solve a number of problems, but it is not a solution that will end all problems. Does the community understand what community policing is and how it works? Does each segment in the community understand its role in community policing and the amount of work to be done? Do citizens have a proper understanding of the police role in the community? Administrators must engage and educate the community to facilitate its involvement.

Employee Understanding and Acceptance of Community Policing

We previously addressed the problem of officer resistance to community policing. Obviously, if a department's community policing efforts are to be successful, rank-and-file officers must be committed to it.

Have Officers Been Properly Trained in Community Policing?

A department cannot expect officers to immediately engage in community policing. Do officers have the skills and knowledge to engage in community policing? What kinds of training do they need? Once officers have been trained, the department must ensure that the training was effective. Did the training result in the desired outcomes? Do officers have not only the skills and knowledge but a commitment as well?

Are Officers Committed to Community Policing?

It is difficult to move officers in a professionally, law-enforcement-oriented department to one where officers emphasize service, order maintenance, and problem solving. However, this is necessary if a department is to become a community policing department. Administrators must ask, Do officers have a commitment to community policing? Are officers properly rewarded when they engage in community policing?

Do Officers Have the Proper Support?

Do officers feel that the department supports their individual efforts to engage the public or solve problems? Are officers given the ability to make decisions about their patrol beats or individual cases to solve problems or assist citizens? Do sergeants and lieutenants support or facilitate their decisions? Managers and supervisors must encourage and support community policing efforts if community policing is going to prevail over the long term.

This section has raised a number of questions that must be asked when a department implements community policing. Addressing these questions allows a department to evaluate the effectiveness of its efforts. No area can be neglected here. If one area is not properly addressed and problems result, there will be problems and issues in other areas. Again, community policing is a comprehensive philosophy that must be ingrained throughout a department.

Summary

This chapter examined the new police paradigm, community policing. Community policing has replaced the professional model of policing as the dominant way police departments operate and are managed. For the most part, community policing is different in that it emphasizes order maintenance and the provision of services to the community. It entails the police department's recognition of the need for and the development of community partnerships. The police need to address problems in the community that cause crime and disorder, rather than merely responding to them. To facilitate community policing, administrators must decentralize authority and give officers and units the ability to engage the community and solve problems.

The majority of police departments have implemented community policing, some more effectively than others. Many departments have employed a number of different strategies in their community policing programs. However, if a department is to be effective in community policing, it must make an effort to comprehensively implement it. This means that every officer and unit in the department has and executes its community policing role. Partial implementation will result in a partially functional program at best.

Finally, a number of organizational impediments make community policing difficult to implement. There must be adequate planning, and when this planning occurs, the administrator must consider the department's structure, the community, and subordinate personnel. The police department is a system where each piece or component affects the others. As such, community policing must be implemented comprehensively.

Study Questions

1. How is community policing implemented at the philosophical level, strategic level, and programmatic level?

2. What are some of the difficulties in implementing community policing?

3. How is the department affected in implementing community policing?

4. How does the relationship with the community change as a result of implementing community policing?

5. How can we evaluate the community's satisfaction with community policing?

6. What can a department do to ensure that officers become committed to community policing?

Net Resources

http://www.communitypolicing.org Community Policing Consortium, a partnership of several leading police organizations in the United States (e.g., PERF, IACP).

http://www.usdoj.gov/cops/home.htm Office of Community Oriented Policing Services, U.S. Department of Justice; provides local law enforcement organizations
with funding to do community policing.

http://www.policing.com/ Community policing website; contains links to several community policing related websites.

References

Bayley, D. H. (1988). Community policing: A report from the devil's advocate. In J. Greene and S. Mastrofski (eds.), *Community Policing: Rhetoric or Reality.* New York: Praeger, pp. 225–238.

Bursik, R. J., and Grasmick, H. G. (1993). Economic deprivation and neighborhood crime rates. *Law and Society Review* 27:263–283.

Cain, M. (1971). On the beat: Interaction and relations in rural and urban police forces. In S. Cohen (ed.), *Images of Deviance.* Baltimore: Penguin, pp. 62–67.

Clarke, R. V. (1992). *Situational Crime Prevention: Successful Case Studies.* New York: Harrow and Heston.

Cordner, G. W. (1999). Elements of community policing. In L. Gaines and G. Cordner (eds.), *Policing Perspectives: An Anthology.* Los Angeles: Roxbury Press, pp. 137–149.

Cornish, D. B., and Clarke, R. V. (1987). Understanding crime displacement: An application of rational choice theory. *Criminology* 25:933–947.

Crank, J. (1990). The influence of environmental and organizational factors on police style in urban and rural environments. *Journal of Research in Crime and Delinquency* 27(2):166–189.

Eck, J., and Spellman, W. (1987). Who ya gonna call? The police as problem solvers. *Crime and Delinquency* 33(1):31–52.

Fogelson, R. (1977). *Big-City Police.* Cambridge, MA: Harvard University Press.

Gianakis, G., and Davis, J. (1998). Reinventing or repackaging public services? The case of community-oriented policing. *Public Administration Review* 58(6):485–498.

Goldstein, H. (1979). Improving policing: A problem-oriented approach. *Crime and Delinquency* 25:236–258.

Greene, J. R. (1987). Foot patrol and community policing: Past practices and future prospects. *American Journal of Police* 6(1):1–15.

Greene, J. R., Bergman, W. T., and McLaughlin, E. J. (1994). Implementing community policing: Cultural and structural change in police organizations. In D. Rosenbaum (ed.), *The Challenge of Community Policing: Testing the Promise.* Thousand Oaks, CA: Sage, pp. 92–109.

Grinc, R. M. (1994). "Angels in marble": Problems in stimulating community involvement in community policing. *Crime and Delinquency* 40(3):437–468.

Hoover, L. (1992). Police mission: An era of debate. In L. Hoover, (ed.), *Police Management: Issues and Perspectives.* Washington: Police Executive Research Forum.

International Association of Chiefs of Police (1990). *Managing the Small Law Enforcement Agency.* Dubuque, IA: Kendall/Hunt Publishing.

Lord, V. (1996). An impact of community policing: Reported stressors, social support, and strain among police officers in a changing police environment. *Journal of Criminal Justice* 24(6):503–522.

Mastrofski, S. (1988). Community policing as reform: A cautionary tale. In J. Greene and S. Mastrofski (eds.), *Community Policing: Rhetoric or Reality.* New York: Praeger.

McDonald, T. D. (1996). Some economic realities of rural criminal justice. In T. McDonald, R. Wood, and M. Pflug (eds.), *Rural Criminal Justice: Conditions, Constraints, and Challenges.* Salem, WI: Sheffield.

Murphy, C. (1988). Community problems, problem communities, and community policing in Toronto. *Journal of Research in Crime and Delinquency* 25(4):392–410.

Parks, R. B., Mastrofski, S. D., DeJong, C., and Gray, M. K. (1999). How officers spend their time with the community. *Justice Quarterly* 16(3):483–518.

Peak, K. J., and Glensor, R. W. (1999). *Community Policing and Problem Solving: Strategies and Practices,* 2nd ed. Upper Saddle River, NJ: Prentice Hall.

Reaves, B., and Goldberg, A. (1997). *Local Police Departments—1997.* Washington: National Institute of Justice.

Rosenbaum, D. (1994). *The Challenge of Community Policing: Testing the Promise.* Thousand Oaks, CA: Sage.

Sadd, S., and Grinc, R. (1994). Innovative neighborhood oriented policing: An evaluation of community policing programs in eight cities. In D. Rosenbaum (ed.), *The Challenge of Community Policing.* Thousand Oaks, CA: Sage.

Spellman, W. (1988). *Beyond Bean Counting: New Approaches to Managing Crime Data.* Washington: Police Executive Research Forum.

Stevens, D. J. (2001). *Case Studies in Community Policing.* Upper Saddle River, NJ: Prentice Hall.

Trojanowicz, R., Kappeler, V. E., and Gaines, L. K., (2002). *Community Policing: A Contemporary Perspective,* 3rd ed. Cincinnati: Anderson Publishing.

Walker, S. (1992). *The Police in America,* 2nd ed. New York: McGraw-Hill.

Walker, S. (1993a). Does anyone remember team policing? Lessons of the team policing experience for community policing. *American Journal of Police* 12(1):33–56.

Walker, S. (1993b). *Taming the System.* New York: Oxford University Press.

Watson, E. M., Stone, A. R., and DeLuca, S. M. (1998). *Strategies for Community Policing.* Upper Saddle River, NJ: Prentice Hall.

Webb, V. J., and Graham, N. (1994). Citizen ratings of the importance of selected police duties. Paper presented at the annual meeting of the American Society of Criminology, Miami, FL.

Webb, V. J., and Katz, C. M. (1997). Citizen ratings of the importance of community policing activities. *Policing: An International Journal of Police Strategy, and Management* 20(1):7–23.

Weisheit, R., Falcone, D., and Wells, L. (1996). Crime and policing in rural and small town America. Prospect Heights, IL: Waveland Press.

Wilson, J. Q., and Kelling, G. (1982). Police and neighborhood safety: Broken windows. *Atlantic Monthly* 29 (March):29–38.

Wilson, O. W., and McLaren, B. (1977). *Police Administration,* 4th ed. New York: McGraw-Hill.

Wilson, W. J. (1987). *The Truly Disadvantaged: The Inner City, the Underclass, and Public Policy.* Chicago: University of Chicago Press.

Yates, D. L., and Pillai, V. K. (1996). Attitudes toward community policing: A causal analysis. *Social Science Journal* 33(2):193–210.

Zhao, J., He, N., and Lovrich, N. P. (1999). Value change among police officers at a time of organizational reform: A follow-up study using Rokeach values. *Policing: An International Journal of Police Strategies and Management* 22(2):152–170.

Part II

Organizational Perspectives

Part II, Organizational Perspectives, consists of two chapters, Foundations of Police Organization and Contemporary Organizational Theories and Management Systems. These two chapters build specifically on the material presented in Chapter 1, and more generally on the other two chapters in Part I. A fundamental understanding of the environmental influences on police organizations is essential to full comprehension of the organizational perspectives presented in Part II.

The foundations chapter (Chapter 4) is devoted to the development of police administration. That is, it examines traditional police administrative practices in terms of how they have evolved to their current status and their implications for a department's operational effectiveness. The contemporary management chapter (Chapter 5), on the other hand, examines a number of administrative and management practices that can be used in conjunction with traditional organizational philosophies; in some cases, options are presented that can be used to replace elements of traditional thinking.

These two chapters in combination present the foundation for understanding police administration. As discussed in Chapter 1, police administration consists of organization and management. This part examines how police departments should be structured. The structuring of a police agency, to a large extent, dictates the department's overall effectiveness. This part provides the basis for understanding and assessing the administrative and managerial activities described in Part III and Part IV. Understanding the remaining chapters in this text depends to a great extent on a thorough and clear understanding of the material presented in these two chapters.

An understanding of these two chapters is especially important in this current era of community policing. The overwhelming majority of police departments in this country have implemented some form of community policing. Some departments have made greater commitments than others to this new form of policing. Regardless, community policing necessitates change on the part of police departments and their personnel. Some of this change is structural alterations in the department. This part, along with Chapter 3, provides a basis for restructuring and successfully implementing community policing.

4

Foundations of Police Organization

Michael Newman/PhotoEdit

Chapter Outline

Introduction

Traditional Police Organization

Classical Organizational Theory
Scientific Management
Weber's Principles of Management

Criticisms of Traditional Police Management
Inconsistency
Authoritarianism
Lack of Innovation
Information Flow Problems
Lack of Motivation

In Defense of Classical Theory

Summary

Learning Objectives

After reading this chapter, you should be able to

1. Understand the roots of classical organizational theory and its relation to bureaucracy.
2. Know how scientific management is applied to organizations today.
3. Determine how the principle of hierarchy or chain of command is used in the police setting.
4. Understand the importance of authority in the police department.
5. Explain how and why specialized units are created in the police organization.
6. Know the deficiencies or criticisms of classical organizational theory.
7. Critique the criticisms or defend classical organizational theory.

T he Columbus, Ohio, Police Department has about 1,800 officers and serves a community of 700,000. The police department has embraced community policing, which has been implemented there for a number of years. To facilitate community policing, the department created the Strategic Response Bureau. The bureau has a staff of nearly 100 officers, whose job is to identify problems in Columbus and help fashion an effective response to them. The bureau consists of three sections. The community liaison section is charged with implementing programs that foster better relations with the community. The enforcement section focuses on problem solving, particularly neighborhood crime problems and specific crime patterns. The investigative section has zone investigators who are assigned to an area or neighborhood; a criminal career liaison unit that targets offenders who commit large amounts of crime; and a criminal information unit that collects data and information that is used to facilitate community policing and other enforcement efforts (Stevens, 2001).

The Columbus Police Department is an example of how the police organization has been affected by the implementation of community policing. The Columbus chief understood that organizational arrangements must be altered so that community policing can be implemented. It is an example of how organization promotes the accomplishment of police goals and objectives. There is a direct relationship among success, organization, and management. This relationship is examined in this chapter.

INTRODUCTION

Police departments are typically organized according to classical organizational principles. Some departments have incorporated innovative or contemporary features such as participative management or community policing into their organizational philosophy, but most departments, especially larger ones, use classical organization to a degree. This chapter is devoted to the discussion of these principles in relation to policing. As noted in Chapter 1, classical organizational theory is the oldest management philosophy in existence today and thereby provides the foundation for any study of organizations. Due to the length of time classical organizations have existed and the depth of study to which they have been exposed, there is a great deal more information on classical organizations than on newer organizational forms.

Classical organizational theory is characterized by a highly ordered or organized structure, and police departments generally adhere to this philosophy of order and structure. The sections that follow outline the tenets of the classical organizational theory and how they are applied in traditional police management. Human relations and contingency theories that came after classical theory are described in Chapter 5. By examining the various theories, the police manager is provided with a variety of ways to manage the police organization. It is the responsibility of the police executive to select internally consistent structural and management philosophies that enable the department to most effectively and efficiently serve the needs of the community.

TRADITIONAL POLICE ORGANIZATION

The *traditional* or *classical police organization* is a quasi-military model. The first modern police department was in London, England, where Sir Robert Peel used the quasi-military model as the basis for organizing the department in 1829. He used the following principles:

1. The police must be stable, efficient, and organized along military lines.
2. The police must be under government control.
3. The absence of crime will best prove the efficiency of police.

4. The distribution of crime news is essential.
5. The deployment of police strength both by time and area is essential.
6. No quality is more indispensable to a policeman than a perfect command of temper; a quiet, determined manner has more effect than violent action.
7. Good appearance commands respect.
8. The securing and training of proper persons is at the root of efficiency.
9. Public security demands that every police officer be given a number.
10. Police headquarters should be centrally located and easily accessible to the people.
11. Policemen should be hired on a probationary basis.
12. Police records are necessary to the best distribution of police strength (Germann, Day, and Gallati, 1978).

Peel's police organizational principles, for the most part, remain ingrained in American policing. They are as applicable today as they were in 1829.

The quasi-military model has long standing in the police community. American police initially adopted this model described to American police managers in 1950 by O. W. Wilson's classic textbook, *Police Administration.* Wilson used classical organizational theory as the basis for how police departments should be organized and managed. During this period, American police service could be dichotomized into the traditional force—plagued by politics, scandal, and poor performance—and the so-called professional or legalistic force—manifesting nonpartisanship, integrity, and technical efficiency. The professional style, advocated by Vollmer (Berkeley), Wilson (Chicago), and Parker (Los Angeles), developed from the reform era and exemplified classic bureaucracy or organizational theory. It is this model that is now referred to as traditional or professional police administration. The professional model of police administration was highly structured and emphasized control. Professional managers implemented this model in an effort to eliminate police corruption and the influence of outside politics. It was reasoned that if police departments operated as the military did, managers could exert enough control to ensure that officers performed according to management's standards.

Prior to professional police management, most police organizations were disorganized, highly political, and ineffective in responding to community needs. Chiefs and sheriffs generally reported to politicians who dictated what the department did. Departments were ineffective in responding to crime. They tended to avail themselves to politicians' whims, and little else was important. Some agencies focused on providing services, because politicians saw this as a way of garnering support in the community (Gaines, Kappeler, and Vaughn, 1999).

CLASSICAL ORGANIZATIONAL THEORY

The two individuals who had the greatest impact on classical theory were Fredrick W. Taylor (1856–1915) and Max Weber (1864–1920). Taylor studied how work was performed. During his time, people often worked until exhaustion. Also, people often were assigned tasks that they did not understand or were incapable of performing efficiently. Thus people often worked ineffectively.

Weber, on the other hand, studied the management structure of successful organizations. He believed that proper structure would lead to more efficiency. Together, these theories spawned bureaucracy.

Scientific Management

Taylor's contribution was in the area of increasing worker productivity by studying work and how it is performed, that is *scientific management*. In short, he believed that scientific principles should be applied to work so that workers would exert the least amount of effort in accomplishing the greatest amount of work. Adherents of scientific management reasoned that if workers worked more efficiently, they would produce a greater volume of product at a lower cost. This would result in a lowering of the product's cost and many more people could afford to purchase the product. Workers could make more money, more consumers could purchase the product, and the company would have greater profits. Taylor's scientific management is used extensively today in business and industry in the form of efficiency studies or time–motion studies.

Taylor focused his efforts on the employee, which was a novel idea during his time. For the most part, employers in Taylor's day gave little if any consideration to workers and their plight. An example of Taylor's scientific management occurred in a rock quarry. Taylor was called upon to increase the rock quarry's productivity. He studied the workers and found that they were often fatigued and could not work effectively during much of the day. After considerable study, he made several alterations to how the work was done. First, he designed different shovels for various types or sizes of stone. He reasoned that different consistencies of stone had varying weights; therefore, the load would be too light when shoveling some types of stone, too heavy when shoveling others. If the weight was too great, the worker would become fatigued and unproductive. To remedy the problem, he had workers use specific shovels for each type of stone. This way he ensured that the weight was not too great and the worker would not become fatigued.

Second, he instituted work breaks to help ensure that workers did not become overly fatigued. The breaks would allow the worker to labor longer periods of time efficiently. To quote Taylor,

> Now, among the various methods and implements used in each element of each track there is always one method and one implement which is quicker and better than any of the rest. And this one best method and best implement can only be discovered or developed through a scientific study and analysis of all the methods and implements in use, together with accurate, minute, motion and time study. (1911:25)

Prior to Taylor, work was somewhat unorganized. The foreman was assigned to a project and his job was to ensure that his men worked. Generally, workers were engaged in numerous tasks that the foreman did not comprehend or have expertise in, and it was difficult for the foreman to supervise or increase worker output. Additionally, job standards were nonexistent. Most workers learned their particular trade by themselves. Thus several workers could perform the same task, with each performing it differently at varying degrees of efficiency.

Taylor felt that improvement would come only if management analyzed tasks and assumed more responsibility. These responsibilities included:

1. Develop a science for each element of a man's work, which replaces the old rule-of-thumb method.
2. Scientifically select and train, teach, and develop the workman, whereas in the past he chose his own work and trained himself as the best he could.
3. Heartily cooperate with the men so as to insure all of the work being done is in accordance with the principles of the science which has been developed.
4. There is an almost equal division of the work and the responsibility between the management and workmen (Taylor, 1911:25).

These tenets were an attempt to provide an orderly manner to work. Taylor's work suggested job planning, which had seldom occurred, and he attempted to have the worker and manager cooperate rather than oppose each other.

Taylor provided one other idea within the scientific management scheme, the concept of functional supervision. Custom had dictated one foreman for each work group. The work group would be responsible for a complete project and for accomplishing a wide variety of tasks. Taylor recognized that it was not possible for one foreman to master all the knowledge required to provide adequate supervision for these varied tasks. He felt there should be a system of functional supervision. *Functional supervision* is practiced by supervisors who are specialized and provide supervision for only those areas of the job in which they have expertise. Each supervisor would master all the knowledge required to provide adequate supervision for a particular facet among the numerous work groups. This had not been done in the past, because it was believed that workers should be responsible to only one supervisor. Taylor felt that functional supervision would increase efficiency since all facets of the job would be brought under the eyes of supervisors who possessed expertise in all relevant areas.

The result of Taylor's scientific management was to emphasize method over workers. The assumption that man is "rational" played a dominant role in his theory. *Rational man theory* dictated that people work for rewards (money) and, when properly rewarded, are productive. If there were mutual benefits, workers and management would cooperate. If there was cooperation, the principal goal of the theory—increased organizational efficiency—would be met.

Scientific management's other principle contributor, Henri Fayol, focused on the management of the organization. He believed there was a universal science of management applicable to all organizations. He recognized that the need for technical knowledge decreased as hierarchical position increased. Managers needed to have a knowledge of how to "manage" the organization, rather than to perform labor. Fayol developed five principles that he felt were imperative if an organization was to be successful:

1. A program of action prepared by means of annual and 10-year forecasts.
2. An organization chart to guarantee order and assure each man a definite place; careful recruiting and technical, intellectual, moral, administrative training of the personnel in all ranks in order to find the right man for each place.
3. Observation of the necessary principles in the execution of command (i.e., direction).
4. Meetings of the department heads of every division; conferences of the division heads presided over by the managing director to insure coordination.
5. Universal control, based on clear accounting data rapidly made available (Dale, 1965:148).

Whereas Taylor attempted to increase efficiency by improving managerial supervision, Fayol attempted to provide a system by which management itself would be more efficiently organized. Operationally, Fayol's principles meant that organizations should engage in long-range planning, establish time lines for work, properly supervise work, and coordinate everyone's activities through coordinative meetings.

Today, scientific management is used throughout business and industry. For example, assembly lines used in manufacturing are based on scientific management. Managers attempt to design jobs that allow the employee to be productive throughout the work shift. Utilization of scientific management in policing might take the form of studying response time to calls for service and redesigning patrol areas to reduce the response time. Other studies might be made of such things as the placement of handcuffs on the uniform to allow for ease of access without jeopardizing the officer's control of the arrest situation.

Weber's Principles of Management

Weber, on the other hand, studied what he termed efficient organizations and attempted to describe them by identifying those principles that made them efficient. He believed that if the principles of efficient organizations could be identified, other organizations could adopt them and become more efficient. At the time, the most efficient organizations in society were the army and the Catholic Church. Weber examined them and described their inner workings. Weber attempted to create a rational management structure so that work processes could be better administered, that is, *bureaucratic management*. Weber was the father of "bureaucracy" insofar as he was the first to describe how the effective organizations of his time functioned. He did not invent bureaucracy, but he studied large, bureaucratic organizations and sought to identify the characteristics that would produce the ideal bureaucracy. Weber (1969) believed the ideal bureaucratic structure is based on a limited number of principles. Weber's principles are discussed here in the context of the police organization:

1. *Well-defined hierarchy of authority.* In every traditional police organization there exist superior–subordinate relations based on authority from the patrol officer to the chief of police. Each person at a higher position or

On the Job

SAN BERNARDINO SHERIFF'S DEPARTMENT
By Sheriff Gary Penrod

Courtesy of Officer Penrod

The San Bernardino Sheriff's Department has the responsibility of policing the largest county in the United States. At 20,157 square miles, San Bernardino County, California, offers a wide variety of geographical regions throughout its desert, urban, and mountain areas. The population of the county is 1.7 million, with approximately half, 824,000, under the jurisdiction of the sheriff. Eleven other police departments serve the rest of the population. The large population has many diverse cultures and different economic levels. This substantially complicates providing police services to the county.

The department has the responsibility of maintaining more than 5,000 inmates in the jails, court security, general law enforcement, specialized investigation, scientific investigation, aviation, and law enforcement training.

The 65 bureaus require 2,450 personnel, 1,540 sworn, to fulfill the mission. There are 16 patrol stations that service the unincorporated areas, with 12 being contract cities. An incorporated city may contract with the Sheriff's Department for law enforcement services instead of having its own police force. The station commander acts as the police chief to the council and city manager.

Rancho Cucamonga Patrol Station and Highland Patrol Station are contrasting contract stations. Each provides full police service for the town with responsibility for traffic investigations and all other matters. The Sheriff's Department supports the contract city with specialized personnel for investigations of narcotics, murder, arson, bomb and explosive investigation, and child abuse as part of the contract. The department also provides hiring, training, risk management, aviation, crime lab, jails, and personnel insurance for contract cities.

Rancho Cucamonga Station has 123 sheriff's personnel serving a population of 125,600 in the 38-square-mile city. The annual budget for 2000 was $10.2 million. The deputies handled 84,000 calls for service and took 14,000 reports. The city has the highest per capita income as well as being considered the safest place to live in the county.

Highland Patrol Station serves a population of 44,450 with 34 sheriff's personnel in the 25-square-mile city. The annual budget is $3 million. The

Continued

deputies handled 31,000 calls for service and took 6,556 reports.

The diversity of operation, locations, population, and the great expanse of the county result in a number of unique challenges to the department's leadership. Strict uniformity in the application of all policies is difficult because each station has distinctive challenges in personnel, location, or population. The size of the county results in some deputies having to drive up to four hours to reach headquarters. Management of San Bernardino Sheriff's Department works hard to overcome the inclination to eliminate discretion because of the separation from the main headquarters. A flexible management style, which pushes authority to the lowest level, is encouraged. Bureau and patrol station commanders are allowed some deviation in policies because of the unique nature of each command. The intention of the policy is followed and, if need, molded to fit the patrol area. Although there is more risk involved by not mandating all issues in a strict style, the department feels that the public receives better and more personal service from its law enforcement. Recent public polls show a high satisfaction rate with the public for San Bernardino Sheriff's Department.

The implementation of community-oriented policing (COP) for the entire department is one example of molding a policy to fit. Most police agencies have a strict model of how COP will work and what it will allow in individual discretion. When the Office of the Sheriff considered requiring all bureaus and stations in the department to do COP, it found that there was no model that fit all places or bureaus. The sheriff determined that a philosophy of COP would be the same, but each area would implement COP to fit its mission and needs. Each commander has implemented COP to meet the needs of his or her command. Consequently, there is some variation in the manner in which COP was implemented, but the spirit of this policy is the same.

The San Bernardino Sheriff's Department prides itself in being innovative and a leader in the policing field. It encourages risk at all levels and holds its members responsible for their actions. Proactive programs such as Crime-Free Multi-Housing for apartment complexes and Clean Sweep for public high schools have dramatically reduced crime and improved quality-of-life issues in these areas. Both of these programs were envisioned by line-level employees and pushed upward. The department's belief in the quality and training of its people allows a management style that rewards innovation yet provides customer and employee satisfaction.

rank has more authority than that person's subordinate. In this fashion everyone is directly supervised and controlled. This authority structure is commonly referred to as a chain of command.

2. *Specialization.* Every person's job is broken down into precise, routine, and well-defined tasks. By dividing tasks among several work groups the

organization becomes more efficient. In the case of police departments, specialization creates units such as criminal investigation, juvenile, traffic, and internal affairs.

3. *Formalization.* There must be a well-established system of rules and regulations detailing workers' duties and to ensure uniformity and reduce discretion. Most police departments have policies and procedures addressing how jobs are performed and what people are supposed to do.
4. *Impersonality of management.* When decisions are made they should be made without regard to personalities or individuals. Decision making should be based on the goals and objectives of the organization.
5. *Personnel decisions based on merit.* Positions should be filled and promotions made according to merit. The department must strive to place the best-qualified persons in the appropriate positions.

Police executives have selected Weber's bureaucratic style for a variety of reasons; consequently, it has had a significant effect on police management. The following sections further describe Weber's principles.

Hierarchy of Authority

The first principle of Weber's bureaucratic model, hierarchy of authority or chain of command, exists in all organizations but is very pronounced in the traditional police department. Military titles are used to identify the incumbents at each level of the organization and to clearly delineate the chain of command to those inside and outside the department. *Hierarchy of authority* or *chain of command* entails the superior–subordinate relationship throughout the department, wherein each individual is supervised by a superior officer. Hierarchy of authority refers to an organization of authority where a supervisor has more "authority" than subordinates but less authority than the superior officer to whom he or she reports. Thus authority is distributed hierarchically in an organization. The purpose of the relationship is to ensure that orders are followed, responsibility is placed with proper individuals, and everyone is aware of their responsibilities via direct supervision.

The chain of command provides the police executive a significant amount of control over the department. It also establishes channels that individuals use to formally communicate information and orders to other individuals throughout the department. For example, in Figure 4–1, the superintendent would give orders to the bureau commanders, who would then pass the orders on to their immediate subordinates, and so on. Information would go up the chain of command in a similar manner. If the chain of command operates properly, it is assumed that officers at each level of the organization will remain informed about departmental activities and responsibilities.

There is no formula or method for determining how many levels of hierarchy should exist in a given police department. Typically, however, hierarchy is added as departments grow in size. Large departments normally have more levels of rank than do smaller departments. Additional personnel require more

Figure 4-1

Chicago Police Department. Organization for command.

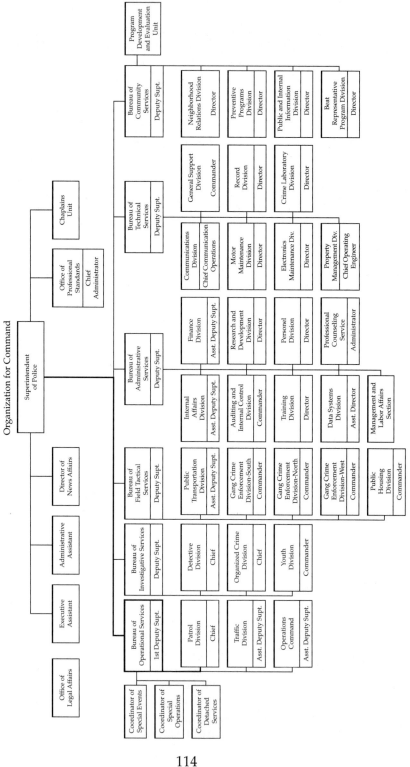

supervisors and managers. Also, larger departments generally have more units such as juvenile services, crime prevention, or auto theft that require supervision and management. For example, the Los Angeles Police Department has more than 200 different specialized units.

A natural problem associated with hierarchy is *excessive layering.* Excessive layering occurs when an organization has too many levels of rank. For example, if a major's rank is created when there are only a few captains in the department, the major's position is excessive or not necessarily needed in the department. Excessive layering results in buck passing, a lack of initiative on the part of managers and supervisors, formalized communications, and overly bureaucratic behavior. The existence of too many managers results in an overlap of responsibilities that eventually distorts how work is performed. Jaques (1990) notes that the creation of rank should result in *real value* being added to the work of subordinates. A hierarchical level should be added only when it improves performance. If performance is not improved, then additional positions or layers are not necessary.

Span of Control.   A number of organizational concepts are subsumed within the principle of hierarchy of authority. One of these concepts, *span of control,* refers to the number of officers or subordinates that a superior supervises without regard to the effectiveness or efficiency of that supervision. Traditional police supervision entails a superior exerting a great deal of control over subordinates. The superior is concerned with subordinates fulfilling responsibilities and completing work tasks, as well as ensuring that subordinates do not engage in behavior that is prohibited by the department. Control of officers by superiors is directly related to the number of subordinates that report to a superior officer—the essence of span of control. Normally a patrol sergeant supervises 6 to 10 patrol officers; the number of officers reporting to a sergeant constitutes the sergeant's span of control. The ratio of officers to superior directly affects the supervisor's ability to control the subordinates. A sergeant who is responsible for 15 officers will devote less time to each officer than the sergeant who is responsible for only 8 officers. Supervisors must be able to devote time and attention to each subordinate without being overly intrusive. The principle of span of control, then, balances efficiency and effectiveness of supervision.

Complexity of work and physical working conditions also affect span of control. The more complex a task or set of tasks, the more supervision required. This is especially true for technical tasks. For example, a detective supervisor who must constantly review reports, cases, and investigations cannot adequately supervise a large number of detectives. Simpler and less complex tasks require less supervision, such as supervising a group of records clerks. The physical working conditions also affect supervision. A supervisor's span of control can be greater when supervising office personnel as opposed to supervising a group of patrol officers since the office workers are confined to a central location, whereas patrol officers are spread over a large geographical area.

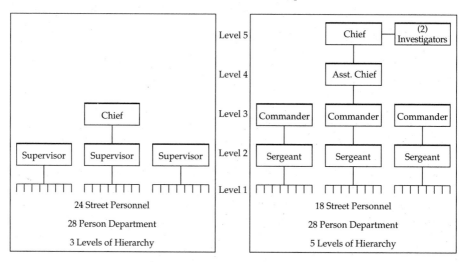

Figure 4–2
Broad span of control.

Figure 4–3
Narrow span of control.

Another consideration relating to span of control is its relation to the chain of command. First, the higher the rank within the chain of command, the smaller the span of control. That is, the ratio of captains per major should be less than the ratio of patrol officers to patrol sergeant. The reason for this is that the higher up the chain of command, the more difficult and complex the problems become. A problem at the major's level would in all probability affect everyone below the major in the chain of command. Consequently, these problems necessitate more consideration, information when making a decision, and time to develop solutions. This necessitates a reduction in the span of control so that commanders and administrators are not overwhelmed with time-consuming problems.

To a great extent, span of control determines the number of levels within the chain of command. The act of decreasing the span of control (reducing the number of officers reporting to a superior officer) will lead to additional levels of rank—making the organization taller and narrower than before (compare the department depicted in Figure 4–2 with the one in Figure 4–3).

The organization shown in Figure 4–2 has three levels of authority while the example in Figure 4–3 has five levels. The number of street personnel is also significantly different. There are 24 street personnel in the department depicted in Figure 4–2; the department in Figure 4–3 has only 18 street officers. Many departments have an overabundance of management and administrative positions as a result of a limited span of control and excessive layering. When the span of control is reduced, it necessarily creates the need for additional supervisors, and when supervisors are created, there normally must be additional management staff to manage them. Also, when more supervisory and management positions are created, the new positions generally reduce the number of police officers at the street level.

Span of control affects team building and participatory management. Too often, critics of close supervision advocate a larger span of control (supervising larger numbers of subordinates) to ensure that supervision does not become oppressive and adversely affect morale. However, it should be realized that an increased span of control diminishes positive interaction between superiors and subordinates. Superiors cannot engage in participatory management, solicit input for operational decisions, or engage in team-building activities if the span of control is so large as to necessitate the superior constantly moving from one subordinate to another when dealing with issues and problems. These issues highlight the need to search for an optimal span of control.

Unity of Command.   The second principle subsumed within hierarchy of authority, *unity of command,* refers to placing one and only one superior in command or in control of every situation and every employee. When a situation occurs necessitating the deployment of police resources (e.g., a hostage, terrorist, bombing, or sniper situation), it is imperative that some individual be responsible and in command of that situation. The unity of command concept is instituted to ensure that multiple or conflicting orders are not issued by several superior officers to the same police officers. For example, patrol officers may be dispatched to a barricaded-person scene. A patrol sergeant may arrive at the scene, deploy personnel, and commence to give other operational orders. The shift lieutenant may subsequently arrive and also issue orders to personnel at the scene. Confusion would most certainly result if the lieutenant issued orders without first ascertaining the actions of the sergeant and attempting to coordinate efforts. This problem is likely to occur in many police situations since the problems encountered by the police may cover large geographic areas: murder scenes, riots, or air and transportation disasters. In every situation, a superior officer should take command and coordinate the activities of all officers to ensure that police efforts are successful.

Another consideration regarding unity of command is to ensure that all police officers are aware of their immediate commander's orders and that the immediate commander is aware of the tasks in which subordinates are involved. That is, every person in the police organization reports to one and only one superior officer, and superior officers follow the chain of command when communicating with subordinate officers. A problem could exist if a patrol lieutenant gave a patrol officer orders without advising or conferring with the patrol officer's sergeant. If this occurred, the sergeant would not be aware of subordinates' activities, which could cause the sergeant problems in terms of deployment of officers or other assignments. Moreover, it could cause friction and conflict between the sergeant and lieutenant or between the sergeant and the patrol officer if the sergeant felt that the lieutenant subjugated the sergeant's authority. When the unity of command principle is followed, everyone involved is aware of the actions initiated by superiors and subordinates.

Finally, there are some instances when a superior exerts authority outside the pyramid of authority. Emergency or tactical situations may arise requiring the services of personnel from several different units within the police department.

For example, a crime scene may require patrol officers, detectives, and crime scene technicians. In such instances it is imperative that one superior be in charge (principle of unity of command). Departmental procedures should dictate how this situation will be commanded. In most police agencies, the patrol commander coordinates and commands activities in the field. In other agencies, the highest-ranking officer takes charge. In situations that require a large number of personnel or last for a long period of time, a command post is established to coordinate activities. All orders and communications to and from the scene are channeled through the command post and the commander to ensure that all activities are fully coordinated.

Delegation of Authority.   Delegation of authority is the third organizational principle within the principle of chain of command. *Delegation of authority* is the assignment of tasks, duties, and responsibilities to subordinates while at the same time giving them the power or right to control, command, make decisions, or otherwise act in performing the delegated responsibilities. As a police department becomes large and complex, it is difficult for a chief to exert control or monitor activities throughout the department. Therefore, to ensure that goals and objectives are being accomplished, the chief must delegate authority to subordinate ranking personnel and hold them accountable to the accomplishment of particular tasks. Delegation presents a problem in some agencies because the administrators and managers delegate responsibility for tasks to personnel below them in the chain of command but fail to give the individual commensurate authority for performance of the task. Proper delegation consists of assigning responsibility with the necessary authority to accomplish the task. Only then can a subordinate be held accountable for task achievement. Moreover, the manager must always remember that ultimate responsibility cannot be delegated; it remains with the delegator.

As an example of delegation of authority, we consider the Chicago Police Department, which has a typical traditional police organizational structure for a very large police agency. Figure 4–4 delineates the organizational structure for the Bureau of Operational Services. The first deputy superintendent in command of operational services delegates authority to the chief in command of patrol, and the chief then delegates authority to an area deputy chief, who then delegates authority to the district commanders. This delegation of authority follows the chain of command and is a method of task assignment wherein specific responsibilities are given to subordinates. Subordinates must not be expected to perform assignments or accomplish objectives unless they have the authority to do so. A patrol district commander who does not have the authority to redesign beat layouts, change shift hours, or change assignments cannot be held accountable for criminal and other police-related activities. That is, individuals must have the authority to plan and make decisions if they are to fulfill organizational requirements.

Delegation of authority is accomplished by two methods: policy formulation and direction. *Policy formulation* refers to the development of general orders, standard operating procedures, and other written documents generated by

Figure 4-4
Chicago Police Department, Bureau of Operational Services.

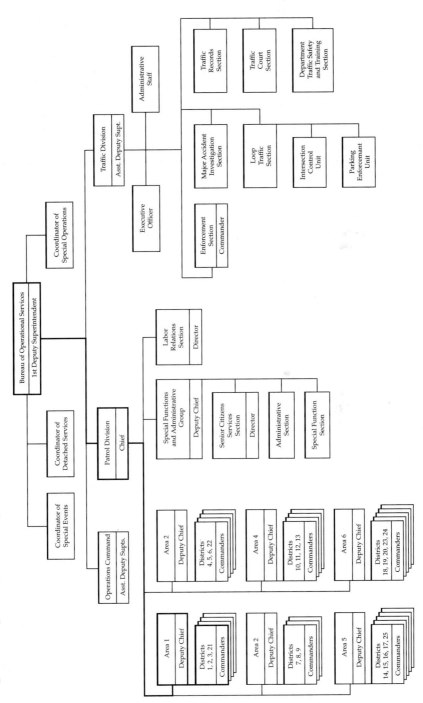

executives within the police department. Generally, the purpose of these is to place responsibility for the accomplishment of specific tasks and activities. For example, many police administrators require that patrol be responsible for the preliminary investigation of crimes, while detectives perform follow-up investigations. The specific requirements of patrol officers and investigative personnel would be detailed in a department procedure. The procedure would also vest certain authority with the patrol and investigative commanders so that activities could be properly supervised. It is most important that police executives ensure that all major activities within the department be spelled out in written policy documents. This is to ensure that there is uniformity in the manner in which tasks are performed. Coordination and control are enhanced since the policies outline unit and individual responsibilities and therefore allow a manager to assess accountability for purposes of disciplinary action when necessary.

Written police policies are supplemented with direction. *Direction* is the orders initiated by the chief, unit commander, or supervisor to guide subordinates' actions toward the accomplishment of some organizational objective. For example, a patrol sergeant may order two patrol units to increase the frequency of patrol in certain sections of their patrol beats in an effort to reduce burglaries. The patrol sergeant is responsible for a geographic area in the jurisdiction; therefore, to effectively control burglary in that section, the sergeant makes individual assignments designed to meet the organizational goal of controlling burglary. Direction is used at all levels of the police organization.

Direction also is used to clarify written directives, which are sometimes general in nature. The commander must periodically supplement and clarify policy to meet situational needs if the department is to remain abreast of changing crime patterns and citizen requests.

Police executives frequently give direction at staff meetings. Chiefs of police meet with their staff and unit commanders to discuss problems and their solutions. This type of format allows for a maximum of discussion so that everyone understands unit assignments. Staff meetings also provide the chief with an opportunity to determine how well individual units are coordinating their activities (to evaluate standard operating procedures) and to determine whether particular programs are working. Some police executives use vertical staff meetings. A *vertical staff meeting* consists of bringing together members from each level of the chain of command within a particular operating unit and soliciting their input for decision making. Vertical staff meetings can enhance morale and keep the commander attuned to problems at the street level, especially if subordinates feel comfortable in sharing their opinions in front of supervisors. However, if subordinates feel threatened in sharing their views, the vertical staff meeting may accomplish nothing. Regardless of the method chosen, police executives should meet regularly with their subordinates to provide them with direction.

Finally with regard to delegation of authority, it is important that the chief hold commanders of departmental units accountable for accomplishing duties and assignments. A chief cannot hold a commander accountable if the commander did not or does not have the proper authority. Once proper authority is dele-gated, commanders should and must be held accountable for their action or failure to act. This means that the chief must ensure that subordinates are doing their jobs. For example, if the clearance rate for felonies is too low, the chief should hold the investigation's commander accountable by asking why such a situation exists. At this point, the commander must be able to assess and report to the chief on the quality of investigations. Of course, there may be problems that are out of the commander's control, but the chief should ensure that this is the case. If an investigation's commander cannot account for changes in clear-ance rates, then the commander may not be in proper control of the unit. If the chief or other administrator regularly inquires into the daily operations of units, unit commanders will be more motivated to stay abreast and remain in close contact with their subordinates. This does not mean that a chief should constantly express concern over operations. However, it may, from time to time, become necessary to replace commanders whose units are not effective. The chief of police must be willing and ready to make this decision. Public interests must come before personal interests. Accountability must be exercised.

Specialization

Police *specialization* refers to division of labor, or job differentiation. As a police department increases in size, it becomes necessary to specialize. That is, it becomes inefficient for everyone to perform all tasks. The police executive must divide the tasks among various work groups or units. Tasks that are different may be performed by different individuals or groups to increase organizational effectiveness. For example, patrol officers perform tasks centering around responding to calls for assistance, making initial contact with citizens, and deterring crime. Traffic officers, on the other hand, investigate accidents, enforce traffic laws, and deploy special equipment such as radar units to apprehend speeding motorists. Each job consists of a number of tasks that are similar in nature. Thus each officer can be assigned certain responsibilities or jobs, can be taught the job, and can perform it efficiently.

When the chief executive is determining how tasks are to be divided, special care must be taken to ensure that the groupings contribute to departmental effectiveness. Generally, tasks are grouped according to four criteria: function, geography, time, and level of authority.

Function. When tasks are grouped according to function, job specialization is created. Function refers to how a particular task is performed and the purpose of performing it. The reason for functional specialization within a police department is usually to relieve patrol of burdensome, time-consuming tasks and to allow them to concentrate on repressing crime and answering calls for service. For example, criminal investigations may take anywhere from one hour to several days to complete, depending on the available evidence and the nature of the case. If patrol officers performed these investigations, they would not be available to perform routine patrol tasks. This is why police departments create detective units. When a police department's level of manpower reaches between 15 to 20 officers, the chief usually creates one or two detective positions. These detectives support patrol by allowing patrol officers to remain on their beats while the detectives investigate crimes.

The major areas of functional specialization are patrol, traffic, criminal investigation, vice, delinquency prevention, communications, records, and staff services such as planning and training. In large police departments there is specialization within the specialized units (see Figures 4–5 through 4–7).

Figure 4–5 is an example of how investigative units within a large police department might be organized. There are three major sections with several units in each section. The primary consideration in determining whether to establish each unit is the volume of workload. That is, these units should be organized only if there are enough cases to justify their existence. A medium-sized police department may only have three units: crimes against persons, crimes against property, and general investigations, with investigators investigating all other crimes. Figure 4–6 provides an overview of how the Bureau of Technical Services is organized, and Figure 4–7 shows how the Bureau of Community Services is organized.

Geography. Many police departments are so large or cover such a large geographic area that it becomes necessary to institute geographical differentiation. In geographical differentiation, a department uses substations or precinct stations as opposed to having all officers work out of a central headquarters. Many police departments use posts, sectors, districts, or precincts. For example, the California Highway Patrol has eight Division Offices, each commanded by a chief and operating as a distinct police organization. Within these eight Divisions, there are a total of 98 Area Offices and 17 Resident Posts. Since the Highway Patrol is responsible for the entire state, it is geographically impossible for all patrol officers to work from a central headquarters. Similarly, the Dallas Police Department divides the city into six divisions as shown in Figure 4–8. Since the department has approximately 2,900 officers, it would be inefficient for them to report to one headquarters. Moreover, since these large departments serve large numbers of citizens over a fairly large geographic area, this decentralization makes the police more accessible to the public. Citizens can go to a neighborhood substation rather than a central headquarters many miles away.

Patrol is usually organized according to geographical differentiation. Patrol officers are assigned to individual beats (the area patrolled by one patrol unit). These patrol officers are assigned to a sergeant who is responsible for a distinct geographic area usually consisting of 6 to 10 beats. The police executive can assure that the jurisdiction is completely covered and can better assign accountability by making officers responsible for specific beats. Figure 4–9 shows the configuration of the 32, beats which are located in the Dallas Police Department's North Central Division. All major police departments use a system or configuration similar to Dallas's division and beat structure.

Figure 4–5

Chicago Police Department, Bureau of Investigative Services.

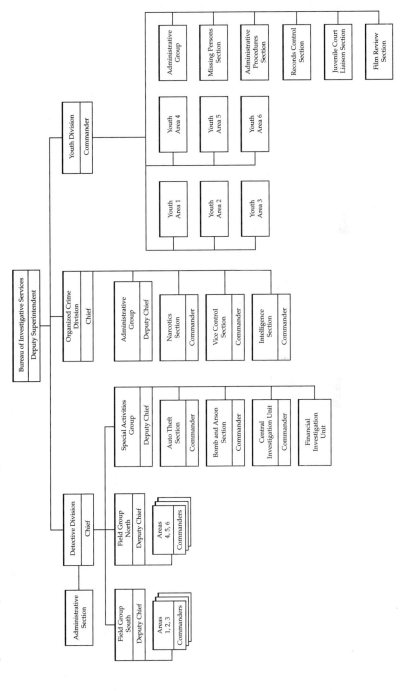

Figure 4-6
Chicago Police Department, Bureau of Technical Services.

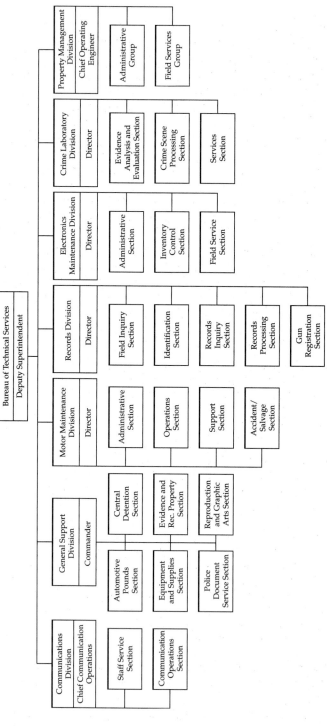

Figure 4–7
Chicago Police Department, Bureau of Community Services.

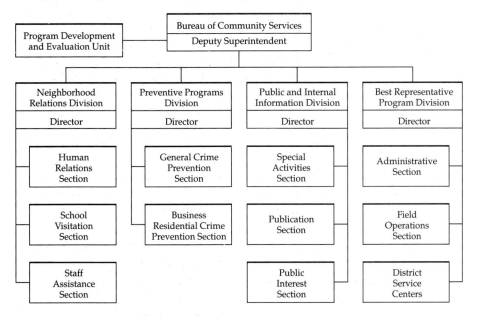

Figure 4–8
Divisional map for the Dallas Police Department.

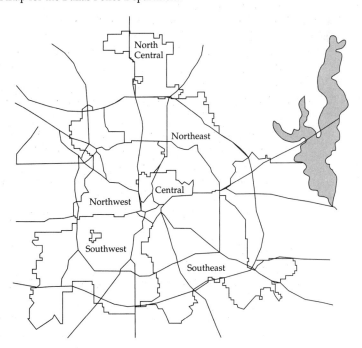

Figure 4–9
Beat map for Dallas Police Department's North Central Division.

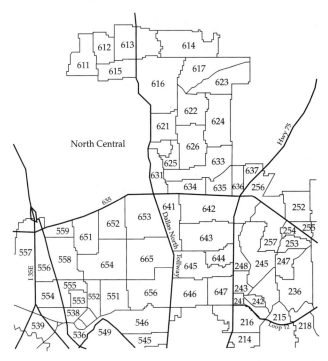

Time. Since police departments are responsible for a jurisdiction 24 hours a day, they must allot personnel into shifts or watches to cover all hours of the day. In most police departments, patrol is divided into three shifts with each shift assigned to an eight-hour period. A few police departments, however, use a 4-10 plan where officers work 10 hours a day, four days a week. This allows for an overlap of shifts during peak activity periods. Some departments even use 12-hour shifts. Regardless, officers are assigned to specific hours to work. The usual time frames and names for shifts are presented in Table 4–1.

From an administrative viewpoint, it is most desirable to have permanent shifts with officers assigned to permanent patrol beats so officers can learn the most about criminal and other activities in their beats. When officers are assigned to permanent shifts, they tend to be more alert and less fatigued, more productive, and less prone to accidents (O'Neill and Cushing, 1991). The police administrator must weigh this benefit against the disadvantage of low morale when officers are assigned to permanent shifts. Officers' morale is affected when they must work permanent shifts that are not in synchronization with their families, or they must work a shift where there is little activity, resulting in boredom (early morning shift). Consequently, most police departments rotate shifts periodically so that officers will not work an undesirable shift for

Table 4–1

Usual Time Frames and Names of Shifts

	Shift Names		
Shift Type	Day (2nd platoon or 2nd watch)	Evening (3rd platoon or 3rd watch)	Night (1st platoon or 1st watch)
Three Separate Shifts	8 A.M.–4 P.M. 7 A.M.–3 P.M.	4 P.M.–12 P.M. 3 P.M.–11 P.M.	12 P.M.–8 A.M. 11 P.M.–7 A.M.
Swing or Relief	An officer works all three shifts in a set pattern over a given number of days.		
4-10 Plan 3 Naturally overlapping shifts	7 A.M.–5 P.M.	3 P.M.–1 A.M.	9 P.M.–7 A.M.
Overlapping Shifts	7 A.M.–3 P.M.	Early 3 P.M.–11 P.M. Late 5 P.M.–1 A.M.	Early 9 P.M.–5 A.M. Late 11 P.M.–7 A.M.

an extended period of time. Shifts should rotate only three or four times a year at most to allow some degree of permanence and reduce the physical and psychological difficulty of adjusting to new shifts.

Shift work presents a number of problems. People have a *circadian rhythm*, or biological clock that regulates all body functions. When the circadian rhythm is interrupted, physiological stress or fatigue results. Some officers are more susceptible to problems from shift work: officers over the age of 50; those who have a second job; those with a heavy commitment at home; those with a history of sleep disorders; those who have an alcohol or drug problem; and those with illnesses such as diabetes, heart disease, or stomach problems.

Other units within police departments also use shifts: traffic, communications, investigations, and so on. Some units may not allocate officers for a full 24 hours, but may use only two shifts, say, traffic and investigations. Detectives in large departments may be organized by function, while detectives in small or medium-sized police departments may be assigned to shifts working all cases that occur during the shift. Detectives may be assigned to two shifts, 7 A.M. until 3 P.M. and 3 P.M. until 11 P.M. It is not necessary, except in the very large police departments, for detectives to work in the early morning hours since it is impossible to conduct follow-up investigations during these hours. Large departments may, however, assign detectives from the various functional units across two or three shifts. These detectives report to a unit supervisor rather than a shift commander.

Level of Authority. Grouping tasks by level of authority directly ties specialization with chain of command and to a degree determines the rank structure within a given police department. It is important to have officers of equal rank at each level of a police department, for example, all division heads are majors or all section heads are captains. This puts all commanders on equal footing in staff meetings or when vying for resources. If the ranks of the various unit heads are unequal, those of a lesser rank are most likely at a disadvantage. On the other hand, unit commanders having equal rank at each level of the chain of command will increase the number of ranking officers to the point that excessive layering would occur in the department. It is important for a department to have only enough ranking personnel to effectively manage the department.

An organizational arrangement that strictly follows the level of authority principle produces an excessive number of ranking officers and violates the principle of span of control. Frequently, ranking personnel have too few subordinates, creating a drain on resources by having too many supervisors. The operations division requires ranking personnel because the majority of the department's personnel is assigned there. However, auxiliary services and administrative services do not require such rank because of fewer personnel.

Conversely, an imbalance of rank at each hierarchical level results when a department is organized so that the fewest possible number of officers hold rank. This imbalance of rank could create control and coordination problems for the chief executive if lower-ranking personnel are not able to effectively represent their units. The positive effect of the imbalance of rank is that it allows the department to have fewer-ranking officers and thereby costs less and allows more flexibility in making assignments.

To summarize the principle of grouping tasks by level of authority, the amount of rank in a given police department should be kept to a minimum, but a department should have enough ranking personnel to ensure that it is adequately commanded.

Functional Specialization: Pros and Cons.   In developing a police department's structure, the amount of specialization within the department must be decided. Advocates of specialization identify a number of advantages to specialization:

1. *Reduces the need for training.* Without specialization every officer would have to receive all types of training; each officer would need training in patrol, selective enforcement, accident investigation, homicide investigation, sex crimes investigation, and so on. This would be very expensive and time-consuming for police departments. Specialization allows administrators to identify those officers who should receive expensive specialized training.

2. *Increases job control.* Specialization places responsibility for specific tasks; therefore, it enables administrators to control the organization more effectively. For example, if the department's crime clearance rate falls, the chief should examine the investigative units. Accountability is vitally important. Functional supervision is the foundation for this process.

3. *Increases job proficiency.* If officers continually perform the same or similar tasks, they become more proficient via repetitive experiences. Functional specialization groups tasks so that officers are assigned a limited number of tasks; therefore, they perform them frequently and thus develop expertise.

4. *Provides career enrichment for some officers.* Assignment to a specialized unit is viewed as a promotion in many departments. Assignment to a specialized unit increases the morale and job satisfaction for officers assigned to the units.

These four factors are the major advantages of job specialization. The primary objective of specialization is to increase operational effectiveness and efficiency. However, disadvantages also result from instituting specialization within police departments. Some of the disadvantages are:

1. *Diminishes territorial coverage.* When specialization occurs and a specialized unit is formed or an old unit is given additional personnel, the officers generally are taken from patrol. As specialization increases, the number of patrol personnel decreases and the amount of territory per patrol beat increases. Also, since specialists are assigned and equipped to perform specific tasks, they are not available for patrol or other duties.

2. *Job dissatisfaction increases.* Increased specialization within a department necessitates limiting the number of tasks an individual officer performs. For example, the most interesting aspects of police work (investigations or stakeouts) are performed by specialists, not patrol officers. As a patrol officer's range of tasks decreases, the likelihood of job dissatisfaction increases. The job may even become boring. Personnel development is also hindered since officers do not experience a wide range of activities and thereby do not develop a clear understanding of other facets of the department and its mission.

3. *Administrative coordination is made more difficult.* Specialization increases the number of units in the organization. Decision makers must consider the impact of any potential decision on all units. Thus decision making and coordination become more difficult to successfully achieve with an increase in units. Suboptimization also occurs—individuals within the various units become more concerned with their units than with the overall police department and its goals. Unit officers pursue their objectives without regard to other units' objectives. Competition sometimes develops and officers may even become hostile toward officers in other units.

Specialization is an important consideration in organizing the police department. The advantages and disadvantages must be weighed in determining whether to specialize and, if so, how much. As the police department grows and becomes more complex, specialization must be instituted to ensure efficient pursuit of organizational goals. However, too much specialization may negate its benefits. Therefore, there can be too little or too much specialization. The general rule to follow is to limit specialization and specialize only if operational effectiveness and efficiency are increased.

Although there are no steadfast rules for determining when and how much to specialize, certain factors should be considered in making the decision regarding specialization. The factors to consider are:

1. *Quality of personnel.* The higher the quality of personnel, the less need for specialization. Competent, well-trained officers can perform a wider variety of tasks than less-qualified officers. As the educational and training level of officers increases, the manager may want to examine the amount of specialization within the department with the intention of reducing it.

2. *Need.* There may be a need for specialization if the performance of certain tasks detracts from the officers' ability to effectively perform their other duties. Additionally, the frequency with which tasks are accomplished, importance of successful completion of tasks, and the necessity of maintaining skills for successful performance of tasks should be considered. Regardless of these factors, administrators should be sure that enough tasks exist to keep the specialists occupied before creating specialist positions.

3. *Departmental goals.* There may be instances where the community expects certain tasks requiring specialists to be performed by the police department. Since the primary responsibility of any police agency is to serve its community, specialization would be justified.

To summarize specialization, the grouping of tasks within the police department is very important. It establishes how the department is organized and how the various units are administered and coordinated by management. The four grouping criteria are (1) function, (2) geography, (3) time, and (4) authority level. These should be considered when organizing the department. There are no steadfast rules for utilizing these criteria in making decisions about how to organize a police department, but the successful administrator will attempt to understand the ramifications of these criteria on the organization and will apply them as the departmental situation dictates.

Formalization

Written rules and regulations are the heart of the traditional police organization because they provide direction and control. The roles, functions, and specific duties of police officers and operational units must be codified and made into a permanent record. For example, patrol officers complete the preliminary investigations and detectives perform the follow-up investigations in most traditional police departments. The exact duties of the officer and detective—where the preliminary investigation ends and where the follow-up investigation begins— should be clearly set out in departmental procedure. Intradepartmental conflict is reduced and organizational effectiveness is enhanced when the department has well-written policies, rules, and procedures because people know what their relative jobs are and how they should be performed.

Police written directives and rules are statements that either prescribe or proscribe employee behavior, the violation of which usually involves the invocation of the disciplinary system; they are synonymous with regulations. Written directives and rules generally follow five forms: policies, procedures, general orders, special orders, and memoranda. A *policy* is general in nature and represents the department's goals and objectives. Policies often represent the department's values. Once the administration identifies its goals and objectives, they should be expressed so that the department's members are made aware of them. An example of a police policy is:

> Truancy by youngsters from the junior high and high schools contributes to societal and police problems. Truant youngsters are more likely to become involved in mischievous or criminal activities. Therefore, this police department will cooperate with other agencies directly involved in combating the truancy problem.

Although this statement is nothing more than a statement of principle, it does establish operating objectives for line units. It shows that the police are interested in repressing crime by keeping truant students in school. It also implies an action by the police—cooperating with school and other officials regarding the problem. It leaves room for the administrator to codify how the police will deal with the problem—a procedure. A policy is an administrative attempt to draw attention to problems and increase departmental efforts toward the alleviation of these problems. All departmental goals should be reduced to policy.

A *procedure* is a document that is specific and applies to the very workings of the police department. Most departments attempt to formulate the "ways" or procedures for accomplishing various tasks within each operational unit. These documents elaborate the specific tasks that individuals within the affected area perform, and they detail, to a degree, how and where those tasks are accomplished. For example, Figure 4–10 presents the Niles, Michigan, Police Department's procedure for using concealable body armor. The procedure outlines when officers are to wear their armor and how they are to store and care for it. All critical police activities should be addressed in written procedures.

A *general order* or *rule* is a directive that is enacted to control some facet of the organization for an indefinite period of time. General orders are similar to procedures in that they specifically outline behavior, but whereas procedures address tasks such as the care of evidence, how to obtain a search warrant, or how to handle a barricaded person, general orders are restrictive in nature and represent rules that must be followed by all officers. For example, Figure 4–11 presents the Gallatin, Tennessee, Police Department's rule on officers' off-duty employment. The order describes what jobs officers cannot hold; how an officer is to receive permission to engage in off-duty employment; circumstances in which officers may use departmentally issued equipment; and the reporting of any incidents that occur during off-duty employment. Orders outline how officers should behave in certain situations, and violations of orders usually result in disciplinary action.

A *special order* is a directive that is temporary in nature, whereas policies, procedures, and general orders are in effect until superseded by a later policy, procedure, or general order. Special orders are usually issued to address special or infrequent events such as parades, the establishment of a temporary special tactical unit, or a situation involving labor disputes. The essence of the

Figure 4–10
Niles, Michigan, Police Department body arms policy.

GENERAL ORDER

Subject:	General Order Number
CONCEALABLE BODY ARMOR	91-3

I.   PURPOSE

To establish a standard for the wearing and use of concealable body armor (protective vests) by police officers while on duty.

II.   PROCEDURE

A.   When any uniformed patrol officer is on duty she/he shall wear concealable body armor (protective vest), which is supplied by the City of Niles, under the uniform shirt.

B.   Exceptions may be made in cases of medical documentation, confirmed by the City Physician.

C.   Non-uniformed sworn personnel shall wear concealable body armor (protective vest) when there are situations, such as plans to make a felony arrest or participating in a raid.

D.   Each officer assigned concealable body armor shall be responsible for the proper care of it.

III.   STORAGE AND CARE

A.   When not in use the vest shall be stored in a clean dry area.

B.   Because of regular wearing the vest will require periodic cleaning. Cleaning and washing shall be as follows:

1.   Outer Cover—wash as often as necessary in cold water using a mild detergent. It may be air or machine dried.

2.   Elastic Straps—wash using the same methods as outer cover.

3.   Ballistic Panels—clean by soaking the panels in a soapy solution and rinsing thoroughly. Air dry before returning them to the covers. Do not machine wash, dry clean, use bleach, or iron.

C.   Service of the vest is important and in the event the vest becomes worn, cut, or torn it must be turned in to be replaced.

D.   An unserviceable cover requiring replacement must be reordered through the quartermaster.

BY ORDER OF:

Charles F. Rogers, Sr.
Charles F. Rogers, Sr.
Chief of Police

---

special order is that it makes temporary assignments and delineates the tasks to be performed while on temporary assignment. Once the duties and tasks, as required by the special order, are carried out, the special order is suspended and all those involved resume their regular assignments.

Finally, this elaborate rule system is supported and reinforced by *memoranda*. The police department is dependent on the use of memoranda. Since the principle of chain of command dictates close supervision, it is necessary for

Figure 4–11

Gallatin, Tennessee, Police Department policy on off-duty employment.

2.6   Secondary or Off-Duty Employment

2.6.1   Any officer wishing to work in a secondary, or off-duty, employment position must receive authorization from the Chief of Police and the Mayor of the City of Gallatin prior to beginning a secondary or off-duty job. Use of departmental equipment, including the officer's uniform and departmental vehicle, in a secondary or off-duty job must have the authorization of the Chief of Police prior to utilization in the secondary or off-duty job.

2.6.2   Off-Duty Coordinator

The Chief of Police will assign an officer to act as the off-duty coordinator. The off-duty coordinator will manage and arrange all requests from the community requesting off-duty officers at an event or other function. The off-duty coordinator will contact interested officers of potential off-duty employment assignments and ensure that authorized events and/or functions are properly staffed with off-duty officers.

2.6.3   Regulations

The hours to be worked and the wage to be paid to the officer will be negotiated with and agreed to between the officer and the business wishing to employ the officer.

No officer will work more than four hours in an off-duty assignment on any day which the officer is scheduled to work for this Department. An officer may work as many hours as he/she prefers to work while on his/her assigned days off.

No officer will work in a position that would lower the image and /or ethics of a police officer. Under no circumstances will an officer work in any of the following types of activities:

A.   Bartender
B.   Taxi Driver
C.   Bouncer
D.   Private Investigator
E.   Body Guard
F.   Polygraph Examiner
G.   Emergency Medical Provider
H.   Private Fire or Codes Inspector
I.   Male or Female Dancer
J.   Hired to Repossess Property
K.   Professional/Expert Witness

No officer will work in police or security-related off-duty employment prior to completion of the Basic Law Enforcement Course at the Tennessee Law Enforcement Training Academy or Prior to receiving certification as a law enforcement officer in the State of Tennessee, as well as successful completion of the Field Training Program.

2.6.4   Suspension of Off-Duty Privileges

All authorization to work in off-duty positions is immediately and automatically suspended whenever the employee is:

A.   Placeed on light duty
B.   Relieved of duty
C.   Injured such that it has become impracticable or dangerous to engage in off-duty employment
D.   On military leave

2.6.5   Report of Off-Duty Incidents

A complete incident report must be filed by an off-duty officer following any police actions taken during the course of, and within the scope of, his/her off-duty employment, with the Chief of Police. This documentation will include the following:

A.   Date and time of incident/accident/injury
B.   Involved person's name, address, and phone number(s)
C.   Name of the involved person's parent or guardian, if a juvenile
D.   Name(s) and phone number(s) of any witness(es)
E.   Complete description of the events and circumstances surrounding the incident/accident/injury

It should be noted that injury is defined in this section as meaning bodily injury and/or property damage.

everyone to be aware of others' activities. Memoranda are used to notify individuals of assignments, orders, and other information. Hence, when there is a problem, the superior can examine the written communications to determine what has occurred. Additionally, the paperwork follows the chain of command; therefore, everyone is kept abreast of activities and commands. This written communications system is a method of controlling the department and ensuring that goals are accomplished.

Two factors mediate formalization: organization size and degree to which work within an organization can be formalized. In terms of size, as organizations become larger there is a natural tendency for them for them to formalize (Robbins, 1990). For example, Miller and Conaty (1987) examined organizational studies that included more than 1,000 organizations and found a high positive relationship between size and formalization. Managers attempt to control employees through rules and direct observation or supervision. As organizations become larger, it becomes more difficult for top managers to observe what is occurring, so they implement rules and regulations to compensate for their decreased ability to directly observe subordinates.

Some work cannot be formalized. Simple, routine tasks are easily formalized, whereas complex nonroutine tasks are not amenable to formalization. For example, it is fairly easy to standardize and formalize the duties performed by police record clerks. Each clerk continually performs an identical set of tasks. Conversely, police officers' jobs are not easily formalized because police officers constantly confront different situations—family disturbances, auto crashes, burglary investigations, and so on. Making formalization even more difficult is that officers must use discretion and situationally respond to community problems. The nature of each task facing officers is dictated by numerous, ever-changing variables that force officers to alter their responses to each situation. For example, it is very unlikely that an officer will respond to two family disturbance calls the exact same way because of the dynamics of the disputes. In reality, police departments cannot totally remove police officer discretion but, at best, they can provide officers with guidelines.

CRITICISMS OF TRADITIONAL POLICE MANAGEMENT

The previous sections detail and describe the organizational principles that are associated with traditional police department management. They depict a managerial structure that to a degree is void of a human dimension and is predicated totally on control. Because all organizations are, theoretically, goal seeking, to some extent control is an essential ingredient. However, an overemphasis on control creates an authoritarian work environment. In reviewing the organizational principles, there is no mention of the individual officers or how they interact with the department. Denyer, Callender, and Thompson (1975) accuse police departments of alienating officers to the point that they are unproductive. Officers need to be treated as human beings, not machines. A number of organizational specialists have devised other methods for managing police which treat officers humanely, creating a police department that is more productive than the traditional police department. In other words, Weber's principles of organization must be mediated with some form of team building.

Guyot (1979) utilized three national surveys to study the management problems of police organizations. She found that there are basically five sets of management problems in policing: (1) lack of management flexibility in personnel decisions; (2) lack of incentives within the rank of police officer; (3) militarism; (4) communication blocked by a tall organizational structure; and (5) insularity. Each of these can be directly linked to the authoritarianism and classical organizational theory. Finally, Franz and Jones examined the military model in police organizations and found:

> Police organizations in our sample did have relatively greater communications problems; there were relatively greater amounts of distrust, particularly of higher echelons in police departments; there were relatively low levels of morale associated with these phenomena and there were lower perceived levels of organizational performance associated with all these factors. (1987:161)

Inconsistency

A number of critics have charged that the preceding principles of organization are inconsistent. Simon (1954) notes that for every principle there is another which when operationalized is contradictory. The principles are not administrative principles, but only criteria for describing and diagnosing administrative situations. Subramanian (1966) agrees:

> For example, according to the principle of span of control the number of subordinates whom a superior can efficiently supervise is limited to, say six. By adopting this in a large organization one would create more levels in the hierarchy than if a larger number, say twelve, was placed under each supervisor. At the same time, there is a contradictory principle which enumerates that administrative efficiency is enhanced by keeping at a minimum the number of organizational levels through which a matter can pass. It is obvious that whenever one seeks to increase efficiency according to the former principle it automatically decreases according to the latter, but there is nothing in the statement of these two principles to indicate which one is the preferred on a given occasion or how the two considerations are to be balanced.

Authoritarianism

The managerial atmosphere surrounding the traditionally organized police department largely is authoritarian. Departmental goals are established by high-level police administrators, and generally without input from lower-level operational personnel. Because authority and power are centralized with the top administrators, persons at lower ranks have not been involved in program development and thus have no stake in program success. Internal communications typically flow downward through the chain of command. The traditional police organization's structure creates decreased morale at lower ranks, and one-way communication creates a perception that the top command is sometimes arbitrary in its action. When officers fail to comply with rules or orders, superiors attempt to motivate them by applying punishment, which negatively affects morale.

Studies of the organizational and individual effects of authoritative management have found that authoritative management is associated with worker alienation and frustration (Franz and Jones, 1987) and low productivity (Likert, 1961; Pfeffer, 1978). Also, authoritative management is associated with organizations that have overly conservative, conforming employees, whose personal growth and adjustment are harmed (Pfeffer, 1978:39–40; Reiser, 1978).

Lack of Innovation

Classical organizations tend to be closed, which stifles innovation. Members of traditional organizations tend to resist changes that challenge the old ways of operating. The organization is unable to cope with environmental changes; therefore, it becomes obsolete and ineffective. Members of classical organizations are also exposed to a conflicting set of expectations—on one hand they must make on-the-spot life-and-death decisions, yet they are allowed little discretion when answering such calls. Formalization oftentimes locks officers into procedures that do not work in every situation. Argyris (1957) states that the chain of command principle tends to make individuals dependent on, passive toward, and subordinate to the leader.

Information Flow Problems

Excessive specialization combined with the hierarchical arrangement generates problems of information flow. Specialization creates additional units or differentiates the organization horizontally while hierarchy creates additional levels (vertical) within each unit. Subsequently, communications emanate from an increased number of sources and must travel through an increased number of offices. This not only slows the travel time of communications, but it also increases the likelihood they will be altered or in some cases completely deleted. This communication filtering creates a situation where employees are unable to receive timely information.

Lack of Motivation

The police officer in the traditional police organization lacks motivation because of psychological deprivation. That is, the organizational setting places police officers in a position where they have no control over their job and are not involved in the day-to-day operation of the department. Officers are assigned tasks but seldom are given an opportunity to make decisions relative to their jobs. The officers are effectively segregated from the higher echelons of the department via the principle of chain of command. Sandler and Mintz

(1978) state that the police paramilitary organization tends to create a sense of demoralization and powerlessness at the lower ranks.

Whereas the chain of command concept inhibits officers' upward communications and contact, specialization inhibits lateral communication. As the number of units increases, the ability to use informal communications channels becomes increasingly difficult. Supervisors and commanders come to expect information to be transmitted formally so that subordinates can be held accountable. This complicates communications to the point where officers sometimes stop communicating.

Specialization also reduces the range of activities performed by officers. With regard to patrol officers, high levels of specialization within the department limits their duties to such a degree that the job fails to challenge them. Patrol officers are assigned a variety of tasks, but when a case becomes complex or interesting, the patrol officer must turn it over to a detective, traffic officer, or another specialist within the police department. This restricts the possibility for the patrol officer to be challenged and stimulated by the job.

The end result of chain of command and specialization is to place patrol officers in a box. They are restricted from becoming involved in managerial activities by the supervisor, and they are restricted from becoming involved in other jobs and tasks because of specialization. Consequently, the officers' involvement in the department becomes rather shallow. They become frustrated, disinterested, and withdrawn. When this occurs, productivity suffers.

IN DEFENSE OF CLASSICAL THEORY

Over the years, there have been a number of critics of classical theory. The previous section summarizes most of their criticisms. Taking these criticisms at face value would indicate that classical theory is doomed to extinction. Its critics portray it as ineffective, demoralizing, and obsolete. It, in essence, could not possibly survive the extremely complex world in which we live.

Yet classical theory remains a viable structural alternative that is used extensively in policing, government, and some areas of business and industry (Goodsell, 1985). Jaques (1990) suggests two reasons why classical theory has persisted. First, it provides the only reasonable structure for ordering large numbers of employees. A police chief can very likely use group decision making or participative management in a 5- or 10-officer department, but a police department consisting of 100, 200, or 1,000 officers must have structure. In other words, large numbers of employees can be effective only if the labor is somehow structured and coordinated. Classical theory is the most expedient, if not the only way to accomplish this task. For example, the New York City Police Department has approximately 36,000 officers. An agency of this size simply cannot be managed without substantial structure.

Second, Jaques (1990) notes that classical theory has survived because it focuses on accountability. Organizations exist to accomplish some purpose; they are created to achieve goals. Every individual's performance in an organization should contribute to the organization accomplishing its goals. Specialization establishes where each activity is placed and who is responsible for its accomplishment. Everyone generally knows who is responsible for making decisions, developing policy, and implementing programs. If an individual or organization fails to meet performance standards, then some remedial action should be taken. In other words, workers and organizations should be held accountable for their performance.

This is particularly true given the history of corruption, politics, and problems with excessive use of force in law enforcement. Although instances of police corruption and excessive force are not commonplace, they do occur frequently enough for administrators to attempt to control officers to prevent their occurrence. The public and elected officials expect and demand that police administrators organize and control their departments so that such problems do not occur.

Traditional organizational theory's acceptance stems from its longevity and from its inherent strengths which have appealed to police administrators. For the most part, classical organizational theory is straightforward and easily understood by all employees. People know where they stand, what is expected of them, and to whom they are responsible. This reduces the possibility of confusion in the workplace as ample direction for the employee exists at all levels. Also, clearly understood lines of communication exist whereby employees are able to communicate with each other.

Finally, exactly how closely police departments adhere to classical organizational principles is questionable. Toch (1999) notes that police departments have evolved and changed over time. He asserts that even though most departments began classically organized, time and interaction with the environment have caused natural evolution, and most departments today are managed using a myriad of organizational principles. On the other hand, Gaines and Swanson (1999) argue that police departments are more lackadaisical in nature, rather than strictly adhering to classical principles. Departments tend to react to problems rather than engaging in problem solving. Routine becomes the cornerstone for bureaucratic police departments.

Summary

The classical organizational model has been present in law enforcement since Sir Robert Peel used the military to model the London Metropolitan Police Department in 1829. Today, it remains as the primary model by which police departments are organized. Its stamina stems from its simplicity and straightforwardness. It is easily implemented and understood by officers throughout the rank structure.

Police departments, because of the nature of their mission in our society, must be organized. Citizens and elected officials have definite expectations that must be fulfilled. The principles of hierarchy, span of control, unity of command, delegation of authority, specialization, and formalization attempt to ensure that the police organization operates efficiently and effectively by constructing a structure which controls and facilitates work.

Although there are a number of criticisms of classical organizational theory, for the most part they focus on two primary classical organizational components: centralization and formalization. In terms of centralization, most argue that classical theory centralizes too much power and authority with top-level administrators. Although classical theory postulates that ultimate responsibility rests at the top, it also recognizes that authority and responsibility are delegated to unit commanders and midlevel managers. Moreover, there is a natural decentralization process as specialization occurs. Authority is naturally diffused among many middle managers. It is questionable whether police departments are more centralized than any other type of organization.

Chapter 5 summarizes postclassical organizational theory. As noted above, classical organizational theory remains as the foundation for police administration. It is important, however, to review other developments and discuss them in terms of their application to law enforcement.

Study Questions

1. Describe the traditional police organization and how today's police organization is different.

2. What is scientific management? The fathers of scientific management are Weber, Taylor, and Fayol. What were their contributions?

3. What are span of control, unity of command, and delegation of authority? How do they relate to the police organization?

4. List the ways in which an organization can have specialization. Give examples of each type in the police setting.

5. What are the criticisms of classical organizational theories?

6. What are the defenses of classical organizational theories as they relate to the police organization?

Net Resources

http://faculty.ncwc.edu/toconnor/205/205lect07.htm Lecture notes on the police military model from North Carolina Wesleyan University.

http://www.lapd.org/organization/lapd_organization_chart.htm LAPD website showing the department's organization chart.

References

Argyris, C. (1957). *Personality and Organization: the Conflict between System and the Individual.* New York: Harper & Row.

Bittner, E. (1970). *The Functions of Police in a Modern Society.* Rockville, MD: National Institute of Mental Health.

Carter, D., and Radelet, L. (1999). *The Police and the Community.* Upper Saddle River, NJ: Prentice Hall.

Dale, E. (1965). *Readings in Management: Landmarks and New Frontiers.* New York: McGraw-Hill.

Denyer, T., Callender, R., and Thompson, D. (1975) The policeman as alienated laborer. *Journal of Police Science and Administration* 3(3):251–258.

Franz, V., and Jones, D. (1987) Perceptions of organizational performance in suburban police departments: A critique of the military model. *Journal of Police Science and Administration* 15(2):153–161.

Gaines, L. K., Kappeler, V., and Vaughn, J. (1999) *Policing in America.* Cincinnati: Anderson Publishing.

Gaines, L. K., and Swanson, C.R. (1999). Empowering police officers: A tarnished silver bullet? In L. Gaines and G. Cordner (eds.), *Policing Perspectives: An Anthology.* Los Angeles: Roxbury Press, pp. 363–371.

Germann, A., Day, F., and Gallati, R. (1978). *Introduction to Law Enforcement and Criminal Justice.* Springfield, IL: Charles C. Thomas.

Goodsell, C. (1985). *A Case for Bureaucracy,* 2nd ed. Chatham, NJ: Chatham House Publishers.

Guyot, D. (1979). Bending granite: Attempting to change the rank structure of American police departments. *Journal of Police Science and Administration* 7:253–284.

Jaques, E. (1990). In praise of bureaucracy. *Harvard Business Review* 68:127–133.

Likert, R. (1961) *New Patterns of Management.* New York: McGraw-Hill.

Miller, G. A., and Conaty, J. (1987). Meta-analysis and the culture-free hypothesis. *Organization Studies* 4:309–325.

O'Neill, J., and Cushing, M. (1991). *The Impact of Shift Work on Police Officers.* Washington: Police Executive Research Forum.

Pfeffer, J. (1978). The micropolitics of organizations. In M. Meyer (ed.), *Environments and Organizations.* San Francisco: Jossey-Bass.

Reiser, M. (1978). Some organizational stresses on policemen. In L. Gaines and T. Ricks (eds.), *Managing the Police Organization.* St. Paul: West Publishing.

Robbins, S. P. (1990). Organization Theory: Structure, Design, and Applications. Englewood Cliffs, NJ: Prentice Hall.

Sandler, G.B., and Mintz, E. (1978). Police organizations: Their changing internal and external relationships. In L. Gaines and T. Ricks (eds.) *Managing the Police Organization.* St. Paul: West Publishing.

Simon, H. (1954). *Administrative Behavior.* New York: Free Press.

Stevens, D. (2001). *Case Studies in Community Policing.* Upper Saddle River, NJ: Prentice Hall.

Subramanian, V. (1966). The classical organization theory and its critics. *Public Administration Review* 44:435–466.

Taylor, F. (1911). *The Principles of Scientific Management.* New York: W.W. Norton & Co.

Toch, H. (1997). The democratization of policing in the United States. *Police Forum* 7(2):1–8.

Weber, M. (1969). Bureaucracy. In J. Litterer (ed.), *Organizations,* Vol. 1. New York: Wiley, pp. 29–31.

5

Contemporary Organizational Theories and Management Systems

Kai Pfaffenbach/The Image Works

Chapter Outline

Introduction

Human Relations Organizational Theory
The Genesis of Human Relations Theory
Human Relations Philosophy
Contribution and Weaknesses of the Neoclassical or Human Relations Model

Contingency Theory: Bridging Classical and Human Relations Theories
Mintzberg's Five Organizational Forms

The Systems Model of Organizational Management
Characteristics of an Open System
Total Quality Management

Summary

Learning Objectives

After reading this chapter, you should be able to

1. Understand how contemporary management theories differ from classical organizational theory.
2. Know the three events that served as the foundation of human relations theory.
3. Explain Mintzberg's five different kinds of organization and relate them to the police department.
4. Understand systems theory and the components of the police system.
5. Discuss total quality management and how it applies to modern police departments and community policing.

R ecently, the Camden, New Jersey, Police Department implemented a plan that decentralized some of the department's operational units. The detective, juvenile, and vice units remained under the central command within the department, while patrol was divided into four district stations. The rationale for the change was that decentralized patrol would allow officers to work more closely with residents. The district stations were given the authority to make decisions about how to identify and solve problems in their respective areas. This change is consistent with community policing and efforts by many police chiefs to push decision making at lower levels, where better decisions can be made by officers who are familiar with the community.

The change, however, had some unintended consequences. The new district stations were a fairly expensive endeavor. As noted in Chapter 3, community policing often requires increases in personnel. This occurred in Camden: the public would have better access to the police only if the district stations were well staffed. This resulted in approximately 16 officers being taken off the street. The new stations also required a substantial amount of equipment such as radios and computers as well as additional facilities. A second problem that arose was that there were some ill feelings between the new community policing officers and other officers. Ultimately, the chief had to make a series of adjustments to ensure that the new district stations operated at the desired level.

This example shows how difficult organizational change can be. It also points out that the police executive must continually monitor the organization to ensure that it allows the department to accomplish its goals. This chapter examines some of the theories that go beyond classical organizational theory, which was discussed in the previous chapter. It provides ideas about how to look at the police department and make changes similar to those made in Camden.

INTRODUCTION

Classical theory is the foundation for American police systems, yet classical organizational theory in policing is somewhat problematic. One problem is that it attempts to use somewhat authoritarian, controlling principles to manage people who generally adhere to democratic values. Additional problems are generated as departments attempt to move to community policing models, which require that subordinates be empowered to have more control over how they respond to problems, crime, and calls for service. The move toward community policing in this country tends to place substantial strain on purely classically organized departments. This chapter provides an overview of the many structural and management innovations that have occurred as a reaction to the rigidity of classical theory. Some have been developed to supplant classical theory; others were meant to supplement it. Most have been implemented in policing, and each has positive and negative points.

For the most part, organizations have been characterized as being mechanistic or organic (Burns and Stalker, 1961). The *mechanistic organization* is a fairly inflexible organization characterized by hierarchy, formalization, and centralized authority. The mechanistic organization is synonymous with classical organization theory. Most theorists would consider traditional police structures mechanistic. *Organic organizations,* on the other hand, are more open organizations that allow employees greater input and responsibility in decision making, especially at the lower levels in the organization. Organic structures supposedly are more responsive to community needs (Kuykendall and Roberg, 1997). This is a critical component of police administration as addressed in Chapter 2.

This chapter provides an overview of a variety of theories that describe the organic organization. As administrative theory developed, theorists came to understand that theories that incorporate organizational theories and management systems would be the most effective. Management practices and systems that exist within organizational structures, to a great extent, are determined by the nature of the organization's structure. Therefore, it seems reasonable to integrate management and organizational theories. Three types of organic theory are human relations theories, systems theories, and behavioral management systems.

HUMAN RELATIONS ORGANIZATIONAL THEORY

The human relations philosophy came about as a reaction to the mechanistic organizational prescriptions of classical organizational theory (Gaines, 1978). It was not until the 1930s and 1940s that the human element was given much consideration in organizations. With the post–World War II business boom, studies were conducted to find ways to improve productivity in the workplace. These studies led to the *human relations philosophy*: management engaged in a social process that combines techniques and people to mutually benefit the organization and the employee.

The human relations philosophy can have a substantial impact on one's understanding of organizations since managers typically spend from 50 to 75 percent of their time dealing with human problems (Huneryager and Heckman, 1967). It functions to motivate people to higher performance, to help us understand people and their relationship to work, and to help people reach their fullest potential. Human relations organizational models are particularly attuned to the behavior of individuals and groups as they operate in the workplace. New insights are provided that are valuable in examining decision making, communication, organizational conflict, problems of individual and organizational change and innovation, leadership, and creativity when the human element is incorporated into administration

The Genesis of Human Relations Theory

Human relations theory developed, to a large extent, as a result of the dissatisfaction with classical management concepts as discussed in Chapter 4. Human relations theory evolved in America during a period of labor unrest, and management embraced the new theory with open arms as a means of solving labor and production problems. It was reasoned that if classical structures did not work, then human relations had to work. In essence, the human relations movement was accepted without any research or proof that it was better (Gaines, 1978).

Human relations theory resulted from the introduction of three theoretical perspectives: the Hawthorne experiments in Chicago, Abraham Maslow's Hierarchy of Needs theory of motivation, and Douglas McGregor's Theory X and Theory Y. This triad of theories serves as the foundation for incorporating people into administrative structures, and other human relations theories build on these three theories.

Hawthorne Experiments

The Hawthorne experiments provided the first glimpse of human relations theory. The Western Electric Company conducted a number of scientific management studies at its Hawthorne facilities in Chicago from 1927 through 1932. The experiments were an attempt to determine the level of illumination (light) and pattern of employee breaks that produced the highest levels of worker productivity. The researchers segregated a group of workers in an area and made numerous and varied changes in the levels of illumination and the length and number of work breaks. It was believed that if the optimal level of illumination and the number and duration of work breaks could be discovered, this information could be used to make employees more productive. Productivity increased as these two variables were manipulated. Ultimately, however, there was no consistent pattern in the changes in production relative to the changes in lighting and work breaks. For example, productivity increased when work breaks were increased, and it increased when work breaks were reduced. The same pattern emerged when illumination was increased and reduced. Given the inconsistencies, the researchers could not discern why productivity was changing. Finally, the increases in productivity were attributed to worker job satisfaction from increased involvement and concern on the part of management. In essence, management's displayed concern for the workers resulted in higher morale and productivity.

Prior to the Hawthorne experiments, employers were not concerned with employees or their feelings. It was assumed that employees followed management's dictates. The Hawthorne experiments spurred a significant change in the relationships between management and employees as management realized that individual workers and the work group itself could have just as much impact on productivity as management. The experiments signaled a need for management to harness worker energy and ideas so that management and workers could mutually benefit.

Maslow's Hierarchy of Needs

Maslow attempted to describe how people were motivated Previously, it was assumed that money was the primary, if not the only source of motivation. Maslow accurately pointed out that there are a number of sources of motivation. He identified and described a hierarchy of five levels of employee needs; in order, from the most basic to the most complex, these needs are physiological, security, social, esteem, and self-actualization. Maslow postulated that as one level of need was satisfied, it was no longer a motivator, and managers had to find other ways of motivating employees. This meant that work had to have some level of collegiality and esteem associated with it. Otherwise, once employees had enough money and job security, they would no longer be interested in their work. In contrast to Maslow, classical theorists had based motivation on financial reward and punishment, which fit into Maslow's lowest-order needs—physiological and security needs. They gave no consideration to any other form of motivation. The human relationists, through Maslow's research on human behavior, attempted to find new ways to achieve higher levels of motivation and productivity. These new ways centered around worker participation and commitment to the job through new management practices. Maslow's Hierarchy of Needs is examined in detail in Chapter 7.

McGregor's Theory X and Theory Y

McGregor (1966) postulated two theories to describe workers. Theory X was based on classical theory while Theory Y was founded on a more humane perception of people. Theory X postulated:

1. Management is responsible for organizing the elements of productive enterprise—money, materials, equipment, people—in the interest of economic ends.
2. With respect to people, this is a process of directing their efforts, motivating them, controlling their actions, and modifying their behavior to fit the needs of the organization.
3. Without this active intervention by management, people would be passive—even resistant—to organizational needs. They must therefore be persuaded, rewarded, punished, controlled—their activities must be directed. This constitutes management's tasks in managing subordinate managers or workers. We often sum it up by saying that management consists of getting things done through other people.
4. The average man is by nature indolent—he works as little as possible.
5. He lacks ambition, dislikes responsibility, prefers to be led.
6. He is inherently self-centered, indifferent to organizational needs.
7. He is by nature resistant to change.
8. He is gullible, not very bright, the ready dupe of the charlatan and demagogue.

In contrast, Theory Y proposes:

1. Management is responsible for organizing the elements of productive enterprise—money, materials, equipment, people—in the interest of economic needs.
2. People are not passive or resistant to organizational needs. They have become so as a result of experience in organizations.
3. The motivation, the potential for development, the capacity for assuming responsibility, the readiness to direct behavior toward organizational goals are all present in people. Management does not end there. It is a responsibility of management to make it possible for people to recognize and develop these human characteristics for themselves.
4. The essential task of management is to arrange organizational conditions and methods of operations so that people can achieve their own goals best by directing their own efforts toward organizational objectives.

Theory X and Y represented two ends of a continuum. Theory X, a classical perception of workers, implied that management must constantly control, punish, and manipulate employees. Theory Y, on the other hand, depicted a worker who was willing to work and failed to be productive only when management failed to provide the proper work atmosphere. The human relationists, based on the Hawthorne experiments, postulated that McGregor's Theory Y was the most

Table 5–1

Argyris's Immaturity–Maturity Changes

Immature Organizational Personality	Mature Organizational Personality
Passivity	Self-determination
Limited behavioral options	Wide range of behavioral responses
Erratic, casual, shallow interests	Complete understanding
Immediate time orientation	Long-term consideration
Subordinate perspective	Collegial position
Lack of self-awareness	Self-control

Source: Adopted from C. Argyris, *Personality and Organization: The Conflict between System and the Individual.* New York: Harper Torchbooks, 1957, pp. 50–51.

accurate account of workers and their potential, and that management practices should focus on the employee rather than the company or production quotas (Likert, 1961; 1967). McGregor's Theory Y was quickly accepted in many management circles because it appealed to our more humane nature, it provided new alternatives to deal with labor strife and unrest, and it served as a positive replacement for classical theory, which, with its repressive methods, was generally viewed as a failure.

Later, Argyris (1957) put forth his Immaturity–Maturity theory, which follows McGregor's theory. Argyris noted that people mature not only chronologically, but also in terms of maturity. Human infants are culturally, socially, and mentally immature. As they become older, they mature. The work setting can either help or hinder the maturity process. When workers are thrust in a Theory X setting, their development is stifled. In some cases, they may even regress as a function of being in a repressive environment. Management, therefore, must provide a work environment that is conducive to people's maturing psychologically. If they are allowed to mature, they will be more productive, according to Argyris. Table 5–1 lists the differences between mature and immature persons.

Today, many believe that police organizations still adhere to McGregor's Theory X. Departments are viewed as mechanistic, authoritarian, and hierarchical in nature. It is doubtful if many departments strictly adhere to Theory X (Toch, 1997). Most departments probably subscribe to a combination of Theory X and Theory Y. They have retained their hierarchical structure and high levels of specialization, giving the appearance of Theory X. However, officers generally exhibit high levels of discretion when dealing with problems and answering calls for service, fitting the Theory Y paradigm. Individual units within departments, such as juvenile services, tactical operations, crime prevention, and narcotics enforcement, also retain substantial autonomy. Central administration may provide units with goals, but the units generally have responsibility for designing the strategies to achieve the goals.

On the Job

FONTANA, CALIFORNIA, POLICE DEPARTMENT
by Chief Frank Scialdone

Courtesy of Fontana, California Police Department

Fontana, California, is located in southern California, 50 miles east of Los Angeles. At the heart of the Inland Empire in San Bernardino County, Fontana is the third largest of nine area cities. Its area is 37 square miles and its population 141,000.

Fontana has been one of the fastest growing cities in the state of California for the past 20 years. Its population during this period tripled from 44,000 to 141,000. This explosive growth has taxed municipal services and has challenged the Fontana Police Department in accomplishing its mission of providing quality service to its residents and businesses.

As the city has grown, three distinct areas whose policing issues and needs require different policing strategies have emerged. The oldest or core area of the city consists of older housing stock with a large number of multifamily developments. The southern portion of the city consists of a wide variety of land uses, including heavy industrial, agricultural, and a large master-plan community. These various land uses are often in conflict, causing unique policing issues. The northern area of the city has developed into an upper-middle-class area nestled in the foothills of a large mountain range. The expectations of the residents in this portion of the city are significantly different from those in the core and southern portions of the city.

Beginning in the mid-1980s, the Fontana Police Department has experimented with different strategies in its community policing and problem-solving efforts. From its early efforts of informal individual employee participation, to lead officers in each patrol beat, and then to a specialized unit handling all community policing activities, the department found that its community policing efforts were relegated to a relatively small number of individuals within the organization and were not coordinated in a departmentwide initiative. To address these organizational issues, the department's Area Commander Program was developed and implemented.

The department determined that its community policing efforts must be housed and coordinated within its largest unit, patrol. At the same time the unique policing needs of the diverse

Continued

areas of the city needed to be addressed. It was determined that an Area Commander Program utilizing patrol lieutenants would serve our needs. It was also recognized, that the staffing levels of our patrol shifts required continued use of patrol lieutenants as watch commanders. It was felt that having the patrol lieutenants serve in both capacities would ensure buy-in by our patrol unit and enhanced coordination of community policing activities between shifts, both of which we felt were critical to our community policing efforts. These assumptions have proved correct, and our patrol unit has become our primary community policing unit.

The three area commanders are scheduled according to the needs of the patrol unit. The three basic shifts of days, evenings, and weekends are staffed. Of course flexibility in schedules is important. Area commanders, whose areas of command correspond to the three distinct areas of our community, are charged with quality-of-life issues and crime trends within their area. Global issues, such as gangs and narcotics, are handled citywide by specific units. All community meetings, regardless of the topic, are coordinated and moderated by the area commander. This has greatly enhanced dialog between the community and all departments of the city.

All other units in the department provide support and serve as resources for the area commanders. Twice-monthly meetings involving all area commanders, division commanders, chief of police and commanders of all specialized units as well as our crime analysis unit are held. Issues are discussed and strategies are developed to address issues as they are emerging. These meetings allow the department's command staff to keep current on community issues and also allow for the coordination of resources among the area commanders.

The City Council and all city departments have embraced the Area Commander Program, leading to a new synergy that has resulted in community-oriented government.

Human Relations Philosophy

Many assumptions about people in the workplace have come out of the human relations movement. They serve to guide the development of policies and objectives within human relations organizations. These assumptions include:

1. Workers are viewed as whole individuals, not just as people who perform certain tasks for the organization but as people with feelings and desires that go beyond the work environment. They have families and friends, belong to many other organizations—educational organizations, religious organizations, social organizations—and have many needs which affect their job performance.

2.   Managers are required to use their experience, intuition, and generalizations from an interdisciplinary perspective to guide them in taking action.
3.   Higher productivity and greater human satisfaction require employee participation in the organization.
4.   Communication is the nervous system of the organization. It provides the stimuli and feedback for action to occur.
5.   The employee has two roles to play at work—a job-oriented role and an informal group–oriented role. The job-oriented role is that which is played in performing the organizational tasks. The informal group–oriented role sets the limits for social interactions in the work environment.
6.   Cooperation in the form of teamwork is an indispensable management practice if the organization is to survive.
7.   Employees are diversely motivated. Satisfaction comes from job accomplishment, recognition, and participation as well as from economic or monetary rewards.
8.   The work situation is a complex social system of interrelated elements.
9.   Human relations management skills can be developed. These skills can be improved through training or awareness, sensitivity, and competency in coping with the human problems of organizations (Huneryager and Heckman, 1967).

Human relations offered a promise for fulfilling the social and self-esteem needs of employees and for solving the problems of interpersonal communication in organizations.

Participatory Management

The primary result of the human relations school has been the implementation of participatory management. *Participatory management* is a management form that in a general sense entails allowing subordinates to participate in decision making and planning, particularly with regard to their own responsibilities and the operation of their own units. It focuses on the operation of each unit within the overall department. Participation is usually encouraged in matters that affect the officer's job performance. For example, participatory management for a patrol shift would occur when the patrol commanders actively seek and utilize information from subordinates about problems and priorities. The commanders meet with their sergeants and officers to obtain information and identify problems and solutions. If changes can be instituted at that level, they are made. If changes cannot be made at that level, the commander may take the problem and suggested solutions to a higher level, a major or assistant chief. Officers would not directly participate at higher levels in the department but would provide some input to these levels since their immediate commanders would advocate their concerns and ideas.

When subordinates' feelings, concerns, and ideas for solutions are expressed to their supervisors and transmitted throughout the upper echelons of the organization by superiors, the process of management is improved. Likert (1961)

Figure 5–1
Likert's linking pin framework.

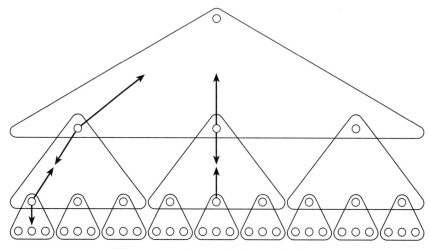

(The arrows indicate the linking pin funtion)

Source: R. Likert, *New Patterns of Management,* New York: McGraw-Hill, 1961, p. 113.

describes this as a managerial linking pin framework (see Figure 5–1). Since each work group consists of superiors and subordinates, information interjected at one point is transmitted upward, downward, and laterally through this *linking pin* network (chain of command). This process allows for the free flow of information, the identification of better solutions to problems, and increased morale since personnel at all levels of the department better understand the perspectives of other people and other units. Its success depends on managers sharing information with superiors and subordinates in a collegial fashion. It essentially consists of teams at the unit level that are coordinated with an information flow through the chain of command.

It is important to note that groups are linked together by several processes: communications, balance, and decision making (Scott, 1996). Communications are important across groups not only as a control and coordination process, but as a mechanism by which people, units, and the overall organization respond to issues and problems. Communications cause parts within an organization to function toward some objective. Balance refers to "an equilibrating mechanism whereby parts of the system are maintained in a harmoniously structured relationship with each other" (p. 266). Work groups negotiate a relationship among and with all other groups, and this relationship must be maintained if the groups are to cooperate with each other. Generally, imbalance results in less cooperation among work groups, and it makes administration more difficult as additional efforts are required to coordinate activities. Finally, decision making is an overarching process that binds groups together. Work groups accordingly focus on two types of decisions, productivity and participation (March and Simon, 1958). The group makes decisions about how much work is to be done, and it decides how involved the group becomes in the overall organization. Seldom is a decision made that affects only one or a few work groups within an organization; decisions usually have an impact on every part of an organization in one fashion or another.

Likert and Scott provide us with a glimpse of how participatory management can be implemented throughout an organization. Participatory management is not something that is easily displayed on an organizational chart, for it is a philosophical notion and a way of conceptualizing the human relationship between management and employee. However, it is easy to recognize the participatory organization by looking at written goals, policies, and procedures statements. These clearly indicate the importance of the human element of the organization and the desire to assimilate the employee into the decision-making process. Generally speaking, the more participatory the organization, the less hierarchical it will appear; it will have fewer levels of hierarchy and may place less emphasis on the superior–subordinate relationship between ranks.

Likert (1967) examined levels of participation in organizations and outlined four management systems based on the level of participation. The four management systems are described in Table 5–2. They range from exploitive-authoritarian to participative. As an organization moves closer to a "participatory" form, it becomes more "open": subordinates have more input into planning and decision making, trust is fostered in the organization, and productivity thereby increases. Police departments with their quasi-military structure often fall into the benevolent–authoritarian management system.

Human Relations Theory and Police Administration

Essentially, there have been two periods of time when human relations theory has been applied to law enforcement. First, in the 1970s, as the police were immersed in the community relations movement, many believed that the police should abandon their quasi-military structure and adopt a more open, employee-centered structure. It was believed that such a structure would facilitate better relations between officers and the public. Second, currently, decentralization and participatory management are mainstays in the community policing movement. It is believed that problem solving and community partnerships, critical ingredients in community policing, can best be facilitated through decentralization and participatory management.

Numerous departments experimented with participatory management in the 1970s. Two such departments, Dayton, Ohio, and Menlo Park, California, are discussed here. In the early 1970s, the Dayton Police Department implemented a democratic model of team policing (Angell, 1978). It was an attempt to move the department into Likert's consultative management system. Officers volunteered for small teams that were assigned to police small geographical areas. The officers then selected their supervisors from a list of volunteers. The officers

Table 5–2

Likert's Organizational Characteristics of Management Systems

Operating Characteristic	Exploitive–Authoritarian System	Benevolent–Authoritarian System	Consultative System	Participative System
Motivation	Economic security marked with fear and threats	Economic and occasionally status rewards coupled with some punishment	Economic, ego, and desire for new experiences; occasional punishment	Economic, ego, and full involvement in the organization and shared power
Communication Processes	Very little and downward	Little and mostly downward	Quite a bit, up and down the organization	Substantial throughout the organization
Character of Interaction–Influence	Little interaction, usually distrustful	Some interaction with caution on the part of subordinates	Moderate interaction and a moderate level of trust and confidence	Extensive collegial interaction with a high degree of trust and confidence
Decision Making	Centralized with top administrators	Policy dictated by top administrators with some decisions resting with midlevel managers	Broad policies made at top with lower echelons having input into programs	Decisions made throughout the organization with lower-level subordinates having input in all decisions
Goal Setting	Goals set by top administrators and orders issued by administrators; directives resisted by subordinates	Goals set by top administrators and orders issued by administrators with some discussion by subordinates	Goals and orders issued after discussion with subordinates; goals and orders have some level of acceptance by subordinates	Goals established through group participation with high levels of acceptance by work group
Control Processes	Formalized controls established by top management with resistance by subordinates	Control rests primarily at the top with resistance from subordinates	Moderate delegation of authority and responsibility with subordinates having some input in performance expectations	Concern for performance throughout the organization coupled with collegiality
Productivity	Mediocre	Fair to good	Good	Excellent

Source: Adapted from R. Likert, *The Human Organization: Its Management and Value.* New York: McGraw-Hill, 1967, pp. 14–24.

were given authority to investigate crimes and generally assume duties that normally were reserved for specialists in the department. The teams met frequently to discuss tactics and assignments, and the teams had the authority to deploy themselves any way they felt that appropriately met the needs of the team's geographical area. Officers could deploy stakeouts, increase patrol, patrol in unmarked units, and engage in crime prevention projects. The teams had almost absolute autonomy in the way they policed their areas. Theoretically, motivation and police productivity would increase as a result of officers' increased involvement. Eventually, the teams were discarded due to problems with middle management, and the department moved back toward a traditional organizational philosophy (Sherman, 1978).

In Menlo Park, the chief of police, two lieutenants, six sergeants, the traffic inspector, and the president of the officers' association decided to redefine the departmental philosophy, organization, and role descriptions. The new philosophy defined the department's professional obligations toward the community, expanded the police role in the community, and redefined the responsibility of the department in relation to its members. The Menlo Park Police Department philosophy statement read:

1. The Menlo Park Police Department is a municipal multi-service organization designed to provide better living and safety for its citizens.
2. Recognizing it must relate and respond to community needs that are dynamic and constantly changing, the department is pledged to recruiting talented personnel who are committed to their fellow man and are free from color and economic bias.
3. While rejecting an authoritarian approach to problem solving, the department is continually involved in enforcement, prevention and education programs designed to control and reduce crime and traffic accidents.
4. The department commits itself to its employees and will make every effort to provide a work atmosphere conducive to personal and career development.
5. Ultimately we hope to provide quality police service at minimum cost to the citizens we serve (Tenzel, Storms, and Sweetwood, 1976:25).

The organization that developed in Menlo Park is depicted in Figure 5–2. In this organization, the providers of police service are central while management and staff assist and coordinate as needed to facilitate service delivery. The department dropped its military rank structure and adopted more contemporary business titles of director, manager, and police agent. The idea was to remove the nuances of the military model from the department and move toward Likert's participatory management system. However, since then, Menlo Park has modified its organizational chart to more clearly reflect the military chain of command as shown in Figure 5–3.

Although a number of departments adopted various forms of human relations theory in the 1970s, eventually they moved back toward the benevolent management system or a traditional organizational structure. There are several possible explanations for this. First, potential liability problems in policing

Figure 5–2
Menlo Park police organization and operational schematic, 1971.

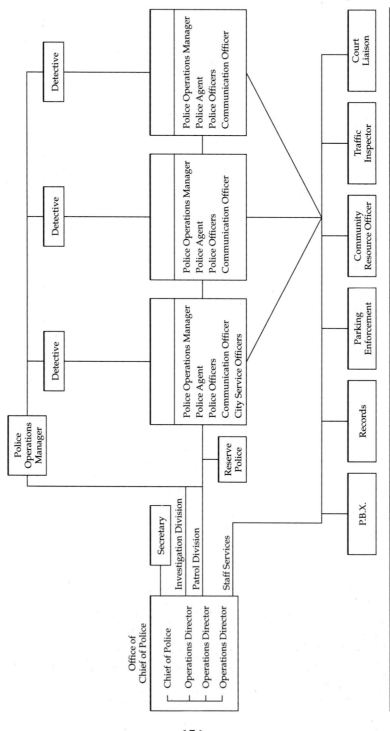

Source: J. Tenzel, L. Storms, and H. Sweetwood, Symbols and Behavior: An Experiment in Altering the Police Role, *Journal of Police Science and Administration* 4, no. 1 (1976), pp. 21–27.

Figure 5-3
Menlo Park police organization and operational schematic, 2001.

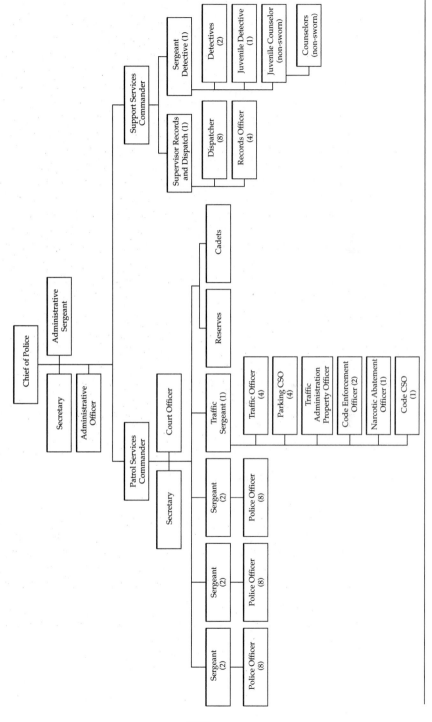

Source: Provided by the Menlo Park Police Department.

place pressure on police administrators to more tightly control their departments. Second, police officers are accustomed to quasi-military organizations, and this history may create a natural affinity for the quasi-military structure. Third, citizens expect the police to respond in a "militaristic" fashion, so there is some pressure for departments to have a military appearance. Finally, it is virtually impossible to operate large organizations, especially government organizations, without substantial structure.

Today, there is a significant movement in policing to again adopt many of the innovations that were experimented with in the 1970s. Much of this pressure comes from departments implementing community policing. Community policing necessitates that officers develop partnerships with residents and engage in problem solving. It is reasoned that the bureaucratic model of benevolent authoritarianism will not facilitate the creation of partnerships or officers engaging in problem solving (Kuykendall and Roberg, 1997). Critics of traditional police administration are calling for departments to decentralize authority so that line officers are free to engage in community policing (Kelling and Bratton, 2000). They claim that police departments should be flattened (the number of levels in the chain of command should be reduced); decrease the amount of specialization to allow officers to be involved in a variety of more interesting duties; reduce the level of formalization, or the number of written rules; and decentralize authority so that lower-level officers and supervisors can make more decisions. Reformers claim that these changes in the police organization would contribute to police being more responsive to the community (Mastrofski and Ritti, 1995; Moore and Stephens, 1992; Stamper, 1992).

Evidence indicates that police administrators do not totally agree with this perspective. For example, Wycoff (1994) found that 61 percent of police administrators in her study reported that there was no need to change the organizational structure of their departments to implement community policing. Similarly, Maguire's (1997) study of departments from 1987 to 1993 found that police departments reduced their height or chain of command, but they increased the level of specialization. He found no differences in structure, however, between departments that had implemented or planned to implement community policing and those that had not implemented the strategy. Since most large departments are already involved in community policing, it appears that administrators feel comfortable with their existing structures to implement the new community policing strategies and tactics.

Many of the police organizational critics fail to comprehend that the police organization has substantially evolved since the 1950s, when the professional model of policing was cemented into American law enforcement. Toch (1997) found that police organizations have substantially changed to allow greater participation by lower-level employees. Reiss (1992) identifies technology, social organization, and the political system as keys in forcing police organizations to change and reshape how they respond to the community. Police departments appear to be far less bureaucratic than their critics believe. Police departments nationally are perhaps more consultative today as opposed to operating within the benevolent authoritarian framework.

Figure 5–4
Operation of a quality circle.

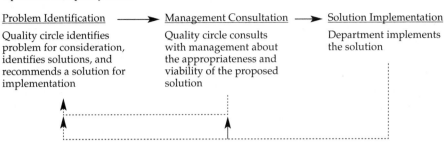

Underline__Problem Identification__   ⟶   Underline__Management Consultation__   ⟶   Underline__Solution Implementation__

Quality circle identifies
problem for consideration,
identifies solutions, and
recommends a solution for
implementation

Quality circle consults
with management about
the appropriateness and
viability of the proposed
solution

Department implements
the solution

Refining Participatory Management: Quality Circles

The quality circle, an outgrowth of human relations theory, is one technique used by managers to involve employees in solving problems within their organization. The *quality circle* consists of a group of highly competent employees who are given a task of solving organizational problems. Quality circles usually consist of nonmanagement volunteers, typically from the same work unit, who meet regularly in small groups to identify and analyze problems and develop recommendations for solving these problems. A facilitator trains quality circle members and leaders in group interaction and problem solving. The facilitator helps the group get under way and provides guidance and help on any problems the circle may encounter. The quality circle leader is often the first-line supervisor but may be a nonmanagement member of the unit. The circle selects the problems it will study. The operation of the quality circle is outlined in Figure 5–4.

The typical operation of quality circles is described by Hatry and Greiner as follows:

> Members are first given training in group interaction and problem-solving techniques. The group then meets weekly to chose the problems they want to work on, to analyze them, and to develop solutions to those problems. They generally meet for an hour during working hours at a location near the work site. The circle leader conducts the meeting and guides the circle through the problem-solving phase. Another circle member records the minutes. The product of this process is a formal presentation of the circle's recommendation to department management, for example, the police chief and perhaps his management team. All circle members participate in the briefing, during which they explain their proposed solution, how they arrived at it, and its estimated cost. If they receive approval of their proposal (and it is within their expertise), they may help to implement the idea. The circle then goes on to examine another problem. (1986:8–9)

Quality circles are expected to improve working conditions and procedures, service efficiency and effectiveness, morale and job satisfaction, and relations with supervisors while costing the organization very little in return. Hatry and Greiner (1986) found that the quality circles did effect numerous minor improvements in working conditions and procedures. The circles also seem to have led to small but identifiable improvements in service efficiency or effectiveness. The evidence from their study indicates that quality circles have had a neutral or positive effect on employee morale and job satisfaction, but the evidence is mixed. The major benefit that was supported by evidence was the improvement in the relationships of supervisors and employees. Another benefit is that the circles have prodded middle managers to solve persistent work problems. As the circle posts its list of potential problems, supervisory personnel frequently scan the list and proceed on their own initiative to alleviate some of the problems identified. The additional training, the chance to contribute to solving problems, and greater authority for the officer were also identified as benefits of circles.

Some of the problems identified in relation to quality circles were "difficulties that emerged from the changes implemented by the circles, additional work with no immediate benefits for circle participants, fear that management would view the circle members as 'complainers,' and increased dissatisfaction with management if it rejected quality circle recommendations" (Hatry and Greiner, 1986:57).

Police quality circles have done little to improve productivity in their departments given the short time frame of operation and the failure of organizations to perform systematic, in-depth assessments of the impacts of quality circles. However, they must demonstrably improve police productivity if they are to be credible and have long-term viability. Hatry and Greiner (1986) believe this may be accomplished under certain conditions. With modification and clarification, seven major recommendations are presented in the following list.

1. Quality circles should be encouraged to tackle significant service delivery operating problems and not just problems of the work environment. For example, they could deal with specific crime problems (such as burglary or drug traffic); problems dealing with use of force (such as defense tactics, flashlights, guns, or batons); prioritization of calls for service; alterations in shift staffing and staff allocation policy; or reducing the number of citizen complaints. Quality circles have focused primarily on improving aspects of the working environment that represent minor irritants and inconveniences but that often have a significant cumulative negative effect on the police officer. Some of the work environment problems that have been addressed are "office lighting and appearance, washroom deficiencies, advance posting of monthly detail rosters, relocation of shotgun lockers, improved security for police substations, and the need for better parking facilities near central headquarters" (p. 19).

2. Quality circles should survey other personnel to obtain their comments and suggestions about problems and possible solutions.

3. To reduce problems of absenteeism, the membership of a circle should be limited to one shift.

4. To increase the breadth of participation and assist in better recommendations, the quality circle should keep supervisors, middle managers, and other unit personnel informed about the subjects they are examining and about the recommendations they are considering. The quality circle

should encourage these persons to provide constructive suggestions as this information is provided and before the circle's recommendations are finalized.

5. The circle facilitator should provide formal training to new circle members and refresher training to longer-term members as a means to develop and maintain group skills and to rejuvenate the circle. This training should consist of brief sessions interspersed throughout the duration of the circle. Too much time spent in training over any one time frame without accomplishing tangible results toward the circle's mission tends to cause members to drop out.

6. Departments should track the status, progress, and impact of circle recommendations on the department. This information should be regularly disseminated throughout the department. To sustain a quality circle, its members must see substantial benefits for the department and receive adequate rewards for their contributions. For example, in the Mesa, Arizona, police department, a quality circle developed a proposal to consolidate several crime prevention pamphlets into one pamphlet. The suggestion saved $3,000 and the members of the circle were nominated to receive awards under the city's suggestion award program.

7. Quality circles should not be established in departments or divisions whose managers want to maintain a tight rein on their employees. They should be introduced only where upper management and most middle managers are willing to experiment with increased participation, are not afraid to give responsibility to lower-level personnel, and do not feel threatened by the potentiality that the circles will directly offer the chief recommendations that do not agree with their own beliefs. Middle and upper-level managers should be thoroughly exposed to participative management concepts before the introduction of quality circles in the organization. The chief must actively support the more open, participative style associated with quality circles if they are to be successful at all.

Quality circles seem to be ideally suited for community policing. One of the defining elements of community policing is problem solving. Rather than focusing on a rapid response to calls for service, the police must concentrate on providing a more substantive response once they are on the scene. The police should identify problems and possible solutions, select a solution, implement it, and then evaluate its results. When this occurs, especially when recurring problems are addressed, the police will more effectively respond to citizens' problems. Quality circles are an excellent mode by which to identify problems and possible solutions.

It must be recognized that the introduction of quality circles in a traditional organization with authoritarian management will threaten that management style and will necessitate a change or modification of the authoritarian style. There must be enough police officials ready and willing to try a more participatory management approach if quality circles are to be feasible in traditional departments.

In summation, participatory management is used to decentralize the police department's command structure at the unit level. Decentralization occurs when decisions are made at the lowest possible point in the department. Benefits include increased intradepartmental communications, improved job satisfaction, and increased productivity. Additionally, this type of management allows police officers to devise strategies and programs that will increase their ability to respond to public needs. Finally, participatory management is a management tool that can be introduced at any level within a police department. Individual commanders can utilize it, or the chief can introduce it department wide by installing management teams.

Contribution and Weaknesses of the Neoclassical or Human Relations Model

The main contribution of the neoclassical or human relations theory was the introduction of behavioral sciences in an integrated fashion into the theory of organization. Managers, as a result of human relations theory, began to study how people behave in the organization. It also provided a systematic treatment of the informal organization, showing the informal organization's influence on the formal structure of organizations. That is, people have an effect on management and the organization.

The human relations model did not demonstrate the high level of research support that was expected. The acceptance of the human relations philosophy was due more to the failures of classical organizational theory than the accomplishments of the human relations movement. Researchers found that informal groups are uncommon as a natural occurrence in organizations and that the majority of workers do not belong to such groups; therefore, the human relations focus on the informal group as a natural phenomenon was ill advised. People are important in an organization, but they cannot function without some level of structure. The concentration of human relationists on social rewards as a sole means of motivation was also found to be ill directed. Research demonstrated that it is necessary for the reward system to consist of both monetary and social rewards—each is an equally important part of the reward system (Gaines, 1978).

CONTINGENCY THEORY: BRIDGING CLASSICAL AND HUMAN RELATIONS THEORIES

Most discussions of classical and human relations organizational theories have been in absolute terms. Many writers assume that they are mutually exclusive and pure in form, although it is very unlikely that they exist in their pure form anywhere. Organizations— even bureaucracies—are vibrant, and they adapt to changes in the environment and workplace. Most organizations, including police departments, consist of degrees of human relations and bureaucracy. For example, police departments were highly structured in the 1950s, but they have evolved and incorporated many human relations elements over the last several decades (Toch, 1997). They tend to have a mix of organizational theories and management styles. The actual structure of a police organization generally is contingent on its mission, its environment, and the composition of its work force.

One of the first to investigate the mix of organizational forms was Woodward (1965), who found that mechanistic structures were more appropriate for mass-production work settings, while organic systems were appropriate for nonrepetitive work environments. Repetitive tasks are best accomplished when they are standardized and controlled. This body of literature seems to indicate that some segments of a police organization are more effective if organized using bureaucratic principles, whereas other segments may be better served if a participatory style is used. For example, some aspects of patrol work such as handling domestic disputes, use of deadly and nondeadly force, and arrest procedures require departments to exert high levels of control. Police officer discretion should be controlled in these cases. On the other hand, an organic unit would be more appropriate for homicide detectives since they require substantial discretion and latitude in procedures when investigating a homicide.

Perrow (1967) in an investigation of a variety of industries reached the same conclusions as did Woodward: Routine technologies require structure, whereas nonroutine technologies must be given some level of flexibility and independence. In an effort to better distinguish routine and nonroutine technologies, he identified the key determinants for structure: (1) the amount of discretion that employees have when completing a task, (2) the amount of authority the employee group has over the work group's goals and work strategies, (3) the level of interdependence among the work group and other work groups, and (4) how dependent a work group is on other work groups for feedback and planning. Using Perrow's determinants, it seems that there are work groups within police departments that should have some level of mechanistic structures, while others require an organic structure.

Along these same lines, Thompson (1967) discussed long-linked technologies. A *long-linked technology* is a process by which individual work groups contribute a part to the total. For example, a long-linked technology in police work is seen when (1) patrol performs the preliminary investigation on a crime and then refers the case to specialists, that is, detectives, and (2) as other units or specialists become involved during the investigation, such as crime scene technicians collecting physical evidence and lab technicians performing analysis of the evidence. Long-linked technologies require more coordination and control because of the interdependence of the units involved in the total process.

Mintzberg's Five Organizational Forms

Organizations can be categorized by their structure. Organizational form generally is dictated by the environment, organizational mission, and work force. Mintzberg (1983) has provided the theoretical framework by which to understand types of organization. He notes that all organizations are composed of five basic elements or groups of people, which are represented in Figure 5–5. Each

Figure 5–5
Strategic parts of a police organization.

type of group may dominate an organization, depending on the organization's nature and activities. The five elements or groups are:

1. *The operational core.* The employees who actually perform the organization's core functions and activities comprise this group. In police departments this includes line officers and civilians who are involved in the delivery of services.
2. *The strategic apex.* The strategic apex consists of top management or those people responsible for administering the organization. Chiefs and their staff generally comprise a police department's strategic apex.
3. *The middle management.* Individuals responsible for units or functions are at the core of middle management. In police departments, middle management consists of unit commanders (e.g., patrol commander or detective commander) and their supervisory staff.
4. *The technostructure.* Every organization has specialists whose responsibility is to control various functions and activities. Police departments have accountants to monitor and control expenditures; computer information systems to report on activities; and planners who write policies. The technostructure is designed to ensure conformity with a preconceived plan of how the department should operate.
5. *The support staff.* Most organizations have technicians who advise management on how to proceed. In police organizations, these include attorneys, consultants who are charged with examining specific elements of the department, and other members of government who may be able to exercise control over departmental decision making.

As noted, each of these groups potentially can dominate an organization. Generally, the group that dominates an organization is determined by the nature of the organization. Group dominance is associated with specific types of organization (Mintzberg, 1983). As a result of groups dominating the organization's activities, organizations evolve into simple structures, machine bureaucracies, professional bureaucracies, divisionalized structures, and "adhocracies" (Greenberg and Baron, 1995).

Simple structured organizations generally exist in small agencies. *Simple structures* are dominated by the strategic apex. They are small, informal organizations with authority generally vested with one or a few people. Most small police departments are dominated by simple structures. Here, the police chief often serves as a line officer as well as the department's executive. The chief retains responsibility for making most if not all decisions. There is little or no specialization or formalization, and the department, for the most part, operates as a small work group. These departments, because of their size and structure, are flexible and able to respond to problems fairly rapidly. Obviously, the primary concern or weakness with such organizations is the ability of the executive. If the chief is skilled, the organization will be successful, on other hand, if the executive is not a skilled administrator, the department may face a number of problems.

The second type of organization, machine bureaucracy, is dominated by a technostructure. The *machine bureaucracy* is adept at performing highly specialized, routine tasks. It is very control-oriented, and consistency of performance is extremely important. Factory assembly lines are perhaps the most common form of machine bureaucracy. However, they also occur in police organizations. For example, records clerks, evidence clerks, dispatchers, and personnel processing warrants are examples of machine bureaucracies in police organizations. These jobs are extremely important, and they require a maximum level of consistency in their performance. Larger police departments will have some units that are operated as machine bureaucracies, but it is doubtful whether any police department uses this form of organization as the principal operating structure. Even though machine bureaucracies are highly efficient, they consist of extremely boring work and tend to dehumanize the employee, a consistent criticism of classical organizational theory.

In a *professional bureaucracy*, power and authority rest primarily with the operational core employees. Perhaps the best examples of professional bureaucracies are hospitals and universities. Doctors and nurses retain authority of the quality of services in hospitals, while professors retain authority for the end product (education) in universities. It is recognized that the professional bureaucrats are highly skilled, and they generally are allowed great discretion in their craft. Administrators in professional bureaucracies tend to support the operational core as opposed to attempting to control it. Guyot (1991) has advocated that police adopt the hospital model as the primary organizational structure. Those advocating participatory management in policing generally envision a professional bureaucracy when doing so.

Today, many police departments operate, in part or wholly, close to a professional bureaucracy. Line officers and supervisors are vested with a high level of police discretion (Brooks, 1997; Walker, 1993); therefore, regardless of amount of effort, it is impossible for administrators to absolutely constrain police behavior. American policing since the 1950s has evolved toward a more participatory model (Toch, 1997).

The *divisionalized structure* is dominated by middle managers and generally consists of a number of autonomous units which are coordinated by a central headquarters. Examples of divisionalized structures in law enforcement are large police departments such as those of Los Angeles and New York City, where captains are responsible for sectors or precincts, and state police organizations, which generally have captains or lieutenants responsible for geographical areas. These middle managers must follow departmental policies and procedures, but they also have a great deal of autonomy in terms of problem solving, decision making, and the allocation of personnel.

Along these same lines, specialized units within most police departments have tremendous autonomy. For example, most narcotics or drug enforcement units, homicide units, selective traffic enforcement units, and community relations units all work independently of other line units and most of the command staff. These units typically operate as professional bureaucracies within the divisional structure. Most large departments are likely to use the divisional structure.

Finally, an *adhocracy* is an organization that is dominated by support staff. Adhocracies most often are teams of professionals working on projects on an ad hoc basis. Planning and development units in large businesses generally operate using this model. They are pure organic structures, and they are formed to create innovation or change. A quality circle is an example of how an adhocracy can be created in a large police department. Other examples of adhocracies in law enforcement include highly specialized enforcement units such as federal or state drug or organized crime task forces.

Mintzberg's organizational forms demonstrate that law enforcement can be organized using a variety of structures. A department's organizational mix often is contingent on a number of factors including size, mission, environment, and work force. However, it should be noted that most police departments, because of size, geographical responsibility, and specialization, use a variety of Mintzberg's organizational forms.

THE SYSTEMS MODEL OF ORGANIZATIONAL MANAGEMENT

Contingency models approach organizations as multidimensional. They emphasize the open construction of organizations, focusing more on organizational processes and outcomes than the human relations model. The contingency approaches attempt to mediate between the classical and human relations approaches. They recognize that organizations are often a mix of the mechanistic and organic, and the key to organizational success is implementing the correct mix at the unit level.

The systems approach to organizational design is rooted in biology. Bertalanffy (1951) noted that all sciences had certain characteristics: (1) the studying

Figure 5–6

Characteristics of an open system.

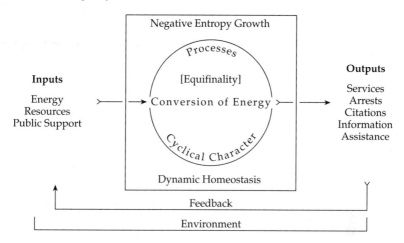

of organisms as a whole, (2) the postulate that organisms tend to strive for a state of equilibrium, and (3) the conclusion that organisms are affected by their environment and affect their environment. In other words, an organization functions the same way that a plant functions. Basically, *systems* consist of a set of interrelated parts or components that work together to achieve a set of overall objectives. Systems theory emphasizes or concentrates on the parts, not the whole. The whole organization is of little consequence since it merely is a sum of the various parts. Thus the classicists and human relationists erred when they concentrated on the implementation of an overarching philosophy. A more accurate way of examining organizations is to study what is occurring within and across the various components.

In Chapter 2, we discussed the importance of police organizations being open to and responding to their environments: The organizational system must be open. It must interact and respond to the environment. Systems are dynamic and ever changing as they respond to their environments. This section expands on the discussion in Chapter 2 and provides more detail about systems components.

Characteristics of an Open System

An open system consists of nine common characteristics (Katz and Kahn, 1966; Robbins, 1990): (1) environmental awareness and importation of energy and resources, (2) conversion of energy into goods and services, (3) outputs, (4) cyclical character of processes, (5) negative entropy, (6) feedback, (7) functional steady state or dynamic homeostasis, (8) movement toward growth and expansion, and (9) equifinality. Figure 5–6 provides a schematic of the open-system process.

Environmental awareness and importation of energy and resources refers to an organization being a part of an overall environment (see Chapter 2). This environment, in turn, has a tremendous effect on the organization in terms of its structure and activities. What a particular police department does is dictated by the needs and desires of the community. There are significant pressures on the police to serve and protect. For example, the bulk of police activities are initiated by citizens' calls to the police requesting some service. If the police fail to respond adequately to these requests, the public may voice its disapproval through the political system. Successful police departments are able to respond to their communities.

Also, a police organization obtains its resources from the community through the political system. If a police department satisfies or meets the demands of the community, the community through the political system very likely will make greater amounts of resources available to the department. On the other hand, if the department is perceived negatively or neutrally by the community, it very likely will have more difficulty in obtaining resources. Regardless, the environment plays a crucial role in an organization's stability and future success.

Conversion of energy into goods and services is the process that occurs when an organization imports energy or resources and then converts them into some form of action. An organization must have resources if it is to function. Energy is used to pay salaries and purchase equipment so that the police department can provide services to its citizens. Once a department receives its allotment of resources, decisions are made as to how they are spent or allocated. This process establishes priorities for the department.

Outputs are the various services a police department provides to the community. The range of services includes arresting criminals, patrolling, keeping the peace, preventing crime, investigating criminal activities, and assisting persons in need. Goldstein (1990) notes that historically the police have not provided a satisfactory level of services to the community and advocates that the police should engage in problem solving rather than superficially responding to calls for service. The police must provide services or outputs which are acceptable to the community and the political system. If they do not, the department very likely will suffer in terms of resources, and there is a possibility that the chief may be forced out of the department.

Cyclical character of processes refers to the nature of work and activities in organizations. Almost all work occurs in cycles or is repetitive in nature. For example, a worker on a factory assembly line will complete a set of repetitive tasks that are part of an overall construction cycle, or what Thompson (1967) describes as a long-linked technology. Engineers when designing a building will exercise a great deal of discretion, but in the end, they generally follow prescribed engineering procedures. The same occurs in a police department. When the dispatcher receives a call, it is dispatched to a patrol officer. If a crime has been committed, the patrol officer will take a report and conduct a preliminary investigation. If the case is not solved by the patrol officer, it is turned over to a detective who completes a follow-up investigation. This chain of events represents a cycle of activities which can be plotted, studied, and understood. Once a work cycle is understood, it can be improved upon and better controlled.

Negative entropy is a process whereby the organization replenishes itself or stores energy. Entropy occurs naturally as organizations move toward disorganization. For example, if the police chief fails to attend to maintaining the department in terms of responding to community needs or remaining technologically current, the department will fall behind and become less functional. Therefore, a department must store resources to be prepared when there are extraordinary demands. Police chiefs should maintain contingency funds for special situations such as crime waves, riots, and natural disasters. Without contingency funds, a department would not be able to respond to such a situation effectively. Along these same lines, a police department must store or amass "good will" within the community. This allows the department to survive whenever an officer makes a decisive mistake such as an accidental shooting or when there is a scandal within the department. A department can weather such events if it has amassed a substantial amount of good will prior to the event.

Feedback is the process whereby the organization monitors the environment to gather information about environmental needs and the organization's performance. Industries and businesses monitor the environment to identify new products and assess how well current products are performing. In the same way, police departments monitor the community to identify needs and adequacy of performance. Police departments generally monitor a number of sources: the news media, citizen groups, and politicians. If a department fails to monitor the community or does so inadequately, it may fail to respond to the community. Moreover, a department's resources or inputs, to some degree, are determined by the adequacy of its outputs, necessitating a cause-and-effect relationship.

Functional steady state or dynamic homeostasis essentially means that organizations function within a set range of behaviors. Activities within an organization consist of a series of cycles; for the most part, departments resist adding, eliminating, or changing the cycles that occur within the organization's boundaries. When events within the environment require an organization to respond, it generally responds using its time-tested approaches or procedures. Organizations over time alter some of their work cycles and add new ones as they respond to the environment. Generally, however, this is a slow, evolutionary process. The management and operational mechanisms within the organization, especially large organizations, are highly resistant to rapid change.

Movement toward growth and expansion refers to the fact that organizations are constantly expanding their boundaries to include more responsibility and authority. Growth of organizations is a natural phenomenon. Part of this process is the result of specialization within organizations. When specialized units are created, their leaders tend to seek to expand the operational boundaries of their units. When boundaries are expanded, the individual units generally receive additional resources. This provides a platform for managers to be promoted to higher levels within the organization. The result of the parts expanding is that the sum or whole organization tends to grow. Thus it is quite natural for police departments to develop new programs and move into new service areas.

Equifinality basically refers the ability to reach a final state by a variety of paths. It was noted that an organization's activities occur in work cycles, or what Thompson (1967) refers to as long-linked technologies. Equifinality means that there are different ways of doing the same job, and the organization must find the "best" path when constructing an activity. Equifinality is concerned with efficiency and effectiveness. For example, a police department must examine all its functions and activities to determine if they are the optimal way of accomplishing stated goals and objectives.

The systems perspective provides a way to examine what is occurring within organizations. Whereas the classicists and human relationists were concerned with an overall philosophy, advocates of systems see the systems approach as an analytical tool by which to better understand the functionality of an organization. Essentially, the systems perspective is an overlay, or blueprint, of an organization. It promotes better understanding of the intricate organizational workings and provides a vehicle by which to make significant alterations.

Total Quality Management

Total quality management (TQM) is a management philosophy as opposed to an organizational structure. Like systems theory, TQM is meant to be integrated into an existing organizational structure, and it can be used in any type of structure (see Spencer, 1994). TQM is a management orientation that ensures that the organization and its members are committed to continuous improvement and to completely meeting customer needs (Schermerhorn, Hunt, and Osborn, 1994). TQM essentially has two philosophical underpinnings: quality and customer orientation. If an organization is to achieve maximum effectiveness, it must ensure that its products and services are of the highest quality. This entails that management closely examine its service or product delivery system and ensure that it operates with "quality" as the overarching objective. It also means that quality is a continuous process that is integrated into every aspect of the organization.

In terms of customers or the consumers of products and services, their opinions of what is important should be the chief determinants of quality. The customer is the most important consideration to an organization, and everything the organization does should be aimed at satisfying the customer. The customer or client is the reason that the organization exists in the first place.

Historical Perspective

To some extent, TQM is rooted in Taylor's principles of scientific management (see Chapter 4). Scientific management, with its emphasis on efficiency, created the first assembly lines. The assembly line resulted in the decomposing of jobs into individual tasks. Workers no longer took pride in or related to the final product; they tended to focus exclusively on their own little niche. This resulted in substantial variation of product and the need for quality control. Quality control as a result of scientific management consisted of inspection of products and elimination or retooling of inadequate products.

Later, after the Hawthorne experiments in Chicago, quality control was operationalized as statistical control. Rather than examining each product as it was produced, batches of products were examined and defects were statistically projected for the total process. Quality meant that the number of defects was below some expected standard. Quality control was relegated to a specialized unit. This meant that line employees and supervisors could focus on quantity and production efficiency as opposed to quality of product. As a result, quality became an adversarial process where operational units would blame each other for shortcomings as opposed to directly addressing the quality problem. Blame supplanted quality.

The Japanese economy and industrial structure was totally devastated as a result of World War II. Deming and Juran introduced the idea of quality to the Japanese as a part of the rebuilding process. Initially they focused on quality control, much as the Americans had. However, they also convinced Japanese management that quality control would ultimately open new markets to Japanese products and was necessary if the Japanese were to compete in world markets. Since the Japanese were rebuilding from the ground up, they were able to incorporate quality throughout their industrial infrastructure. Quality in Japanese products increased at a exponential rate.

American and other Western manufacturers did not invest in quality. The 1950s witnessed a significant increase in the consumption of goods and services. Consumers essentially bought everything that was available in the marketplace. The Japanese, as a result of the quality of their products, gained the competitive edge in markets such as electronics, automobiles, and photography equipment by the 1970s. In many cases, "made in America" came to mean inferior goods. American and other Western corporations began their own pursuit of quality in the 1980s. Many American corporations become competitive in the 1990s in the quality arena. For example, in 1992 the Ford Taurus outsold the Honda Accord to become the leader in domestic car sales. The Americans were finally able to compete with the Japanese in the automobile market (Dean and Evans, 1994).

Deming's Philosophy

Deming believed that quality could be improved by reducing the uncertainty and variability in the manufacturing process. He believed that the work system, not the worker, was the primary cause of most problems in the workplace. If an organization focused on improving quality, then productivity would follow. To this end, Deming developed 14 points to guide management:

1. Create consistency of purpose with a plan.
2. Adopt the new philosophy of quality.
3. Cease dependence on mass inspection.
4. End the practice of choosing suppliers based solely on price.
5. Identify problems and work continuously to improve the system.
6. Adopt modern methods of training on the job.
7. Change the focus from production numbers (quantity) to quality.

8. Drive out fear.
9. Break down barriers between departments.
10. Stop requiring improved productivity without providing methods to achieve it.
11. Eliminate work standards that prescribe numerical quotas.
12. Remove barriers to pride of workmanship.
13. Institute vigorous education and retraining.
14. Create a structure in top management that will emphasize the preceding 13 points every day (Ross, 1995: 5).

As Hradesky notes, "TQM is a philosophy, a set of tools, and a process whose output yields customer satisfaction and continues improvement" (1995:2). TQM is a management system because it not only focuses on the management or organizational structures themselves, but it moves beyond and focuses on how work is accomplished and outputs (goods and services) are received by consumers.

TQM and Police Administration

Hoover (1996), upon examining how TQM might apply to police administration, advises that it essentially encompasses three primary areas: culture, customers, and counting. *Culture* refers to the internal operating philosophy of the organization; *customers* are clients, or those citizens who consume an organization's product or receive its services; and *counting* refers to increasing the element of accountability and understanding within an organization in terms of how it operates and provides goods and services to its constituents. These three areas, when integrated into a police management philosophy, result in a much more powerful organization in terms of efficiency, effectiveness, and responsiveness.

Culture.   Culture refers to the matrix of values that reside within an organization. It is a matrix because as an organization becomes larger, so does the number of constituent groups within the organization, and each group, along with each individual, has its own set of values. Although many of these values overlap the values of other groups, there are unique values among work groups. For example, detectives and patrol officers often have different viewpoints about what is important, and business leaders and minority residents within a city often disagree about what the police should be doing. Thus the police organization is pulled in a number of directions as different values compete for dominance.

Historically, the police organizational value system has focused on maintaining the status quo, and organizational structure was more important than most other matters. Police departments were quasi-military institutions that emphasized their own importance over the citizens they served or even the employees who were responsible for accomplishing goals and objectives. TQM, as a philosophy, totally reverses this trend. Under TQM, the citizen or consumer of police services is most important, followed by the work force, and, last, management. In order to accomplish this, the department must change management practices so that all employees, from the patrol officer to the chief's staff, emphasize serving the citizenry. This means that the traditional organizational culture in most police departments must be drastically altered so that citizen satisfaction and the quality of services rendered to citizens dominate both management and line officers' thinking. It also means that police managers must recognize the importance of the line police officer. Management must come to see supporting officers as an organizational imperative.

Management must not only refocus on citizen consumers, but also empower employees with the ability to better respond to citizen needs. In the past, police leadership was defined as establishing goals and work standards for employees. Once work standards were established, management undertook to ensure that employees complied with them. Under TQM, leadership is seen as giving officers and first-line supervisors the authority to make some decisions that traditionally were reserved for high-ranking officers. Management must vest line officers and units with the authority to do their jobs. Second, management under TQM is seen as a mechanism to facilitate, rather than control, the activities of officers and units. Here, management must ensure that officers have the resources and support to do the job. This requires that officers be allowed to network and work with officers from a variety of line police units as well as other units of government and private agencies. TQM means that officers are able to pursue a wide variety of alternatives when they are attempting to solve problems. Finally, as management and officers pursue goals and objectives, they both must emphasize total quality.

Customers. Fairly recently, starting with Goldstein (1979), we began to recognize that the police have failed to provide the best possible services to the public. Indeed, it may be said that, in many instances, law enforcement's response to citizen needs has been inadequate (Goldstein, 1979, 1990). The police's overemphasis on efficiency and rapid response has in many departments turned officers into nothing more than glorified call takers. That is, officers respond as quickly as possible to calls for service and crimes, but once on the scene, they routinely provide a minimum level of service to the citizen. Officers focus on answering calls, rather than solving problems. They often feel that they cannot devote much time to individual calls, because they must return to their patrol cars and prepare to respond to the next call. Consequently, the police in many jurisdictions concentrated on sufficiency of service rather than citizen satisfaction. TQM mandates that the citizen come first. The police must ensure that citizens receive the best possible police service. This should be a police department's highest priority.

Counting. Counting refers to the fact that police organizations must focus on the important rather than the mundane. Historically, police officers were evaluated by the number of arrests made, citations issued, or cases cleared, or by the amount of stolen property recovered. At best, such measures are only rough estimates of police performance. Statistics can be easily manipulated. All officers know where they can write large numbers of citations in a short period of time, or where they can go to observe for violations to make easy misdemeanor arrests. But such activities do not result in "good" law enforcement. Indeed, there may be little relationship between numbers of police activities and good police service (Bayley, 1996; Stephens, 1996).

An increasingly larger number of police agencies are attempting to counter this problem with citizen surveys and meetings. Skogan (1994) provides a number of examples of the police collecting direct feedback from citizens as a method of evaluating police effectiveness. Officers in Oakland and Houston used a series of home visits by officers to gather information about crime and drug problems as well as feedback on police performance. Baltimore deployed ombudsman police officers in some areas. These officers met with citizens and used questionnaires to collect information about problems and citizen satisfaction with the police. Birmingham and Madison added police substations in an effort to provide citizens more accessibility to the police. Police departments throughout the United States are implementing programs that attempt to provide higher levels of service and measure citizen opinions about the adequacy of the services provided. Further, departments are targeting public housing and other areas that heretofore generally have been disenfranchised from the police.

TQM as a management philosophy is a vehicle for implementing community policing; indeed, a number of departments that are implementing community policing already use various elements of TQM. The defining elements of community policing are community partnerships and problem solving. Basically, community policing dictates that the police work more closely with citizens in identifying and solving their problems. In this instance, citizens become clients who must be satisfied. The idea of problem solving represents a new level of quality for police work. As discussed above, it means the police do a better job of responding to crime and other problems.

Regardless, it should be noted that TQM is not easily implemented. TQM like so many other concepts is easily described, but implementation is much more complex. Swiss (1992) notes that governmental service organizations, such as the police, have much more difficulty in implementing TQM than private enterprise, where the profit motive makes it much easier to implement and measure TQM. Moreover, government has a number of operational constraints that private enterprise lacks. For example, government cannot always select or refuse the clients it serves. Political necessity often places parameters on what a public agency can or cannot do. Civil service and other personnel laws confine administrators, and they cannot adequately reward employees or sufficiently empower them. Finally, public bureaucracies do not have the flexibility to shift direction as service needs or requirements change. Many bureaucratic constraints are not a function of the organization itself but are mandated by law or tradition. A great deal of what police departments do is dictated by law and government as opposed to police chiefs.

Nonetheless, various TQM attributes have been implemented. Hoover (1996) surveyed 200 Texas police managers and found that they were doing reasonably well applying TQM culture principles and moderately well in focusing on customers or clients, but little effort was being exerted in measuring how well departments were responding to citizen needs. Although the implementation of TQM is somewhat hampered in law enforcement, there are several areas on which police administrators can focus: (1) developing better mechanisms for gathering information about client or citizen satisfaction, (2) doing a better job of tracking and evaluating performance, (3) working toward continuous improvement rather than reacting to crises, and (4) attempting to implement higher levels of participatory management throughout the police organization. As Hoover found, the police now use only moderate levels of TQM, but the philosophy has great potential to improve American law enforcement.

Summary

Chapter 4 focused on police organizational management from the perspective of traditional police management. Classical theory, as described in Chapter 4, serves as the foundation for most police organizations. It entails a substantial amount of structure and focuses on the organization rather than the employee or citizens who are served by the police. When police departments focus inward (closed system), they often fail to adequately serve the public. Therefore, purely classical organizational theory is inappropriate for law enforcement.

This chapter focused on managing the police organization using human relations, contingency or mixed models, and systems models. Each perspective represents a distinctly different view of how a police department should be managed. The traditional principles represent a prescribed outline by which to organize the department, emphasizing control and strict task assignments. Contemporary styles of management, on the other hand, recognize the need to involve all organizational participants in the task of managing and working. Unlike classical principles, it emphasizes openness, communications, and group involvement. (The informal organization, which is an important part of the human relations organization, will be discussed at length in Chapter 7.)

Perhaps the best way to understand police organizations is to review Mintzberg's five organizational forms. They clearly show that organizational structure is contingent on a number of factors. Police organizations are a mix of classical and contemporary forms and, in Likert's terms, reside more in the consultative category as opposed to being benevolent-authoritarian. Police administrators must construct or fashion the organization which best allows the department to serve its community. This may entail experimenting with a variety of forms and the creation of a "matrix organization" where there are a variety of specialized units addressing a variety of problems.

Study Questions

1. What is human relations organizational theory? What are the three theories which lead to its development?

2. How does human relations theory differ from traditional or classical organizational theory?

3. What is the impact of human relations theory on American law enforcement?

4. Relate Mintzberg's five organizational forms to a police department.

5. What are the parts to an organizational system and how do they relate to one another and the total organization?

6. What is total quality management and how would it work in a police department?

7. What is the relationship between human relations theories and community policing?

Net Resources

http://deming.eng.clemson.edu/pub/tqmbbs/cases/ Deming's principles as related in Total Quality Management.

http://www.scit.wlv.ac.uk/university/scit/modules/cp4414/lectures/week2/manage/ sld003.htm Read more about management theory in the 20th century.

http://www.mapnp.org/library/systems/systems.htm#anchor117156 Read more about systems theory.

References

Argyris, C. (1957). *Personality and Organization: The Conflict between System and the Individual*. New York: Harper & Row.

Bayley, D. H. (1996). Measuring overall effectiveness. In L. Hoover (ed.), *Quantifying Quality in Policing*. Washington: Police Executive Research Forum, pp. 37–54.

Bertalanffy, L. (1951). General systems theory: A new approach to the unity of science. *Human Biology*, 23:302–361.

Brooks, L. (1997). Police discretionary behavior: A study of style. In R. Dunham and G. Alpert (eds.), *Critical Issues in Policing: Contemporary Readings*. Prospect Heights, IL: Waveland Press, pp. 149–166.

Burns, T., and Stalker, G. (1961). *The Management of Innovation*. London: Tavistock.

Couper, D. C., and Lobitz, S. H. (1988). Quality leadership: The first step towards quality policing. *The Police Chief* 55(4):79–84.

Dean, J. W., and Evans, J. R. (1994). *Total Quality: Management, Organization, and Strategy*. St. Paul: West Publishing.

Gaines, L. (1978) Overview of organizational theory and its relation to police administration. In L. Gaines & T. Ricks (eds.), *Managing the Police Organization*. St. Paul: West Publishing.

Goldstein, H. (1979). Improving policing: A problem-oriented approach. *Crime and Delinquency* 25:236–258.

Goldstein, H. (1990). *Problem-Oriented Policing.* New York: McGraw-Hill.

Greenberg, J., and Barron, R. A. (1995). *Behavior in Organizations,* 5th ed. Englewood Cliffs, NJ: Prentice-Hall.

Guyot, D. (1991). *Policing as though People Matter.* Philadelphia: Temple University Press.

Hatry, H. P., and Greiner, J. M. (1986) *Improving the Use of Quality Circles in Police Departments.* Washington: U.S. Department of Justice, National Institute of Justice.

Hoover, L. (1996). Translating total quality management from the private sector to policing. In L. Hoover (ed.), *Quantifying Quality in Policing.* Washington: Police Executive Research Forum, pp. 1–22.

Hradesky, J. L. (1995). *Total Quality Management Handbook.* New York: McGraw-Hill.

Huneryager, S., and Heckman, I. (1967) *Human Relations in Management.* New Rochelle, NY: South Western Publishing.

Katz, D., and Kahn, R. L. (1966). *The Social Psychology of Organizations.* New York: Wiley.

Kelling, G. L., and Bratton, W. J. (2000). Implementing community policing: The administrative problem. In W. Oliver (ed.), *Community Policing: Classical Readings.* Upper Saddle River, NJ: Prentice Hall, pp. 258–268.

Kuykendall, J., and Roberg, R. (1997). *Police Administration.* Los Angeles: Roxbury Press.

Likert, R. (1961) *New Patterns of Management.* New York: McGraw-Hill.

Likert, R. (1967). *The Human Organization: Its Management and Value.* New York: McGraw-Hill.

McGregor, D. (1966) The human side of enterprise. In W. Bennis and E. Schein (eds.), *Leadership and Motivation.* Cambridge, MA: MIT Press, pp. 5–16.

Maguire, E. R. (1997). Structural change in large municipal police organizations during the community policing era. *Justice Quarterly* 14(3):547–576.

March, J., and Simon, H. (1958). *Organizations.* New York: Wiley.

Mastrofski, S. D., and Ritti, R. (1995). Making sense of community policing: A theory-based analysis. Presented at the American Society of Criminology Meeting, Boston.

Mintzberg, H. (1983). *Structure in Fives: Designing Effective Organizations.* Englewood Cliffs, NJ: Prentice Hall.

Moore, M. H., and Stephens, D. (1992). Organization and management. In W. Geller (ed.), *Local Government Police Management.* Washington: International City Managers Association.

Perrow, C. (1967). A framework for the comparative analysis of organizations. *American Sociological Review* 32:194–208.

Reiss, A. (1992). Police organization in the twentieth century. In M. Tonry & N. Morris (eds.), *Modern Policing.* Chicago: University of Chicago Press.

Robbins, S. P. (1990). *Organization Theory: Structure, Design, and Application.* Englewood Cliffs, NJ: Prentice Hall.

Ross, J. E. (1995). *Total Quality Management.* Delray Beach, FL: St. Lucie Press.

Schermerhorn, J. R., Hunt, J. G., and Osborn, R. N. (1994). *Managing Organizational Behavior,* 5th ed. New York: Wiley.

Scott, W. G. (1996). Organization theory: An overview and an appraisal. In J. Shafritz and J. Ott (eds.), *Classics of Organization Theory*, 4th ed. Belmont, CA: Wadsworth, pp. 264–273.

Sherman, L. (1978). Middle management and police democratization: A reply to John E. Angell. In L. Gaines and T. Ricks (eds.), *Managing the Police Organization*. St. Paul: West Publishing, pp. 119–129.

Skogan, W. (1994). The impact of community policing on neighborhood residents: A cross-site analysis. In D. Rosenbaum (ed.), *The Challenge of Community Policing: Testing the Promises*. Thousand Oaks, CA: Sage.

Spencer, B. A. (1994). Models of organization and total quality management: A comparison and critical evaluation. *Academy of Management Review* 19(3):446–471.

Stamper, N. (1992). *Removing Managerial Barriers to Effective Leadership*. Washington: Police Executive Research Forum.

Stephens, D. (1996). Community problem-oriented policing: Measuring impacts. In L. Hoover (ed.), *Quantifying Quality in Policing*. Washington: Police Executive Research Forum, pp. 95–130.

Swiss, J. E. (1992). Adapting total quality management (TQM) to government. *Public Administration Review* 52(4):356–362.

Tenzel, J., Storms, L., and Sweetwood, H. (1976) Symbols and behavior: An experiment in altering the police role. *Journal of Police Science and Administration* 4(1):21–27.

Thompson, J. D. (1967). *Organization in Action*. New York: McGraw-Hill.

Toch, H. (1997). The democratization of policing in the United States: 1895–1973. *Police Forum* 7(2):1–8.

Walker, S. (1993). *Taming the System*. New York: Oxford University Press.

Woodward, J. (1965). *Industrial Organization: Theory and Practice*. London: Oxford University Press.

Wycoff, M. (1994). *Community Policing Strategies*. Unpublished Report, Police Foundation.

Part III

People in the Police Organization

Part III, People in the Police Organization, explores the interactions among organizational units and the people who reside within the police organization. Whereas Part II focused on how to build a police department, the chapters in Part III attempt to describe how to treat people and how they will behave in the police department setting. Understanding the dynamics of organizational behavior is a critical component of a police administrator's job. Administrators accomplish organizational goals and objectives through and in conjunction with other people. Hence a firm grasp of these dynamics is critical.

Chapter 6, Police Leadership, explores one of the primary interactive relationships between superiors and subordinates within an organization: leading people toward goal accomplishment. It reviews styles of leadership, including contingency approaches to leadership and transformational leadership. Special attention is also given to the process by which people ascend to the position of chief.

Employee motivation is addressed in Chapter 7, People in the Police Organization. Because no one best way to manage exists, the reader is presented with a number of theories and explanations for motivation in organizations. As we point out in the chapter, employees have different aspirations, expectations, and needs. This entails dealing with subordinates differently. That is, the effective administrator will vary leadership styles and techniques to suit particular people and accomplish goals. This chapter provides an overview of how to identify the correct fit between subordinate motivation and administrative leadership.

Communication, negotiation, and conflict resolution are addressed in Chapter 8. Communication represents the nervous system for any organization. That is, people, whether they are administrators or line police officers, must be constantly apprised of what is happening and what is expected. This organizational requirement necessitates that efficient and effective communication procedures exist within the police agency. Similarly, conflict is a behavior which is an almost constant occurrence. As people and units interact and work within an organization, conflict will certainly arise. Negotiation and ultimate resolution of conflict are extremely important, because if conflict is allowed to fester for any length of time, it will soon negatively affect the operations of the department. Chapter 8 therefore provides a number of practical techniques for dealing with conflict and communication problems in police organizations.

Stress, which is addressed in Chapter 9, has become recognized as one of the most important personnel issues confronting police administrators in a number of years. It was only in the last decade that researchers and administrators began to recognize the existence and effects of job stress on police personnel. Indeed, police administrators themselves must deal with their own sources of stress, which we address as well. Not only are the implications of job stress addressed, but a number of stress-reducing programs are explored. The chapter provides the reader with a number of alternatives to the development of a total stress reduction and treatment program within a police department.

An overview of police human resource management is presented in Chapter 10. Human resource management is one of the most important administrative functions performed by police administrators. Regardless of how well a department is organized, it will be only as effective as the quality of its personnel. A number of personnel functions are therefore discussed: civil service, equal employment opportunity, recruitment, selection, training, performance appraisals, and promotions. Both theoretical and practical applications are discussed. The purpose of this chapter is to provide the reader with a starting point from which to develop a comprehensive and effective personnel system.

Chapter 11, Labor Relations, explores the world of police unionization and employee organizations. Some states have statutes requiring that jurisdictions officially recognize and negotiate with employee unions or professional associations. Other states allow this to occur, and, consequently, a number of jurisdictions must, to some extent, bargain with employee groups. Labor relations clearly play an important role in police administration, and Chapter 11 explores issues and problems confronting police administrators in labor relations.

Again, Part III emphasizes the people within the police organization. It is of critical importance that the administrator understand the implications and functions associated with this organization dimension. A police department is a system, and a system is only as good or effective as its weakest part. Understanding the people aspect of administration is one step toward strengthening every part of the police system.

6

Police Leadership

Michael Newman/PhotoEdit

Chapter Outline

Introduction

Leadership and Power

Leadership: Theories and Processes

Styles of Leadership
Likert's Leadership Systems
Downs's Bureaucratic Leadership Styles

Two-Factor Theories of Leadership
Stogdill and Coons's Ohio State Leadership Studies
Blake and Mouton's Managerial Grid

Contingency Approaches to Leadership
Fiedler's Leadership Style and Work Situation Model
House and Mitchell's Path–Goal Theory of Leadership
Hersey and Blanchard's Situational Leadership
Applying Contingency Leadership

Transformational Leadership

The Police Chief as Leader
Police Chief Tenure
Ascending to the Position of Chief

Summary

Learning Objectives

After reading this chapter, you should be able to

1. Understand the differences among leadership, power, and authority and how they are applied in the police organization.
2. Identify the different styles of leadership that occur in the police organization.
3. Know the two-factor theories of leadership and how they can be applied in the police department.
4. Understand the contingency approach to leadership and the factors that affect how a police administrator can make decisions.
5. Understand transformational leadership and how it can be used to change the organization, particularly when implementing community policing.
6. Discuss the role the police chief plays and how personnel become police executives.
7. Understand the tenure issues facing police chiefs and the politics involved in their dismissal.

In October 2001, Anthany Beatty was appointed police chief in Lexington, Kentucky. Prior to becoming chief, he had served the department for more than 20 years and had achieved the rank of major. He had served as the commander for one of the department's sections for several years. His appointment as chief completely changed his world. He immediately found that his new job differed vastly from his old position. In his old job he was responsible for the operation of a section within the police department. He spent most of his time working with other unit commanders, supervising the units under his command, and reporting to the chief about his section's activities. In his new position, he was not only responsible for the whole department and its activities, but he also became the primary spokesperson for the department. He was suddenly inundated with requests to make public presentations and to meet with community leaders. In addition to providing leadership for the department, he had a newfound leadership role in the community. He had to constantly balance the needs of the department with the demands of the community.

This example shows how the police chief has a number of leadership roles. He or she must lead the department, ensure that it operates effectively, and be a leader in the community. Thus leadership is one of the primary roles that a police chief must assume. He or she must perform this role well. If the community is neglected, the department may suffer in terms of public support. On the other hand, if the chief is not a good leader in the department, operations may slide and problems develop. This chapter explores a number of theoretical and practical aspects of leadership.

INTRODUCTION

Over the course of history, we have been fascinated and inspired by leaders. Indeed, when we examine any historical event, we tend to focus on the leaders and their deeds. This fascination with leaders indicates that people shape the past and present. They are the catalyst for action and change. They also bring stability into our lives. Citizens depend on all sorts of leaders, be they national leaders such as the president or local leaders such as a mayor, pastor, or other community leader, to guide, direct, and inspire them. Following is a natural phenomenon in a complex, pluralistic society, and leaders' ability to lead is determined, to a great extent, by the degree to which they are accepted by followers (Barnard, 1968).

The police chief is a leader who is recognized and respected in most communities. Citizens see the police chief as an individual who leads the forces that protect them. The police chief is seen as a person who has the knowledge and ability to deal with citizens' problems. Members of the police department, on the other hand, see the police chief as the individual who represents them in government by advocating for the department when battling for resources. The chief also sets the department's direction by establishing its goals. Police chiefs are more than figureheads; they are leaders.

The term "leadership" has many meanings. Some managers view good leadership as telling subordinates what to do. Others believe that good leadership is getting along with their subordinates. Both of these definitions are too narrow. When leadership is viewed from such narrow perspectives, it is unlikely that productivity can be achieved and sustained. A more adequate definition of *leadership* is "the process of directing and influencing the task-related activities of group members" (Stoner and Freeman, 1992). If we accept this definition, leadership appears to consist of several components: people, power, and influence.

First, people are involved in the leadership process. There are subordinates, or followers, to whom leadership is directed. In some cases, a leader is attempting to influence or work with a large number of subordinates, and in other cases, the work group might be quite small. The leaders, in order to be successful, must strive to influence people.

Second, leadership involves the distribution of power. *Power* is the ability to influence or control others. In Chapter 4, we discussed hierarchy and the distribution of authority. Power and authority are distributed hierarchically in the chain of command. Officers possessing higher rank have more power and authority than those of a lesser rank. Leaders derive power from a variety of sources, including coercion, reward, legitimacy, expertise, and association (French and Raven, 1959). Although groups of people are not powerless, they generally are subordinate to their leader and accept their leader's influence.

Finally, leadership entails influence over subordinates' attitudes and behavior. The ability to influence is best understood by examining what Bernard (1968) called the *zone of indifference*. He notes that there are three classifications of directives that a leader might give:

1. *Clearly acceptable directives.* These orders are unquestionably accepted by subordinates. They are recognized as part and parcel of the job.
2. *Questionable orders to subordinates.* These are unusual orders such as a patrol sergeant requesting an officer to remain at one location during a shift, which the officer very likely will question unless the circumstances are adequately explained.
3. *A directive completely outside the bounds of acceptability.* These are very unlikely to be accepted. For example, a detective supervisor may direct investigators to patrol when not actively investigating a case.

If a leader's directives are within the zone of indifference, then they very likely will not have adequate influence on subordinates.

Given this perspective, it can be seen that leadership is an interactive process with leaders and followers affecting each other. Barnard (1968) noted that leadership is delegated "upward," which is contrary to the organizational principles discussed in Chapter 4. His point is that a leader can be successful only when he or she is accepted by subordinates. Thus the relationship between the leader and those being led is critical.

Organizations have both formal and informal leaders. *Formal leaders* are those that are placed in positions of leadership by the organization. They are vested with authority and responsibilities by virtue of the position they hold. For example, patrol sergeants, as part of their position, have specific responsibilities.

Some of these responsibilities include directing officers in their squad in terms of assignments and following of procedures when answering calls. Formal leaders may or may not possess leadership skills. For the most part, they depend on their "authority" to lead people. *Informal leaders* are those individuals within the work group who have no position or authority, but who are recognized by their peers as individuals who have knowledge and can provide assistance outside the chain of command. Informal leaders are seen as having a modicum of power but no recognized authority. Informal leaders will be discussed in more detail in Chapter 7. Successful police departments generally promote informal leaders to formal leadership positions.

LEADERSHIP AND POWER

Power is the foundation of leadership. It is the ability to influence the behavior of others. McClelland and Burnham (1976) in their research found that power is essential to an executive. Power is the essential ingredient in one's ability to accomplish tasks through the work of others. To this end, people receive power as a result of their position within the organization, and they receive power as a result of their personality or who they are. There are three types of positional or organizational power:

1. *Reward power.* Reward power refers to the ability to control valued resources within the organization. An individual who has the capacity to provide others with something of value—a salary increase, a better assignment, access to new equipment, and so on—has reward power. Reward power should not be used to bribe, but as a way of rewarding subordinates for loyalty and dedicated service.
2. *Coercion power.* Coercion power is the opposite of reward power. Coercion power is embodied in one's ability to punish others. Coercion or punishment is usually associated with an organization's disciplinary procedures. However, it also includes the ability to withhold rewards—not allow subordinates to have merit raises, be assigned a new patrol vehicle, or given a choice assignment. Coercive power, like reward power, should not be used frivolously. Its use has long-lasting effects on the individual and possibly the organization.
3. *Legitimate power.* Legitimate power refers to the power people receive as a result of their position within the organization. Legitimate power is vested with one's authority. This power is hierarchical. Persons of higher rank have greater or more legitimate power than those below them. Legitimate power is not unrestricted; it is restricted to those matters that pertain to the position within the organization. Generally, subordinates recognize their leaders' legitimate power.

Reward, coercive, and legitimate power represent the power which an organization bestows on the individual. These sources of power are viewed as tools to be used to motivate and manage subordinate work groups. There are two types of personal power:

1. *Expertise power.* Expertise power refers to officers' knowledge or ability to perform some specialized task. Police work consists of a number of highly specialized skills such as accident reconstruction, ability to operate computers, knowledge of drugs and drug testing, ability to write grant proposals, or the ability to maintain a unit budget. Expertise is gained through training, education, and tenure on the job.
2. *Referent power.* Referent power is the ability to influence as a result of one's association with other powerful figures in the organization such as a captain, major, or assistant chief and people external to the department such as a council member, influential business leader, or civic leader. Such associations are developed through friendship, past working relationships, the subordinate having abilities that are valued by the powerful sponsor, or kinship. Sponsors often consider it in their best interests to see that their prótegés develop and succeed in the department.

Expert and referent power derive from the individual's personality and standing within the organization. Informal leaders acquire power through expertise and reference, while formal leaders accumulate power from all sources. Classical organizational theory (as discussed in Chapter 4) assumes that power is proportionately distributed with one's authority. However, power is a commodity that is distributed unevenly within a department. Administrators and managers acquire and depend on different mixes of power. For example, one survey of managers revealed that they preferred to use expert power, and the least desirable form of power was coercive power (Kipinis et al., 1984). This seems to indicate that managers would rather develop positive relations with subordinates than force compliance on them. Power is a critical component of the managerial mix and it is a necessity for accomplishing goals and objectives within the police agency.

Power is not a static commodity. An individual's power can increase and decrease. Some officers methodically attempt to gain more power in an effort to improve their position within the department. Kanter (1977) identified four ways in which people can acquire power within an organization. First, they can acquire it through the "performance of extraordinary activities." Officers who solve high-profile crimes, make a large number of arrests, or are able to complete a complicated project within the department very likely will witness an increase in their organizational power. Second, people can gain power through "higher visibility." Officers in positions such as media relations, planning, or training have increased visibility and an increase in their relative power. Third, when officers demonstrate their relevance to the department by "solving a perplexing problem," they increase their power. For example, an officer with computer skills may facilitate the implementation of a new, complicated computer system, or an officer may solve a series of burglaries that has raised the community's ire. Finally, officers can increase their power through "sponsors." Here, officers attempt to associate themselves with more powerful members of the department.

Finally, the pursuit and accumulation of power is not always positive. In 1513, the Italian philosopher Machiavelli wrote a book titled *The Prince*. In it, Machiavelli outlined a ruthless strategy for seizing and holding power. *Machiavellianism*, as it is known today, is the manipulation of others within the organization to achieve and hold power and use that power for personal, rather than organizational, benefits. Machiavelli believed that a few simple rules could be followed to accomplish this objective. Three have application to this discussion:

1. Never show humility, as arrogance is far more effective when dealing with others in the organization.
2. Only weak people subscribe to morality and ethics. Powerful people feel free to deceive whenever it suits their ends. The ends always justify the means.
3. People are successful when they are feared.

It is unsettling to think that such self-serving individuals exist in organizations. However, Machiavelli's philosophy is alive and well today. Ilgen and Moore (1987) found that when large numbers of people are tested to determine the extent to which they subscribe to Machiavellian principles, there are many who possess high levels of the attribute. They generally are ambitious, have no organizational ethics, and will do almost anything to climb the organizational ladder. They are able to exist because most people are unwilling to complain about their misdeeds. Machiavellian leaders are generally successful in the short term, but ultimately they run afoul of the organization. Their behavior is also detrimental to the organization and its employees. Power should be used for positive or organizational purposes, not for individual gain.

Research examining Machiavellian leadership in policing is limited. Girodo (1998) examined leadership styles among police leaders in various police positions. He found that the Machiavellian style of leadership was the most frequently used leadership style among police leaders who worked in administration. It seems that police managers who deal with administration use strategic interpersonal relations, power, and control to carry out management functions. The Machiavellian style of leadership may appeal to or fit the "traditional" police personality that is predicated on traits such as dominance and forcefulness. Furthermore, one might hypothesize that implementing community policing would result in a reduction of Machiavellianism in policing, but in fact it may present more opportunities for unscrupulous managers to manipulate and garner power.

LEADERSHIP: THEORIES AND PROCESSES

What makes a good leader? When asked this question most people respond that effective leaders possess a certain set of desirable traits or qualities: intelligence, self-confidence, fairness, charisma, honesty, persuasiveness, and aggressiveness, for example. One could possibly conjure up several hundred traits that an effective leader should possess. The problem with looking at leadership in terms of leadership traits is that when effective leaders are compared or examined, they

On the Job

KENTUCKY STATE POLICE

By Commissioner Ishmon F. Burks

Courtesy of Commissioner Burks

Leadership is one of the most important commodities that an administrator or manager can possess. Leaders lead people. It is the most significant, the most challenging, and the most rewarding responsibility one can ever have. To this extent, leadership is the center of gravity for a police department. Leadership can result in successes or it can result in failures. Thus leadership is an active process that molds an organization and stimulates it to progress.

How do police leaders lead? Good leaders

- Lead with strength and compassion.
- Understand that the other half of leading is listening and understanding.
- Lead from the front and by example.

- Inspire and lift organizations to new and higher levels of performance.
- Recognize the need for change before the lack of change evolves into an emergency situation.

The Kentucky State Police is an agency with approximately 1,000 sworn officers serving the Commonwealth of Kentucky. It is a state police, which means that our troopers have police powers and jurisdiction over all areas in the state. The number of officers, the geographical size, and the fact that the department is a full-service police agency complicate the leadership process. Generally, a good leader tries to maintain contact with as many of his or her subordinates as possible. Such personal interaction facilitates communication, understanding, and motivation. However, this is not possible in the state police. Therefore, as commissioner, I must influence my staff and encourage them to apply leadership skills throughout the department.

Outstanding leaders make people and organizations better. The best leaders appear to have an extraordinary understanding of human nature; emotional intelligence is the sine qua non of leadership. To a great extent, good leaders must prepare themselves to assume leadership roles. One does not become a leader overnight, but the path to leadership is paved with training, thoughtfulness, and a genuine interest

Continued

in improving both the organization and its human resources.

It is important to note the difference between a leader and a manager. These two terms are often used interchangeably—so often that we lose sight of how different they are and at the same time how they complement each other. Defining yourself as a leader or a manager in a department will in a number of ways determine outcomes. The leader has a vision for the department and will outline a path to be taken. The leader is constantly looking into the future and pushing the department forward. On the other hand, a manager is someone who manages things. Managers manage time; they manage budgets; they manage human resources; they manage information; and they manage daily processes that occur in a police department. Although a good leader must focus on these management activities, he or she cannot allow them to become all-consuming. The leader must not become a bureaucrat, but must focus on providing direction to the organization.

Finally, regardless of leadership style or level of leadership, there are at least two character traits the leader must possess if the department is to realize its full potential. Leadership will require that you think through how you will lead, and ultimately you must articulate your leadership or command philosophy. There are two personal qualities that must dominate the leader's thinking. First, excellence is an attitude. Excellence is not automatic, but everyone and every organization has the capacity to have it. How we treat our work and other people affects excellence. We must aim beyond mediocrity or trying to meet minimum standards; we must always set our sights high. Second, leadership means that a leader must have courage. Courage secures all other virtues. Safety cannot be ensured without an act of courage. Leaders have to instill courage in their subordinates.

Finally, good leaders must ensure that the departmental culture embraces leadership. Everyone from the trooper to the commissioner must exercise leadership. When this occurs, the department is successful.

possess different sets of traits, and they possess these traits in differing degrees. Also, an encyclopedic list can emerge from leadership trait research. Seldom does any leader possess all the requisite or identified traits. This trait method of studying leadership does not lend itself to a definitive conclusion. It is difficult to gain an understanding of leadership by examining leadership traits. Leadership can be better understood by examining how leaders approach the act of leadership.

Perhaps an economical way of summarizing the leadership trait literature is to examine the skills required of a police executive. Basically, executives need human relations or people skills, visionary or conceptual skills, and technical skills. Managers require people skills if they are to effectively interact with subordinates, peers, and superior officers. A large part of the leadership process is the ability to relate to others. Second, successful police administrators are

Figure 6–1
Mix of leadership skills.

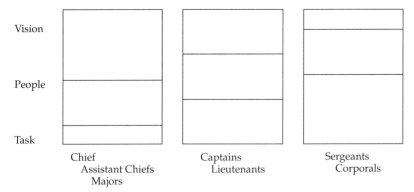

visionaries. They understand that the future brings change and new challenges. They strive to anticipate those changes and prepare the department for them. Third, managers must possess conceptual skills. Effective managers must have a vision of the future for the organization. They must be forward-thinking and have an idea of where the organization should go and how it can get there. Managers must also be technically proficient. Today, technology is a central part of any organization. The information age requires that managers in all professions be able to obtain and use technical data and information.

As shown in Figure 6–1, police administrators, middle managers, and supervisors require differing levels of these skills depending on their position within the chain of command. A police chief, assistant chiefs, and majors must have a vision and be able to conceptually plot the department's course. Since these top administrators deal primarily with policy issues, people or human relations skills and technical expertise are less important. Police middle managers, on the other hand, are responsible for the implementation of policies and programs. They must have some degree of vision, technical expertise, and people skills. They deal with people and programs and must make them come together in a cogent fashion. Police supervisors, on the other hand, must have good people or human relations and task or technical skills. The people skills are required to effectively deal with subordinates and citizens, and the task knowledge is necessary to provide officers the proper guidance and supervision as they perform police duties. The mix of skills changes from one level to the next in the chain of command.

STYLES OF LEADERSHIP

A number of studies have examined the styles of leadership used by persons in leadership positions. *Style* refers to actual leadership behavior and actions toward employees as opposed to innate qualities which a person might possess. Several theories of leadership are presented in the following sections. Each theory categorizes leader behavior in a slightly different manner.

Figure 6–2
Likert's leadership style continuum.

Explotive- Authoritarian	Benevolent- Authoritarian	Consultative	Participative
Low ———— Employee decision making involvement and interaction ———▶ High			

Likert's Leadership Systems

In Chapter 5, we examined Likert's management systems (1961, 1967) in terms of organizational theory and the levels of participation subordinates have in the organization. Likert's management systems are a good way to conceptualize the differences across organizational theories. Here, we discuss Likert in terms of the leadership styles he identified as a result of his research. Likert examined a number of industrial plants in an attempt to discover the styles of leadership used by various managers. He was primarily interested in finding those leaders who were successful and determining why. Likert identified four distinct leadership types: exploitive-authoritarian, benevolent-authoritarian, consultative, and participatory. Figure 6–2 shows these types in a continuum from low employee involvement to high involvement and interaction.

Exploitive-Authoritarian Leadership

The exploitive-authoritarian leader has no confidence or trust in subordinates, and subordinates are not allowed to provide input into decisions. Policies and decisions are formulated by top management and filter down the chain of command. There is little superior–subordinate interaction, and when there is, it is usually negative or directive in nature. Superiors generally attempt to motivate subordinates through fear, threats, and punishment (coercive power). Employees become frustrated and join together in informal groups to protect themselves from top management and to oppose unpopular policies. The exploitive-authoritarian style of leadership thwarts motivation and causes officers to concentrate only on attaining minimum productivity levels.

Critics of the professional model of policing suggest that the exploitive-authoritarian style is used in that environment (see Roberg and Kuykendall, 1997). This style of leadership is obviously inappropriate in policing since police officers' work activities cannot be highly or easily controlled due to the types of activities performed and the high degree of discretion officers must have when dealing with crime and calls for service. Moreover, first-line supervisors seldom provide close supervision of officers, which is a key component of the exploitive-authoritarian style. If this style of leadership exists in law enforcement, it exists in only a few isolated cases.

Benevolent-Authoritarian Leadership

The benevolent-authoritarian style is somewhat more positive than the exploitive-authoritarian style. Here, the bulk of policies and decisions are made by top management and are distributed by the chain of command, but sometimes managers and supervisors listen to subordinates' problems. There is more interaction between first-line supervisors and line employees than in the exploitive-authoritarian style. Superiors frequently are willing to listen, but they continue to make all the decisions. Subordinates still view superiors with caution and distrust, but not to the point that they oppose organizational goals. They feel somewhat frustrated since they have little input into daily activities, especially those which directly affect them.

This style of leadership permeates many traditionally organized police departments and is responsible for many of the motivational problems in these departments. (Authoritarian leaders may gravitate to police work because the enforcement aspect of policing is, to a great extent, authoritarian and this type of individual is attracted to policing.) Many officers working under this leadership style concentrate on accomplishing their assigned tasks but seldom go beyond their assigned duties due to the lack of encouragement and the possibility of getting into trouble with their superiors. Hence there is no external motivation to succeed, which is a necessary part of a successful organization. There are no statistics on the extent to which leadership styles exist in police organizations, but the majority of police leaders very likely are benevolent-authoritarian or consultative.

Consultative Leadership

The consultative style of leadership is a process whereby management establishes goals and objectives for the organization or department with subordinates making some of the decisions on methods of goal achievement (strategic and tactical decisions). The relationship between superiors and line personnel is relatively positive as problems and possible solutions are discussed openly and freely. Employees are encouraged to become involved by providing input into some decisions and unit goals. Positive rewards are emphasized and punishment is used to motivate only in extreme cases.

Whole or parts of police departments formally or informally adhere to this leadership style. This is especially true in larger police departments where operational units have a great deal of autonomy (Toch, 1997). For example, the leadership style in drug units often is collegial. Officers in drug units very likely have substantial discretion in how they attack an area's drug problem. This style of leadership tends to emphasize involvement and esteem rewards and leads to a more positive motivational climate.

Participative Leadership

The participative leadership style denotes subordinates having input not only into tactical decisions but also into policy formulation. It is a team approach whereby everyone has input in the organization's goals and objectives and operational strategies and tactics. The participative style insinuates that police officers provide direct input into what the department should be doing. Witte, Travis, and Langworthy (1990) found that officers at all levels within police departments favored the use of participatory management, but only those officers in administrative positions felt that they were allowed an adequate level of participation. All other officers believed that they were not allowed adequate participation in decision making and strategic planning.

The chief of police should attempt to use this strategy where possible, but it should be remembered that it is not always appropriate. As discussed in Chapter 2, citizens have a vested right to provide input through the political system into the setting of police goals and objectives. There are times and situations where citizen and police perceptions of what is most appropriate are not congruent. It is at such points that the chief must ensure that the public is properly represented and must convince police personnel to follow a public-oriented policy line (disagreements on policy usually center around law enforcement versus service provision roles). However, if there is a high degree of trust within the police organization, this may be only a minor problem. In the vast majority of cases, subordinates should be allowed to have some level of input into policy decisions. This could be accomplished through vehicles such as quality circles and departmental hearings regarding new policies. Such actions would maximize a police department's human resources and create a positive motivational environment.

Police organizations must move toward the latter two styles of leadership. Approximately 80 percent of any police department's budget is devoted to salaries for personnel, and personnel represent an important resource in police agencies. These resources must be used to their maximum advantage. Police administrators can no longer be content merely to ensure that all calls are answered; they also must ensure that quality services are provided. The consultative and participatory styles of leadership create a positive motivational atmosphere in which officers are more likely to be concerned about doing an excellent job in accomplishing objectives.

Downs's Bureaucratic Leadership Styles

Close examination of Likert's leadership styles would lead one to assume that leadership is strictly a matter of authority and subordinate participation in decision making. Downs (1967) upon examining bureaucratic organizations developed a typology of leadership based on a leader's effort and orientation within the organization. He identified four styles of leadership: the styles used by (1) climbers, (2) conservers, (3) zealots, and (4) advocates. *Climbers* are ambitious and generally unethical people who use every opportunity to further their careers (i.e., they are Machiavellian). They actively recruit sponsors to help further themselves. They will take on extra duties to gain attention or approval from superiors, and they willingly sacrifice subordinates to better themselves. They look for every opportunity to promote themselves. Most police departments have a few climbers who constantly are involved in internal politics for their self-promotion.

Conservers essentially are bureaucrats who strive to maintain the status quo. They work themselves into a position within the organization, and they get comfortable by thoroughly understanding the tasks and policies associated with the position. They settle in and seldom seek promotion. They expend a great deal of energy resisting change and innovation. Conservers usually are older and become classic bureaucrats, ensuring that policies are followed to the letter regardless of circumstances. *Zealots*, on the other hand, are organizational members with a mission. They generally have a narrow special interest and a great deal of energy, which they focus on that interest. They often neglect their duties as they focus almost exclusively on their crusade, sometimes so adamantly that they tend to antagonize others. In the end, they tend to be unproductive leaders. In police organizations, zealots often find their way into specialized units that match their interests. Finally, *advocates* are those leaders who care only about their sphere of influence—their particular unit. When dealing with outsiders, they look at only what is good for their unit and seldom compromise even for the greater good. They are just as zealous as zealots, but rather than focusing on an issue, they focus on their domain. Advocates in police departments often refuse to cooperate with other units and are often at odds with members of other units in the department.

Downs's styles of leadership theory focuses on how various leaders react in the organization. They do not consider subordinate input or participation but concentrate on their idiosyncrasies and personal agendas. Each type is plentiful in police departments, and each type presents a unique set of problems.

TWO-FACTOR THEORIES OF LEADERSHIP

In looking at Likert's continuum of leadership style, one gets the impression that he was overly concerned with how leaders deal with people and had little concern about the leader's attention to organizational goals. There are in fact many leaders who concentrate all their efforts on keeping their subordinates happy, frequently disregarding goals. Likert's most important point was that people are an organization's most vital asset and no organization can maximize its productive potential without ensuring that leadership is conducive to motivation. However, organizational goals and objectives cannot be neglected in favor of better relations with employees. Other leadership theorists described leader behavior in a two-dimensional perspective, where people and goals receive equal attention.

Stogdill and Coons's Ohio State Leadership Studies

Stogdill and Coons (1957) identified two dimensions of leader behavior: initiating structure and consideration. *Initiating structure* refers to the leader's behavior in emphasizing organizational goals by delineating the relationship between the leader and the subordinates when establishing well-defined patterns of organization, communication, and procedure. *Consideration*, on the other hand, refers to the leader's behavior in emphasizing the friendship, mutual trust,

Figure 6–3
Two dimensions of leadership.

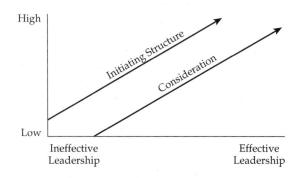

warmth, and respect relationship between the leader and subordinates. Their theory states that a leader must balance the two perspectives in order to be effective. Stogdill and Coons's two dimensions are displayed in Figure 6–3.

Stogdill and Coons studied leadership behavior by asking employees to describe their leaders' behavior and by asking leaders to give their self-perceptions about their own leadership style. They found that initiating structure and consideration were distinctly separate dimensions. A leader's behavior could be described as a mix of these two dimensions. For the first time, leader behavior was plotted on two separate axes instead of on a single continuum. Stogdill and Coons found that both dimensions were vital if leadership was to succeed. Not only must there be a positive relationship between the leader and subordinates, but subordinates must be led toward the accomplishment of specific goals and objectives.

Blake and Mouton's Managerial Grid

Blake and Mouton (1964) named the leader behavior associated with each quadrant of the Ohio State leadership study. The result was their *managerial grid,* which is superimposed on the Ohio State leadership findings in Figure 6–4. Leaders may fall anywhere in one of the four quadrants or the central part of the grid in Figure 6–4, depending on their leadership qualities and behavior. Here, both structure and consideration are examined.

> *Team Leaders.* The most effective leaders fall in the upper-right, or team, quadrant and are strong in both consideration and structure. The team manager accomplishes work through committed people. In the police organization, there is an interdependence of the officer and manager through a "common stake" in the organization's mission, which leads to a relationship of trust and respect on which true authority is based. It represents the quintessence of leadership in that managers working at this level should be able to maximize results by working with subordinates.

Figure 6–4

The Managerial Grid figure.

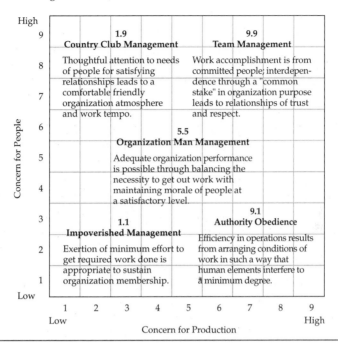

Source: from *The Managerial Grid III: The Key to Leadership Excellence,* by Robert R. Blaek and Jane Srygley Mouton. Houston: Gulf Publishing Company, Copyright © 1985, page 12. Reproduced by permission.

Task Leaders. Those falling in the task (lower-right) quadrant are overly concerned with tasks, often disregarding the needs of subordinates. (This type of leader would be an exploitive-authoritarian or benevolent-authoritarian in Likert's scheme.) Task managers arrange work conditions in such a way that human considerations interfere minimally with work efficiency—getting the job done with the least amount of energy and effort. Task managers see work, not people, as being extremely important. Task leaders, as a result of their uncaring attitudes, frequently have motivational problems with their subordinates. Task leaders are sometimes effective for short-range projects, but they experience insurmountable difficulties in the long term.

Country Club Leaders. Country Club leaders (top-left quadrant) are primarily interested in remaining friends with subordinates regardless of organizational consequences. The country club manager pays thoughtful attention to the needs of officers to engender satisfying relationships. Work or organizational goals are not important to this type of leader. These managers allow subordinates' feelings and needs to interfere with the organizational mission. Even though this leader attends to subordinate needs, the country club manager frequently has motivational problems because subordinates see that the work is not being accomplished.

Impoverished Leaders. The impoverished leader (lower-left quadrant) is not overly concerned about goals or people. The impoverished manager exerts only that minimum amount of effort necessary to get required work done so that the manager can remain employed in the agency. Some officers and commanders spend each day at work doing only what they are told to do or what they have to do. This type of leader spends most of his or her time avoiding decision making, staying out of trouble, and being inconspicuous in the organization. This manager is more of a bureaucrat than a leader and is very similar to what Downs termed a conserver. Obviously, little is accomplished when this type of leader is in control. Motivational problems develop because subordinates become frustrated about not having any direction.

Organization Man Leaders. Blake and Mouton included a fifth or central portion of the grid, the organization man. The organization man balances the necessity to produce organizational results while maintaining the morale of people at a satisfying level. This type of leader is moving in the right direction but is not willing to exert maximum effort or has not learned to achieve at the highest levels.

Swanson and Territo (1982) attempted to investigate the extent to which Blake and Mouton's various styles are utilized by police managers. They surveyed police managers and found that almost 40 percent of the participants reported that they used the team style of leadership as their primary form of leading. Some 27 percent reported the task style as their primary form of leadership, 14 percent reported using the impoverished style, 11 percent reported using the organization man form, and only 8 percent said they were country club managers. Swanson and Territo's research indicate a variety of styles being used by police leaders. It is interesting, however, that the predominant style is the team style. This research tends to indicate that police managers are not as authoritarian as some of the human relationists believe.

The two-factor theories of leadership provide a basis for understanding the complex process of leadership. They emphasize the need to moderate between consideration and the task at hand. To this end, the effective leader must use consideration when attempting to get officers to attain departmental goals and objectives. When consideration of employees and tasks are not equally and highly important to the leader, as in task management, it is doubtful that personnel will be effective.

CONTINGENCY APPROACHES TO LEADERSHIP

The previous sections examined trait and two-factor theories of leadership, which provide a good understanding of the leadership task. However, these theories are deficient in that they do not consider the impact of the environment and other external forces on a leader's behavior. It is simplistic to assume that a police manager has to worry only about subordinates and the task at hand. In fact, a number of extraneous variables affect a leader's ability to lead and the style of leadership which should be utilized. In other words, leadership is contingent on a number of factors, and these factors must be considered when choosing a leadership style.

To this end, Stoner and Freeman (1992) identified the following factors that dictate leadership style:

1. *Leader's personality, past experiences, and expectations.* Leaders enter situations with a history. Some leaders have numerous and varied leadership experiences; others have few. Some leaders have personalities that are conducive to motivating subordinates. Some leaders are achievement-motivated and have high expectations for the organization and their subordinates. The sum total of a manager's personality has a substantial impact on the how he or she leads and the degree of success.

2. *Superiors' expectations.* All leaders are bounded by demands and expectations. Police chiefs are accountable to other governmental officials, and police middle managers and supervisors answer to superior officers in the chain of command. Superiors largely dictate subordinates' job requirements. Superiors also affect leader style. Research tends to indicate that subordinates, to some extent, assume their immediate superior's leadership style.

3. *Job requirements.* The implications of type of task on management style was discussed in Chapter 5. Some tasks or jobs, because of their complexity or importance, require close supervision, whereas simple tasks allow the leader to give subordinates an inordinate amount of freedom. The job at hand definitely affects leadership style.

4. *Subordinates' characteristics.* Subordinates' educational and training experiences as well as their job expectations to a degree dictate leadership style. Highly qualified employees require little direction, whereas minimally qualified workers necessitate that the leader provide increased levels of direction.

5. *Peer expectations.* Police departments are composed of numerous work groups, and these work groups must cooperate and work together. Moreover, each manager within a department has expectations of other managers. These expectations often limit what managers can do and how they do it.

6. *Departmental culture and politics.* The organizational environment plays a key role in leadership. An organization's culture places numerous expectations and limits on what incumbents can do. Leadership behavior, to a great extent, is limited by culture and politics.

The contingency approach, as depicted in Figure 6–5, consists of a number of internal and external factors which affect leadership. A number of leadership theories have attempted to include these factors.

Figure 6–5
Contingency approach to effective leadership.

Basically, *contingency leadership* consists of identifying the environmental and employee factors that are most important in a given situation and then utilizing the most appropriate style of leadership for the situation. Three contingency models are presented and discussed: Fiedler's leadership style and work situation model, House and Mitchell's path–goal theory, and Hersey and Blanchard's situational leadership model.

Fiedler's Leadership Style and Work Situation Model

The first to discuss the contingency approach to leadership was perhaps Fiedler (1978). He postulated that the work group's success or effectiveness is determined by the demands of the situation and the leader's style of management. What makes Fiedler's theory interesting is that he states that leaders cannot easily adapt and change leadership styles to meet the demands of the situation. Personality may limit people's behavioral responses to situations. For example, can leaders be employee-oriented in one situation and authoritarian in another? Fiedler believed that good leaders could manage situations to the point that they better matched the leader's skills. A strong leader will manage a situation differently from a weak leader. Both potentially can achieve the same results by manipulating the structure to match their leadership skills. Unlike other leadership theories, Fiedler focused on changing the structure or problem rather than style of leadership applied.

There appear to be some data to support Fiedler's assertion. Swanson and Territo (1982) upon investigating Blake and Mouton's managerial grid found that about 27 percent of the police managers in their study reported having a task-oriented leadership style, 8 percent reported having a country club style, and 14 percent reported having an impoverished style. In other words, a full 50 percent of the police managers reported having extreme management styles. One must wonder whether it is possible for these managers to make a 180-degree shift in their leadership styles, and if they are able to do so, how effective would they be in using a management style that is completely the opposite of their primary style?

Fiedler perceived leadership to be a dichotomy consisting of task-oriented managers who are less concerned with human relations and human relations–oriented managers who are considerate of others and fairly permissive in the

Figure 6–6

Matching leadership style and situation: summary predictions from Fielder's contingency theory.

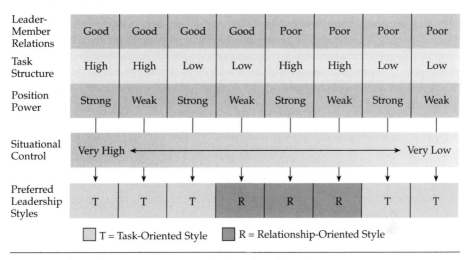

Leader-Member Relations	Good	Good	Good	Good	Poor	Poor	Poor	Poor
Task Structure	High	High	Low	Low	High	High	Low	Low
Position Power	Strong	Weak	Strong	Weak	Strong	Weak	Strong	Weak
Situational Control	Very High ←							→ Very Low
Preferred Leadership Styles	T	T	T	R	R	R	T	T

☐ T = Task-Oriented Style   ■ R = Relationship-Oriented Style

Source: J. R. Schermerhorn, *Management*. New York: John Wiley & Sons, 1996, p. 327.

workplace. He determined type of manager by having respondents describe their *least preferred co-worker (LPC)*. Respondents who described their LPC in negative terms were classified as task-oriented, while those who described their LPC favorably were grouped as relationship-oriented managers.

The quality of leadership, according to Fiedler, is determined by three dimensions: leader–group relations, task structure, and leader's power. Leader–group relations is the most important dimension. If the leader gets along with the work group, there is less dependency on power and authority. Task structure is the second most important dimension. If the performance of a task is clearly delineated so that everyone knows what is expected, the leader has less difficulty in getting subordinates to comply with organizational expectations. On the other hand, if performance of the task is not clear, there is a measure of ambiguity in work group members' roles. The ambiguity easily leads to disagreement, and the leader's authority is more easily called into question. Finally, leaders have varying levels of power. More powerful leaders are better able to cope with an adversity that may occur when relations with the work group are deficient or when there is task performance ambiguity.

As shown in Figure 6–6, there are eight possible combinations or leadership situations based on strong and weak leader positions (power), structured and unstructured tasks, and good and poor relations between the leader and the work group. After studying more than 800 work groups in an effort to determine the style of leadership that was the most successful, Fiedler found that task-oriented leaders were most effective in extreme situations where the leader had a great deal of power and influence or where the leader had very little power and influence. Relationship-oriented leaders were most effective where they had moderate power and influence. Fiedler's data show that there are some conditions under which certain kinds of leaders are not effective. Figure 6–6 summarizes the environmental conditions as they relate to the two types of leader.

Fiedler's model suggests that the leader's style should be matched to the situation. As administrators make decisions about where to assign midlevel managers and supervisors, the nature of the task, the leader's power, and relationships with subordinates should be considered. It appears that if administrators can match these dimensions more accurately, organizational performance should improve.

House and Mitchell's Path–Goal Theory of Leadership

A popular contingency approach to leadership is House and Mitchell's (1974) path–goal theory of leadership. Path–goal theory is rooted in Vroom's (1964) expectancy theory of motivation, which is discussed in the following chapter. House and Mitchell established two general propositions for path–goal theory: (1) subordinates accept leader behavior and find it motivating if they believe that the leader behavior is instrumental in satisfying their immediate or future needs and (2) when employees are productive, leaders satisfy subordinate needs by providing guidance, support, and rewards. All employees have needs, be they financial, recognition, or some kind of new assignment. They are motivated to work if they believe that they will be appropriately rewarded, and the reward goes to satisfy their needs. For example, young officers often have a need for recognition. They will be motivated if their sergeants and lieutenants are aware of their good work and publicly recognize it. An older officer may have a desire to transfer from patrol to criminal investigation. He or she will be motivated to work harder if the work enhances the chance of the transfer. In short, path–goal theory postulates that the leader plots a course and guides subordinates toward achieving organizational objectives. Figure 6–7 depicts the two paths that result in positive or negative organizational and personal outcomes.

Leaders choose how to deal with any given situation and employee. No one best style of leadership is appropriate for every situation. Leadership is more complex than selecting a particular style and adhering to it. Leaders must be flexible in selecting one of several styles of leadership dependent on the situation. Four styles are available:

1. *Directive.* The leader lets subordinates know specifically what is expected of them by giving explicit guidance.
2. *Supportive.* The leader sets a friendly tone for subordinates so that employees know the leader is concerned for their well-being and is approachable should they encounter any problems.
3. *Participative.* The leader consults with subordinates, soliciting their suggestions and taking those suggestions into consideration when making decisions.
4. *Achievement-oriented.* The leader sets challenging goals, expecting subordinates to perform at their highest level.

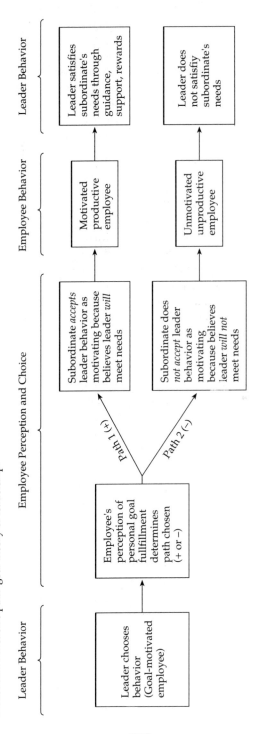

Figure 6–7
House and Mitchell's path–goal theory of leadership.

Leader Behavior   Employee Perception and Choice   Employee Behavior   Leader Behavior

Leader chooses behavior (Goal-motivated employee)

Employee's perception of personal goal fullfillment determines path chosen (+ or –)

Path 1 (+)

Path 2 (–)

Subordinate *accepts* leader behavior as motivating because believes leader *will* meet needs

Subordinate does *not accept* leader behavior as motivating because believes leader *will not* meet needs

Motivated productive employee

Unmotivated unproductive employee

Leader satisfies subordinate's needs through guidance, support, rewards

Leader does not satisfiy subordinate's needs

Each of these leadership styles is appropriate under certain conditions, and a leader may use all of them when motivating subordinates. Thus leadership behavior is contingent on the characteristics of the subordinates (subordinates possess different needs and motives) and the environment (the entire situation at hand). Not only must leaders tailor their style of leadership to a given situation, but they may also use different styles for different subordinates within their command to account for individual differences.

Hersey and Blanchard's Situational Leadership

Hersey and Blanchard (1988) described contingency leadership in terms of situational leadership. They posited that leadership is based on the interplay of (1) the amount of guidance and direction given by the leader, (2) the amount of emotional support provided by the leader, and (3) the maturity of subordinates in terms of their ability and willingness to take responsibility for directing their own behavior in performing a specific task. The model of situational leadership presented here combines their idea of situational leadership with the leadership perspective presented by Blanchard, Zigarmi, and Zigarmi (1985) in the popular book *Leadership and the One Minute Manager*.

Situational leadership matches the leader behavior to the level of employee development and the task to be performed. Leader behavior has directive and supportive components. *Directive behavior* focuses on tasks and consists of several dimensions: specifying the goals people are to accomplish; organizing the work situation for people; setting time lines; providing specific directions; and specifying and requiring regular reporting on progress. *Supportive behavior* focuses on the leader's relationship with the subordinate and has these dimensions: providing support and encouragement, involving people in give-and-take discussions about work activities, facilitating people's interaction with others, seeking out and listening to people's opinions and concerns, and providing feedback on people's accomplishments. Supportive and directive behavior are combined in various manners to create four leadership styles: directing, coaching, supporting, and delegating. Each style has characteristic behaviors and decision-making styles. The employee's job and psychological readiness to perform organizational tasks dictates the appropriate style. Employee readiness is determined by assessing competence and commitment. Competence is the degree of job knowledge or skills the employee exhibits. Commitment is a measure of psychological readiness or the motivation and determination on the part of the employee to accomplish organizational tasks. The leadership styles (S1 to S4) are directly matched to the employee development levels (M1 to M4), as seen in grid form in Figure 6–8.

Directing

Directing is the appropriate leadership style when dealing with a new employee or an employee who is starting a new task. In this style the leader directs the employees' behavior by telling them what is to be done, showing them, watching them, and giving them positive reinforcement as they progress in accomplishing the task. The employee in such an instance has little competence but is

Figure 6–8

The situational leadership model.

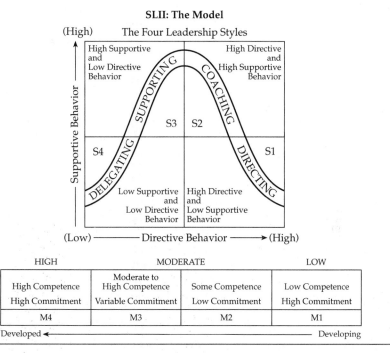

SLII: The Model

(High)   The Four Leadership Styles

High Supportive and Low Directive Behavior

High Directive and High Supportive Behavior

SUPPORTING   COACHING

S3   S2

S4   S1

DELEGATING   DIRECTING

Low Supportive and Low Directive Behavior

High Directive and Low Supportive Behavior

(Low) ———— Directive Behavior ———→ (High)

Supportive Behavior

HIGH	MODERATE		LOW
High Competence	Moderate to High Competence	Some Competence	Low Competence
High Commitment	Variable Commitment	Low Commitment	High Commitment
M4	M3	M2	M1

Developed ◄——————————————————— Developing

Source: Situational Leadership ® is a registered trademark of the Center for Leadership, Escondido, CA. Used with permission. All rights reserved.

highly motivated to perform. The new police employee is an excellent example of the employee needing a directing style of management. The supervisor's task is to develop the employee to be a competent police officer, capable of performing the police function without direction. This style would also be appropriate for use with a new sergeant. The lieutenant would appropriately use the directing style until the sergeant begins to develop competence in the role of supervisor. The directing mode is also appropriate when veteran officers are transferred to new assignments or when officers are assigned specific tasks that they previously have not performed.

The directing style requires that the leader personally know how to handle situations and tasks. It requires that the leader be able to separate each task into its various parts and to establish appropriate performance objectives for the employee's development level. When using the directing style, the leader makes the decisions.

Coaching

Coaching is the appropriate leadership style when dealing with employees who have developed some degree of competence but may have a lowered commitment to the organization as a result of job frustration or the novelty of the

job diminishing. These employees often question their abilities and feel inse-cure on the job. The leader must provide direction and supervision because these officers need praise to build their self-esteem, support to know that the leader has confidence in them, and involvement in decision making to build their commitment. As the leader continues to use the coaching style with these employees they will become more competent and gain commitment.

Supporting

Supporting is the appropriate leadership style when dealing with employees who are highly competent—that is, who know how to perform the police tasks that are required of them—yet waiver in commitment. Sometimes the variable commitment is due to a lack of confidence in their abilities or frustrations expe-rienced on the job; on other occasions it is due to insufficient motivation. The supporting style does not entail extensive direction because employees have the requisite skills. The supporting style requires the leader to praise the employee in specific terms and immediately after the accomplishment. Such praise should be for the regular day-to-day activities the officer performs well. The purpose is to demonstrate to the officer that the leader knows the officer is doing a good job and that the leader appreciates the officer's productivity. The supportive leader is also a good listener, using reflective or active listening, and serves to facilitate or make the officer's job easier or less frustrating by provid-ing all the essential coordinative support efforts. If the leader appropriately supports the individual officer, that officer should eventually develop to be both highly competent and highly committed.

Delegating

Delegating is the appropriate leadership style for dealing with those employ-ees who are both able and willing to work by themselves with little supervision or support. These employees are highly competent and highly committed. The leader turns over the day-to-day decision making to these employees. This does not mean that the leader shows no interest in them and no longer evaluates what they are doing. Too often leaders who have employees who are highly developed forget that these employees need recognition and praise. They need to be listened to and facilitated in performing their work. If these employees are ignored, there is the potential that their commitment may diminish and they will revert to a state of variable commitment. To ensure that this does not occur, the leader should continue to provide some degree of support but little direc-tion to these employees. Too much direction will cause the competent employee to question the leader's faith in the employee's skills and ability.

Praise and Positive Reprimands

Situational leadership as presented by Hersey and Blanchard (1988) builds on two other popular books: *The One Minute Manager* (Blanchard and Johnson, 1982) and *Putting the One Minute Manager to Work* (Blanchard and Lorber, 1984).

In combination they emphasize the use of rewards and redirection for those employees who are still developing. Through goal setting and observing the achievement toward those goals, the leader praises behavior that is moving in the right direction while redirecting the employee in those areas where the employee is not performing competently. Reprimand or punishment is reserved solely for those employees who are clearly competent but who are under-achieving. In reprimanding, the leader approaches competent, developed employees specifically with what they have done wrong, how the leader feels about the behavior (e.g., disappointed, angry, irritated, betrayed), and why the behavior is so disturbing (e.g., the officer always performs well in this task, is highly responsible, is always on time, is always dependable). Positive repri-mands such as this emphasize what the officer has done wrong instead of how the officer was treated.

Kuykendall and Unsinger (1982) investigated police leadership styles rela-tive to an earlier leadership scheme developed by Hersey and Blanchard. They surveyed 155 police managers from California and Arizona to determine whether their dominant leadership style was telling, selling, participating, or delegating—or if a dominant style existed at all. They found the predominant style to be selling (51 percent), which is similar to coaching as used in the cur-rent model. A large number of the respondents, 45 percent, had no dominant style. None of the police managers adopted delegating as their dominant style. Kuykendall and Unsinger also found that the police managers were most effec-tive when using a leadership style that had a high task emphasis. The police managers often failed to use the appropriate leadership style when the situation called for them to delegate or support. This finding indicates that police man-agers have some difficulty in changing leadership style to meet the situation.

Applying Contingency Leadership

Clearly, the contingency approach incorporates many aspects of the other lead-ership and motivation theories. It requires that leaders pay close attention to subordinates' needs—the leader must ensure that a work situation and subse-quent rewards allow individuals to satisfy their needs. The leader also must treat everyone equitably. Treating everyone fairly while using different leader-ship styles to motivate different individuals may appear to be a contradiction, but it must be accomplished. The leader walks a fine line here, using different rewards, making assignments, and counseling officers. The key is to give each officer the necessary individual attention so that the officer perceives that he or she is a necessary part of the department.

Another consideration of contingency theory is that leaders must be adap-tive in their behavior. Most people's behavior, especially leadership behavior, is based on the types of leadership to which they have been exposed. Leaders tend to lead as they have been led. They also tend to continue to behave as they have behaved in the past. It would be quite difficult for an authoritarian or directive leader to lead in a situation demanding a supportive or participatory style of leadership. Leader behavior does not change overnight! Police administrators should give a great deal of consideration to assigning leaders to positions that match their innate leadership styles. For example, a directive leader should command the riot squad or tactical unit. The situations confronting these units generally require directive leadership. Conversely, an achievement-oriented leader might be assigned to a planning unit or a vice unit. In such a situation this type of leader would probably obtain the greatest results since the responsibilities of these units are somewhat ambiguous and results are based on what the leader is able to accomplish. Administrators should attempt to match subordinate commanders' personalities with the demands of the particular unit. Moreover, efforts should be made to develop the skills of all leaders within the department so that they become more flexible and develop better leading skills. Police departments should also consider selecting people for leadership positions on the basis of their leadership potential.

TRANSFORMATIONAL LEADERSHIP

The previous sections provide a road map to understanding the evolution of leadership theory and thought. Leadership is an important component in police administration, so we should constantly search for a more effective understanding of leadership within the police department. The leadership theories discussed thus far, for the most part, focus on leadership as a process with various theories incorporating a number of factors or dimensions that have an impact on the leadership process. Theory evolves from simple formulations that focus on the leader to more complex models that incorporate a host of work group, organizational, and environmental factors.

The two-factor theories and contingency theories downplay the importance of the leader, whereas the trait theories discussed at the beginning of the chapter focus solely on the leader. Even though the environment, work group, and organizational factors are important in the leadership process, the catalyst for organizational goal attainment remains with leaders. Thus renewed attention has emphasized the leader as the focal point for organizational change and revitalization. A substantial part of the impetus for this movement rests with House and Mitchell's path–goal leadership theory, which postulates that the leader plots a course and simply helps guide subordinates as they achieve organizational objectives.

Bass (1985) described leadership as transactional. *Transactional leadership* is a process of daily exchanges between leaders and subordinates in which the leader uses contingent rewards, active management, passive management, and laissez-faire techniques to accomplish work in the organization. Bass notes that transactional leadership consists of two key components. First, subordinates understand the nature of rewards and work. That is, they understand what management expects of them, and they understand the benefits of meeting management's expectations. Second, management-by-exception is the mode by which superiors deal with work and workers. *Management-by-exception* describes a situation in which superiors concentrate on problems and problem

employees rather than micromanaging all aspects of the job. Management-by-exception allows managers to focus on what they consider important aspects of work as opposed to focusing on all aspects of work

One form of transactional leadership is transformational leadership. *Transformational leadership* is the process by which the leader attempts to broaden the interests and horizons of subordinates and move the organization in a new direction. A key component of transformational leadership is charisma, where the focus is on leadership as a mechanism to accomplish work. *Charisma* is the ability to interact with subordinates and inspire them with organizational objectives. Charismatic leaders often energize an organization by articulating a vision for the organization. Followers become enthusiastic about the leader and his or her ideas and work hard to support them. Charisma is an exclusive form of leadership and perhaps is not sustainable over extended periods of time, but it is quite useful in attempting to motivate subordinates to work toward a new goal. For example, the implementation of community policing is best accomplished by a transformational leader. The objective of transformational leadership is not so much to oversee the daily operation of the organization as to stimulate change or movement in some predetermined direction. In this instance, the manager is more of a change agent than a manager. Transformational leadership is used to transform the organization into a more effective body.

Transformational leadership can be an effective method to transform a stagnant police agency into a more effective department. It is also an effective tool by which to implement new programs such as community policing. Schermerhorn (1996) identified the qualities of transformational leaders as:

1. *Vision.* Having a clear sense of direction, communicating the direction to others, and developing a level of enthusiasm among subordinates for the direction.
2. *Charisma.* Having the ability to interact with subordinates and inspire them toward organizational objectives.
3. *Symbolism.* Offering special awards and holding ceremonies to recognize excellence and identify heroic or outstanding performance.
4. *Empowerment.* Delegating truly challenging work and helping others develop.
5. *Intellectual stimulation.* Creating an atmosphere whereby subordinates begin to think about problems and use their creativity to solve them.
6. *Integrity.* Being honest and open to all members of the organization and consistently adhering to a high standard of ethics and morality.

A leader who possesses these characteristics can transform an organization. Generally, it is vital for a newly appointed police chief to be a transformational leader. The new police chief is judged by all sorts of standards; thus it is important for him or her to make an impression within the organization as quickly as possible. A transformation style of leadership can certainly provide a new chief time to accurately evaluate the department and establish a regime of management practices.

THE POLICE CHIEF AS LEADER

The preceding sections presented information on the theoretical aspects of leadership. The various theories are provided as a road map for administrators to use when they are attempting to understand and develop their relationships with subordinates. The various leadership theories when taken in combination suggest that the leadership process is complicated. An administrator, to be a good leader, must be skilled in applying the right leadership techniques to situations and subordinates. If this is accomplished with precision, the leader and the organization will be more successful. Furthermore, law enforcement is a unique profession. As such, the task of policing plays a key role in the leadership style assumed by the leader.

Most leaders develop a leadership style which they use the majority of the time. They generally select one that is comfortable and works for them. Sheehan and Cordner (1995) identified four primary styles of leadership exhibited by police executives. To a great extent, these styles are focused either internally, attending to managing or running the department, or externally, focusing on the external political activities required of a police chief. A chief, depending on the situation, may use one or more of these styles when managing the department. The four leadership styles are:

1. *Administrator.* Administrators are executives who turn their attentions inward. They concentrate on the inner workings of the department, and they generally adhere to classical organizational tenets and expend a great deal of energy planning, directing, staffing, controlling, and organizing the internal workings of the department. Because they see autonomy as an important ingredient to success, they generally fail to read some the problems within the environment as they occur.

2. *Top cop.* Top cops, somewhat like administrators, turn their attentions inward. The difference is they emphasize leadership rather than management. Top cops see leadership as being actively involved in police operations. They are more likely to take charge of situations and make their presence known in the field. Top cops are generally well liked by the rank-and-file officers because of their involvement in field activities. Top cops, however, generally neglect to attend to many of the department's management requirements. They do not spend a great deal of time in planning, controlling, staffing, or organizing.

3. *Politician.* Politicians turn their attention outward. Politicians, like top cops, do not attend to the managerial aspects of the department. They prefer to interject themselves into community and political affairs. They expend a great deal of energy acquiring personal power through affiliation with community leaders. They abdicate management responsibilities to lower-level subordinates and seldom give them adequate attention.

4. *Statesman.* Statesmen are attentive to both internal and external affairs. They understand the importance of working with community leaders, but they do not see it as their consuming responsibility. At the same time,

they understand the importance of managing the department through planning, directing, staffing, controlling, and organizing. They have the capacity to delegate both internal and external responsibilities. They are skilled at evenhandedly running their departments and working with community and political leaders.

Stamper (1992) provides support for Sheehan and Cordner's typology of police chiefs. In a survey of large police departments, Stamper investigated chiefs in terms of their leadership or external orientation as opposed to their managerial or internal orientation. He found that chiefs generally scored higher on leadership (external orientation) than on managerial functions. However, their subordinates reported that the chiefs in the study actually emphasized internal management functions more than they reported. Stamper notes that management functions generally overwhelm chiefs, and they tend to perform external leadership functions or interact with the community in their spare time. Unlike Sheehan and Cordner, Stamper does not believe that a police chief in a large department can adequately attend to internal and external leadership duties.

Stamper believes that the police leadership problem can be solved with the implementation of a modified management system. He suggests that the police chief delegate the vast majority of the internal management responsibilities to an assistant chief. When this occurs, the chief can devote ample time to external leadership duties, which generally are considerable. When most people have a problem or complaint, they expect to and attempt to talk with the chief. The chief's office is constantly inundated with calls and requests for appointments from people who expect him or her to resolve their problems. Even when these requests are delegated to a subordinate, they generally require some time and effort on the part of the chief. At the same time, the chief must meet with elected and appointed political officials such as council members or heads of other departments and attend to civic organizations such as civic clubs and neighborhood associations. The police chief is the primary political contact between the department and community.

When the chief delegates substantial responsibility for running the department to a subordinate such as an assistant chief, the chief must communicate his or her vision of the department to the assistant chief. This provides the assistant chief with perceptual parameters when making management decisions. The subordinate's actions should mirror the chief's vision of the department. Additionally, the chief can routinely review subordinate management decisions and provide guidance about what should be done and how it should be accomplished.

Police Chief Tenure

Although a great deal can be said about police chief leadership style, it should be noted that most chiefs serve for very short periods of time, and that a chief's departure as chief often has little to do with leadership style. For example, Mahtesian (1997) recently examined the longevity of chiefs in the nation's larger departments and found only one chief with tenure greater than five years. He found that Cleveland had fired three chiefs in a four-year period.

Police chief terminations generally are not the result of ineffectiveness or corruption; rather, police departments today must satisfy too many constituents within the community. The police cannot adequately satisfy all the groups that vie for police attention and services. When the police fail to attend, or inadequately attend, to constituent needs, this becomes a factor in the political process. Over time, the sum of these failures or inadequacies reduces public support, and mayors and city managers often see replacing the chief as a way of garnering public support. Most police chiefs basically are in a no-win situation.

Lower-level police managers often contribute to this process. Doug Hamilton, former police chief in Louisville, once noted that many midlevel commanders operate under the philosophy that "nothing good can happen to me until something bad happens to you [the chief]." Ambitious managers often see the removal of the chief or a general shakeup of the chief's staff as the most likely way of being promoted. They engage in politics to expedite a shakeup. The primary mode of operation here is to engage community leaders and city council members and solicit their support for advancement. At the same time, they usually demonize or severely criticize the chief and his or her programs. For example, district or precinct commanders may tell council members that problems in their districts are the result of the chief's failure to respond or provide the precinct with adequate resources. Renegade managers constantly tell community leaders and politicians how they and their constituents would be treated better if they had more resources or were in charge.

Another source of attack on police chiefs is police unions or employee organizations. Police chiefs must often implement policies which restrict police officer discretion. Points of contention usually revolve around issues such as discipline, use of force, police pursuits, and the treatment of citizens, especially minorities. This often causes animosity between the officers and the chief. If union leaders are sufficiently annoyed with the chief and believe they have enough clout, they often resort to public attacks on the chief. For example, in 1997, the Louisville Fraternal Order of Police (FOP) evaluated the chief by giving officers a questionnaire that examined a number of personal and administrative dimensions. The FOP then issued a scathing report on the chief's performance. However, only a few members of the FOP saw the returned questionnaires and there was no control over who responded or how many questionnaires could be completed by an officer. An independent commission appointed by the mayor conducted an impartial citizen survey and found that the chief and department were well respected by the community and generally rated the chief quite high on all categories.

The police chief often faces attack from a number of directions. To say the position of chief is tenuous is an understatement. For example, Tunnell and Gaines (1996) investigated police chief tenure in Kentucky and found politics to be a significant factor in police chief turnover. Table 6–1 presents data on why police chiefs vacated their office. They found that a full 44 percent left because of political pressure and an additional 9 percent were demoted within the department. An additional 30 chiefs, or 26 percent, left for personal reasons.

Table 6–1

Reasons Given for Predecessor Chiefs' Departure from the Department

Reason	Number	Percent
Personal reasons	30	26.5
Retired after successful service	20	17.7
Terminated by the government	20	17.7
Resigned due to political pressure	19	16.8
Retired due to political pressure	11	9.7
Demoted within the department	10	8.8
Died	3	2.7

Source: K. Tunnell, and L. K. Gaines, Political Pressures and Influences on Police Executives: A Descriptive Analysis. In G. Cordner and D. Kenney, eds. *Managing Police Organizations,* Cincinnati: Anderson Publishing, 1996, p. 11.

Although a number of reasons could account for this group's decision to leave office, it is conceivable that politics played a role. Along these same lines, research indicates that the average tenure for police chiefs is less than six years (Enter, 1986; Mahtesian, 1997; Witham, 1985).

Obviously, the working relationship between the chief and political executive can be a difficult one, and considerable effort from all parties must be exerted if it is to be positive. Regoli and his colleagues (1986a, 1986b) found that the most important factors contributing to chiefs' job satisfaction were autonomy, job security, salary, and job conditions. However, police chiefs seldom are able to achieve autonomy, and the other key factors are largely dependent on their relationship with the governmental executive. Perhaps a former superintendent of the police in Chicago best sums the chief–governmental executive relationship:

> The chief's ability to serve as a major municipal policy maker—and even his ability to run a police department free from the most outrageous kinds of partisan political incursions—is largely dependent on local idiosyncrasies rather than on the scientific application of immutable principles concerning the police chief–mayor relationship (Brzeczek, 1985:55).

It becomes clear that doing a good job or attempting to nurture a good working relationship with governmental officials will not always suffice to allow a chief to remain in office. Bill Bratton, former commissioner of police in New York City, received national publicity for substantially reducing crime, but was forced out of office after only 27 months because he received more publicity than the mayor. Sometimes, job stability is a matter of extenuating circumstances well beyond the reach of the chief.

Ascending to the Position of Chief

Research indicates that there are a variety of paths to become chief. Enter (1986) upon surveying a number of chiefs developed a typology which distinguished the various paths. First, the Ultimate Outsider (A) is one who has had experience

Cleveland Police Chief Mary Bounds is sworn in by Cleveland Mayor Michael R. White. Bounds was the city's first female police chief.

Tony Dejak/AP Photo

with a federal law enforcement agency or the military immediately prior to becoming a police chief. Only 1.7 percent of Enter's respondents fit this category. Second, the Ultimate Outsider (B) is one who becomes police chief after having served as an executive in another type of criminal justice agency (e.g., a prosecutor who is appointed as chief). Again, only 1.7 percent fit this type. Third, the Multi-Agency Career Path individual is one who has had experience with a variety of police and nonpolice agencies. This accounted for 5.5 percent of Enter's sample. Fourth, the Insider is one who, being promoted through the ranks, ultimately attains the rank of chief. Seventy-nine percent of Enter's sample were Insiders. Finally, the Outsider is one who has had a career with two or more police agencies. This type constituted 28 percent of the group.

Enter examined his police chief types in relation to several departmental and demographic variables and found that the Ultimate Outsiders (A) were appointed chief in the least amount of time (2 years) while Insiders took an average of 22 years to become chief. The Ultimate Outsiders (A) had the longest police executive tenure, with an average of 14.63 years service, while the Multi-Agency type had the shortest tenure with a mean of just under 2 years. Insiders generally were not as well educated as the other types of police executives.

In a similar line of research, Crank et al. (1986) and Regoli et al. (1990) identified career stages through which police chiefs progress. From the initial appointment through their first two years, new chiefs go through a "crisis stage" in which they attempt to identify the boundaries of their power and authority. Here they attempt to learn how they mesh with the government and other governmental officials. Second, during the third and fourth years, chiefs go through an "interregnum stage" in which they attempt to identify their power bases and begin to take charge of the department and its operations. Third, during years five through nine, chiefs go through an "institutional stage" in which they become entrenched and continue their own programs and policies. Fourth, chiefs go through a "concretion stage" during years 10 through 14 in which they gain support from the department and community. Here, they continue to fine-tune their programs, but they generally fail to adopt new ones. Finally, chiefs go through a "demise stage" some time after their fifteenth year. At this point they have accomplished most of their goals and are content to rest on their laurels as their upcoming retirement approaches. However, as noted above, most chiefs' tenure is less than six years.

Summary

This chapter addressed the very important concept of leadership. Leadership is by no means simple in its application, and to a great extent people's ability to lead is dependent on the power they possess. People obtain power from a number of sources. Individuals seek power to achieve personal as well as organizational goals. A balance between personal and organizational goals must be maintained. Power must be used appropriately. Power without integrity is tyranny.

If the police agency is to maximize its productivity potential, administrative officers in leadership positions must be capable and have the requisite skills necessary to perform adequately. Leadership is not static and does not consist of a finite number of traits, but it is an ongoing process which requires the constant attention of police administrators. As a process, it requires that the leader understand those who are being led, the situation, and the environment. Leadership is very much an art. Experience and intuitive understanding are required to successfully apply the many theories of leadership. If leadership was a science, a simple formula or recipe would demonstrate how techniques and ingredients are mixed to produce motivated employees. Leadership is not a science; therefore, artists who perceive the subtleties of human behavior are an essential element in leadership.

Finally, it should be noted that the police chief is the department's ultimate leader. He or she exists in a political process. The chief is exposed to a variety of demands and pressures. Recently, it seems that chiefs have substantial difficulty retaining their jobs. This is due in part to the fact that police departments cannot solve all of society's problems, but nonetheless, the police chief is often held accountable for all failures. The police chief often serves as a convenient scapegoat. Regardless, the police chief must understand and work within the confines of the political system.

Study Questions

1. What kinds of power can police leaders possess? List situations in which each might be appropriate and explain why.

2. What are Likert's styles of leadership and how do they relate to policing?

3. What are two-factor theories of leadership and how do they differ from Likert's styles of leadership?

4. How does contingency leadership differ from other kinds of leadership theories? How can they be applied in the police setting?

5. What are transactional and transformational leadership?

6. What are the primary duties of a police executive and how might they be best managed?

7. What is the tenure of a police chief? What problems await the newly appointed police executive?

Net Resources

http://www.slopoa.org/developing_police_leadership.htm Article posted by the San Luis Obispo Police Officers Association on developing police leadership.

References

Barnard, C. (1968). *The Functions of the Executive.* Cambridge, MA: Harvard University Press.

Bass, B. M. (1985). Leadership: Good, better, best. *Organizational Dynamics* 13(3):26–40.

Blake, R., and Mouton, J. (1964). *The Managerial Grid.* Houston: Gulf Publishing Co.

Blanchard, K., Zigarmi, P., and Zigarmi, D. (1985). *Leadership and the One Minute Manager.* New York: William Morrow.

Blanchard, K., and Johnson, S. (1982). *The One Minute Manager.* New York: William Morrow.

Blanchard, K., and Lorber, R. (1984). *Putting the One Minute Manager to Work.* New York: William Morrow.

Brzeczek, R. J. (1985). Chief–mayor relations: The view from the chief's chair. In W. Geller (ed.), *Police Leadership in America: Crisis and Opportunity.* New York: Praeger.

Crank, J., Culbertson, R., Poole, E., and Regoli, R. (1986). Cynicism and career stages among police chiefs. *Justice Quarterly* 3:343–352.

Downs, A. (1967). *Inside Bureaucracy.* Boston: Little, Brown.

Enter, J. (1986). The rise to the top: An analysis of police chief career patterns. *Journal of Police Science and Administration* 14(4):334–346.

Fiedler, F. E. (1978). Contingency model and the leadership process. In L. Berkowitz (ed.), *Advances in Experimental Social Psychology,* Vol. 11. New York: Academic Press, pp. 60–112.

French, J. R., and Raven, B. (1959). The bases of social power. In D. Cartwright (ed.), *Studies in Social Power.* Ann Arbor: University of Michigan Press, pp. 150–167.

Girodo, M. (1998). Machiavellian, bureaucratic, and transformational leadership styles in police managers: Preliminary findings of interpersonal ethics. *Perceptual and Motor Skills* 86:419–427.

Hersey, P., and Blanchard, K. (1988). *Management of Organizational Behavior: Utilizing Human Resources,* 5th ed. Englewood Cliffs, NJ: Prentice Hall.

House, R. J., and Mitchell, T. R. (1974). Path–goal theory of leadership. *Journal of Contemporary Business,* Autumn, pp. 81–97.

Ilgen, D. R., and Moore, C. F. (1987). Types and choices of performance feedback. *Journal of Applied Psychology* 72:401–406.

Kanter, R. M. (1977). *Men and Women of the Corporation.* New York: Basic Books.

Kipinis, D., Schmidt, S. M., Swaffin-Smith, C., and Wilkinson, I. (1984). Patterns of managerial influence: Shotgun managers, tacticians, and bystanders. *Organizational Dynamics* 12:60–65.

Kuykendall, J., and Unsinger, P. (1982). The leadership styles of police managers. *Journal of Criminal Justice* 10:311–321.

Likert, R. (1961) *New Patterns of Management.* New York: McGraw-Hill.

Likert, R. (1967) *The Human Organization.* New York: McGraw-Hill.

Mahtesian, C. (1997). Mission impossible. *Governing Magazine,* January, pp. 19–23.

McClelland, D., and Burnham, D. (1976). Power is the great motivator. *Harvard Business Review* 54(2):100–110.

Regoli, R., Crank, J., and Culbertson, R. (1986a). The consequences of professionalism among police chiefs. *Justice Quarterly* 6(1):47–67.

Regoli, R., Crank, J., and Culbertson, R. (1986b). Police cynicism, job satisfaction, and work relations of police chiefs: An assessment of the influence of department size. *Sociological Focus* 22(3):161–171.

Regoli, R., Culbertson, R., Crank, J., and Powell, J. (1990). Career stages and cynicism among police chiefs. *Justice Quarterly* 7(3):593–614.

Roberg, R., and Kuykendall, J. (1997). *Police Management,* 2nd ed. Los Angeles: Roxbury Press.

Schermerhorn, J. R. (1996). *Management,* 5th ed. New York: Wiley.

Sheehan, R., and Cordner, G. W. (1995). *Police Administration,* 3rd ed. Cincinnati: Anderson Publishing.

Stamper, N. H. (1992). *Removing Managerial Barriers to Effective Police Leadership.* Washington: Police Executive Research Forum.

Stogdill, R., and Coons, A. (1957). *Leader Behavior: Its Description and Measurement.* Ohio State University, Bureau of Business Research.

Stoner, J. A., and Freeman, R. E. (1992). *Management,* 5th ed. Englewood Cliffs, NJ: Prentice Hall.

Swanson, C. R., and Territo, L. (1982). Police leadership and interpersonal communications styles. In J. Greene (ed.), *Police and Police Work*. Beverly Hills, CA: Sage.

Toch, H. (1997). The democratization of policing in the United States: 1895–1973. *Police Forum* 7(2):1–8.

Tunnell, K., and Gaines, L. (1996). Political pressures and influences on police executives: A descriptive analysis. In G. Cordner and D. Kenney (eds.), *Managing Police Organizations*. Cincinnati: Anderson Publishing, pp. 5–18.

Vroom, V. (1964). *Work and Motivation*. New York: Wiley.

Witham, D. C. (1985). *The American Law Enforcement Chief Executive: A Management Profile*. Washington: Police Executive Research Forum.

Witte, J. H., Travis, L. F., and Langworthy, R. H. (1990). Participatory management in law enforcement: Police officer, supervisor, and administrator perceptions. *American Journal of Police* 9(4):1–24.

7

People in the Police Organization

Michael Newman/PhotoEdit

Chapter Outline

Introduction

The Individual in the Organization

Theories of Motivation

Content/Need/Humanistic Theories of Motivation
Maslow's Hierarchy of Needs
Herzberg's Motivation–Hygiene Theory
McClelland's Achievement, Power, and Affiliation Motive Theory
Summary of Humanistic Theories

Behavioral Theories of Motivation
Adams's Equity Theory
Expectancy Theory

A Comprehensive Theory of Motivation

The Dynamics of Group Behavior

Culture and Police Work
The Police Culture
The Competing Cultures in Policing

Summary

Learning Objectives

After reading this chapter, you should be able to

1. Explain the concept of motivation and its importance in the police department.
2. Understand the difference between content and behavioral theories of motivation.
3. Understand the various motivational theories and how they might be applied in the police setting.
4. Formulate and apply a comprehensive motivational plan for a police department.
5. Understand how group behavior and dynamics affect officer motivation.
6. Appreciate the police culture and its implications for police management.
7. Understand the various cultures that exist in the police department.

R ecently, a new captain was assigned to manage one of the department's patrol watches. The officers on the watch had a reputation for being unproductive and treating citizens unprofessionally. The chief assigned the captain to solve the problems and take actions to improve the work relations on the shift. The captain soon learned that a number of the problems facing the watch were rooted in the culture of the officers assigned to the shift. Officers believed that they had been treated unfairly by their commanders in the past. They were opposed to community policing, which had recently been implemented in the department. They saw it as creating more work and not improving the police department's ability to respond to crime and citizen concerns.

After diagnosing the problem, the captain began meeting with officers in groups and individually. He took a number of actions to remedy the problem. First, he had officers from other units to attend role call and highlight some of the success stories from their community policing efforts. He began to praise them when they did a good job, especially when dealing with the public. He examined the distribution of officers' days off and attempted to do a better job of accommodating everyone, rather than just giving ideal schedules to a few officers. He encouraged officers to apply for training opportunities, especially those that were seen as prestigious. He started backing officers when they answered calls for service to show them that he was concerned with their well-being and working conditions.

After a rough initial period, the captain's efforts began to pay off. The culture of the work group changed. Officers began to trust the captain and respect his ideas about how the shift should operate. Officers' motivational levels increased as the captain began showing concern and rewarding their efforts. Stronger bonds began to develop among everyone on the patrol watch.

This example shows how motivation can affect police productivity. It also shows how leadership can affect motivation. When motivational problems exist, actions and adjustments must be made to change the work group atmosphere. If motivational problems are not addressed, unit productivity surely will suffer.

INTRODUCTION

A police department, like any other organization, depends on its supervisors and managers to lead and motivate line officers to achieve the department's goals. Individuals and groups in each community have expectations of their police department, and the police executive must strive to ensure that the department is productive in meeting those expectations. Productivity in policing is difficult to define and measure but nevertheless depends to a great extent on the interpersonal management activities of leadership and motivation. No organization, regardless of its nature, can reach its productivity potential without good leadership and motivated employees.

This is particularly true in police organizations where services are provided in an environment that ranges from indifference to hostility. It is very difficult to maintain productivity and motivation when police officers are exposed to the many frustrations that are generated by having to enforce laws, such as traffic offenses, that place the typical law-abiding citizen in a position of being viewed as a criminal, or to provide direction and assistance to citizens who are unwilling to accept direction and assistance. It indeed is a difficult task to keep officers on target when confronted by such hostilities.

This chapter focuses on officer behavior. It is difficult to design an organizational structure or establish a predominant leadership style without developing a firm understanding of how subordinate officers react in the organizational setting. This chapter begins with a brief discussion of people and organizations. How well individuals adjust to the organization and their personalities affects how well they can be led and their productivity. Next, motivation theories are examined in depth, starting with humanistic theories and moving on to behavioral theories. Here we provide a foundation for understanding how to get people to work and be productive. Finally, the organizational culture is discussed. Work group culture, especially in police departments, plays an important role in determining how productive individual employees are.

THE INDIVIDUAL IN THE ORGANIZATION

Everyone is different to some extent. That is, everyone has a unique personality. People have their own behavioral characteristics, idiosyncrasies, and worldviews—all of which must be taken into consideration by effective leaders. Differences among people is one of the foundations of contingency leadership theories, as discussed in Chapter 6. Hersey and Blanchard's (1988) situational leadership model, as discussed in the previous chapter, is predicated on differences among subordinates. It therefore seems that if we can develop a better understanding of people within the organization, we can develop better leadership styles or better match leadership to the people being led.

An interactionist perspective is perhaps the best way to understand work behavior. An *interactionist perspective* implies that behavior is the result of one's personality and the nature of the situation or job (Greenberg and Baron, 1995). Like the contingency theories of leadership, the interactionist perspective dictates that although a given situation will help fashion people's behavior, their responses will not be uniform since each individual's personality will also have some impact on his or her behavior. For example, if two officers are dispatched to a family disturbance, their reaction to the situation may very well be quite different. Police administrators attempt to ensure uniform responses to such calls through training and the promulgation of procedures; but nonetheless, there very likely will be, at a minimum, subtle differences in how the two officers respond to the disturbance.

The nature of police work dictates that not everyone is suited to be a police officer. Police agencies must strive to select people whose personalities meet the demands of the job. In this regard, departments must endeavor to achieve a person–job fit as depicted in Figure 7–1. Police administrators must determine what constitutes good performance, identify police officers who are good performers, and then attempt to design a selection system that selects applicants

Figure 7–1

Person–job fit in law enforcement.

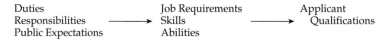

Duties	Job Requirements	Applicant
Responsibilities	Skills	Qualifications
Public Expectations	Abilities	

who are like the good performers. As discussed in the chapter on Police Human Resources Management, most personality testing at the police selection stage has been designed to identify those who are unfit for service. The person–job fit paradigm dictates that police agencies concentrate on identifying those who will be good performers. The difference between these two perspectives is the middle group, which might be characterized as mediocre or average. When a department concentrates on selecting out unfit candidates, the mediocre applicants remain in the selection pool. On the other hand, if the selection process focuses on identifying the good performers, a larger number of the mediocre candidates will be excluded from the selection pool.

There has been considerable research on the working personality. This research is flawed, much like the trait theories of leadership, in that most employees only approximate, rather than fit, the ideal type as described in the listing of traits. However, five employee traits consistently appear in any listing, and these should be considered when selecting employees (Greenberg and Baron, 1995). These traits are a natural fit for police work:

1. *Extroversion.* Police officers should be somewhat extroverted. They must be outgoing so that they engage people and work with them.
2. *Agreeableness.* Police officers should be gentle, cooperative, and forgiving. Irritable, ruthless, inflexible, uncooperative people tend to be bad employees and bad police officers.
3. *Conscientiousness.* Employees, especially police officers, should be dedicated to their work, organized, and self-disciplined.
4. *Emotional stability.* Police officers must be calm, poised, and secure. People who are anxious, emotional, or depressed have difficulty coping with the rigors of police work.
5. *Openness to experience.* Police officers must be worldly. They must be imaginative, sensitive, and to some extent polished.

These personality traits provide a sound foundation for any employee. In combination, they are a general description of who should be in the police service. Even though it is virtually impossible for all employees to meet all of the criteria, the criteria provide a direction to begin the selection process.

Values play a key role in determining if a person is a good employee. *Values* are "global concepts that guide actions and judgments across a variety of situations" (Schermerhorn, Hunt, and Osborn, 1994:159). Values are specific ideas about right and wrong, limited by an individual's personality. Employees' values must be congruent with the organization's. To some extent, employees and the organization must be like-minded. For example, Raelin (1987) notes that the values of people who grew up in the 1960s include defiance of authority, participation in decision making, a sense of social justice, and a desire to serve society. Obviously, a defiance of authority would not be conducive to police work, but the other values of this generation are fairly congruent with the nature of police work. Along these same lines, many police executives today complain that applicants for police service lack a work ethic. Again, an applicant without this value would be a poor police officer.

Leadership and motivation are important in making a police department successful. However, a leader cannot lead and motivate employees unless the employees' values and personality meet the demands of the organization. Thus, as discussed in Chapter 10, the police department cannot be successful without first employing the "right" kinds of people.

THEORIES OF MOTIVATION

Motivation is a complex phenomenon. Some police managers measure their subordinates' motivation in terms of the degree to which they support their leader. Other managers measure motivation in terms of daily attendance or sick leave abuse. Still others see motivation in terms of productivity such as the number of traffic citations written. Such measurements only partially explain the phenomenon of motivation. *Motivation* generally refers to "the set of processes that arouse, direct, and maintain human behavior toward attaining some goal" (Greenberg and Baron, 1995). This definition implies that motivation comprises several elements. First, "arousal" refers to getting subordinates interested in working or doing something. Some people are self-motivated and do not require a stimulus from a supervisor, whereas others require direction or prodding. Second, this definition implies that people make choices about their behavior. They make choices about the amount and quality of their work. Management, through policies, direction, and consultation, can assist employees in making the correct choices. Finally, motivation is about maintaining productive behavior. Leaders must strive to have their subordinates working constantly to achieve goals.

There are two general types of theory explaining how police officers may be motivated: humanistic and behavioral. The *humanistic theories* focus on human relations, employee potential, or the internal will or drive in the person. According to humanistic theories, motivation comes from within, necessitating that police agencies select personnel with the right values and attitudes. Humanistic theories are also referred to as content or need theories.

Behavioral theories, also called process or instrumentality theories, attempt to explain behavior through the process of reinforcement. A common criticism of humanistic theories is that they are descriptive and do not capture the dynamics of people as they interact with the work environment. As officers perform day-to-day activities they receive rewards or punishment for their endeavors. Behavioral theorists postulate that these rewards and punishment eventually mold subordinates' behavior.

Figure 7–2

Basic premise of humanistic theories: factors leading to motivated versus frustrated employees.

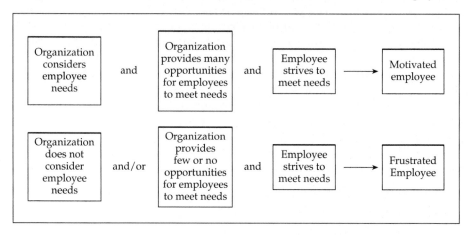

Schermerhorn, Hunt, and Osborn (1994) point out that behavioral and content theories of motivation are not necessarily at odds, and they can be merged into a global theory explaining motivation. The content theories are directly linked to explaining job satisfaction, while the behavioral theories more accurately explain work efforts and performance.

CONTENT/NEED/HUMANISTIC THEORIES OF MOTIVATION

Content/need theories postulate that people possess various internal needs and that they will seek to satisfy their needs through their work. It is important that organizations consider employee needs and provide an opportunity for satisfying their internal needs. If the opportunity is available and people are working toward satisfying their needs, they will be motivated. Conversely, if no opportunity exists and their needs are blocked or thwarted, they will become frustrated (see Figure 7–2).

Need frustration is exhibited in three unproductive forms of organizational behavior: (1) resignation—the individual abandons hope and becomes passive; (2) fixation—the individual continues to exhibit the same behavior, to be concerned with the same problems, and fails to grow emotionally in terms of the job; and (3) rationalization—the individual is not concerned with work and blames any shortcomings on others or factors out of his or her control. When officers exhibit these behaviors, the supervisor should be able to recognize them and take action in assisting the frustrated employee in getting back on track.

The content theory of motivation requires the organization to develop a work climate which allows individuals to seek and achieve their internal needs. Motivation and productivity cannot exist without a positive work climate.

Figure 7–3
Maslow's Hierarchy of Needs.

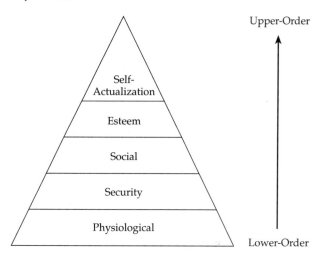

Maslow's Hierarchy of Needs

One of the first content theories of motivation was Maslow's (1943) Hierarchy of Needs. Maslow postulated that there is a hierarchy of needs in which individuals progress from lower needs to higher needs as shown in Figure 7–3.

According to Maslow, a lower-order need must be partially fulfilled before the next higher need is activated. Therefore, more than one need may be experienced at the same time. When a lower-order need is satisfied, it no longer serves to motivate the individual, and the individual progresses to the next need category. As the individual progresses up the need structure it is increasingly difficult to satisfy needs. Hence some people remain at a particular need level while others continue to progress, grow, and move up the need structure. It is also possible to move backward or drop to lower levels of needs as a result of significant life events such as loss of job, divorce, or serious personal illness. The individual would then restart the progression of needs. Finally, some individuals are content to remain at a particular need level, not attempting to satisfy higher-order needs.

Physiological Needs

The most basic needs are the physiological needs: food, clothing, adequate shelter, and water. The fulfillment of physiological needs is usually associated with salary. That is, people use their income to purchase those things necessary to satisfy physiological needs. It is important, therefore, for police departments to pay officers a salary that sufficiently meets these needs. If they do not, the attrition rate for officers may be quite high, or officers may become more interested in part-time jobs or other sources of income than they are in their primary police duties.

Although many police departments have made significant strides in pay increases over the past two decades, it appears that salaries may remain a problem. For example, Reiss (1988) found large numbers of officers working part-time jobs. He found during one period that 47 percent of Seattle's police officers had work permits (departmental permission for a part-time job) and 53 percent of Colorado Springs's officers worked off-duty in uniform. These work patterns surely point to a pay problem. Police administrators should frequently evaluate the department's pay schedule considering the rate of inflation and salary levels in the private sector to ensure that the department's salary structure is competitive and that officers are provided a quality standard of living.

Security Needs

Security needs are the conscious and subconscious desires to develop continuity in life. People want to ensure that their physiological needs will continue to be satisfied in the future. Traditionally, the need for job security has been considered to be a prime motivator for many people entering police work. This premise is especially true during periods of high unemployment. Those aspiring to become police officers know that society will always need the police, thus the position of police officer is a secure position.

Satisfaction of the security need is accomplished through civil service regulations in most agencies. Civil service protects officers from being arbitrarily dismissed. The need for job security also serves to keep officers from quitting the force—it is a difficult decision to leave a secure job. On the other hand, the need for physical security serves as an obstacle to some individuals who enter police work. Some perceive policing to be too dangerous and opt for safer vocations. For others, physical security needs are met when the police department provides adequate training in defense tactics and firearms, provides dependable backup in emergency situations, and provides quality equipment.

Social Needs

Once physiological and security needs have been satisfied, social needs dominate an individual's motivation concerns. People are social beings; they need to interact, socialize, and be accepted by others. Membership in a police department to a great extent satisfies the social need. Officers belong and interact within departmental units, police social events, and fraternal organizations. A number of researchers have noted the high degree of socialization that occurs in police work groups (e.g., Ahern, 1972; Lundman, 1980; Reiss, 1971; Skolnick, 1966).

Sayles and Strauss (1966) identified a number of needs that are satisfied by group membership. Group membership provides companionship, combating feelings of isolation that may breed discontentment and poor efficiency. The group provides a source of identification and values that set the limits for acceptable and unacceptable behavior. Police peer groups may attempt to protect the less productive officers by restricting the number of citations each officer should write. In this instance, group values conflict with organizational goals. The group

On the Job

FRANKFORT POLICE DEPARTMENT

By Ted Evans

Courtesy of Chief Evans

The City of Frankfort, as the capitol of the Commonwealth of Kentucky, is home to a variety of activities that normally are not present in other cities around the state. The fact that Frankfort is the state's capitol complicates my job as chief of police and results in duties for our officers that frequently are not performed by officers in other cities. Police officer motivation is critical to the Frankfort Police Department.

The department currently has an authorized force of 61 sworn officers—a relatively small police department for a state capitol city. The department serves a resident population of approximately 28,500 people, plus an additional 5,000 to 7,000 state government employees who commute into the city daily from surrounding communities. When the state legislature meets, several thousand transient people come to the city to conduct business and lobby legislators and their staffs. The additional population results in additional demands for police service from the department. When the state legislature is in session, the department and its officers are frequently in the public eye as the additional news outlet coverage converges on the city. The political expectations and media scrutiny that result create pressure and stress for the officers, which affects their motivation and job satisfaction.

As police chief, it is my responsibility to ensure that officers' motivational levels are consistently high. I must constantly evaluate the officers' performance, identify problems, and provide solutions. Motivational levels ebb and flow and are very susceptible to external events and actions as well as internal department activities. I think this is especially true during the present era of community policing.

Because the department is relatively small, I am able to meet and talk with a majority of the officers on a regular, if not daily, basis. This enables me, in turn, to communicate directly with the officers about identified problems and enables me to dispel or counter the ever-present internal rumors. Face-to-face communication is reassuring to officers and offers the most effective way to discuss department activities and plans. Clear communication is a critical part of police administration.

Continued

Community policing has resulted in the department's implementation of a number of programs and activities designed to allow and encourage police officer engagement with the public that they serve. This is often stressful for officers because it represents a departure from the traditional policing norm. Police officers are often resistant to change. They develop ideas about how policing should be done, and they often view change as inefficient or detracting from their concept of their duties. However, community policing has provided a number of opportunities for officers to become more involved in the department and the community. Community policing has resulted in a wider variety of assignments and performance expectations in the department's operations (patrol) division. Implementation of bicycle patrol, neighborhood and school liaison, canine handling, and other community policing activities offers Frankfort police officers duties that they find challenging and exciting, which in turn generates new enthusiasm for the job. Community policing in Frankfort has resulted in officers having contact with a wider variety of citizens in the community and on a level that promotes mutual understanding and involvement with each other.

As the police chief, I also influence motivation by working for and looking after the best interests of the officers. I am the primary contact point between the police department and the rest of city government. Issues come before the city's legislative body that affect the department and the officers expect me, as police chief, to act in their interest. I lobby for better salary and benefits, better equipment, and additional resources. When officers see me advocating for them, they develop a greater investment in the goals and objectives of the police department. The officers begin to view the department as a team, and teamwork is critical to successful community policing in Frankfort.

In summary, I believe that police officer motivation is of major importance in police management and administration. As the chief of police, I must make every effort to positively motivate officers and identify and address issues that detract from positive motivation or the result will be poor job performance and a reduced effectiveness of the department's community policing efforts.

values can also augment or assist in accomplishment of organizational goals. The group provides the individual an opportunity for creativity and initiative in striving to achieve the goals of the peer group. The group often serves to provide assistance to the individual in solving technical or personal problems. The social or peer group also provides the officer some degree of protection from management. This is especially true in departments that are unionized. Regardless, bonds developed among group members aid them in crisis or difficult situations. The social need is extremely important in policing, where the work can be monotonous or boring at times and dangerous at other times.

Esteem Needs

Esteem needs are dominant for individuals who have met their social needs. Hersey and Blanchard (1988) noted that esteem or recognition needs take two primary forms, prestige and power. In Chapters 4 and 5, traditional police management was contrasted with more contemporary practices such as participatory management. A principal criticism of traditional police management is that a quasi-military structure did not allow subordinates to fulfill esteem needs. In the traditional organization, subordinates are given orders and their participation in planning or decision making is rather limited. Participative management, on the other hand, allows for participation by subordinates, especially in those areas which directly affect them.

A participative style of management helps subordinates to satisfy their esteem needs: they come to feel important (prestige) and have some control (power) over their own destiny. Power also refers to the need to exert control or influence over others. Power may by one of the primary driving forces (needs) for individuals seeking promotion. The need for power is also evident in the unionization process: Individuals without rank have the desire to accumulate enough power to intervene into the formal management structure. Regardless of the form the esteem need takes—power or prestige—satisfaction of the esteem need is important to police officers.

Administrators must develop avenues to fulfill this need if officers are to be highly motivated. The need for esteem is difficult to satisfy. Few police officers ever feel that they have received the proper recognition for their work. This is most likely a result of the failure by most police agencies to provide recognition for superior performance. Managers should acknowledge good performance on a daily basis. Witham notes that this strategy is the only proper and sensible approach for police leaders:

> Many successful leaders have adopted a simple habit that directly influences their superior performance: the ability to say "thank you" to their co-workers. These leaders understand that their job is to give credit to subordinates for their contribution. They realize that hoarding praise or stealing credit from others makes them and their organizations losers (1985:62).

Self-Actualization Needs

Maslow's highest need category is self-actualization—the need to make the most of one's life—self-fulfillment, accomplishment, and achievement. Maslow notes that very few people achieve this final need; most people remain concerned with lower-level needs. For the police officer in a traditional police agency, self-actualization is possible only upon promotion, through highly specialized functions such as detective, or through special skill development such as marksmanship. Yet in the department that uses a participatory management style, it is possible that competent, committed officers might be given a mission and the capacity to fulfill the mission, which might result in self-actualization.

Figure 7–4
Motivational pattern where security needs dominate.

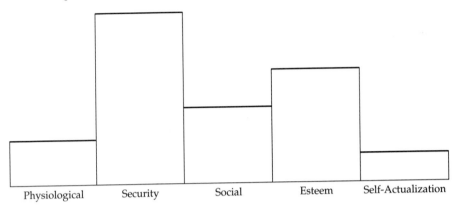

| Physiological | Security | Social | Esteem | Self-Actualization |

Application to Employees in General

Maslow's Hierarchy of Needs is useful in assisting the manager to understand the needs that generally are most important for employees. The needs presented earlier have varying degrees of dominance for employees. That is, physiological needs are the strongest for persons whose needs for food, shelter, or clothing have not yet been somewhat satisfied. Once physiological needs are somewhat satisfied, security needs dominate as need motivators for employees. When security needs have been somewhat satisfied, esteem needs become the strongest need. Finally, as esteem needs are somewhat satisfied, the employee's need for self-actualization dominates the need structure. Employees can become stuck at a need level if that need is not sufficiently satisfied for them.

Maslow did not intend for the Hierarchy of Needs to be universally applicable but to be considered as "a typical pattern that operates most of the time" (Hersey and Blanchard, 1988:29). There are exceptions to the typical pattern. These exceptions are evident in individual motivational differences.

Application to an Individual Employee

Maslow's Hierarchy of Needs should not be considered as a strict hierarchy because individuals are motivated differentially. There are numerous such patterns and everyone has a distinct pattern. Figure 7–4 depicts the motivational state of an individual. The columns show the magnitude of importance for a given need. Individuals following the pattern in Figure 7–4 would be most concerned with security needs. These individuals are not as motivated by other needs. They are more interested in job security or stability and retirement or disability benefits than in being allowed to make decisions about their work (esteem need). Esteem needs are more important than social needs for this individual. Physiological and self-actualization needs are relatively equal and unimportant for this individual.

A partial explanation for differential need patterns may be that the individual has experienced need frustration due to himself or herself, others, or the organization. If such need frustration exists, Alderfer (1972) suggests that the individual will compensate by redirecting his or her attention to meeting a lower-level need. Differential need patterns complicate the leadership task; leaders must develop different rewards for different people. Each person must be considered as an individual with his or her own variations in needs.

Herzberg's Motivation–Hygiene Theory

Another well-known humanistic theory is Herzberg's (1968) Motivation–Hygiene theory. Where Maslow's Hierarchy of Needs can be viewed to some degree as a continuum across which an individual transverses, Herzberg identified two primary groups of factors that affect one's productivity: motivation and hygiene factors. He arrived at these factors by interviewing workers to determine what they found to be satisfying and dissatisfying about their jobs. Basically, Herzberg discovered that dissatisfaction—*hygiene factors*—referred to the work environment, whereas satisfaction—*motivation factors*—referred to the work itself. This finding also applies to police officers: they frequently are dissatisfied with the work environment—close supervision, perceived unfair policies, salary disparities, and the status of policing—but enjoy police work. Herzberg's theory is outlined in Figure 7–5.

Herzberg's hygiene factors include the organization's policy and administration, supervision, work conditions, salary, relationships with peers and superiors, status, and security. Motivators (satisfiers) include individual achievement, recognition, responsibility, growth, and work itself. For Herzberg, satisfaction is not the opposite of dissatisfaction. Job satisfaction (motivation) and dissatisfaction (hygiene) are two different human dimensions. Both must be considered in the work environment. For example, police officers who have excellent hygiene factors in the form of salaries, benefits, equipment, and relations with supervisors would not be dissatisfied. Even though they are satisfied, they are not necessarily motivated to do a good job. To motivate (satisfy) the officers, the managerial practices should allow the officers some degree of job control, responsibility, and achievement.

If a department uses some form of participatory management to give officers latitude in performance of their duties (enhancing their esteem needs) but salaries and benefits are substandard, officers will be motivated but somewhat dissatisfied with the job. Even though they are dissatisfied, these officers may perform many police tasks well because they receive gratification (motivation) from the work itself. Routine or mundane tasks, however, would receive little attention from these officers due to their job dissatisfaction. Herzberg postulates that managers must recognize and provide opportunities for officers to fulfill both hygiene and motivation needs.

In comparing Maslow's Hierarchy of Needs and Herzberg's Motivation–Hygiene Theory, it is evident that both essentially focus on the same concerns. Herzberg's hygiene factors are conceptually similar to Maslow's physiological,

Figure 7–5
Herzberg's Motivation–Hygiene Theory

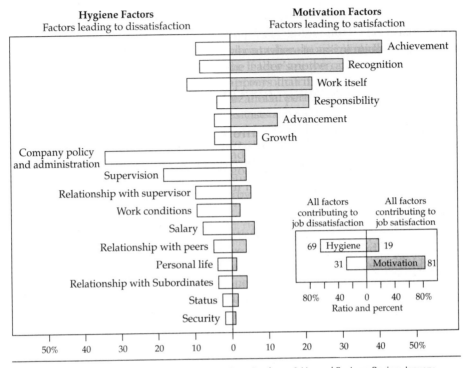

Source: F. Herzberg, One More Time: How Do You Motivate Employees? *Harvard Business Review*, January–February 1968, © Fellows of Harvard College; all right reserved.

safety, and social needs, and the motivation factors approximate Maslow's esteem and self-actualization needs. Maslow's Hierarchy of Needs theory has been interpreted by many to imply that once a need is satisfied, it is no longer an important consideration. Herzberg clearly notes that both hygiene and motivational needs must be considered constantly by the police manager if a high degree of motivation is to be maintained.

McClelland's Achievement, Power, and Affiliation Motive Theory

McClelland (1964), another humanistic theorist, believed that individual needs were acquired over time and as a result of experience. He identified three motives or needs that are important to an individual within an organizational environment:

1. *Need for achievement*—the need to succeed or excel. Some individuals must have standards or benchmarks to separate success from failure, and they have an internal force (motivation) that drives them toward accomplishment.

2. *Need for power*—the need to exert control over one's environment. Some individuals have an internal desire to make decisions and ensure that others abide by those decisions.
3. *Need for affiliation*—the need to establish and maintain friendly and close interpersonal relationships (social need).

Individuals who have a compelling drive to succeed are more interested in personal achievement than the rewards for their success. Such people have a desire to do things better; they seek situations where they can attain greater personal responsibility; they quickly volunteer for complex, challenging assignments. As they work through an assignment they must have immediate and continuing feedback on their performance. If not carefully monitored and controlled, such individuals may develop into the "working personality" known as the workaholic.

McClelland notes that power and affiliation needs are closely related to managerial success (see Chapter 5). Successful managers have a greater need for power and a lower need for affiliation. This type of individual is willing to take charge of a situation and act without undue regard for the social implications of decisions. However, if the need for power overshadows the affiliation need, managers may become Machiavellian, concentrating on their own success rather than the organization or its personnel.

McClelland's theory has implications for police management. The administrator should identify the high achievers and place them in positions where their attributes would best meet the department's needs. Some positions call for affiliation-oriented people while others require achievers. When there is a crisis situation, a problem area within the department, or a new program is being developed and implemented, the administrator should ensure that planning and operations are handled by a high achiever. This internally motivated individual will take charge and work single-mindedly to ensure that the assignment is completed successfully.

Some might argue that McClelland's theory overemphasizes authoritarian police management practices by emphasizing the need for task-oriented managers as opposed to managers who are concerned with how their subordinates feel about them. To the contrary, task-oriented managers are not necessarily authoritarian. Authoritarian leaders often are more concerned with form than substance. That is, they frequently are caught up in making decisions and imposing their rules in an exercise of power while they give little regard to the task at hand. Said somewhat differently, they tightly control activity to the neglect of results. These managers often are no more successful in attaining organizational goals than commanders who are overly concerned with how well they are accepted by their subordinates. McClelland's successful manager is also an achiever who is goal-directed and will do what is necessary to accomplish a given task. In most instances the achievement of goals is impossible without high motivation within the work group. Therefore, the high achiever must maximize the resources of subordinates in order to be effective; this necessitates not only keeping an eye on unit achievement, but also looking after the higher-order needs of others within the work group.

Summary of Humanistic Theories

The content theorists attempt to explain behavior in terms of internal drives. Interestingly, the humanistic theorists raise a number of questions. For example, how many needs are there? How many must be satisfied? Is there a hierarchy of needs? Which needs are most important? Are needs consistent across occupations? and How can managers satisfy needs? It is no simple matter to apply humanistic need theories. The administrator must, according to these theorists, provide avenues whereby subordinates can achieve their internal needs. Such a move would require better selection procedures for unit assignments, the opportunity for officers to have input into decision making, and a work climate where officers' pay and benefits are at least adequate.

BEHAVIORAL THEORIES OF MOTIVATION

Behavioral motivational theories are also considered process theories since these theories are founded on the law of effect and involve a process of motivation. This law does not attempt to differentially explain behavior but only to provide a probability estimate of an observable relationship. It states, "Rewarding behavior increases the probability it [the behavior] will be repeated, and punishing behavior decreases the probability it [the behavior] will be repeated" (Likert, 1967:12). In essence, people learn behavior as a result of past experience. If someone performs a specific task and is rewarded for it, it is highly probable that the individual will repeat the task.

Whereas the content theorists attempt to explain behavior (motivation) in terms of instincts (needs), the behavioral theorists attempt to explain motivation in terms of learned behavior. The content theorists perceive motivation as being a product of early socialization, whereas the behavioral theorists see motivation as a product of the immediate environment. Many behavioral theorists totally discount the importance of instincts or drives. Expectations are based on people's past learning experiences in terms of rewards and punishments. Skinner (1971) noted that people who do not learn are not motivated, and people who are not motivated do not learn; that is, people who lack motivation did not learn to be motivated. Thus it appears that the behavioral theorists view motivation as something that can be formed by management and management practices.

Adams's Equity Theory

Adams attempted to explain behavior in terms of perceived inequity as follows:

> Evidence suggests that equity is not merely a matter of getting "a fair day's pay for a fair day's work," nor is inequity simply a matter of being underpaid. The fairness of an exchange between employee and employer is not usually perceived

Figure 7–6
Equity theory applied.

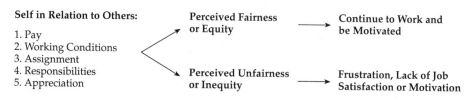

by the former purely and simply as an economic matter. There is an element of relative justice involved that supervenes economics and underlies perceptions of equity or inequity (1963:422).

In other words, as shown in Figure 7–6, a person's perceptions of equity are based on that person's effort (productivity) and rewards (salaries, benefits, etc.) in relation to others' efforts and rewards. Police officers may not be as concerned with their salaries as they are concerned with how much they make in relation to their peers, subordinates, and superiors.

Inequity can exist in several ways. An officer assigned to patrol may perceive inequity when comparing his or her work status, duties, and tasks to another officer who is assigned to community relations. The inequity here would consist of the working conditions and the perceived value of the job done. Another inequitable situation may exist when officers compare their job status with the status of their superiors. For example, a patrol officer may view the patrol captain as not being productive or having any real responsibilities. The officer may believe the captain spends too much time at headquarters, seldom venturing into the field; thus the officer may perceive the captain's contribution to the organization as less important than the subordinate officers' contributions. The officer may become cynical due to the perceived inequities of pay and productivity of the captain in relation to the officer's situation.

Several possible causes of inequity exist within any police department: how specialized assignments are made, how days off are assigned, the quantity and quality of work among officers in a given rank, and the outcomes of various intradepartmental conflicts. An officer may attempt to compensate in those areas where inequity is perceived. That is, officers may decrease their output or effort to achieve a balance of work and compensation in relation to others. On the other hand, officers may increase their efforts in order to receive some of the rewards that other officers are receiving, although this adjustment disappears if the desired reward is not forthcoming.

The police manager must realize that real and perceived inequity play an important role in the motivation process. Individual officers' morale is frequently affected where real or perceived inequity exists. There are three general ways by which a manager can attempt to decrease the effects of perceived inequity within the police agency.

First and foremost, the manager should ensure that no real inequitable work situations exist. Some individuals in the rank structure may have fewer assignments and responsibilities than others. Such a situation could be due to personnel shortages, work patterns shifting among individuals and units over time, or superiors delegating an increasing amount of their work to subordinates. The police administrator must periodically examine these work and task patterns to ensure that work is distributed equally. If the department has job descriptions, policies, and procedures outlining the responsibilities of various personnel and units, the administrator will be able to maintain closer control over organizational activities. However, such prescriptive mechanisms should be used with caution since they limit the subtlety of management and employee discretion that are necessary in effective police organizations.

A second manner by which to reduce perceived inequity is through a sound program of job rotation. A great deal of the perceived inequity within a police agency comes from the members of one unit not understanding the activities of other units. For example, patrol officers often criticize detectives for doing too little work and for stealing patrol officers' cases. The fact that many patrol officers do not understand the duties of detectives and the interworkings of the investigative unit may be the cause of this criticism and perceived inequity. At some point in officers' careers, they should be assigned to every operational and staff unit in the police department. This would help officers develop a clear understanding of the role and activities of each unit and should help resolve potential misunderstandings and conflicts.

A third way to reduce (perceived) inequity is through supervision. The supervisor is responsible for identifying officers with motivation problems and deriving solutions to those problems. Inequity or perceived inequity is a dominant factor in many motivational problems since officers tend to examine their own well-being, benefits, and quality and quantity of assignments in relation to their fellow officers. The supervisor must possess a good understanding of counseling theory and skills as he or she sits down with an officer and discusses the officer's problems. The success of the supervisor depends largely on how well he or she can assist the officer in putting the problem in proper perspective. The supervisor must assist the officer to recognize the activities and contributions of others if the officer is to overcome the feelings of inequity. Since the problem often is primarily one of perception rather than reality, it is imperative that the officer be led to this understanding rather than merely being told how things are. Good supervision is a key to good motivation.

Expectancy Theory

Several expectancy theories have been developed. Perhaps the most popular ones are those by Vroom (1964) and Porter and Lawler (1968). Expectancy theory is similar to equity theory in that both theories consider motivation as a consequence of the work environment. Equity theory states that individuals examine their work and rewards relative to others, and if equity exists, officers

Figure 7–7
Expectancy theory.

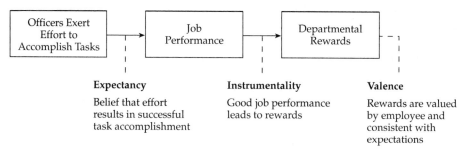

are motivated. Expectancy theory, on the other hand, postulates that individuals are motivated only when their reward is sufficient; the reward is sufficient when it is equal to or greater than the effort exerted by the individual. Both theories view motivation in terms that are, for the most part, extraneous to the individual—the leader and the management environment control the individual's motivation in equity and expectancy theory.

Expectancy theories identify three beliefs that workers have: expectancy, instrumentality, and valence. *Expectancy* is an individual's belief that effort will result in acceptable performance. This may not always be true. For example, a detective may spend numerous hours investigating a case but not be able to solve it. In this instance, the detective's work did not result in the desired outcome, and he or she may become frustrated and not motivated. Work then must also be instrumental. *Instrumentality* refers to workers' belief that their performance will be rewarded. When officers work hard and are productive, they have expectations as to what the department will do for them or how it treats them. Vroom (1964) argues that individuals decide to act based on the expected valences of outcome. The *valence of outcome* refers to the officer's perception that his or her productivity will result in a positive outcome or reward. A valence of outcome is positive when the officer perceives that the reward is equal to or greater than the amount of effort and productivity; this influences the officer toward action (motivation). A valence of outcome is negative when the reward does not meet the officer's expectation relative to the effort exerted; this leads to frustration and influences the officer toward inaction. In deciding whether to attempt a task and how much effort to exert, the officer will evaluate the anticipated reinforcement that will result from his or her action or inaction: Is the reinforcement worth the amount of effort exerted? Figure 7–7 shows how expectancy theory works.

At this point, it is worthwhile to mention Herzberg. A police manager usually is unable to motivate officers using hygiene rewards of salary, policies, or working conditions which are established as a result of civil service laws or governmental policies. This means that the manager must depend on motivational rewards such as praise, better or more challenging assignments, more responsibility, and additional training or developmental opportunities. The police manager must interact with subordinates and use his or her limited resources to ensure that there is a positive valence for each officer's efforts.

It is generally recognized that rewards are more effective as motivators than is punishment. Punishment has only a short-term impact on behavior, whereas rewards affect behavior for longer time periods. For expectancy theorists, the important consideration when using rewards is whether the reward matches the subordinate's effort. The reward must be strong enough to appear worthwhile in relation to the effort expended by the employee. Tasks requiring similar amounts of effort should receive relatively equal rewards (equity theory). For example, the reward of praise and recognition should be no greater for clearing a major case such as a homicide or rape than it is for clearing a burglary if the effort required to solve these cases is approximately the same, considering that generally it is more difficult to solve a burglary case than a homicide case. Typically, however, the clearance of a homicide or rape gets wide recognition while the equally challenging burglary clearance generally goes unnoticed. Supervisors must develop and provide rewards that approximate the officer's effort in all types of cases that are considered important in achieving the organization's goals. Otherwise, officers may be inclined to avoid or exert less effort in these less-rewarded cases such as larceny or burglary. Therefore, motivation can be lost or reduced by inadequate or unequal reward systems.

Behavior must be rewarded consistently. All too often police administrators are inconsistent with their rewards. For a reward to be effective and produce future desired results, it must be given consistently. If a supervisor rewards an officer by praising him or her for a good investigation, the officer will probably exert an equal or greater effort in future investigations. If the sergeant fails to praise future efforts, the officer may view them as no longer important to the superior and when later assigned such tasks will tend to expend less time and energy on them. Thus an officer's motivation is dependent on the superiors' abilities to motivate in a consistent manner.

A COMPREHENSIVE THEORY OF MOTIVATION

The two types of motivational theory that have been discussed to this point— humanistic and behavioral—are limited in scope. Each fails to recognize the strengths of the other. This section brings these together with other notions to develop a more comprehensive and complex approach to motivation.

There are three general sources of motivation: the individual, the organization, and their interaction. A comprehensive theory of motivation considers each of these motivational sources and their relationship to behavior. The following four points set forth a comprehensive theory of motivation:

1. An individual's level of motivation is determined by a combination
    of forces in the individual, the work environment, and the leader.
    Various assignments such as patrol, criminal investigation, juvenile,
    crime prevention, and internal affairs provide individuals with different

motivational opportunities. Leadership behavior bonds the individual and the work environment. The leader can inhibit or increase motivation and productivity.

2. Individuals make decisions (choices) about their behavior. Individuals exert a great deal of control over their own productivity. Formal or informal minimum production standards should be established. Most officers are aware of the minimum amount of work they must accomplish without getting into trouble with their superiors. When officers are not motivated they tend to produce at this minimum level. However, if officers can be motivated, there is a high probability that productivity will subsequently exceed this minimum level.

3. Individuals have different needs, desires, or goals. This point was made by the content and process theorists. If managers understand the needs of individuals under their command, the proper leadership style and reward structure can be developed to enhance productivity.

4. Individuals decide to be productive based on their expectation that they will be rewarded appropriately. If a reward does not fit an individual's particular need, it will not be effective. Moreover, the reward must be equal to the effort exerted and rewards must be distributed equitably with respect to individual tasks and employees. In essence, officers' choices are guided by the departmental reward system.

The content and process theorists made important points in terms of how to motivate police officers, but viewed alone any one of those theories is too simplistic to explain motivation. Too often commanders and supervisors view motivation in simplistic terms. This is a major error because motivation is an extremely complex managerial process. All attributes of the process must be considered if subordinates are to be motivated. To this end, one cannot concentrate on one theory or one type of theory. Supervisors must incorporate the complete range of motivational theories into their management style if they are to be successful. The comprehensive theory of motivation provides a basis for this to occur.

Thus far, motivation has been discussed. The police department cannot maximize its productivity potential unless officers are motivated. An officer's motivation is, to a great extent, dependent on a number of factors. One of the most important factors is organizational context in which behavior occurs. A key element of this organizational context is the group. The group is the microsetting in which people work, and it has a significant affect on individual behavior. The following section examines the work group.

THE DYNAMICS OF GROUP BEHAVIOR

A *group* is a collection of people who interact with each other, have a stable pattern of relations, share goals, and perceive of themselves as related (Forsyth, 1983). Individual behavior cannot be understood without examining the behavior within the context of the group. Few people are not influenced by the dynamics of a group. To avoid the influence of groups, one must not belong to groups. This is a virtual impossibility in our society. Groups are inevitable, and they touch everyone. Groups can have both positive and negative consequences on the individual. Groups develop a collective personality and affect behavior. For these reasons, it is of vital importance for police managers to understand groups and learn to work with them.

Essentially, two broad types of group exist: formal groups and informal groups. *Formal groups* typically are the organizational units within an organization. They are created by the organization, usually through specialization, to achieve objectives. Examples of formal units in a police department are the juvenile unit, third patrol shift, crimes against persons investigative unit, and crime prevention unit. Each of these is a task group. *Task groups* are groups that have the responsibility for specific tasks or line activities. *Command groups*, on the other hand, include supervisors and managers as well as line employees. A command group can consist of a task group and its sergeants and lieutenants. Other formal groups include *committees* such as quality circles or task forces that are created to address specific problems or issues. Committees may be permanent or temporary in nature.

Informal groups are those groups that are formed as a result of social interaction. Examples of informal groups are bowling teams, church groups, membership in clubs, and neighborhood groups. Informal work groups tend to form in and around formal groups. Numerous informal groups exist in police departments. A patrol shift may have several informal groups as members with common interests socialize into groups. Unlike formal groups, informal groups are not created deliberately but tend to evolve naturally.

When groups form they go through a four-stage development process (Donnelly, Gibson, and Ivancevich, 1995). The first stage is *mutual acceptance*. When groups are initially formed, members are somewhat distrustful or uneasy about their companions. This uneasiness causes members to seek to engage others, and eventually a mutual bond is developed. The second phase is *decision making*. Here members learn to trust the judgment of other members of the group. For example, younger patrol officers often seek the advice of experienced patrol officers and generally place greater value in their opinions than in the opinions of their sergeant or lieutenant. The third phase is *motivation*. Once group members come to trust each other, they find that cooperation generally reaps greater rewards than dissension. They learn to work together toward common objectives. The final stage of group formation is *control*. Upon achieving trust and cooperation, the group begins to establish norms or rules. Such norms generally are based on past experiences or explicit directives by superiors or informal group leaders. The group then uses informal sanctions to enforce its norms. For example, if a young officer writes more citations than the other members of the group, the officer is advised that it makes the others look bad. If the behavior continues, the group may shun or ostracize the overzealous officer. This developmental process occurs in both formal and informal groups.

Members of the group, as well as the group itself, assume a variety of work and social roles. Role ambiguity sometimes occurs as the group attempts to sort through information and determine its role within the organization. *Role ambiguity* is the confusion people have about their roles when they do not have definite information about what is expected of them. Here, members of the work group have a *perceived role,* or their understanding of what the organization expects of them. There is a *sent role,* which is information passed on to the group by supervisors and administrators about performance expectations. Finally, there is the *enacted role,* which consists of what people actually do. If there are good communications and agreement between the group and supervisors, the perceived role, sent role, and enacted role will all be the same.

Role ambiguity in policing can be seen in community policing. Many police departments have implemented community policing, but there is little consistency in its application. This has resulted in ambiguous sent roles. Greene, Bergman, and McLaughlin (1994) noted that there has been a great deal of resistance to community policing by line officers, and a good deal of the resistance is the result of officers' being unsure of what is expected of them. Police managers must ensure that individual officers and work groups have a clear mandate in terms of organizational expectations.

Group cohesiveness is an important part of the group process. *Group cohesiveness* is the degree to which group members remain together. Highly cohesive groups tend to cooperate more within the group, have better participation in group work activities, and are absent from their jobs less (Cartwright, 1968). It appears that the primary factor determining cohesiveness is the size of the group (Van Fleet and Peterson, 1994). As groups become larger, they become less cohesive. Larger groups are more difficult to coordinate, and their larger size allows for numerous smaller competing groups to form. This fact should guide police administrators as they create work groups. Work groups should be small enough to maintain their focus on goals and objectives.

When work groups achieve cohesiveness, they work as a team. Katzenback and Smith (1993) defined a *team* as "a group whose members have complementary skills and are committed to a common purpose or set of performance goals for which they hold themselves mutually accountable." This definition demonstrates the importance for supervisors to ensure that group cohesiveness and team spirit be maintained. When the group works as a team, it will be most productive.

Along these lines, Stoner and Freeman (1992) identified four ways to keep teams focused. First, managers can introduce competition. Police managers often attempt to motivate their subordinates through competition. This competition may be in the form of comparing their unit's numbers of citations or arrests with those of other units. The manager attempts to strive toward some goal by beating another similar unit in the department. Second, managers increase what Stoner and Freeman call "interpersonal attraction." Here, managers attempt to increase the relative prestige of the unit. Any police department has a small number of units that many police officers desire to join. In some cases, this desire is the result of the nature of the unit's objectives such as narcotics or criminal investigation, but in other cases the desire is the result of officers knowing that the officers assigned to the unit are professional, friendly, and accommodating. Units will become more cohesive as their prestige in the department increases. Third, managers can increase the level of interaction within the group. Supervisors can increase camaraderie by working closely with subordinates and increasing communications with them. Superiors should meet periodically with units and discuss unit activities and the department as a whole. Police officers like to be in the loop. Finally, managers "establish common goals and clearly understood and defined roles" for the team and its members. When officers have a shared vision about their jobs, they tend to be much more productive.

Contingency leadership dictates that the leader consider the individual, the situation, and the work to be completed when deciding on how to lead in a given situation. The nature of the work group certainly is a key factor in decision making and contingency leadership. The leader must employ techniques that complement the group as well as the individual. Specifically, the leader should work to ensure group cohesiveness and ensure that work objectives are defined for and accepted by the members of the group.

CULTURE AND POLICE WORK

Schein defined *culture* as "the pattern of basic assumptions that a given group has invented, discovered, or developed in learning to cope with its problems of external adaptation and internal integration" (1985:9). Cultures emerge as a result of people's efforts to manage uncertainty or to thwart chaos. Culture provides meaning and order to everyday life. Culture is a social system which provides its members with information about what is right and wrong, and it provides its people with a set of collective goals. Cultures exist at various levels within our society, including within organizations (Trice and Beyer, 1993).

Schein (1985) advises that organizations have two levels of culture. First, there is the *observable culture.* This is what outsiders see when they observe a culture. It may consist of language, dress, and activities. Schein notes that the observable culture manifests itself through:

1. *Stories,* which are oral histories that dramatize incidents and members of the organization.
2. *Heroes,* whose accomplishments or exploits transcend time; their deeds are immortalized in stories and they serve as role models for current employees.
3. *Rites and rituals,* which are the formal and informal activities in the organization that celebrate members' accomplishments and serve to motivate members of the culture.
4. *Symbols,* which are the language and nonverbal expressions that communicate the important themes and features of the organization.

Underneath the observable culture is the core culture. The *core culture* comprises the values and underlying beliefs that guide behavior. The police have an observable culture: they wear uniforms, use a police language, and are engaged in a set of unique activities. Outside observers often readily comprehend the police observable culture. However, they often do not understand the core cultural values that underlie the observable culture.

The Police Culture

Most of the literature examining the police culture, belief systems, and values has pointed to a monolithic culture where members of a department share a common set of values (Ahern, 1972; Barker, 1999; Reiss, 1971). Perhaps the best way to understand the police culture is to examine police officers' worldview. A *worldview* is developed through the a socialization process and it represents the standard by which the police officers tend to view people and situations. In an anthropological examination of the Los Angeles Police Department, Barker found that officers' careers spanned five phases, which to a great extent are dictated by the police culture. Phase one, *hitting the streets* consists of an officer's first three years. This phase is divided into three stages. First, officers receive academy training, which acquaints them with the formal organization with its rules and procedures. Second, there is an initiation in which they are assigned to a watch and get a taste for policing. Third, they absorb the norms of the informal culture and learn the realities of police work.

The second phase, *hitting their stride,* is approximately a five-year period where they work, gain confidence, and learn the job in terms of both formal and informal norms. During this phase, officers also develop discontent with certain aspects of the job, which they find outside their "perceived roles." The third phase of an officer's career is *hitting the wall.* This phase lasts for roughly four years, and it is a period of stress and continued disillusionment. Officers are generally dissatisfied with their jobs. The fourth phase, *regrouping,* is a period where officers reevaluate their lives, begin to cope with their careers, and develop a strategy for retiring. Finally, officers go through a *deciding-to-retire* phase. Here officers ruminate endlessly over whether to retire. They weigh their options and ultimately leave the police department. Officers for the most part maintain a set of core values across the five phases of their careers.

To some extent, the police develop and maintain a worldview of us-versus-them across their careers (Gaines, Kappeler, and Vaughn, 1999; Skolnick, 1966). An underlying belief among the police, especially those in larger cities, is that the police are under siege, and they have little support from the public. They see themselves as standing alone in the war against crime and drugs.

This worldview is substantiated through a value system which promotes separation and protection from the public. Values central to the police worldview are bravery, danger, secrecy, solidarity, and isolation. Bravery is an important element in the police worldview because it sets officers apart from other citizens in our society. It is a source of importance within the culture. The danger associated

Officers have informed discussion after roll call.
Michael Newman/PhotoEdit

with police work also legitimizes the importance of the police, and it is used as a basis for isolationism. Secrecy and solidarity refer to how line police officers treat or view others. Officers sometimes have a "siege mentality" whereby they feel that police administrators, or "the brass," and citizens are out to get them. Officers protect themselves by refraining from giving up information, and they always support their fellow officers regardless of the nature of the situation.

This worldview is largely a product of the professional era of police management that permeated American law enforcement in the 1950s and 1960s. The quasi-military model of the period emphasized control of police discretion through close supervision and isolation of the police from the public as a means of reducing police corruption. Police officers were discouraged from getting close to citizens during this period. It was believed that if police officers became close to the citizens they policed, it would eventually lead to corruption.

This worldview is diametrically opposed to the precepts of policing today, especially community policing. Today, the police are encouraged to become involved, individually and collectively, with citizens and neighborhood groups. The police are attempting to build partnerships with citizens so that they can jointly solve community crime and disorder problems. Obviously, the professional era values that remain in many departments hinder this process. Police administrators must endeavor to change the values and culture so that community partnerships and helping relationships are valued.

The Competing Cultures in Policing

Reuss-Ianni (1983) conducted an observational study of the New York City Police Department (NYPD) that lasted more than 18 months. She concluded as a result of her study that the best way to characterize the culture, at least in the NYPD, was as two distinct cultures, a street-cop culture and a management-cop culture. The two cultures, are increasingly at odds, particularly regarding the implementation of departmental policies and procedures aimed at controlling officer discretion.

The street cops long for the "good old days of policing" where the police were respected and possessed almost total discretion on how to do the job. They see themselves as the "thin blue line" that protects citizens from the crime and drug elements. Since the police are in a no-win situation, they must sometimes resort to extralegal measures to deal with problems, as in the Rampart Division scandal in Los Angeles. When this occurs, they see management and society failing to support them. In Southerland and Reuss-Ianni's (1992) analogy the police see management moving from a family model to a factory model. Under the family model, managers and street cops have a singular view of the world and take care of each other. The newly installed factory model produces a bureaucratic relationship where officers are constantly being limited in and judged by their actions. It appears that management cops have grasped the idea of community policing or at least understand the politics of communities. The street cops, on the other hand, have failed to progress and attempt to retain a worldview that is no longer contemporary or constructive.

There also appear to be cultural divisions among police supervisors. Van Maanen (1989) studied supervisors in a large police department and found two cultures: the station house–sergeant culture and the street-sergeant culture. The station house sergeant focuses on quotas, ensures that paperwork is completed on time, and attempts to keep officers within the bounds of departmental policies and procedures. The station house sergeant is a bureaucrat who is distant and most comfortable behind a desk. He or she is loyal to the management cops who administer the department. The street sergeant, on the other hand, basically is a police officer with rank. Street sergeants try to be "one of the boys." They see themselves as more police officer than supervisor. They sometimes compete with line officers for arrests and become directly involved in working cases. Van Maanen notes that both types of supervisor are unpopular because the station house sergeant is seen as someone who follows the rules and gets officers in trouble, while the street sergeant is seen as someone who intrudes in officers' cases and frequently tries to steal their credit.

There are even cultural divisions among the police officers. Perhaps the most notable divisions occur around race and sex. Haarr (1997) conducted a study of cultural stratification among police officers in a police department. She found that officers tend to socialize and choose work partners based on race and sex. She found that white male officers tended to communicate and work primarily with other white male officers. African-American officers tended to form work groups among themselves but had higher levels of communications with other types of officers than did white males. Finally, female officers tended to confide in other female officers throughout the department, primarily because their numbers were so low. Haarr's study shows that integration in police work groups is far from complete, and, unfortunately, segregation and distancing are due to race and sex as opposed to some social or occupational factor.

A large measure of this stratification is the result of police work traditionally being viewed as "man's work." Many rank-and-file police officers see police work as being tough and dangerous and as an occupation that only men can perform adequately. The American policing culture attempts to preserve traditional Anglo-American, masculine values (Martin, 1990). Displays of masculinity, sexism, and aggression are seen as primary modes of operation, especially when officers deal with problems (Hale and Wyland, 1993). Kappeler, Sluder, and Alpert (1998) note that this culture is propagated largely through the selection process, whereby officers are selected according to white middle-class male standards.

The police culture is an important administrative consideration. It, to a great extent, dictates behavior. If a police leader is attempting to have subordinates do something at odds with the department's culture, the leader will very likely encounter considerable difficulty. In some cases, the leader must be able to change the organizational or group cultural values before progress toward goals can be made. This is done through leadership. For example, community policing emphasizes community empowerment and building partnerships with the community. These objectives are inconsistent with the traditional culture in many police departments. It may be necessary for the police leader to change the department's culture before endeavoring to work more closely with the community. Such situations call for transformational leadership; as discussed in the previous chapter. Regardless, culture has a substantial impact on leadership, and motivation and is a prime consideration to the police leader.

Summary

This chapter focused on the staff aspect of the police department while the previous chapter examined leadership. However, leadership and the effects of leader behavior are to a great extent influenced by the motivational levels of employees, the dynamics of departmental work groups, and the department's culture. Leadership cannot be discussed without also considering employee motivation and work group structure.

There are two types of motivational theories: content theories and behavioral theories. The content theories attempt to explain motivation through needs and values. That is, people have a variety of needs, and they will work to fulfill them. Leaders can motivate subordinates by providing them opportunities to fulfill or satisfy their needs. The primary content motivational theories are Maslow's Hierarchy of Needs, Herzberg's Motivation–Hygiene theory, and McClelland's achievement, power, and affiliation motives theory. The behavioral theories attempt to explain motivation as a result of the individual interacting with the work environment. Work must be instrumental in the worker receiving a reward, and the reward must be fair or equitable. Of course, the individual's personality is the mitigating factor in motivation. One's personality dictates how one interprets the many cues and stimuli in the work environment, and the leader must consider those being led and the situation in which leadership is being applied. The primary behavioral theories are Adams' equity theory and expectancy theory.

From a macro perspective, it must be remembered that the work group and organizational culture play an important role in motivation and goal accomplishment. The work group and organizational culture place parameters on behavior. In some instances, the organizational culture and informal group norms have more influence on officers' behavior than does the formal organization. Leadership and motivation represent a subset of the total work picture. Indeed, if leaders are to be effective, all of these factors must be considered and controlled.

Study Questions

1. What is the relationship between motivation and leadership in the police organization?

2. There are two types of motivational theory, content and behavioral. How do they compare with each other?

3. How does Herzberg's Motivation–Hygiene Theory differ from Maslow's Hierarchy of Needs? How do these theories explain police officer behavior?

4. How does expectancy motivational theory explain behavior, and how does it relate to the various contingency leadership theories discussed in Chapter 5?

5. How does community policing relate to the various theories of motivation?

6. There are formal and informal work groups in police organizations. How do they affect leadership and goal accomplishment?

7. Describe the work culture in police organizations. What types of culture exist in police departments?

8. What are the five phases of a police officer's career?

Net Resources

http://www.mpli.org/mpi/index.html Massachusetts Police Leadership Institute. An institute ran by the University of Massachusetts at Lowell and the Lowell Police Department.

http://www.police forum.org Police Executive Research Forum. An organization devoted to enhancing police management practices and operations.

http://www.theIacp.org The International Association of Chiefs of Police. Largest police executive organization in the world.

References

Adams, J. (1963) Toward an understanding of inequity. *Journal of Abnormal Psychology* 67(5):422–436.

Ahern, J. (1972) *Police in Trouble*. New York: Hawthorn Books.

Alderfer, C. (1972) *Existence, Relatedness and Growth: Human Needs in Organizational Settings*. New York: Free Press.

Barker, J. C. (1999). *Danger, Duty, and Disillusion: The Worldview of Los Angeles Police Officers*. Prospect Heights, IL: Waveland Press.

Cartwright, D. (1968). The nature of group cohesiveness. In D. Cartwright and A. Zander (eds.), *Group Dynamics: Research and Theory*. New York: Harper & Row, pp. 91–109.

Donnelly, J., Gibson, J., and Ivancevich, J. (1995). *Fundamentals of Management*. Chicago: Irwin.

Forsyth, D. L. (1983). *An Introduction to Group Dynamics*. Monterey, CA: Brooks/Cole.

Gaines, L., Kappeler, V., and Vaughn, J. (1999). *Policing in America*, 3rd ed. Cincinnati: Anderson Publishing.

Greenberg, J., and Baron, R. (1995). *Behavior in Organizations*. Englewood Cliffs, NJ: Prentice Hall.

Greene, J., Bergman, W., and McLaughlin, E. (1994). Implementing community policing: Cultural and structural change in police organizations. In D. P. Rosenbaum (ed.), *The Challenge of Community Policing*. Thousand Oaks, CA: Sage, pp. 92–109.

Haarr, R. N. (1997). Patterns of interaction in a police patrol bureau: Race and gender barriers to integration. *Justice Quarterly* 14(1):51–85.

Hale, D., and Wyland, S. (1993). Dragons and dinosaurs: The plight of patrol women. *Police Forum* 3:1–8.

Hersey, P. and Blanchard, K. (1988). *Management of Organizational Behavior: Utilizing Human Resources*, 5th ed. Englewood Cliffs, NJ: Prentice Hall.

Herzberg, F. (1968). One more time: How do you motivate employees? *Harvard Business Review*, January–February, pp. 27–35.

Kappeler, V., Sluder, R., and Alpert, G. (1998). *Forces of Deviance: Understanding the Dark Side of Policing*. Prospect Heights, IL: Waveland Press.

Katzenback, J. R., and Smith, D. K. (1993). The discipline of teams. *Harvard Business Review* 71(2):111–120.

Likert, R. (1967). *The Human Organization*. New York: McGraw-Hill.

Lundman, R. (1980). *Police and Policing: An Introduction*. New York: Holt, Rinehart and Winston.

McClelland, D. (1964). *The Achieving Society*. Princeton: Van Nostrand Reinhold.

Martin, S. (1990). *On the Move: The Status of Women in Policing*. Washington: The Police Foundation.

Maslow, A. (1943). A theory of human motivation. *Psychological Review* 50:370–396

Porter, L. W., and Lawler, E. E. (1968). *Management Attitudes and Performance.* Homewood, IL: Irwin.

Raelin, J. A. (1987). The 60's kids in the corporation: More than daydream believers. *Academy of Management Executive* 1(1):21–30.

Reiss, A. (1971). *The Police and the Public.* New Haven: Yale University Press.

Reiss, A. (1988). *Private Employment of Public Police.* Research in Brief. Washington: National Institute of Justice.

Reuss-Ianni, E. (1983). *Street Cops and Management Cops.* New Brunswick, NJ: Transaction Books.

Sayles, L., and Strauss, G. (1966). *Human Behavior in Organizations.* Englewood Cliffs, NJ: Prentice Hall.

Schein, E. H. (1985). *Organizational Culture and Leadership.* San Francisco: Jossey-Bass.

Schermerhorn, J., Hunt, J., and Osborn, R. (1994). *Managing Organizational Behavior,* 5th ed. New York: Wiley.

Skinner, B. F. (1971). *Beyond Freedom and Dignity.* New York: Knopf.

Skolnick, J. (1966) *Justice without Trial: Law Enforcement in a Democratic Society.* New York: Wiley.

Southerland, M., and Reuss-Ianni, E. (1992). Leadership and management. In G. Cordner and D. Hale (eds.), *What Works in Policing?* Cincinnati: Anderson Publishing, pp. 157–178.

Stoner, J., and Freeman, R. (1992). Management, 5th ed. Englewood Cliffs, NJ: Prentice Hall.

Trice, H. M., and Beyer, J. M. (1993). *The Cultures of Work Organizations.* Englewood Cliffs, NJ: Prentice Hall.

Van Fleet, D. D., and Peterson, T. O. (1994). *Contemporary Management,* 3rd ed. Boston: Houghton Miffin.

Van Maanen, J. (1978). Observations on the making of policemen. In P. Manning and J. Van Maanen (eds.), *Policing: A View from the Street.* Santa Monica, CA: Goodyear Publishing, pp. 292–308.

Van Maanen, J. (1989). Making rank: Becoming an American police sergeant: In R. G. Dunham and G. P. Alpert (eds.), *Critical Issues in Policing: Contemporary Readings.* pp. 146–151. Prospect Heights, IL: Waveland Press.

Vroom, V. (1964) *Work and Motivation.* New York: Wiley.

Witham D. (1985). *The American Law Enforcement Chief Executive; A Management Profile.* Washington, DC: Police Executive Research Forum.

8

Communication, Negotiation, and Conflict Resolution

Lionel JM Delevingne/Stock Boston

Chapter Outline

Introduction

Communication
Purposes of Communication
Symbols, Context, and Perception

Manners and Modes of Communication
Formal Communication
Informal Communication
Verbal Communication
Nonverbal Communication

The Communication Process

Barriers to Communication
Physical Barriers
Psychological Barriers
Other Barriers

Keys to Effective Communication

Communication Networks

Technological Advances in Communication

Conflict
Types of Conflict
Sources of Conflict
Types and Sources of Conflict Facing Police Administrators
Conflict Resolution Strategies
Alternative Conflict Resolution

Negotiation
Power
Time
Information
People Smartness
Planning
Implementing the Negotiation Process

Summary

Learning Objectives

After reading this chapter, you should be able to

1. Understand the importance of communication, negotiation, and conflict resolution from an administrative perspective.
2. State the purposes, manners, and modes of communication.

253

3. Explain the communication process.

4. List the many barriers to communication.

5. Understand what it takes to become an effective communicator.

6. Understand communication networks as well as technological advances in communication.

7. List the types and sources of conflict.

8. Know the methods for dealing with conflict.

9. Understand the negotiation process.

10. List several tools for effective negotiation.

P olice officers in the New York City Police Department have been classified as "street cops" and "management cops" (Reuss-Ianni, 1983). Street cops, the lowest-ranking officers, generally are patrol officers. Management cops, on the other hand, are those holding a rank of sergeant or higher—most often lieutenants, captains, and chiefs. It is frequently the case that street cops are critical of management cops. A typical sentiment heard among street cops is "We do *real* police work, putting bad guys in jail." Street cops view management cops as possessing a different set of goals and pursuing a different set of priorities; management cops are not viewed as of the same "brotherhood" as street cops (Barker, 1999). Invariably this rift that exists between street cops and management cops breeds conflict and communication problems. Accordingly, police administrators must develop the tools to address such problems. These tools are the focus of this chapter.

INTRODUCTION

Human relationships are vitally important to police organizations. Police supervisors and administrators must deal with peers, subordinates, and superiors to accomplish the goals related to their positions. Police officers are constantly involved with people in a variety of situations. Just about everything an officer does involves people. Police personnel must know how to communicate effectively and how to negotiate if they are to be productive. This chapter examines the interpersonal relations that people develop in the police setting. Three components are examined: communications, negotiations, and conflict resolution. This chapter essentially prepares the reader to be a more effective member of a police organization.

COMMUNICATION

Communication is the transmission or exchange of information between a sender and one or more receivers to reach a common understanding (O'Reilly and Pondy, 1979). One person cannot communicate alone, even when utilizing a written format. There must be a receiver to complete the act of communication. Communication does not occur until the message is received and read or heard, and its meaning is understood.

Purposes of Communication

The purpose of communication is to achieve understanding between two or more people. The sender may wish to express an opinion, idea, or attitude; the sender may wish to prompt action from the listener; or the sender may wish to provide support or further insight to actions that have been initiated by some other person, component of the organization, or external source.

Communication also serves to achieve departmental goals. Police administrators can increase efficiency through communication. This is done by learning about new technologies and procedures, implementing them in the organization, and communicating to subordinates how to use them. Communication also improves service quality. Administrators need to communicate to subordinates the importance of service quality and impart the tools necessary to achieve it. Good communication also improves responsiveness. This is especially true in law enforcement, where interactions between law enforcement officials and members of the public occur regularly. Finally, communication encourages innovation. Dissatisfaction with the status quo needs to be expressed to those in a position to call for change. Likewise, police managers need to communicate their intentions when new strategies are adopted.

Despite the many reasons for and advantages of communicating properly, careful attention needs to be given to a number of factors before the communication process begins. The following elements must be weighed when selecting the appropriate method for any given communication.

1. The purpose of the sender.
2. The organizational position, perceptions, nonverbal behavior, and listening skills of the sender and receiver or receivers.
3. The message to be sent.
4. The methods by which the message may be sent.
5. The possible interpretations of the message content by the receiver.
6. The action the sender wants the receiver to take in response to the communication.

Communication must be viewed as a process, and each element in the process must be considered if the communication is to be effective.

Symbols, Context, and Perception

All communication consists of symbols and context. *Symbols* are the words, gestures, and pictures that give meaning to another person. Consider the word "crime." By itself, the word "crime" has little meaning. However, the reality of crime lies in the meaning we attach to the word. *Context* gives more information about the symbol. It places "crime" in some framework that has specific meaning for an individual person. Context is the environment in which the symbol is used. In the context of a poor, urban, minority-dominated neighborhood, the term "crime" has a meaning different from its meaning in a corporate context. The former is generally viewed as serious, whereas the latter is usually viewed as less serious.

Similarly, the words "weapon" "police," "cruiser," and "gun" can have very different meanings for different people. If the context is not specified in the communication (this is particularly true of written communication), the context is left to the imagination of the receiver of the communication, and the receiver's experiences will serve to set the symbol in the context of familiarity. This is important in written reports and directives police leaders use to communicate departmental policy to police officers. It is also especially critical in police communications with the public, which may have an entirely different frame of reference.

Another way to understand the importance of symbols and context is in terms of perception. *Perception* is "the process through which people select, organize, and interpret sensory input to give meaning to their surroundings (Schiffmann, 1990). Personality, attitudes, values, prior experiences, and other factors all influence people's perceptions of certain phenomena. This inevitably affects the way people make sense of communication. In other words, symbols— the building blocks of communication—mean different things to different people. Effective communication acquires sufficient meaning only when the sender leaves as little to the receiver's imagination as possible.

The symbolic aspect of communication can also be understood in terms of *inferences*. Whenever symbols are interpreted on the basis of one's assumptions and not on the basis of fact that has been presented, an inference is made (Davis and Newstrom, 1985). If communication is to be effective, the context must not be left to the imagination and therefore to the inferences of the receiver.

Symbols and context are therefore an important part of communication, but the message must also be transmitted to a receiver. To accomplish the message transmission, one must first select a manner and mode of transmission. Several manners and modes exist. The following section presents a discussion of informal and formal communication; verbal and nonverbal communication; and spoken, written, and technological communication modes. These are different manners and modes of communication, and each has a bearing on the effectiveness of communication.

MANNERS AND MODES OF COMMUNICATION

There are several ways to describe and classify communication. This section covers two ways of classifying communication: formal versus informal communication and verbal versus nonverbal communication. Neither classification is necessarily independent of the other. For example, it is possible to communicate informally through verbal channels. Alternatively, it is possible to communicate formally through nonverbal channels.

Formal Communication

Formal communication is communication that occurs within the framework of the formal organization. The formal organization (chain of command) provides the communication channels for formal communication. These formal channels are designed by the organization, known by everyone in the organization, and illustrated by the organization chart. The lines connecting the positions indicate the formal channel of communications (see Figure 8–1). The vertical lines are the chain of command. It is through this chain of vertical communication that formal communication goes up and down the organization from the chief to the police officer.

Vertical communication is "communication that involves a message exchange between two or more levels of the organizational hierarchy" (Bartol and Martin, 1998:461). Two different types of vertical communication can be identified. These are downward communication and upward communication. *Downward communication* occurs when information flows from a higher level to one or more lower levels in the organization. Katz and Kahn (1966) observed that downward communication includes information from one of five categories: (1) job instructions; (2) job rationales; (3) procedures, practices, and policies; (4) feedback on individual performance; and (5) efforts to encourage a sense of mission and encourage dedication toward organizational goals. For example, when the chief signs a new departmental policy, it will be distributed "down" to all members of the department.

Upward communication occurs when information flows from lower levels to one or more higher levels in the organization. Seeger (1983) identified five types of information that flow upward through organizations: (1) reports of progress on projects; (2) reports of problems and situations requiring help from supervisors; (3) new developments within the work unit or organization; (4) suggestions for improvement; and (5) information about employee attitudes, morale, efficiency, and satisfaction.

Horizontal communication "is lateral or diagonal message exchange either within work-unit boundaries, involving peers who report to the same supervisor, or across work-unit boundaries, involving individuals who report to different supervisors" (Bartol and Martin, 1998:463). The horizontal lines in Figure 8–1 connect members in this chain and determine formally allowed communication among peers. For instance, the four sergeants under each shift commander can formally communicate among themselves but not with the sergeants serving under either of the other two shift commanders. Similarly, the seven police officers serving under a sergeant can formally communicate with each other but not with officers supervised by any other sergeant.

Research shows that administrators spend about one-third of their communication time in horizontal communication (Kiechel, 1991; Stech and Ratliffe, 1985). Horizontal communication usually falls into the following categories: (1) task coordination; (2) problem solving; (3) information sharing; (4) conflict resolution; and (5) peer support (Reich, 1987). According to Bartol and Martin,

Figure 8–1
Formal communication channels.

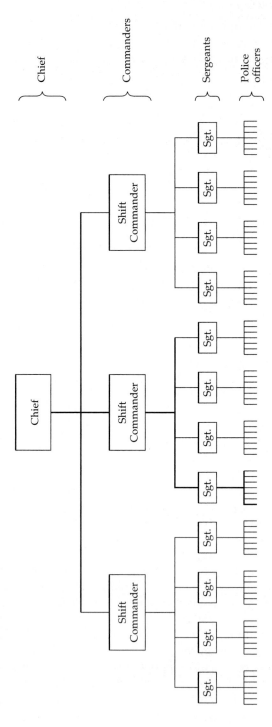

"Horizontal communication can take many forms, including meetings, reports, memos, telephone conversations, and face-to-face discussions between individuals" (1998:463).

Legitimate organizational modes of communication (such as memoranda, called meetings, and telephone conversations) are used to transmit messages along the formal lines of communication. However, only a small percentage of the total communication that occurs between organizational members is transmitted through the formal communication channel (Massie and Douglas, 1981). The remainder of communication occurs informally.

Informal Communication

Informal communication occurs within the framework of the informal organization. The informal organization exists to fill the gaps left by the formal structure. Massie and Douglas characterize informal communication channels as "emergent": they "arise to fill needs not met by the formal channels" (1981:353). Informal communication channels are used and recognized by those who need them. It is not necessarily true that all managers or employees use informal channels. Such channels exist in every organization, so managers are aware of their existence. However, management is seldom privy to the content of information that flows through informal channels. Informal communications channels constantly develop and change, and they are used by a variety of organizational participants when the need arises. They are developed to transmit sensitive or personal information. The messages carried by the informal system of communication are usually oral, rarely written.

Informal communication is used regularly in policing. For example, when an officer investigating a case believes another officer may have some helpful information, the investigating officer typically bypasses the chain of command (formal communication channel) and contacts the officer directly to ask for assistance. The formal channel is considered too burdensome and often results in responses that are too late to be of use in the investigation.

The "grapevine" or "rumor mill" is one of the most frustrating forms of informal communication to managers. It emerges spontaneously to disseminate information throughout the organization. The items carried by the grapevine are random. They appear to be whatever sounds interesting to those sending the information. Sometimes the information is factual. Other times the information is partially factual and partially fabricated. Most frustrating for the manager are the occasions in which the information is merely created to provide what others want to hear (rumors). The grapevine can be positive when the information transmitted is relevant or needed. Nevertheless, officers will typically be upset to some degree because such information should have been disseminated through formal communication channels; they should not have had to hear it through the grapevine. Low morale is frequently attributable to the rumors circulating in the police department.

On the Job

Riverside, California, Police Department
Communication, Negotiation, and Conflict Resolution

By Chief Russ Leach

Courtesy of Chief Leach

Effective communications begin with personal credibility. The value of virtually any form of human communication, verbal or nonverbal, oral or written, is measured by the willingness of the listener to understand and believe the message. Personal integrity gives rise to credibility, the cornerstone of effective communications. Effective communicators first build rapport and confidence by demonstrating that they are trustworthy. Bridging the credibility gap therefore requires that the listener know something about you, that what the listener knows inspire trust, and that the rapport that results stimulate the listener to believe in what is being promoted.

Modern police methods encourage officers and managers to engage in consensus building and problem solving. Most police agencies embrace the philosophy of community partnerships and understand that these partnerships are strengthened by open and candid communications between the public and its officers. The agency responsibility, therefore, extends to each of its members, requiring that everyone be skilled as an effective listener and a truthful spokesperson. Police agencies concurrently understand that effective community partnerships cannot form without a demonstration of personal credibility and integrity. The success of community policing philosophy depends on personal relationships formed between community members and officers. To complete this process, police agencies are strictly accountable for courteous, respectful, and consistent treatment of others. We earn the trust of one another and our community by holding ourselves accountable to our principles and our commitments.

In the public sector, validation of core values is institutionalized more by repetition than any other method. Opportunities to persuade are afforded in many venues—public relations, recruitment, promotion, community meetings, training, campaigns, policy, and procedure. Imaginative and recurring statements of mission, purpose, and anticipated outcomes by leaders tend to reinforce the ideal of a shared vision by all.

Finally, listeners respond to persons or organizations based on what

Continued

they know about them. If they have little background information, they tend to formulate a response based on their own knowledge and value sets, often leading to misperception and miscommunication. It is the skillful communicator, therefore, who provides a sense of history and familiarity in the message he or she promotes.

I feel that a Native American proverb translates this idea best: "What you do means so much more than what you say, that what you say doesn't matter anyway."

Verbal Communication

Verbal communication has been defined as the "written or oral use of words to communicate" (Bartol and Martin, 1998:446). Each form of verbal communication is found throughout police organizations.

Oral Communication

Oral communication is speech. Oral communication can occur face-to-face with one person or with a group of people. Face-to-face communication may be with employers, employees, peers, or with persons external to the organization. Committees are one form of oral group communication. Roll call or after-shift briefings are a form of group oral communication often used in police organizations.

Oral face-to-face communication is generally thought to be the most effective of the modes of communicating. Hitt, Middlemist, and Mathis explain its effectiveness. In face-to-face communication,

> nonverbal messages can be used to convey additional important information. It also provides immediate feedback and the chance to clarify any misunderstandings. But there is no permanent record of the message, so much of it may be forgotten. If the same message must be conveyed to many others, the other receivers are unlikely to get the same message because there is no permanent record (1979:321–322).

Oral communication can also occur from a distance through the use of various technological means of transmission. The telephone is the most frequently used means for distant oral communication in most organizations. Suggestions concerning the use of the telephone for communication are presented in the section on negotiation. The most frequently used means of distant oral communication in a police department is the radio. The same concerns regarding the transmission and understanding of the received message that are true for telephone conversations apply to radio communications. Essentially, even though they are two-way communications, they are so limited in the amount of time one can communicate that they effectively serve as one-way communications.

Oral communication can also be transmitted by videotape or television. These are very useful tools in combating the grapevine or rumor mill in organizations. The chief of police tapes messages to be played at roll call or presents information live by closed-circuit television. Satellite telecommunications are also being used to train officers by teleconferencing (interactive televised conferences).

Written Communications

Written communication is another form of verbal communication that occurs from a distance. Written messages—memoranda, standard operation procedures, training bulletins, letters—provide a permanent record of the message and ensure that every receiver gets the same message. However, there is no guarantee that everyone will interpret the message accurately. Written communication does not allow feedback or nonverbal clarification. It is critical that the writer provide as much detail as possible to reduce the interpretation flaws resulting from perceptual differences between the sender and those who receive the communication.

Written messages, until recently, were generally transmitted through some form of mail process, either an internal mail system or the federal postal system. Currently, computerized telecommunication, especially e-mail, offers the technological means to transmit written messages and receive immediate feedback. With e-mail and other electronic modes of written communication, two people can type in information that is displayed on the other person's computer screen. The two can continue to ask each other questions and give responses until they are satisfied that they understand each other. This information can then be captured in a word processing file for review at a later time. Such a mechanism has potential for utilization between administrators and managers within a police organization, particularly for those agencies with decentralized district or precinct stations. Many departments now have mobile digital computer terminals in their police cars. Dispatchers send calls and information such as driver's license checks or checks for warrants via the terminals. Many departments have installed these terminals because radio waves could not handle the volume of traffic.

Another fairly recent innovation in written messages is the advent of the electronic bulletin board, where messages can be left for retrieval at a later time by another party using a computer. Here officers would periodically access terminals for information updates. Crime information or activities for a department's patrol beats could be posted, and officers would periodically retrieve the information. The bulletin board is not used to dispatch calls or transmit emergency information.

Nonverbal Communication

Nonverbal communication refers to behaviors such as the inflection of the voice, emphasis given to words, gestures, behavior, or expressions of the body that impart information to a receiver. In other words, nonverbal communication is "communication by means of elements and behaviors that are not coded into words" (Bartol and Martin, 1998:446). Often, nonverbal communication is unintentional on the part of the sender. Nonetheless, the nonverbal cues "indicate the communicator's emotions (e.g., anger, fear, joy)" (Hitt, Middlemist, and Mathis, 1979:320). Also, nonverbal communication is an inadvertent part of face-to-face communications.

Nonverbal communication, relative to verbal communication, is the most common form of communication. Research estimates that between 65 and 93 percent of what is communicated is nonverbal in nature (Birdwhistell, 1970; Mehrabian, 1972). Important categories of nonverbal behavior include kinesics, proxemics, paralanguage, and object language.

Kinesics, the academic study of "body language," refers to gestures, facial configurations, and other body movements. This field of study has generated some interesting applications in policing for interviewing and interrogation. Detectives often observe the body movements of suspects for clues to the veracity of their statements. Body language, as it is generally labeled, adds to and complicates other nonverbal and verbal communication (Robbins, 1979).

Proxemics concerns the influence of proximity and space on communication. For example, if a police administrator makes a habit of standing versus sitting in a particular setting, this can have a bearing on the effectiveness of communication. Proxemics also relates to comfort zones and personal space; people who are "close talkers" can sometimes intimidate the person they are intent on sending a message to, whereas the communication sent by someone who maintains a distance will probably be received differently.

Paralanguage has to do with the vocal aspects of communication. This includes the volume and tone of language. People who talk loudly are more likely to be heard. As a result, their communications are more capable of being understood by the recipient of the message. Inflections and emphasis on certain words often provide valuable information about the message.

Object language, according to Bartol and Martin (1998:447), "is the communicative use of material things, including clothing, cosmetics, furniture, and architecture." In other words, objects can be used to communicate things about you. This communication usually occurs in conjunction with other modes of nonverbal communication. People often consider the dress or appearance of the person communicating when they weigh the importance of the message communicated. A police officer will likely give a well-dressed citizen more credence than a homeless complainant.

The manner and mode of communication are critical to the success of any effort to communicate. However, to effectively transmit the message, it is also important to understand the process that occurs in communication.

THE COMMUNICATION PROCESS

Simple communication consists of three steps: (1) a sender transmits (2) the message to (3) a receiver. The actual communication process is much more complicated, however. The following figures and discussion are designed to present many of the specifics. Figure 8–2 offers an overview of the process.

Figure 8–2
The communication process.

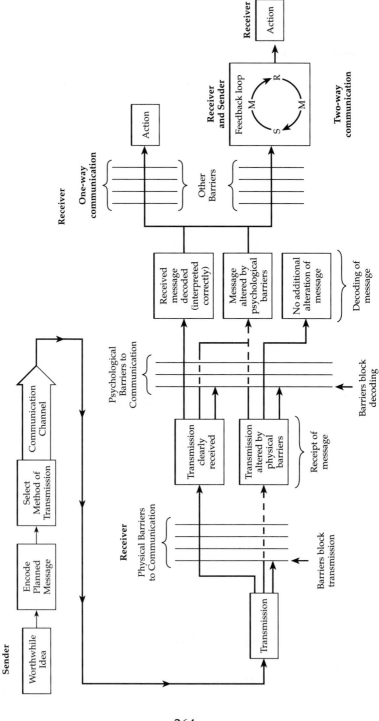

Communication begins with the development of a worthwhile idea the sender wishes to transmit to the receiver. The sender must then transform this idea into a planned message. This step is accomplished by *encoding,* or determining suitable words, pictures, tables, or charts for use in transmitting the idea to the receiver. The sender then selects the method for transmitting the encoded planned message. The message is then transmitted. For example, a supervisor who needs to talk with an officer about being late to work has a message to transmit, that is, the officer has been late to work and the supervisor wants the behavior to stop. The idea is there, but the message might be ineffective. The supervisor must develop a planned message that will result in the appropriate response by the officer. A supervisor who is concerned with getting the organizational purposes accomplished and maintaining a good relationship with the employee will probably decide to begin by asking the officer why he or she has been late. The supervisor will then proceed on that basis to inform the officer why it is important to be on time.

The next consideration in the communication process is the physical barriers that intervene to interfere with the successful accomplishment of communication. These physical barriers to communication are detailed in a later section. If the physical barriers are not strong enough to block the communication, a message will be received. Receipt of the message does not guarantee understanding. There is the possibility that a physical barrier may have caused the message to be distorted or words to be incorrectly transmitted. Receipt of messages depends on the perceptual and attentive skills of the receiver (i.e., listening, hearing, seeing, and feeling). The receiver, as well as the sender, must strive to ensure that communications are received accurately.

On receipt of the message, the receiver *decodes* or *interprets,* the message. It is at this point that the psychological barriers to communication may intervene. Psychological barriers include receiver conditions that inhibit the accurate receiving and decoding of messages. For example, an officer may previously have had negative experiences with a sergeant, and these experiences can serve as a psychological barrier to effective communications. Psychological barriers and the receiver's perception (acceptance or nonacceptance) of the information being transmitted play an important role in the efficacy of the decoding process.

Communication can be one-way or two-way. One- and two-way communication processes become different once decoding occurs. One-way communication proceeds to action, whereas two-way communication proceeds to feedback before taking action. Whenever feedback results from communication, the process is categorized as two-way. *Feedback* is the provision of questions requiring clarification or statements from which the sender can determine whether the communication has been received and interpreted in the manner the sender intended. If a commander gives several subordinates an order, then the commander has initiated a one-way communication. Conversely, when a supervisor asks questions or requests input from officers, a two-way communication is initiated.

The feedback loop, also known as the communication loop, is generally present in two-way communication. It is a back-and-forth pattern in which the speaker sends a message and the receiver generates a response to the speaker so that the speaker can adjust the next message to fit the previous response. This process allows for better understanding by both parties. It also allows the adjustment of the message to fit the understanding of the receiver.

Action is the last step of the communication process. This step is the utilization of the information or message received. The effectiveness of the communication can be evaluated by the action taken as a result of the message. If the communication is successful, the subsequent action will meet the goal or objective (intent) of the sender.

A useful tool in assessing the communication process is the Rule of Five. The *Rule of Five* refers to the set of five receiver steps in the communication process. The sender wants to ensure that the receiver accomplishes these five steps. If they are accomplished, the communication is judged successful. The five receiver steps are (1) receive, (2) understand, (3) accept, (4) use, and (5) give feedback to the sender. The Rule of Five is more likely to be successfully accomplished with two-way communication.

BARRIERS TO COMMUNICATION

There are several types of interference that may limit the receiver's understanding of the transmitted message. These obstacles are called *barriers to communication*. Barriers to communication may totally block a communication, filter part of it out, or give it incorrect meaning. There are two primary categories of barriers: physical and psychological.

Physical Barriers

The typical physical barriers that may come to mind are such things as distracting noises that drown out a vocal message. Other examples of physical barriers to communication are distances between the people communicating, walls, static interference with radio messages, and physical impairments of the individuals (e.g., speech impediments or hearing loss). Physical barriers distort the received message.

Another physical barrier that is often disregarded is communication overload. *Communication overload* occurs when people "receive more communication inputs than they can process or than they need" (Davis and Newstrom, 1985:453). Katz and Kahn describe Miller's categories of response to or results of information overload:

> Miller [classified information input overload] into the following seven categories: (1) omission, failing to process some of the information; (2) error, processing information incorrectly; (3) queuing, delaying during periods of peak load in the hope of catching up during lulls; (4) filtering, neglecting to process certain types of information, according to some scheme of priorities; (5) approximation, or cutting categories of discrimination (a blanket and nonprecise way of responding); (6) employing multiple channels, using parallel channels, as in decentralization; and (7) escaping from the task (1966:231).

Communication overload can result from receiving too much information at one time for it to be processed effectively. It can also result from the generation of too much information over a period of time, or from having to handle too many types of information in a short period of time. For example, managers often face communication overload due to the necessity for them to deal with many subordinates, peers, and the memos, letters, reports, telephone conversations, e-mail, and face-to-face interactions that are associated with management.

Psychological Barriers

Filtering is a process in which part of a message is omitted by either the sender or the receiver. Filtering, sometimes called omission, can be intentional or unintentional. When filtering is unintentional, it is usually the product of receivers hearing what they want to hear. People have biases, preconceived notions, or organizational needs, and there is a tendency for people to dismiss or omit information that is counter to these preestablished ideas. In other words, people do not like "bad" news. The sender as well as the receiver can be guilty of producing this barrier. For example, an officer may omit details or information when explaining a problem to his or her sergeant. Another example relates to the Drug Abuse Resistance Education program: There is ample data that substantiates the ineffectiveness of DARE programs, but if such information is communicated to a DARE officer, it is doubtful that he or she will listen or accept the information. As Massie and Douglas note, "If a manager is not careful, there may be a free flow of only those messages that contain little information" (1981:360).

Perceptual disorders also contribute to communication failure. Four common problems of perception that may act as barriers to communication are stereotyping, the halo effect, projection, and perceptual defense. These are explained by Hitt, Middlemist, and Mathis (1979) as follows:

1. *Stereotyping* is labeling an individual as belonging to a particular group and then attributing to that person all the characteristics one thinks are common to the group.
2. *Halo effect* is observing one or two characteristics of a person and then developing conclusions about other characteristics of that person without observing them.
3. *Projection* is taking one's feelings of guilt or failure and placing the blame on someone else.
4. *Perceptual defense* is not seeing, hearing, or perceiving anything that might disturb us. It is the act of protecting our mental image.

Such perceptual disorders can affect both the sender and the receiver of a message. These distortions can interfere greatly with interpersonal communication. Because both the sender and receiver have perceptions of each other, the potential for perceptual distortion is great.

Cognitive dissonance is another of the psychological barriers that can interfere with effective communication. Davis and Newstrom describe cognitive dissonance as

> the internal conflict and anxiety that occurs when people receive information incompatible with their value systems, prior decision, or other information they may have. Since people do not feel comfortable with dissonance, they try to remove or reduce it. Perhaps they will try to obtain new communication inputs, change their interpretation of the inputs, reverse their decision, or change their values. They may even refuse to believe the dissonant input, or they may rationalize it out of the way (1985:75).

Other Barriers

Barriers that fall into this category may affect the communication process as it reaches the point for action to be taken. *Timing* is one of these barriers and entails releasing information at the wrong time. Another barrier in this category is *routing,* or sending the message to the wrong person or group of people. *Semantic* barriers arise from the limitations of the symbols used to communicate. Symbols have a variety of meanings, and the parties to communication choose from among these many meanings. Misunderstandings or distortions of the message occur when the wrong meaning is selected. Feedback helps to overcome this barrier. *Experiential* barriers also limit the ability of one to effectively communicate. A receiver who has not experienced the event under consideration does not have a frame of reference to judge and evaluate the incoming information. Finally, *listening* is often a weak link in two-way communication, because many people do not actively work at listening well. "Listening is a conscious, positive act requiring will power. It is not a simple, passive exposure to sound" (Davis and Newstrom, 1985:437). As such, this is a crucial barrier to communication. Without effective listening, the message cannot be adequately processed.

KEYS TO EFFECTIVE COMMUNICATION

The barriers to effective communication have been presented. This section outlines some of the approaches that may be taken to overcome the barriers and achieve an effective level of communication.

Listening is perhaps the most critical of the communication activities. Listening should include active participation in the communication process. That is, the receiver should actively clarify points and seek additional information when necessary. Good listening entails the establishment and use of the feedback loop. Fairness, openness, and "straight talk" will reduce the incidence of distortion. Words should be selected with care to avoid emotionally loaded terms that will cause the receiver to jump to incorrect conclusions. This is particularly important when dealing with sensitive issues such as disciplinary actions, use-of-force investigations, or post-shooting investigations.

The sender can also do several things that will assist in breaking down the barriers to good communication. Simple, clear language and multiple channels (appealing to all five senses) will help to increase the accuracy and clarity of the message. Managers should also "repeat the message and reinforce words with action. Managers . . . [can also] use direct, short lines of communication and ensure that competent individuals (good communicators) are in communication centers" (Hitt, Middlemist, and Mathis, 1979:328).

Communication can be improved by using appropriate communication modes. Police administrators often depend solely on written communications to transmit information. Administrators and commanders must use multiple communication modes to effectively impart information. New communications technology provides excellent opportunities that never before were available.

Another matter for the attention of administrators and managers is understanding the forms of communications networks and how they operate. This is the topic of the next section.

COMMUNICATION NETWORKS

Communication networks have a dynamic influence on the nature of group communication. A *communication network* is the number and arrangement of the various communications channels that exist. They must be managed or they may generate misunderstanding and a reduction in organizational effectiveness through communications breakdowns, filtering, or the interjection of inaccurate information into the system. The network establishes the relationships between people and their relative power and leadership. Communication networks also have important effects on the emergence of informal group leaders. The effects depend on the type of network used. Hitt, Middlemist, and Mathis observed the following:

> Individuals who occupy central positions are likely to emerge as high-status members, or group leaders. This often happens even when they have characteristics that would normally prevent them from becoming informal group leaders . . .
>
> Many networks do not have central positions . . . these networks make it difficult for a leader to emerge, and this difficulty may cause conflict among group members who want to become central persons . . .
>
> Managers often use this knowledge when communicating with employees. Informal group leaders can facilitate communication if they receive the message first. But if another group member receives the message before the leader, competition between the leader and this member may result. The informal leader may purposely create misunderstanding to weaken the other member's position as a central person in the communication network (1979:325–327).

Figure 8–3 depicts the most notable forms of network. These are only a few of the networks that can exist. For simplicity, no more than four-person networks are shown. In reality, the number of persons in a network can be much larger.

Figure 8–3
Communication networks.

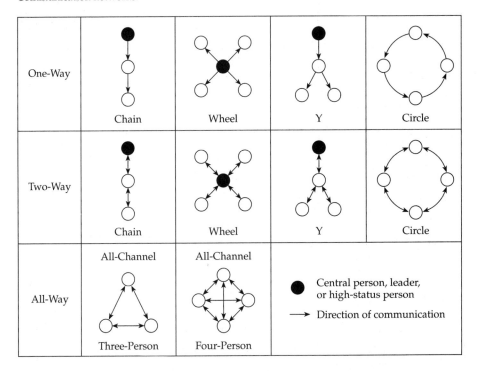

The wheel and Y networks are consistent with and appropriate for formal organizations. The leader initiates communication in these networks. The circle and all-channel networks illustrate communication that is more likely in informal groups or in neoclassical forms of organization. In one-way communication, the network allows for no feedback or upward communication.

As the number of communicators increases, the number of channels grows in geometric instead of arithmetic proportion. For example, in the three-person all-channel network there are 6 channels, but in the four-person all-channel network there are 12 channels. It is clear that small groups are necessary if the all-channel network is to be used due to the increased demands on management to control such communication networks.

It is apparent from this discussion that there is a need for police administrators to manage communications. Communications, formal or informal, are a rudimentary management tool without which nothing could be accomplished. Administrators disseminate information, policies, and orders through communications, and they determine the status of the department (compliance with policy and orders) through the same communications channels. One might mistakenly view communications as a simple management process; however, as the department increases in size, communication becomes more complex and demanding. If the administrator does not constantly consider, monitor, and evaluate communication networks and information flow, managerial effectiveness could be altered through communication breakdowns. Communication is extremely important and should receive appropriate managerial consideration.

TECHNOLOGICAL ADVANCES IN COMMUNICATION

Numerous changes in information technology have given administrators new abilities to communicate with others quickly. E-mail is increasingly being used as a tool for communication. Similarly, many agencies are beginning to make use of the World Wide Web to communicate with citizens and other people outside the department. In addition to computer technologies, many agencies have begun to use closed-circuit television combined with other modes of communication to transmit important message between different locations.

Since the mid-1990s, e-mail has become one of the most common forms of communication in police agencies and other public organizations (Milward and Snyder, 1996). E-mail offers advantages over traditional forms of communication. For example, the communication it provides is almost instantaneous. E-mail also provides for information to be transmitted to numerous people at the same time. It also allows relatively secure communication, and even the most technologically incapable person can figure out how to use e-mail with minimal effort. Finally, it helps reduce communication lag and provides for the transmittal of time-sensitive information. In all, e-mail is cheaper and swifter than printed correspondence.

Of course, where there are advantages, there are also disadvantages. For example, supervisors may be inclined to use e-mail communication in preference to face-to-face contact, which makes the communication process less personal. Another problem concerns the seriousness with which e-mail messages should be viewed. Are they to be viewed as "mail" in the traditional sense, or is the information

Officer checks driver's license using MDT computer in his patrol car.

Michael Newman/PhotoEdit

transmitted through e-mail offhanded or less important? Any ambiguity here can be damaging to the communication process. E-mail is an invaluable tool nowadays, but it should not supplant traditional modes of communication. Performance reviews, criticisms, reprimands, and other forms of "sensitive" information should probably be sent through traditional channels (Markels, 1996). Overall, however, e-mail and other forms of electronic communication should improve and enhance the way information is shared and transmitted in law enforcement agencies.

Another way law enforcement agencies are changing their modes of communication is through the World Wide Web. A growing number of agencies have developed home pages that provide information on goals, personnel, organizational layout, and so on. Departments are also using the Web to communicate more directly with citizens via the department's home page. This form of communication is largely one-way, and it differs from the communication discussed in this chapter in that it typically targets individuals outside the police organization rather than within it. Even so, the Internet provides a powerful means to communicate important information about police organizations.

CONFLICT

Fundamental to an administrator's ability to resolve conflict is his or her ability to communicate effectively. A substantial amount of conflict is the result of poor communications skills, and when conflict occurs, it is best resolved by a good communicator. Research and practical experience shows that conflict is inherent in all organizations (Litterer, 1966; Schmidt and Kochan, 1972). This is especially true in public organizations such as police agencies because the goals of different stakeholders such as managers and subordinates are often at odds with one another.

Conflict can be defined as "discord that arises when the goals, interests, or values of different individuals or groups are incompatible and those individuals or groups block or thwart each other's attempts to achieve their objectives" (Jones, George, and Will, 1998:501). For example, if a new police chief is appointed with the mission of clearing up a department's tarnished image, and he or she proposes significant changes in the way things are done, conflict will almost certainly follow.

Change in public organizations is fraught with problems, and it is difficult to change the status quo. Thus, when new administrators revise and change traditional policies and procedures, they invariably encounter resistance. The ability to manage such conflict is an indispensable administrative asset. And the best tool at an administrator's disposal to manage conflict is communication.

Despite its dark side, conflict does not necessarily have to be destructive. The cause of the conflict and how it is viewed can ultimately determine whether it will be viewed as beneficial or destructive. The negative type of conflict—that which builds animosities, depletes energies, and divides individuals and groups—has detrimental effects on organizational health. However, positive conflict can do such things as stimulate interest, prevent stagnation, encourage creativity, provide a group identity, and create and sustain solidarity (Goser, 1956).

Types of Conflict

Several types of conflict arise in organizations. Putnam and Poole (1987) identified four primary types of conflict: (1) interpersonal conflict; (2) intragroup conflict; (3) intergroup conflict; and (4) interorganizational conflict.

Interpersonal conflict is one of the more common types of conflict. It occurs when individual members of the organization come into conflict because of goals and values that are at odds with one another. Interpersonal conflict could occur, for example, when a police administrator supports the values inherent in community policing, but one of his or her subordinates does not.

Intragroup conflict occurs when there is tension and rivalry within a particular group in the police organization. When officers in the patrol division are divided over the allocation of resources, the result is intragroup conflict. Another example of intragroup conflict would be disagreement among members of a collective bargaining unit. For example, conflict between patrol and criminal investigation may occur when detectives fail to recognize patrol officers' contributions to a successful investigation.

Intergroup conflict is conflict that occurs between two or more groups. Sticking with the collective bargaining example, when there is disagreement between the union and administration, intergroup conflict results. Alternatively, when different divisions within a particular agency disagree, intergroup conflict is a result.

Interorganizational conflict is conflict that arises across organizations. For example, if a county sheriff disagrees with a municipal police chief in that county, interorganizational conflict occurs. Many media depictions of the law enforcement profession have consistently portrayed rampant interorganizational conflict. Movies and television often suggest that there are rivalries between federal officials—the "feds"—and local law enforcement, despite the fact that such rivalries are relatively isolated and uncommon.

Sources of Conflict

Conflict in police organizations arises from a number of sources. At least eight sources of conflict can be identified: (1) incompatible goals and time horizons; (2) overlapping authority; (3) task interdependence; (4) status inconsistencies; (5) scarce resources; (6) communication failures; (7) individual differences; and (8) incompatible procedures for rewarding and reprimanding performance (Pondy, 1967; Wall and Callister, 1995; Walton and Dutton, 1969). Each of these eight sources of conflict is depicted in Figure 8–4.

Incompatible Goals and Time Horizons

By now you well know that law enforcement organizations are grouped in divisions based on the many tasks that need to be performed on a day-to-day basis. Numerous divisions can have incompatible goals and time horizons, especially in large departments, and this frequently causes organizational conflict. For example, conflict between a traffic division and a community-policing unit can arise. The goal of the traffic division is to enforce traffic laws—inconveniencing many citizens, causing police–public relations to suffer. On the other hand, the

Figure 8–4

Sources of conflict.

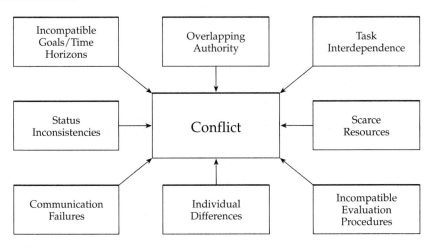

community policing unit may have among its central goals the desire to improve police–community relations. Both divisions—the traditional traffic division and the new and responsive community policing division—pursue largely different goals, in the same organization, and at the same time. The result can be conflict between officers within each division, not to mention tension, conflict, and confusion among citizens who are targeted by each activity. Other divisions within police departments—for example, the SWAT team, narcotics—are charged with duties that sometimes run at odds with the "softer" side of policing.

Time horizons can differ in police organizations as well. For example, a new police chief may be brought in and asked to encourage a change in departmental philosophy from a traditional approach to a community approach. Inevitably, such a change can be effected only with time and hard work. At the same time, as the highest-ranking official in the department, the chief is also responsible for the more short-term task of managing the crime problem and demonstrating effectiveness in this regard. The time horizons associated with each task differ considerably; a natural result is conflict.

Overlapping Authority

The flipside of incompatible goals and time horizons is overlapping authority, a situation that arises when two or more division or department heads claim authority for the same tasks or duties. Highly bureaucratic organizations, with clear lines of authority and a well-defined separation of duties, are less likely to face conflict arising from overlapping authority. However, if an agency is not organized in such a manner, a result may be conflict. Conflict resulting from overlapping authority may be a feature of highly decentralized police organizations characterized by shared authority, minimal supervision, and diverse responsibilities. Such conflict most often occurs among operational units.

Task Interdependence

Another source of organizational conflict is task interdependence, which occurs when several individuals, groups, teams, or divisions are dependent on one another. Conflict is almost inevitable when more than one person is charged with the same task. This is not to say teamwork should be discouraged, however. Rather, it is important for the administrator to have an awareness of the potential for conflict in group situations.

Two types of task interdependence can be identified. The first is *sequential interdependence*. This type of interdependence exists when one unit or division is dependent on the activities of another unit or division. Sequential interdependence in police organizations sometimes exists between police officers and detectives. With some exceptions, detectives are dependent on patrol officers to complete the report and preliminary investigation on crimes. Detectives often complain that some of these investigations are substandard, causing the detectives more work. The second type of task interdependence is *reciprocal interdependence*. This type of interdependence exists when individuals or groups are mutually interdependent. Members of a drug task force, usually consisting of officers from several departments, are reciprocally interdependent. That is, they are all required to work together toward a primary goal.

Status Inconsistencies

This type of conflict can occur when the "status" associated with particular ranks is not clear. Does a community outreach officer enjoy the same status as a patrol officer? If not, the result is conflict associated with status inconsistencies. Status inconsistencies are not common in organizations characterized by clear lines of authority and explicit horizontal and vertical lines of communication.

Scarce Resources

Resource shortages plague police departments all around the country, not to mention other public organizations. Police administrators are the people most likely to confront conflict arising from resource scarcities. Among their duties, as we have seen, is the task of budgeting. This involves ensuring that appropriate divisions and units each receive their share of a limited supply of funding and equipment. The fact that some units and divisions receive more or less funding and equipment than others can lead to destructive organizational conflict, hostility, animosity, frustration, and inadequacy.

Communication Failures

Communication failures occur for a number of reasons. As we have seen already in this chapter, communication failures can occur because of physical and psychological barriers. Timing, experiential barriers, and other problems can also interrupt effective communication. A result of communication failure, then, is conflict. When considering conflict that arises from communication failure, it is important to take into account the parties to the communication. If one party dislikes, distrusts, or resents the other, communication failures can be particularly destructive. On the other hand, communication failures between parties who get along regularly are less likely to result in conflict (Bartol and Martin, 1998:498).

Individual Differences

All organizations have differences among individuals. Differences in personalities, backgrounds, experiences, values, and other factors are frequent sources of conflict. One job of administrators is to minimize the negative organizational consequences associated with individual differences. Diversity is advantageous to all organizations, but the downside of diversity—conflict—needs to be minimized so the destruction and disarray it can cause is never realized.

Incompatible Evaluation Procedures

Incompatible procedures for rewarding and reprimanding performance is the last source of organizational conflict that we consider. For example, systems that reward competition in situations calling for cooperation can result in conflict. Punishment procedures can have much the same effect, especially when they are inconsistent, incompatible, and inappropriate. Another task of the administrator, then, is to ensure that performance is rewarded (or reprimanded) consistently and responsibly.

Many other sources of conflict exist. Police organizations, while sharing many characteristics of business and other government agencies, are also unique entities. The conflict they face can stem from sources not identified in this brief review. However, what has been offered here is an overview of common sources of conflict facing all organizations. Astute and learned administrators need to identify sources of conflict in their agencies and take steps to ensure that conflict is managed constructively. As we have seen, conflict does not have to be destructive; there is such a thing as good conflict. Another administrative task, then, is to distinguish between positive and negative conflict, then seek to minimize the harmful effects of negative conflict. Many strategies are available for doing this, as the next section of this chapter attests.

Types and Sources of Conflict Facing Police Administrators

First, police administrators are faced with dealing with employee conflict. In particular, problem employees—those who continually act in an objectionable fashion—are found in virtually all organizations. The administrator needs to answer the question, Is it better to get rid of the problem employee or attempt to modify his or her behavior? If the administrator does not act, the problem employee can reduce the department's effectiveness and take a toll on the organization.

Conflict can also exist between one police department and another. Disputes over such things as jurisdictional authority and who takes charge at accident scenes sometimes occur. As an example, an automobile accident occurred on a

California freeway on-ramp that happened to be connected to a road separating two counties. The California Highway Patrol reported that it was not responsible for the investigation because the accident was not on the highway. One county sheriff agency said the accident should be handled by the other county and vice versa. The result was a mild dispute between three police agencies, each refusing to investigate the accident.

Conflicts with the public are also frequent and unavoidable. Indeed, all law enforcement officers (not just administrators) are intimately familiar with the fact that they cannot make everyone happy. Because of the confrontational nature of many police activities and because of the media's tendency to paint the police in an unfavorable light at times, police administrators often find themselves embroiled in controversy. People routinely file complaints and air their grievances in very public ways. The result is that a certain segment of the population is always dissatisfied, even if their dissatisfaction is totally misplaced. Consider, for example, what has happened to the image of the Los Angeles Police Department in the wake of the Rampart Division scandal. Despite the fact that a few officers were responsible for a number of abuses, the whole department of nearly 10,000 officers suffered an image and morale problem.

Police administrators must be cognizant of several other sources of conflict, such as conflicts between management and subordinates, conflicts between the chief and other elected or appointed officials, and conflicts between unions and administrators. Whatever form, however, conflict is an inevitable feature of the organizational life that police administrators need to be prepared to deal with. To an extent, administrators need to develop a "thick skin," knowing that they can never do quite enough to satisfy everyone inside and outside the organization.

Conflict Resolution Strategies

Numerous tools and strategies are available for reducing and resolving conflict (Lewicki and Litterer, 1985; Thomas, 1992). Some are quick fixes and likely to encounter minimal opposition; others require more work on the part of both parties to the conflict and are relatively extreme in nature. Conflict resolution strategies include (1) altering the source of the conflict; (2) appealing to third parties; (3) adopting an interpersonal conflict-handling approach; (4) increasing diversity awareness and skills; (5) practicing job rotation or temporary assignment; (6) using permanent transfers or dismissals; and (7) changing organizational structure and/or culture.

Altering the Source of the Conflict

Whenever possible, the best tool for reducing conflict is to alter the source of the conflict. If we consider the sources of conflict mentioned above, this strategy would involve taking steps to ensure that goals are compatible, that authority does not overlap, that task interdependence is not detrimental to the organization, and so on. Unfortunately, these solutions may be prohibitively time-consuming or expensive. Nonetheless, examining goals and clarifying units' responsibilities sometimes can reduce conflict. Clarity of goals often reduces uncertainty and conflict.

Appealing to Third Parties

This conflict reduction strategy comes from mediation, arbitration, and litigation origins. Where possible, it is desirable for a dispute between two parties to be resolved by those two parties. However, in some situations it is necessary to call on a third party such as a judge or mediator. This occurs when the disputing parties reach an impasse and can no longer communicate constructively and effectively.

The administrator sometimes can act as the third party. For example, if conflict exists between one or more organizational divisions or unit, the administrator is the first person to attempt to resolve this conflict. There are instances where third-party mediation is helpful. Examples include conflicts between a police department and another department. The police department as a result of community policing may attempt to clean up a neighborhood. Third-party mediation may be needed to gain the cooperation of the sanitation department in the project. Also, third-party mediation is sometimes required to settle grievances filed by the union against the department.

An Interpersonal Conflict-Handling Approach

This conflict resolution strategy places the administrator in something of a third-party role. He or she attempts to mitigate the conflict through one of five possible approaches, each of which draws on his or her interpersonal skills (see Rahim and Magner, 1995; Reitz, 1987; Thomas, 1977). These approaches, according to Bartol and Martin (1998) are (1) avoiding, (2) accommodating, (3) competing, (4) compromising, and (5) collaborating. The first approach, *avoiding,* is not desirable, as it involves ignoring or suppressing the conflict in hopes that it will disappear on its own. *Accommodating* is a strategy where the administrator lets the opposed party have its way rather than continue with the conflict. The *competing* approach is where the conflict is pushed to resolution. The conflict is controlled, but efforts are made to ensure resolution. *Compromising* encourages each party to make some concession so that a mutually satisfactory solution can be achieved. Finally, *collaborating* encourages working together rather than making concessions.

Increasing Diversity Awareness and Skills

As discussed in Chapter 2, diversity issues are important in police departments. Administrators can take steps to increase diversity awareness and skills. This strategy may prove particularly helpful when conflict arises from peoples' backgrounds. For example, an older officer may feel resentful of having to report to a younger officer who happens to be her supervisor. Alternatively, a Hispanic police officer might feel singled out or isolated in a largely white police department. The plight of women in police agencies over the last several decades has improved substantially yet remains another example of a diversity-based conflict problem (Haarr, 1997; Hale and Wyland, 1999). Conflict that arises from these and similar situations can most likely be reduced by appropriate training and awareness education. Of course, this conflict resolution strategy may not work where diversity concerns are not the primary source of the conflict.

Practicing Job Rotation or Temporary Assignment

A slightly more invasive conflict reduction strategy involves moving people to different assignments or practicing job rotation. Sometimes conflicts arise because people simply cannot get along or fail to understand the work activities and demands placed on them by others. In such situations an administrator might elect to rotate the person into another position or assign him or her temporarily to another division in order to minimize conflict. This solution should not be viewed as disciplinary. Rather, job rotation and temporary assignment can expand the officer's knowledge base and appreciation of other divisions or units, which ultimately will improve the situation when the officer is transferred back to his or her original position.

Administrators may have difficulty in adopting this conflict resolution strategy, however, as the bureaucratic, civil service orientation of many police agencies may make position changes difficult. Moreover, administrators who adopt this strategy should be aware that temporary assignments and transfers can result in status inconsistencies, another source of conflict that we have already reviewed.

Permanent Transfers or Dismissals

Perhaps the most extreme disciplinary measure to reduce conflict involves transferring someone permanently, taking disciplinary action such as a suspension, or dismissing the person altogether. This option should be viewed as a last resort. More often than not, conflict that is identified early on can be resolved without such a serious approach. Administrators should first exhaust all other options before resorting to permanent transfer or dismissal. Dismissals due to less-than-legitimate reasons can cause legal headaches for the administrator as well as the entire organization.

Changing Organizational Structure and/or Culture

One of the more difficult approaches to conflict resolution involves altering the structure of the police organization and/or its culture. If either approach is adopted, the administrator should be aware that change of this nature often comes with considerable difficulty, especially in police agencies. As we have seen, police agencies are often resistant to change. Consider the difficulties police agencies have faced in changing organizational culture from a professional model to a community model (Trojanowicz, Kappeler, and Gaines, 2001).

Some agencies have succeeded, but the evidence for large-scale changes of this nature is somewhat limited. Similarly, attempts to change the structure of American police agencies, particularly in ways that are commensurate with the community policing paradigm, have failed miserably in a great many agencies (Maguire, 1997). Wholesale organizational change, like permanent transfers and dismissals, should be viewed as a last resort. More than likely, conflict can be resolved with a less invasive approach.

Ultimately, the appropriate conflict resolution strategy will depend on two things: (1) what the administrator is comfortable with or willing to do and (2) the nature and source of the conflict. The primary tool used by administrators to resolve conflict is negotiation, which is a form of leadership. Negotiation is one of the most important weapons in the administrative arsenal. Accordingly, the remainder of this chapter focuses on the topic of negotiation.

Alternative Conflict Resolution

There is a major movement afoot, not just in law enforcement, to seek out alternative means of conflict resolution. Generally, the motivation behind this movement is to minimize the confrontational and costly nature of traditional dispute resolution. For example, disputing parties can pursue, or even be forced to pursue mediation before heading to court. Civil trials are particularly costly and time-consuming, so many people have begun to advocate alternative conflict resolution strategies. Whatever its form, alternative conflict resolution is very much akin to an appeal to third parties, as addressed above. One important example of alternative conflict resolution traces its origins to community policing.

Since community policing is designed to, among other things, improve a police department's image and responsiveness, many departments have taken steps to offer mediation in situations where conflict between the department and community arises. As McGillis observes, "As American society becomes increasingly more diverse and complex, and as conflicts of all sorts—from interpersonal disputes to conflicts between groups and organizations—grow, the work of [mediation] programs . . . can be of great assistance in helping citizens address and resolve troubling and potentially escalating conflicts." To this he adds, "Mediation provides disputants with the opportunity to communicate face-to-face, enables disputants to see each other as human beings rather than abstract opponents, and provides opportunities to identify common ground that can lead to the resolution of conflict" (1998:13).

Cooper offers some important recommendations as to how police officers can serve as mediators between citizens who experience conflicts with one another:

> As a component of community policing, mediation should be used by patrol officers when responding to calls for service . . . If patrol officers address interpersonal disputes through mediation, many of the goals of community policing are satisfied. Patrol officers play the role of mediator or third party who assist disputants to fashion their own resolutions to conflicts. In these ways, the officer is defined as a "helper," championing a central community policing objective: citizen empowerment (1999:5).

In other situations involving conflict between police officers and the public, alternative conflict resolution can also prove valuable. In the new era of policing, there is more the police can do than just tell the public what to do. To the extent citizens perceive problems with the police, the police should become problem solvers and depend on the citizenry for input that helps establish mutual satisfaction for both parties.

NEGOTIATION

Negotiation is a particular form of communication. *Negotiation* is the establishment of a feedback loop used to exchange and refine ideas, exert leadership, and engage in decision making. Negotiation is a fact of everyone's life. For example, young people negotiate daily with their parents over how late they can stay out, where they can go, or whether they can use the car. Children negotiate things such as the use of television and when they must go to bed. Spouses typically negotiate household chores and activities. In the workplace, employees and managers negotiate work schedules, vacations, salaries, and the amount and type of work to be performed. Each negotiation consists of people who want to resolve some issue or conflict with another person. Some conflicts are severe, whereas others are relatively minor in nature. The issues

NYPD officer counsels citizens.
Richard Lord/PhotoEdit

involved in the negotiations might be of extreme importance or, in some cases, insignificant. Negotiation guarantees that needs and desires will be heard and that at least a portion of the request is fulfilled. Often when we are engaged in a negotiation, we do not call it negotiating; we may call it compromising, working it out, resolving a problem, reaching an understanding, or coming to a joint or mutual decision. Regardless of what the process is called, the result is negotiation.

Police officers and managers find themselves in conflict situations every day when they negotiate an outcome with another person or persons. The result of their negotiations can often be vitally important to an individual's life or to the organization's success. These negotiations have three possible results. First, one party can get what it wants while the other party gets nothing. This result is called *win–lose*. Second, both parties can stubbornly hold out for what they want while neither gets any part of what they want. This result is called *lose–lose*. Third, both parties get some part of what is important to them. The result is a compromise, or *win–win*. The last outcome is considered the best result in negotiations.

Principled negotiation, developed by the Harvard Negotiation Project (Fisher and Ury, 1981), and Cohen's (1980) negotiation methodology are two examples of how negotiations should occur. Each of these authors encourages the win–win negotiation style, wherein neither party loses. The principle of win–win is to not use negotiation skills to intimidate or hurt others. Instead, both parties should make mutual gains during the process.

Police supervisors can use this form of negotiation in establishing work schedules and work assignments such as deciding on days off, vacation schedules, and shifts to be worked by the various employees. Police supervisors can use win–win negotiation in jointly establishing individual goals and objectives with subordinates, and administrators can use it in obtaining the budget they need for the department. Police officers can use it in dealing with hostage takers, barricaded individuals, and other uncooperative persons. Any time there is a disagreement or a conflict, negotiation skills are the best technique for dealing with the situation.

Cohen (1980) identified three crucial variables to negotiation: (1) power, (2) time, and (3) information. Negotiating successfully depends on one's ability to analyze information, time, and power to affect behavior and meet one's needs as well as the other party's needs.

Power

Power is often thought of negatively. The negativism associated with power is related to either the way power is used or the goal of power. Power used in a manipulative, coercive, or dictatorial manner is abusive. It is power over someone or something instead of power to accomplish some goal. Power is also perceived negatively when the goal of power is seen as being corrupt or exploitative (i.e., Machiavellian).

Despite its potential to be abused or used improperly, power enables us to achieve our goals, protect ourselves, and have control over our lives. When we fail to understand the uses of power or fail to use power to control our lives, the result is a feeling of powerlessness. Powerless people respond negatively to their world. They become apathetic, and then others have to carry their load in the organization. The resultant unmotivated police personnel do not contribute to the department's productivity. Powerless people often become hostile and try to tear down what they cannot control and do not understand. For example, a police officer who is frustrated with the courts for placing an offender on probation when the police officer thought "hard time" in prison was warranted will sometimes resort to circumventing the system through "street justice." Such hostile action, taking the law into one's own hands and thereby abusing the power of a police officer, occurs because the officer feels powerless to help the community.

The ingredients of power must be understood and practiced. Power does not come from reading, but from practicing its proper use. The police administrator must learn to appropriately use power in dealing with subordinates, other department or agency heads, the mayor or other governmental administrators, and external entities. The situation in dealing with each of these will be different and will require careful selection of power-establishing techniques. As we have seen, the police administrator may have to negotiate with other agency heads or other police commanders over the allocation of scarce resources. In such a situation, the administrator must be careful to present a powerful stance in terms of asking for the resources that are needed (initiating structure). At the same time, the administrator must be careful not to harm relationships (concern for people) by playing the power issue too hard, that is, by being overly aggressive or bullying others to give in to his or her demands. This clearly defines the difference between the win–win approach to negotiation and the win–lose approach. The administrator wants to get as much as possible while allowing other parties to reach goals. In dealing with external entities (e.g., vendors), a stronger power stance can and should be taken. For example, in negotiating the purchase of supplies and equipment, or in negotiating for capital construction, the police administrator will be much more concerned with the needs of the police organization than with the needs of the salesperson. Without a position of power, the likelihood of getting a favorable deal on purchases is extremely low. This is not to say that salespeople's needs should be completely overlooked, for often it is by giving them something that is important to them that the administrator can get the best deal for the organization.

An understanding of the sources of power is essential to the proper utilization of power. In Chapter 4, we discussed organizational power. Here we examine the use of power within the context of negotiations. The challenge is to recognize the source of power and properly use it in meeting legitimate goals for personal or professional development. Cohen (1980) identified a number of sources of power when negotiating. Several of these power sources are discussed next, and these strategies or tactics should always be considered when negotiating.

The Power of Competition

The value of what we have or can do increases when there is competition for it. The value of police service to the community becomes much higher when it is a scarce resource. Should a rash of street robberies occur in a particular community, for example, the members of that community would want a highly visible police presence in their area. Thus the value of a police presence increases. But with the overall number of police officers remaining constant, competition between communities in the city increases. Such competition can be used by police administrators in seeking to increase personnel or equipment or supply items in the budget. A skillful negotiator can create competition and thereby develop options when entering into a negotiation. Managers who negotiate without options are treated lightly and seldom are successful.

The Power of Risk Taking

Risk taking involves mixing common sense and courage, calculating the odds before taking risks. However, it is important to take optimum or moderate risks. As Cohen observed, "Before chancing anything, calculate the odds to determine whether the potential benefits are worth the possible cost of failure. Be rational, not impulsive. Never take a risk out of pride, impatience, or a desire to get it over with" (1980:64).

Police managers and supervisors are often faced with risk-taking situations. Many police departments are extremely bureaucratic and are highly resistant to change. When unit commanders or supervisors attempt a new program or even suggest a new program, they are taking a risk. Such actions or suggestions usually confront superiors who are locked into the old way of doing things. When to risk is an individual decision. It should be a decision based on thought, not compulsion.

The Power of Commitment

Getting commitment from others to join in risk taking disperses the overall risk. Risk is shared by the entire group. Commitment from a group creates much more power than an individual. An example of the power of commitment is the labor union movement. People in a united front usually have the power to achieve their goals. This form of power is also useful in creating organizational change. The successful change agent will get others involved by giving them a "piece of the action" from the change—they will gain something of value from the change. Involvement brings commitment, and commitment brings power.

The Power of Expertise

When others believe or perceive that an administrator possesses knowledge and skill, they will be likely to treat him or her with respect. If the administrator establishes credentials early in the negotiation process, his or her statements may not even be challenged. Asking intelligent questions is more important than being able to speak at length on a subject in most negotiation situations. Polite irreverence, combined with persistence and questions, is an important negotiating ability.

The Power of the Knowledge of "Needs"

In all negotiations there are two things at stake: (1) the specific demands that are stated openly and (2) the real needs of the other side, which are rarely stated. The administrator's job as a negotiator is to establish a reasonable estimate of the other side's needs. The challenge is to satisfy the real needs of the other side. Then and only then will their demands be met. If these needs are not met, the other side will continue to negotiate new demands. Recognizing real needs takes practice and insight into human behavior.

The Power of Investment

Another powerful tool in negotiation is getting the other person to invest time, energy, or resources. Such investments cause people to be less willing to give up on the negotiation and more willing to settle for less than they had originally intended. At the beginning of each encounter, it is important to approach people collaboratively, working together with them as partners sharing the investment. Difficult negotiation items should be kept to the end of the negotiation, after the other side has a substantial time and energy investment in the negotiation.

The Power of Rewarding or Punishing

Cohen pointed out that people will never negotiate unless they're convinced they can and might be rewarded or punished. Moreover, it is important to avoid transforming oneself into a paper tiger. The perception that an administrator is willing to exercise his or her power may prevent a potential aggressor from taking an opportunity to act.

The Power of Identification

Getting others to be able to identify with the administrator's position is an important aspect of one's negotiating ability. To do this, the administrator must act professionally and reasonably when dealing with others to gain their loyalty, respect, and cooperation. It is essential to be understanding and empathetic to others' needs, hopes, desires. Such conduct engenders respect and support from others. The power of identification plays a significant role in most negotiations and decision-making situations. Identification can be a negative factor, however, especially for an administrator who is power hungry, untrustworthy, or undependable.

The Power of Morality

Most Westerners are raised to have the same moral and ethical values. Often this moral code can be used to one's benefit in negotiations. This is particularly true when there is an issue of fairness or justice. Here, the negotiator appeals to the opponent's sense of right and wrong. This type of appeal will not always work with people who have different values stemming from different cultures, but it may prove particularly valuable for issues on which there is a moral consensus.

The Power of Precedent

Precedent can be a hindrance or a help to negotiation. Precedents, or past events, establish trends and mind sets for accomplishing goals. A precedent should not become an excuse not to change—or an excuse to change. If a precedent is outdated or inapplicable to current conditions, then the precedent should not be followed. However, if the precedent fits current needs, it should be given maximum attention. All assumptions relative to precedents should be considered and tested. Frequently, precedents are used in negotiations to strengthen positions. The effective negotiator should always use them when they substantiate or solidify a position and carefully analyze them when they are used by others.

The Power of Persistence

Lack of persistence is a common failure among negotiators. One must be tenacious because persistence is the quality that gives power its strength. When police officers fail to be persistent with suspects, informants, or witnesses when investigating cases, the outcome can be less than satisfactory.

The Power of Persuasive Capacity

Logic, or reasoning capacity, is what we usually rely on to make things happen. However, logic by itself seldom wins in negotiating. According to Cohen, three additional strategies are important: (1) state a position so that others will understand it; (2) provide overwhelming evidence to support your position; and (3) when possible, do what meets with current needs and desires of the other side. If the other side is to be persuaded, it is important for the administrator to demonstrate the immediate relevance and importance of what his or her position is.

The Power of Attitude

A large part of the negotiation process is attitude. The successful negotiator generally has a relaxed, open attitude toward the process and his or her opponents. Negotiating is essentially knowing when to give and when to take. An objective attitude, coupled with experience in negotiating, allows for this process to occur.

These 13 of Cohen's elements of power can be quite useful to police administrators, managers, supervisors, and officers. Their usefulness varies, depending on the type of negotiation situation that presents itself. The second variable in negotiation is time.

Time

Most people speak of negotiation as if it had a definite and unchangeable beginning and ending. Such a concept of negotiation sets one up for failure. Deadlines for negotiations should be viewed as flexible. The negotiator must ensure that his or her deadline is set after the other side's deadline since significant concessions and settlements are most likely to occur just prior to the deadline.

Since deadlines are usually self-imposed, they can be flexible, allowing negotiators to use more patience. Deadlines imposed by others may also be negotiable. Some questions that help clarify the effects of missing deadlines are: What will happen if I allow the deadline to pass without acting? How likely is it that a penalty or detrimental action will result? How severe will the punishment be? The negotiator should always evaluate and weigh the risks associated with deadlines. This allows the negotiator to better understand his or her position.

Even though deadlines should be viewed as flexible, it is wise not to leave them indefinitely open-ended. To do so implies that the administrator is stalling, buying time, or otherwise trying to avoid negotiating on important issues. A reasonable timeline coupled with responsiveness and responsibility can improve the negotiation process. It should be pointed out, however, that the type of negotiating situation determines the time element of negotiating.

Information

Successful negotiation and decision making depend on adequate information. Why then do we so often go into negotiation events without needed information? Because we see negotiation situations as limited events. We seldom anticipate that we will need information until a crisis occurs. Police administrators and managers often get caught in an emergency negotiation situation which they are ill prepared to deal with because they lack necessary information.

Negotiation is not an isolated event; it is a process that usually encompasses days, weeks, or even months before the participants meet. It is during this time that a negotiation strategy should be prepared. Even in a police emergency such as a riot or natural disaster, police personnel should have anticipated emergency conditions and developed contingency plans. Contingency planning may be a formal plan or it may exist only in the thoughts of the personnel. Whatever the case, being caught without information in a strategic negotiation is a sign of ill preparedness. Police intelligence gathering and assessing of the environment can aid in filling weak information links. This information gathering should begin as early as possible.

Prior to the actual negotiation, there should be an exchange of information. This exchange of information may be a mutual exchange, in which each side provides the other with information, or only one side may disseminate information. There must be an attempt to build two-way trust through mutual risk-taking behavior in which one side gives information to foster trust.

Another reason for sharing information is to ensure that the other side does not get surprised during the negotiation event. People generally react negatively to a proposal when it is first stated. They need time to consider it and adjust their thinking. If they are given sufficient time to consider the proposal and are furnished with new information later, there is an increased possibility of acceptance. Therefore, new ideas should be presented slowly and in small doses. This is particularly true when presenting a proposal that will directly impact a group of employees. For example, a chief wanting to implement participative management should present the concept slowly in small doses to the upper and midlevel managers who will be most affected by the change. Proposals for changing employee benefit packages should also be presented in the various stages of development so that employees can comment on the plans and have sufficient time to consider the proposals.

Awareness of and ability to use power, time, and information effectively is only one part of successful win–win negotiation. Win–win negotiation also depends on knowing human behavior, or being "people smart." Another element of successful win–win negotiation is planning. The last element is successful implementation of the negotiation process. The following sections are devoted to the issues of people smartness, planning the negotiation, and successfully implementing the negotiation process.

People Smartness

People smartness requires people to understand themselves and others. People smartness is the ability to know how others behave—being able to correctly identify how people act, what their needs are, and how they are motivated. Why is people smartness important in negotiation? Negotiation requires one person to deal directly with another. The success of the negotiation depends to a large degree on how well the parties understand each other and relate to each other. People have different styles for dealing with others, perceiving information, making decisions, and interpreting events. It is important that we recognize these differences, understand our own style, figure out the other person's style, and adjust our behavior to fit the other person's frame of reference. Only by doing this can we hope to gain mutual understanding and know the other side's feelings, needs, and interests.

There are many theoretical groupings of personality styles. The one used here describes three distinguishable basic motivation patterns in which people strive for rewards and gratification. The theoretical grouping of personality styles considered here is part of Relationship Awareness Theory (Porter, 1973). Each style has strengths which, when carried to the extreme, become weaknesses. No pattern is inherently superior to any other, and every individual experiences all three basic motivations at one time or another. We often find others hard to understand. As we learn to recognize how we are motivated and how others are motivated, we are better able to relate to them and understand them. Therefore, our negotiations with them become more successful.

Analytic-Autonomizing Style

The characteristics of this style are liking to be independent and self-sufficient; valuing planning and an orderly approach; disliking emotionalism; respecting logic, facts, and wisdom; and viewing the self as needing to be more trusting and considerate. People with this style have the following strengths: they are analytic, cautious, methodical, and fair. However, if taken to the extreme, the strengths become weaknesses. These weaknesses include nitpicking, suspiciousness, rigidity, and a lack of feeling.

Assertive-Directing Style

People with this style like to control and get things done through others; like to compete and win; dislike gullibility and indecisiveness; and view themselves as needing to be more considerate. Their strengths are ambitiousness, competitiveness, self-confidence, and forcefulness. These strengths become weaknesses when taken to the extreme. The assertive-directing person must guard against becoming ruthless, combative, arrogant, and dictatorial.

Altruistic-Nurturing Style

These people like to be genuinely helpful; care about others' feelings and well-being; dislike selfishness and anger; and view themselves as needing to be more assertive. Their strengths are supportiveness, trusting nature, adaptability, and optimism. When carried to the extreme, these strengths can also become weaknesses. These weaknesses can come in the forms of submissiveness, gullibility, spinelessness, and impracticality.

Every person has a characteristic interpersonal style that has strengths and weaknesses. The weaknesses are the strengths used to excess (e.g., a person who is supportive under any and all circumstances carries supportiveness to its extreme—submissiveness, which is viewed as a weakness in management and in negotiation). The characteristic interpersonal style may also change when the person is under stress or pressure.

Why is personality type important in negotiation? People with the same style tend to get along better, negotiate more easily, and in general have a better working relationship than people of different styles. Those people who have a good blend of each style tend to do the best in relating to people with differing interpersonal styles.

Negotiators should be primarily concerned with examining the interpersonal style of the "other side" in light of their own interpersonal style. This is important because one's interpersonal style determines how one perceives another person's actions. If the negotiator knows his or her style as well as the competitor's style, the negotiator can make adjustments in negotiating strategy and gain insights into the opposition's perspective.

Agreement comes much easier if the parties have a mutual interpersonal style on which to base the negotiation. Communication is much easier in such a circumstance, and this makes it easier to get others to be forthcoming with their true feelings, needs, and interests. If negotiators are aware of the other side's interpersonal style and can develop a better understanding of where the opposition is coming from, they are in a much better position to suggest an option that will be mutually beneficial. This will yield a win–win negotiation.

Planning

Planning is essential to win–win negotiation. The plan sets forth the strategy for success in the negotiation. Several elements are involved in planning the negotiation. First, *understand the problem* associated with the negotiation. Why is the negotiation taking place? What are the participants trying to accomplish? Negotiators must set their goals for the negotiation and determine their priorities. Determination of creative options or alternatives is an important part of this process. Second, *gather information* to determine who the other side's key person is and what that person's feelings, needs, and interests are regarding the negotiation. Third, *determine if the necessary ingredients* for a negotiation exist. In making such a determination the following questions must be answered: Is the issue at stake negotiable? Is the other side willing to negotiate? Is there an established trust relationship between us and the other side and a desire to make a decision on this issue? and Is the issue worth our time and energy to negotiate? Fourth, administrators need to plan to *ensure the support* of those around them. This entails communicating and leading the group toward the recognized objective. Finally, *set the psychological tone* for the negotiation. Setting the tone entails considering the issue at hand as well as the psychological composition of the competitor. Successful negotiation cannot be completed without this planning process.

Implementing the Negotiation Process

The success of a negotiation lies in the details. Items that appear to be inconsequential can mean a lot to the final outcome. This section examines successful negotiation and offers some hints in negotiation decision making.

Agendas are very important to successful negotiation. It is critical to have a written agenda and provide copies to all participants. If someone else has determined the agenda, it is necessary to get it in writing, making copies for all parties. In many instances negotiations are informal; it is important that an agenda be established so that the administrator addresses all significant points.

In meeting people, negotiators need to learn as much as possible about them. This is especially true if the negotiator has not previously met them. Questions need to be asked, with particular attention to (1) obtaining information; (2) ensuring that appropriate information is provided; (3) discovering the personality of the other person; and (4) showing that one is interested in the other person.

When talking with others in negotiations, it is important to take time to think, particularly when answering the questions posed by the opposing party. Negotiators often fail to utilize their evaluation time, responding impulsively instead. Such impulsiveness is counterproductive. Information should be shared on a reciprocal basis, not volunteered.

Negotiation is a matter of information, time, and power, as discussed in the previous pages. Negotiation is a leadership process that managers use on a daily basis. Law enforcement officials, from the officer to the chief or sheriff, are constantly negotiating a variety of situations. Negotiation skills are required whether the situation is formal (e.g., union negotiations) or informal (e.g., when the chief discusses budget matters with the mayor or city manager).

Summary

This chapter examined communication, negotiation, and conflict resolution—skills that effective police administrators must possess. Effective leaders must be able to communicate with their subordinates, deal with conflict, and negotiate favorable positions for their units, divisions, and personnel. Communication is a process that is often taken for granted, but it is a process fraught with problems and pitfalls. The administrator can communicate more effectively when he or she understands potential problems and takes action to eliminate them. Planning is vital in communication.

As discussed in this chapter, conflict is ever-present in the police department. It is a natural consequence of people working and interacting with each other. Conflict detracts from the organizational mission. It causes people to lose concentration and thus fail to give their full attention to the mission at hand. Therefore, the police administrator must take measures to recognize its existence and, when it exists, take definitive action to eliminate it. Sometimes this is an arduous, time-consuming process; nevertheless, it must be done.

Finally, this chapter addressed negotiation. Negotiations occur in most of the interactions that we have with other people. To an extent, it is the direct application of leadership: getting things done through others. Negotiation is the process frequently used by leaders to motivate subordinates to achieve organizational objectives. A good leader must be skilled negotiator, and this is accomplished by understanding the negotiation process and using it effectively.

Study Questions

1. Define communication. What constitutes good communication?

2. What are the purposes of communication?

3. Why are context, perception, symbols, and inference important concepts in discussions of communication?

4. How are formal and informal communication similar and dissimilar?

5. How are verbal and nonverbal communication different? What are the characteristics of each? How do oral and written communications differ?

6. Distinguish between horizontal and vertical communication. What are the purposes of each?

7. Describe the communication process. How are one-way and two-way communication related to the concept of feedback?

8. What are the common barriers to communication? How can they be overcome?

9. What are the various types of verbal and nonverbal communication? How do they differ? Which is more desirable? Which is more frequently used?

10. What are the primary barriers to communication? Why is it important that administrators recognize these barriers?

11. Describe the various communication networks. Which would work best in a quality circle? Why? Describe settings in which each might be used successfully.

12. What is conflict? What are the main types of conflict? How do they differ? What are the sources of conflict?

13. What are the primary conflict resolution strategies? How does each relate to the others? Which is most desirable?

14. Define negotiation and discuss its importance in daily life and in policing. How is negotiation related to the issue of leadership?

15. How does win–win negotiation differ from the win–lose style? When is negotiation most likely to result in lose–lose? What are the consequences of lose–lose negotiation?

16. Why is power an important element to account for in negotiation?

17. Briefly discuss each of the sources of power which should be considered when negotiating. Give an illustration of why each is important to successful negotiation.

18. How does the successful negotiator use time and information?

19. What is people smartness? Why is it important to be people smart in negotiating? Describe the three personality styles presented in the chapter and how each might approach negotiation.

20. What are the primary considerations in planning for the negotiation and in implementing the negotiation process?

Net Resources

http://www.keylinecompany.com/behav_assess.html Learn more about your own communication style at this site.

http://www.mediationworks.com/mti/mam.htm Another website for training in conflict management and mediation.

http://www.portalpoint.com/ A website for mediation and conflict resolution training.

References

Barker, J. C. (1999). *Danger, Duty, and Disillusion: The Worldview of Los Angeles Police Officers*. Prospect Heights, IL: Waveland.

Bartol, K. M., and Martin, D. C. (1998). *Management*, 3rd ed. New York: McGraw-Hill.

Birdwhistell, R. (1970). *Kinesics and Context*. Philadelphia: University of Pennsylvania Press.

Cohen, H. (1980). *You Can Negotiate Anything*. Toronto: Bantam Books.

Davis, K., and Newstrom, J. W. (1985). *Human Behavior at Work: Organizational Behavior*, 7th ed. New York: McGraw-Hill.

Fisher, R., and Ury, W. (1981). *Getting to Yes: Negotiating Agreement without Giving In*. New York: Penguin Books.

Goser, L. A. (1956). *The Functions of Social Conflict*. Glencoe, IL: Free Press.

Haarr, R. (1997) Patterns of interaction in a police patrol bureau: Race and gender barriers to integration. *Justice Quarterly* 14(1):53–85.

Hale, D. and Wyland, S. M. (1999). Dragons and dinosaurs: The plight of patrol women. In L. Gaines and G. Cordner (eds.), *Policing Perspectives*. Los Angeles: Roxbury Press, pp. 450–458

Hitt, M. A., Middlemist, R. D., and Mathis, R. L. (1979). *Effective Management*. St. Paul: West Publishing.

Jones, G. R., George, J. M., and Will, C. W. L. (1998). *Contemporary Management*. New York: McGraw-Hill.

Katz, D., and Kahn, R. L. (1966). *The Social Psychology of Organizations*. New York: Wiley.

Kiechel, W., III. (1991). The art of the corporate task force. *Fortune*, January 29, pp. 104–105.

Lewicki, R. J., and Litterer, J. R. (1985). *Negotiation*. Homewood, IL: Irwin.

Litterer, J. A. (1966). Conflict in organizations: A reexamination. *Academy of Management Journal* 9:178–186.

Maguire, E. R. (1997). Structural change in large municipal police organizations during the community policing era. *Justice Quarterly* 14:547–576.

Markels, A. (1996). Managers aren't always able to get the right message across with e-mail. *Wall Street Journal*, August 6.

Massie, J. L., and Douglas, J. (1981). *Managing: A Contemporary Introduction*, 3rd ed. Englewood Cliffs, NJ: Prentice Hall.

Mehrabian, A. (1972). *Silent Messages*. Belmont, CA: Wadsworth.

Milward, H. B., and Snyder, L. O. (1996). Electronic government: Linking citizens to public organizations through technology. *Journal of Public Administration Research and Theory* 6:261–275.

O'Reilly, C. A., and Pondy, L. R. (1979). Organizational communication. In S. Kerr (ed.), *Organizational Behavior*. Columbus, OH: Grid.

Pondy, L. R. (1967). Organizational conflict: Concepts and models. *Administrative Science Quarterly* 2:296–320.

Porter, E. H. (1973). *Strength Development Inventory*. Pacific Palisades, CA: Personal Strengths Publishing.

Putnam, L. L., and Poole, M. S. (1987). Conflict and negotiation. In F. M. Jablin, L. L. Putnam, K. H. Roberts, and L. W. Porter (eds.), *Handbook of Organizational Communication: An Interdisciplinary Perspective*. Newbury Park, CA: Sage, pp. 549–599.

Rahim, M. A., and Magner, N. R. (1995). Confirmatory factor analysis of the styles of handling interpersonal conflict: First-order factor model and its invariance across groups. *Journal of Applied Psychology* 80:122–132.

Reich, R. B. (1987). Entrepreneurship reconsidered: The team as hero. *Harvard Business Review,* May–June, pp. 77–83.

Reitz, H. J. (1987). *Behavior in Organizations,* 3rd ed. Homewood, IL: Irwin.

Reuss-Ianni, E. (1983). *Two Cultures of Policing: Street Cops and Management Cops*. New Brunswick, NJ: Transaction Books.

Robbins, S. (1979). *Organizational Behavior: Concepts and Controversies*. Englewood Cliffs, NJ: Prentice Hall.

Schiffmann, H. R. (1990). *Sensation and Perception: An Integrated Approach*. New York: Wiley.

Schmidt, S. M., and Kochan, T. A. (1972). Conflict: Towards conceptual clarity. *Administrative Science Quarterly* 13:359–370.

Seeger, J. A. (1983). No innate phases in group problem solving. *Academy of Management Review* 8:683–689.

Stech, E. and Ratliffe, S. A. (1985). *Effective Group Communication: How to Get Action by Working in Groups*. Lincolnwood, Il: National Textbook.

Thomas, K. W. (1977). Toward multidimensional values in teaching: The example of conflict behaviors. *Academy of Management Journal* 2:484–490.

Thomas, K. W. (1992). Conflict and negotiation processes in organizations. In M. D. Dunnette and L. M. Hough (eds.), *Handbook of Industrial and Organizational Psychology*. Palo Alto, CA: Consulting Psychologists Press, pp. 651–717.

Trojanowicz, R., Kappeler, V., and Gaines, L. K. (2001). *Community Policing: A Contemporary Perspective*. 3rd ed. Cincinnati: Anderson Publishing.

Wall, J. A., Jr., and Callister, R. R. (1995). Conflict and its management. *Journal of Management* 21:515–558.

Walton, R. E., and Dutton, J. M. (1969). The management of interdepartmental conflict: A model and review. *Administrative Science Quarterly,* March, pp. 73–84.

Zander, A. (1982). *Making Groups Effective*. San Francisco: Jossey-Bass.

9

Managing and Responding to Stress

Wayne E. Newton/PhotoEdit

Chapter Outline

Introduction

Stress
The Nature of Stress
Symptoms of Stress

Stress and the Police Administrator
Sources and Antecedents of Stress for Police Administrators
Career Stages and Stress among Administrators

Stress and the Police Officer
Sources of Stress for Police Officers
Critical Incidents
Police Career Stages and Stress

The Effects of Stress in Policing
Health-Related Problems
The Police Officer and the Family
Differential Responses to Stress

Managing the Stress Problem
The Individual and Stress
Stress and the Police Organization

Strategies for Responding to Stress
Proactive Strategies
Reactive Strategies
Wellness Programs
Employee Assistance Programs

Summary

Learning Objectives

After reading this chapter, you should be able to

1. State the nature and symptoms of stress.
2. Understand the sources of stress for police administrators
3. Understand the sources of stress for officers not in administrative ranks.
4. Understand the effects of stress on health and family.
5. State the differential responses to stress.
6. Develop strategies for responding to stress.
7. Explain the consequences of stress for police organizations.

Prior to January 1995, the New Orleans Police Department had the distinction of being one of the most corrupt departments in the nation. One of the responses to this problem was the hiring of a new chief, Richard J. Pennington, former chief of operations with the Washington, D.C., Metropolitan Police Department and an African-American. Shortly after being appointed to his position, Chief Pennington issued a plan containing 10 major reform elements. His plan included the creation of the Public Integrity Division to root out internal corruption. He also established an early warning system to identify and monitor the behavior and conduct of problem officers. New hiring standards were established for police recruits. He also implemented community policing in high-crime public housing developments.

When radical change such as this is pursued—in this case by a chief hired from outside the department—resistance and stress are common results. The stress and tension between the new chief and the rank and file, for example, can take its toll on the agency as well as the new administrator. Research has also shown that when the new police chief is a minority, stress levels can be compounded. In this vein, the focus of this chapter is on the problem of police stress.

INTRODUCTION

Occupational stress has been the subject of much discussion for several decades. The police literature reports a great deal of research regarding the effect of job-related stress on police personnel, their families, and police organizations. There is common agreement that stress can be a negative, debilitating force, which, if left uncontrolled, can adversely affect police administrators, individual officers, and ultimately entire departments (Stotland, 1991). This chapter examines stress in each of these settings.

STRESS

Stress has both biological and psychological effects on its victims. Stress is associated with a number of health problems and diseases: cardiovascular disease, ulcers, and high blood pressure. For example, Jacobi (1975) found police medical compensation claims to be six times higher than the rate of other occupations, with 50 percent of the police medical claims for high blood pressure. Fell, Richard, and Wallace (1980) examined health data for Tennessee and found police officers had significantly high rates of premature death and admissions to hospitals. Stress can also cause a number of psychological or personality problems: anxiety, depression, alienation, and general morale and motivation problems. For example, Maslach (1976) reported that in one year, 1,500 New York City police officers required psychiatric care for stress problems. Stress in the workplace must be viewed as a significant problem, and management must take steps to reduce its occurrence and effects.

The Nature of Stress

Selye (1981), one of the foremost authorities on *stress,* defines it broadly as anything that places an adjustive demand on the organism. This definition allows stress to be either positive or negative. Selye calls positive stress "eustress" and negative stress "distress."

Eustress

Eustress is a stressful event that does not threaten or harm the individual but is pleasurable, challenging, or exciting. For example, the stress created by beginning a new and challenging job or assignment could qualify as eustress. The new police officer experiences eustress when going on patrol for the first time. Experienced officers usually experience eustress when changing to a new assignment such as criminal investigation. This form of stress is positive and actually heightens motivation.

In fact, all jobs require a certain level of stress for incumbents to be proficient or productive. For example, a football player must experience a level of stress (be keyed up) before he operates at his best. Job demands, goals, expectations, and controls must be present for individuals to be productive in the work setting. When this necessary and productive stress does not exist, the organization suffers.

Distress

Distress is the form of stress discussed in this chapter. It can be defined as a harmful stimulus, that threatens the functioning of the individual or is likely to overload the capacity of the individual to cope with environmental stimuli. Distress may result from such things as an extraordinarily high caseload, assignment to a high-crime area, being provided equipment that is inadequate, or having a supervisor who fails to provide support. All organizations contain job assignments or situations that are threatening to individuals, and it is these assignments or situations that create the greatest demands.

Allen, Hitt, and Greer (1982) note that stress is best conceptualized as an inverted U-curve. The inverted U-curve denotes that performance will rise with an increase in stress to a point where it becomes dysfunctional. At that point, increases in stress result in proportional decreases in performance. Those who are familiar with algebraic concepts might see this more clearly as a parabolic relationship. It is represented in Figure 9–1.

Selye formulated what he called the *general adaptation syndrome* (GAS) to describe the process by which stress incapacitates an individual who is unable to successfully cope with it. The syndrome consists of three distinct stages: (1) alarm, (2) resistance, and (3) exhaustion.

> **Alarm stage.** The alarm stage occurs when the individual is confronted by a threatening or stressful situation. Physiological reactions to this situation include the release of adrenaline into the blood and an increase

Figure 9–1
Relationship of performance to stress.

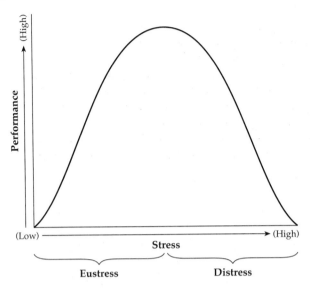

in cardiovascular activity. The individual becomes psychologically and physically prepared for the threat. If the threat subsides, the individual returns to a normal state.

Resistance stage. If the threat continues, optimal bodily resources are mobilized. The body attempts to defend against the stressor. The person also takes steps to mitigate the stressor's detrimental effects.

Exhaustion. Finally, if the individual is not able to defeat or manage the threat, the body may resist until it reaches a state of exhaustion, is where there are no remaining resources to cope with the threat. The individual then becomes unable to function properly.

Stress, essentially, is a problem of incompatibility between a person and the environment. Stress occurs when the individual is overwhelmed by negative environmental factors or when the environment fails to provide for or meet the individual's needs. Every person has a unique set of skills, abilities, experiences, and personality, and every job, within the context of the environment, requires the employee to possess a certain set of skills, abilities, experiences, and personality. When the person does not match the job, a potential result is heightened stress. Violanti and Marshall refer to this situation as the dilemma of "occupational necessity vs. personal considerations" (1983:383).

Effective stress management requires that the symptoms of stress be recognized. Within a police organization, no one party should be burdened with the responsibility for recognizing these symptoms. Rather, it is vital that all persons who function in administrative and management capacities be able to spot the signs of stress and identify possible methods for alleviating the distress. The symptoms must be acknowledged and ameliorated before they develop into excessive problems for both the stressed person and those who must associate with him or her.

Stress is a problem of the individual, but it is not and cannot be isolated within that single person. All forms of stress spill over to affect the relationships the stressed individual has with others, whether they are one-on-one or group relationships. Therefore, stress is a critical problem for individuals, administrators, and organizations on the whole. Minor stress may accumulate, bringing about major stress, which may lead to a serious physical or emotional breakdown. Prolonged stress can cause wear and tear on the body, and its effects may be irreversible if not treated quickly.

Symptoms of Stress

There are five generally recognized categories in which stress symptoms may appear. From the least serious to the most serious, these are (1) physical, (2) intellectual, (3) emotional, (4) social, and (5) spiritual. Police personnel are regularly exposed to environmental stimuli that may bring about stress reactions in these categories. Individually, or in conjunction with one another, these symptoms can bring about a condition known as burnout, which is discussed briefly at the end of this section.

Physical Symptoms

Physical symptoms of stress are usually the first to be recognized. Ulcers, headaches, backaches, frequent colds, sexual problems, and a general reduction of energy are the typical physical symptoms. The first symptom to appear is fatigue, a general, all-around tiredness. Officers who display physical symptoms of stress seldom engage in any systematic exercise or nutrition program.

Intellectual Symptoms

Intellectual symptoms are exhibited in a general loss of sharpness in thinking and problem solving. Creativity may diminish. There may be cynicism toward innovative or different strategies for accomplishing work. Statements such as "That will never work" or "We've tried something like that already" reflect cynicism that is symptomatic of stress. Officers who are manifesting intellectual symptoms of stress seldom have a hobby or any other mode of intellectual relaxation such as reading, playing chess, or listening to music.

Emotional Symptoms

Emotional symptoms are recognized by examining the general positive or negative aspects of one's emotional life. Is the officer's basic approach to life optimistic or pessimistic? Is the officer generally happy or unhappy? One of the common emotional symptoms is the overinvestment of energy in one's job with

On the Job

TROY, NEW YORK, POLICE DEPARTMENT

By Commissioner Mark L. Whitman

Courtesy of Commissioner Whitman

The position of chief executive for a law enforcement agency is one of the most demanding jobs in government. The expectations society places on the men and women in these positions are extraordinary and oftentimes unrealistic. Most CEOs are appointed after successfully holding a series of increasingly responsible positions in one or more law enforcement agencies. Although the ascent to the position of police chief, director, superintendent, or commissioner is the result of a long and distinguished career, there is nothing that quite prepares one for the seat in the front office except experiencing it.

Law enforcement executives must learn how to increase their ability to influence others, to maximize cooperation and work toward common goals, to apply various leadership approaches to the demands of the position, and to analyze their leadership strengths and weaknesses.

Before my current tenure as the police commissioner of a 115-sworn-member police department in Troy, New York, I served as the police chief in Hornell, New York, for a 22-person police department—both highly unionized departments. I have observed similar characteristics within the policing culture regardless of the agency size. Troy is a 300-year-old city situated along the Hudson River; once a manufacturing mecca, it now suffers from rust belt syndrome. Troy is the home of Uncle Sam and the birthplace of the industrial revolution, and it houses three well-known colleges or universities, adding to an already diverse community. Troy has suffered from financial problems to the point of nearly experiencing bankruptcy and currently is under the control of the State Comptrollers Office.

In addition to the financial woes of Troy, political officials interest groups, police unions, and the general public have steadily increased their demands on the law enforcement CEO throughout my years as a law enforcement executive. None of this has presented more of a challenge than keeping the job interesting for the work force.

A primary motivational factor impacting any agency is employee burnout. Employee burnout is actually more of a cultural fallacy than an objective constant. "Burnout has never been

Continued

created by the job; burnout is the result of an attitude." It is important to provide the best possible workplace for your members. This includes but is not limited to the tools required to do the job; clean and sufficient work sites; and good uniforms, salary, and benefits. Those valued extrinsic tangible concerns are not enough, however. The CEO must clearly deal with the intrinsic values of the membership. For example, the CEO must have the ability to participate in the decision-making process that affects the member. This is critical to the success of the organization's mission. The CEO must be a risk taker, allowing his or her members to participate in policy development and change, especially where it impacts those performing the tasks. Allowing the members to participate in the decision or the initial planning phase will expedite the buy-in process and retain member motivation.

I have observed that the most successful police administrator is the one who enthusiastically relinquishes control and provides autonomy to members to do the job. The law enforcement CEO today must be a risk taker and must accept the responsibility for the programs that fail. He or she must never

fear change and must constantly promote healthy change, including sharing of the decision-making process.

Not all ideas are brilliant and none are stupid, regardless of where they may emanate from. The successful administrator must not "shoot the messenger." President John F. Kennedy said on leadership, "In order to go along, you have to get along." This is true at international government levels and equally important to emphasize at the law enforcement agency level.

As cities, towns, villages, and society as a whole change, so must the successful law enforcement CEO. He or she must constantly review policy and procedures of day-to-day priorities. The law enforcement chief must remain flexible in management style, stay in touch with organizational members, and communicate openly with the department and the community in which it functions. It is important for each of us to remember the objective of providing the finest and highest level of professional service to the community in which we operate. No greater challenge faces today's administrator than that of employee relations and motivation.

very little interest in anything outside of work. When the dreams and expectations of work are lost, feelings of helplessness may result, and symptoms of depression may be displayed. Officers who have varied interests apart from work appear to have a built-in buffer against these symptoms reaching a severe state. When problems arise at work, they have other aspects of life that offer satisfaction.

Social Symptoms

Social symptoms are connected to the officer's feelings of isolation versus feelings of involvement. There are several key questions to ask in attempting to recognize these symptoms. Do others understand this officer's feelings of fatigue, frustration, anger, or disillusionment? Is the officer free to share these feelings with others, or does such behavior seem inappropriate? What type of support system does the person perceive as being available? Is there someone outside work who will listen? Officers suffering from serious social symptoms may not want to burden someone else with their problem; they may feel it is an imposition or they may fear rejection. The net result is self-imposed isolation.

Spiritual Symptoms

Spiritual symptoms are related to the degree of meaning one feels or perceives is present in life. Many officers have noble expectations when they enter their chosen profession, policing. If and when they realize that these expectations will never be fulfilled, there may be a void in their lives. A large part of who they are and what they have dreamed of being is now missing. The challenge to overcoming the spiritual symptoms of stress is to create new meaning for their lives. This process begins by developing meaningful interests outside work. Officers need to ask, answer, and implement the response to the question: What can be changed in my job to make it more meaningful? If the meaning for life is lost, the officer is left in a critical stress condition referred to as "burnout."

Burnout

Burnout is the progressive loss of idealism, energy, purpose, and concern that results from the conditions of work. According to Veniga and Spradley, burnout is "a debilitating psychological condition brought about by unrelieved work stress" (1981:6). Burnout can also be understood as the final stage of mental or physical exhaustion, where the individual is no longer able to cope with the job (see Silbert 1982).

Veniga and Spradley (1981) identified five features of job burnout. The symptoms vary between individuals, but they usually include (1) job dissatisfaction, (2) inefficiency at work, (3) fatigue, (4) sleep disturbance, and (5) escape activities (e.g., daydreaming). When an officer exhibits all five symptoms, burnout can be said to have reached its most serious state.

More (1998) pointed out that there are four *stages* through which the symptoms of burnout manifest themselves: (1) the honeymoon/enthusiasm stage, (2) the fuel shortage/stagnation stage, (3) the chronic symptoms/frustration stage, (4) the crisis/apathy stage, and (5) the hitting-the-wall/intervention stage. In the first stage, the officer reacts enthusiastically to the challenges of the job. This is followed by the realization that the job is not as exciting as previously thought; routine sets in, and the officer may tend to view the job as boring. This may be followed by feelings of intense and seemingly irresolvable apathy and frustration. Pessimism can follow, and the officer can come to be plagued by feelings of self-doubt. In the "hitting-the-wall stage," the officer may reach his or her wits' end, perhaps turning to alcohol and drugs to relieve the feelings of failure and anger that have built up over time.

It should be underscored that frustration and stress build progressively to create the condition of burnout. A burned-out police officer is one who displays extreme symptoms of stress. The job of police administrators and managers, then, is to recognize the early warning symptoms and take action to assist police personnel to cope effectively with their frustrations and stress so that burnout is avoided.

It is also imperative that police managers and administrators look for these symptoms in themselves. They are not immune from the symptoms. Burnout at the administrative and managerial levels in a police organization can lead to organizational stagnation and a generally unhealthy organizational climate. Indeed, stress itself—short of burnout—can have detrimental effects on police administrators, as the following section attests.

STRESS AND THE POLICE ADMINISTRATOR

Early research found that administrators have the same stress problems as lower-ranking police officers. Hillgren, Bond, and Jones, upon examining stress among police administrators, noticed "the marked similarity between the sources of stress identified by police officers for themselves, and those identified by chief administrators for themselves. Both groups indicated that pressures from city officials, the courts, and the community were most troublesome" (1976:447).

Recently, a growing body of research has identified significant differences in the levels of stress and varieties of stressors experienced by police administrators compared to their subordinates. Clearly, the administrative role is a broad one, so it is only natural that police administrators be potentially more susceptible to stress than lower-ranking officers in the police department. This is compounded by the fact that administrators are charged with managing and responding to stress among lower-ranking officials throughout their agencies (e.g., by implementing employee assistance programs).

Sources and Antecedents of Stress for Police Administrators

Crank and his colleagues (1993:313) asked, "Are there broad features of the occupation or role of police executives that affect their perceptions of stress?" They asked 1,120 police executives to respond to a series of statements measuring the extent of the job-related stress they reportedly experienced. The researchers identified four sources of stress for police executives: (1) position, (2) educational attainment, (3) control over the hiring process, and (4) decision-making autonomy.

> **Position.** The law enforcement executive's position—chief or sheriff—was found to contribute to stress. Even though police chiefs are usually appointed officials, sometimes subject to replacement on a whim, the researchers found consistently higher levels of stress among sheriffs.

Crank and his colleagues offered no explanation for this phenomenon, but one possible reason that sheriffs reported more stress than chiefs was linked to the need to please a wide range of constituents and ensure one's reelection.

Educational attainment. "The direct effects of education on role stress derive from the skills and knowledge that better equip an executive to cope with the complexities of leadership and administration" (Crank et al., 1993:315). In other words, education is linked to stress. Police executives with high school diplomas or less reported higher levels of stress than their college-educated counterparts.

Control over the hiring process. The researchers also found that police executives who perceived a greater level of control over the hiring process reported lower levels of stress. This finding is consistent with a century of professionalization endeavors that have attempted to "rationalize" police administration and give police executives more discretion in the hiring process.

Decision-making autonomy. Not surprisingly, the literature suggests that autonomy is inversely related to stress. Administrators who can make decisions without being subject to other constraints (such as the mayor's approval) should be less likely to report stress. Crank and his colleagues found precisely this; decision-making autonomy was linked to lower levels of stress among police executives.

In another study, Crank, Regoli, Hewitt, and Culbertson (1995) identified several additional sources of stress for police executives. These were (1) legitimacy issues, (2) organizational complexity, (3) belief in public service, and (4) ethnicity.

Legitimacy issues. The extent to which powerful actors inside and outside the police organization perceive the police agency as "legitimate" was thought to contribute to stress. The following legitimacy issues were found to affect stress: (1) public and media relations; (2) relationships with other criminal justice officials; (3) budget considerations, personnel retention, and unions; and (4) minority and female hiring (Crank et al., 1995).

Organizational complexity. Clearly, some organizations are more complex than others. Large-scale police organizations contain several divisions and levels, some of which spread across a large geographic area. It is the job of the police executive to maintain some degree of control over these various entities. Accordingly, functional complexity may explain stress among police executives.

Belief in public service. Crank and his colleagues predicted that "a commitment to public service would be negatively associated with negative aspects of a chief's working psychology" (1995:157). In other words, executives who were not committed to their work, those who did not believe in public service, would presumably report higher levels of stress.

Ethnicity. The researchers also hypothesized that minority police executives would be more prone to stress. This would presumably occur because of their historically underrepresented status within police organizations. "As representatives of groups who have entered police work only recently, they may feel greater performance pressures" (Crank et al., 1995:157).

The results of Crank, Regoli, Hewett, and Culbertson's (1995) study indicate that the institutional and organizational features of police executives' occupational environment (e.g., belief in public service, concern with minority hiring, personnel relations, public relations, and relations with other criminal justice officials) explain stress more readily than individual characteristics (e.g., ethnicity and years of experience).

Still other research suggests that stressful events for police administrators include making amends to the public for mistakes made by subordinates (Kroes, Hurrell, and Margolis, 1974). Moreover, meting out discipline was found to be particularly stressful in one study of stress among police administrators (Kroes, Hurrell, and Margolis, 1974). More recent studies have also found that the tasks of motivating employees, building morale, appraising performance, communicating effectively with people in the department, and making interventions in subordinates lives when personal problems reach high levels caused significant stress (Norvell, Belles, and Hills, 1988). Standfest (1996) summarized the problem of stress among police executives by noting that it stems from their location in the department's hierarchy. People on all sides make constant demands on them.

Career Stages and Stress among Administrators

Crank, Regoli, and Culbertson (1986) examined cynicism among police chiefs at various stages throughout their careers. Their research is important in the present context because cynicism can be understood as a reaction to the stress associated with police administration. The stages were as follows:

1. Crisis (0 to 2 years).
2. Interregnum (3 to 4 years).
3. Institutionalization (5 to 9 years).
4. Concretion (10 to 14 years).
5. Demise (15 years and above).

The five stages are to be viewed as cumulative. That is, they build on each other; demise is the last stage in the cynicism process.

Crisis. The crisis stage begins when a new police chief enters office. It is during this stage that the new chief must confront many challenges, such as clearing up a department's tarnished public image. As Regoli and colleagues observed, "The chief's authority to produce mandated change in the departmental structure, street-level policies, or delivery of services is constrained by political leaders . . . and by existing pockets of authority within the department, such as union leaders and entrenched middle-management personnel" (1990:595–596). For example, if the chief plans a radical change such as the implementation of computer-driven crime statistics (called COMPSTAT), or some other aggressive mechanism to ensure accountability for lower-level supervisors, he or she is likely to face considerable resistance from others within the department who perceive this approach as too harsh.

Interregnum. During the interregnum stage the chief has established authority but not a firm grasp on the whole department. What makes this stage unique, then, is that it is characterized by struggles between the new chief and opposing groups that have resisted change during the first two years. If the chief survives this stage and becomes a "player," then the chief is said to have learned three lessons. First, he or she comes to understand the practical aspects of administration. Second, he or she knows which policies will be received favorably by opposing groups. Finally, he or she will have a grasp of the consequences associated with change. As Regoli et al. observed, "Throughout this stage, the chief has continuously learned the importance of flexibility in adjusting to situational contingencies" (1990:596).

Institutionalization. Chiefs who survive to the institutionalization stage can claim more successes than failures, or they would have been ousted (or would have chosen to leave) at some point during an earlier stage. At this point, many of the chief's new policies and procedures have been implemented, and most resistance has been overcome. Some changes continue to face resistance, but the chief has essentially become "institutionalized," a familiar and lasting figure within the police organization.

Concretion. Chiefs who make it to this stage are well-known figures not only in the police agency, but in the community. The concretion stage is viewed, in part, as a time for renewing outmoded policies and procedures. Chiefs sometimes refocus their efforts and pursue new agendas. Some resistance will be encountered, but chiefs surviving into the concretion stage have successfully overcome the most stubborn forms of resistance, as evidenced by their tenure in office.

Demise. Chiefs who survive into the demise stage have basically made careers out of administration. Having spent several years moving up through the ranks in one department or another, most chiefs in the demise stage are approaching retirement age. Most, if not all, of the changes they pursued throughout the previous 15 or so years have been accomplished. "As they gradually relinquish power, they relax their informal relations with subordinates and persons outside the department" (Regoli et al., 1990:597).

The evolution from one stage to the next is thought to be brought about by unique features of the administrative role. Regoli and his colleagues (1990) found that cynicism varies depending on such factors as department size, perceived autonomy, professional commitment, and education. Additionally, stress was a significant factor found to influence cynicism, particularly during the middle stages of a police chief's career (interregnum, institutionalization, and concretion).

STRESS AND THE POLICE OFFICER

Aside from dealing with their own stress, police administrators are also responsible for managing the stress problem among their subordinates within the police agency. The sources of stress for line officers are different in many respects, and administrators must have an awareness of them so measures can be taken to reduce the negative consequences of stress.

Sources of Stress for Police Officers

Police officers are required to provide the public a wide variety of services. Many of these services are rendered in areas that are threatening to the officers. The tasks themselves frequently are dangerous, and the circumstances surrounding the delivery of the service might be unpleasant or undesirable. A number of researchers have examined police stress and found four general categories of police stress: (1) organizational and administrative practices, (2) the criminal justice system, (3) the public, and (4) stressors intrinsic to police work (Webb and Smith, 1980).

Organizational and Administrative Practices

Organizational and administrative practices as sources of stress are a two-way street. We saw in the previous section that administrators face stress when implementing new policies and effectuating change. This is because resistance is often encountered when administrators disrupt the status quo. However, lower-ranking police officials must respond to changes and mandates imposed from above. This becomes especially problematic when there is tension between superiors and subordinates. Stotland (1991) found that criticism, rejection, or derogation by their sergeants was a significant source of stress for officers. Also, sergeants' unwillingness to support officers in "official trouble" is extremely stressful.

Work in bureaucratic police organizations is often found to be extremely frustrating and stressful due to the self-serving, slow, and unresponsive nature of such organizations. Even though there is evidence that police management styles are becoming less authoritarian (e.g., with the advent of community policing), there is no significant movement away from the bureaucratic organizational structure which continues to predominate in police organizations in the United States and around the world (Crank and Caldero, 1991).

Stress factors that officers identify as endemic to law enforcement organizational structures include excessive paperwork, red tape, lack of participation in decision-making processes that directly affect them, antiquated promotional policies, disciplinary regulations that require them to maintain significantly higher personal and moral standards than are expected of civilians, irregular duty hours (shifts), departmental management policies that are unfair or unreasonable, insufficient opportunity for advancement, inadequate direction from supervisors, and conflicts between articulated expectations and the factors on which officers are evaluated (Lord, Gray, and Pond, 1991; Storch and Panzarella, 1996).

Another organizational and administrative factor thought to contribute to stress among police officers is agency size. Researchers have suggested that informal relationships in smaller police organizations may contribute to reduced stress (Regoli, Crank, and Culbertson, 1989). Morash and Haarr (1995) support this contention. They found a positive relationship between stress and organizational size. Officers in large police organizations experienced more stress than their counterparts in small agencies. Brooks and Piquero (1998) note that large departments place many more demands on officers. These demands emanate from a variety of sources, including citizens, the criminal justice system, management, and the increased levels of danger that are generally present in larger departments.

The Criminal Justice System

Kroes, Margolis, and Hurrell (1974) examined stress among Cincinnati police officers. They interviewed 100 police officers, and 56 percent of the respondents noted that courts were stressful. No other category in their survey was deemed to be as stressful by the officers. Officers identified a number of problems associated with the courts: rulings restricting police procedures, dismissing cases and giving lenient sentences for offenders, having to appear in court on days off or during off-duty time, and the lack of respect shown police officers by court and prosecutor personnel. More recent studies suggest that giving court testimony can be particularly stressful for police officers as well (e.g., Brooks and Piquero, 1998; Sigler, Wilson, and Allen, 1991).

The corrections system is also bothersome to some police officers (Brooks and Piquero, 1998). A great deal of concern is related to corrections' inability to rehabilitate criminals and to the likelihood that offenders will serve only a small portion of their sentences. Lax or overly tolerant parole officers who allow parolees to commit numerous infractions before revoking parole are another source of concern to the average police officer. Often it appears that the criminals are "back out on the street" before the police officer can finish the arrest report.

The Public

In Chapter 2 we discussed the police–public relationship. For the most part, it appears that the public accepts and supports the police. However, the police erroneously tend to believe that the public disapproves of them and the work they are doing. As one officer observed, "Anytime you deal with the public they have certain images, stereotypes, and expectations of you . . . most people aren't happy to see the police, as it is usually some sort of negative contact" (Crank and Caldero, 1991:345). This lack of approval is a source of stress to many police officers. For example, Kroes, Margolis, and Hurrell (1974) note that 22 percent of the officers in their study were bothered by the public's apathy and lack of support for the police while 16 percent identified the police officer's negative image as stressful. The police tend to believe that the public views them negatively regardless of how the public actually views them.

Perceived stress attributable to the public may be exacerbated by the media's occasional (or possibly frequent, depending on your perspective) tendency to portray the police in a negative light. Many people form their opinions of the police not so much from direct encounters, but from reports in the newspapers and on television about police activities. Negative press coverage, then, can serve as a significant source of stress for many police officials (Brooks and Piquero, 1998).

Disapproval, criticism, and apathy represent one area of public attitudes toward the police. Another area is danger. The police face potentially dangerous situations almost on a daily basis (Bayley, 1976). Although most officers do not face danger on a regular basis, the potential is ever-present. The police officer never knows when an encounter with a citizen will result in an armed confrontation. This possibility shapes training, patrol preoccupations, and operating procedures. It results in a mutual apprehension between citizens and the police when they come into contact.

Stressors Intrinsic to Police Work

Police officers are required to make decisions that may result in serious negative consequences for the lives and the property of others. They are also frequently placed in a work environment in which they consistently must deal with pain, crime, poverty, and citizens in despair. This "task environment" can be seen as a significant source of stress for police officers (Crank and Caldero, 1991).

Police are forced to deal with the worst problems of society and the worst elements of society while being expected to relate in a positive manner to all persons with whom they come in contact. The emotional toll of such stress is further compounded by the fact that many of the life-affecting decisions must be made instantly. This creates such intense situations that the police officer can become emotionally crippled. Even the mere anticipation of danger can have detrimental effects on the individual (Crank and Caldero, 1991).

Sewell (1981) examined stress by looking at individual stressors rather than classes of stressors. He developed the Law Enforcement Critical Life Events Survey to determine which stressors were the most stressful. Table 9–1 lists the 25 most stressful critical life events according to the police officers in his survey.

Other features of the police job can contribute to stress. Shift work, boredom on the job, and performing nonpolice duties can cause disillusionment and frustration, precursors to stress and burnout. In addition, the threat of civil liability

Table 9–1

The Twenty-Five Most Stressful Law Enforcement Critical Life Events

---

 1. Violent death of a partner in the line of duty
 2. Dismissal from the force
 3. Taking a life in the line of duty
 4. Shooting someone in the line of duty
 5. Suicide of an officer who is a close friend
 6. Violent death of another officer in the line of duty
 7. Murder committed by a police officer
 8. Duty-related violent injury (shooting)
 9. Violent job-related injury to another officer
10. Suspension
11. Passed over for promotion
12. Pursuit of an armed suspect
13. Answering a call to a scene involving violent nonaccidental death of a child
14. Assignment away from family for a long period of time
15. Personal involvement in a shooting incident
16. Reduction in pay
17. Observing an act of police corruption
18. Accepting a bribe
19. Participating in an act of police corruption
20. Hostage situation resulting from aborted criminal action
21. Response to a scene involving the accidental death of a child
22. Promotion of an inexperienced/incompetent officer over you
23. Internal affairs investigation against you
24. Barricaded suspect
25. Hostage situation resulting from a domestic disturbance

Source: J. Sewell, Police Stress. *FBI Law Enforcement Bulletin* 50, no. 4 (1981), pp. 7–11.

is a significant source of stress for many police officers. This is especially true nowadays, as many people seem to resort to litigation at the drop of a hat. The paradox for police officials is that they must work tirelessly to control crime, but they must also avoid stepping over the line that separates appropriate conduct from misconduct.

Finally, Lawrence's (1984) Police Stress Inventory identified four sources of stress for police officers: the courts, administration, the public, and equipment. We have already considered the first three sources of stress, but equipment, Lawrence claimed, ranked highly in police officers' appraisals of job-related stress. Concerns over having the latest equipment or faulty equipment, having plenty of cars, maintaining one's personal equipment, being able to use a weapon proficiently, and so on weighed heavily in the stress equation.

Critical Incidents

A major source of stress in police work concerns the possibility of becoming involved in critical or traumatic incidents. According to Stevens, a critical incident "refers to any high-risk encounter with officer–civilian contacts when officers reasonably believe they might be legally justified in using deadly force,

An injured New York Police Department officer lies on the ground after clashes with mourners attending funeral services for unarmed police shooting victim Patrick Dorismond.

James Keivon/Getty Images

Table 9–2

Officers' Rank Ordering of 14 Critical Incident Stressors

 1. Harming or killing an innocent person
 2. Harming or killing another officer
 3. Killing of another officer by a citizen
 4. Hate groups and terrorists
 5. Riot control
 6. Barricaded persons
 7. Hostage takers
 8. Disturbed offenders
 9. High-risk warrants
10. Sniper incidents
11. Killing criminals
12. Hot pursuit
13. Using excessive force
14. Protecting VIPs

Source: D. J. Stevens, Stress and the American Police Officer. *The Police Journal* 72, no. 3 (1999), pp. 247–259.

regardless of whether they use such force or avert its use" (1999:247). Examples of critical incident stressors include apprehending disturbed persons, serving warrants against dangerous persons, providing riot control, or dealing with hostage takers and barricaded suspects. Table 9–2 ranks 14 critical incident stressors in order of their seriousness, according to a sample of police officers.

One of the most stressful events that a police officer can experience is a shooting in which the officer critically wounds or kills another person, or in which a fellow officer is killed or critically wounded. Most experts agree that many good police officers leave policing because of postshooting trauma, which can have longlasting effects on the police officer. However, not every officer who is involved in a shooting has a traumatic reaction. The postshooting trauma reactions are almost equally divided among mild reactions, moderate reactions, and severe reactions (Solomon, 1988). Carson (1982) examined the trauma of a shooting incident. He noted that officers involved in shootings experience emotional or psychological numbing. Essentially, there are five stages of coping that an officer experiences when involved in a catastrophic event. These stages do not last for any particular length of time; they may be experienced in various orders, and one or more may be omitted. The phases are:

Denial. The person does not want to believe what has happened. This stage is usually very brief in officer-involved shootings.

Anger and resentment. This is usually nonspecific or vaguely directed at the person shot for making the officer act as he or she did. This stage is usually short-lived, though it may return at various times during the adaptation process.

Bargaining. This stage involves the officer's wishing the bullet could be pulled back into the gun. It may be due to the officer's being worried about reprisals from the department.

Depression. This stage lasts the longest. The severity of the depression is dependent on the personality of the officer, the amount of trauma involved in the incident, the agency's response to the incident, the officer's social network, and other factors.

Acceptance. This stage has been reached when the event begins to be integrated into the officer's life or the officer makes the transition from being totally preoccupied with the event to merely acknowledging that it took place.

Carson (1982) found that the symptoms of postshooting trauma were most intense for the first 48 to 72 hours following the event, although the various reactions would come and go for some time after. The officer experiences a number of symptoms. Almost immediately the officer feels isolated, depressed, and agitated and exhibits abruptness in behavior. Other symptoms of trauma may occur immediately or later and continue for a period of time. The officer may experience a heightened sense of danger or vulnerability, fear and anxiety about future encounters, anger or rage, nightmares, sleep difficulties (insomnia, sleep disturbances, or escaping through sleep), guilt, emotional numbing, emotional withdrawal from others, sexual difficulties, physical problems (e.g., headaches, indigestion, muscle aches, diarrhea, or constipation), or anxiety reactions (e.g., difficulty concentrating, excessive worry, irritability, nervousness) (Solomon, 1988). The officer may continually think about the incident and frequently have flashbacks. Officers tend to neglect their families and duties, become consumed by the incident, and increase their alcohol consumption. They may begin to examine their values and consider giving up law enforcement as a career.

Occasionally, stress arising from critical incidents can lead to a condition known as post-traumatic stress disorder (PTSD). McHenry defines PTSD as "a condition which sets in following a traumatic event with which the sufferer cannot cope. It has been described as an event outside the usual human experience, one which is experienced in a markedly distressing way, with intense fear, terror, bewilderment and a sense of helplessness" (1995:18). According to McHenry symptoms of PTSD can include (1) persistent and recurring memories of the event, (2) loss of interest and feelings, (3) problems sleeping and concentrating, and (4) hypervigilance. In the wake of particularly traumatic incidents, it is advisable to treat potential PTSD problems before they get out of control. If early treatment is offered and utilized, many of the long-term negative effects of PTSD can be prevented or eliminated.

Police Career Stages and Stress

We have already seen that police administrators go through various stages with respect to stress and job cynicism. In another study, Niederhoffer (1967) found that police officers go through a series of four stages during their careers. These stages were based on adjustment to police work:

1. Alarm stage (0 to 5 years).
2. Disenchantment stage (6 to 13 years).
3. Personalization stage (14 to 20 years).
4. Introspection stage (20 years and over).

Violanti (1983) used Neiderhoffer's career stages to explain the stress process in police work.

> **Alarm stage.** During the alarm stage the young police officer is exposed to the realities of police work. All recruits coming into police work have conceptions about what police work is about, and usually police work turns out to be something other than what they imagined. The rookies are faced with the experiences of police work: the death and injuries from crime and accidents; hostility from suspects, victims, and other uncooperative citizens; the extended periods of boredom during patrol; and the massive paperwork requirements. The alarm stage is when officers initially cope with the newness of the job and question their ability to be good police officers. During this stage of their careers, officers generally lack self-confidence, which is stressful in itself.
>
> **Disenchantment stage.** The disenchantment stage is characterized by bitter disappointment. It is a time when officers realize and accept that they are unable to do anything about the problems of society and the bureaucratic interworkings of the police and criminal justice

systems. Officers become extremely cynical and tend to distrust everyone around them. Niederhoffer notes that this cynicism is one of the primary coping tools used during this stage.

Personalization stage. During the personalization stage, officers tend to focus outward, away from the police department and police work. It is during this stage that job stress begins to subside. Personal goals, rather than police work, tend to dominate the individual's interests. The officer no longer fears failure, and the demands of being a police officer are taken in stride.

Introspection stage. After 20 years of service, police officers tend to be relatively secure in their jobs. They have experienced most of the undesirable situations and problems associated with police work and are able to cope with them with relatively little difficulty. Officers know that retirement is close, and they can leave just about any time they want to. This gives them a degree of independence, which greatly reduces stress.

The police career stages provide insights into how police officers will interact with the department and the environment. It appears that all officers will experience some stress during the first 13 years. Officers' personality and departmental support will, to a large part, determine how stressed the officers will become as they progress through their careers.

THE EFFECTS OF STRESS IN POLICING

For the most part, it is recognized that job stress negatively affects the department as well as the individual officer. The department is affected in terms of lowered productivity and increased officer absenteeism, injuries, and turnover. Several of the problems that can be associated with stress are discussed in the following sections.

Health-Related Problems

As noted at the beginning of the chapter, stress contributes to a number of diseases and debilitating conditions. There has been a great deal of research examining police health problems and stress. In examining the general health of police officers, Grencik (1975) found that 15 percent of the officers had high cholesterol; triglycerides were high in 27 percent of the officers; and 56 percent of the officers were from 6 to 20 pounds overweight, while 28 percent were more than 21 pounds overweight. These general health conditions have been shown to lead to an increased susceptibility to coronary heart disease. These data indicate that officers tend to neglect their health when they are faced with stress.

Jacobi (1975) examined workmen's compensation cases and found that police officers submit six times more claims than other employees. Some 30 percent of the claims were for lower back pain, and another 50 percent were for high blood pressure. Blackmore (1978) reviewed a National Institute of Occupational

Safety and Health (NIOSH) study of 2,300 police officers in 29 departments and reported 36 percent of the officers had serious health problems.

Blackmore (1978) reported on another NIOSH study that examined hospital admissions and death certificates. The study indicated that police work was ranked seventeenth out of 130 occupations relative to health problems. In a similar study, Richard and Fell (1975) examined a sample of 23,976 Tennessee workers which included 168 police officers. They found that police officers had more health problems than workers in other occupations, particularly digestive and circulatory problems.

These studies tend to indicate that police officers generally are not as healthy as they should be. Some of this can be attributed to shift work and irregular eating, sleeping, and exercise habits. Police officers appear to have a significant number of health problems, many of which have been associated with stress.

The Police Officer and the Family

Researchers have long recognized the negative effects police work has on the family. A number of terms and descriptions have been used to describe the problem: marital discord, child-rearing problems, sexual promiscuity, loss of nonpolice friends, and divorce (Terry, 1981). Police officers are faced with a gamut of family problems, and they may experience these problems to a greater extent than people in other occupations.

Several police stress researchers have examined the divorce rate for police officers and found it to be excessively high. Blackmore (1978) reported that 37 percent of the officers in a study with 2,300 officers had serious marital difficulties. He reported on another NIOSH study which found that 22 percent of the police officers sampled have been divorced at least once, as compared to a national average of 13.8 percent at the time of the study. Police officers who were married prior to entering police work had the highest divorce rate, 26 percent, while those marrying after becoming a police officer had a divorce rate of 11 percent. However, Davidson and Veno (1978) pointed out several flaws in Blackmore's research and concluded that divorce rates among police officers may be no higher than those of the general population.

Other studies on police divorce have questioned whether police officers experience high divorce rates relative to the general population. That is, these researchers note that divorce is high in our society and police divorce rates are no higher than the divorce rates for other occupations. For example, Terry (1981) examined a number of studies which found police divorce rates to be lower than or the same as the general population. These data tend to indicate that police marriages are no different from other marriages, and that police families are better able to cope and adjust to the stress of police work.

Territo and Vetter (1981) examined stress in the police family and identified several factors that contribute to family problems: (1) changing work schedules, (2) emotional exhaustion, (3) negative public image, (4) overprotection of the spouse and family, (5) hardening of emotions, (6) sexual problems, (7) identity problems, and (8) problems with children.

Changing Work Schedules

Most police departments require officers to rotate work shifts. Shifts have a psychological and physiological impact on the employee. Police officers typically are required to work evenings, when spouses and children are at home, and during weekends and holidays. This results in extensive disruption in the home life and prohibits the planning of family activities. Police officers subsequently are unable to participate in family activities or even spend an adequate amount of time with the family. This leads to communication problems and ultimately feelings of isolation.

Emotional Exhaustion

When they are at home, police officers are generally emotionally exhausted. While on the job, they are constantly bombarded with negative situations and problems, most of which are unsolvable. By the time they return home, this frustration has led to psychological exhaustion. They frequently do not have the energy to cope with problems and issues at home and tend to withdraw or isolate themselves from the family, which only compounds the family problem. Family members view this behavior as rejection and become angered. This situation frequently escalates into a confrontation between the officer and family members.

Negative Public Image

Police officers have a great deal of difficulty socializing with nonpolice acquaintances. People continually tell officers how they unjustly received a traffic citation or how their home or business was burglarized and the police did nothing to solve the case. Police officers tend to avoid nonpolice people as a result of such negativism. This has an isolating effect on the family, and the family comes to resent the officer's reluctance to socialize with their friends. These social problems create a substantial amount of stress in the family.

Overprotecting the Spouse and Family

Police work requires officers to be cautious and observant of the things which occur around them. They develop an innate need to know. This carries over into the family where the officer becomes overly concerned with the actions and whereabouts of family members. Family members come to view this behavior as restrictive and untrusting. Ultimately, conflicts develop, which increase the level of stress in the family.

Hardening of Emotions

One of the primary coping mechanisms used by police officers to deal with the problems and stress of the job is the hardening of emotions. They attempt to detach and isolate themselves emotionally from the negative happenings in the environment. It is impossible to turn this emotional detachment on and off and subsequently it is carried over to the home. Family members are faced with someone who appears to be uncaring, impersonal, and unwilling to participate in family matters. The police officer must exert a great deal of effort to overcome this problem but oftentimes is too emotionally exhausted to find the strength and determination necessary to effectively deal with the family.

Sexual Problems

The hardening of emotions, emotional exhaustion, and other problems will take their toll on the officer over time (Somodevilla, Baker, Hill, and Thomas, 1978). Emotional estrangement develops when intimacy and loving subside within the marriage. Over time, the problem becomes more difficult and can ultimately lead to open hostility. Infidelity also becomes a problem.

Identity Problems

As the two-paycheck family has become increasingly prevalent in the United States, male police officers often have had difficulty coping with their wives' outside interests. Additionally, working women develop new friendships that require the family to socialize in new circles. This places an additional strain on the police officer. As both spouses increasingly attend to their jobs, there is less energy available to make the marriage work. The husbands of female officers may have similar difficulty accepting their wives in the nontraditional role of police officer.

Problems with Children

Police officers tend to feel that they live in a fishbowl where everyone constantly examines what they do. Police officers, since they are involved in law enforcement, have strong feelings about what their children can and should do. They tend to be stricter than other parents and have little patience when the children misbehave. This becomes a critical problem when the children are adolescents. The teens frequently rebel against their restrictive parents, which increases the problem. Unfortunately, police officer parents tend to view juvenile problems as a reflection on themselves.

Differential Responses to Stress

The individual is a key ingredient in the stress process. That is, the amount of stress an individual experiences depends largely on how well the individual copes with the stress situation. Violanti (1983) emphasizes that stress is a matter of perception. Stress is said to occur only if the individual *perceives* that social demands cannot be adequately handled; otherwise, that individual is not threatened by the anticipation of failure and will not experience stress. From this point of view, stress is a personal experience depending on the social and psychological attributes of each person.

One of the stress research issues is the individual's cognitive appraisal of stress (Lawrence, 1984). That is, we are interested in how an individual comes to define a situation as being stressful. Two officers could be placed in a situation, and one might become stressed while the other effectively copes with or manages the situation. Understanding why some individuals become stressed while others do not has implications for police selection and training as well as for dealing with stressed police officers.

Since stress is recognized as a person–environment fit problem, it would appear that there is a need to determine what types of officers "fit" into the police work environment. Every person has a distinct set of needs and values that drive the individual. The needs, to a degree, dictate behavior while values serve to restrict behavioral choices. If the environment is incongruent with a person's needs and values, the result is stress.

A number of researchers have examined individual and personality variables in relation to success in the workplace and the police field. Opton and Lazarus (1967) found that individuals who were socially inhibited, introverted, submissive, insecure, or passive were more likely to be bothered with stress. French and Caplan (1970) found that persons who have a high need for social approval experienced more stress. Conversely, persons with high self-esteem are better able to cope with stressful situations (Mechanic, 1974). Personality is an important consideration in the study of stress, as a person's personality will dictate how the individual will respond to the specific stress situation.

In short, some people respond badly to stress, while others seem to thrive on it. Police officials respond differently to stress not just because of the stressors they face, but because of enduring features of their personalities. Two famous cardiologists, Friedman and Rosenman (1994), attributed the differences to "Type A" and "Type B" personalities.

People with *Type A* personalities are described as competitive, ambitious, driven, and always rushed. These are the people who feel pressed to do the most with their lives. Thus they place huge demands on themselves to accomplish a lot in a short amount of time. They seem to have little time for hobbies or other personal affairs, choosing instead to focus on work-related accomplishment. They crave recognition, attention, and positive reinforcement for their actions. Not surprisingly, people with Type A personalities suffer from stress. Type A police officers may be more prone to the negative effects of stress than Type B personalities.

The *Type B* personality is the exact opposite of Type A. Type B people are more relaxed, passive, nonaggressive, and patient. They take more time to relax, and they take pleasure in activities such as exercise and hobbies. People with Type B personalities tend to be less obsessed with success, and they tend to deal more effectively with stressful situations. On the contrary, people with Type A personalities have been shown to be much more prone to developing coronary heart disease, with an increased risk of suffering heart attacks, as well as other physiological problems. The characteristics of Type A and Type B personalities are summarized in Table 9–3.

The Type A–Type B distinction is both comforting and disconcerting. On the one hand, it is informative to know that different individuals respond in different ways to stress. This suggests that we should spend more time analyzing personalities than identifying the features of police work most likely to cause

Table 9–3

Differences between Type A and Type B Personalities

Type A	Type B
Always rushed, never enough time in the day	Little sense of time urgency
Constantly impatient	Relaxed, makes time for fun
Cannot cope with leisure time	Can relax without feelings of guilt
Obsessed with measuring success	Not overly concerned with achievement
Competitive	Not very competitive
Difficulty dealing with stress	Deals more effectively with stress
Little time for intimate relationships	Values intimate relationships
Always distracted by a focus on tasks	Attentive, concerned with what others say

stress. On the other hand, it is not very reassuring to know that some officers will respond more severely to the already high-stress environment of police work. People with Type A personalities should be most attuned to what can be done in terms of managing and responding to stress.

MANAGING THE STRESS PROBLEM

The Individual and Stress

Individuals develop strategies for dealing with threats, stress, or conflict situations. These strategies are called "coping." *Coping* is a form of problem solving that is designed to protect the individual's well-being in situations in which the person does not clearly know what to do. Coping is the means used to gain control of situations that are threatening. Sometimes coping strategies (such as attack, inaction, or a defense mechanism) are used to reduce the perceived threat.

Haarr and Morash (1999) examined gender, race, and coping with occupational stress in policing. They found a variety of coping mechanisms that police officers used in reaction to stress. They include such reactions as, (1) changing job assignments, (2) escaping by ignoring the situation or avoiding people, (3) expressing feelings of anger or hurt, (4) taking action such as seeking professional help, (5) forming racial bonds, (6) blowing off steam with co-workers, and (7) seeking support from co-workers, family members, and others. They found that, for the most part, males and females used the same coping mechanisms, except that women tended to use escape more frequently than men.

Obviously, police officers are not always going to be able to successfully deal with stress through personal coping mechanisms. The police department must become involved, especially in instances where the source of stress is endemic or traumatic for the officer involved. Support for the stressed officer is helpful. Departmental support, operating in conjunction with individual coping mechanisms, offers an effective means of combating the detrimental effects of stress. Figure 9–2 details this process.

Figure 9–2
The stress process.

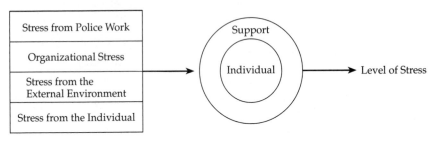

Eisenberg (1975) observes that police departments use one of five alterna-tives when dealing with an officer whose behavior has deteriorated as a result of stress: ignore the officer, hide or transfer the officer, fire the officer, retire the officer on disability, or rehabilitate the officer. The first three alternatives occur too frequently in policing. They essentially do nothing to solve the problem. In these instances, police executives completely abrogate their responsibility as administrators. In some cases, officers must be given a disability retirement, but when this alternative is used, it usually indicates that the department has allowed the problem to exist for an extended period of time without doing any-thing about it. Police departments have a basic moral obligation to attempt to help or rehabilitate any officer who is suffering from stress. Moreover, when departments fail to address stress and treat stressed officers unfairly, personnel are left to conclude the administration has little concern for their welfare. The result is that morale throughout the department suffers.

Stress and the Police Organization

There is little a police administrator can do about external stressors, which are created by sources outside the police agency, but a great deal of influence can be exerted on the stress situations that result from internal policy and procedure. Police executives can take a proactive role in managing the stress experienced by officers in their department. Greller (1982) suggests that the police depart-ment can identify the events that are under the department's control and that have the potential to cause significant stress. They can then target those elements for change. The immediate targets should be those administrative stressors that are unrelated to field duties but that occur within the department and are under the department's control. Elements to be considered are the promotion system, the system of deployment and distribution of personnel, shifts and shift assign-ment, personnel benefits, training, policy and procedures statements, supervi-sory techniques, and control procedures. A proactive role in managing police stress will require police executives to take a broad view of the work environ-ment and to assess the stressfulness of the events that confront the members of the police department.

White and Marino (1983) conducted an exploratory analysis of the causal relationships among organizational stressors and police stress. Specifically, attitudes of influence, norm observance, and trust in management were each found to be related to perceived stress. Attitudes of influence referred to perceived freedom and control in work-related activities. The term "norm observance" alluded to by White and Marino refers to the perception that upward mobility within the organization is the result of superior performance and ability. White and Marino suggest that perceptions of nonadherence to norm observance can be resolved through administrative action involving the clarification and adherence to policies regarding transfer and promotion. The intent, evaluative dimensions, and procedures of the performance evaluation system must also be clarified, and must be tied directly to the distribution of rewards if the individual officer is to be motivated to alter behavior.

Trust in management involves the perception that the organization's management acts in the best interests of the officers. White and Marino (1983) identified ways to reduce the stress resulting from mistrust in management. First, clear lines of communication and authority should be established to facilitate the discussion of officers' concerns and grievances. Second, work groups, supervisors, and administration should meet regularly so that officers have access to management to discuss policies and procedures. Finally, officers should be involved in decisions that affect work activities.

Hart, Wearing, and Headey's (1995) study found that police organizations are more responsible for stress among line officers than police work itself (i.e., the task environment). They argued that police administrators should place greater emphasis on improving their "organizational health." They advocate the use of clinical and organizational psychologists to mitigate the detrimental effects of police stress.

In another study, Standfest (1996) advocated a four-stage approach to dealing with stress among law enforcement executives. The four stages are (1) assessment, (2) planning, (3) action, and (4) follow-through.

> **Assessment.** In this stage, police executives should determine what problems affect personnel within their department. The following questions should be addressed: Are there policies and procedures within the agency that cause stress? Are there physical features of the department that contribute to stress? What can be done to improve the quality of life within the department?
>
> **Planning.** Once stressors have been identified, administrators must find ways to deal with problems. As Standfest (1996) observes, "Any action taken must show a good faith effort on the part of the agency and the city to address the problems faced by managers and supervisors."
>
> **Action.** Once problems have been identified and solutions proposed, administrators should take steps to implement the necessary changes. Studying problems and talking about them are not helpful; administrators need to put the wheels of change in motion. Problems must be addressed seriously and enthusiastically, or morale will suffer.

Follow-through. Initiating action does not ensure the action will succeed. Administrators need to go back to the people affected by the change to determine whether it is working. Is the stress waning, or is there something else management should do to alleviate the problem?

STRATEGIES FOR RESPONDING TO STRESS

Webb and Smith (1980) examined stress prevention and alleviation strategies. They make the important distinction between proactive and reactive strategies. *Proactive strategies* are designed to prevent the development of stress, whereas *reactive strategies* attempt to deal with eliminating sources of stress or alleviating their consequences. If a department is to deal successfully with the stress problem, it must implement both proactive and reactive strategies (Lowenstein, 1999). Many agencies have implemented employee assistance and wellness programs. These are briefly touched on toward the end of this section.

Proactive Strategies

Training

Webb and Smith (1980) identify two types of training and education program that are useful in preventing stress. First, training should be developed to provide officers with the skills and knowledge necessary to satisfactorily carry out the duties and responsibilities of the job. Too often, such important or critical subjects receive only cursory attention or are presented incorrectly in training academies. For example, Taylor (1982) notes that trainers often inadequately combine theory and practice in the academy, causing the trainee to misunderstand the subject matter, which ultimately causes problems during application. Efforts should be made to ensure the total subject matter content is addressed.

Second, training should be provided that assists officers to know themselves. Here officers learn about their own limits, needs, reactions, and abilities. These programs are frequently referred to as stress inoculation. They are based on the notion that people who understand themselves are better able to deal with others and their problems. For example, Das (1986) examined police training on the subject of ethics. He concluded that officers who understand and value ethical police behavior can better deal with the public and themselves. This type of training is critical to reducing an officer's propensity toward stress.

Selection Procedures

As we have seen, the distinction between different personality types suggests that there are stress-prone individuals, but it is unclear if they can be identified during the selection process. However, there are a number of researchers who believe stress-prone applicants can be identified (Hillgren and Bond, 1975). Roberts (1975) developed a program for the San Jose Police Department that he believes identifies people who are particularly vulnerable to stress. There has been little research in this area, and there is a need to explore the subject more extensively. However, the assumption is that applicants who have high self-esteem and are extroverted are better able to cope with the stress of police work. Moreover, people who know the value of relaxation, recreation, and exercise (among other things) may be less prone to becoming victims of stress.

Career Development

Officers tend to place too much emphasis on being promoted. Subsequently, when officers fail to be promoted after a reasonable term of service, they experience stress. Schwartz and Schwartz (1975) suggested that police departments should establish nonpromotion positions with increased responsibilities and status. An alternative is the generalist approach, where patrol officers are involved in a wide range of activities, as in recent attempts to implement community policing. Still another alternative is for the department to emphasize the importance of patrol work. Regardless of modality, the department must take steps to ensure that the status and prestige associated with the various jobs and positions within the department are fairly equal. When officers believe there is inequity or a difference in status, they become more susceptible to stress.

Spouse Programs

Spouse programs are extremely important because if there is stress in the family, it will be carried over to the job. Also, stress in the family tends to interact with the stress on the job, and each exacerbates the other. Territo and Vetter (1981) identified a number of strategies to reduce stress in the family.

Orientation programs for spouses are designed to assist spouses in understanding police work. Such programs should provide information about the department's operations, levels of command, and daily duties of police officers. The program allows spouses to ask supervisors and administrators questions clarifying uncertainties and misconceptions. When spouses have a better understanding of police work, they are able to communicate and empathize with their husbands' and wives' problems and concerns. John Stratton (1976, 1978), a psychologist for the Los Angeles County Sheriff's Department, expanded on the orientation program concept and developed a complete training course for spouses. The program is outlined in Table 9–4.

Spouses, upon completion of such a program, are better able to communicate with their husbands and wives and eliminate or reduce some of the friction and stress at home.

Police departments should implement interview programs with the spouses of police applicants. As noted earlier, the highest police divorce rate is for officers who are married before becoming police officers. The interview should be conducted in the applicant's home, and should be designed to help determine the compatibility of the couple with the rigors of police work. Sometimes officers can better manage problems if they anticipate and clearly understand them. Also, if the couple's lifestyle is not compatible with police work, it is easier to make the decision early in the application process.

Table 9–4

Couples-Based Stress Prevention Program

I. Didactic group presentations (8 weeks)
Weekly two-hour sessions
    1. First hour: stress management education
    2. Second hour: group shares thoughts and experiences

II. Support groups
Peer mentors provide ongoing support after didactic presentations
    1. Peer support provides continuity

Another valuable program is the ride-along program. Here, spouses are allowed to ride with their husbands or wives while on duty to become familiar with actual police operations and situations. The program allows the police officer's spouse to experience the job and to discuss actual calls or police activities. The experience is valuable when the police officer is experiencing job stress since the spouse acquires a better understanding of how to relate to the problems of police work and can empathize with the officer. Recently, because of legal issues and potential conflict-of-interest problems, spousal ride-along programs have been curtailed in some jurisdictions.

The firearms safety program is another program that a department can implement to reduce stress. As police officers progress in their careers, they frequently are apprehensive about their families' safety while they are working. A firearms safety program provides officers with a sense of security and reduces stress.

Physical Fitness Programs

It is generally recognized that physical exercise helps mediate the effects of stress. Also, a high level of general fitness tends to ward off the effects of stress, as physical fitness helps to improve mental fitness. Departments have experimented with various programs. The Lexington, Kentucky, Police Department purchased a gymnasium for its officers, while the Bowling Green, Kentucky, Police Department pays officers' membership fees to a local health club. Such programs provide officers with access to health facilities.

Providing opportunity does not ensure that officers will participate in fitness program. Some departments now require officers to maintain a certain level of fitness. They periodically test officers to determine their level of physical fitness. Generally, programs such as these are developed to enhance officer preparedness or productivity; however, they also help officers to deal with job stress.

Reactive Strategies

Proactive strategies are useful in reducing stress before it occurs or becomes a problem for officers. Reactive strategies are used when officers have achieved a level of stress that inhibits performance. Management should ensure that officers

Officers in training lift weights to improve physical ability.
Michael Newman/PhotoEdit

are involved in reactive programs as soon as stress becomes a problem. Too often, officers enter such programs when it is too late—after there are manifest emotional or psychological problems at work or in the home.

Counseling

Counseling is one of the most effective means of handling stress and other problems experienced by police officers. Historically, police officers avoided counseling because they felt it showed weakness or they were afraid the department's administration would use it as an excuse to take disciplinary or other action against them. In essence, the pressure to be emotionally tough held sway. According to Shearer (1993), the hesitancy among officers to resort to psychological counseling may be due to (1) "fear of losing the respect of fellow officers, and being branded as emotionally weak or inadequate" (p. 96) and (2) fear that disclosing stressful experiences will adversely affect the stressed officer's fitness report and chances for promotion. Fortunately, over the years and as the result of a number of successful programs, police managers and officers have come to view counseling as a means of managing stress.

Counseling can be general in nature or can focus on specific problems like alcohol abuse, or family problems, or on traumatic situations such as post-shooting anxiety, severe injury in the line of duty, or the death of a partner. General counseling should be available for officers who feel the need for help. Often, employee assistance programs require officers to meet some predetermined criteria (e.g., a certain number of disciplinary actions, a shooting incident, documented drug or alcohol abuse, divorce or death of a spouse) before receiving services. However, such criteria discourage officers from receiving help when they need it and before the problem becomes severe.

Departments in Boston, Dallas, Oakland, and other cities have instituted peer counseling utilizing police officers as the counselors. Police officer counselors have a better working knowledge of problems and frequently are trusted by their fellow officers. The Boston program started with officers volunteering to work with fellow officers who have drinking problems; however, officers soon started coming to the counselors to discuss other problems. The counselors quickly realized they needed additional counseling skills and contacted Boston University, which provided courses in counseling for them. Boston now has a well-established stress program helping hundreds of officers (Donovan, 1985).

To reduce fear of reporting stress and fear of participating in counseling, Shearer (1993) advocates trust between counselors and clients, confidentiality of communication, a supportive therapeutic environment, and similar techniques to encourage law enforcement officials to share their problems without fear of reprisal. Tolerance and awareness by administrators will ensure the future vitality of counseling programs.

Debriefing after Critical Incidents

A number of factors determine how well the officer is able to cope with critical incidents. Some of these factors are the actual severity of the incident itself, the amount of control the officer had over the situation, support from the family and the department, professional support from someone like a psychologist, how the event is handled by the media, how the department handles the incident, and the personality of the officer. Critical incidents are extremely complicated and are most difficult in terms of coping.

The goal of intervention in postshooting situations, for example, should be to allow the officer to verbalize concerns about the incident, perhaps numerous times, in a nonthreatening atmosphere. Carson (1982) suggests that officers and supervisors should use active listening skills and avoid statements such as "I know how you feel." Monday-morning quarterbacking, joking, or congratulating the officer on the shooting should be avoided. Instead, it is important to demonstrate a caring attitude for the officer after a shooting incident. Officers should be treated as human beings, not as suspects. The officer should be allowed to work back into service at his or her own speed. Several departments require the officer to contact the department psychologist soon after a shooting. Such a requirement takes the responsibility for seeking help off the officer and makes it easier to accept professional help.

Table 9–5

Ten Common Reactions to Critical Incidents

1. Feeling jumpy, anxious, moody
2. Having difficulty concentrating and making decisions
3. Having trouble going near the scene of the critical incident or places that trigger memories of the incident
4. Having trouble being around people
5. Having trouble being alone
6. Feeling helpless and abandoned
7. Having relationship problems and family troubles
8. Feeling anger and resentment
9. Feeling guilty and powerless
10. Having flashbacks

Many departments have recognized the problems officers face in postcritical incident trauma and have developed programs to assist officers in managing the trauma. Departments have begun to acknowledge that critical incidents of many types cause stress to police officers. Pierson (1989) notes that departments should seek to identify critical incidents and prepare plans for dealing with the debilitating psychological problems that follow such incidents.

Table 9–5 highlights some of the common reaction to highly stressful critical incidents. In some cases, people may feel extremely overwhelmed and unable to cope with the demands of the job. They may experience numbness, shock, abandonment, and helplessness. Some officers may have trouble sleeping; others may stay away from work or turn to drugs or alcohol. Still others might take their stress out on their families as a means of coping. Police administrators can effectively manage critical incident stress by formulating clear policies and procedures that provide for a sensitive response for troubled workers.

Generally, *critical incident debriefing* consists of some variations on four stages: (1) defusing, (2) debriefing, (3) critiquing, and (4) reviewing (adapted from Bell, 1995; Curtis, 1995; Dyregrov, 1997). The defusing session is a short, nonconfrontational meeting of the officers affected by the incident with a "defuser." The defuser explains the likely reactions the officers will have to the incident as well as providing information on how the workers should take care of themselves in order to overcome the negative consequences of stress. These sessions should be held immediately after the incident. Debriefing sessions are essentially extended defusing sessions, but they occur well after the critical incident. In these sessions the affected employees are further taught how to manage stress and promote the recovery process.

After the initial defusing and debriefing sessions, the character of the critical incident debriefing takes on a more administrative tone. For example, a critiquing session is when employees and supervisors work together to review all aspects of the critical incident; this is usually done several days after the incident. These sessions are designed to uncover deficiencies in the way the incident was handled and to provide solutions so that similar problems will not occur. Finally, the administrative review stage is when administrators conduct a board review of the incident. This review is designed to identify corrective steps that can be taken in future critical incidents.

Mitchell and Bray (1990) outlined a seven-stage model for *critical incident stress debriefing* (CISD). Leonard and Alison (1999:145–146) describe each of the stages:

1. *Introduction.* Ground rules are established, confidentiality is emphasized, and participants are urged to talk if they wish.
2. *Facts.* Participants are asked to describe what happened during the incident from their own perspective. This helps to give a total picture of what happened.
3. *Thoughts.* Participants describe their first thoughts about the event. The discussion now becomes more personal.
4. *Emotions.* Participants discuss their emotional reactions.
5. *Assessment.* Physical and psychological symptoms are noted and discussed.
6. *Teaching or education.* Stress reaction and responses and coping strategies are discussed.
7. *Reentry.* Participants ask questions, team leaders summarize what has occurred, advise participants that they can contact team members if they wish, and draw the debriefing to a close.

Leonard and Alison found support for the efficacy of critical incident stress debriefing for officers involved in shootings. According to their research, a group of officers that "received CISD showed a significant reduction in anger levels and greater use of some specific adaptive coping strategies" (1999:144). In another study involving officers who responded to the scene of a plane crash, however, researchers found no differences in stress levels among officers who went through CISD and those who did not (Carlier and Van Uchelen, 1998). More research is necessary.

Wellness Programs

Many agencies have adopted wellness programs to prevent and reduce the negative effects of stress. *Wellness* has been defined as "an integrated and dynamic level of functioning oriented toward maximizing potential, dependent on self-responsibility" (Robbins, Powers, and Burgess 1991:8). This definition suggests that individuals should take steps to prevent stress, rather than reacting to it. Moreover, wellness programs recognize that administrators cannot control or prevent all stressors that their subordinates face. Accordingly, police officers should take steps to ensure a healthy lifestyle.

There are several dimensions to wellness. Anspaugh, Hamrick, and Rosato (1991) identify five dimensions to wellness: (1) spiritual, (2) social, (3) emotional, (4) intellectual, and (5) physical. Each dimension is important to a healthy way of life. Each dimension should receive equal attention, as overcommitment to one or another will reduce the beneficial effect.

Spiritual wellness. This dimension includes the individual's ethics, values, and morals. Spiritual wellness comes with self-reflection and an awareness of one's beliefs and attitudes toward colleagues and others.

Social wellness. Social wellness discourages isolation and antisocial behavior. People should have social skills, interact with people in their environments, form intimate relationships, and share their feelings. As we have seen, communication is one of the most important steps in being able to overcome the stress problem, especially when reacting to critical incidents.

Emotional wellness. Emotional wellness goes hand in hand with spiritual and social wellness. People should have an awareness of the problems that face them, be honest in their appraisals of what is happening in their lives, and be able to communicate those feelings effectively with colleagues, family, and friends.

Intellectual wellness. Intellectual wellness is achieved through learning. If people to fail to absorb new information, they cannot fit in an ever-changing world. Improved knowledge also equips people with an awareness of their surroundings, minimizes tendencies to hold uninformed, sometimes negative opinions of certain phenomena, and otherwise equips them with the psychological tools to better do their jobs.

Physical wellness. Physical wellness is achieved with exercise and diet. People should take steps to eat nutritious food and stay in shape through cardiovascular exercise. Physical wellness also comes with the avoidance of tobacco and alcohol and other substances that are harmful to one's health.

Spiritual, social, emotional, and intellectual wellness are usually the responsibility of the individual. Police departments do take steps to encourage communication and emotional health (e.g., by offering counseling), but it is usually easier to encourage physical wellness. For example, the Kansas City, Missouri, Police Department implemented a weight control program (North, 1993). The chief believed that slimmer, fitter police officers would be healthier and better able to do their jobs. The California Highway Patrol was another agency to adopt physical standards for its officers (Craig, 1981). All signs suggest that this is a growing trend.

In a recent study, Church and Robertson (1999) reported that the majority of state police agencies maintained wellness programs. Not surprisingly, many varieties of wellness programs were reported, and many agencies failed to adopt "comprehensive" wellness programs, but Church and Robertson's research indicates that wellness programs are increasingly gaining acceptance. Wellness programs are particularly advantageous because, as these authors observed, "Treating mental and physical fitness problems on an on-going basis can prevent the loss of many valued officers" (p. 306). Church and Robertson concluded by suggesting that a sound, comprehensive wellness program should provide for each of the following components: (1) physical fitness; (2) stress management; (3) psychological and mental health; (4) nutrition and diet; and (5) alcohol and chemical dependency treatment and education. In addition, "Law enforcement agencies, whether federal, state, or local, which lack a wellness program, should investigate programs of other agencies and adopt aspects of those programs to fit their needs" (p. 310).

Employee Assistance Programs

Increasingly police departments are implementing employee assistance programs (EAPs) to assist officers with problems stemming from stress. Such programs are used to "humanize" the police department and increase productivity (Perry and Cayer, 1992). Employee assistance programs can take many forms. Some examples include psychological counseling, chemical dependency treatment, and stress mitigation.

EAPs are frequently employed to help identify and treat employees with chemical dependencies to drugs and alcohol and other problems. Chemical dependency is a serious problem in policing. Some studies estimate that nearly 25 percent of all police officers are currently experiencing problems with chemical dependency compared to 10 percent in the general work force (Glossick, 1988). The risk that such officers pose to themselves and to public safety is immense.

Chemical dependency in policing is certainly not a new phenomenon, and some say that it is not a problem at all. Police have been encouraged to drink as in the legendary custom of "choir practice." Peer pressure to "have a few" after the conclusion of a shift is standard practice in many police organizations. Glossick (1988) notes that officers also abuse both legal prescription drugs and illegal street drugs. Addiction to both alcohol and drugs can be a problem and should be of concern to any police agency. Figure 9–3 shows the progressive deterioration of the chemically dependent person's behavior and the typical crisis points that occur in the person's deterioration.

When an officer is using illegal drugs, a strong case can be made for terminating the officer. However, when the officer is an alcoholic or is abusing legal prescription drugs, administrators will have more difficulty making a case for termination. The officer may successfully claim that the chemical dependency is job-related. In such cases, the officer will be given a second chance. The administrator then has an obligation to assist the officer to make the change necessary to successfully maintain employment with the department through treatment of the dependency. This can be accomplished through educational, intervention, and detection programs to identify chemically dependent officers and refer them to treatment program.

An effective EAP must include a commitment by the department to help officers stop drinking or using drugs and to deal with the medical, psychological, social, and spiritual problems that accompany the disease. Treatment should be provided by a multidisciplinary team specializing in addictive diseases.

Figure 9–3

How a chemically dependent employee behaves.

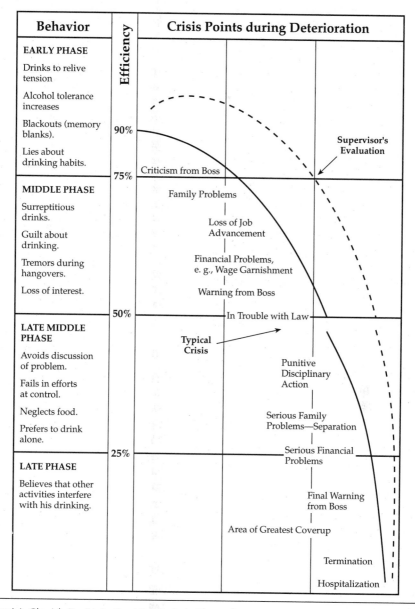

Behavior	Efficiency	Crisis Points during Deterioration
EARLY PHASE Drinks to relive tension Alcohol tolerance increases Blackouts (memory blanks). Lies about drinking habits.	90% 75%	**Supervisor's Evaluation** Criticism from Boss
MIDDLE PHASE Surreptitious drinks. Guilt about drinking. Tremors during hangovers. Loss of interest.	50%	Family Problems Loss of Job Advancement Financial Problems, e. g., Wage Garnishment Warning from Boss In Trouble with Law
LATE MIDDLE PHASE Avoids discussion of problem. Fails in efforts at control. Neglects food. Prefers to drink alone.	25%	Typical Crisis Punitive Disciplinary Action Serious Family Problems—Separation Serious Financial Problems
LATE PHASE Believes that other activities interfere with his drinking.		Final Warning from Boss Area of Greatest Coverup Termination Hospitalization

Source: J. L. Glossick, Don't Let a Good Cop Go Bad—Chemical Dependency Is Treatable, *Police Chief* 55, no. 10 (1988), p. 89.

Physicians and nurses provide 24-hour-a-day medical care for managing the physical symptoms of the dependency. Therapists, licensed in treating chemical dependency, develop and implement the individualized treatment plan of each officer. An intensive 28-day program, occurring in a special addiction recovery setting, incorporates treatment of the various aspects of the chemical dependency and involves group, family, and individual therapy; educational lectures and films, and stress management skills.

Aftercare for the EAP is divided into two periods. An intensive aftercare period for the first six months consists of the patient and family attending weekly sessions to work on the goals that were set just prior to the discharge from the formal program. Here the officer continues to work on self-awareness, assertiveness, problem-solving skills, and sober living skills. Near the end of the intensive aftercare period the officer meets again with the treatment team and decides on goals for the secondary phase, which lasts 18 months and consists of the officer and family attending monthly aftercare meetings, unless more frequent meetings are necessary (Glossick, 1988).

Summary

This chapter examined stress in the police environment. Stress is universally recognized as a factor that contributes to a number of personnel and productivity problems. Police administrators cannot expect officers to exist in a negative work environment for long periods of time without experiencing stress problems. Therefore, they should establish a safety net through stress reduction programs. Money spent on such programs will reap greater benefits through better personnel and increased productivity.

In the past, police administrators did not appreciate the implications and impact stress had on the organization. Because of recent research, they now should understand how it can negatively affect the department. With this in mind, the department should have a variety of problems in place to treat stress. Some of these programs should be proactive in nature to prevent its occurrence; others should be reactive to treat existing stress. A department should have a comprehensive approach in dealing with stress. Otherwise, stress-related problems will persist.

Study Questions

1. What is the difference between eustress and distress, and how do they relate to police productivity?

2. Describe Seyle's general adaptation syndrome. How is it related to the issues of eustress, distress, and stress management?

3. Describe the sources of stress for police administrators. How do these differ from the sources of stress for nonadministrative personnel?

4. Describe each of the four categories of stress symptoms for police officers. How do critical incidents factor into the stress equation?

5. What are the career stages administrators go through during their careers? How do these differ from the career stages for police officers?

6. Describe the effects of police stress on health.

7. Do people respond differentially to stress? If so, why?

8. Describe the effects of police stress on the police family.

9. What are the stages an officer goes through in postshooting trauma? How is the stress of the shooting incident complicated for the officer by the use-of-force investigation? What are some of the normal stress reactions to postshooting incidents? What can management and administration do to help reduce the negative effects of postshooting stress?

10. How does the police organization contribute to the stress police officers feel? Discuss the proactive and reactive ways the police organization can assist officers in managing stress.

11. What strategies are at managements' disposal for dealing with the problem of stress?

Net Resources

http://www.copkiller.net/ A website for critical incident stress management and training.

http://www.help4cops.netheaven.com/ A website devoted to post-traumatic stress disorder, stress, anxiety, and depression in the law enforcement community.

http://www.icisf.org/ Website for the International Critical Incident Stress Foundation, Inc.—an organization dedicated to the prevention and mitigation of stress in law enforcement.

http://www.policestress.com/ Another website for more information on police stress.

http://www.policestress.org/signs.htm Common signs and signals of stress.

References

Allen, R. D., Hitt, M. A., and Greer, C. R. (1982). Occupational stress and perceived organizational effectiveness in formal groups: An examination of stress level and stress type. *Personnel Psychology* 35:359–371.

Anspaugh, D. J., Hamrick, M. H., and Rosato, R. D. (1991). *Wellness: Concepts and Applications.* St. Louis: Mosby.

Bayley, D. (1976). *Forces of Order: Police Behavior in Japan and the United States.* Berkeley: University of California Press.

Blackmore, J. (1978). Are police allowed to have problems of their own? *Police Magazine* 1(3):47–55.

Brooks, L. W., and Piquero, N. L. (1998). Police stress: Does department size matter? *Policing: An International Journal of Police Strategies and Management* 21(1):600–617.

Carlier, I. V. E., and Van Uchelen, A. J. (1998). Disaster-related post-traumatic stress in police officers: A field study of the impact of debriefing. *Stress Medicine* 14:143–148.

Carson, S. (1982). Post-shooting stress reduction. *Police Chief*, October, pp. 66–68.

Church, R. L., and Robertson, N. (1999). How state police agencies are addressing the issue of wellness. *Policing: An International Journal of Police Strategies and Management* 22(3):304–312.

Craig, G. (1981). Physical maintenance project: California Highway Patrol develops physical maintenance standards. *Police Chief* 48(11):26–27.

Crank, J. P., and Caldero, M. (1991). The production of occupational stress in medium-sized police agencies: A survey of line officers in eight municipal departments. *Journal of Criminal Justice* 19:339–349.

Crank, J. P., Regoli, R. M., and Culbertson, R. G. (1986). Cynicism and career stage among police chiefs. *Justice Quarterly* 3:341–352.

Crank, J. P., Regoli, B., Hewitt, J. D., and Culbertson, R. G. (1993). An assessment of work stress among police executives. *Journal of Criminal Justice* 21:313–324.

Crank, J. P., Regoli, R., Hewitt, J. D., and Culbertson, R. G. (1995). Institutionalization and organizational antecedents of role stress, work alienation, and anomie among police executives. *Criminal Justice and Behavior* 22(2):152–171.

Das, D. (1986). Police training in ethics: The need for an innovative approach in mandated programs. *American Journal of Criminal Justice* 11(1):62–87.

Davidson, M. J., and Veno, A. (1978). "Police stress: A multicultural interdisciplinary review and perspective, Part I." *Abstracts on Police Science*, July/August: 190–191.

Donovan, E. (1985). The Boston police stress program. *Police Chief*, February, pp. 38–39.

Eisenberg, T. (1975). Labor–management relations and psychological stress: View from the bottom. *Police Chief*, November, pp. 54–58.

Fell, R., Richard, W., and Wallace, W. (1980). Psychological job stress and the police officer. *Journal of Police Science and Administration* 8(2):139–144.

French, J., and Caplan, R. (1970). Psychosocial factors in coronary heart disease. *Industrial Medicine* 39:383–397.

Friedman, M., and Rosenman, R. H. (1994). *Type A Behavior and Your Heart*. New York: Knopf.

Glossick, J. L. (1988). Don't let a good cop go bad—Chemical dependency is treatable. *Police Chief* 55(10):86, 88–90.

Greller, M. (1982). Taking a department-wide approach to managing stress. *Police Chief*, November, pp. 44–47.

Grencik, J. (1975). Toward an understanding of stress. In W. Kroes and J. Hurrell (eds.), *Job Stress and the Police Officer: Identifying Stress Reduction Techniques*. Washington: U.S. Department of Health, Education, and Welfare.

Haarr, Robin N., and Morash, Merry (1999). "Gender, race, and strategies of coping with occupational stress in policing." *Justice Quarterly* 16(2):303–306.

Hart, P. M., Wearing, A. J., and Headey, B. (1995). Police stress and well-being: Integrating personality, coping, and daily work experiences. *Journal of Occupational and Organizational Psychology* 68(2):133.

Hillgren, J., and Bond, R. (1975). Stress in law enforcement: Psychophysiological correlates and legal implications. *Journal of Forensic Psychology* 25-32.

Hillgren, J., Bond, R., and Jones, S. (1976). Primary stressors in police administration and law enforcement. *Journal of Police Science and Administration* 4(4):445–449.

Jacobi, H. (1975). Reducing police stress: A psychiatrist's point of view. In W. Kroes and J. Hurrell (eds.), *Job Stress and the Police Officer: Identifying Stress Reduction Techniques.* Washington: U.S. Department of Health, Education, and Welfare.

Kroes, W., Margolis, B., and Hurrell, J. (1974). Job stress in policemen. *Journal of Police Science and Administration* 2(2):145–155.

Kroes, W. M., Hurrell, J. J., and Margolis, B. (1974). Job stress in police administrators. *Journal of Police Science and Administration* 2(4):381–387.

Lawrence, R. (1984). Police stress and personality factors: A conceptual model. *Journal of Criminal Justice* 12(3):247–263.

Leonard, R., and Alison, L. (1999). Critical incident stress debriefing and its effects on coping strategies and anger in a sample of Australian police officers involved in shooting incidents. *Work and Stress* 13(2):144–161.

Lord, V. B., Gray, D. O., and Pond, S. B., III. (1991). The Police Stress Inventory: Does it measure stress? *Journal of Criminal Justice* 19:139–149.

Lowenstein, L. E. (1999). Treating stress in the police force. *The Police Journal* 72(1):65–74.

McHenry, C. (1995). Stress in the Police Service: Preventing the long-term effects of trauma. *Occupational Health Review* July/August, pp. 17–20.

Maslach, C. (1976). Burned-out. *Human Behavior* 5.

Maynard, P., and Maynard, N. (1982). Stress in police families: Some policy implications. *Journal of Police Science and Administration* 10(4):302–314.

Mechanic, D. (1974). Social structure and personal adaptation: Some neglected considerations. In G. Coelho, D. Hamburg, and J. Adams (eds.), *Coping and Adaptation.* New York: Basic Books, pp. 32–44.

Mitchell, J., and Bray, G. (1990). *Emergency Services Stress.* Englewood Cliffs, NJ: Prentice Hall.

Morash, M., and Haarr, R. (1995). Gender, workplace problems, and stress in policing. *Justice Quarterly* 12:113–140.

More, H. W. (1998). *Special Topics in Policing,* 2nd ed. Cincinnati, OH: Anderson.

Moyer, I., and Hopper, D. (1983). An exploratory study of "role distance" as a police response to stress. Paper presented at the annual meeting of the Academy of Criminal Justice Sciences, San Antonio, Texas.

Neiderhoffer, A. (1967). *Behind the Shield: The Police in Urban Society.* New York: Doubleday.

North, J. (1993). KC police fight fat along with crime. *Kansas City Star,* February 3, p. B1.

Norvell, N., Belles, D., and Hills, H. (1988). Perceived stress levels and physical symptoms in supervisory law enforcement personnel. *Journal of Police Science and Administration* 16(2):75.

Opton, E., and Lazarus, R. (1967). Personality determinants of psychophysiological response to stress: A theoretical analysis and an experiment. *Journal of Personality and Social Psychology* 6:291–303.

Perry, R. W., and Cayer, N. J. (1992). Evaluating employee assistance programs: Concerns and strategies for public employees. *Public Personnel Management* 21(3):323–333.

Pierson, T. (1989). Critical incident stress: A serious law enforcement problem. *Police Chief* 56(2):32–33.

Regoli, R., Crank, J., and Culbertson, R. (1989). Police cynicism, job satisfaction, and work relations of police chiefs: An assessment of the influence of department size. *Sociological Focus* 22(3):161–171.

Regoli, R., Culbertson, R. G., Crank, J. P., and Powell, J. R. (1990). Career stage and cynicism among police chiefs. *Justice Quarterly* 7(3):593–611.

Reiser, M. (1973). *Practical Psychology for Police Officers*. Springfield, IL: Charles C. Thomas.

Richard, W., and Fell, R. (1975). Health factors in police job stress. In W. Kroes and J. Hurrell (eds.), *Job Stress and the Police Officer: Identifying Stress Reduction Techniques*. Washington: U.S. Department of Health, Education, and Welfare.

Robbins, G., Powers, D., and Burgess, S. (1991). *A Wellness Way of Life*. Dubuque, IA: William C. Brown.

Roberts, M. (1975). Job stress in law enforcement: A treatment and prevention program. In W. Kroes and J. Hurrell (eds.), *Job Stress and the Police Officer: Identifying Stress Reduction Techniques*. Washington: U.S. Department of Health, Education, and Welfare.

Schwartz, J., and Schwartz, C. (1975). The personal problems of the police officer: A plea for action. In W. Kroes and J. Hurrell (eds.), *Job Stress and the Police Officer: Identifying Stress Reduction Techniques*. Washington: U.S. Department of Health, Education, and Welfare.

Selye, J. (1981). *Stress without distress*. Philadelphia: Lippincott.

Sewell, J. (1981). Police stress. *FBI Law Enforcement Bulletin* 50(4):7–11.

Shearer, R. W. (1993). Police officer stress: New approaches for handling tension. *Police Chief*, August, pp. 96–99.

Sigler, R. T., Wilson, C. N., and Allen, Z. (1991). Police stress and teacher stress at work and at home. *Journal of Criminal Justice* 19:361–370.

Silbert, M. (1982). Job stress and burnout of new police officers. *Police Chief* 49:46-48.

Solomon, R. M. (1988). Post-shooting trauma. *Police Chief* 55(10): 40, 42, 44.

Somodevilla, S., Baker, C., Hill, W., and Thomas, N. (1978). *Stress Management in the Dallas Police Department*. Dallas: Psychological Services Unit, Dallas Police Department.

Standfest, S. R. (1996). The police supervisor and stress. *FBI Law Enforcement Bulletin* 65(5):7.

Stevens, D. J. (1999). Stress and the American police officer. *The Police Journal* 72(3):247–259.

Storch, J. E., and Panzarella, R. (1996). Police stress: State-trait anxiety in relation to occupational and personal stressors. *Journal of Criminal Justice* 24(2):99–107.

Stotland, E. (1991). The effects of police work and professional relationships on health. *Journal of Criminal Justice* 19:371–379.

Stratton, J. (1976). The law enforcement family: Programs for spouses. *FBI Law Enforcement Bulletin* 45(3):16–22.

Stratton, J. (1978). Police stress: An overview. *Police Chief* 45(4):58–62.

Taylor, M. (1982). Police training: Towards a new model. *The Police Journal* 55(3):219–230.

Territo, L., and Vetter, H. (1981). *Stress and Police Personnel.* Boston: Allyn and Bacon.

Terry, W. (1981). Police stress: The empirical evidence. *Journal of Police Science and Administration* 9(1):61–75.

Veniga, R. L., and Spradley, J. (1981). *How to Cope with Job Burnout.* Englewood Cliffs, NJ: Prentice Hall.

Violanti, J. (1983). Stress patterns in police work: A longitudinal study. *Journal of Police Science and Administration* 11(2):211–216.

Violanti, J. (1992). Coping strategies among police recruits in a high-stress training environment. *Journal of Social Psychology* 132(6):717–729.

Violanti, J., and Marshall, J. (1983). Police stress: The empirical evidence. *Journal of Police Science and Administration* 11(4):389–394.

Webb, S., and Smith, D. (1980). Stress prevention and alleviation: Strategies for the police. *Criminal Justice Review* 5(1):1–15.

White, S., and Marino, K. (1983). Job attitudes and police stress: An exploratory study of causation. *Journal of Police Science and Administration* 11(3):264–274.

10

Police Human Resources Management

Paul Conklin

Chapter Outline

Introduction

The Human Resources System
Civil Service
Equal Employment Opportunity and the Human Resources System

The Job Analysis

Recruitment and Selection
Recruitment of Police Human Resources
Selection of Police Officers
Model Selection Procedure

Police Training
Academy Training
Probationary Period
Field Training Officer Program
In-Service Training

Performance Appraisal

Promotions
Historical and Legal Aspects of Promotion
Components of Promotion Systems

Assessment Centers
In-Basket Exercise
Leaderless Discussion Group
Role-Play Exercise
Presentation Exercise
Tactical or Problem-Solving Exercise

Summary

Learning Objectives

After reading this chapter, you should be able to

1. List the components of the police human resource system.
2. Understand the components of the civil service system and how they affect officers.
3. Be familiar with the various components in the police selection process.
4. Distinguish between academy training, field training, and in-service training.
5. Understand how police performance is evaluated.
6. Discuss the police promotion process.
7. Explain the components of a police assessment center and how it operates.

A newly appointed police chief understands that community policing has become the dominant philosophy of American policing in the majority of departments in the United States. One of the chief's responsibilities is to incorporate sufficient community policing principles into the department to ensure that the department is an effective community policing department. Changing to community policing from the old professional model entails a great deal of work and planning. One important area of change facing the new chief is human resources management, or personnel administration. The new chief asks staff members to identify changes that should be made in the human resources system. After several meetings they make the following recommendations:

1. Have psychologists perform the psychological screening of new officers to ensure that applicants can communicate effectively with people, are not rigid in dealing with people, and can analyze situations to solve problems.

2. Ensure that community policing is incorporated in training for recruits and in-service officers.

3. Modify the performance evaluation form to emphasize and reward community policing behaviors.

4. Include information on community policing on the promotion reading lists and ensure that promotion exercises contain questions about it.

This example shows how complicated and comprehensive the human resources system is. Human resources is the key to an effective police department. If any one piece of the system is lacking, the whole department may be affected. Police administrators must strive to ensure that the human resources system is the best possible.

INTRODUCTION

Thus far, this book has addressed a number of important organizational and management issues that affect the operation of a police agency. No matter how well a department is organized, it is effective only insofar as its people are able to manage and carry out police duties and responsibilities. Effective police agencies, then, are well-organized and well-staffed, on the principle that good people cannot function effectively in a poorly structured department and a well-organized department cannot be effective without qualified personnel.

Mathis and Jackson define *human resource management* as "the design of formal systems in an organization to ensure the efficient use of human talent to accomplish the organizational goals" (1997:4). Police departments must maximize their "human capital" so that the department successfully meets citizens' expectations. Human resource managers must ensure that employees are capable of performing in accordance with today's expectations, and they must also develop programs that will prepare them for tomorrow's changes—changes that include promotions, reassignments, and an evolving work environment.

This chapter examines the people aspect of police administration—human resources management. The motivation and leadership chapters focused on how to maintain quality within the department through management practices. Good management practices aid in maintaining productive employees. Human resources (HR) management on the other hand, deals with selecting, placing, and promoting personnel within the department and developing a formal system of maintaining quality personnel and performance. HR practices are used to ensure that the right people are placed in each position and that they maintain sufficient skills and job knowledge to perform their jobs. The key, then, is the development and implementation of procedures that allow the department to achieve this objective. These procedures emphasize selecting and maintaining quality human resources.

The HR function is a management function, although HR specialists are not directly involved in supervising people. Human resources specialists are indirectly involved in management by establishing a framework to improve employee relations and productivity. To this end, HR activities interface the work environment and facilitate work. These personnel interfaces include work analysis, staffing, training and development, performance appraisal, compensation, and maintenance. HR specialists develop numerous programs by which to accomplish these processes.

HR administration is not a simple concept or operation. It is complex, involving a large number of people, many of whom are external to the police department, and these people are involved in a large number of tasks or functions. *HR administration* should be considered a system composed of numerous components such as police administrators and government executives, including mayors, city managers, council members, and judges. All of these people, to some degree, affect the development and application of HR policies in a police department. Citizens also affect HR administration by placing demands and expectations on the police department and government in general.

THE HUMAN RESOURCES SYSTEM

Human resources administration can be understood more clearly by examining the various participants involved in the human resources function. Figure 10–1 shows a typical police-political organization for a municipal police agency.

The key participants shown in Figure 10–1 are police administrators, municipal government executives (the specific executives and the degree to which they exert influence on human resources policies vary from jurisdiction to jurisdiction depending on the type of government), and civil service commissions. These are the primary actors, but others play a significant role in human resources administration without being part of the formal system. For example, federal and state courts affect a city's HR policies through the interpretation of state and federal laws (Gaines, Kappeler, and Vaughn, 1999). State legislatures and Congress alter municipal HR policies by passing state and federal laws dictating how cities should hire, promote, and pay employees. Most notably, equal employment laws have modified municipal human resources policies and directly affected the work environment.

Figure 10–1

Agencies and persons involved in police personnel administration.

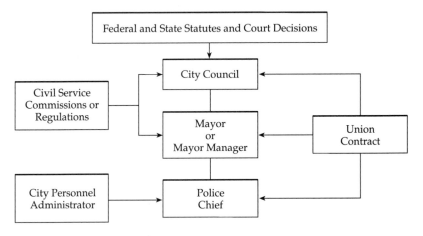

Generally, the HR function is handled in one of two ways for a police agency: internally or externally. An internal operation is one in which the HR function is housed inside the police agency and most of the operations are carried out or controlled by police officials. In external operations, most of the HR activities are handled or supervised by a civil service commission or a city human resources department. Presently, most police personnel activities are handled by external agencies or at least shared with external agencies. External agencies are used because federal and state legislation has significantly complicated HR management, and persons with HR administration expertise are required to perform these duties. Only large departments have internal HR operations. Almost all small departments use an external HR operation since it is more economical for smaller cities to centralize these functions.

In the externally controlled system, the HR department advertises positions, supervises the testing of police applicants and those officers participating in promotion examinations, manages the retirement system, coordinates insurance programs, and maintains HR records. This does not mean that the police department is not involved in HR administration. The central HR agency is responsible for coordinating the process, and therefore utilizes the police department's services and expertise. For example, the department will probably perform the background investigations for applicants, establish oral interview boards, and initiate and oversee disciplinary actions. Even though the HR agency has overall responsibility for HR activities, the police department is extensively involved.

Civil Service

Civil service is a system whereby employees are hired, retained, advanced, disciplined, and discharged on the basis of merit; in police departments, this system has displaced the patronage system. Although the term civil service is frequently used, it is seldom fully understood because its application across state and local jurisdictions is not uniform. Even though two police departments may have civil service, the actual duties and responsibilities of the respective civil service commissions may vary. When state legislatures mandated civil service, they usually did so by establishing broad guidelines that were applicable to local governments. The respective local governments often were free to expand civil service coverage into areas not addressed by the legislature. State legislatures compounded this inconsistency by mandating different levels of coverage for the various classes or types of jurisdictions within the state. For example, the type and extent of civil service coverage for Kentucky police departments depends on the class or size of city. Thus to fully understand a particular jurisdiction's civil service system, one must examine the state and local legislation as it applies to the specific jurisdiction.

Historical Aspects of Civil Service

Initially, civil service was instituted as an effort to reform policing and to enhance professionalism. For example, in 1917 Republicans gained control of the government in Louisville, Kentucky, from the Democrats. The result was that 300 police officers from a force of 429 were dismissed, and no one above the rank of sergeant survived the political purge (Fosdick, 1969). During the first half of the last century, this type of political intervention was commonplace in almost every major city. Politicians controlled the police and what the police did. Who they arrested depended largely on the whims of the controlling politicians. Essentially, the police were minions who helped the political machines remain in power. Civil service was one of the mechanisms legislated by state governments in an attempt to curb the corruptive abuses of local politicians. Civil service resulted in the establishment of hiring standards that prevented politicians from hiring their unqualified friends and provided employees protection by preventing wholesale firings. Consequently, police officers were given some degree of autonomy in the performance of their duties with the advent of civil service.

The *Pendleton Civil Service Act*, which took effect in 1883, was the first permanent legislation enacting civil service. This act was the result of three significant political occurrences. First, in 1881 Charles Guiteau assassinated President James A. Garfield; according to Cayer, this act "became a dramatic symbol of the evils of spoils"(1975:24). Guiteau was an unsuccessful seeker of political patronage, who killed President Garfield when he did not receive the patronage position he felt was due him. Second, the U.S. Supreme Court's decision in *Ex parte Curtis* in 1882 upheld a law passed in 1876, forbidding the assessment of political contributions from federal government workers. Essentially, the Court upheld the conviction of a U.S. Treasury Department employee, who was also the treasurer of the New York Republican Party, for attempting to solicit contributions from federal employees. Third, in 1882 the Republicans sustained substantial losses in the national elections. As a result, support for the passage of the Pendleton Act increased in order to protect

Republican civil servants from the Democrats when they assumed power in the White House. The Pendleton Act applied only to the federal government. Today, approximately 90 percent of civilian employees working for the federal government are covered by civil service. Civil service at the state and local levels has evolved slowly and the extent of coverage varies across jurisdictions. For example, deputies in many sheriff's departments across the country do not have any civil service protection.

Roles of Civil Service

To understand civil service, one must comprehend the various roles the civil service commission can assume. Greisinger, Slovak, and Molkup (1979) identify four such roles: policy formulation, administrative and advisory, adjudicative, and regulatory (see Figure 10–2).

> The *policy formulation* role refers to the civil service body participating in or being wholly responsible for formulating HR policies. Here the civil service commission may be responsible for setting minimum qualifications for entry-level positions or establishing the criteria and procedures for disciplinary actions in the police agency.
>
> The *administrative and advisory* role refers to the civil service body advising government on what the HR policies should be and how they should be implemented, or in some cases administering the HR function within government.
>
> The *adjudicative* role refers to the civil service commission having administrative hearing powers. The civil service commission, in this instance, hears or rules on cases involving human resources actions such as dismissals or suspensions. The commission often has final decision-making authority on the outcome of such hearings except in the case of an appeal. However, in many cases where the police department conducts the disciplinary hearing, the civil service commission hears the appellate case and makes the ultimate disposition.
>
> The *regulatory* role refers to the civil service commission monitoring or reviewing HR rules and regulations as they are developed within governmental agencies. In these cases, the commission determines what is acceptable, but it cannot promulgate policies and procedures. Regulatory commissions tend to constrain police effectiveness by inhibiting change.

These are the four roles or functions that the civil service commission may assume in a particular jurisdiction. The civil service commission may not perform all four functions, but it may be responsible for any one or more of them. A given legislative body may legislate one or more of these roles to its civil service commission. It is for this reason that there is not a uniform application of civil service. A number of cities do not use civil service commissions but manage

Figure 10–2
Roles assumed by a civil service commission.

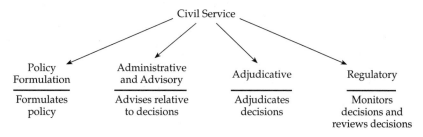

these functions through a central HR agency. In other cities, where the civil service commission is not given responsibility for all four functions, the remaining ones are usually housed in a central HR agency. The end result is the same when either a civil service commission or a central HR agency is used because all four HR functions are administered external to the police organization.

Negative Side-Effects of Civil Service

Although civil service provides a number of positive benefits to employees, it does have negative side-effects. Civil service rules contribute to organization stagnation. Critics of civil service see it as a mechanism protecting the incompetent and unproductive. When the civil service commission becomes involved in promulgating rules and adjudicating violations of those rules, the authority to control the organization is removed from the police administrator. For example, in one case the Louisville, Kentucky, Police Department fired a detective for cause. The detective was later reinstated by the Civil Service Commission. Many felt that the commission overstepped its responsibility, emphasized political expediency and individual rights over the right of government to administer governmental activities, and created a situation in which the chief could not exert adequate control over the department. Also, there is some evidence that civil service commissions are less strict than police administrators in disciplining police officers. Civil service may make it more difficult to discipline and sometimes control officers, making it more difficult to control the police department.

Another problem with civil service commissions is that they are not totally immune to politics, counter to the very reason they were formed. They may attempt to go outside the boundaries of their authority to implement policies that are contrary to the good of the police administration. Commission members may identify with members of the police department or other key persons in the community and may allow those associations to affect their decision making. It is important for the civil service commission to follow the rule of law and be impartial in their deliberations.

Equal Employment Opportunity and the Human Resources System

Equal employment opportunity (EEO) has many meanings, but one thing is clearly understood—EEO has definitely affected the workplace. Views of EEO are wide-ranging, and regardless of viewpoint, EEO is a volatile issue that frequently is misinterpreted and misunderstood. Some view it as overburdening and complicating the HR function; others view it as hampering their chances of promotion or entry into the police profession; still others view it as the vehicle that enables minorities to better cope with discrimination. Regardless of viewpoint, EEO is a body of laws, administrative rules, and court decisions that affect and mold HR administration.

The following sections examine several key EEO areas: civil rights, discrimination against the disabled, and sexual harassment against employees. These three areas are of primary concern to human resource managers and police administrators.

Civil Rights Legislation and Court Decisions

Title VII of the 1964 Civil Rights Act establishes the basis of fair employment practices. The act in Section 703A mandates that it is unlawful for an employer to fail to hire, refuse to hire, discharge any individual, or otherwise discriminate in any other manner against any individual with respect to employment compensation, terms, conditions, or privileges because of race, color, religion, sex, or national origin. In 1972, Title VII was amended to establish the *Equal Employment Opportunity Commission (EEOC)*, which was given the authority to "intervene on behalf of affected individuals" and to "file suit against businesses or governmental entities in cases of discrimination." Individuals no longer had to bear the burden for taking action against their employer—the federal government would intervene on their behalf. This opened the door for increased litigation and clearly delineated the EEO law through court decisions.

Griggs v. Duke Power Company (1971) was the first case to really define discrimination as promulgated in the act. Griggs, an African-American laborer, applied for a higher-paying labor position within the Duke Power Company. Transfer and promotion decisions were based on applicants possessing a high school diploma and passing a professionally developed aptitude test. Griggs and a number of other African-American employees were denied the positions because they could not meet the qualifications. The Supreme Court ruled that the high school diploma and test requirements were not related to the position which Griggs sought.

Prior to *Griggs*, the standard the Supreme Court used in determining discrimination cases was whether there was intent to discriminate: if there was no intent, there was no discrimination. However, the Court in the *Griggs* case decided that Title VII not only prohibited "overt or intentional discrimination," but also prohibited practices that were intended to be "fair in form" but were discriminatory in practice. A second point established in the case was the

On the Job

LEXINGTON–FAYETTE URBAN COUNTY DIVISION OF POLICE
The Chief's Perspective

By Chief Anthony Beatty

Courtesy of Chief Beatty

The Lexington–Fayette Urban County Division of Police is a metropolitan police agency with 500 sworn personnel and 250 civilian support personnel. The city covers 284 square miles and is situated in the central bluegrass region of Kentucky. The chief of police is responsible for administering the final phase of the selection process, promotions, and discipline. The real challenge for the Lexington Division of Police is sustaining quality police service with a lean officer-to-population ratio of 1.9:1,000. This agency provides a broad spectrum of services to the community, including patrol, traffic, investigation, community services, canine, mounted patrol, bicycle patrol, neighborhood officers, and other services.

In Lexington, Equal Employment Opportunity (EEO) and recruitment plans are updated annually to ensure that goals are adjusted to account for new hires and that ineffective recruiting methods are modified. Police agencies face many obstacles while attempting to be effective in recruiting minority and female candidates. They also experience negative media attention, cultural pressure, and interagency recruiting competition for the same candidate pool. Lexington's recruiting efforts serve a dual purpose by targeting specific population groups while educating the public on the agency's role in the community. Minority candidates are recruited by networking with local community groups, churches, civic leaders, and universities that have a large minority enrollment. Representatives from these groups and institutions participate in this agency's Recruiting Committee, which provides continuing input on recruiting. Although starting salaries are comparable to those of regional agencies, Lexington emphasizes its expectations for professionalism, appearance, demeanor, and esprit de corps. The goal is to attract a diverse group of candidates who are receptive to the overall agency philosophy.

The Lexington Division of Police conducts its own state-certified basic academy and annual in-service training. All new officers are required to complete a basic academy, regardless of prior

Continued

academy attendance, to ensure continuity in the delivery of service and facilitate the adoption of the agency's philosophy. To increase the likelihood for successful completion of basic training, the Mentoring Program was established. Participation in this program helps the recruit and his or her family acclimate to the training process. Those recruits relocating from other cities are provided assistance in locating housing and other services. However, the most beneficial outcome of the Mentoring Program is the coaching that increases the opportunity for the successful completion of academic and practical training requirements.

It is difficult to identify a police executive who is completely satisfied with the performance appraisal system utilized by his or her agency. Standard appraisals that equate with a "one size fits all" format are seldom appreciated by the officer receiving the evaluation. Generic evaluations are criticized for their lack of specificity and acknowledgement of employee accomplishments. The Lexington–Fayette Urban County government recently adopted a performance appraisal system that will base a portion of each pay raise on ratings received for specific performance criteria. Appraisals will be specific to each job category and further customized to recognize tasks unique to specialized assignments. The employee assists in establishing the rating criteria, while the supervisor determines criteria for measuring how well each task is performed.

The Lexington Division of Police utilizes a promotional process for the selection of sergeant, lieutenant, and captain. To qualify for participation, a candidate must meet minimal service, education, and disciplinary requirements. Candidates must successfully pass a written exam in order to proceed to the oral board. An oral board uses questions to narrow the pool of successful candidates eligible to participate in an assessment center. The assessment center ranks candidates based on performance on written tests, practical exercises, verbal response/presentation, as well as the other areas. The use of multiple testing methods as part of the promotional process helps to ensure that all candidates compete in a fair manner. As the final step in the promotional process, a candidate is selected from the top of group of candidates (Rule of Five) based on an oral interview.

The role of the Lexington Division of Police in human resource management is one that in interdependent on the city's Division of Human Resources to make the process of selection, appraisal, and promotion of personnel a professional process. As administrators, it is incumbent on chiefs to ensure the human resource processes for which the agency is accountable are conducted in a manner beyond reproach.

requirement that if there is adverse impact against a protected class, it was the defendant's responsibility to show that a practice was job-related or there was a *business necessity* to use the practice. Griggs was not selected for the job he sought because he did not have a high school diploma or pass the placement test. The Court reasoned that the job standards were not useful in identifying "qualified laborers." To avoid being found in violation of Title VII, the Duke Power Company had to prove that the job requirements (high school diploma and test results) effectively distinguished those who could perform the job from those who could not perform it. This shift in burden of proof made it easier for employees who were discriminated against to win a lawsuit since they no longer had to prove that a test or practice was not job-related. The case made HR administration much more difficult for employers, since they had to be able to prove their selection standards were job-related.

Washington v. Davis (1976) shows how agencies can go about validating their selection procedures. The Davis case involved the hiring of police officers in Washington, D.C. The issue in this case was a reading comprehension and aptitude test given to applicants. The applicants read and were tested on material that would be learned in the training academy. The problem with the test stemmed from a disproportionately higher number of minority applicants being rejected as a result of the test. The Supreme Court ruled that the department did not discriminate unfairly because the test was job-related. The police department met the job-relatedness standard by showing a relationship between test scores and performance in the training academy. Applicants who scored high on the test did well in the academy. The department also established a relationship between training academy score and police officer performance. Officers who had high academy scores received higher performance evaluations once on the job. The police department was able to show a direct relationship between the test and officer performance.

The *Davis v. Dallas* (1985) case is another example of the court's acceptance of valid selection criteria in policing. In this case, the Dallas Police Department requirement of a minimum education of 45 college hours with a C average from an accredited university was challenged and upheld. The U.S. Court of Appeals held that the college education requirement, while discriminatory against minorities, was valid because of the "professional" nature of policing, the risk to the public if police act injudiciously, and the responsibility held by the police. Other professions' educational requirements have established legal precedent for such requirements. The case also stated that to validate college education as a job qualification, an agency does not have to follow the EEOC guidelines of quantitative empirical analysis but can base job relatedness on the "qualitative demonstration of the complexity of the police task, the public risk associated with policing, and the use of expert opinion to support these issues" (Carter, Sapp, and Stephens, 1988). The *Davis* decision also upheld the department's prohibition of marijuana usage as a reasonable limitation for the job of police officer, even though the standard had adverse impact on minorities.

In 1989, the U.S. Supreme Court rendered its decision in *Wards Cove Packing Co. v. Atonio*. This case was the culmination of several other legal decisions, and it significantly changed how discrimination was applied. The Court, fearing that businesses would adopt informal hiring quotas as a means of avoiding litigation, attempted to establish new standards that would make self-imposed quotas more difficult. First, the Court stated that plaintiffs must identify the employment practice that caused adverse impact and show how the practice caused discrimination. Theretofore, plaintiffs had to show a statistical under representation only. Second, the employer could offer evidence that the practice met the legitimate employment goals of the employer. This diminished the Griggs standard of business necessity to one of business justification; that is, did the employment practice serve, in a significant way, the legitimate employment goals of the employer (*Wards Cove*, p. 659)? *Wards Cove* effectively made it easier for employers to prevail in discrimination lawsuits. The case dramatically changed the legal definition of discrimination from its origin in *Griggs*.

The *Civil Rights Act of 1991* was an attempt by Congress to reverse the *Wards Cove* decision and to redefine civil rights back within the parameters of *Griggs*. The act requires that employers show that an employment practice is "job-related for the position" and consistent with "business necessity" if disparate impact occurs. Disparate impact is when members of a protected class are not adequately represented in the selection process. The act reaffirms the use of statistical comparisons to establish discrimination. The act also prohibits the use of race, color, religion, gender, or national origin in the employment process.

Second, the act prohibits the use of race or gender norming or other statistical adjustments. In the past, employers have used systems that added points or changed the passing point for minorities or females relative to majority candidates. Such procedures now are strictly prohibited as a result of the 1991 Civil Rights Act. This makes it more difficult for an employer to use written tests and physical agility tests because adverse impact is usually present in such testing. In the past, employers avoided problems by making adjustments or having different passing scores for adversely affected groups (Gaines, Costello, and Crabtree, 1989).

EEO in Perspective.   Generally, the courts use one of three procedures or tests to determine whether a department is discriminating against a protected class:

1. *Population comparisons:* The court examines the percentage of minorities in the population relative to the percentage of minorities on the department.
2. *Four-fifths rule:* The courts examine selection policies to ensure that minority passing rates are at least four-fifths the passing rate for majority candidates. For example, if majority candidates have a 50 percent pass rate, minorities must have a 40 percent success rate (four-fifths of 50 percent).
3. *The McDonnell Douglas rule:* The court determines whether (a) an applicant is from a protected class, (b) the applicant was qualified for the position but was rejected, and (c) the employer continues to advertise for the position (*McDonnell Douglas v. Green*, 1973).

Historically, population comparisons and the four-fifths rule have been the predominant methods used in police discrimination cases.

The various court decisions and legislation regarding EEO have subsequently established broad guidelines for HR systems. It is important to note that minority parity or equal representation is not required as a result of EEO, but if a department's selection procedures result in inequality, the department must be able to prove that its selection procedures are job-related and valid, and that it has adequate affirmative action programs which attempt to address any imbalances. This is a difficult task and few departments have attempted the necessary research on their selection procedures. Thus when no research findings are available and there is adverse impact, the department is in an indefensible position.

Negative Effects of EEO. Many police departments do not have adequate minority or female representation in their ranks. These departments, when faced with litigation, stand to sustain substantial monetary and public relations losses. EEO judgments tend to stigmatize a police department, its chief, and its personnel: It is extremely difficult to overcome their effects. Furthermore, the loss of trust as a result of an EEO suit will affect how citizens respond in other areas. People, especially those from the minority community, may be less likely to report crimes or provide information to police officers.

Many police administrators have criticized Congress and the courts for forcing them to hire "unqualified" minorities as a result of court-imposed quota systems. Indeed, Mahtesian (1996) criticizes quotas and diversity hiring for allowing individuals with criminal records to join police departments. He cites examples involving the Miami and Washington, D.C., departments where individuals with prior criminal histories were hired and later were accused of criminal conduct while on the job. He equated the problem to pressures on police officials to hire minority officers. However, it should be noted that departments nationwide have successfully recruited minority candidates who performed equally with majority candidates. When departments experience difficulties in hiring so-called unqualified minorities, it is the result of departments failing to adequately recruit qualified minorities. The recruitment of minorities cannot be haphazard, but a well-executed recruitment plan must be in operation. Furthermore, if departments such as those of Miami and Washington, D.C., had maintained adequate affirmative action programs over time, there would not have been pressures to hire large number of minorities at one time, a situation that is conducive to numerous hiring problems.

In the past, courts used quota systems as the primary remedy when discrimination occurred. For example, in *Johnson v. City of Albany, Ga.* (1976), the court placed the city under a permanent injunction that remained in effect until 1994. The court determined that if the city would not effectively hire and promote African Americans on its own, then a quota system would be a logical remedy to ensure that African Americans receive fair treatment. Another interesting example of court-ordered quotas occurred in Philadelphia. In *United States v. Philadelphia* (1980), the court entered a consent degree requiring the department to hire females in 30 percent of the next 2,670 openings. Next, in *Pennsylvania v. O'Neill* (1983), a consent degree required that 12 percent of the next 2,442 new hires be African American. Finally, in *Alvarez v. City of Philadelphia* (1990), the court required the department to hire 107 bilingual officers. *Albany* and *Philadelphia* show how complicated and intrusive hiring quotas have been.

Positive Effects on Police Management.   The positive effects of EEO on police management must be recognized. First, many police agencies actively recruit minorities and women where they did not in the past. Minorities and women must be represented if departments are to effectively serve their respective communities (Balzer, 1976). Second, and most important, EEO has caused departments to refine their selection and promotion procedures and, in some cases, initiate validation studies. A police department must select qualified officers regardless of race or sex. Prior to EEO, many selection procedures were arbitrary, political, and even haphazard in nature. Some departments did not use tests; selection and promotion were based on politics and administrative fiat. Majority candidates are receiving as much benefit from EEO as minorities, since selection and promotions in many departments are now based more on ability than on other factors such as politics.

Discrimination against the Disabled

In 1990, Congress passed the *Americans with Disabilities Act (ADA)*, which forbids discrimination against the disabled. An estimated 43 million Americans have some type of disability. Many are of working age, desire to work, but are unable to obtain employment. The ADA is designed to protect these individuals in the workplace.

Specifically, the ADA prohibits discrimination against applicants with disabilities who can perform the essential functions of the job. A disability, according to the ADA, is "a physical or mental impairment" that "substantially limits" one or more "major life activities." A record of having a disability must exist, or the individual is protected if he or she is regarded as having a disability. For example, if an applicant has only one kidney or is missing several fingers, the applicant cannot be rejected if he or she can perform the essential functions of the job. Prior to passage of the ADA, police agencies routinely rejected applicants with these medical problems. Furthermore, even if the applicant cannot perform the essential functions, the department must attempt to provide a reasonable accommodation to assist the disabled person. A reasonable accommodation may include a special schedule, new assignment, training, or the purchase of special equipment (Schneid and Gaines, 1991).

It is the obligation of the police department to identify the essential functions of the job. Essential functions are job-related and of a "business necessity" to the department. The essential functions are generally identified by a job analysis (which is discussed below). Examples of essential functions include running up a set of steps, being able to subdue a suspect, being able to see a license plate at a distance, or being able to communicate with citizens. Once the essential functions are identified, the department must develop appropriate tests to screen applicants to determine if they can perform the essential functions. Acceptance or rejection cannot be based on a disability. In fact, a police department cannot require that applicants receive medical examinations until the applicants have been given a provisional job offer. This is to prevent applicants from being rejected because of the results of such an examination based on a disability.

The ADA requires that police departments and other employers develop sophisticated selection procedures. Selection cannot be a haphazard process. Selection procedures must mirror the job, and they must accurately advise police administrators if a candidate can function as a police officer. Once candidates prove that they can perform the essential functions of the job by passing a department's tests, the department cannot deny employment.

The ADA protects several classes of persons who prior to the act routinely had been excluded from law enforcement. First, the ADA protects persons infected with human immunodeficiency (HIV). Individuals who test positive for virus HIV are protected even if symptoms are not present (Snyder, 1991). For example, in *Doe v. District of Columbia* (1992), the court ruled against the District of Columbia Fire Department for its outright rejection of an HIV-infected applicant, and in *Tanberg v. Weld County Sheriff* (1992), the sheriff's department was ordered to pay compensatory damages to a reserve officer who had been discharged after testing HIV seropositive. The protection of HIV-seropositive individuals concerns law enforcement officials because of the possibility of spreading the disease during a scuffle with a suspect or upon becoming injured while performing some other activity such as investigating an automobile crash. It is unlikely the courts will accept this as a justification for not employing HIV-seropositive individuals, however, because HIV is rarely spread in this fashion.

The ADA also provides protection to "rehabilitated" drug addicts. A drug addict is deemed rehabilitated if he or she successfully completes a rehabilitation program. The framers of the ADA dictated that employers adhere to the *Drug-Free Workplace Act of 1988.* This act encourages drug testing in the workplace, and it was believed that a well-designed workplace drug testing program could detect those who were using illicit drugs, which could result in the errant employee's termination. The act does not protect persons who have committed drug-related crimes. Most drug addicts have sold drugs, and rather than deal with the rehabilitation issue, most departments are refusing to hire rehabilitated addicts based on their past crimes.

The ADA substantially affects police selection and officer retention practices. It requires that departments give due consideration to individuals with disabilities, and an individual can be rejected only if he or she cannot adequately perform the job. For example, in *Bombrays v. Toledo* (1993), an insulin-dependent diabetic applicant was rejected by the Toledo, Ohio, Police Department as a health and safety risk. Bombrays was denied employment because the department had a policy of not hiring diabetics. The court held that a blanket policy violated the act and that diabetics must be considered on a case-by-case basis to determine whether they can perform the essential functions of the job. However, in *Champ v. Baltimore County* (1995), the court decided in favor of the department. Champ had lost the use of one of his arms as the result of an on-duty motorcycle accident. Champ was placed on disability leave and he filed suit. The court held that the department was justified because Champ could not perform one of the essential functions of the job, effecting a physical arrest. The court also ruled that there was no reasonable accommodation that the department could make for Champ.

Sexual Harassment in Policing

Sexual harassment of employees in the workplace has long been a human resources problem. However, in 1991 sexual harassment came to the forefront as a public and occupational issue when University of Oklahoma law professor Anita Hill testified at a congressional hearing considering Clarence Thomas for appointment to the U.S. Supreme Court. Professor Hill's description of Thomas's behavior as sexual harassment caused everyone to question how women were treated in the workplace, and it resulted in a substantial increase in the number of sexual harassment complaints.

Sexual harassment is "actions that are sexually directed, are unwanted, and subject the worker to adverse employment conditions or that create a hostile work environment" (Mathis and Jackson, 1997:154). Legally, sexual harassment emanates from Title VII of the 1964 Civil Rights Act, which prohibits discrimination as a result of gender. However, it was not until 1977 that sexual harassment was ruled to be illegal under Title VII (see *Barnes v. Costle*, 1977). Prior to *Barnes*, sexual advances were considered merely "personal proclivity, peculiarity, and mannerism," which did not affect employment and therefore did not violate Title VII (*Corne v. Bausch and Lomb*, 1975).

In 1986, the U.S. Supreme Court in *Meritor Savings Bank v. Vinson* clarified the issue of sexual harassment by specifying two distinct types of sexual harassment: (1) quid pro quo and (2) hostile work environment.

Quid pro quo sexual harassment exists when there is a tangible economic detriment as a result of a refusal to succumb to sexual advances. Economic detriment can refer to any job condition or benefit including work schedule, promotion, overtime, assignment, or other working condition. Thus, when an employer or superior insinuates that some working condition may be affected by the refusal to submit to sex or other affections, quid pro quo sexual harassment has occurred.

Hostile work environment, on the other hand, refers to situations in which unwelcome sexual conduct has the effect of "unreasonably interfering with an individual's work performance or creating an intimidating environment" (*Hall v. GHS Construction Co.*, 1988). The harassment must be "sufficiently severe or pervasive, so as to alter the conditions of the victim's employment and create an abusive working environment" (*Meritor Savings Bank*). Later, in *Harris v. Forklift Systems* (1993), the U.S. Supreme Court identified three factors that should be considered in determining whether a hostile work environment exists:

1. Was the conduct physically threatening or humiliating as opposed to being just offensive?
2. Did the conduct reasonably interfere with the employee's work performance?
3. Did the conduct affect the employee's psychological well-being?

Numerous court cases illustrate that what may be a playful joke to one employee may be offensive and hostile to another. Actions such as commenting on dress or appearance, allowing pornography or lewd pictures into the workplace, continued sexual or social requests to another employee, and telling sexually suggestive jokes can contribute to the creation of a hostile workplace. Anyone in the police organization can create a hostile work environment. Once a situation comes to the attention of administrators, they must immediately exert every effort possible to correct or eliminate the situation.

Sexual harassment has been a widespread problem in law enforcement. For example, in 1993 the California legislature passed a statute requiring that all peace officers receive sexual harassment training. The law was enacted after several police agencies faced large judgments as a result of sexual harassment. The Los Angeles Sheriff's Department paid $4.5 million in 1992. The Long Beach Police Department paid $3.1 million to two female officers, and the Santa Clara Sheriff's Department paid $700,000 to a female deputy in 1991. In 1992, the San Diego Police Department paid $90,000 to a woman deputy who had her shirt doused with water (Public Safety Personnel Research Institute, 1993).

Police departments have gone to great lengths to cover up and deny the existence of sexual harassment. A New York City Police Department case exemplifies this behavior. In 1983, a female probationary police officer alleged that a male officer took her firearm and raped and sodomized her. The following day, the officer threatened to kill her if she reported him. Upon being raped, the officer received a medical examination. Medical officials reported the crime to Nassau County Police. At the reporting, she deliberately gave the wrong date for the rape and did not tell officials that her assailant was a police officer, although she later identified the officer who had raped her. Police officials stated that the officer passed a departmental polygraph and the complainant officer's polygraph was not completed. She also reportedly was asked to sign a blank piece of paper that later was made into a withdrawal of charges. The Nassau County Police charged her with criminally filing a false accusation, and subsequently the NYPD suspended her and then terminated her employment. No one from Internal Affairs talked with her prior to the suspension. She brought suit in U.S. District Court and ultimately was awarded $264,242 (*Sorlucco v. New York City Police Dept.*, 1992).

Police departments must take action to avoid sexual harassment problems. First, they must implement policies that define and forbid such conduct. Segal (1992) notes that such policies should contain the following elements:

1. Instructions on how to report complaints, including how to bypass a supervisor if he or she is involved in the harassment.
2. Assurances of confidentiality and protection against retaliation by those against whom the complaint is filed.
3. A guarantee of prompt investigation.
4. A statement that disciplinary action will be taken against sexual harassment up to and including termination of employment.

Second, departments should implement training and education programs so that all officers know what sexual harassment is and know the department's position when it occurs. This includes supervisory training that advises supervisors of their obligations when sexual harassment is reported to them or otherwise comes to their attention. Third, when there is a report of sexual harassment, the department must immediately investigate it and take corrective action if it indeed occurred. Finally, the department must ensure that no retaliatory actions are taken against anyone who reports sexual harassment (Robinson et al., 1993).

THE JOB ANALYSIS

Civil service, EEO-related legislation, and court decisions establish the parameters of police human resources administration; the job analysis forms its foundation. *Job tasks* are the building blocks of organizations and constitute the primary units of work for individuals, groups, and units within a police department. The job analysis identifies these primary units and the relative importance of the tasks to the job. Gatewood and Feild defined *job analysis* as a "purposeful, systematic process for collecting information on the important work-related aspects of a job" (1988:245). Job analysis consists of three elements: (1) identifying the job; (2) determining its content, including tasks, duties, responsibilities, working conditions, and ascertaining the skills and characteristics required of workers to perform it successfully; and (3) writing a job description and specifications or qualifications.

The job analysis, then, is a method to identify what incumbents do in the department's various positions or assignments. Information can be collected by a variety of methods: observation, questionnaires, interviews, or an examination of case histories or work products. Regardless of method, the job analysis attempts to identify all the tasks performed by incumbents on the job. Examples of tasks performed by police officers are arresting suspects, writing citations, investigating accidents, handling family disturbances, investigating criminal activity, testifying in court, and resolving crisis situations. Once the tasks are identified, the researchers attempt to gather data about the individual tasks: how often the tasks are performed, how critical the tasks are, what the consequences of inadequate performance of the tasks are. The job analysis is also concerned with determining the knowledge, skills, and abilities (KSAs) required to perform the tasks. The specific information about the tasks varies, depending on the eventual uses of the analysis. Figure 10–3 charts the job analysis process.

Once the instrument is developed, it is administered to officers currently holding positions at the level being analyzed. Generally, large numbers of officers are asked to respond to the questionnaires or to provide information. For example, when Ohio did its statewide job analysis, 3,828 officers from 477 agencies were sampled. Responses from the questionnaires were tabulated and tasks were rank-ordered in terms of frequency of performance and task importance. These rank-ordered tabulations then gave the administrator information relative to what officers do and its importance. These formalized results allow administrators to write job specifications, develop performance appraisals, write promotion and selection tests, develop training curricula, and establish career development plans. Table 10–1 lists the 10 most important tasks performed by sergeants in the Lexington, Kentucky, Police Department.

The importance of the job analysis is exemplified in the number of court decisions over the years that have been related to job analysis. In a number of court

Figure 10–3
The job analysis process.

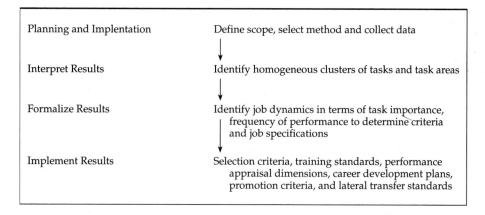

Planning and Implentation	Define scope, select method and collect data
Interpret Results	Identify homogeneous clusters of tasks and task areas
Formalize Results	Identify job dynamics in terms of task importance, frequency of performance to determine criteria and job specifications
Implement Results	Selection criteria, training standards, performance appraisal dimensions, career development plans, promotion criteria, and lateral transfer standards

Table 10–1

Top 10 Tasks Performed by Lexington Sergeants

1. Supervise subordinates in the performance of their duties.
2. Review and approve various departmental reports and transport reports to HQ.
3. Keep superiors appraised of ongoing situations.
4. Listen and respond to citizen complaints.
5. Provide information and assistance to citizens.
6. Disseminate information to subordinates.
7. Conduct roll call.
8. Observe subordinates in handling calls and other duties.
9. Issue duty assignments.
10. Maintain current knowledge specific to assignment.

decisions, the courts invalidated selection and promotion procedures due to the lack of or faulty job analysis. The court in *Chance v. Board of Examiners* (1973) rejected a cursory job analysis when only duty statements were used. In *Vulcan Society v. Civil Service Commission* (1973), the court rejected personnel tests because there was no job analysis. In *Kirkland v. Department of Correctional Services* (1974), the court rejected a cursory job analysis consisting of job audits; outdated materials; one-paragraph job specifications; and knowledge, skills, and abilities statements that reflected the content of the test rather than the job.

Selection criteria and tests as well as promotion tests should be based on a job analysis. The *Griggs* case requires that any test reflect the nature and content of the job. This can be done only with a valid job analysis. For example, a written selection test should test an applicant's ability regarding the job requirements of a police officer. Finally, if departments are sued as a result of the ADA, a job analysis will be necessary for the department to successfully defend itself.

RECRUITMENT AND SELECTION

Administrators often view recruitment and selection as one continuous process. However, if a department is to be effective in acquiring human resources, the police administrator must view them as two distinct processes, and the selection process cannot begin until the recruitment process has been adequately completed. *Recruitment* is defined as the development of a pool of sufficiently qualified applicants from which to select officers. The key to recruitment is ensuring that the applicant list provides a sufficient number of "qualified applicants," since no selection process can be effective without an adequate pool of qualified applicants. *Selection*, on the other hand, refers to identifying those in the applicant pool who will be chosen for police service. Thus recruitment is a critically important part of the HR system.

Recruitment of Police Human Resources

The first step in recruitment is determining the type of person needed by the department. In other words, what should be the department's minimum standards? The job analysis identifies the important tasks, and requisite job knowledge, skills, and abilities (KSAs) can be developed by analyzing the tasks. When we say minimum standards, we are referring to identifying those qualities or KSAs that an applicant must possess to successfully function as a police officer. As dictated in the *Griggs* case, standards must reflect job requirements.

These minimum standards must be specified and must guide recruitment efforts. Recruiters use these standards to counsel and discuss hiring with potential applicants. The recruiters can advise potential applicants of their probability for success in the hiring process. Minimum standards vary from one agency to another, and in addition to skill and ability information, these minimum standards contain other jurisdictional requirements such as residency, citizenship, or possession of a valid driver's license.

An important issue in recruiting officers is minority and gender-focused recruitment. Police departments must attempt to ensure that minorities and women are represented in the applicant pool. Many police departments have a minority and female recruitment program as a part of their overall recruitment programs. For example, Langworthy and his colleagues (1995) found that 91 percent of the departments in their study had minority recruiting programs, and 52.7 percent had programs that focused on female applicants. Such programs are essential if a department is to maintain racial and sexual parity. Doerner (1995) found that female officers, especially African-American women, had a higher attrition rate than white men. This means that departments must recruit increasingly larger numbers of women if they are to maintain some semblance of representation. Minority and gender recruitment programs assist in achieving and maintaining adequate representation.

Race and sex are not the only issues to consider when developing a recruitment program. McKay (1996) in a study of 37 Texas police departments found that more than half of the departments implemented programs that specifically attempted to recruit college graduates. Many departments visit and make presentations on college campuses in order to attract college graduates. A number of departments also have college incentive pay, offering higher salaries to applicants with college credit. Such programs illustrate the importance and kinds of recruitment programs which can be implemented.

The recruitment of police officers frequently is guided by the economy. During periods when the economy is sluggish and there is higher unemployment, police departments have a relatively easy time attracting qualified applicants. However, when the economy is good and unemployment is low, police departments, like all employers, have difficulty attracting good applicants. During the recent period of strong economy, police departments throughout the country had difficulty recruiting applicants. Many departments implemented nationwide recruiting programs while others expanded their recruiting regions. Others implemented bonus programs for officers who identify and recruit new officers. It is important for departments to not lower their selection standards when it becomes difficult to acquire new officers. It is better to work shorthanded than to hire officers who might become problems later in their careers.

Residency Requirements

Today many departments have dropped their residency requirements and recruit nationwide. Several larger cities, however have maintained residency requirements, which they believe assist in maintaining a racial and ethnic balance within the department. When a department recruits from the community it serves, it is likely to obtain an applicant pool that reflects the makeup of the community. Many smaller departments also recruit exclusively within the community—a reflection of local politics. A department should recruit from the largest possible area to maximize the potential qualified applicant pool.

One problem that exists when a department recruits from outside the jurisdiction is attrition. There seems to be a higher attrition rate among officers who join departments that are located long distances from their homes. Over time there is a tendency for them to resign from the department and return to their home area and seek a job. Regardless, if a department is to maximize its recruiting potential, there should be no residency requirement with the exception that all applicants be a citizen of the United States.

A related issue is residency once an applicant has joined the department. A number of departments require officers to reside within the jurisdictional boundaries, a policy that is resisted by many officers, especially in jurisdictions that have few middle-class neighborhoods and where adequate, affordable housing is unavailable. Jurisdictions have these residency requirements for two reasons. First, they are seen as contributing to a jurisdiction's tax base. When government employees reside outside a jurisdiction, property and sales tax revenues are lost (Gonzalez, Mehay, and Duffy-Deno, 1991). Second, residency requirements result in more officers in a jurisdiction, which ultimately will help reduce crime. Officers have more contact with citizens and are available to observe what is happening when they are out in the community. However, in a related study, Murphy and Worrall (1999) did not find that a residency requirement enhanced citizen satisfaction with the police. Although a residency requirement may lead to more contact, it does not appear that this increased contact leads to more positive appraisals by citizens.

Age Requirements

Age requirements at the entry level for police departments refers to a minimum and a maximum age. The vast majority of departments have a minimum age requirement of 21 years; some departments have had lower minimum age requirements ranging from 18 to 20 years of age. The minimum age should not be lower than 21 since younger applicants generally lack maturity for the job.

Many departments have maximum age requirements, usually ranging between 35 and 38, and will not hire applicants over the maximum age. In 1967, Congress passed the Age Discrimination in Employment Act (ADEA). The ADEA was intended to prevent discrimination against older Americans and prohibits a maximum age requirement for employment. Initially, the ADEA was applied to law enforcement agencies; however, they have since been exempted from the act by Congress, and departments are free to establish maximum age requirements.

Education Requirements

The vast majority of police agencies require a high school diploma or its equivalent; however, many departments require some college or even a college degree. Table 10–2 provides a breakdown of educational requirements in American policing. In 1973, the National Commission on Criminal Justice Standards and Goals recommended that departments adopt a requirement of a four-year degree by 1982. This goal, in the vast majority of cases, was not met because of a perceived shortage of college-educated applicants, the discriminatory effect on minorities, and a fear that the department might miss otherwise qualified candidates (Carter, Sapp, and Stephens, 1989). Today, however, it appears that there is an ample supply of college-educated applicants with the numerous criminal justice college programs. In terms of the discriminatory effects of requiring a college degree, minorities statistically are at a disadvantage since a larger percentage of the white population possess college degrees. However, there is an overriding public interest, and police agencies must employ only those individuals who can adequately perform in today's complex society. The courts have upheld the high school diploma requirement even though the requirement is discriminatory (*Arnold v. Ballard*, 1975; *Castro v. Beecher*, 1972). In *Davis v. Dallas* (1985), Dallas's 45-college-credit requirement was upheld. The court noted that the department had sufficiently linked successful performance to the educational requirement. Departments should move toward adopting a four-year college requirement, and any discriminatory effects the requirement may have can be overcome with an active minority recruitment program.

Table 10–2

Minimum Educational Requirements for New Officer Recruits in Local Police Departments, by Size of Population Served[a]

Population Served	Total with Requirements	Percentage of Agencies Requiring a Minimum of:			
		High School Diploma	Some College[b]	Two-Year College Degree	Four-Year College Degree
All sizes	97	86	4	7	1
1,000,000 or more	100	75	25	0	0
500,000 to 999,999	100	85	11	4	0
250,000 to 499,999	98	73	13	9	2
100,000 to 249,999	100	81	9	3	7
50,000 to 99,999	100	72	11	17	1
25,000 to 49,999	100	78	9	9	4
10,000 to 24,999	98	84	5	7	3
2,500 to 9,999	100	90	2	7	1
Less than 2,500	94	85	4	5	0

[a]Percents may not add to total because of rounding.
[b]Nondegree requirements.

Source: Bureau of Justice Statistics, *Local Police Departments, 1993*, NCJ-148822 (Washington, DC: U. S. Department of Justice, 1996), p. 5, Table 7; *Sourcebook of Criminal Justice Statistics 1996*, p. 40.

Ample evidence suggests that college-educated police officers outperform their less-educated peers. For example, Krimmel (1996) found that in self-assessments, college-educated officers rated themselves higher than those without a college education. Carter and his colleagues (1989) believe that college-educated officers are better prepared to successfully confront the many complex and difficult human situations that occur in police work. Shernok (1992) found that college-educated officers are less authoritarian and place a higher value on ethics. Dantzker (1996) found that officers with a college degree had higher levels of job satisfaction during the first five years of their careers, but in subsequent years their job satisfaction declined at a faster rate than officers without degrees. Finally, Kappeler, Sapp, and Carter (1992) found that officers with college education received fewer citizen complaints than their less educated counterparts. Thus a number of arguments support the recruitment of applicants who possess a college degree.

Height and Weight Requirements

Most police departments had minimum height requirements in the past. These requirements have been found to be discriminatory against women, Asians, and Latinos. With few exceptions, police departments have lost court cases involving the height requirement. For example, the court in *Vanguard Justice*

Society v. Hughes (1979) noted that the Baltimore Police Department's height requirement of 5 feet, 7 inches, which excluded 95 percent of the female population and 32 percent of the male population, was a prima facie case of gender discrimination. The court, in *Mieth v. Dollard* (1976) summarized the outcome of most cases:

> The 5'9", 160 pound height and weight requirements set by the Alabama Department of Public Safety for the job of state trooper were not rationally related to achievement of any legitimate state interest contentions that exclusion of women from employment as state trooper was intended for their protection and for the protection of the public was not sufficient to justify minimum height and weight limitations, which had effect of excluding all women, since not only do women not need protectors but there was no record evidence that a woman could not perform the duties of a patrol officer. . . . Evidence failed to establish . . . that tall officers hold advantage over smaller colleagues in effectuating arrests and administering emergency aid; furthermore, contention that tall officers have a psychological advantage was not, as measure of job performance, sufficient constitutional justification for blanket exclusion of all individuals under specified height (418 F.Supp. 1169).

Today, police departments do not have minimum height requirements. Many, however, have requirements that an applicant's weight must be proportionate with his or her height. This requirement is aimed at eliminating applicants who are too obese.

Vision Requirements

Many departments' vision requirements are based on tradition rather than need. It was long argued that a police officer should have relatively good vision since there always was the potential for officers to lose their glasses or contact lenses during an altercation with a suspect, rendering the officer helpless. Good and Augsburger (1987) found that 50 percent of the officers in their study experienced spectacle dislodgement, with a average of 4.09 occurrences during their careers. Strict vision requirements eliminate many otherwise well-qualified applicants. Sheedy (1980) noted a person with 20/200 uncorrected may be able to adequately function as a police officer, depending on the type of vision problem. Since the ADA potentially protects anyone rejected because of vision requirements, it is important that departments establish such standards judiciously.

The Recruitment Process

The department's entry requirements and testing procedures should be detailed in recruitment literature. Such literature provides potential applicants with information to help them determine whether they are qualified. If an applicant is not qualified and can readily make that determination, it will save the applicant and the department's recruiters time and effort.

The police department must aggressively recruit to ensure that the applicant pool has an adequate number of qualified applicants. Often police administrators are too passive in their recruitment; they are content to allow applicants to come to them as opposed to seeking qualified applicants. This results in the department's sometimes not having enough highly qualified applicants in the applicant pool, which becomes more problematic during periods of high employment and is especially important with regard to minorities. Police departments should follow the example set by private enterprise; a business or industry seeking applicants spares no effort or expense in recruitment.

A department should emphasize its positive aspects or attractions during recruitment. In effect, a department must sell itself. Job attractions include the department's benefit package, working conditions, possibility of advancement, and the professional aspects of the department. A department should also emphasize the intangible aspects of being a police officer. For example, policing is an important part of our society and police officers receive a great deal of intrinsic reward from their work. Efforts to educate potential applicants about police work are likely to pay off in generating candidates' interest about the profession. Candidates must want to apply before they will actually apply.

The department's reputation plays an important role in recruitment. If a department has a bad reputation, applicants are likely to apply to other departments or seek employment in other fields. Even a department that can pay the highest salaries will find its recruitment efforts greatly hampered by a bad reputation. Thus a department's community relations are extremely important, and continuous efforts are necessary to constantly upgrade the department's image. This is a prerequisite to a good recruitment program.

Once the recruitment effort begins, the department must attain maximum exposure. This includes advertisement in the media, visits by recruitment teams, and the active involvement of all officers in identifying potential applicants. The department should develop a recruitment brochure describing the department, its policing philosophy, the rewards and benefits of being a police officer, and the department's salary and benefits. The recruitment brochure should serve as the primary information source for applicants. Maximum exposure to the recruitment program will produce the maximum number of applicants; therefore, the boundaries of the recruitment efforts should be as large as possible.

Selection of Police Officers

Over the years, police selection has consisted of a variety of tests, measurements, and exercises. These range from management prerogative, where the chief interviews candidates and makes the selection decision based on his or her judgment, to an assessment center, where candidates are subjected to a battery of tests measuring a wide range of knowledge, skills, and abilities. The selection process is the most important component in the human resources system. If the department does not select highly qualified candidates, the department, in all likelihood, will be forced to retain substandard officers for years. An agency should spare no expense or effort in selecting officers.

The key to selection is the job analysis, which identifies in fairly precise terms the selection requirements. Case law, as discussed earlier, dictates that selection be based on a job analysis. Selection is generally a multistage process whereby candidates are tested in a number of areas. Components usually included in the selection process are a written exam, physical ability test, character or background investigation, medical examination, and psychological screening oral interview.

Written Examinations

The written examination generally is the first test administered to police applicants who make it to the selection process. The written test is fairly inexpensive and is used to eliminate the largest number of applicants. For example, when the Kentucky State Police announces that it is hiring, it usually will get 1,000 to 1,500 applications for approximately 100 positions. It is impossible for the agency to process 1,000 or so applicants through the total selection process. The written test is used to reduce the applicant pool to a manageable number.

The written examination is the hurdle that screens out the most applicants and has been the subject of the most court litigation. Historically, police agencies used a variety of written tests ranging from intelligence tests to departmental or community-specific tests. For example, O. W. Wilson (1950) in the first edition of his book *Police Administration* recommended an intelligence quotient of 112 as a minimum standard for police service. The *Griggs* case, in effect, prohibits the use of such tests when adverse impact occurs. It is easily argued that police officers should have a high IQ or be intelligent. Measuring intelligence or IQ is more difficult. What kind of intelligence does a particular IQ test measure? Will a person with an IQ of 120 be a better officer than one with an IQ of 100? These questions cannot be answered definitively, but there is evidence that IQ is positively associated with police academy performance (Kenney and Watson, 1996). The problem with such tests is that to validate or link the test results to actual performance, as is required by *Griggs*, is impossible. These IQ tests provide abstract measures of the person rather than measuring actual ability or aptitude.

Many departments use tests developed specifically for police selection. One such test is marketed by the International Personnel Managers Association (IPMA). This test is advertised as a multijurisdictional police aptitude test. A nationwide job analysis was used to validate the test when it was first developed. It tests for knowledge and skills that are prerequisites for police work using items that are examples of actual police work. It has six subscales:

- Ability to learn and apply police information.
- Ability to remember details (names, descriptions, and facts).
- Verbal ability.
- Ability to accurately complete forms.
- Ability to interpret maps and accident diagrams.
- Ability to use judgment and logic.

Police departments use this test or similarly constructed tests because the tests appear to be job-related.

Gaines and Falkenberg (1998) investigated the IPMA's test and found a number of problems. First, like almost all police written selection tests, it had adverse impact on minorities. Second, there was an overrepresentation of "easy" items on the test, calling into question the test's ability to identify qualified applicants. Third, although the test contained six subscales, a statistical analysis found that items on the test did not necessarily correspond to the subscales, raising a validity question. Finally, the test was highly correlated or related to education, indicating that the test may be measuring education rather than police aptitude. It is doubtful that the IPMA test is any different from other purchased tests, and they should be used with caution in selecting police officers.

Physical Ability Testing

A concern to police managers in the selection process is the physical strength or agility of police candidates. In the past, departments used height and weight requirements as a measure of physical ability. The police had to be big and strong to deal with the perceived physical dangers of the job. In the early 1970s some departments had minimum height requirements of six feet and taller. However, the courts have ruled these height requirements to be discriminatory against females, Asians, and Latinos, and departments abandoned height requirements for some form of physical ability testing. Martin (1990) found that 80 percent of the municipal departments and 84 percent of state-level departments had physical ability testing as a part of the selection process. Physical ability combines both strength and agility measures to give an overall measure of the physical ability of police personnel.

The New York City Police Department adopted a physical ability test that consisted of three events: (1) run stairs/restrain, (2) a dummy drag, and (3) a wall climb/obstacle course (Jordan and Schwartz, 1986). The California Commission on Peace Officer Standards and Testing developed a test consisting of (1) a body drag-lift using a 165-pound dummy, (2) a six-foot fence climb and run, (3) a chain link fence climb and run, (4) an agility run, (5) a body lift and carry using a lifelike dummy, and (6) a 550-yard run (Berner and Kohls, 1982).

Physical ability testing, like the old height requirements, posed the problem of adverse impact on females. Hernandez (1981), investigating the adverse impact of the physical ability testing for deputy sheriffs, found that females were four times more likely to fail than males. At issue is the lack of any scientific way of establishing and justifying cutoff scores (Gaines, Falkenberg, and Gambino, 1996). In other words, what is a reasonable time to run 550 yards? For example, in *Harless v. Duck* (1980) the court ruled the Toledo, Ohio, Police Department's physical ability test invalid. The test required applicants to do 25 situps, 15 pushups, a six-foot standing broad jump, and a 25-second obstacle course. The court noted that although the job analysis disclosed a need for physical ability, it did not define the amount required for the job, and the test was developed through an intuitive process with no justification for the exercises and the pass/fail criteria used by the department.

To counter these problems, many departments moved to a health-based physical ability testing system. The most popular health-based program was developed by the Aerobics Institute in Dallas. It involved five physical areas: (1) cardiovascular capacity, generally measured by a 1½-mile run; (2) upper-body strength, measured by pushups or a bench press; (3) abdominal strength, measured by situps; (4) body-fat composition, usually measured with body calipers; and (5) flexibility, measured by a toe-touch exercise. Gender discrimination was avoided by using male and female norms. For example, a department might establish the 50th percentile as the cutoff. That means that males would have to score at the midpoint on an event using the scores of males; females would be compared to other females' scores. This system generally identified those who were physically capable of being police officers.

In the mid-1990s this system was largely abandoned because of the Civil Rights Act of 1991. The act forbade the use of gender-based norms. Many departments reinstituted physical ability tests and continued to face the problems of establishing valid cutoff scores. However, in 1996, the Eighth Circuit of the U.S. Court of Appeals rendered a decision in *Peanick v. Morris* that allowed the continued use of health-based testing. The defendants in the case successfully argued that gender-based norms did not violate the Civil Rights Act of 1991. The court ruled that even though cutoffs for males and females were different, the norms were used to establish that males and females were at the same level in terms of physical health. A number of departments have abandoned the agility tests and again are using health-based testing.

There is some question about the relevance of physical ability screening in law enforcement. Maher (1981) argued that such tests do not represent realistic job samples because the various tests relate to aspects of the job that are seldom performed. Police work is fairly sedentary coupled with very infrequent bursts of physical activity. In *Blake v. City of Los Angeles* (1979), the court forbade the use of the police department's physical ability test because it discriminated against females. In addition to questioning the test's validity, the court noted that for decades the department had successfully hired officers without the benefit of a physical ability test. Finally, Gaines and his colleagues (1996) examined a Kentucky State Police selection system in which no physical ability test was administered but obese applicants were screened out. At the end of the academy experience, all cadets' performance far exceeded any minimum standards as the result of intensive physical training.

Background/Polygraph Examination

Most departments use a background or character investigation, and an increasing number use the polygraph to screen applicants. This phase of the selection process is very important since past behavior is a good predictor of future behavior and police departments must select individuals who have good character.

The *background investigation* consists of reviewing official records and interviewing the applicant's past employers and acquaintances to determine the applicant's fitness for service. The background investigation focuses on the following areas: criminal history, employment record, sociability, mental and emotional conditions and history, personal integrity, education, and medical history. The candidate's history of drug and alcohol use is also an important part of the background investigation. All of these areas should be thoroughly investigated by reviewing all available records and interviewing as many people as possible. If there is a question about an applicant's integrity or suitability, the hiring decision should be made in favor of the department: The applicant should not be hired.

The amount of detail and effort put into the background investigation varies among departments as these investigations are time-consuming and expensive. Too often, officers spend too little time and contact only convenient references when doing the investigation. The background must be a complete and exhaustive examination of the applicant's past if it is to serve its purpose. All desirable and undesirable applicant traits must be uncovered, since an applicant's work and social behaviors while on the police force will be very similar to his or her behaviors before entering into police service. The background investigation will shed light on the candidate's motivation, productivity, and competence, whereas the polygraph will primarily examine behavioral problems.

The *polygraph examination* is used to determine the veracity of statements and information provided by applicants during the hiring process and to uncover past criminal or unacceptable deviant behaviors. The Employee Polygraph Protection Act of 1988 bars the polygraph in most employment screening, but government agencies are exempted from the act, allowing its use in policing. Some states, including Michigan and Pennsylvania, prohibit its use in police applicant screening. Horvath (1993) upon examining its use in law enforcement found that police administrators believed that it resulted in (1) more honest answers on applications, (2) higher-quality employees, and (3) fewer undesirable applicants being hired.

The polygraph examination should be considered a separate phase from the background investigation. These two phases focus on two very different areas. The polygraph addresses areas that normally cannot be readily examined during the background investigation. A background investigation cannot yield recent information or information that only the applicant would know. The polygraph enables the investigator to gain information about the applicant's behavior and character. It is used to validate information on the application, discover criminal behavior, identify past work-related problems, and examine morals. Generally, the applicant is questioned about past use of drugs, involvement in reported and unreported criminal activity, social and work relationships, and sexual practices. Table 10–3 shows the areas addressed most frequently during the polygraph examination.

In many cases, this information can be obtained only through the polygraph examination. The polygraph should not supplant the background investigation, since the background investigation is used to gather detailed information that cannot be gleaned from a polygraph. For example, the polygraph may develop

Table 10–3

Areas Tested During Polygraph Examination

Honesty	97.3
Criminality	100.0
Sexual Preference	25.0
Aggression	48.6
Racism	24.3
Loyalty	18.9
Sexism	21.6
Motivation	16.2
Phobias	10.8

Source: R. Langworthy, T. Hughes, and B. Sanders, "Law Enforcement Recruitment, Selection, and Training: A Survey of Major Police Departments in the United States." Paper presented at the Annual Meeting of the Academy of Criminal Justice Sciences, Boston, MA, 1995.

information about an applicant's being fired or stealing while on the job, but it does not produce information about the candidate's work performance and relations with other employees and supervisors.

Frequently, the most vital information gained from a polygraph examination does not come from the polygraph results but from the preexamination interview. Since applicants know they are about to be tested, they tend to be more honest during this interview. For example, during a preexamination interview, the examining officer asked the applicant when he last smoked marijuana. The applicant replied that he had smoked some in the parking lot because he was nervous about taking the test. Rejection of the applicant was based on the applicant's statements, rather than on the polygraph results. This example also illustrates how the polygraph is instrumental in obtaining information about applicants that otherwise would be inaccessible.

Drug use is the leading problem resulting in the rejection of applicants. It is increasingly more difficult to find qualified applicants without a history of drug use. Consequently, departments are developing drug use policies for applicants. These policies usually focus on (1) recency of use, (2) patterns or frequency of use, (3) types of drug used, and (4) involvement in the sale or distribution of drugs. Departments have different standards, and to a large extent the standards are determined by whether a department can recruit enough applicants. Many departments use mandatory drug testing to supplement drug entry standards. Thus departments have a mechanism to ensure that candidates who previously used drugs have discontinued their use.

Some departments use honesty tests to augment the polygraph examination. Two leading tests in this area are the Reid Report and the Stanton Survey. Sample questions on these surveys include:

Have you ever told a lie?
Would you tell your boss if another employee was stealing?
Is it all right to borrow company equipment and return it later?

These tests are designed to identify applicants who are dishonest. Such tests are criticized because many believe they are not reliable in identifying those who may be dishonest. However, coupled with the results of the polygraph and psychological tests, they can be very revealing. Honesty testing is particularly relevant where polygraph testing is prohibited.

Medical Examination

The importance of hiring medically sound candidates cannot be overstated. If an employee is not medically fit, the employee's performance is directly affected, and there is an increased potential that the candidate will retire early on an injury retirement or incur medical costs that will substantially affect the department's health care costs. Every applicant should be given a complete and thorough medical examination to determine whether the applicant is suffering from any disqualifying diseases or ailments.

The Americans with Disabilities Act (ADA) protects applicants with disabilities and has substantially complicated the selection process. As a result of the ADA, a department cannot require a medical examination until a provisional job offer has been given to the candidate. That is, applicants are hired if they pass the medical examination. This is to prevent departments from using information about minor medical conditions in other selection tests such as the oral interview.

The medical examination should be designed to discover any physical abnormalities or medical condition such as back problems or high blood pressure that might render the applicant physically unqualified for duty. As required by the ADA, any disqualifying medical problem must be related to the applicant's inability to perform the essential functions of the job. Drug testing is also becoming a standard part of the medical evaluation in the selection process. Special care should be taken to monitor the medical evaluation. Applicants who take drugs to control for hypertension have been known to have friends provide urine specimens to conceal the ailment or drug use.

Departments are increasingly developing more thorough medical or health testing procedures to ensure that applicants are fit and will remain fit during their tenure as police officers. For example, the Alexandria, Virginia, Police Department is using a health-based system. Applicants are screened in terms of total fitness. Blood is analyzed for cholesterol and triglycerides, body fat composition is measured, and candidates' fitness in terms of cardiovascular and lung disease is measured. Departments using a health-based system maintain that they have a financially vested interest in hiring healthy personnel since healthy officers are more productive, use less sick time, and are less prone to injuries. However, such programs may be challenged on the basis of the ADA.

Psychological Examination

Psychological screening is another critical phase in the selection process. In *Hild v. Bruner* (1980) the court found a city negligent for not using psychological screening. When a department hires an officer who has mental problems, and the officer subsequently harms a citizen as a result of the problem, the city bears some responsibility. Mills (1983:57) notes there are two different screening ideologies: the search for psychopathology in the applicant and the search for positive traits. The search for applicant *psychopathology* entails examining the applicant for disorders such as emotional instability, excessive dependency needs, paranoid tendencies, sexual identity problems, schizophrenia, lack of self-confidence, depression, and neurotic or psychotic tendencies. If these problems are found, the applicant is disqualified. The *positive trait* method attempts to identify the "ideal" police candidate. Applicants are examined for motivation, sensitivity, stability under stress, leadership ability, maturity, flexibility, integrity, extroversion, and self-assertiveness. Positive trait screening is the most effective selection technique since it identifies those who are potentially good officers rather than rejecting the unqualified.

Psychologists and psychiatrists use a number of tests to evaluate police candidates. For example, Johnson (1990) in a survey of psychological screening of police applicants in New Jersey found 60 different tests being used. The Minnesota Multiphasic Personality Inventory (MMPI), California Personality Inventory (CPI), Rorschach Ink Blots, Figure Drawings, and Sentence Completion are some of the most frequently used tests that attempt to measure psychopathology, while the Inwald (Shusman, Inwald, and Kantz, 1987) is a test used in law enforcement to identify positive traits, or "screen in" applicants. The department should make arrangements with a licensed psychologist or psychiatrist to perform psychological assessments. The department should arrange to retain all data relating to this testing for use in follow-up studies to establish the predictive validity of the tests. For example, an increasing number of officers are applying for stress-related disability retirement, yet there have been few studies to determine if they were susceptible to stress when they entered the department.

The Model Selection Procedure

Figure 10–4 presents a model selection procedure for police departments. The arrangement of the various screening phases follows two principles: Institute the phases that screen out the greatest number of candidates early in the procedure, and place the most expensive procedures at the end of the process. Thus the model attempts to economize the process as much as possible. For example, the medical and psychological examinations are the most expensive and the background investigation is expensive in terms of personnel's time. The written test is followed by a physical ability test since it is relatively inexpensive to administer, and it disqualifies a fair number of applicants.

The final phase before selection and probationary employment is the oral interview. Police departments have used two different oral interview methods.

Figure 10–4
Model selection procedure.

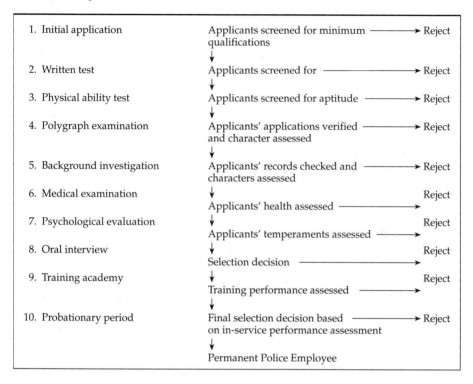

First, some agencies rate each candidate on predetermined traits and the out-come becomes part of the ranking scores. Here traits such as motivation, appearance, work history, judgment, and initiative are measured. Whether the oral interview is valid and reliable enough to adequately serve this purpose is highly questionable (Doerner, 1997; Gaines and Lewis, 1982). However, oral interviews remain a mainstay in police selection as they are seen as a way of getting a "close look" at applicants.

In the second method, the oral interview is used to make the selection deci-sion. At this point the department has usually gathered adequate data on all the candidates and now must simply decide which ones should be hired. The purpose of the interview is not to obtain information but to possibly clarify existing infor-mation. The previous selection phases (application through background) should have created an exhaustive, detailed database on each candidate. The members of the oral interview board must sift through this information, noting deficiencies and exemplary characteristics, and then use this information to structure the interview. Candidates can be made to explain deficiencies, inconsistencies, or omissions. Eventually, the interview board will produce a list of candidates ranked in terms of their desirability, from which appointments will be made.

The final two phases of selection, recruit training or basic academy training and the probationary period, are not normally considered part of the selection process. However, the quality of police officers might be enhanced if these steps were formally considered part of selection. After the probationary period is successfully completed, the police officer becomes a permanent employee of the police organization.

POLICE TRAINING

The last two decades have seen a drastic improvement in the quality and quantity of police training. A number of states have set minimum training standards and developed regional and statewide training academies to serve departments that do not have the resources for their own programs. Departments are paying more attention to curriculum, training methods, and facilities development.

There are two types of ongoing police training: in-service or career development training and academy training. *In-service training* is used to constantly update the skills and knowledge base of veteran officers. Since new techniques of operations and management are constantly being developed, efforts must be made to keep all officers current. *Academy training* is the initial training an officer receives, and it serves to orient new officers to the department, indoctrinate them about the department's goals and objectives, and provide them with the necessary skills and knowledge required for the job. Both types of training are vital to a department's well-being.

Academy Training

Academy training, which is the training that occurs immediately after an officer is hired, varies in length. Table 10–4 provides a breakdown of academy training time and field training time by department size. The average academy time is 425 hours, and it appears that the larger cities require more training than smaller jurisdictions. Academy training is a critical part of HR administration, because if recruits are not properly trained, they will not function adequately as police officers. Great care must be given to developing the training program. Curricula should be based on a job analysis to reflect the actual work environment. Other sources of curriculum-building information include interviews with officers and supervisors, analysis of performance appraisals, review of goals and objectives, and forecasts of future needs. The training curriculum should be evaluated continually and kept current.

Two general types of basic police academy are in use today. First, there are those that are operated by a police department or a statewide police training agency. Usually an applicant must be hired before being sent to one of these academies. Second, a number of states, including California, Ohio, and Minnesota, have academies in community colleges where potential applicants can receive basic academy certification at their own expense. Students in these programs often receive an associate degree when they receive their police academy

Police officers at range target practice.
Bob Daemmrich/Stock Boston

Table 10–4

Training Requirements for New Officer Recruits in Local Police Departments, by Size of Population Served

Population Served	Percentage of Agencies Requiring Training	Average Number of Hours Required*	
		Classroom Hours	Field Training Hours
All sizes	90%	425	215
1,000,000 or more	100	865	311
500,000 to 999,999	100	757	396
250,000 to 499,999	100	727	551
100,000 to 249,999	99	630	498
50,000 to 99,999	100	494	435
25,000 to 49,999	100	492	393
10,000 to 24,999	98	468	305
2,500 to 9,999	93	455	204
Less than 2,500	83	352	105

*Computation of average number of training hours required excludes departments not requiring training.

Source: Bureau of Justice Statistics, *Local Police Departments, 1993,* NCJ-148822 (Washington: U.S. Department of Justice, 1996), p. 5, Table 8: *Sourcebook of Criminal Justice Statistics 1996,* p. 40.

Table 10–5

California Basic Academy Requirements

Subject Area	Training Hours	Subject Area	Training Hours
Ethics and Professionalism	8	Crimes in Progress	16
Criminal Justice System	4	Handling Disputes	12
Community Relations	12	Domestic Violence	8
Victimology/Crisis Intervention	6	Unusual Occurrences	4
Introduction to Law	6	Missing Persons	4
Crimes against Property	10	Traffic Enforcement	22
Crimes against Persons	10	Traffic Investigation	12
General Criminal Statutes	4	Preliminary Investigations	42
Crimes against Children	6	Custody	4
Sex Crimes	6	Physical Fitness	40
Juvenile Laws	6	Weaponless Defense	60
Controlled Substances	12	First Aid/CPR	21
ABC Law	4	Firearms/Chemical Agents	72
Laws of Arrest	12	Information Systems	4
Search and Seizure	12	Persons with Disabilities	6
Concepts of Evidence	8	Gangs	8
Report Writing	40	Crimes against the Justice	4
Vehicle Operations	24	Weapon Violations	4
Use of Force	12	Hazardous Materials	4
Patrol Techniques	12	Cultural Awareness	24
Vehicle Pullovers	14	**Total**	**599**

certification. The community college system has evolved in an effort to provide an increased number of qualified police applicants and to reduce the costs to police departments for training officers. The direct and indirect costs of hiring an officer and sending him or her to an academy are approximately $40,000. Applicants who have academy certification represent substantial savings for the department.

Table 10–5 presents a breakdown of the basic training curriculum for California police officers. This curriculum, developed by the California Police Officer Standards Training Commission, attempts to provide to officers the knowledge, skills, and abilities required for the job. The curriculum contains a number of domain areas and comprehensively addresses the job of police officer.

Kirkpatrick (1977) elaborated four criteria by which to evaluate the effectiveness of training. First, what were the trainees' reactions to the training? Did they accept it as being valid and were they motivated as a result of it? Training must make an impression on the trainees if it is to be effective. Second, was there learning? Did the trainees internalize the facts? Not only must the facts be presented, but they (training techniques) must be presented in such a fashion that trainees are able to understand and learn the information. The third criterion is resulting behavior. Learning the information does not ensure that trainees will use it. After training, good field supervision is essential to ensure that knowledge and skills are adequately applied. Finally, Kirkpatrick notes that training is evaluated by its results. It may be that officers apply their knowledge and skills, but the desired results are not produced. This points to a deficiency in the training program. Evaluating training is a complicated, time-consuming process, but it is necessary if a department is to have an effective training program.

Buerger (1998) notes an underlying problem of academy training: Applicants come to the job with preconceived notions about police work that are usually developed from news stories, fictional books, and movies. They come into the job expecting to do "police work," not "community service" or "problem solving." Buerger notes that police trainees find "skills training" such as firearms training, evidence collection, or driving to be interesting and deemed important. Training in such areas a ethics, community responsibility, and the proper role of the police is seen as boring and unimportant. Skills training is engaging and captures recruits' attention. The nonskills training is routinely provided through lectures in a "cold, preachy fashion." This problem calls into question the ability of a department to adequately train and instill community service and problem-solving values in recruits. Police agencies compound this problem by placing more training emphasis on skills areas. For example, Edwards (1993) found that state police agencies tend to place less emphasis on "values" training and devote an inordinate amount of training time to police proficiency training.

The way training material is presented is just as important as curriculum development. Police trainers in the past overrelied on lectures and the use of videos. Many academies utilized a militaristic system that produced a stressful atmosphere. As Birzer notes, "This structured approach, which emphasizes mastery and obedience, puts undue stress on students and does not encourage effective learning or support the community policing mission" (1999:17). Birzer likens many academy training techniques to techniques used to "teach children," which are hopelessly ineffective in teaching adults. Training should include as much role playing, problem solving, and simulation as possible. Outside expert speakers, such as representatives from the NAACP, public defender's office, and ACLU, should be used to provide a broad perspective to recruits. The police are involved in numerous areas of social control that are controversial to many police officers, and outsiders can enhance the recruit's understanding of these issues. Trainees should be encouraged to actively participate by asking questions and debating issues since such interaction enhances learning and understanding. This better understanding leads to more effective decision making and problem solving on the part of officers once they are assigned to the field. This is extremely important as departments continue to implement community policing.

Probationary Period

The final phase of basic training is the probationary period. The *probationary period* varies in length but usually lasts for approximately 12 months. This period is not only a training period but also serves as a part of the selection process. New officers are further trained and evaluated in terms of their ability to apply the skills and knowledge taught during academy training. If they are not able to perform adequately, they can be terminated "without cause" from the department during the probationary period. The objective of the probationary period is not to terminate officers but to improve their performance. However, termination may be necessary if officers do not function at an acceptable level. Generally, the method by which probationary officers are evaluated during probation is the field training officer program.

Field Training Officer Program

Since the first formal field training officer (FTO) program was established in San Jose, California, in 1972 (McCampbell, 1987), many departments throughout the United States have initiated FTO programs. As shown in Table 10–4, new officers spend an average of 215 hours in FTO training. The FTO program has become important in helping to ensure the quality of the police recruit training process. Most agencies that have FTO programs have adapted the San Jose model to meet their own needs. Figure 10–5 is a flow chart of the San Jose FTO program.

The FTO program is designed to ensure that recruits have the basic competencies to perform as police officers. This is accomplished through a formalized program to evaluate new officers. Once the recruits graduate from the basic training academy, they are assigned to work under the supervision of a *field training officer* (FTO). The FTO trains the officers by allowing them in actual street experiences to apply the principles they learned in the classroom setting. New officers thus are taught to apply academy material and to handle themselves on the street. The FTOs supervise, instruct, and evaluate the new officers. The decision to retain new officers is based on the FTO's evaluations. Figure 10–6 is an FTO evaluation form used by the Houston Police Department. This formalized evaluation system enables a department to make a more accurate decision on a recruit's suitability for police work.

McCampbell (1987) made the following recommendations concerning the management and administration of FTO programs.

1. The FTO program should be considered a normal part of the selection and training process and the FTO program should be designed to provide the organization with the best possible police officers.
2. In large organizations, patrol should be given administrative control over the FTO program because of the close interrelation between the FTO program and the patrol function.
3. The recruit should be assigned to several FTOs during the field training program to reduce the possibility of bias and personality conflicts and to allow several experienced trainers to evaluate the recruit.
4. All FTO training should be planned, standardized, and logically sequenced.
5. Each skill should be demonstrated and explained to the recruit by the FTO. The training guide should clearly separate and state the elements necessary for mastery of the skill. The recruit should be required to consistently and satisfactorily perform a skill before the FTO certifies competency on the skill.

Figure 10–5
San Jose field training process.

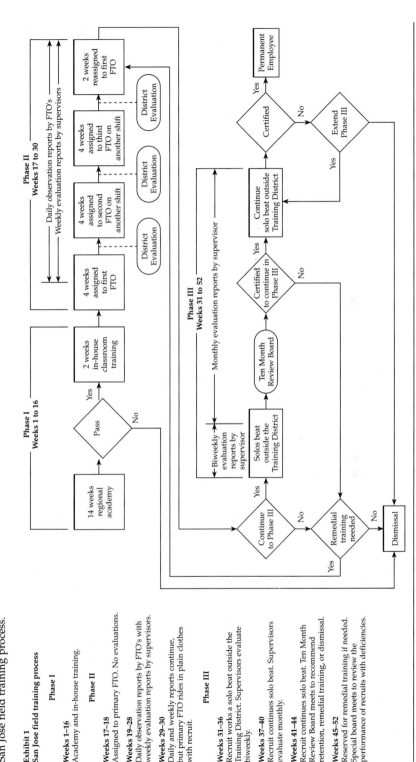

Exhibit 1
San Jose field training process

Phase I

Weeks 1–16
Academy and in-house training.

Phase II

Weeks 17–18
Assigned to primary FTO. No evaluations.

Weeks 19–28
Daily observation reports by FTO's with weekly evaluation reports by supervisors.

Weeks 29–30
Daily and weekly reports continue, but primary FTO rides in plain clothes with recruit.

Phase III

Weeks 31–36
Recruit works a solo beat outside the Training District. Supervisors evaluate biweekly.

Weeks 37–40
Recruit continues solo beat. Supervisors evaluate monthly.

Weeks 41–44
Recruit continues solo beat. Ten Month Review Board meets to recommend retention, remedial training, or dismissal.

Weeks 45–52
Reserved for remedial training, if needed. Special board meets to review the performance of recruits with deficiencies.

Source: M. S. McCampbell, *Field Training for Police Agencies: The State of the Art*, Washington: U.S. Department of Justice, National Institute of Justice, 1987, pp. 4–6.

379

Figure 10–6

Houston Police Department, field operations command—field training and performance evaluation program.

Phase Six Daily Evaluation Report

DAY _____ WEEK 1 2 3 DIVISION _____ SHIFT 1 2 3 4 5 DATE _____ 19 _____

PROBATIONARY OFFICER _____ EMP. NO. _____ CLASS NO. _____

PERFORMANCE EVALUATOR _____ EMP. NO. _____

Evaluation Categories	Performance Levels							
	Worst		Minimally Acceptance			Best		

Orientation

1. Appearance _____ 1 2 3 4 5 6 7 NO.
2. Acceptance of criticism _____ 1 2 3 4 5 6 7 NO.
3. Attitude toward police work _____ 1 2 3 4 5 6 7 NO.
4. Use of common sense and good judgement _____ 1 2 3 4 5 6 7 NO.

Knowledge

5. Of department policies and procedures _____ 1 2 3 4 5 6 7 NO.
6. Of common Texas penal code offenses _____ 1 2 3 4 5 6 7 NO.
7. Of common Houston City ordinances _____ 1 2 3 4 5 6 7 NO.
8. Of commoon Texas traffic laws _____ 1 2 3 4 5 6 7 NO.

Performance

9. Use of key map _____ 1 2 3 4 5 6 7 NO.
10. District orientation/response time _____ 1 2 3 4 5 6 7 NO.
11. Driving skills _____ 1 2 3 4 5 6 7 NO.
12. Appropriate use of the radio _____ 1 2 3 4 5 6 7 NO.
13. Radio: listens and comprehends _____ 1 2 3 4 5 6 7 NO.
14. Routine forms: accuracy and completeness _____ 1 2 3 4 5 6 7 NO.
15. Reporting writing: organization and details _____ 1 2 3 4 5 6 7 NO.
16. Report writing: grammar/spelling/neatness _____ 1 2 3 4 5 6 7 NO.
17. Self-initiated field activity _____ 1 2 3 4 5 6 7 NO.
18. Managing calls of service _____ 1 2 3 4 5 6 7 NO.
19. Conducting searches and/or seizures _____ 1 2 3 4 5 6 7 NO.
20. Officer safety _____ 1 2 3 4 5 6 7 NO.
21. Prisoner and/or mental patient management _____ 1 2 3 4 5 6 7 NO.
22. Control of conflict _____ 1 2 3 4 5 6 7 NO.
23. Execution of evidentiary techniques _____ 1 2 3 4 5 6 7 NO.

Relationships

24. With citizens _____ 1 2 3 4 5 6 7 NO.
25. With police personnel _____ 1 2 3 4 5 6 7 NO.

NO.–Not Observed

FIELD TRAINING ADMINISTRATION OFFICE USE ONLY

CONTROL NO. _____ MONITOR _____

ENTERED _____ CHECKED _____

CHECKED _____ RECEIVED _____

RECEIVED _____ RETURNED _____

Figure 10–6
(Concluded)

All formal evaluation categories receiving a score of less than 4 (minimum acceptable) must have specific documentation of each substandard performance. The documentation MUST contain the following: time, location, nature of incident, incident report/ticket number and a description of the probationary police officer's performance. Attach copies of unacceptable work samples to this report.

Cat. Nos. _____

_____

_____

_____

_____

_____

_____

_____

_____

_____

_____

(should more space be required, use supplemental form)

List specific strengths displayed by the probationary police officer during this day.

Cat. No. _____

_____

_____

_____

_____

_____

_____

_____

_____

_____

_____

Were there any weaknesses identified during this day in categories NOT BEING FORMALLY EVALUATED? If so, specifically document and indicate below the numerical score that would be assigned to that category for the day in the space provided. (NOTE: Do not assign a score to the front of this report.)

Cat No. _____ Score _____ _____

_____

_____

Cat No. _____ Score _____ _____

_____

_____

I CERTIFY that this is an accurate account of the probationary police officer's performance during this day.

_____
Signature—Field Performance Evaluator

I CERTIFY that I have recieved this report and found it in compliance with program standards.

_____
Signature—Field Training Supervisor

6. The FTO should evaluate the recruit daily using a standardized evaluation form that has been reduced, as much as possible, to a checklist-type form.
7. A job task analysis for the patrol officer position should be the basis for the recruit's performance evaluation.
8. The FTO position should be clearly defined, preferably by a job task analysis for the position of FTO, to include the responsibilities of the FTO as trainer and as patrol officer.
9. The FTO should be selected from a pool of highly motivated volunteers. On selection the FTO should receive a minimum of 40 hours of training before being allowed to act in the official capacity of FTO.
10. Some form of extra compensation should be offered to FTOs to ensure that the most qualified are attracted and retained in the FTO position.
11. Agencies should perform annual evaluations of their FTO programs.

McCampbell's research found that FTO programs were associated with a reduction in civil liability complaints and a significant decrease in the number of successful discrimination judgments against departments. FTO programs seem to improve police–community relations and the internal climate within the police organization by ensuring that new officers follow the letter and spirit of departmental policies.

In-Service Training

Another important part of police training is in-service training for veteran officers. Laws are constantly changing, new departmental procedures are implemented, new expertise is needed, and old skills require reinforcement. Police departments must ensure that officers remain up-to-date in terms of their job knowledge and skills. Many states now mandate a minimum number of training hours per year for police officers. For example, police officers in Kentucky must receive 40 hours of certified in-service training per year. Officers can receive in-service training in a variety of ways. First, they may receive it in-house, if the department's training unit offers in-service courses. Second, they can be sent to a regional or state academy, which generally offers a large variety of in-service courses. Third, officers can be sent to an institute that offers specialized training programs, such as the Southern Police Institute, Southwestern Law Enforcement Institute, or Northwestern Traffic Institute.

In-service training should be institutionalized so that all officers have to attend courses periodically. The department's HR office should maintain records of performance appraisals, negative police incidents, and information on citizen complaints. The department should use this information to help structure in-service training. In this sense, in-service training is used not only to update officers but also to correct deficiencies within the department. The departmental HR office should also ensure that officers are sent to in-service training that is relevant. That is, there is little need to send a patrol officer to radar school if the patrol officer is not assigned to perform radar enforcement. In-service training should be matched to officers' assignments.

A critical part of in-service training is supervisory and managerial training. Officers frequently are promoted and expected to perform as sergeants or higher without additional training. There is an inherent assumption that these officers have learned the necessary skills and knowledge to perform these new jobs while on the job. This is not the case. It can be argued that working for a supervisor or manager or serving in that capacity will not provide the necessary skills and knowledge an officer needs when promoted. All newly promoted officers should be required to attend and pass a rigorous course focusing on supervision, motivation, leadership, planning, communications skills, and police operations. Departments cannot rely on experience and on-the-job training as a means of developing good supervisors or managers. Moreover, refresher courses addressing these topics should be mandatory each year.

In summary, training is an important part of police management. Administrators should take every step necessary to ensure that all officers have the requisite knowledge and skills to successfully perform their jobs. This requires the development of a comprehensive training plan whereby it is ensured that the department's human resources are prepared to meet the challenges confronting today's police departments.

PERFORMANCE APPRAISAL

An important element in the administrator's effort to maintain quality police services is the performance appraisal. Performance appraisals are a formalized process where by supervisors provide subordinate officers with feedback on their performance. In other words, the performance appraisal is used to identify and evaluate officers' strengths and weaknesses. This information is used in a number of HR functions.

Performance appraisals are used in several areas affecting employees' salary, status, and benefits. They include

1. *Formalized feedback to employees.* Performance appraisals are used to provide officers with feedback about their performance. They note strengths and weaknesses, and they are intended to lead to increased productivity. Even veteran officers need this type of feedback periodically.
2. *Training.* Performance appraisals can identify problems in the department and training deficiencies. For example, officers may not be following a departmental procedure because they have not been trained in it or do not adequately understand it.
3. *Horizontal job changes.* Transfer or selection of officers to a specialized unit such as criminal investigation, domestic violence, or crime prevention can best be accomplished by examining officers' performance in key areas. Commanders of specialized units should examine past performance appraisals to see if officers possess the experience and skill for the new job area.
4. *Compensation.* Many police departments require officers to achieve a certain score before receiving annual pay increments or merit pay increases.

5. *Disciplinary actions.* Consistent poor performance appraisals are justification in many departments to take disciplinary action. In some departments, officers can be terminated as the result of consistent negative performance appraisals.

Each of these areas represents important human resource actions in the police organization. They demonstrate the importance of the performance appraisal process.

Figure 10–7 is the performance appraisal form of the Albany, Georgia, Police Department. Notice that the form is divided into topical areas, and each topical area has a number of specific statements or performance areas. Although the form does not capture information about the "total" job, it does examine all the "important aspects" of policing. The department took extra care to include officers' performance in community policing. The inclusion of community policing statements in the rating form not only allows the department to measure officers' performance in community policing but also sends a statement to officers as to its importance. The performance appraisal helps provide everyone a common frame of reference about the department's goals and objectives.

Cascio and Bernardin (1981:211–212) examined court cases centering around performance appraisals and found that the following criteria must be met for a performance appraisal system to be acceptable:

1. Appraisals must focus on performance standards as identified by a job analysis.
2. Performance standards must have been communicated to and understood by employees.
3. Ratings should be based on specific clearly defined dimensions as opposed to undefined, global dimensions.
4. The rated dimensions should be behaviorally anchored and these ratings should be supported by objective, observable behaviors.
5. Abstract dimensions such as loyalty or honesty should be avoided unless they can be defined in actual observable behavior.
6. Rating scale anchor statements should be logical and brief.
7. The appraisal systems and the ratings of the individual raters must be reliable and valid.
8. Any system should contain an appeal mechanism for employees who disagree with their ratings.

The major problem with performance appraisals is that raters are sometimes subjective in their ratings. *Rater error* can result from such subjectivity. There are several types of such subjectivity problems: (1) *halo effect,* where the rater tends to judge subordinates on one factor that the rater deems important, and this one factor affects all the rating categories; (2) *constant error,* where some raters are too hard or easy on all of their ratings and ratings are skewed relative to other raters; (3) *recency,* where a recent activity or event rather than performance from the total rating period is judged or has undue influence on the ratings; (4) *biases,*

Figure 10–7
Albany Police Department performance evaluation form.

Directions: This form contains several rating section which are distinguished by roman numerals. Each roman numeral designates a rating category. The rater will provide a numerical score for each category. **A score of 1 through 7 or 10 must be justified in the comments section by the rater.**

The rating categories should receive a rating from 1 to 10, with 10 being the highest score. A score of 8 or higher for a rating category is considered passing. The numerical scores are defined as follows:

1–6	Unsatisfactory performance
7	Marginally satisfactory performance
8	Average performance
9	Above-average performance
10	Outstanding performance

Additionally, each rating category has a series of statements. These statements represent key tasks or job activities within each of the rating categories. Their purpose is to assist the rater in understanding and evaluating the rating categories. The rater should place a "–" in the space for needs improvement, a "0" for neutral or average, and a "+" for excels for each of these statements. These scores or notations are used to assist the rater in determining the rating category score.

RATING CATEGORIES

I. _____ **Relationships with Departmental Supervisors**

a. _____ Amenable to suggestions and criticisms
b. _____ Openly discusses problems and issues with superiors
c. _____ Keeps superiors informed of problems, incidents, and activities
d. _____ Follows supervisors' direction

II. _____ **Relationships with Other Officers**

a. _____ Has good relationships with officers in unit and other units
b. _____ Willingly shares information with other officers regarding crime and other police activities
c. _____ Backs up or assists officers on calls, investigations, and other activities
d. _____ Displays an understanding and acceptance of diversity among co-workers

III. _____ **Relationships with Citizens**

a. _____ Does not have too many unjustified complaints from citizens
b. _____ Tends to handle officer–citizen interactions appropriately
c. _____ Displays an adequate understanding and acceptance of diversity

IV. _____ **Police Activities**

a. _____ Displays an adequate knowledge of laws, ordinances, and policies when performing police work
b. _____ Performs unit activities, e.g., patrol, criminal investigation, traffic
c. _____ Has an adequate level of activity, e.g., arrests, citations, response time
d. _____ Maintains issued equipment

Figure 10–7
(concluded)

V. _____ **Attendance**

   a. _____ Is not tardy for duty

   b. _____ Does not have any unapproved absences, e.g., fail to report, abuse of sick time

   c. _____ When present for duty is ready in terms of alertness, uniform, and demeanor

   d. _____ Actively participates and successfully completes police training activities

VI. _____ **Judicial Functions**

   a. _____ Appropriately uses legal procedures, e.g., domestic violence, arrest, DUI

   b. _____ Effectively obtains and serves warrants and other court documents

   c. _____ Is an effective witness in judicial hearings and trials

VII. _____ **Community Policing**

   a. _____ Effectively attempts to develop partnerships with various government entities, other police units, and community groups

   b. _____ Successfully solves crime, disorder, and other police–community problems

   c. _____ Serves as a resource person in the community

VIII. _____ **Discipline and Ethics**

   a. _____ Has not committed acts which have required disciplinary action

   b. _____ Has not committed acts which have required excessive supervisory counseling

   c. _____ Where applicable, generally follows departmental policies and procedures

   d. _____ Generally displays ethical behavior and integrity

IX. _____ **Reporting and Communicating**

   a. _____ Completes reports on a timely basis

   b. _____ Reports are complete, well written, and relatively free of spelling and grammatical errors

   c. _____ Reports are legible

   d. _____ Demonstrates effective verbal communication skills

X. _____ **Use of Force and Driving**

   a. _____ Effectively makes arrests and uses physical force appropriately

   b. _____ Displays appropriate levels of skills regarding police weaponry in field and training situations

   c. _____ Regular and high-speed driving records show ability and good judgment where the rater is prejudiced against an individual or individuals because of personality, gender, race, or appearance; and (5) *unclear standards,* where the rater is unclear about the rating dimensions' meaning and the ratings become somewhat haphazard.

The most effective method to reduce rater error and build a reliable performance appraisal system is to train raters about the system and have management closely monitor the process. Rater training is extremely important because training helps raters better understand the activity that is being rated and the exact meaning of the dimensions and scales as they apply to the department. Specifically, raters should be trained on the activity and levels of productivity that are expected in each area. Such training tends to reduce rater errors and is recognized by the courts as a way to increase reliability and validity of the performance appraisal system.

Management should monitor the performance appraisals process by cross-comparing the ratings of various raters and by comparing the ratings officers receive to their organizational measures of productivity. Raters should be required to explain ratings when an officer who is highly productive in terms of positive citizen contacts, arrests, convictions, citations issued, and low or no usage of sick time receives a lower rating than a less productive officer. When raters know managers are reviewing ratings, they tend to be more consistent and reliable in their ratings.

In summary, performance appraisal is a key component in the HR system. Great care must be taken in managing its operation and the use of information it produces. If the system is ineffective, there will be errors in a number of HR decisions and officers' morale will be adversely affected.

PROMOTIONS

A police department's promotion system is critical in the sense that it is used to advance officers to higher ranks or leadership positions. Bad promotion decisions can have lasting effects on a department. If a department promotes incapable personnel, the productivity of complete units within the department will be affected through inferior leadership. Promotions also have been the focal point for a number of EEO-related cases. Like police selection, police promotion systems have been found to be discriminatory. Administrators must strive to develop a system that is able to identify capable individuals while remaining within the tenets of EEO laws.

Historical and Legal Aspects of Promotion

Equal employment opportunity litigation has had a profound effect on promotions. A number of departments were forced to use court-imposed promotion systems to achieve adequate minority representation at the various rank levels. As a result courts have been criticized for interfering in local and state government and for forcing police departments to promote individuals who are inferior (Glastris, 1994). EEO is a reality that police departments must face.

The government does not force police departments to promote the unqualified. It is questionable whether the minorities being promoted are unqualified or even less qualified than other officers being promoted if the promotion system is unable to accurately make fine distinctions among a group of candidates. Furthermore, departments must recognize EEO's potential impact and ensure their applicant pools include qualified minorities. This is accomplished through aggressive recruitment, career development, and training programs for officers at all levels. If departments must fill higher-level positions with unqualified minorities, it indicates that the department has weaknesses in other HR programs.

The problem of developing a sound promotion system is compounded because one of the principal factors affecting a department's morale is promotions—or the lack of promotions. Morale is generally lowest immediately preceding and following promotional examinations. The morale problem's fires are fueled by rumors and perceived and real departmental politics. In the past, promotion systems were riddled with political intrigue: cliques and political elites vied for power and control of the department through promotions. Oral interview boards and performance appraisal scores have been adjusted or controlled, written examinations have been compromised, and promotion lists have been adjusted. EEO and court actions have been primary factors in reducing promotion politics and advancing the sophistication of promotion systems. In this regard, everyone has benefited from EEO since promotions are now geared toward ability rather than politics. Today, more than ever, qualifications dominate promotions.

Departments have employed a variety of promotional schemes. Promotional components include performance appraisals, written examinations, oral interview boards, seniority, training and education, and veteran's preference points. Most departments have systems composed of several components, rather than relying on only one component such as a written examination. For example, a study conducted by the International Association of Chiefs of Police and the Police Foundation found that 55 percent of the agencies used a written test, 35 percent used an oral interview board, and 46 percent used a performance appraisal. Each component in a promotion system is given a weight and the scores from the components are combined for a final ranking. Departments using performance appraisals and oral boards as components of the promotion process must exercise care since these components are the most susceptible to manipulation. Some organizations require additional education for officers seeking promotions. For example, San Diego has a 60-credit requirement for promotion to sergeant and lieutenant. Sacramento, California, instituted a bachelor's degree requirement for promotion to lieutenant.

Any promotion system must be based on a job analysis to identify the critical tasks, skills, and abilities required by the position. Once these are identified, promotion components or tests can be developed to measure candidates' aptitude. The job analysis also is used to develop the weights for the various tests and components. For example, if a performance appraisal is used in the promotion system, its weight or proportion of the total promotion score should depend on the weight (criticality and frequency) of the traits measured by the performance appraisal in relation to all the traits measured in the total promotion system. If a weighting system is not deployed in this fashion, the promotion system is less likely to identify the best-qualified applicants and is susceptible to EEO challenges.

Components of Promotion Systems

As noted, a variety of tests or components have been used in promotion systems. Some are more appropriate than others, and all have advantages and disadvantages.

Written Examinations

The written examination is a critical part of the promotion system since there is a wide range of knowledge that promoted officers must possess—knowledge about law, departmental procedures, leadership theory, and so on. The written test must be developed to measure these important knowledge areas. Departments frequently provide for candidates a reading or study list of police-related textbooks, penal code, and departmental policies from which the tests are developed. The police-related textbooks generally are in the areas of criminal investigation, police supervision, and police administration. The test items should focus on important aspects of the job, and they should be written by people with expertise in test writing so the test will be reliable.

Performance Appraisals

The performance appraisal is a common component of a promotion system since it measures how well a person does a job as opposed to measuring the person's knowledge. A candidate may have knowledge, but that does not necessarily mean the candidate can use it. If performance appraisals are used for promotion, they must be job-related: they must measure important job dimensions of the rank that the officers are attempting to be promoted to as opposed to their current rank level. For example, if a performance appraisal is used for promotion to sergeant, qualities exhibited by sergeants, rather than officers, should be used as the rating dimensions.

Oral Interview Board

The oral interview board, although commonly used in promotions, is a troublesome or questionable component. The problem is that the process is superficial and raters generally are not presented with ample opportunity for an in-depth evaluation of the candidates' potential. Moreover, some of the information gained in the interview may not be job-related but is used in the ratings. Common dimensions used by boards are leadership, decision making, and aptitude, which are extremely difficult to measure in the oral interview setting. Rating decisions tend to be based on limited data. Moreover, as the number of candidates increases, it becomes more difficult for the raters to cross-compare candidate responses (a reliability problem).

In general, the oral interview board should not be used unless a refined systematic approach is used. This includes the specification of rating dimensions in terms of behavior, development of a behaviorally anchored rating scale, and the implementation of rater training prior to any ratings.

Seniority

Seniority is frequently a part of promotions. Seniority should be used in two ways. First, a minimum seniority level should be required for eligibility to participate in the promotion testing. Common seniority requirements are five years at officer level to compete for sergeant and one to two years at other levels before being able to compete for the next higher rank. This on-the-job training requirement is important since experience is one of the best teachers in law enforcement. Second, should a tie occur on the promotion list, seniority should be used to determine the first to be promoted. Candidates, however, should not receive seniority points. Seniority does not necessarily mean an officer is better; it means he or she has been around longer. All parts in a promotion system should be based on some measure of candidates' knowledge, ability, or aptitude.

Education and Training Points

Candidates should not be given points for their college education or training. If candidates learned as a result of their education or training experiences, it should be reflected in their performance on the various tests. For example, Roberg and Laramy (1980) found college hours to significantly improve candidates' performance on written examinations. Education and training are intended to increase officers' ability and performance, and ability and performance should be measured by other means in the promotion process. Nevertheless, departments may appropriately establish educational and training benchmarks that must be attained before officers can compete for promotion, as noted earlier.

Situational Tests

A number of departments are using situational tests in which candidates are required to perform job-related tasks on which they are then evaluated. For example, candidates may be required to counsel a problem employee played by a role player. Raters evaluate each candidate's communication, decision-making, supervision, and analytical skills as they apply to the situation. This controlled interview is effective since raters evaluate not only what the candidate knows but also what he or she does when confronted with the situation. Moreover, since the situation is controlled, the appropriateness or inappropriateness of specific actions can be judged beforehand. Situational tests are very reliable and valid if properly constructed, and they should be used where possible.

Discipline

Finally, discipline should play key role in the promotion process. That is, if an officer has been disciplined he or she should not be allowed to participate in the promotion process. For example, the Cincinnati Police Department's guidelines will allow an officer to seek promotion as long as he or she has not been demoted in the last year. Such a policy allows officers to compete for promotion if they have been suspended or fined as a result of some deviant or inappropriate act. Most police departments will not allow an officer to compete for promotion if he or she has had any type of discipline within the last year. This is perhaps the best policy.

ASSESSMENT CENTERS

The assessment center is perhaps the most accurate method of selecting and promoting personnel. It has gained popularity for promotion but is only now being considered a viable option for selecting new police employees. The discussion here is directed primarily toward its use for promoting employees, but some of the same exercises are used in selecting police officers. An assessment center uses multiple tests or measures to assess a wide range of candidates' knowledge, skills, and aptitude. It refers to a process, not a place. Ross notes, "The task of an assessment center is to measure those behaviors which have been determined by the job analysis to be important for successful job performance in that particular job" (1979:44). The assessment center is developed from the job analysis and evaluates candidates on a larger number of traits or dimensions than do traditional test procedures. Ross identified seven criteria a procedure must meet to be considered an assessment center: (1) multiple techniques must be used; (2) multiple assessors must be used; (3) outcomes must be based on pooling information from techniques and assessors; (4) evaluations are made at a separate time from the observation of the measured behavior; (5) simulation exercises must be used; (6) dimensions or criteria measured are a result of a job analysis; and (7) techniques used are designed specifically for measuring the desired dimensions. If a testing process does not meet these criteria, then it is not considered an assessment center.

An assessment center is a complicated, comprehensive evaluation process. A number of tests or components have been used in assessment centers: in-basket exercises, leaderless discussion groups, management games, objective tests, interviews, individual presentations, writing and research assignments, and role-playing exercises. An assessment center's components depend on what the assessors are attempting to measure, which is determined by the job analysis. The job analysis identifies the important tasks required for the job. Assessors then construct tests or exercises to measure candidates' aptitude in relation to the tasks. A better understanding of the assessment center is gained by examining the exercises commonly used in its implementation.

In-Basket Exercise

In the in-basket exercise, candidates are given a set of written documents similar to those he or she must process on the job. These documents include telephone messages, scheduling problems, correspondence from citizens, information requests from other units in the department, and requests from officers.

The candidate must work through or process the documents as though he or she held the actual position in the department. Departmental procedures dictate how each of the matters should be processed, and these procedures are used to determine the correct responses. Dimensions usually measured include decision making, planning, written communication skills, supervision, and scheduling.

Leaderless Discussion Group

The leaderless discussion group attempts to simulate a police staff meeting at which participants are given a problem to solve. For example, the department may be experiencing an increase in crime in a specific area. The candidates would be asked to make recommendations as to how the department should address the problem. Candidates relative contribution to the task is measured in terms of verbal communication, planning, decision making, and problem analysis.

Role-Play Exercise

In the role-play exercise, the candidate generally interacts with a role player regarding a specific problem. For example, the candidate may be assuming the role of a sergeant who must counsel an officer whose productivity is low. The role player is provided a scenario to follow to ensure that each candidate receives the same responses. Assessors observe the interview and rate the candidate in terms of supervision, human relations, verbal communications skills, and planning.

Presentation Exercise

For the presentation exercise, candidates are asked to make a public presentation before the rating panel. It may be a news release to reporters, a presentation before a civic group, or a training presentation before a group of officers. Usually, the candidates are provided with information about the topic to ensure that all the candidates possess a baseline of information. They are then given time to prepare the presentation. They are graded on their presentation and how they respond to follow-up questions. Criteria such as verbal communications skills, conflict resolution, training ability, and leadership are evaluated.

Tactical or Problem-Solving Exercise

A tactical or problem-solving exercise can be written or oral. Candidates are given tactical problems which they must solve. For example, sergeant candidates may be told that dispatch has received a report of a barricaded person with a hostage. At this point, the candidate is told he or she is the only supervisor available to respond to the situation. The candidate is then instructed to advise what actions he or she would take using normal departmental resources. The best actions according to departmental policies and resources would have been previously scripted for the raters, and the raters would use that information to evaluate each candidate's response. Candidates can be evaluated on factors such as leadership, planning, decisiveness, and interpretation of departmental policies.

The assessment center is more accurate than other methods since the assessment center allows for the collection of more information about the candidates. Moreover, the assessment center measures what candidates do in simulated situations as opposed to asking them what they would do, which is the level of measurement in written tests and oral interview boards. Obviously, selection and promotion decisions are more accurate when more variables and information are considered. A number of departments—including those of Columbus, Georgia; Ocala, Florida; Kansas City, Missouri; Savannah, Georgia; Rochester, New York; Lexington, Kentucky; and the Federal Bureau of Investigation—have used assessment centers for promoting their employees.

Summary

This chapter focused on a number of important human resources issues confronting today's police manager. Again, a properly designed and implemented police human resources administration system is vital to the operation of a police agency. No matter how well the department is organized, it will be effective only to the extent that qualified personnel are working within the structure. The human resources administration function is extremely complex given the legal constraints governing its operation; nevertheless, the manager must ensure that every effort is made to recruit, select, and promote the best possible personnel. Moreover, there must be an effective evaluation and career development system in place to maintain quality personnel.

The police HR system works within the larger governmental and legal system which places a number of requirements and constraints on HR policies. Title VII of the 1964 Civil Rights Act and the 1991 Civil Rights Act specifically restrain how police departments hire and promote police officers. The proper operation of the HR component requires continuous study and consideration. It cannot be haphazard, for it is one of the most important management components within police administration.

Study Questions

1. What is human resource management and how does it affect police administration?

2. How does Title VI of the 1964 Civil Rights law affect police human resource management?

3. How is information from a job analysis used to structure promotion tests and performance appraisals?

4. What do you believe is the best police selection system?

5. What are the components of a police promotion system and how do they fit together?

6. What is sexual harassment?

Net Resources

http://www.lapd.org/organization/hrb/human_main.htm The Los Angeles Police Department's Human Resource Management web page provides interesting information about personnel issues.

http://www.policecareer.com/ Police Career provides information on police testing procedures.

http://www.mcoles.org/ The Michigan Commission on Law Enforcement Standards provides information on state mandated training activities.

References

Alvarez v. City of Philadelphia, 98 F.R.D. 286 (E.D. Pa. 1990).

Arnold v. Ballard, 390 F. Supp. 723 (1975).

Balzer, A. (1976). A view of the quota system in the San Francisco Police Department. *Journal of Police Science and Administration* 4(2):124–133.

Barnes v. Costle, 561 F.2d 983 (D.C. Cir. 1977).

Berner, J., and Kohls, J. (1982). *Patrol Officer Physical Performance Testing Manual.* Sacramento: Police Officer Standards and Training.

Birzer, M. (1999). Police training in the 21st century. *FBI Law Enforcement Bulletin* 68(7):16–19.

Blake v. City of Los Angeles, 595 F.2d. 1367 (9th Cir. 1979).

Bombrays v. Toledo, 849 F. Supp. (ND Ohio 1933).

Buerger, M. E. (1998). Police training as a pentecost: Using tools singularly ill-suited to the purpose of reform. *Police Quarterly* 1(1):27–64.

Carter, D., Sapp, A., and Stephens, D. (1989). *The State of Police Education: Policy and Direction for the 21st Century.* Washington: Police Executive Research Forum.

Carter, D. L., Sapp, A. D., and Stephens, D. W. (1988). Higher education as a bona fide occupational qualification (BFOQ) for police: A blueprint. *American Journal of Police* 7(2):1–27.

Cascio, W. F., and Bernardin, J. (1981). Implications of performance appraisal litigation for personnel decisions. *Personnel Psychology* 9:211–226.

Castro v. Beecher, 459 F.2d 725 (1972).

Cayer, N. J. (1975). *Public Personnel Administration in the United States.* New York: St. Martins Press.

Champ v. Baltimore County, 884 F. Supp. 991 (1995).

Chance v. Board of Examiners, 3 FEP 673 (1973).

Corne v. Bausch and Lomb, 390 F. Supp. 161 (D. Ariz. 1975).

Dantzker, M. L. (1996). An issue for policing: Educational level and job satisfaction. In J. Kenney and G. Cordner (eds.), *Managing Police Personnel.* Cincinnati: Anderson Publishing, pp. 115–132.

Davis v. City of Dallas, 777 F.2d 205 (1985, cert. *denied* May 19, 1986).

Doe v. District of Columbia, 61 LW 2022, 59 FEP Cases (BNA) 363 (D.D.C. 1992).

Doerner, W. G. (1995). Officer retention patterns: An affirmative action concern for police agencies? *American Journal of Police* 14(3/4):197–210

Doerner, W. G. (1997). The utility of the oral interview board in selecting police academy admissions. *Policing: An International Journal of Police Strategy and Management* 20(4):777–785.

Edwards, T. (1993). State police basic training programs: An assessment of course content and instructional methodology. *American Journal of Police* 12(4):23-46.

Fosdick, R. B. (1969). *American Police Systems,* rpt. ed. Montclair, NJ: Patterson Smith.

Gaines, L. K., Costello, P., and Crabtree, A. (1989). Police selection testing: Balancing legal requirements and employer needs. *American Journal of Police* 8(1):137–152.

Gaines, L. K., and Falkenberg, S. (1998). An evaluation of the written selection test: Effectiveness and alternatives. *Journal of Criminal Justice* 26(3):175–183.

Gaines, L. K., Falkenberg, S., and Gambino, J. (1996). Police physical agility testing: An historical and legal analysis. In D. Kenney and G. Cordner (eds.), *Managing Police Personnel.* Cincinnati: Anderson Publishing, pp. 25-41.

Gaines, L. K., and Forester, C. W. (1983). Recruit training processes and issues. In C. Swank and and J. Conser (eds.), *The Police Personnel System.* New York: Wiley.

Gaines, L. K., Kappeler, V., and Vaughn, J. (1999). *Policing in America,* 3rd ed. Cincinnati: Anderson Publishing.

Gaines, L. K., and Lewis, B. (1982). Reliability and validity of the oral interview board in police promotions. *Journal of Criminal Justice* 10(4):63–79.

Gatewood, R. D., and Feild, H. S. (1998). *Human Resource Selection.* Fort Worth: Dryden Press.

Glastris, P. (1994). The thin white line: City struggles to mix standardized testing and racial balance. *U.S. News and World Reports* 117(7):53–54.

Gonzalez, R. A., Mehay, S. L. and Duffy-Deno, K. (1991). Municipal residency laws: Effects on police employment, compensation, and productivity. *Journal of Labor Research* 12(4):440–452.

Good, G. W., and Augsburger, A. R. (1987). Uncorrected visual acuity standards for police applicants. *Journal of Police Science and Administration* 15(1):18–23.

Greisinger, G., Slovak, J., and Molkup, J. (1979). *Civil Service Systems: Their Impact on Police Administration.* Washington: U.S. Department of Justice.

Griggs v. Duke Power Co. 401 U.S. 424, 433 (1971).

Hall v. GHS Construction Co., 842 F.2d 101 (8th Cir. 1988).

Harless v. Duck, 619 F.2d 611 (1980).

Harris v. Forklift Systems, 114 S. Ct. 367 (1993).

Hernandez, E. (1981). Physical agility remedial training. *Journal of Police Science and Administration* 11(1):42–45.

Hild v. Bruner, 496 F. Supp. 93 (1980).

Horvath, F. (1993). Polygraph screening of candidates for police work in large police agencies in the United States: Survey of practices, policies, and evaluative comments. American *Journal of Police* 12(4):67–87.

Johnson, E. (1990). Psychological tests used in assessing a sample of police and firefighter candidates: An update. *American Journal of Police* 9(4):85–92.

Johnson v. City of Albany, Ga., 413 F. Supp. 782 (1976).

Jordan, D., and Schwartz, S. (1986). NYC's physical performance testing program. *Police Chief Magazine* 53(6):29–30.

Kappeler, V., Sapp, A., and Carter, D. (1992). Police officer higher education, citizen complaints, and departmental rule violations. *American Journal of Police* 11(2):37–54.

Kenney, D. J., and Watson, S. (1996). Intelligence and the selection of police recruits. In J. Kenney and G. Cordner (eds.), *Managing Police Personnel.* Cincinnati: Anderson Publishing, pp. 3–24.

Kirkland v. Department of Correctional Services, 374 F. Supp. 1361 (S.D.N.Y. 1974).

Kirkpatrick, D. L. (1977). Evaluating training programs: Evidence vs. proof. *Training and Development Journal,* November–December, pp. 9–12.

Krimmel, J. T. (1996). The performance of college-educated police: A study of self-rated police performance measures. *American Journal of Police* 15(1):85–96.

Langworthy, R., Hughes, T., and Sanders, B. (1995). Law enforcement recruitment, selection, and training: A survey of major police departments in the United States. Presented at the annual meeting of the Academy of Criminal Justice Sciences, Boston.

McCampbell, M. S. (1987). *Field Training for Police Agencies: The State of the Art.* Washington: U.S. Department of Justice, National Institute of Justice.

McDonnell Douglas v. Green, 414 U.S. 811; 94 S. Ct. 31 (1973).

McKay, B. W. (1996). Recruitment practices. *TELEMASP Bulletin* 3(6):1–15.

Maher, P. (1981). Police physical ability tests: Can they ever be valid? *Public Personnel Management Journal* 13:173–183.

Mahtesian, C. (1996). The big blue hiring spree. *Governing,* January, pp. 28–31.

Martin, S. (1990). *Women on the Move? A Report on the Status of Women in Policing.* Washington: Police Foundation.

Mathis, R. L., and Jackson, J. H. (1997). *Human Resource Management,* 8th ed. St. Paul: West Publishing.

Meritor Savings Bank v. Vinson, 474 U.S. 1047 (1986).

Mieth v. Dollard, 418 F. Supp. 1169 (1976).

Mills, R. B. (1983). Psychological, psychiatric, polygraph, and stress evaluation. In C. Swank and J. Conser (eds.), *The Police Personnel System.* New York: Wiley.

Murphy, D. W., and Worrall, J. L. (1999). Residency requirements and public perceptions of the police in large municipalities. *Policing: An International Journal of Police Strategies and Management* 22(3):327–342.

Peanick v. Morris, 96 F.3d 316 (1996).

Pennsylvania v. O'Neill, 100 F.R.D. 354 (E.D. Pa. 1983).

Public Safety Personnel Research Institute (1993). *Fire and Police Personnel Reporter.* No. 93-8.

Roberg, R., and Laramy, J. E. (1980). An empirical assessment of the criteria utilized for promoting police personnel: A secondary analysis. *Journal of Police Science and Administration* 8:183–187.

Robinson, R. K., Allen, B. M., McClure, G., and Duhon, D. (1993). Sexual harassment in the workplace: A review of the legal rights and responsibilities of all parties. *Public Personnel Management* 22(1):123–135.

Ross, J. D. (1979). A current review of public sector assessment centers: Cause for concern. *Public Personnel Management* 8:41–46.

Segal, J. A. (1992). Seven ways to reduce harassment claims. *HR Magazine,* January, pp. 84–85.

Sheedy, J. E. (1980). Police vision standards. *Journal of Police Science and Administration* 8(3):275–285.

Shernock, S. (1992). The effects of college education on professional attitudes among police. *Journal of Criminal Justice Education,* Spring, pp. 71–92.

Schneid, T. D., and Gaines, L. K. (1991). The Americans with Disabilities Act: Implications for police administrators. *American Journal of Police* 10(1):47–58.

Shusman, E., Inwald, R., and Kantz, H. (1987). A cross-validation study of police recruit performance as predicted by the IPI and MMPI. *Journal of Police Science and Administration* 15(2):162–169.

Snyder, D. A. (1991). *The Americans with Disabilities Act.* Portland: Labor Relations Information System.

Sorlucco v. New York City Police Dept., 971 F. 2d 864 (2d Cir. 1992).

Tanberg v. Weld County Sheriff, 787 F. Supp. 970 (D. Colo. 1992).

United States v. Philadelphia, 499 F. Supp. 1196 (E.D. Pa. 1980).

Vanguard Justice Society v. Hughes, 471 F. Supp. 670 (1979).

Vulcan Society v. Civil Service Commission, 5 FEP 1229 (1973).

Wards Cove Packing Co. v. Atonio, 57 U.S.L.W. 4583 (U.S. June 5, 1989).

Washington v. Davis, 96 S. Ct. 2040 (1976).

Wilson, O. W. (1950). *Police Administration.* New York: McGraw-Hill.

11

Labor Relations

Michael Douglas/The Image Works

Chapter Outline

Learning Objectives

After reading this chapter, you should be able to

1. Relate the labor movement to police administration.
2. Discuss the impact of strikes on American police.
3. Understand the unionization process and how unions are formed
4. Distinguish unions from other organizations such as fraternal orders.
5. Elaborate on the issues in the police organization that cause employee discontent and lead to unionization.
6. Understand the phases of the negotiation process.

E ach year the San Bernardino, California, Professional Police Association conducts a salary study comparing the pay of police officers throughout California. The association collects information on the beginning salary, salary steps, and maximum pay that officers in other jurisdictions earn. Once this information is compiled, the association distributes it to its members, provides press releases to the media, and makes copies available to government leaders and politicians. This information is the basis of one of the primary methods used by police employee groups to pressure government for salary and benefit increases. The association essentially launches a campaign to raise support for wage increases.

This example shows how unions work to increase members' wages. Union members expect their union to work for them, and this expectation often places the union at odds with the police chief and other government officials. The relationship between the union and management is surveyed in this chapter.

INTRODUCTION

Labor relations has different meanings depending on orientation, position, and relationship to the organizational structure. For the purpose of this chapter, *labor relations* refers to the manner in which peaceful solutions can be found to the mutual problems of employers and employees. Effective police labor relations require the establishment of harmonious relationships between employers and employees, allowing them to work together for the common good of the organization, its employees, and the public. To develop and sustain good labor relations, police administrators and managers must be aware of the historical and current issues involved in police unionization, collective bargaining, strikes, and grievance procedures.

Police executives and managers today face the necessity of realistically dealing with police unions and other employee organizations that use union tactics. In the decade of the 1960s, police throughout the United States mounted the sort of militant campaigns that had not been seen since the Boston police strike of 1919. The police movement toward unionization that began in the 1960s was prefaced by job actions of other public sector employees—teachers, postal workers, firefighters. Essentially, the police observed other occupations making advances in wages and other benefits through unionization and felt union tactics were the only way to increase their standard of living to a reasonable level. The conscience of the criminal justice community and the general public was shocked by police collective actions. "Blue flu," work slowdowns or speedups, and walkouts were used by police in a united effort to become recognized as a viable force, having legitimate authority to negotiate to obtain their demands. Police actions of the 1960s and 1970s made police employees a force to be reckoned with.

THE POLICE LABOR MOVEMENT: A HISTORICAL PERSPECTIVE

A *labor union* is an organization that represents dues-paying workers for the purpose of negotiating with employers concerning issues that are of importance to workers. Examples of such issues are employee benefits, wages, structure of the work week, disciplinary actions, and conditions of employment. Labor unions are not a recent phenomenon; they have existed in this country since the late 1700s. For example, as early as 1790, skilled craftsmen (shoemakers, tailors, and printers) organized into trade unions, posting minimum wages and visiting shops to ensure that members did not accept lower wages and fees. Unions and union membership grew until 1837, when a major depression caused a decline in membership. In 1869, a group of tailors met and formed the Knights of Labor, a union that ultimately became involved in political and social reform. It had 100,000 members by 1885 and expanded to 700,000 the following year as the result of winning a major strike against the railroad. The Knights of Labor essentially went out of business in 1893 after losing a number of strikes and because of leaders' insistence on focusing on political and social reform.

In 1886 Samuel Gompers helped found and became first president of the American Federation of Labor (AFL). The AFL consisted of skilled workers and focused its attention on "bread-and-butter" issues. The AFL grew rapidly until the end of World War I, when its membership exceeded 5.5 million. By the mid-1930s, the union had declined to fewer than 3 million members as a result of the postwar depression, the renewed resistance of employers to unionism, and the death of Gompers. Union membership continued to periodically increase and decline. By 1955 union membership was up to approximately 34 percent of the workforce, but by the mid-1990s less than 20 percent of the workforce were union members (Mathis and Jackson, 1997).

The decline in unionization has several causes. First, management recognized the power unions wielded and took a proactive stance against them. Second, salaries and benefits in a number of job sectors came to be viewed as fairer and more rewarding than they had been in the past. Third, manufacturing jobs, the traditional backbone of unions, were exported to other countries in great numbers. Fourth, federal and state laws were enacted that provided for a safer workplace and protected employees from some arbitrary employer actions. Finally, high employment and prosperity reduced the need for unions. Today, many workers feel they do not need unions to protect them

The Early Police Union Movement

Police employee groups started forming as early as the Civil War. These early groups were fraternal organizations rather than unions. The goal of the fraternal organizations was primarily to ensure the provision of employee assistance (death benefits and welfare insurance) to their members. Police officers did not actively unionize until the passage of civil service reform, which gave them some degree of job protection. Between 1890 and 1915, officers in most of the large departments formed employee organizations, many of which still exist today. Juris and Feuille (1974) note that since the cities and departments were politically controlled, these early police groups attempted to use political leverage rather than collective bargaining to achieve their goals.

A number of police groups attempted to affiliate with the early American Federation of Labor. In 1897, the AFL rejected a petition by special police in

Cleveland, Ohio, for a local chapter. However, by 1917, the AFL reversed its position and allowed police charters, and in September 1917 there were 37 charters with a membership of more than 4,000 police officers, mostly in small and medium-sized cities. One of these early charters was issued to the Boston Police Department. The Boston police went on strike when the city refused to recognize the union. This strike created negative public reactions throughout the nation. The strike caused the AFL to revoke all its police charters, and it had a chilling effect on the police labor movement, effectively stalling it for 20 years.

The Boston Police Strike

The Boston police strike was not the first strike by police officers in this country, but it was the most dramatic in terms of loss of life, destruction, and public attention. In 1889, the Ithaca, New York, police force of five officers walked off the job because of a pay reduction. Cincinnati, Ohio, experienced a police strike in 1918 after the chief fired four officers for meeting to discuss a pay increase of $300 a year. In Cincinnati, as a result of the chief's actions, 450 officers joined in a strike and did not return to work until the director of public safety agreed to consider reinstating the discharged officers.

The Boston police strike was significant because it involved more than 1,100 police officers, several lives were lost as a result of rioting, and immense property damage was suffered. Looting began on the first day of the strike, and property damage amounted to more than $1 million. The Massachusetts State Guard was called in on the second day of the strike, and immediately three persons were killed as the guard attempted to suppress a riot in South Boston.

A number of conditions precipitated the strike:

> The morale of Boston policemen prior to the strike was low because of distressingly inadequate working conditions, among which were vermin-infested station houses, wages too low for the post–World War I inflationary period, working hours ranging between seventy-three to ninety hours per week, a requirement that officers pay for their uniforms, and the use of favoritism in assigning officers to the best positions. (Burpo, 1971:3–4)

Yet the immediate cause of the strike was the refusal of Police Commissioner E. V. Curtis to recognize the union. He had prohibited officers from joining the union and had filed charges against several officials of the union. A citizens' committee mediated a settlement between the commissioner and the officers which included their giving up the union charter. The commissioner ignored the settlement and suspended a dozen officers. As a result, three-fourths of the Boston police force went on strike (Levine, 1988).

The strike lasted four days, after which, on "orders from Governor Calvin Coolidge, the Commonwealth dismissed the strikers and destroyed the union" (Levine, 1988:335); 1,100 police officers lost their jobs. Entry standards were lowered to enable the department to quickly recruit replacement officers.

President Woodrow Wilson severely condemned the police and the strike, saying

> A strike of policemen of a great city, leaving that city at the mercy of an army of thugs, is a crime against civilization. In my judgment the obligation of a policeman is as sacred and direct as the obligation of a soldier. He is a public servant, not a private employee, and the whole honor of the community is in his hands. He has no right to prefer any private advantage to public safety. (Ziskind, 1940:49)

Governor Coolidge also condemned the strike, stating, "There is no right to strike against the public safety by anybody, anywhere, anytime" (Ziskind, 1940:49). Both equated policing with military service. Unionism was incompatible with policing because police have the same obligation as soldiers to give their undivided allegiance to safeguarding their community.

Although the strike resulted in police officers losing their jobs, the strike did result in significant gains for Boston police. Salaries were increased by $300, officers were no longer required to purchase their uniforms, and a pension system was created. The newly hired officers were able to reap the benefits of the strike.

Management traditionally has used the Boston police strike as a weapon to combat unionization. Robert Kliesmet, president of the International Union of Police Associations (AFL-CIO), has been critical of using the Boston strike to resist the police labor movement:

> Never mind that chiefs and politicians have parlayed the Boston horror story into negotiation and management styles that have retarded police salaries and the development of genuine professionalism while turning police departments into fiefdoms for chiefs who could hardly administer their way home let alone a large complex organization—fiefdoms in which talented, earnest, and idealistic young persons turn into cynical, bitter officers who start looking toward retirement when barely out of the academy. (1985:283)

The Boston police strike had a profound effect on the police labor movement. It solidified politicians' and the public's positions against police unions and organizations. It essentially halted police collectivism for nearly two decades, and it was not until the 1960s that the police labor movement began to achieve the same status as private sector unions.

Police Employee Organizations and Unionization

Historically, police employee organizations have been local in nature, designed to serve the purposes of the local police personnel. Many of these organizations have retained their local autonomy while others have associated with national unions. The association with national unions has occurred primarily in strongly labor-oriented states. Several fraternal organizations, such as the patrolman's benevolent associations (PBAs) and the Fraternal Order of Police, have served as quasi unions providing guidance and leadership, but leaving the negotiating arrangements to local agency personnel.

Fraternal Organizations

The Fraternal Order of Police (FOP) was founded in 1915 with the purpose of achieving civil service protection and better pension benefits for police. The FOP emerged in Philadelphia, Cincinnati, Cleveland, Detroit, and other mid-western and mid-Atlantic cities. Today it is a configuration of approximately 2,000 local lodges in 44 states with 290,000 members. It is primarily located in the southern and north central states. The FOP allows all members of a department, regardless of rank, to join lodges, thus reducing some of the administrative resistance to its activities.

The FOP is adaptable in the manner it represents its members, partly because states are inconsistent in what police groups can do. The FOP provides a flexible, locally controlled structure that gives local lodges the freedom to develop and serve its membership based on local needs and local laws. A number of the lodges serve as the primary bargaining unit for the department and its officers. In other jurisdictions, usually in states where collective bargaining by the police is statutorily prohibited, the lodge serves as a benevolent organization. This type of lodge may issue press releases about departmental policies, officer working conditions, or crime problems. Lodge officials must resort to the political process to pressure government officials in order to effect desired changes. The FOP lodges often support political candidates who are sympathetic to their causes, which makes them a strong political force in the community.

Another fraternal organization is the police benevolent association (PBA). PBAs can be found in northeastern cities, particularly in New York and New Jersey. As an example, the PBA has long been the primary bargaining unit for the New York City Police Department. In addition to being the primary bargaining unit, PBAs often operate service programs for their membership. The New Jersey PBA provides its members with dental plans and operates an assistance fund for families of officers who are killed or injured in the line of duty. Many PBA activities parallel union activities, but the PBAs are locally organized and fairly independent.

In Texas, the Combined Law Enforcement Association of Texas (CLEAT) represents 90 affiliated associations with 11,500 police officers. CLEAT works with its affiliate associations to form political action committees, support candidates in local and statewide elections, and lobby the state legislature. CLEAT has worked to pass a variety of legislative bills affecting the police: health care for retired officers, death benefits for officers killed in the line of duty, elimination of residency requirements for police officers, and prohibition of the use of polygraphs in police internal investigations, it has also enhanced local associations' position to bargain with governments.

Police Unions

The American Federation of Labor (AFL) reemerged in the 1940s in the police labor movement. In 1941, the AFL established police chapters in Denver, Colorado; Hartford, Connecticut; and Flint, Michigan. Other departments quickly followed suit: New Britain and New Haven, Connecticut; Joliet, Illinois; St. Paul, Minnesota; Omaha, Nebraska; Asheville and Durham, North Carolina; Portland, Oregon; Chattanooga, Tennessee; and Port Angeles, Spokane, and Tacoma, Washington (Burpo, 1971). Today, there are a number of unions associated with the AFL-CIO representing police officers.

The International Brotherhood of Police Officers (IBPO) was started in 1964, in Cranston, Rhode Island, after the city terminated several officers who were protesting the leaking of a promotional examination to some of the candidates. Its chapters are located primarily in New England. The IBPO touts itself as the largest police union in the United States. It has been active in supporting a number of its officers by providing legal assistance and filing a variety of lawsuits relative to local police issues. The IBPO is associated with the National Assembly of Government Employees, which includes correctional officers and paramedics.

The American Federation of State, County, and Municipal Employees (AFSCME), an affiliate of the AFL-CIO, represents about 1.3 million workers and 100 affiliated associations. A number of departments from throughout the country with about 32,000 police officers are represented by AFSCME. AFSCME has been strongest in the East and Midwest.

The International Brotherhood of Teamsters has actively attempted to organize the police. In the mid-1970s it was reported that the Teamsters represented 200 police organizations of various sizes (Matzer, 1977). The Teamsters see police departments as a strong source for membership but must compete with a variety of other unions and associations.

The National Association of Police Organizations (NAPO), located in Washington, D.C., is an umbrella organization for an estimated 4,000 police unions and fraternal organizations. NAPO is not a union per se but provides a lobbying service for its subscribing members, which primarily are police unions and local police associations. NAPO helps to present a solid front for police organizations in the nation's capital.

Police unionization is limited to a large extent by legal constraints on collective bargaining. *Collective bargaining* is the action of an organization in bargaining for or acting as a negotiating agent on behalf of a group or collective of employees. Several states and municipalities have laws prohibiting collective bargaining, thus effectively eliminating unions. Reaves and Goldberg (2000) found that collective bargaining is authorized in 37 percent of the police departments in the United States. Larger departments are more likely than smaller agencies to have collective bargaining. They also found that 46 percent of departments are represented by a police union, while 28 percent are represented by a non-police union. Seventy-six percent of all departments have some type of police association or fraternal organization.

It is apparent that police organizing has been a fragmented affair. Even when unions are involved, bargaining has remained a local phenomenon focusing on local issues and problems. Complicating the bargaining problem is the fact that there may be several different employee groups within a given police

On the Job

Reno, Nevada, Police Department
Mighty Unions at the Bat

By Assistant Chief Ron Glensor

Courtesy of Assistant Chief Glensor

I would guess that the mighty Casey would have liked at least one more swing at the plate in his attempt to win the game for his Mudville Nine. The odds are very good that he would have gotten a hit. In these days of strong police unions with collective bargaining, state bill of rights legislation, and tough contract negotiations, officers enjoy many added steps to the grievance and discipline appeals process. Like Casey, odds are lopsidedly in the officer's favor to have grievances mediated or discipline reduced. The potentially harmful effect of this situation for the leadership and management of police agencies is troubling and deserves attention.

My concerns began 10 years ago as a young patrol captain. I recall a case in which an officer had a second avoidable accident within a year. The discipline for these cases without mitigating circumstances was a "departmental letter of reprimand." I was surprised when the officer decided to appeal to my level and quickly informed me that his plans were to appeal before the chief of police. While he never disputed his culpability, he simply felt that as he progressed up the chain of appeals, the chances for a lesser punishment increased. The officer said he thought the chief would mitigate it as lawyers do with "nuisance lawsuits." This was the beginning of worse times ahead.

Just consider the opportunity for appeals in a disciplinary case that recommends time off as its discipline. A sergeant or internal affairs officer conducts the investigation and presents a recommendation to the officer, often accompanied by a union representative and union attorney in many cases. If the officer disagrees with the discipline, the next steps for appeal may include an area captain, division deputy chief, chief of police, and city manager.

And that's not the end. Some states also allow for binding arbitration. In this case an arbitrator is agreed upon by

Continued

both sides. It is important to mention that arbitrators are independent contractors and their livelihood is dictated by their balance of decisions between labor and management. Right and wrong is often diluted in the arbitrator's desire to mediate the discipline and "give a little" to both sides. Although binding arbitration is meant to be final, I've seen many situations in which unions have disagreed with arbitrators' decisions and successfully brought their cases before hearings with state employee or labor management relations boards. If the officer is still not satisfied, cases may be brought to district courts in the form of a lawsuit. To say the least, it may take years to resolve some issues, further aggravating labor–management relations.

Some people may not see a problem with what's been discussed thus far. But, let us consider the potentially harmful impacts on organizations. If one agrees that the organizational culture is strongly influenced by its recognition of right behavior and its control of wrong behavior, then a potentially serious problem exists when controls are weakened. For example, research shows that it is uncommon for an officer to be convicted of a criminal act in many jurisdictions. Research shows that judges and juries are typically lenient with officers. On several occasions following high-profile cases against officers, I've heard other officers comment in hallways and briefings the day after the court's decision, "Well that's another thing I can do and not get fired."

It is no wonder to me that ethics is at the forefront of major concerns for police administrators. Whenever an officer uses a victory in an administrative appeal or court decision to rationalize wrongful behavior, a dangerous situation exists. The media are also used effectively by unions to fuel the battle between labor and management. I recall a situation when a police union published the year's "wins against management" in a local paper. By law, the agency was prevented from responding to the article because it involved personnel issues. This left many readers with the opinion that the organization was wrong. This is just another example in which wrongful behavior could be rationalized, resulting in harm to the organization.

It should be clear that I am troubled about the state of law enforcement and the potentially negative impact of unions in the disciplinary and grievance process. As the rights of management continue to dwindle in contract negotiations and through state legislation, fewer controls of officers' behavior will result. While there is much attention on ethics these days, most deals with the individual's recognizing and overcoming personal ethical dilemmas. I would suggest that equal attention be paid to the other factors, like unions, that may have significant impact on employee behavior. Regardless of one's position on this subject, I hope that the concerns expressed provoke more critical debate of the issues by the field.

agency. Employee groups such as supervisors, detectives, African-American officers, female officers, and Hispanic officers have each formed separate collectives in some of the larger departments. The existence of multiple unions or employee associations complicates the police executive's job in collective bargaining and negotiations. Regardless, efforts must be made to ensure that each group's issues are recognized and dealt with.

CAUSES OF POLICE UNIONIZATION

Police unionization has been the result of several economic and social factors. Officers, in many instances, believed unions were the only mechanism to achieve economic security, receive respect from departmental administrators, and have some degree of control in their lives. Indeed, in some police departments police officers believed that working conditions were oppressive, wages were substandard in comparison to other departments and similar jobs in the community, and that management in general had no concern for their well-being. Burpo (1971) identified five common objectives sought by police employee organizations:

1. Recognition of the organization.
2. Better economic benefits.
3. Better job conditions.
4. A voice in management policies.
5. In some cases, professionalization of the police.

Generally, no one problem led to efforts to install collective bargaining, but working conditions were deficient across the board. However, in many cases wages and employee benefits became the focal point for officers since they are more tangible and more easily comprehended by rank-and-file officers. In essence, police officers attempt to secure a better life through unionization.

One point is obvious: Police unions do not form when working conditions are satisfactory. Collective bargaining reduces the potential for arbitrary decision making and serves as a internal check against the misuse of power by police administrators (Bell, 1981). If labor disputes are to be avoided, employees must believe that management operates in a fair and equitable manner and that employee concerns are given proper consideration. Bell notes, "Collective bargaining in the police field has not developed due to one isolated incident. It has grown over the past decades due to numerous problems but generated from one general area—management; that is, the problem of management itself" (1981:299).

Historically, management problems have been pervasive and distributed across all types of department, especially those that adhere to a quasi-military structure. The National Advisory Commission on Criminal Justice Standards and Goals (1976:17) identified a number of management issues: (1) lack of decisive leadership by the police executive; (2) failure of the police chief executive to understand his role and how to do his job; (3) poor organization of the agency; (4) lack of a management system and follow-up controls; (5) lack of training for personnel engaged in specialized activities; and (6) failure of the police chief to define and establish priorities and objectives. These management problems collectively create a negative working environment, which, more or less, can push officers toward union membership and collective bargaining.

It should also be noted that community policing has been causing a measure of conflict between police managers and line officers. First, community policing on its face is somewhat nebulous and officers have difficulty understanding it. It also represents a "new" way of doing things. A number of officers are having difficulty committing to it. For example, Greene and his colleagues (1994) examined community policing in Philadelphia and found substantial officer resistance. Second, community policing requires an improved working relationship with the community. Many officers see departmental efforts to forge community partnerships as being soft on crime or as being outside the purview of police responsibilities. Police unions have been highly resistant to efforts that mandate public accountability, especially when civilian review boards have been involved.

MANAGEMENT'S VIEW OF UNIONIZATION

Management traditionally views labor relations as *rights*. That is, management has the right to manage and employees have the right to resign if they are dissatisfied with management. Management has the sovereign right to manage and any reduction in this right not only detracts from the administrator's ability to manage, but it also reduces the department's ability to protect life and property. Administrators contend that ultimately someone must make decisions, and those decisions cannot be made through extensive discussion or by vote.

Specifically, managers see unions attempting to control or at least have approval over management policymaking. For example, the union in Minneapolis attempted to require periodic promotions regardless of vacancies. This move would have bloated the department's management structure. In other jurisdictions unions have attempted to influence personnel allocation, assignments to specialized units, assignment to shifts, and even the type of uniform worn by officers. Not only have unions attempted to control policy; in some instances they have attempted to control the chief. In Prince George's County, Maryland, police unions became involved in the chief's selection process, which ultimately resulted in the selection of an "insider." In Montgomery County, Maryland, the union established a "union watch" to scrutinize the actions of their chief, Robert diGrazia (Bouza, 1985). Recently, the Louisville FOP lobbied to have a popular captain promoted to chief. They were successful, but he was terminated within a year after giving a departmental award to an officer who was involved in a questionable shooting.

Management typically views the union as a negative force within the police organization that attempts to procure financial gains and control over administrative policymaking without regard to the best interests of the department or the community. Too often an unproductive adversary relationship develops between management and the union. This is regrettable since the administration and the union frequently have mutual interests and common problems. Both sides spend too much time and energy establishing power bases and conquering new organizational territory rather than working on police problems.

THE POLICE UNION: A DEVELOPMENTAL PROCESS

Not all police departments are represented by a union or employee organization. Carter and Sapp (1992) surveyed all police departments with 100 or more officers and found that 52 percent of the responding departments had a collective bargaining agreement. Smaller departments are less likely to be unionized and probably have an even lower percentage of departments with contracts.

Police departments become unionized through a developmental process. Sapp (1985) identified three phases in the development of police unions. This model of union development can be used to understand the dynamics of the organizational and interpersonal relationships that occur as the union develops. Sapp's model is concerned with the same things administrators undergoing unionization are concerned with: (1) the goals of labor, (2) changes that are likely to occur, (3) the tactics that will be used, and (4) the concerns that exist at any given time within any labor group. The three phases of union development are

1. *The initial phase.* The initial phase encompasses the period of organization of the union through the period where it is recognized as a collective bargaining unit by the employer.
2. *The consolidation phase.* The consolidation phase begins when the union, gains a degree of acceptance by management and police officers and seeks to consolidate its position and power.
3. *The institutionalized phase.* This is the final phase in the development of the police union where the union becomes almost an integral part of the organizational structure of the employing agency.

Sapp identifies three areas that are involved in the union development process: organizational, goal attainment, and administrative. This process is depicted in Figure 11–1.

The *organizational* area relates to the resolve of the union members in terms of commitment and participation and in terms of departmental factors such as goals, structure, and management style. Generally, officers in departments where morale is low have a higher commitment to unionization. In essence, organizational areas consist of how departmental members interact with the department itself. During the initial phase of unionization, union membership is attempting to organize itself and the relationship between the union and the organization could be characterized as an adversary relationship in which there is a general absence of trust, and in which the members have a strong commitment to the union instead of the organization. As the union develops into the

Figure 11–1
Factors in union development.

Organizational Factor	Stage of Union Development		
	Initial	Consolidation	Institutionalized
Organized structure	Weakly differentiated	Somewhat differentiated	Strongly differentiated
Legitimacy	Minimal	Limited	Extensive
Trust	Minimal	Limited	Extensive
Scope of membership	Limited	Substantial	Near universal
Member participation	Near universal	Substantial	Limited
Membership commitment to union goals	High	Moderate	Low
Organizational goals	Toe hold	Growth	Maintenance
Nature of activities	Controversial	Controversial	Largely non-controversial
Scope of activities	Narrow	Limited	Extensive
Goal Attainment Factors			
Relationship with management	Polarization, adversary	Interaction	Cooptation, compromise
Dominant task orientation	Recognition and negotiation	Compensation issues	Fringe benefits, working conditions
Negotiating posture	Inflexible	Moderately flexible	Flexible
Conflict resolution focus	Grievance procedures	Mediation and fact-finding	Binding arbitration
Impasse resolution focus	Strikes	Job actions	Mediation
Political action	Minimal	Limited	Extensive
Administrative Factors			
Union staff	Minimal	Expanding	Limited
Fiscal resources and budget	Minimal	Limited	Extensive
Membership dues	Minimal	Limited	Extensive
Dues checkoff	None	Limited	Extensive

Source: A. Sapp, 1985, Police unionism as a developmental process. In A. Blumberg and E. Niederhoffer (eds.): *The Ambivalent Force*, 3rd ed., New York: Holt, Rinehart and Winston, pp. 414–417.

institutional stage, relations become more relaxed and there is a renewed interest in and commitment to policing.

Goal attainment factors relate to what the police union wants to achieve. These factors evolve around economic issues, management style, and policy issues. During the initial phase, the union generally is rather inflexible and

Los Angeles police officers try to understand what Mayor Richard Riordan is trying to convey during his announcement of significant police reform measures during the midday role call at the Los Angeles Police Rampart Station.

David McNew/Getty Images

uncompromising relative to most issues and exerts the greatest amount of energy toward being recognized as the employees' legitimate representative. As the union progresses into the institutional phase of development, the union leadership learns to work with management and to compromise on issues. Increased attention is given to procuring better working conditions and benefits as opposed to ensuring that the union is recognized. Finally, the union tends to use more moderating tactics such as political pressure, lobbying, and arbitration as opposed to strikes, work stoppages, and work slowdowns.

Finally, *administrative* factors relate to the economic development of the union—the collection of dues and other support. Traditionally, management has been able to thwart union development by prohibiting the union from collecting dues through a paycheck deduction or checkoff plan. During the initial phase of union development, the union has few resources at its disposal, and the union must expend a substantial amount of effort becoming financially solvent. As the union progresses to the institutionalized phase, it develops financial security through the orderly collection of dues. It also procures a staff which carries out union business.

Sapp's model shows the natural progression of union development. Some departments remain at the initial stage of development, where officers are represented by a loosely configured, weak union or association and are impeded by management resistance and statutes. Others progress to the institutionalized stage, where they regularly work with management on problems and issues. As shown in Figure 11–1, there are a great deal of resistance and a number of problems between management and labor during the initial phase of unionization; however, if a union is to move toward the institutionalized phase, both employees and management must grow. That is, both sides eventually focus on what is best for everyone, as opposed to what is best for their side, and both sides must be willing to cooperate and compromise, as opposed to being entrenched on issues and resisting change.

PROFESSIONALISM AND THE UNION

Obviously, opinions on the effect of unions on police professionalization differ. Administrators generally see unions as being antiprofessional, concentrating on benefits and controlling management's ability to respond to community needs. In essence, they initially see unions and the labor movement as totally objectionable and as the antithesis of professionalization. Labor, on the other hand, views unions as a method by which to spur the development of professionalization. Unions become a vehicle through which communication channels are opened and management becomes accountable not only to the union, but also to the public through the union.

Kliesmet (1985) notes that police chiefs typically have an "elitist" view of professionalism, viewing it as the bureaucratization of policing. Efficiency, effectiveness, and productivity are seen as the tenets of professionalism and are accomplished through close supervision, policies, and control. If this is the true meaning of professionalism, then unions are the opponents or natural enemies of professionalism. However, professionalism is a much broader concept. *Professionalism in policing* incorporates a universal understanding and commitment toward protecting and serving the public.

If the police administrator views the labor union as a potential source of support and as a means to allow participation in management, much conflict will be averted. Many police unions were formed to oppose unreasonable policies and attitudes of the chief; however, others were formed with the approval of the chief and for the express purpose of indirectly accomplishing things that the chief could not legally or politically achieve. Salerno (1981) indicates that police unions do not generally want to take over the administration of the department; they are interested in improving the overall situation of their members and in raising the overall quality of police service.

Police unions also provide the employee with a sense of belonging that is often lacking in large, impersonal police agencies. The union provides the officers with a platform to express their views and attain personal and collective goals. "The solidarity of a union gives strength to individuals who would ordinarily not have the knowledge or courage to speak their minds" (Salerno, 1981:39). The union also allows more information to become "public," forcing management to rely more on planning and program implementation and less on arbitrariness.

Although there is a positive side to unions, the costs associated with unionization should be weighed. Juris and Feuille (1973) in an early study of police unions noted that the greatest impact of police unions has been shared decision making in the allocation of monetary and human resources. That is, employee benefits frequently are considered before needed new programs. In the same vein, unions often attempt to control or place restrictions on the chief when allocating and distributing personnel. For example, unions typically fight for two-officer cars even though research shows that one-officer cars are more productive and probably safer (Pate, Ferrara, Bowers, and Lorence, 1976; Spelman and Brown, 1984). This also diminishes a department's ability to respond to citizen needs. Juris and Feuille also found that unions systematically interfered with the quest for professional status by objecting to and resisting programs such as lateral transfers, higher education requirements, affirmative action programs, higher standards for recruitment, and master patrol officer programs.

THE COLLECTIVE BARGAINING PROCESS

Public sector collective bargaining effectively came into being in the 1960s. In 1962, President John Kennedy issued Executive Order 10988, which gave limited collective bargaining rights to federal employees. This move, more or less, reflected local sentiment as a number of jurisdictions previously had allowed public employees to collectively bargain. For example, Robert F. Wagner, mayor of New York City, had issued a similar order for New York City employees in 1958, and in 1959, Wisconsin was the first state to enact a public sector labor relations law, which mandated collective bargaining for cities. Soon thereafter, a number of states, including California, Connecticut, Delaware, Massachusetts, Michigan, Oregon, and Washington, gave limited collective bargaining rights to government employees. By 1985, some form of legislation dealing with public employees had been passed in 40 states.

The details of the collective bargaining process can be found in the National Labor Relations Act. The act does not apply to public employees, but many jurisdictions have modeled their labor statutes after it. The National Labor Relations Board, which was established to govern the act, hears cases and delivers rulings. These rulings generally are used as precedents in public arbitration and labor litigation.

Collective bargaining is the process whereby the employer and employees, represented by a recognized union, negotiate a formal written agreement over wages, hours, and conditions of employment (Burpo, 1971:265). According to the National Labor Relations Act,

> to bargain collectively is the performance of the mutual obligation of the employer and the representative of the employees to meet at reasonable times to confer in good faith with respect to wages, hours, and terms and conditions of employment, or the negotiation of an agreement, or any question arising thereunder, and the execution of a written contract incorporating any agreement reached if requested by either party, but such obligation does not compel either party to agree to a proposal or require the making of a concession.

Figure 11–2

The collective bargaining process.

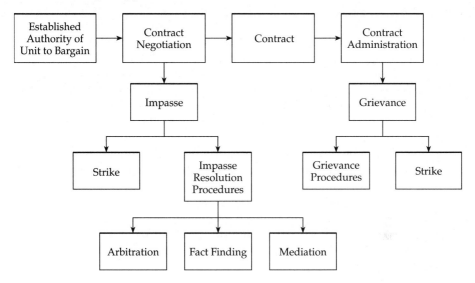

The collective bargaining process must be understood if the administrator is to have the necessary information for approaching negotiation with police collective bargaining agents. The process as depicted in Figure 11–2 is a relatively simple process involving four major steps: establishment of the authority of the unit to bargain collectively, negotiation of the contract, formalization of the written contract, and administration of the contract provisions. Kearney (1984) presents the most detailed and clearest description of the collective bargaining process. The following paragraphs briefly touch on the main points of the process presented in his book.

Authority of the Unit to Bargain Collectively

It is important to determine which group or groups of employees compose the bargaining unit and whether the union has the authority to act on behalf of that employee group. A successful union receives certification as the bargaining representative or bargaining agent for the employee group and, under most circumstances, the union will possess exclusive rights of representation for the group.

Representation or certification is generally determined through a union drive and election. This process consists of five steps: (1) initial contact, (2) signing of authorization cards, (3) hearing, (4) campaign, and (5) election. The *initial contact* occurs when union officials contact members of the work force, attempting to develop an interest in the union. An organizing committee is frequently established to assist in the recruitment efforts. In the *authorization cards* step, the union distributes authorization cards to employees. If 30 percent of the work force signs the cards, a union election is held. The 30 percent requirement is a benchmark set by the National Labor Relations Act. Most state statutes follow the 30 percent requirement, however, some jurisdictions have a petition process and different percentages of employee support or interest are used. During the *hearing phase*, two questions are answered. First, has the required 30 percent of the work force signed the authorization cards? Management examines the cards to determine whether everyone signing the cards is a member of the targeted group, and the exact number in the targeted group. Second, what is the bargaining unit? In some instances, more than one union or employee organization is attempting to represent the employee group. Also, at this point, it must be determined which employees are being organized. For example, most police departments have separate unions or employee organizations representing sworn officers and civilian employees. The *campaign* step is where union representatives and supporters campaign for the union while management attempts to convince employees to vote against unionization. During this step, management often makes concessions in an effort to thwart unionization efforts. Finally, during the *election*, workers determine whether they are going to be unionized and which union represents them.

Contract Negotiation

The next step after union recognition is the heart of collective bargaining, negotiation of the contract between union and management. What happens here largely determines the context of labor relations during the next one to three years or the length of the contract. Burpo, DeLord, and Shannon (1997) advise union representatives that negotiations are a "no-holds-barred" ordeal, and the union should take every action possible to ensure that the union wins. Thus the negotiation process can be extremely confrontational, and both sides must be prepared to negotiate for their positions.

Labor law has established categories of items that are subject to the bargaining process: mandatory, voluntary, and illegal bargaining items. *Mandatory* items are basic labor concerns such as pay, hours, rest periods, layoffs, transfers, and benefits. If brought to the negotiating table, both sides must address these items. *Voluntary* items are neither mandatory nor illegal items, but they become a part of the bargaining process only through an agreement by management and the union. For example, management practices usually fall into this category. *Illegal* items are those items that cannot be negotiated as a result of law. For example, a state may have a prohibition against police strikes. The union cannot attempt to include or exclude this provision in the contract.

As an example of negotiation, Sandver (1987) studied the negotiation that occurred in the Plain County, Ohio, Sheriff's Office. The following issues were presented to management by the union to be negotiated:

Union recognition	Grievance and arbitration procedure
Union security	Discipline
Union rights of representation	Safety and health
Nondiscrimination	Wages
Holidays	Uniforms

Sick leave	Probationary periods
Leaves and leave of absence	Overtime and hours of work
Health insurance	Management rights
Life insurance	No strike
Bidding on job vacancies	Duration
Layoff and recall	

As can be surmised from this list, the union attempted to force management to negotiate many wide-ranging employee benefits and working conditions, as well as union recognition. It is advantageous to the union to select as many areas for negotiation as possible. This allows the union to give up some items while retaining those that are most important to the membership.

Bargaining typically follows several stages (Glueck, 1976). First, each side presents its demands. Here the two sides generally are far apart on a number of issues. Second, after deliberation, there is a reduction in demands, generally through trading off on issues. Third, subcommittee studies are completed. Here the two sides establish joint committees to study specific issues and demands. The subcommittee attempts to work out an agreement, and if an agreement cannot be reached, the committee then tries to move closer to agreement and identify issues that either side is willing to negotiate or compromise. Fourth, an informal settlement is reached. Representatives check informally with the group they represent to obtain approval on the informal settlement. In some cases, the group rejects the compromise, and the process of negotiation continues. If the two sides cannot reach agreement, there is an impasse. An impasse generally requires that impasse resolution procedures be initiated. If there is agreement, a contract is drafted and signed by the parties.

A very common and serious problem in negotiation is the bargaining away of management prerogatives. Bouza notes that "the only inherent rights of management are those labor does not bargain away from them" (1985:270). Examination of union contracts in a number of jurisdictions points to instances where management seemed to be "asleep at the wheel" during negotiations. They willfully bargained away management rights for a reduction in economic demands. Once management rights are bargained away, it is extremely difficult to regain them through the negotiation process. Management must critically analyze all aspects of union proposals and clearly understand what is at stake before coming to an agreement.

Another common problem in negotiations is that there is a temptation to offer benefits that are not requested by the union. All negotiating alternatives should be carefully evaluated and their impact on the organization considered. Many of the negotiations should be conducted on a quid pro quo basis whereby the department does not give anything up without receiving something in return. For example, increases in benefits could be coupled with employee increases in productivity or assurances that management rights are protected. Collective bargaining in essence is nothing more than bargaining, and when only one side bargains, the eventual outcomes become one-sided or win–lose. However, there are cases in which an issue is mutually beneficial. An increase in the starting pay for officers would benefit officers and the department, since the department may be in a position to attract better-qualified police applicants.

Management must be prepared to negotiate and take it seriously. Management must determine who will do the negotiating, what the issues are, and what the limits of the negotiations will be. Management should attempt to identify the "real issues" prior to negotiating. Although both sides may identify numerous issues and demands, but usually, each side has only a limited number of real or important concerns. Management should attempt to "cost out" all contingencies. This enables management to understand the ramifications of any concessions made in the negotiations.

It is most important that management be represented at the bargaining table by someone who is trained in negotiation. Inexperienced negotiators are not able to comprehend the process and deal with the other side during negotiations. In the past, a number of jurisdictions have delegated negotiation to a city attorney or midlevel administrator who ultimately had to face the union's professional negotiator. When this occurs, the jurisdiction usually loses. If the jurisdiction does not have a competent, well-trained negotiator, someone within government should be trained in negotiation and union activity.

Historically, central governmental administrators have been the principal negotiators. The police chief should ensure that the department is represented in the negotiation and in the preplanning. Government officials generally do not fully understand the interworkings of the police department and may be too willing to negotiate away management prerogatives in lieu of financial benefits. They too often are more concerned with the negotiated cost of the contract than with the operating effectiveness of the department once the negotiation has been completed.

Impasse

An *impasse* indicates that the contract negotiation has broken down. An impasse usually occurs when one side is demanding more than the other will offer. When this occurs there are two possible approaches for resolving the situation: job action and implementation of impasse resolution procedures. The next paragraphs will discuss the usual impasse resolution procedures. Even where departments are unionized, they are usually not allowed to strike as a matter of law. However, officers in a number of departments have participated in illegal strikes. Job actions and strikes will be addressed in later sections. In lieu of striking, some bargaining agents have submitted issues to the state legislature for resolution of the impasse or to the voters in the form of a referendum.

Impasse Resolution Procedures

Basically, there are three impasse resolution procedures that are commonly used in collective bargaining: mediation, fact finding, and arbitration. An impasse can occur when negotiating the contract or later, when interpreting the provisions of the contract. Generally, the law determines which procedures are used in a particular jurisdiction.

Mediation

Mediation may be the most frequently used form of third-party intervention in public sector labor disputes. Upon impasse in contract negotiation, mediation may be requested by either party. Mediators are selected by the parties from approved lists; or, if no list exists, a mediator who is mutually acceptable is selected. Mediators are also appointed under specific conditions of law. *Mediation* is a highly informal impasse resolution process. Records are not kept so one is forced to rely mostly on anecdotes in order to gain an understanding of what transpires.

The purpose of mediation is to keep the parties at the bargaining table and avoid lengthy stalemates. The goal is to reach a settlement that is widely accepted among the parties' constituents. Basically, the mediator examines the situation, analyzes data and factual information about the jurisdiction, and eventually recommends possible solutions to the impasse. The mediator essentially attempts to facilitate information flow and communication between the two parties. The mediator has no formal authority over either side; therefore, the mediator cannot force a settlement on the participants. Mediation ends when a settlement is reached, one of the negotiating parties requests that the mediator disengage in the process, the mediation time has expired, or the mediator feels that he or she cannot assist the parties in arriving at an acceptable contract.

Fact Finding

Fact finding normally can be initiated by either party to the negotiation. An individual fact finder or a panel of three members may be appointed. Fact finding usually is initiated only after mediation has failed, but mediation is not necessarily a prerequisite to fact finding. *Fact finding* is a formal proceeding that operates as a quasi-judicial hearing of the positions of the parties. A written record of the facts and events and a written recommendation for settlement are produced as a result of fact finding. This process is like mediation in that it provides no finality; however, since there are a degree of formality and a written recommendation that often is public record, parties generally give the outcome more credence.

Arbitration

Arbitration in any of its forms is the most controversial impasse resolution procedure short of a strike. Like fact finding, arbitration involves a formal, quasi-judicial setting where each party presents evidence supporting its position to a single neutral or multimember board. Issues that can be arbitrated generally are dictated by law. There are two types of arbitration, voluntary and compulsory. In *voluntary arbitration*, both parties must agree to the arbitration process, and once this occurs, the decision of the arbitrator is binding. In *compulsory arbitration*, the parties are forced into arbitration by law and the arbitrator's decision is final and binding on the parties.

One of the criticisms of arbitration is that when some parties believe that arbitration will be used, they tend to not bargain to reach a settlement but more or less attempt to solidify their positions. For example, the union will inflate its demands and management will deflate its concessions, since these moves will give them a better position in arbitration. Arbitrators' decisions are based on the submitted proposals, thus a side has more advantage when its proposal is more extreme. For example, a union may want a salary increase of 30 cents an hour, but it will ask for 50 cents an hour hoping the arbitrator will decide on the 30 cents. Management may be willing to accept the 30 cents but might propose a nominal or no increase to reduce the arbitrator's final decision.

The skill level of the arbitrator is extremely important in arbitration. For example, a highly skilled and knowledgeable arbitrator will have an understanding of the jurisdiction's financial capabilities and the area's "going rate" for wages and benefits. In other words, the arbitrator's objective is to determine real market value of a given item and whether government can afford it. A skilled arbitrator will cut through much of the rhetoric and force both sides to take positions that are fact-based, credible, and defendable.

Iris (1999) examined arbitration decisions in the Chicago Police Department. He found that arbitrators routinely cut in half the discipline imposed by the department. This was done in spite of elaborate investigations by the department and the fact that many of the cases involved officer misconduct in high-profile excessive force allegations. These findings question the fairness of arbitration outcomes and question how well administrators can maintain discipline in their departments when arbitration is not evenhanded.

In *final-offer arbitration*, the arbitrator receives the two sides' proposals and selects the one that appears most equitable for both parties. In essence, it is an "all-or-nothing" proposition for the issue at arbitration, and it forces both sides to be realistic in their demands. This form of arbitration can occur on a single item, several items, or the entire package, depending on the jurisdiction. Connolly (1986) found that final-offer arbitrations are involved in only 10–15 percent of the contract settlements, but they tend to have influence on all contracts. A number of states, including Wisconsin, Michigan, Iowa, Massachusetts, and Ohio, now use final-offer arbitration to deal with this problem (Sandver, 1987).

In most instances, both parties want to avoid arbitration since the judgment is final and subsequently there is a greater potential for losing. Thus the threat of arbitration frequently encourages both parties to compromise and settle issues.

Content of Police Collective Bargaining Agreements

Carter and Sapp (1992) examined the collective bargaining contracts for cities with a population of 50,000 or more or those having a police force of 100 or more officers. They attempted to determine the kinds of clauses contained in the contracts. They found that 84 percent of the contracts contained sections dealing with management rights or management prerogatives. These clauses recognize the chief's authority and responsibility to manage the department. A large number of the contracts contained strong language that clearly vested the chief with the authority to make decisions in numerous administrative areas.

Approximately 89 percent of the contracts contained clauses that defined grievances. An overwhelming majority of the clauses limited or restricted grievances to issues arising out of the interpretation of the contract. This means that officers cannot grieve an issue that is not addressed in the collective bargaining agreement. Such a policy likely leads to strife among the officers and efforts to include new areas in future negotiations. It would seem more productive to both sides if grievances were defined more broadly. The contracts allowed for grievances to be resolved in a variety of manners. The predominant method (83 percent) was arbitration. A few of the departments required that grievances be resolved internally or by a government entity.

The contracts contained a variety of provisions relative to discipline. Twenty-four percent of the contracts contained a police officer bill of rights. This number was low because 19 states have enacted police officer bill of rights laws, and it is no longer necessary that they be included in collective bargaining agreements. A full 90 percent of the contracts contained some type of disciplinary appeal clause allowing officers to have their disciplinary cases heard at several levels. A large number of contracts (37 percent) allowed the disciplinary procedure to be reviewed through arbitration. This is an area that unions typically concentrate on to protect members. For example, Iris (1999) documents how a number of police unions have fought civilian review boards and pushed to include stringent evidentiary standards and requirements in collective bargaining agreements.

Many contracts contain language affording management the prerogative to make staffing changes. Such staffing changes include flexibility in assigning patrol officers across shifts, days, and beats. Labor prefers that staffing be permanent or based on seniority. Some 72 percent of the contracts gave management the right to make such decisions, while 27 percent of the contracts contained no mention of staffing. Based on a similar study by Rynecki and Morse (1981), management has actually improved its position in this area. It seems that management has been able to retain most of its authority in this area.

Layoff of officers is a critical concern to police unions. Eighty-four percent of the contracts had language relating to police officer layoffs. About half of the contracts dictated that any layoffs would be based on seniority, with newly hired officers laid off first. Several of the contracts established standards that must be met for the department to lay off officers. In about half of the contracts seniority was required as the primary or an important consideration in shift assignments, transfers, promotions, and other personnel actions. Thus the unions view seniority as the fairest criterion for a number of human resources decisions.

The contracts generally had several provisions relating to the use of sick time. Sixty-one percent of the contracts required officers to provide the department with notice of being sick. For example, many departments require officers to notify the department at least two hours before the start of a shift. More than half of the contracts specified when a department could demand documentation for sick time, and 24 percent of the contracts elaborated additional circumstances (pregnancy, family illness, funeral leaves, and medical appointments) when officers could use sick time.

Training and education are typically addressed in collective bargaining agreements. Only 25 percent of the contracts had provisions relating to mandated training for officers. This small percentage is explained by the facts that training is broadly accepted by officers and generally mandated by state statutes. College tuition reimbursement was addressed in 41 percent of the contracts, and education incentive pay was included in 42 percent of the contracts. Finally, 13 percent of the contracts had a provision for an educational leave of absence.

Police collective bargaining contracts address a variety of issues beyond wages and benefits. They serve as an operational blueprint for the union and department. They also have substantial authority and must be followed by both parties.

Contract Administration

Contract administration entails the application and interpretation of the broad terms of the contract on a day-to-day basis. This stage is the true test of the maturity and soundness of the relationship between the union and management.

A collective bargaining agreement may be well administered by each party or it may be poorly implemented. The union may attempt to force interpretation of the contract to its advantage by picketing, walkouts, or job slowdowns. Similarly, management may ignore the terms of the agreement and attempt to impose terms and conditions of employment unilaterally. Conflict and controversy are inherent in any labor–management relationship. The key to a healthy and stable employment relationship, however, is to manage conflict and controversy over the implementation of the contract in a peaceful manner, with due consideration of the rights and responsibilities of each party.

The chief administrator has the responsibility for ensuring that his or her subordinates understand and abide by the contract. The negotiating team members can be used to distribute the document and explain it to other managers and supervisors. It is critical that supervisors understand the particulars of the negotiated contract since they may establish a precedent that is not in the best interest of management if they misinterpret the contract. Supervisors essentially apply the contract to employees.

A contract that is acceptable to all sides is the result of successful negotiation. Collective bargaining can assist police administrators to accomplish this goal if the administrator understands negotiation and utilizes the tools available. Aggressive management interested in implementing new and better ways of providing police services will inevitably find the bargaining process restrictive. In the best of worlds, the police manager would prefer to make decisions in an unfettered manner, but in the bargaining world, many important decisions must be cleared by the police officers' representative. The manager's goal is to obtain an agreement that meets both the need to make bargains and the desire to make decisions with minimum expense and time. Because the impact of collective bargaining on management freedom is so extensive, it is important to draft carefully and negotiate artfully a contract that protects the vital interest of police management.

GRIEVANCES

A *grievance* is "an allegation by employees or employers of a violation of rights to which the party has been entitled by a collective bargaining agreement, federal or state law, past practice, or company rules" (Gordon and Miller, 1984:118). This usually results from some conflicting interpretation regarding the negotiated agreement or a conflict where no agreement exists. Labor contracts are not inclusive, and numerous details about the job are not addressed in the contract. Some provisions are too general or vague and are open to interpretation, which can result in grievances. After the grievance is filed there are two possible outcomes: strike or initiation of grievance resolution procedures. Strikes will be covered in the next section. A brief discussion of grievance resolution procedures follows.

The Grievance Procedure

The grievance procedure generally is spelled out in the contract or in departmental policies. Actions to be taken and the time frame for completing them are spelled out in strict guidelines. The following steps are found in most grievance procedures:

1. Discuss the issue with the immediate supervisor. This generally is done informally.
2. If the grievance is not settled at the supervisor level, the officer then writes a memorandum outlining the grievance to his or her commander. The commander then acts on the grievance within a specified time.
3. If the grievance is not satisfactorily resolved at the commander level, it is forwarded to the chief of police.
4. If the chief is unable to reach an agreement with the officer, the grievance is forwarded to the city manager's office.
5. If the grievance remains unresolved at the city manager level, it is usually subject to arbitration.

Police administrators and city officials will examine the contract during their reviews. If the supervisor's actions have violated the contract, the grievance will be settled in favor of the officer. The officer will contact his or her union representative, who will review the contract to ensure that the officer's grievance is within the bounds of the contract. In many cases, the grieved issue is not covered by the contract or the contract is vague in terms of the rights and procedures. If this occurs, union representatives will attempt to negotiate a settlement. If a settlement is not reached, the issue is arbitrated.

Bowers (1973) identifies five basic sources of grievances:

1. Supervisory antagonism of employees, including such behavior as sarcasm, open criticism in front of other employees, discrimination, and needling.
2. Failure to consistently and equitably enforce contract terms, including allocation of overtime, seniority, leave time, hours of work, time for union business, and outside employment.

3. Failure to properly comply with contract terms, which may relate to pensions, longevity payments, overtime payments, and educational incentive pay.
4. Failure to counsel employees and to maintain a two-way flow of communication.
5. Poor working conditions, including such factors as favoritism, equipment, and departmental facilities.

LaVan, Katz, and Carley (1993) examined grievances by public safety employees. They found the decisions on the grievances arbitrated were split fairly evenly between the department and labor. Work assignments received the highest number of grievances, 23.2 percent; 22 percent of the grievances were related to hiring practices; wages and benefits, discipline, and union activities each accounted for approximately 15 percent; and performance evaluations accounted for 7 percent. The high number of grievances as a result of work assignment can be explained by the fact that police work is labor-intensive across 24 hours and during holidays. Officers attempt to obtain better shifts and days off. The high number of grievances as a result of the hiring process is the result of applicants being dissatisfied with employment standards or findings from the background, psychological, or polygraph examinations.

The grievance procedure is the primary mode by which to resolve issues in any organization; therefore, all police agencies should have such a procedure as a matter of management practice. When a department does not have a grievance procedure, the only option available to employees for resolving a problem is some type of job action, which is costly to the city and the department. Litigation as an option does not resolve the problem but applies a legal end to the dispute. Litigation can be very expensive for both parties. Other options available to the employee do not resolve problems; they tend to ignore them or make them worse. Such options are resignation from the department or exhibiting dissatisfaction through some other means such as minimal productivity. Regardless, these options are all costly to the department and the community. The grievance procedure provides an avenue for problem resolution. Grievance procedures also tend to stimulate good management practices, since there is always the possibility for review.

Use of Courts to Solve Labor Problems

Schachter (1980, and 1981) analyzed the ways police unions use the judicial system to influence departmental policy. She indicates that "frequent use of the courts to solve labor problems may diminish the unique deference now paid judicial verdicts" (1981:28). The courts also carry a different function than do mediators or arbitrators. The courts limit the opportunity for compromise: their function is to apply law and not to make peace between the parties, thus their decisions are very specific.

For example, the City of New York altered the police selection system in such a fashion that it became easier for African Americans and Puerto Ricans to be selected. At the time, both groups were underrepresented on the department. The changes effectively reduced the number of whites that would be hired by the department. The Patrolmen's Benevolent Association filed suit and was able to invalidate the new system. In effect, the PBA was able to use the courts to change management policy without having to resort to negotiation. The courts, effectively, have become the battlefield in a number of instances, and by using the courts, the union is able to avoid political problems within the department and in the community.

JOB ACTIONS AND STRIKES

A minority of the states allow for arbitration, which means that in the majority of states, there is no ultimate authority to decide impasses. In these states, the union may be subject to a take-it-or-leave it attitude on the part of the government. When this occurs, the police union may resort to some type of job action or, in some cases, a strike. Strikes are not a desirable outcome. Strikes by police officers can be extremely damaging to the public they are sworn to protect and to the police union as well.

Police Strikes

Police strikes are infrequent today, but during the decades of the 1970s a number of police departments throughout the country went on strike. Gentel and Handman (1979) examined the strikes in San Francisco (August 18–21, 1975), Tucson (September 22–28, 1975), Oklahoma City (October 23–26, 1975), Las Cruces, New Mexico (February 3–March 5, 1976), and Youngstown, Ohio (September 28–October 2, 1976). They found that the strikes were different in some ways. They occurred in cities of various sizes, they lasted for various periods of time (3 to 33 days), some strikers won raises while others lost their jobs, and some strikers wore flowers in their holsters while others shot out street lights.

Gentel and Handman (1979) found a number of problems that contributed to the strikes. There was widespread job dissatisfaction within the police departments. Police management systems tended to be benevolent-authoritarian, which adversely affected morale. The cities were experiencing financial problems and therefore could not pay officers what they thought they deserved. The police did not accept this position because most of the cities continued to fund numerous other projects, which infuriated the police. The cities contributed to the strikes through ineffective negotiations. The cities almost always waited to the last minute to begin negotiations. They often had inexperienced negotiators who did not know what to do or what to propose. There was poor communication between city officials and the police union before and during the negotiations. City officials attempted to politicize the problem by making statements to the public and media, which often angered the rank and file. A number of mayors and city council members tried to further their own political careers by criticizing police demands. Finally, none of the cities had any mechanisms in place to deal with an impasse.

During that period, numerous cities were facing dire economic times and had few resources to fund better police salaries and benefits. More recently, governments had less difficulty in funding police requests as a result of better economic conditions. Also, police executives today are much more sophisticated and are better able to deal with police officers and police unions.

Police Job Actions

In addition to striking, the police have used a number of other job actions to communicate their discontent over a contract or grievance. They have used tactics to bring public or economic pressure on the government and public attention to their cause. Moreover, job actions are more acceptable than strikes, since strikes often create a great deal of public animosity. Union leaders recognize that it is much easier to negotiate a more favorable contract if the police are supported by the citizenry (Burpo, DeLord, and Shannon, 1997).

One tactic frequently used by the police is work "slowdowns" and "speedups." When engaging in work slowdowns, officers commonly write fewer traffic citations or stop writing citations. The object here is to place financial pressure on the government to come to contract terms. In 1997, the New York Police Benevolent Association initiated a work slowdown following an impasse in contract negotiations. The job action cost the City of New York $2.3 million in two months. Management then put pressure on officers to write more tickets. The PBA responded by accusing the administration of enforcing ticket quotas, which resulted in a number of public relations problems for the department (Cooper, 1997). Interestingly, after the Rampart Division scandal, Los Angeles police response time increased and crime increased precipitously. Burpo and his colleagues (1997) noted that work slowdowns can be counterproductive. Since the public in general is opposed to the issuance of traffic citations, a work slowdown may engender public support for a continued impasse.

Work speedups is another ploy sometimes used by the unions. Here officers make arrests and write citations for violations that they normally disregard. They essentially flood the courts with offenders. The object is to create administrative problems for the criminal justice machinery. This tactic causes substantial ill-will among the public, but it is intended to antagonize and place pressure on the administration to come to an agreement with the union.

Police unions use a number of public forums to communicate their message and pressure the administration into an agreement. One common method of voicing discontent is a vote of no confidence for the police leader. In 2000, the New York State Police Investigators Association had a vote of no confidence for the state police superintendent as the result of a dispute concerning overtime for investigators. The Fitchburg, Massachussetts, Police Department voted no confidence in their chief three times in nine years. They basically accused the chief of being a dictator. The union commented, "No confidence in Chief Gallant, in his moral character, in his leadership, in the example he sets, in his ability to impose discipline fairly, and in his ability to place the interests of the Fitchburg Police Department above his own petty, vindictive interests" (Nugent, 2000).

Votes of no confidence can place significant pressure on a police chief, especially if he or she has other political problems. Politicians adverse to the chief seize such information and attempt to use it to cause the removal of the chief.

Unions sometimes resort to picketing to voice their displeasure with contract negotiations. The Cranston, Rhode Island, police officers' union solicited the support of teamsters, teachers, and other AFL-CIO unions to picket a congressional candidate who had opposed a police contract while on the city council. In other cases, police unions have picketed city hall, city council meetings, and other public facilities to garner support for their positions. For example, Newport, Kentucky, police officers and their families crowded a city council hall to express their displeasure over a delay in negotiating a new contract. The Los Angeles Police Protective League threatened to demonstrate at the 2000 Democratic presidential convention as a means of pressuring the city to negotiate an acceptable contract.

The New York City Patrolmen's Benevolent Association ran full-page newspaper ads advising people that they should not join the NYPD. The ads were the result of a dispute over salaries. NYPD officers were paid about $10,000 a year less than officers in nearby Suffolk County. The ads came at a time when the department was having difficulties in recruiting applicants.

Another tactic commonly used by unions is salary surveys. Table 11–1 reproduces a salary survey conducted by the San Bernardino County, California, Safety Employees' Association. The comparisons are based on the top step for deputies and include all types of compensation provided deputies: base salary, incentive pay, longevity pay, uniform allowance, and insurance package. Several of the departments in the survey were compensated at a rate higher than that of San Bernardino County. The San Bernardino deputies were paid 26.31 percent less than Oakland police officers. Only one sheriff's department, San Diego County, paid less, but six county departments offered better compensation packages. Police officers in the City of San Bernardino were compensated 7.55 percent more than their deputy counterparts. The survey helped the deputies win a better contract when they negotiated with the County Board of Supervisors.

As can be seen, the police can be very innovative in voicing their problems with management. Some of the tactics used by organized labor are probably more effective than going out on strike. Essentially, when there is an impasse, labor attempts to deploy tactics that will keep the pressure on the administration. The administration, on the other hand, attempts to deflect the pressure by presenting their position to their constituents and at the same time pressuring the union into a more reasonable settlement.

Summary

This chapter examined the police labor relations movement in terms of problems, strategies, and current trends. Although slow to develop, police unions and employee groups play a critical role in police administration in many jurisdictions. The primary cause of police unionization has been employee dissatisfaction

Table 11–1

San Bernardino Sheriff Deputy Salary Comparison: Total Compensation, Deputy Sheriff/Police Officer–Top Step

Jurisdiction	Salary	Incentive	Longevity	Uniform	Retirement	Insurance	Total	Lead/(Lag)
City of Oakland	$5,035	$252	$156	$54	$495	$532	$6,524	26.31%
City of Santa Ana	4,694	704	0	0	486	482	6,366	23.25
City of San Jose	5,167	388	0	56	0	588	6,199	20.02
City of Ontario	4,385	200	636	71	307	460	6,059	17.31
County of Orange (4)	4,945	300	0	0	236	453	5,934	14.89
City of Long Beach (1)	4,547	400	0	0	495	470	5,912	14.46
City of Los Angeles	4,704	141	400	54	0	545	5,844	13.15
City of San Francisco	4,689	281	0	0	373	500	5,843	13.13
County of Los Angeles	4,588	574	0	83	0	489	5,734	11.02
City of Fresno	4,754	333	0	53	0	461	5,601	8.44
City of San Bernardino	4,484	150	0	42	421	458	5,555	7.55
City of Chino	4,318	246	0	40	302	608	5,514	6.76
City of Sacramento	3,622	855	25	63	411	475	5,451	5.54
City of Fontana (3)	3,919	392	235	58	274	558	5,436	5.25
County of Riverside (2)(4)	4,406	243	0	56	424	330	5,403	4.61
County of Ventura	4,186	302	0	56	409	442	5,395	4.45
State of California (CHP)	4,107	200	329	43	329	372	5,380	4.16
City of Redlands	3,475	781	174	75	313	525	5,343	3.45
City of Rialto	4,331	219	0	75	303	386	5,314	2.88
County of Sacramento	3,820	764	0	63	209	455	5,311	2.83
City of San Diego	4,352	180	0	50	357	308	5,247	1.59
County of Kern	4,028	483	0	53	205	425	5,194	0.56
County of San Bernardino (SB)	*4,137*	*331*	*0*	*50*	*306*	*341*	*5,165*	
City of Montclair	4,155	0	0	45	374	532	5,106	-1.14
City of Colton	3,846	169	77	53	373	562	5,080	-1.65
City of Barstow	3,987	138	0	75	279	600	5,079	-1.67
City of Upland	4,062	0	30	37	365	528	5,022	-2.77
County of San Diego	3,857	289	0	63	379	291	4,879	-5.54
City of Adelanto	2,945	0	265	25	148	420	3,803	-26.37
Average without SB Co.	$4,268	$315	$83	$46	$299	$470	$5,497	

Notes:
(1) Retirement amount includes $50.00 per month that the city contributes to deferred comp.
(2) Incentives based upon salary and longevity.
(3) Longevity does not apply to those hired after 1990.
(4) Uniforms are fully provided by agency.

428

with management and management practices. Therefore, if management conscientiously treated employees with dignity and respect, allowed them to be involved in operational planning and decision making, and attempted to acquire a reasonable standard of living for employees, there would be no need for unions. Furthermore, where unions exist, if management attempted to develop a cooperative relationship with the union, many labor relations issues could be resolved before they become problems.

Today, a number of departments have some form of union. Since the 1970s, a period of labor strife and police strikes, administrators and labor leaders in numerous departments have come to develop a cooperative relationship. Although unions can and some do infringe on management prerogative, for the most part, they focus on pay and benefit issues. Administrators through solid negotiating can preserve management's ability to make those decisions that are critical to the effective operation of the department. Management and labor can work together to provide the community with the services it deserves.

Study Questions

1. Define "labor relations." Discuss the importance of labor relations for effective police management.

2. Trace the historical development of the police labor movement in America.

3. What is the significance of the Boston police strike for the American police labor movement?

4. Define "collective bargaining." What is the relationship between collective bargaining and police unions? Does a union have to be the collective bargaining agent? Explain your answer.

5. Discuss the five common objectives sought by police employee organizations.

6. Describe the traditional relationship between management and unionization.

7. Describe the process by which a police labor union develops.

8. How do administrators and union members view professionalism as it relates to unionization?

9. Describe and discuss the four major steps in the collective bargaining process and their components.

10. What are the differences between mandatory, voluntary, and illegal bargaining items?

11. Administratively, why is it important to safeguard management prerogatives in bargaining collectively? How might this be accomplished?

12. Define "impasse." Compare and contrast the impasse resolution techniques of mediation, fact finding, and arbitration.

13. What is the difference between voluntary and compulsory arbitration? Define "binding arbitration."

14. How is final-offer arbitration different from other forms of arbitration? Evaluate the positive and negative aspects of final-offer arbitration for resolving an impasse.

15. Define "contract administration." Why is successful contract administration important?

16. Define "grievance." Discuss the sources of grievances.

17. Describe a grievance procedure. Why are administrators typically opposed to developing grievance procedures? What are the alternatives to grievance procedures? Evaluate the consequences of each on the governing body and on the police organization.

18. Discuss the contributing causes of police strikes. How might police administrators avoid or avert a strike? Which of these means should generally be most effective and most productive for the organization?

Net Resources

http://www.napo.org/ Visit the National Association of Police Organization for information on police unions.

http://www.ncpso-cwa.org/ Visit the National Coalition of Public Safety Officers for information on police labor issues.

http://www.officer.com/unions.htm Visit officer.com for police issues and employee organization information.

References

Bell, D. (1981). Collective bargaining: Perspective for the 1980s. *Journal of Police Science and Administration* 9(3):296–305.

Bopp, W. J., and Wiatrowski, M. (1982). Police strike in New Orleans: A city abandoned by its police. *Police Journal* 55(2):125–135.

Bouza, A. (1985) Police unions: Paper tigers or roaring lions? In W. Geller (ed.), *Police Leadership in America: Crisis and Opportunity*. New York: Praeger.

Bowers, M. (1973). *Contract Administration*. Gaithersburg, MD: Public Safety Labor Relations Center, IACP.

Brennan v. Kock, 564 F. Supp. 322 (S.D.N.Y., 1983).

Burpo, J. (1971). *The Police Labor Movement: Problems and Perspectives*. Springfield, IL: Charles C Thomas.

Burpo, J., DeLord, R., and Shannon, M. (1997). *Police Association Power, Politics, and Confrontation.* Springfield, IL: Charles C Thomas.

Carter, D., and Sapp, A. (1992). A comparative analysis of clauses in police collective bargaining agreements as indicators of change in labor relations. *American Journal of Police* 12:17–46.

Connolly, M. (1986). The impact of final-offer arbitration on wage outcomes of public safety personnel: Michigan vs. Illinois. *Journal of Public Negotiations in the Public Sector* 15:251–262.

Cooper, M. (1999). Nassau County Officials to seek 207 police layoffs in fiscal crisis. *New York Times* (April 12):B5.

Dessler, G. (1984). *Personnel Management.* Reston, VA: Reston Publishing.

Gentel, W., and Handman, M. L. (1979). *Police Strikes: Causes and Prevention.* Gaithersburg, MD: IACP.

Giacopassi, D. J., and Sparger, J. R. (1981). The Memphis police strike: A retrospective analysis. *Southern Journal of Criminal Justice* 6(2):39–52.

Glueck, W. (1976). Labor relations and the supervisor. In G. Newport (ed.), *Supervisory Management.* St. Paul: West Publishing.

Gordon, M., and Miller, S. (1984). Grievances: A review of research and practice. *Personnel Psychology* 37(1):117–146.

Greene, J., Bergman, W., and McLaughlin, E. (1994). Implementing community policing: Cultural and structural change in police organizations. In D. Rosenbaum (ed.), *The Challenge of Community Policing: Testing the Promises.* Thousand Oaks, CA: Sage.

Igleburger, R., and Angell, J. E. (1971). Dealing with police unions. *The Police Chief* (May): 50–55.

Iris, M. (1999). Police discipline in Chicago: Arbitration or arbitrary. *Journal of Criminal Law and Criminology* 89(1):215–244.

Jacobs, J. (1985). Police unions: How they look from the academic side. In W. Geller (ed.), *Police Leadership in America: Crisis and Opportunity.* New York: Praeger.

Juris, H., and Feuille, P. (1973). *Police Unionism: Power and Impact in Public Sector Bargaining.* Lexington, MA: D.C. Heath.

Juris, H., and Feuille, P. (1974) Employee organizations. In O. G. Stahl and R. A. Staufenberger (eds.), *Police Personnel Administration.* North Scituate, MA: Duxbury Press, pp. 203–226.

Kearney, R. C. (1984). *Labor Relations in the Public Sector.* New York: Marcel Dekker.

Kliesmet, R. (1985). The chief and the union: May the force be with you. In W. Geller (ed.), *Police Leadership in America: Crisis and Opportunity.* New York: Praeger.

LeVan, H., Katz, M., and Carley, C. (1993). The arbitration of grievances of police officers and fire fighters. *Public Personnel Management* 22(3):433–444.

Levine, M. (1988). A historical overview of police unionization in the United States. *Police Journal* 61(4):334–343.

Mathis, R., and Jackson, R. (1997). *Personnel: Human Resource Management.* St. Paul: West Publishing.

Matzer, J. (1977) Labor–management relations. In B. Garmire (ed.), *Local Government Police Management.* Washington: International City Managment Association.

National Advisory Commission on Criminal Justice Standards and Goals (1976). *Police.* Washington: Government Printing Office.

Nugent, P. (2000). Police vote no confidence in chief again. *Worcester Telegram and Gazette* (February 25):B1.

Pete, T., Ferrara, A., Bowers, R., and Larence, J. (1976). *Police Response Time: Its Determinants and Effects.* Washington: Police Foundation.

Pfuhl, E. H., Jr. (1983). Police strikes and conventional crime. *Criminology* 21(4):489–503.

Reaves, B., and Goldberg (2000). *Local Police Departments, 1997.* Washington: Bureau of Justice Statistics.

Ritchey, F. J., Wilson, M., Hamby, R., and Trigg, B. (1983). Public perceptions of a police strike in a southern city. *Journal of Police Science and Administration* 11(1):90–96.

Rynecki, S. B., and Morse, M. J. (1981). *Police Collective Bargaining Agreements: A National Management Survey,* rev. ed. Washington: Police Executive Research Forum and National League of Cities.

Salerno, C. A. (1981). *Police at the bargaining table.* Springfield, IL: Charles C Thomas.

Sandver, M. (1987). *Labor Relations: Process and Outcomes.* Boston: Little, Brown.

Sapp, A. (1985). Police unionism as a developmental process. In A. Blumberg and E. Niederhoffer (eds.), *The Ambivalent Force,* 3rd ed. New York: Holt, Rinehart and Winston.

Schachter, H. L. (1980). Police unions, the judicial system and the development of police department policy: A research note. *Criminal Justice Review* 5(1):9–97.

Schachter, H. L. (1981). Fiscal crisis and police union bargaining: The case of New York. *Criminal Justice Review* 6(2):23–30.

U.S. Department of Labor (1976). *Collective Bargaining Agreements for Police and Firefighters.* Washington: Government Printing Office.

Ziskind, D. (1940) *One Thousand Strikes of Government Employees.* New York.

Part IV

Control Processes in Police Management

Control often has a negative connotation within the organizational setting because it is associated with authoritarian administrative practices. Merely hearing the word "control" causes many people to become apprehensive and withdrawn. Neverless, organizational control is a very important part of administration. Within this context, *control* refers to managing the police department and keeping it on an even keel in accomplishing its goals and objectives. Control is important also from the perspective that any organization requires incremental adjustment with the passage of time, and control is a primary mechanism for recognizing the need for such change.

This section begins with Chapter 12, Control and Productivity in the Police Setting. We discuss the roles, levels, and types of control. We also pay special attention to the control process, which involves determining areas to be controlled, the establishment of standards and expectations, and the measurement of performance. Chapter 12 also delves into productivity, a dimension that increasingly is playing an important role in police management. We examine the theoretical dimensions of productivity in terms of what the department is doing in relation to its goals. A productive department is one whose activities coincide with the needs of the community. Individual unit and officer productivity are also examined.

Chapter 13 examines planning, programming, and budgeting in the police administrative setting. Planning, programming, and budgeting are the mechanisms that administrators use to exercise broad control over the police department. Planning is essentially a control process in that a department consciously determines its goals and then develops a plan to ensure that the goals are accomplished. Programs are the results of planning and represent the practical steps that are taken to achieve goals. Finally, budgeting is an integral part of planning in that no matter how effective the plan is, it is of little utility if the department does not have the fiscal resources to fund it.

Chapter 14 is about accountability in the police organization. We organize this chapter into two sections: internal and external accountability mechanisms. Among the internal accountability mechanisms we consider are internal affairs,

Compstat, and codes of ethics. These are areas over which the police administrator has a great deal of control. However, police organizations must also be held accountable to external forces such as politicians and citizens. Thus we focus on the roles of civilian review, citizen complaints, civil liability, accreditation, and other mechanisms in the accountability process.

Finally, Chapter 15 examines change in the police organization. Because the community and environment are constantly changing, the police agency must also constantly change and remain abreast with the community and environment to be effective. This chapter examines a number of trends and possible problems that will confront police departments in the immediate future. The reader will better understand the complexities of policing and police management with a thorough grasp of this chapter.

In summary, control is an important administrative function. The police department is a system with a number of integrated parts. Control assists the administrator in coordinating these numerous parts, and it enables the administrator to develop mechanisms which will alert him or her to problems. Again, although control is often viewed as something negative, it should be regarded as an integral part of police administration.

12

Control and Productivity in the Police Setting

A. Ramey/Stock Boston

Chapter Outline

Introduction

Control
Management by Exception
The Roles of Control
Levels of Control
Types of Control
The Control Process

Productivity
Productivity Defined
Uses for Productivity Measures
Measuring Productivity
Improving Police Productivity
Strategies for Improving Police Productivity

Summary

Learning Objectives

After reading this chapter, you should be able to

1. Understand the roles of control.
2. List the levels of control.
3. Understand the various types of control.
4. Explain the control process.
5. Understand performance evaluation and methods of corrective action.
6. Understand the definition of productivity.
7. Measure productivity.
8. Discuss how to improve productivity.

I n Volusia County, Florida, sheriffs' cars are fitted with videocameras that record routine traffic stops. A study of more than 148 hours of videotape gathered from the cars documented that although only 5 percent of the drivers on the stretch of I-95 patrolled by sheriff's deputies were minority, nearly 70 percent of the motorists stopped by the police were minorities (Brazil and Barry, 1992). The sheriff soon came under fire for allowing this practice to persist.

The racial discrepancy revealed in the department's history of traffic stops exemplifies the difficult balance that needs to be struck between control and productivity. On the one hand, law enforcement administrators are responsible for controlling their subordinates to avoid painting an unpleasant image for the agency. On the other hand, law enforcement officials must be productive in their endeavors to control crime. According to some, a necessary but unfortunate by-product of crime control is the inconvenience some people will suffer. But opponents say that no amount of crime control justifies unfair treatment of citizens.

Accordingly, this chapter begins with a discussion of organizational control then moves into productivity, issues of paramount importance to the police administrator.

INTRODUCTION

Organizational control is an important issue in policing. Administrators must control the department to ensure that departmental goals are achieved and that officers are not engaged in inappropriate behavior or activities that otherwise undermine the effectiveness of the department. This chapter focuses on control from the perspective of making the department as effective as possible in achieving its goals and objectives. Chapter 14 examines police accountability and problems that occur when officers act outside the boundaries of prescribed police procedures. This chapter also addresses the issue of police productivity. A central part of control is ensuring that officers and departmental units are productive and that their productivity addresses departmental goals and objectives.

CONTROL

The infrastructure of a good police department includes defined goals and objectives; an organizational structure; appropriate technology; and sufficient, competent personnel. With such a foundation in place, efficient accomplishment of goals and objectives depends substantially on effective control. Wieland and Ullrich define control in its most basic form: "obtaining behaviors desired by the organization" (1980:105). With respect to police administration, *control* is the process of regulating organizational activities so that performance conforms to expectations (Brand and Scanlan, 1995). Here, expectations refer to those held by the department's administrators as well as those held by the department's constituency.

Decisions related to control are among the most difficult that must be made by police executives. Control is expensive in that it requires the investment of personnel and resources to supervise, manage, and inspect. Administrators should weigh the potential costs of control against the potential benefits when making decisions regarding control plans and implementation. Also, maintaining a balance between undercontrol and overcontrol is a challenge. *Excessive control* seriously reduces employee initiative and morale. It can create suspicion, secrecy, and other dysfunctional organizational behavior. It also results in organizational stagnation since decision making is centralized, and decisions consequently are not made on a timely basis. Police organizations are thought to employ excessive control because of their quasi-military nature. On the other hand, *inadequate control* reduces the probability of successful organizational performance. That is, police departments will not efficiently and effectively pursue their goals. Thus deciding on how much control to initiate in the department is critical.

Both formal and informal constraints influence the control function. *Formal constraints* are expressed in constitutions, laws, ordinances, administrative guidelines, budgets, union contracts, and legal documents (e.g., a complaint) and opinions. The granting authorities that provide the department its legitimacy impose these formal constraints. As government establishes agencies and departments to serve its citizens, it also provides them with duties and responsibilities. The agency and department heads must control their units to ensure these duties and responsibilities are met.

Informal constraints stem from a range of things, including the power of special interest groups and political elites, the community's history and tradition, and social and political conditions within the area. Communities develop expectations of their police, and the police must strive to meet these expectations. The combination of formal and informal constraints affecting a chief and the department establishes parameters for decision making and organizational control efforts.

Management by Exception

An important constraint on the chief's ability to control the organization is the physical impossibility of the chief's personally monitoring all activities within the department and adjusting every action that deviates from what is desired. A chief will attempt to overcome this constraint by delegating authority and responsibility to lower-level commanders and concentrating on those areas that require the chief's attention or where the greatest potential harm exists.

The chief ultimately is responsible for what occurs in the department. The government, whether a city council or a state legislature, vests the chief with categorical authority for operating the department and ensuring that it achieves its legislated mandates. The chief then delegates authority to lower-level managers, commanders, and supervisors, each accountable to a higher authority within the department. The chain of command or hierarchy of authority represents a primary control mechanism whereby officers within each unit are accountable to a superior.

Police executives can narrow the range of potential problems by identifying areas where the greatest *potential deviance* exists, then concentrating their control efforts on those areas. In other words, the chief can identify those persons within the department who are most likely to seriously deviate from public expectations; those activities where serious deviation is most likely to occur; or those units that are most likely to deviate. The chief can then focus control efforts on these individuals, activities, or units. Consequently, a rational system for maintaining sufficient control can be instituted. Examples of areas that require more thoughtful control systems include training, use of force, handling of evidence, pursuit driving, and undercover operations.

The control system should be as automatic as possible. Automatic control requires the establishment of criteria and conditions to facilitate (1) self-control by police personnel and (2) routine processes (such as continuous review of employee reporting) to detect variations from standard performance expectations and implement corrective action. Where automatic methods are not practical or where a safety net is needed to address potential failures of self-regulation, the chief should delegate the authority for controlling routine matters to lower-level police managers and supervisors. The top executive should reserve only nonroutine matters of control for attention. This technique of reserving top executive attention for those few instances involving significant deviations from anticipated performance is *management by exception*. Police administrators must ensure the establishment of policies, procedures, and rules that allow and facilitate exceptional issues to surface for executive attention; otherwise, the job of the police administrator quickly becomes overwhelming.

The Roles of Control

Control procedures assist managers in dealing with administrative challenges. Bartol and Martin (1998:512-513) describe five administrative challenges that can be dealt with by appropriate control mechanisms: (1) coping with uncertainty, (2) detecting irregularities, (3) identifying opportunities, (4) handling complex situations, and (5) decentralizing authority.

Coping with Uncertainty

Thompson (1967) identified three sources of uncertainty for organizations: (1) technical, (2) managerial, and (3) institutional. *Technical uncertainty* arises from performance of daily functions. In the case of police agencies, these functions include, but are not limited to, patrol, investigation, and service delivery. Police work is becoming increasingly technical. New techniques in evidence collection and processing and changes in the laws relative to arrest, search, and seizure make policing rather complex. Administrators must strive to ensure that all officers are using the most advanced technological knowledge if the department is to be effective.

Managerial uncertainty arises during the course of attempting to coordinate the activities of various units and ensure that they have adequate resources to get the job done. The Los Angeles Police Department has more than 200 distinct operational units, each charged with a set of goals and objectives. Coordinating these units to ensure cooperation and reduced duplication of services is a monumental task. It often creates confusion and problems for the police executive.

Finally, at the *institutional level*, organizations deal with elements of the environment over which they have no formal authority. These elements include law, public interest, and the political sentiment and activities within a department's political jurisdiction. In sum, because police agencies are public entities, managers must cope with uncertainty arising from numerous sources. Control procedures help mitigate the detrimental effects of uncertainty within organizations. On the other hand, a lack of control almost guarantees that uncertainty will reach dangerous levels.

On the Job

ALBANY, GEORGIA, POLICE DEPARTMENT

By Chief Bobby Johnson

Courtesy of Chief Johnson

Albany is located in southwest Georgia and has a population of approximately 78,000 and a geographical area of about 57 square miles. The city is located in a rural area and serves as a center for the region in terms of shopping, medical services, and transportation. Much of the surrounding area is engaged in agricultural activities. The department serves a diverse population.

The police department currently has 214 officers. Officers have a substantial workload and answer between 140,000 and 150,00 calls for service each year. The department's supervisors and managers are constantly working and planning new and innovative ways to serve the public. Along these lines, the department is geographically divided into four districts, with a total of 15

patrol beats. A lieutenant is assigned to each district to manage the department's community policing efforts. The lieutenant works with officers and detectives in developing and implementing proactive policing programs at the neighborhood level. This arrangement allows the department to be proactive in addressing citizen problems, crime, and disorder.

Productivity is an important part of policing, especially today when some departments are experiencing reductions in the growth of their budgets. A number of departments have seen substantial increases in workloads, without a proportionate increase in resources. When this occurs, a department must maximize its resources so that public services do not suffer.

The Albany Police Department has enacted several measures to increase productivity and enhance services to the public. First, we have implemented community policing. Rather than creating a number of special units to deliver community policing services, we have made it a priority in all operational units, especially patrol. This was accomplished by providing all of our officers and supervisors with COP training. As noted, the department responds to a large number of calls. By having patrol officers involved in community policing, they are able to work on problem solving and community partnerships between calls. The COP

Continued

lieutenant serves as a resource to assist them with projects. When a problem or community policing project requires more time or effort than patrol officers have available, the lieutenant can coordinate efforts to ensure that the project is completed.

Another way in which the Albany Police Department has enhanced its productivity is by applying for and receiving a variety of state and federal grants. For example, the department received the Weed and Seed Grant from the U.S. Justice Department. This grant has allowed the department to pay overtime to several officers who focus on the city's drug problem. Although all Albany police officers engage in drug enforcement, the Weed and Seed officers are there to focus on long-term problems. If officers are able to eliminate a problem and the number of calls for service shows a corresponding reduction, the department in the end will be much more productive. The department received Local Law Enforcement Block Grants, which funded the purchase of equipment. This equipment was used to make the work of officers easier and less time-consuming. The department hired several officers as

a result of the Universal Hiring Grant from the Office of Community-Oriented Policing Services. for new officers. The department has a Juvenile Mentoring Program (JUMP) that involves mentoring at-risk kids. Thus one way the department has attacked the productivity problem is to acquire additional resources from outside sources. These external funds have been extremely important to our ability to serve the city.

Finally, the department has attempted to be more productive by shifting its priorities. Historically, police departments have measured productivity by the numbers of arrests, citations, and calls answered. These measures do not evaluate the essence of policing: citizen satisfaction with the police. Today, we place greater emphasis on how we are viewed by the public. Our community policing lieutenants periodically evaluate citizen perceptions of the police and collect input from citizens in terms of perceived problems. The department then incorporates this input into its planning process in hope that the department will do a better job in serving the citizens of Albany.

Detecting Irregularities

Control also assists administrators in detecting irregularities. The range of potential irregularities is almost limitless; however, some leading irregularities include poor service quality (perhaps evidenced by an increase in the incidence of citizen complaints), deficient functioning within operational units, and increasing employee turnover. Effective control mechanisms provide for the early detection of irregularities. Early detection helps ensure that small problems do not mushroom out of control. When problems grow to significant levels before irregularities are noticed, change or corrections can prove difficult. Control, then, helps administrators identify problems so steps can be taken to minimize harmful consequences.

Identifying Opportunities

Control also helps administrators identify opportunities. As Bartol and Martin observed, "Controls also help highlight situations in which things are going better than expected, thereby alerting management to possible future opportunities" (1998:512). If, for example, a police agency targets a high-crime public housing complex with aggressive enforcement efforts and succeeds in driving out the criminal element, it will probably gain a measure of favor with law-abiding citizens residing in the same complex. This favor may serve as an opportunity, as concerned residents may be more willing to notify the police of potential problems in an effort to preserve the safety of their surroundings.

Handling Complex Situations

Control procedures are especially important for handling complex situations. Control enhances coordination, particularly in large organizations. Control helps administrators keep track of the various elements within the organization, to be sure that they are well synchronized, on task, and doing what they are supposed to be doing. For example, a traffic accident involving the spilling of hazardous chemicals presents a dangerous situation. A number of units and different agencies become involved in the problem. A variety of tasks, including evacuation, traffic control, and proper cleanup of the chemicals, must be accomplished. This cannot be accomplished safely without proper control. Policing is an extremely complex occupation, so administrators need to have control mechanisms in place to ensure that the delivery of services occurs satisfactorily and within established parameters.

Decentralizing Authority

Control also provides administrators with the ability to decentralize command. This requires some explanation. What is required is delegation of authority. In essence, this involves decentralizing decisions, or moving them out to the margins of the organizational hierarchy, where they can be more readily and reasonably made. This process has to occur with controls, however, and with measures to ensure the accountability of those subordinates whose duties include making important decisions. As Bartol and Martin observed, "With controls, managers can foster decision making at lower levels in the organization but still maintain a handle on progress" (1998:513). The ability to maintain a handle on progress, or to control decentralized decisionmaking, then, is an important aspect of control. Control provides for decentralization only inasmuch as it keeps the agency on track, in pursuit of its mission and its goals.

Levels of Control

Lorange, Morton, and Ghoshal (1986:12) point to three levels of control in organizations: (1) strategic control, (2) tactical control, and (3) operational control. Attention to each level of control increases the probability of realizing organizational goals and objectives (Schreyoff and Steinmann, 1987; Simons, 1995). Accordingly, each level of control is addressed in the following sections.

Strategic Control

According to Bartol and Martin, strategic control "involves monitoring critical environmental factors to ensure that strategic plans are implemented as intended, assessing the effects of organizational strategic actions, and adjusting such plans when necessary" (1998:515). Strategic control requires looking into the future and taking steps to ensure that the organizations' goals and objectives are being developed and maintained and that they can continue this way.

Consider strategic planning, as discussed in Chapter 13. Police departments implement numerous strategies to address a wide array of problems. Police managers must exert some measure of control in the department to ensure that these strategies are properly implemented and the desired results are obtained. Community policing, which dominates police strategic thinking today, encompasses a wide variety of programs. If community policing is to be effective, police managers must exert control over units to ensure that they are implementing community policing in a fashion that addresses the community's and the department's needs.

Tactical Control

Tactical control can be defined as "a control type that focuses on assessing the implementation of tactical plans at departmental levels, monitoring associated periodic results, and taking corrective action as necessary" (Bartol and Martin, 1998:515). Whereas strategic control primarily involves upper-level administrators embracing large expanses within the department, tactical control generally involves middle-level managers and specific operational units.

Tactical control essentially evolves around ensuring that programs function properly. For example, in the past drug units concentrated on amassing numbers of arrests. Today, drug eradication programming focuses on eliminating drugs in a particular area or hot spot. Managers must ensure that narcotics officers concentrate on problems rather than giving their full attention to accumulating arrests, which has little impact on the drug problem.

Operational Control

Operational control is the lowest level of control. It occurs where individual officers are responsible for carrying out the programs and policies decided on from above. Sergeants are typically responsible for operational control. They provide feedback about what is being done, what works and does not, and they call attention to potential problems and negative reactions. For example, patrol supervisors ensure that patrol beats are properly staffed, that officers use the correct amount of force when making arrests, and that officers follow the department's policies when answering a domestic violence call. Traffic supervisors ensure that traffic officers properly investigate traffic crashes and issue traffic citations at those locations where accidents are most likely to occur. Detective supervisors ensure that detectives completely follow up cases, correctly collect and process evidence, and prepare their cases for presentation in court.

The community policing elements of police–citizen interactions, partnerships, and problem solving are instructive here. These elements are basically community policing in practice, and they provide guidance on how officers should respond to calls for service and work with residents. From an operational control standpoint, supervisors train and guide officers in daily tasks with a mind to having more positive interactions with the public, attempting to partner with citizens and citizen groups, and solving problems as opposed to merely responding to them.

Types of Control

Administrators exercise three primary types of control: (1) output control, (2) behavior control, and (3) clan control (Jones, George, and Hill, 1998). Police administrators are, to varying extents, responsible for exercising each type of control. Output control is perhaps most important, but the other types of control are essential for managing a smooth-running law enforcement agency.

Output Control

Output control first involves choosing a performance standard. This standard is selected to measure efficiency, effectiveness, fairness, or any other goal the administrator deems desirable. An example of an output standard in policing is the crime rate. The incidence of particular crimes is a standard against which law enforcement effectiveness is gauged. Alternatively, the incidence of citizen complaints can be used to measure fairness, among other outcomes. Implementing productivity measurements assists managers in implementing output control. The issue of productivity is discussed at greater length below.

Behavior Control

Behavior control is another type of control. Jones and his colleagues point out that "managers can develop an elegant organizational structure with highly appropriate task and reporting relationships, but it will work as designed only if managers also establish control systems that allow them to motivate and shape employee behavior" (1998:280). Hence the need for behavior control. Behavior control can be accomplished in several ways, but three mechanisms of behavior control stand out: (1) direct supervision, (2) management by objectives, and (3) rules and standard operating procedures (Jones et al., 1988).

Obviously, direct supervision is difficult for police administrators; patrol and related functions take place far from the watchful eyes of management. However, direct supervision is accomplished through the chain of command. Sergeants are responsible for making assignments, ensuring that officers produce according to department standards, and guaranteeing programs are implemented as planned. Supervisory standards often are the department's rules and regulations, and specific assignments relate to the objectives that officers should achieve as a result of their assignments. Supervision that is too intrusive can stifle motivation and officer productivity. However, most supervision is instructive and collegial, which results in higher levels of subordinate job satisfaction.

Clan or Employee Group Control

Jones and colleagues define clan control as "control exerted on individuals and groups in an organization by shared values, norms, standards of behavior, and expectations" (1998:285). Clan control goes hand in hand with the notion of organizational culture, the values, expectations, and standards that shape how individuals within the organization interact with one another. Clan control is unwritten and informal, whereas output and behavioral control are somewhat more concrete, codified, and quantifiable.

Clan control derives from the training and socialization processes, where recruits internalize organizational values and norms. This type of control is important because it makes control possible in situations where administrators cannot be present. In addition, subordinates will focus on the goals and mission of the organization when one set of values is internalized. Unfortunately, in policing, there is evidence of two relatively distinct cultures—the culture of administrators and the culture of subordinates—which makes clan control problematic. When these cultures are at odds, clan control becomes difficult to accomplish.

The Control Process

Managers and supervisors perform the vast majority of the control functions in a police department. Departmental regulations enumerate the acceptable standards and expectations for behavior. Effective organizational control cannot be achieved at any level of the organization without a strong superstructure of clear and comprehensive standards and expectations that are thoroughly understood and accepted by police personnel. Rank-and-file officers often complain about policies and procedures being overly restrictive, but rules essentially outline how everyone is to perform their assigned tasks and responsibilities.

The control process, as depicted in Figure 12–1, involves four essential elements: (1) determining areas to be controlled; (2) establishing of standards and expectations; (3) measuring performance; and (4) taking corrective action to bring back into line behavior or operations judged to be significantly divergent from established requirements. The remaining sections are devoted to presenting these four elements in detail.

Determining Areas to Be Controlled

It almost goes without saying, but administrators need to choose among areas to control. Choices are necessary because to exert control over all organizational elements, especially the many elements found in contemporary law enforcement agencies, is time-consuming, expensive, and perhaps impossible. Choices regarding who and what to control are also essential because subordinates will become resentful if they perceive "excessive" control over their every action. Several of the chapters in this book identify and discuss the primary duties of police administrators, the areas where they are most responsible for making important decisions and directing subordinates in the pursuit of organizational goals and objectives.

Figure 12–1

The control process.

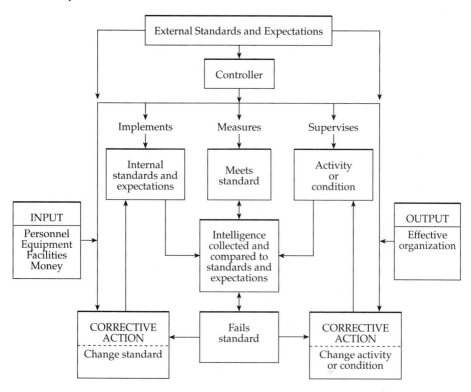

Establishing Standards and Expectations

Appropriate, well-defined standards and completely understood expectations are essential to effective control. The standards for behavior must be understood by personnel and supported by commanders and supervisors. Continuous reinforcement ensures that personnel remain committed to them. Effective enumeration of standards substantially reduces control problems in a police agency.

Organizational goals, unit objectives, and operational plans provide overall guidance for the exercise of control in police operations. Standards and expectations deserve attention because they are the measuring devices against which police behavior is evaluated. For discussion purposes, the following review will be divided into *external* standards and expectations (those established outside the organization) and *internal* standards (those which the organization formally defines as guidelines for agency control purposes). In reality there is considerable interplay and overlap between these two types of standards and expectations.

External Standards and Expectations.   Since police have been vested with a great deal of authority and discretion in maintaining social order, preventing criminal acts, and apprehending suspected law violators, public expectations and standards related to the use of this authority are high. The regulation of police employees is much more stringent than that leveled against private business employees or other public officials. Items about police abuse of authority and failure to protect citizens appearing in the news media attest to this high level of public scrutiny.

The sources of police regulations are varied. Laws, professional standards of conduct, and court decisions are three means through which police conduct and the training relevant to police conduct are regulated. Federal and state constitutions contain prohibitions related to arrest, search, seizure, privacy, and other invasions of citizens' rights. Substantive and procedural law contains additional standards for the guidance of police discretion. Professional organizations such as the International Association of Chiefs of Police, Police Foundation, National Organization of Black Law Enforcement Executives, and Police Executive Research Forum have contributed additional standards of conduct in the areas of ethics, pursuit driving, use of deadly force, equal treatment of minorities and women, and personnel selection. These standards are widely accepted by police officials and judicial bodies.

Internal Standards and Expectations.   External standards serve as a framework for controlling police behavior and as a basis for guiding management control efforts. However, there are numerous expectations and requirements on police behavior that cannot be left to external devices. Hence the police executive should develop internally written documents that define appropriate standards and expectations. If these internally defined standards are not adequate or relevant to police responsibilities for the jurisdiction, they will be widely ignored, and will be ineffective as control devices. Consequently, a great deal of thought and effort should go into developing the department's internal written directives.

The documents that guide the operational activities of the organization are organized by three general categories:

1. *Policies*—The broadest and most flexible statement of operational principle enumerates the department's mission and goals.
2. *Procedures*—Comprehensive statements about the general approach to be followed in addressing operational situations.
3. *General orders or rules and regulations*—Precise, specific, directives concerning the behavior of organizational employees.

Wasserman, Gardner, and Cohn (1973:18-22) list 12 specific steps for sound development of standard police policies:

1. The department should acknowledge and discuss the role of discretion in police work.
2. All policies should embody a commitment to democratic values, to the legitimacy and appropriateness of constitutional limitations, and to the fundamental goals of community service and responsiveness.

3. The department should use the policymaking process as a framework in which to examine or set basic goals and priorities.
4. The department should use the policymaking process to explore new roles and areas of service that traditionally have not been considered police business.
5. The issues to be addressed should be carefully considered, especially during early efforts at establishing policy.
6. The department should develop and enforce a strict policy governing the use of deadly force.
7. The department should involve beat officers in policy development.
8. The department should experiment with community participation in policy development.
9. The department must circulate policy to its members in a form that makes it useful, comprehensive, and credible.
10. The department should use the policymaking process to eliminate petty rules.
11. The department should take advantage of the experience of other cities.
12. The department should adopt a process of regular, automatic policy review so that outdated, inappropriate policy is eliminated or replaced.

Police administrators basically use four methods in developing formal policies and written guidelines: (1) policies developed by professional organizations such as the International Association of Chiefs of Police or a state training agency are incorporated into the department's procedural guidelines; (2) a police official or planner is given the responsibility of reviewing the police operations and written guidelines; (3) policymaking task forces, usually consisting of both nonpolice and police members, are established to assist a planner in developing the guidelines; and (4) community-based teams of police officers working in conjunction with other social service agencies and residents of the community write the guidelines. Community policing has resulted in increased use of the latter two methods, which leads to more comprehensive policies and perhaps a higher commitment on the part of officers.

Directives and guidelines that are internalized by police officers reduce the amount of time management must spend on the control function. Therefore, the development of guidelines that are to a degree acceptable to the rank-and-file officers should be a goal of management. To produce such guidelines, administrators should permit and encourage active subordinate participation in their development. Since operational personnel generally have the most pertinent experience to handling the problems covered by rules, they should be encouraged to contribute to rule development. Officers who have participated in the rule-making process subsequently have a thorough grasp of the meaning and implications of established guidelines, and they are more likely to exert peer pressure to comply with the rules.

Documentation of standards and expectations (1) provides a yardstick against which supervisors can measure actions and (2) provides a basis for learning appropriate self-control. Rules and regulations are not only an instrument of discipline; they are training tools that should be used by everyone in the department to improve the collective performance of the department. Moreover, supervision and direction supplement written standards. Each officer is directly responsible to a superior officer, who ensures that work standards are met and who interprets standards and provides direction when necessary.

Without appropriate guidance, first-line supervisors—those who are responsible for observing the condition of facilities, equipment, and personnel—subjectively choose and prioritize the standards they enforce, the variables they use to assess the extent to which standards are met, and the nature of the measurements required. Supervisors generally will agree with the command staff on the critical areas to be evaluated. However, differences can occur as performance areas are selected and subordinates are being observed. An older, militaristic supervisor may select variables such as hair and sideburn length. A supervisor who is traffic oriented may use a subordinate's citation production as a measure for control. A supervisor who is committed to the "rule of law" may use arrests as a variable for determining whether corrective action should be taken to control an employee.

Without clear direction for control, not only is there a lack of agreement on priorities and measurements for control, but the variables used in measuring will not be made explicit. Subordinates will be left to determine for themselves the priorities and variables to be used by each supervisor in assessing performance.

High-Risk Activities.   Nowhere is the importance of clearly articulated standards and expectations more apparent than in the area of high-risk activities. Law enforcement officials are often called upon to engage in any number of inherently risky activities (e.g., service of search and arrest warrants, pursuits, or hostage situations). High-risk situations pose danger to officers and citizens, and when handled inappropriately, they may result in death or injury and expose the department to high levels of liability. It is critical that departments have thoughtful policies that protect officers and citizens and lead to the successful end of a high-risk incident. Policies and procedures here are instructive and are used to guide and coordinate police responses, reducing danger to all parties involved.

One high-risk area of law enforcement where clearly defined policies and procedures are of paramount importance is the use of deadly force. Shootings can be particularly taxing on administrators. Contrary to the Hollywood image, officer shootings are followed by investigations to determine whether the force was justified. Sometimes, shootings are followed by critical media commentary and public outcry. Clear policies governing deadly force can minimize these and other consequences of officer shootings. Researchers have found that restrictive departmental firearms policies not only reduce the number of shootings by officers (Geller and Scott, 1992; Meyer, 1980) but change the nature of those shootings (Fyfe, 1979; Sherman, 1983). Evidence also suggests that restrictive policies governing deadly force promote a safer working environment for officers (Blumberg, 1997).

Another high-risk law enforcement activity is high-speed pursuits. Pursuits have become relatively controversial in recent years. Critics cite the threat posed to innocent bystanders; law enforcement officials cite the need to apprehend fleeing criminals. Carefully articulated pursuit policies can help achieve a balance between these two conflicting notions as well as reduce physical and financial risks for law enforcement officials (Alpert, 1997). All pursuits involve substantial risk, but restrictive policies improve tactical knowledge and advanced preparation, not to mention decreasing and controlling risk. Alpert (1997) identifies four essential elements of a pursuit driving policy: (1) clear and understandable written guidelines; (2) specific training geared toward reinforcing the policy, using examples of risk assessment; (3) a detached supervisor who takes control over the pursuit so as to minimize personal involvement by the officer pursuing the suspect; and (4) accountability, including criticism, feedback, and corrective action as needed. Administrators as well as their subordinates benefit from policies of this nature because restrictive policies can minimize the potential for injury to innocent parties, civil liability, public outcry, and other threats to organizational survival.

Measuring Performance and Maintaining Control

A variety of processes are used to collect information for measuring organizational and personnel performance. The collection of data must be consistent with control needs and the ability of the organization to use the data to facilitate decision-making and control actions. Data collection should be comprehensive, addressing all aspects of the department. The information-collecting repertoire available to police administrators for organizational control includes (1) line supervision techniques, (2) staff inspections, and (3) audits and research.

Line Supervision. Police departments are organized using a number of structural techniques, including chain of command, span of control, unity of command, and the exception principle, for controlling the department and its activities. These arrangements facilitate supervisory observations and evaluation, known in management as line or authoritative inspection. *Line inspection* involves the inspection of subordinates, activities, equipment, and physical facilities over which the manager or supervisor has responsibility. Supervisors, commanders, and managers observe and review subordinate performance, whether that performance is related to an officer giving information to a citizen or to one investigating a crime. They inspect equipment to ensure that it is properly functioning and that officers carry only the equipment or weapons that are authorized by departmental policies. They also inspect or observe police activities to ensure that they result in desired outcomes.

This process might be viewed as negative in that it centers on close supervision. However, supervisors must follow up on activities to ensure that they are properly carried out. In some cases, problems may develop even when officers follow proper procedures. In these cases, the department's procedure may be defective. First-line supervisors are in the best position to report problems and recommend changes in procedures.

Supervisors observe subordinate behavior, or the results of behavior, and gauge the extent to which it matches established standards. In those instances where the behavior constitutes only a minor misconformity, the supervisor is expected to take corrective action to ensure conformity. The supervisor does this preferably through positive supervisory practices. *Positive* disciplinary methods to control subordinate behavior include instruction and reassignment of responsibilities, which are usually sufficient to obtain changes in behavior. When positive disciplinary methods are ineffective or when the misconduct is substantial, police supervisors normally have to resort to disciplinary measures (discussed in Chapter 14).

Police supervisors not only possess the capacity for direct observation for detecting police misbehavior, but they can also use reporting systems that have been developed for controlling police organizations. Daily activity reports are frequently required of all field officers, including specialists. Patrol officers initiate "daily activity reports." Figure 12–2 is a copy of the daily activity report for the St. Michaels, Maryland, Police Department. These reports provide a running record of all activities performed by an officer during the work period (front) and a summary of the officer's total activities (back). These reports may also include information about the officer's equipment and other facts that a supervisor can use for evaluation and control. Specialists such as investigators are usually expected to prepare daily plans on which they organize their anticipated workload at the beginning of each day. These plans are then filed with a supervisor who can refer to them during the course of the workday. Specialists also complete daily reports that compile information about their activities. A detective's daily report may require information on the numbers of arrests, witness interviews, stolen property recovered, drugs seized, and interrogations.

Although this record keeping builds an organizational memory that is essential to the successful accomplishment of the police job, it is obviously equally important to the intelligence collection aspects of organizational control. Downs (1967) points out that employee reports inform high-level officials about what is happening, remind each subordinate that he or she must meet certain standards of performance, and encourage subordinates to carry out the desired performance—or at least to report having done so.

These compliance-inducing functions, according to Downs, account for what sometimes appear to be excessive reporting requirements for employees of bureaucracies: "Even if 90 percent of all such reports are never looked at, they may still have a potent effect in causing compliance with the bureau's standards" (1967:145–146).

Staff Inspections.   Staff positions are established in large departments for the purpose of examining and evaluating line operations. The authority of staff personnel to conduct inspections is derived from the chief. In essence, staff inspectors are the "eyes and ears" of the chief, and their job is to ensure that the department is in compliance with established standards. Units responsible for

Figure 12–2
St. Michaels Police Department: Officer's daily activity report.

ST. MICHAELS POLICE DEPARTMENT

Officer's Daily Activity Report

OFFICER	BADGE NO.	DAY OF WEEK	DATE

EQUIPMENT NO.	ON DUTY: FROM	TO	TOTAL HOURS

ODOMETER READING   TOTAL MILES   EQUIPMENT CONDITION START   EQUIPMENT CONDITION FINISH
START   FINISH

Log of Activities

TIME RECEIVED	TIME COMPLETED	TIME CONSUMED	SOURCE OF COMPLAINT	LOCATION, TYPE OF ACTIVITY AND ACTION TAKEN
				Approved by:

Chief of Police

Continued

Figure 12–2
(Concluded)

Officer's Daily Activity Report

Meter Tickets _____   State Traffic Citations _____

Ordinance Tickets _____   Municipal/State Infractions _____

Written Warnings _____   Traffic Arrests _____

Security Awareness _____   Criminal Arrests _____

ERO's _____

Suspicious persons/vehicles/circumstances observed:

_____

_____

_____

_____

Lookouts (things or people to look out for):

_____

_____

_____

_____

Messages for other officers/next shift:

_____

_____

_____

_____

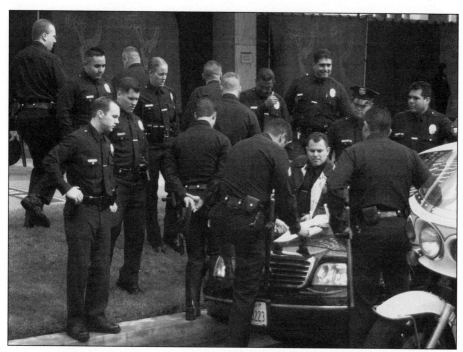

Los Angeles police officers review security locations before the start of the 53rd Annual Primetime Emmy Awards at the Shubert Theater.

Vince Bucci/Getty Images

staff activity are in essence extensions of the chief, and as such their commanders and personnel are neither responsible for the performance of the operations being inspected nor answerable to the commanders of those units.

Nearly all specialized staff units, including personnel, training, records, communications, planning, criminalistics, and internal affairs, perform limited staff inspection functions. These units continuously review the activities of operational units and personnel. For example, records unit clerks review, process, and use reports and records generated by police employees; personnel unit specialists review employee evaluations that have been completed by line supervisors; and the planning unit evaluates the progress and consequences of planning implementation by line operations. Such functional inspections normally occur in an unobtrusive, cooperative fashion, which supports line operations. Variations from the expectations and standards are generally called to the attention of middle managers or first-line supervisors. Only in instances of repeated uncorrected deviation from standards or in situations with serious consequences do officials in these units bring operational deviancy to the attention of the chief.

In addition to inspections by specialized units, large police departments also need a specialized staff inspection system devoted exclusively to the accumulation and transmission of information concerning the operations and activities. The most common organizational arrangement instituted exclusively for operational surveillance and the conduct of formal inspections is the staff inspection unit.

The *staff inspection unit* is normally situated structurally independent of line command either inside the chief's office, as in the case of a small or medium police agency, or as a major unit that reports directly to the chief. Regardless of physical location, the commander of the staff inspection unit usually has direct access to the chief.

A staff inspection unit's sole responsibility is periodic evaluations of departmental possessions, personnel, and activities. In essence, its activities supplement line inspection activities. It conducts well-planned, comprehensive assessments of the police operations, rather than focusing on detecting or investigating the occasional indiscretions of police employees. Some departments, including the Los Angeles Police Department, do, however, charge the inspection unit with periodic *single-function inspections* to determine the state of a narrow phase of a unit's responsibility. Such a single-function inspection involves a "biopsy approach," where a single situation or area such as a crime, arrest, or traffic report is chosen at random and subjected to detailed analysis, including the interviewing of all parties involved in the situation.

Police administrative authorities generally agree that a staff inspection unit should emphasize the correction of deficiencies rather than only reporting such information to the chief. Consequently, a staff inspection unit spends considerable time planning for comprehensive inspections and disseminating the plans well in advance of the actual inspection. This advance notice provides line commanders with the opportunity to identify and correct problems prior to the actual inspection. Unannounced inspections by a staff inspection unit are viewed as undesirable by most authorities, who maintain that the primary purpose of inspections is to bring the organization into line with policies and management expectations. Others hold to the opinion that "scheduled inspections bring scheduled results," and they make a practice of conducting unscheduled and unannounced inspections. Although surprise staff inspections should be an option for dealing with unique, serious problems in the command system, the practice causes suspicion and ill-will between line operations and staff inspections, which may be unnecessary in a police agency that has a history of sound management.

Inspection plans include the identification of all areas and items to be inspected and the identification of who is responsible for the inspection. Staff inspection personnel are either specialists assigned exclusively to inspections or employees temporarily reassigned from other specialized units in the department. The use of permanent rather than temporary inspectors is normally associated with larger departments. Even when inspections are being performed by staff inspectors, written instructions and guidelines covering the areas and specifics of inspectional responsibility are essential elements of an efficiently organized staff inspection process. These instructions and guidelines are rooted in policies, procedures, and rules. Special training and briefings are particularly important in situations where personnel are temporarily reassigned from noninspectional units.

Following the completion of the initial inspection, it is considered good practice to draft a confidential report of the findings for review by the commanders of the units that were evaluated. This action is designed not only to ensure the accuracy of the findings, but also to stimulate quick correction of any deficiencies. In instances where commendable situations are found, reports should contain appropriate commendations. After a reasonable review and comment period, a general report is normally made to the chief and command personnel. These reports should also be provided to staff units such as planning and training so they can evaluate the need to make changes in their unit activities.

Audits and Research.   Audits and research are the most neglected areas of information collection available to police managers. The techniques for accumulating information through audits and research may be neglected because the techniques are not well understood or the skilled people needed to perform these services are not available. Audits and research are valuable because they collect and analyze quantitative data related to operational performance. Given that many departments now have automated dispatch systems and computerized records management systems, there is a wealth of information to facilitate audits and research.

Typical examples of research and audits include ratios of arrests to convictions, personnel hours worked to incidents handled, vehicles to personnel, personnel to workload, error rate to reports, and response time to calls. Mapping allows research in specific neighborhoods and individual programs that target specific problems. Single- and dual-dimension auditing and experimental research designs are essential to the evaluation of police programs and strategies. Such quantitative research has been used over the past 30 years by researchers to compare such strategies as one- and two-officer patrols, proactive and reactive patrolling, vehicle and walking patrols, and traditional policing and community policing arrangements. Although the findings from such studies have stimulated discussion and changes throughout the police field, they have failed to stimulate police officials to recognize the potential value of quantitative research as an instrument of information collection for control purposes.

At a more basic level, however, the police administrator should constantly review statistics that are generated by the normal activities of the department. Statistics relating to such area clearance rates, calls answered, arrests, response times, and citations issued provide the administrator a fairly accurate picture of the department's productivity. The administrator should watch for shifts and drastic changes in these statistics. Accounting for such changes should be a high priority, since they might signal that a problem exists. In essence, these statistics can serve as an early warning system for the executive.

Unfortunately, the potential of quantitative research is yet to be grasped by most police administrators. It is usually viewed as an expensive exercise that far too often produces embarrassing results for the police agency, documenting the failure of strategies that have been advocated by police officials. There is a need to better integrate the techniques of audits and research into management processes. These techniques ultimately will enhance a police department's productivity.

Taking Corrective Action

The final stage in the control process is corrective action, which consists of the supervisory or management measures undertaken to bring unacceptable conditions in line with standards and expectations. It is aimed at rectifying impediments to optimum organizational performance. Basically, when a defect is observed or identified, management must take corrective action as quickly as possible. If the defect is not corrected, irreparable damage to the department might occur or the behavior may become institutionalized.

The first step in the corrective action process is to ensure that the problem is fully identified and understood. Sometimes managers treat symptoms of problems rather than dealing with the actual problems. For example, if an officer is using an abnormally large amount of sick time, the problem might be with the officer or it might be indicative of improper supervision. In other words, the officer might be reacting to negative working conditions. In some instances, the department might have unreasonable expectations. For example, officers are able to perform the preliminary investigation on a large number of simple cases such as burglaries or larcenies relative to cases such as rapes or robberies. Essentially, the types of cases should be considered in determining the caseload for officers. It is extremely important that the problem be completely understood before taking action.

Guyot identified a three-step process for problem identification: "(1) circle the problem, consult people and records which have information about the problem; (2) write a clear statement of the problem; and (3) analyze the problem, seeking out multiple solutions" (1977:324). If such a procedure is used, line units will be more successful in attempting to correct problems.

Once the problem is fully understood, a plan of action must be developed. As Guyot noted, all alternatives should be explored in developing the action plan, with positive alternatives being given first consideration. For example, an abusive officer's behavior might better be corrected through retraining than through taking disciplinary action. The problem and alternatives should be discussed in detail with the officers involved. Such candid discussions provide better information about the problem and proposed solution and, generally, a commitment from the officers involved.

PRODUCTIVITY

All successful organizations, public or private, must be able to provide quality goods and services at a cost affordable to the consumer. When a private sector business fails to emphasize quality or to provide its product at a reasonable cost, the public may not buy its goods, causing bankruptcy or some other drastic measure. Free market competition eventually forces businesses that desire to be high achievers to provide quality products or services at a competitive price. To this end, managers of such a company constantly compare methods of manufacturing, measure public perceptions of the company and its products, recruit the best possible personnel, and generally attempt to continually improve the company's ability to compete in the marketplace.

Within the public sector, and particularly in policing, this keen competition and search for new, innovative, cost-effective procedures has not been seen. The supply of governmental services largely has been idiosyncratic, depending on the availability of funding and the political atmosphere. Today, community policing dominates police services. Community policing emphasizes problem solving and the building of community partnerships. Police departments that emphasize community policing must also continue to provide a wide array of services that are associated with traditional policing. The modern police department therefore is responsible for innumerable services to the community, which complicates the measurement of productivity.

Productivity Defined

The National Commission on Police Productivity defined *productivity* as "the return for a given unit of input" (1973:1). To increase productivity means to get a greater return for a given investment. Productivity is the relationship between the resources used and the results obtained. Resources include personnel, capital, technology, machinery, land, energy, or anything that can be combined by the application of managerial intelligence into an end product of some kind. Results of such efforts can be goods or services (Kuper, 1975). A general indication of the level of productivity for a particular police department would be the ratio of outputs produced (services provided to the public, criminals apprehended, and the amount of crime prevented) to the resources expended (operating budget, use of property and equipment, etc.).

According to the National Commission on Police Productivity (1973), increased police productivity can be achieved in four general ways.

First, increasing productivity means improving current practices to the best level known, to get better performance without a proportionate increase in cost. Here the concern is to do things better, for example, to reduce the length or number of reports patrol officers must complete, to reduce officers' court time through planned scheduling of officers and their court days, or to change supervisory leadership styles to motivate officers and increase their productivity. Police administrators must systematically review what the department is doing and how it is done to determine if improvements can be made.

Second, increasing productivity means allocating resources to activities that give the highest return for each dollar spent. Police personnel must be assigned to programs that most effectively achieve departmental objectives. For example, in the Differential Police Response Program civilians are trained to take police reports over the telephone when the situation does not require the presence of a sworn officer and the citizen requesting services is satisfied with this approach. This procedure substantially reduces a department's workload and allows for the reallocation of resources. Police administrators must not only prioritize goals and objectives but also examine and place priorities on how goals and objectives will be achieved.

Third, given the uncertainties of police work, increasing productivity means increasing the probability that a given goal will be met. Police managers must set priorities and concentrate on achieving them. This is extremely difficult considering the numerous, constantly changing responsibilities facing police departments, but it can be achieved through careful planning and program implementation. It means that the department must focus on individual problems rather than generally responding to each new problem or issue. For example, if a tavern has a high number of calls, the police should take action to reduce the calls. Intensive enforcement or liquor license suspension might be effective. If the problem with the tavern is resolved, the department is productive since officers can spend their time on other activities.

Finally, increasing productivity in police work means making the most of the police personnel's talent. Hersey and Blanchard (1982) reported that research shows that employees can work at approximately 20 to 30 percent of their potential without being fired! Employees' productivity can be increased to 80 to 90 percent of their potential through proper management practices. Management must work to develop a work environment that motivates officers and implement a management structure that goes beyond officers viewing their jobs solely as "call taking" or "case managing."

To this end, Hyde (1985) developed the notion of the "productivity environment." Managers have identified *inadequate resources, inappropriate organizational structure,* and *insufficient motivation* as the three most common impediments to productivity, and these were discussed in detail in previous chapters. Inadequate resources and organizational structure typically contribute to motivation problems. If people are to be productive, they must work in an environment that is conducive to performance. The police department is a system and all three of the above areas must be continuously addressed if the department is to be productive.

Uses for Productivity Measures

In discussing planning in Chapter 13 we detail the need to collect information to monitor programs. These measures can serve as *productivity indexes,* which are defined as those measures that the police executive collects and uses to determine the ratio of outputs to input. The prudent manager usually develops some measures by which to monitor the personnel and programs within the command. Hatry (1979) identified several general uses for productivity indexes:

1. By identifying current levels of productivity, measurement can indicate the existence of particular problems.
2. When productivity is measured over time, measurement can indicate the progress or lack of progress in improving productivity.
3. When collected by geographical areas within a jurisdiction, productivity data can help identify areas in particular need of attention.
4. Measurement can serve as a basis for evaluating specific activities. Measurement may indicate activities that need to be modified or personnel who need special attention, such as training or selection practices.
5. Measurements of existing productivity can provide agencies with the information necessary to set productivity targets. Actual performance can subsequently be compared to the targets to indicate degree of accomplishment, for example the stated goal of burglary reduction of 35 percent or reducing drug trafficking in a neighborhood.
6. Performance incentives for both managerial and nonmanagerial employees might be established.
7. Measurement of data can be used for in-depth productivity studies on ways to improve specific aspects of productivity, such as the appropriateness of new programs over old ones.
8. Productivity measurement information can be a major way to account for government operations to the public. Accountability is a growing concern that refers not only to the legal use of funds but also to the broader question of what is actually being accomplished by government operations.

The net effect of using productivity indexes is to improve the ability of the department to serve the public. Once developed, they aid the police manager in controlling the activities and operation of the department and in providing better services to the public. The development of productivity measures cannot be haphazard but must be systematic, examining all aspects of the police organization.

Productivity studies have led to changes in a number of departments. For example, the Augusta, Georgia, Police Department now contracts for its police car maintenance at a substantial saving. The Kentucky State Police uses case screening and closes cases with little probability of being solved early so that personnel can spend more time on cases with a higher probability of being solved. The Cottage Grove, Oregon, Police Department uses volunteer senior citizens trained in crime prevention to mark citizens' property and recommend security measures. The Scottsdale, Arizona, Police Department uses police assistants to perform a number of the routine tasks that higher-paid police officers were once required to perform. The San Bernardino, California, Police Department contracts jail and booking operations with a private security agency.

Measuring Productivity

It is more difficult for public organizations to define and measure productivity than it is for private corporations. Private corporations generally produce a product or service that is tangible and more easily measured in terms of output versus input. Private corporations have outputs such as televisions, automobiles, toys, computers, Internet services, and books. On the other hand, public organizations produce intangible services such as clean streets, assistance to the needy, and security in the city.

Police organizations that measure productivity are able to identify problem areas and priorities that need improved efforts. One traditional measure of police productivity is the Uniform Crime Reports (UCRs) compiled by the Federal Bureau of Investigation. Police departments from across the nation collect crime-related information and report it to the FBI for inclusion in the UCRs. Congress frequently refers to these reports to determine how effective the nation's police forces are in combating crime. If there are drastic increases in crime rates, additional resources are sometimes made available to the police. Of course, crime is only one dimension of the police role (as discussed in Chapter 2), and others such as the provision of services, citizen satisfaction with the police, and maintaining order also must be measured.

After deciding to measure police productivity, an administrator must decide which indexes to collect. That is, whose productivity will be measured and how? Typically, every individual, unit, and activity within the department would be measured. Indexes should be developed for every activity so that the administrator can evaluate and adjust departmental operations. Thus, within a typical police department, productivity can be measured at several levels.

Traditional Measures of Police Productivity

Productivity is an issue that permeates the department and thus can be measured at a number of levels. The following sections outline how officers, units, and departments traditionally have been assessed in terms of productivity.

Individual Officer Productivity.　Administrators and supervisors alike have a need to examine the productivity of individual officers to ensure that unit and departmental goals are being accomplished. Some officers are more productive than others are. Walsh (1985), in a study of patrol officer felony arrests, found that approximately 10 percent of the officers made approximately 57 percent of the felony arrests. Obviously, there are vast differences in the productivity rates of individual officers. These differences may be due to the characteristics of the work situation (officer assigned to a high-crime/activity area as opposed to a low-crime/activity area), or they may be due to officer characteristics. A commander should examine the average response times for all officers, number of citations issued, number of police calls for service answered, and number of felony and misdemeanor arrests for officers. This is not to say that disciplinary action should be taken against those officers who are below average. However, if the average number of citations per month is

15 and a particular officer consistently writes 2 or 3 per month (well below the average), some action is needed. These types of statistics are useful to the commander in deciding on training programs; career development programs; counseling; and, sometimes, disciplinary action.

The traditional method of evaluating an officer's performance has been the performance appraisal. Here abstract traits such as dependability, demeanor, cooperation, citizen contacts, and driving ability are measured. These are subjective measures made by supervisors who may not possess enough information to make accurate judgments. How an officer performs at roll call may be entirely different from performance at a domestic violence call. Moreover, such measures generally do not relate to actual performance; they relate more to intrinsic qualities of the officers that only indicate how the officer should be able to perform.

Performance appraisals generally have failed to measure performance and increase productivity. Edwards (1983) noted that the performance appraisal process has become so entangled in legal restrictions and bureaucratic red tape that it is quite ineffective. Performance appraisals remain abstract and have little effect on officer or agency performance. Police administrators must work to devise performance systems that will change officer behavior and channel their efforts toward departmental goals.

More accurate productivity indexes must be used if the police manager is to monitor officers' activities. The following measures are among those that can be utilized (Hatry, 1979; Hirsch and Riccio, 1974; National Commission on Police Productivity, 1973):

1. *Time spent at work.* One important measure of individual officer productivity is time at work. That is, if individual officers take an inordinate amount of sick time, they are not productive. When officers or groups of officers exhibit high sick time usage, the manager must investigate its causes. Causes usually include job dissatisfaction, poor working conditions, or personal problems such as alcohol abuse or domestic problems. Regardless of cause, management should investigate and take corrective action.

2. *Arrest rates/citations issued.* Patrol commanders frequently use these rates to compare the productivity of their subordinate officers. However, when using these measures the police manager should exercise caution to avoid giving the appearance of establishing quotas. Officers working different areas will have different arrest rates due to variations in workloads and calls for services. Also, officers working different hours—day shift compared to night shift—will exhibit varying arrest rates. Even though it is difficult to compare individual officers' levels of productivity, supervisors should inquire into those cases in which officers have low levels of arrests or citations.

3. *Percentage of arrests that lead to convictions.* One important measure is the percentage of arrests that result in convictions. A low conviction rate may indicate an officer is making poor-quality arrests or the officer needs

skills development in the area of investigation or court presentation. However, the supervisor must realize that some types of cases are more easily investigated and presented in court than others, and this must be taken into consideration.

4. *Citizen complaints against officers.* This measure evaluates the public's acceptance of police actions. When complaints are filed, supervisors must take immediate action to investigate their validity. Citizens frequently complain about officers not because they do something wrong but because of the way they performed some task. For example, an officer's manner may appear to be gruff or insensitive when dealing with a citizen's problems. Officers should constantly be counseled and trained in dealing with the public to overcome such problems. Moreover, officers who handle large numbers of disturbance or fight calls will probably receive more complaints than other officers.

These four measures are among those most frequently used to evaluate officer productivity. The supervisor will usually develop measures that match the task at hand. There are no limitations on what to measure; the supervisor must only ensure that indexes comprehensively measure what subordinates do. Retaining accurate information on officer activities is an important control mechanism to the supervisor and manager. For example, the Ocala, Florida, Police Department applied management by objectives to the beat level. The officer and supervisor confer on objectives and how they are measured. This type of management plan not only helps direct officers toward departmental goals and motivates them, but it also allows for the implementation of a productivity measurement system that has broad-based agreement.

In the Community Patrol Officer Program (CPOP) initiated in New York City, supervisors monitor where officers go and whether they spend their time appropriately and productively. They establish monthly work plans with each officer and agree on priority problems the officer will focus on and the strategy and tactics to be used. The work plans are reviewed regularly to determine if progress toward solving problems is being made and if officers are doing what they are supposed to do. Productivity measures in CPOP include identifying and interacting with residents; amount of time spent in different homes, stores, offices, and at community meetings; number of people enlisted to help correct problems in the community; and success in marshaling police and nonpolice resources to deal with a problem on the beat. The number of officers' arrests and summonses was not considered a useful indicator of productivity and effectiveness for CPOP officers (Weisburd, McElroy, and Hardyman, 1988). These examples show that productivity measures vary depending on the organizational emphasis.

The most effective way to develop and retain individual officer productivity information is through a standardized reporting system. This is usually accomplished through some type of officer daily or weekly activity report, as discussed previously. Officers record their activities on these reports, which are used to compile monthly and yearly statistical summaries. Figure 12–3 is an

Figure 12–3
Daily field activity report.

DAILY FIELD ACTIVITY REPORT

1. OFFICER'S NAME, RADIO NUMBER	2. DATE	3. DAY	4. VEHICLE	5. TTL HRS	6. REMARKS
KING R.R. 202	11-14-78	TUE	6876	11	NO SPARE TIRE - VEHICLE NOT SERVICED

	7. TIME REC.	8. TIME CLEAR	9. MIN USED	10. SRC	11. LOCATION	12. TYPE OF ACTIVITY	NAME	OR SUMMONS
A		1700	15		GCPD	ROLL CALL/VEHICLE INSPECTION		
B	1710	1750	40	DIS	4111 S. BANNOCK	PRIOR BURGLARY OFFENSE REPORT	JONES	OR 79-316472
C	1803	1812	09	OFF	TABOR AND CHEROKEE	TRAFFIC STOP/COLC LIC# PP6171 IMPROPER TURN SUMMONS	KESSLER	TS T1001
D	1825	1840	15		LAMPLIGHTER	CODE 7 COFFEE		
E	1908	1920	12	OFF	3500 S. DELEWARE	SUSPICIOUS SUBJECT F.I. CARD	BARNES	1 F.I.
F	1955	2010	45	DIS	701 W. KANSAS KING SOOPERS	ADULT SHOPLIFTER O.R. PENIAL SUMMONS MISDM ARREST	WALLACE	22631 79-31650
G	2025	2157	70	F	GCPD JAIL	BOOKING PRISONER	WALLACE	
H	2250	2245	15	DIS	ST. CATHERINES HOSPITAL-E.R.	DISTURBANCE ASSIST UNIT 201		ASSIST 79-31680
I	2250	0010	80	DIS	4219 S. 4TH	DISTURBANCE - MENTAL CASE STOOD BY FOR AREA MENTAL HEALTH WORKER - INCIDENT RPT	SHERWOOD	79IR-316818
J	0015	0025	10	I	MENTAL HEALTH CENTER	TRANSPORT SUBJECT TO MENTAL HEALTH CENTER	SHERWOOD	
K	0105	0115	10	SPV	STEVENS PARK	MEET SGT. JONES I CK REPORTS 2-O.R. 1-I.R. 1-P.S. 1-T.S. 1-F.I. 1-M.A.	JONES Jones	
L	0120	0200	40	DIS	MAIN AND PINE	PROPERTY DAMAGE ACCIDENT (SPV ASSISTED) DUI ARREST – ACCIDENT REPORT-SUMMONS	WELLS	572632 79-36195
M	0200	0205	5	L	TO G.C.P.D.	TRANSPORT PRISONER	WELLS	
N	0205	0400	175	L	G.C.P.D.-JAIL	BOOKING AND PROCESSING PRISONER	WELLS	
O		0400				END OF WATCH R.R. King		
P								

	SOP	WT	TTL
13. OFFENSE RPT	2	5	10
14. INCIDENT RPT	1	3	3
15. H&R ACCIDENT RPT	0	5	
16. P.P ACCIDENT RPT	0	3	3
17. ACCIDENT RPT	1	4	4
18. ACCIDENT SUMMONS	0	4	
19. RADAR SUMMONS	0	3	
20. TRAFFIC SUMMONS	1	4	4
21. PENAL SUMMONS	1	3	3
22. PARKING SUMMONS	0	1	
23. WARNING SUMMONS	0	1	
24. WARRANT ARREST	0	5	
25. FELONY ARREST	0	20	
26. MISDMR ARREST	1	4	4
27. PETTY ARREST	0	3	
28. D.U.I. ARREST	1	5	5
29. DETOX	0	4	
30. MISC. DETENTION	0	4	
31. F.I.	1	2	2
32. DEF VEHICLE	0	2	2
33. TOTAL			35
34. ASSIGNED CALLS	4	1	4
35. ASSIGNED ASSISTS	1	1	1
36. OFF. INITIATED	2	3	6
SPV. NAME Sgt. Jones			

465

example of an officer's daily report as used by the Englewood, Colorado, Police Department. The Englewood form differs from the St. Michaels form in that it contains a point system for activities.

First, the form compiles the officer's activity for the day. The supervisor or manager can examine officers' reports and quickly determine productivity levels for any given category of police activity. Second, the form contains a weighting system whereby each category of activity is given a certain number of points, for example DUI arrests =5 points. The points represent the degree of importance or priority placed on an activity. The Kentucky State Police uses a similar scheme, but the weighting system is based on the average time it takes an officer to accomplish a given task, for example, an officer is given 15 minutes (or points) for writing a traffic citation, or 60 minutes for investigating a property damage accident. Thus in Englewood the manager examines an officer's total points, whereas the Kentucky State Police manager will examine the percentage of an officer's time working in relation to patrol time.

There are distinct advantages to using such productivity monitoring systems. First, officers and supervisors must focus on the complete range of police activities and responsibilities as opposed to one or two categories of police work. Including all types of activity on the form serves as a reminder of the range of police responsibilities. Second, managers can exert a degree of control over officers through the examination of periodic summaries. Supervisors are able to identify officers whose productivity deviates from the productivity of other officers in the unit in terms of total activity and those officers who tend to reconcentrate their efforts on other work areas or activities. Finally, officers are more goal-directed because the form designates what is expected of them. Managers can manipulate goals by increasing or decreasing the relative weights assigned to the various police activities. They can cause officers to focus on specific problems by increasing the points given for these activities.

When constructing a daily activity monitoring system, administrators must ensure that all types of activity are included. If some activities are omitted, the officers will tend not to perform them. Officers will become "credit conscious," attempting to maintain a satisfactory level of points. Activity is easily monitored with computer-aided dispatch systems and records management systems that are fairly common in police departments today. Departments are able to generate reports showing the progress of all officers and units.

Individual Unit Productivity. Unit productivity is monitored using the officers' daily reports. Commanders can compile weekly, monthly, and annual summaries of their unit's activity through this reporting system. These reports can then be compared with reports covering previous periods of time to determine changes in units of work performed and demands for services. These comparisons provide the unit commander with a better understanding of work trends and staffing needs.

As noted above, individual officer daily reporting systems can be devised for every unit in a police department. Typically, managers utilize these systems in patrol but not in specialized units. The commander of criminal investigations, for example, should use a system to monitor cases worked, cases cleared by arrest, reports filed, witnesses interviewed, stolen property recovered, court presentations, and convictions. The commander of community relations similarly should record information on the number of public speaking engagements, businesses and residents signed up for operation identification, tours of police facilities, and business security checks. Each commander should comprehensively monitor the activities of the unit. Since chiefs delegate responsibility for unit operation to the commanders, the unit commanders should at least have input into if not direct control over the development of the system.

This command monitoring system is most important in ensuring that the unit and the department are goal-effective. The unit commander can take unit summaries and compare them to unit and departmental goals and objectives as well as summaries for previous periods. Officers' activities must be goal-directed. The unit commander can make changes in the allocation of staff and assignments using these comparisons between unit activity and unit objectives. The commander must ensure that the unit is providing services that are necessary to the public and fit into the scheme of departmental responsibilities.

Productivity of Dissimilar Units. The chief and other top administrators may want to compare the productivity of particular units in dissimilar divisions. For example, the assistant chief in charge of operations may want to compare the productivity of the individual patrol shifts or watches with the productivity of some of the criminal investigation units. This is particularly important when personnel allocation decisions are made. Also, since numerous units are involved in achieving the same goal (e.g., detectives and patrol officers are involved in repressing or eliminating crime), the commander may want to evaluate the productivity of the various units within the command before assigning new programs to one of the operational units.

This task is difficult since the goals and activities across dissimilar units are usually totally different. For example, as discussed above, productivity measures for detective units are different from those used in patrol, making comparison of the two units a complicated process. When such comparisons are desired, the basic productivity measure of time can be used (efficiency). Daily logs divulge patrol officers' in-service time (responding to and answering calls for service and self-initiated activities) and detectives' uncommitted time (the time they are not investigating a case). Administrators should attempt to ensure that all officers, regardless of unit assignment, have about the same percentage of uncommitted time.

Measures of Departmental Productivity. The sum of the numerous productivity measurements compiled for units within a department constitutes a measure of how well the department is performing. Administrators must constantly monitor their departments' successes and failures so that adjustments can be made to ensure that the department meets the needs of the community. Information gained as a result of the monitoring is used in strategic and tactical planning.

It is extremely difficult to measure the productivity of a particular police department since there are no standards for comparison. Generally, departments compare their productivity indexes with other comparable departments in the region or with previous years' statistics. Such comparisons are not totally accurate since no two cities are exactly alike, and the population makeup, economic conditions, and other social factors within a given city change from one year to the next. Thus such comparisons should be considered in light of possible changes and differences in populations. Moreover, the goals and objectives of a given department may change from one year to another, making such comparisons inadequate. Regardless, the following are some of the more frequently used indexes:

1. *Number of police officers per 1,000 population.* Police and government administrators frequently compare the level of personnel or budgets with other cities or previous years. Personnel requirements, however, cannot be based on population. It is quite possible for one city with a 250,000 population to be adequately served by a forced of 300 officers, whereas another city of the same size would be inadequately served by a police force of 400 officers. Personnel requirements are based on need, and need is usually determined by crime, socioeconomic, and demographic factors. Subsequently, when such comparisons are made, the results should be used with caution.

2. *Crime rates.* Crime rates have occasionally been used and compared among cities in an effort to measure the productivity of the police. Again, crime rates are unique for individual cities since crime is caused by socioeconomic conditions and therefore should used with caution. Administrators also examine crime rates from one year to another. Since most police activities are seasonal, month-to-month comparisons are not always valid. Populations change and shift yearly, and the comparison of present crime statistics with those of previous years should be used cautiously.

3. *Apprehension rates.* An important productivity index that a chief should monitor, especially for felony cases, is apprehension rates. Sudden changes in these rates usually indicate a need to reexamine policies or procedures. Any significant decrease in these measures should be fully investigated. Additionally, these measures can be used to evaluate policy changes. If a department moves from the use of specialized detectives to patrol teams to investigate crime, apprehension rates for the department can be used to compare the effectiveness of the old and new procedures.

4. *Citizen perceptions of security and satisfaction with the police.* An important measure of police productivity is how well the police are able to project a positive image and make the citizens feel that their city is safe. If people feel unsafe and their freedom of movement is inhibited, then police productivity must be improved in terms of apprehension of criminals and repression of crime.

5. *Average response time for calls for service.* Even though research indicates that response time has little impact on apprehension rates (Pate, Ferrara, Bowers, and Lorence, 1976; Spelman and Brown, 1996), it is important that police officers respond promptly to all calls. Of course, response time to felonies and injured-person calls should be as short as possible, but response to routine police matters should also be accomplished without undue delay. The public frequently evaluates the police on how fast they respond, rather than what the officers do once on the scene. Response times can be reduced to a minimum through proper allocation and distribution of personnel.

These measures represent an effort to quantify departmental productivity. However, they are inadequate since they do not effectively measure how well the department serves the community, and they examine a limited number of police activities. A more robust method of measuring a department's productivity would be a subjective examination of how well the department achieves its goals. For example, the production of traffic citations is of little use to the police department unless the citations are contributing to a goal—reduced accidents. Therefore, each unit commander must examine unit goals, set work priorities, and ensure that officers' activities are goal-directed as opposed to being activity-directed. Productivity management is an integral part of operational planning.

Contemporary Measures of Police Productivity

Measures of productivity examine the police organization at the micro level. That is, productivity is measured by examining the many "pieces" that compose the whole. The traditional view assumes that the many pieces constitute an accurate picture of the department, and as long as officers and units are productive, the department will be efficient and effective. Although the foregoing measures are informative and helpful, they do not always provide a true picture of the department's productivity.

Spelman (1988) compared traditional measures of police productivity to "bean counting." He notes that traditional measures evaluate police activity but do not communicate how productive a department is. Narcotics arrests illustrate his point. Traditional policing measured a narcotics unit's productivity by the number of arrests and convictions and the amount of drugs seized. Consequently, the narcotics unit would focus on generating arrests and seizing drugs. The unit would essentially net as many arrests as possible. Strategically, however, this policy likely had little impact on the narcotics problem. The arrests would be interspersed throughout the jurisdiction, and there were always other drug dealers to take their place. Community policing and problem solving have caused the police to focus on a problem area and to alleviate the problem, as opposed to generating contacts and arrests. In the case of drugs, the police concentrate on a particular drug market using a variety of tactics until the problem has been significantly reduced or eliminated. Concentrating on a geographical area may not generate as many arrests as traditional strategies, but it does result in specific areas having fewer drug and crime problems. When the police concentrate on problems, rather than bean counting, they eventually will have a more profound impact on crime and disorder in the community.

Thus a better measure of police productivity is how well the police were able to respond to specific problems in the community. Did police activity improve the quality of life in the community? Alpert and Moore (1998) note that the police must devise and implement specific, comprehensive strategies for each problem the department identifies in the community. Such strategies cut across a number of police operational units and represent a comprehensive attack on problems. The ability of a department to solve problems, regardless of their nature, is perhaps one of the most effective measures of police productivity.

To this end, Spelman and Eck (1987) identified five degrees of effectiveness the police should consider: (1) totally eliminating the problem, (2) reducing the number of incidents (crime and disorder) that occur as a result of the problem, (3) reducing the seriousness of the incidents, (4) implementing police procedures that more effectively handle incidents, and (5) "co-actively" dealing with the problem by enlisting the assistance of an agency that is better suited to deal with the problem. Essentially, some problems cannot be solved, but the police can take action that will reduce the problem. The point here, however, is that departments must articulate a goal for each problem identified, and the goal should point to a desired level of performance (what constitutes success).

A second overarching measure of police productivity is citizen satisfaction with police services. Although citizen satisfaction or approval of the police was studied for a number of years by academics, it really did not affect police thinking until after the Flint, Michigan, Foot Patrol Studies (Trojanowicz, Kappeler, and Gaines, 2001). The Flint studies revealed that fear of crime and satisfaction with the police, not crime per se, had a major impact on citizens' lives. Also, when the police attend to fear of crime and citizen satisfaction, they ultimately will be able to deal more effectively with crime problems. Bayley (1994) postulates that the police may possess more ability to affect "subjective" measures of crime such as fear than crime itself. The idea of attending to citizen satisfaction with police services is consistent with the "broken windows" perspective of policing (Kelling and Coles, 1996). The fabric of society is undermined through the accumulation of disorder and crime, and the police must deal with the *effects* of disorder and crime (citizen perceptions) as well as with crime. For these reasons, it is important for the police to monitor and consider citizen attitudes toward the police and crime.

Citizen surveys are fairly widespread today. For example, they are a part of the National Crime Survey that is distributed to a cross section of American households, and numerous departments perform them regularly. These surveys can tell a department where problems are and what kinds of problems exist. Departments can customize surveys for different neighborhoods. For example, departments can query residents in public housing or an area that has

Figure 12–4

Management concerns related to productivity.

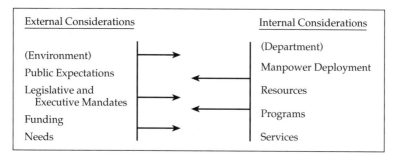

a gang problem. Most surveys indicate that traffic and disorder, rather than crime, dominate citizens' perceptions of problems. Since citizens are the consumers of police services, the police should attempt to ensure that they provide those services that best reduce citizen concerns and problems.

Improving Police Productivity

Improving police productivity is a difficult task for the police manager. The problem is that there are no simple answers to the difficult questions. Productivity is a complex issue requiring complex planning and managerial actions to make improvements. Numberous internal and external factors that affect a department's productivity. Figure 12–4 depicts the complex nature of productivity.

A police department is a large, complex conglomeration of people, units, and activities that, at times, is most perplexing even to the most skilled police managers. Advances in productivity require that attention be given to all aspects of the department. The sheer volume of the work necessary to have an impact on productivity can intimidate the manager. Thus the manager must search for some natural starting places when attacking the problem.

Morgan (1975) identified four criteria that should be used to identify where productivity can be improved. First, he notes that police managers should give special consideration to "operations that involve large numbers of employees who perform routine and repetitive tasks" (p. 135). For example, police officers perform a number of routine tasks such as directing traffic, investigating minor property damage automobile accidents, and taking reports. A number of police departments have devised strategies to perform these functions at a reduced cost. Departments have hired police assistants to handle such routine tasks more efficiently. Essentially the police assistants are civilians who are paid at a lower rate than sworn officers and perform many tasks that were historically assigned to patrol officers. Several departments have hired retired officers who want to work part-time as investigative assistants without police powers. They perform a number of the case preparation activities such as record checks before the case is assigned to an investigator. Some departments have them perform background investigations for police applicants. Departments across the country now take minor reports by telephone as opposed to sending an officer to the scene to take a report. Programs such as these allow a department to reduce the number of officers or not have to hire additional officers. The police manager must examine all police activities that are routine and repetitive to determine whether they can be accomplished at a lower cost or if they are even necessary.

Functions that require a large number of hours are another area the manager can study for productivity improvement. Personnel must be allocated based on need. Approximately 60 percent of a police agency's personnel is generally allocated to patrol. More personnel can be made available if productivity is increased by using civilians, eliminating clerical work, reducing court time through efficient scheduling, reducing excessive time on patrol, using crime analysis and crime mapping to direct patrol activities, and reducing response time. It is important for the police manager to examine what officers are doing in a particular assignment. Patrol officers spend an inordinate amount of time performing administrative tasks, and if these tasks could be reduced or streamlined, then officers could spend a greater proportion of their time on more essential police tasks.

Police managers should closely examine functions that normally result in work backlogs. These backlogs may have a significant impact on the effectiveness of other operations and outcomes. The backlog of physical evidence examination by lab technicians affects detectives' ability to clear cases. A number of crime labs report that they are not notified when cases are plea-bargained or settled out of court. The result is that technicians examine a substantial amount of evidence that is never used in court. An effective notification system would reduce lab technicians' workload and allow technicians to analyze court-bound evidence on a more timely basis.

Another example of backlogging is the number of cases assigned to detectives for investigation. Backlogs of cases assigned to detectives force detectives to give only a minimal amount of time to each case. There is substantial research that shows that a department's clearance rate may improve through case screening, where detectives do not investigate cases that have a low probability of being solved (Brandl and Frank, 1994). Criminal investigation managers can reduce workload by effectively assigning cases and ensuring that detectives concentrate their efforts on those cases that have a probability of being solved.

The final area that Morgan (1975) identified as having great potential for productivity improvement is high unit costs. For example, drug units frequently request the purchase of highly sophisticated equipment that is quite expensive relative to other police equipment. The police manager should constantly evaluate such requests to determine if they are cost-effective. Moreover, agencies in the same region could share both the cost of the equipment and its use. Training is another area that necessitates examination. Departments send officers to expensive specialized training courses when it may be less expensive to hire trainers to come to the department to train several officers or to develop online training courses. All expenditures should be examined to determine their appropriateness in relation to the total operation of the department.

Strategies for Improving Productivity

Although all aspects of the productivity issue should be examined, there are strategies that the police manager should consider. Holzer (1973) identified five strategies or catalysts that may be used to enhance productivity: productivity bargaining, capital investments, awareness of innovation, management audit, and principles of management.

Basically, *productivity bargaining* refers to "negotiating increased productivity with police employee unions or fraternal organizations" (Holzer, 1973:464). The police manager cannot afford to make strategic decisions without giving due consideration to rank-and-file police officers. Police unions and other employee groups within the department have a recognizable impact on police productivity. The police manager must gain the cooperation of employees rather than embroiling them in controversy. The police manager must sell programs to officers before they are implemented. This ultimately will lead to more productivity and less turmoil in the department.

A prime example here is police traffic units. Many of these units have informal quotas where traffic officers write a limited number of citations. Examining the dispatch logs on where and when traffic citations are issued evidences this fact. We often find that traffic officers write most if not all of their tickets within a two- to three-hour span of time in essentially the same location. The remaining part of the shift becomes unproductive. Along these same lines, some traffic officers concentrate solely on producing traffic citations. These officers fail to run warrant checks or perform field investigations to investigate possible crimes, because it detracts from their informal quota of tickets. All units in a police department have idiosyncrasies that can be addressed to improve productivity.

Where possible, the police administrator should use principled negotiations when dealing with unions and employee associations. In conducting *principled negotiations,* the negotiators attempt to remove personalities from the negotiations and focus on issues (Covey, 1990). This is not always possible because negotiations seldom focus on one issue; other issues and programs often become embroiled in the negotiations. When executives cannot gain compliance through principled negotiations, as Burpo, DeLord, and Shannon (1997) advise, negotiations with unions should be quid pro quo. Here, management should make union gains in salaries and benefits contingent on commitment to departmental programs and increased employee productivity. Both sides should compromise and work for an outcome that benefits the department and the public.

Perhaps a useful example of productivity bargaining is how a number of departments are addressing police officer physical fitness. Police administrators have long recognized that police officers who are physically fit are more productive. They take less sick time and are more physically capable of performing a variety of police activities. A number of police departments have negotiated mandatory physical fitness standards for officers in return for the department's providing up-to-date physical fitness facilities or paying officers' membership fees in health clubs. Such an arrangement is not overly costly and results in fewer injuries to officers, reduced sick time, and an increase in officer productivity.

Capital investment plays an important role in productivity. Police work is increasingly becoming more technical, and departments must acquire the necessary equipment to be productive. Today, computers are playing an important role in resource allocation, crime trend and pattern identification, and productivity monitoring. Portable robbery alarms and high-tech surveillance equipment can be used to replace several patrol officers in high-crime areas. The police manager must examine needs and, where possible, supplement traditional methods of policing with automation to reduce costs. As technology becomes available, the police should consider its application.

Another strategy used today to increase productivity is the *management audit*. A management audit differs from a financial audit in that the management audit focuses on the efficiency and effectiveness of operations in terms of productivity. The audit usually examines how personnel are allocated, management style, distribution of rank, task assignments within the department, and the reporting system. Usually, but not necessarily, an outside independent agent performs the management audit. This outside agent can provide the police manager with fresh ideas and new perspectives on how the department can be better operated. The department staff inspector is an internal agent who can perform this function on a routine basis to ensure that operations are progressing as planned. Regardless of how it is performed, the management audit is an important management process that enables management to monitor and improve operations.

Finally, the sound application of *principles of management* enhances productivity. The importance of organization, management, leadership, and motivation was discussed in previous chapters. Management is a factor that greatly affects productivity. It can either enhance or detract from a department's performance. Therefore, the police manager cannot depend on traditional methods of management but must look for better, more appropriate management practices. This is especially true in an era of community policing when officers are expected to perform a wider variety of tasks in the community.

The five strategies to improve productivity represent a philosophy that the police manager must incorporate into departmental planning. If managers within a department do not proactively seek ways of improvement, then the department becomes stagnant, and stagnation leads to a situation in which the department is ineffective in meeting community needs.

Summary

Organizational control and the management of police productivity are two of the most critical activities undertaken by administrators and supervisors. They are also two of the most complex and abstract administrative functions. This chapter provided guidance on the executive's role, the process of control, the potential dysfunctional consequences of excessive or inadequate control, and how productivity may be managed. These functions are central to police administration because they conceptually equate to how the police interact with the public.

The executive's role in control and productivity is one of providing leadership and guidance regarding what to control, what is important for the organization to achieve, and how the organization fits into the broader framework of society. The chief and administrative staff are directly involved in control by means of the exception principle; otherwise, the chief delegates control to managers and first-line supervisors who perform nearly all the control functions.

The administrator must also maintain control over the control process itself. Otherwise, the control process can become an instrument for creating the very problems it was designed to correct. Employees cannot achieve organizational goals if they expend too much time and energy in activities designed to provide operational control. Neither can the chief expect morale and motivation to remain high under these conditions. Too much control implies distrust of employees. The executive must balance the need for control with the need for an organizational climate that is challenging and motivating.

Improving police productivity represents a philosophy to which every police manager should adhere. Every police department is expected to provide more services than the budget allows. Therefore, the police manager must learn to obtain the greatest results for the dollar spent. All aspects of the department should be examined when attempting to improve productivity, and efforts to make improvements should be systematic, touching all parts of the department.

Study Questions

1. Why is the concept "management by exception" so critical to administrative control in a police department?

2. What are the sources of the various standards and expectations used for control purposes in police departments and why are they important?

3. What are the functions and processes for line and staff inspections?

4. What are audits and how do they assist the police administrator in controlling the police organization?

5. Define "productivity" as it relates to policing.

6. What is a "productivity index"? Discuss the general use of productivity indexes identified by Hatry.

7. What problems are presented by the typical measures of individual officer and unit productivity? Be sure to consider community policing as well as traditional police arrangements.

8. If you were a police chief, what techniques and strategies would you use to improve productivity and then to maintain it at a high level?

Net Resources

http://www.andromeda.rutgers.edu/~ncpp/ National Center for Public Productivity provides information on how to improve organizational productivity.

http://www.policeforum.org The Police Executive Research Forum provides information on some of the latest studies in policing.

http://www.sourceuk.net/articles/f00963.html Constable John Newing provides information on police productivity.

http://www.vera.org Visit the Vera Institute for information on police and criminal justice productivity.

References

Alpert, G. (1997). The management of pursuit driving. In R. G. Dunham and G. P. Alpert (eds.), *Critical Issues in Policing: Contemporary Readings,* 3rd ed. Prospect Heights, IL: Waveland Press, pp. 547–564.

Alpert, G., and Moore, M. (1998). Measuring police performance in the new paradigm of policing. In G. Alpert and A. Piquero (eds.), *Community Policing: Contemporary Readings.* Prospect Heights, IL: Waveland Press, pp. 215–232.

Bartol, K. M., and Martin, D. C. (1998). *Management.* New York: McGraw-Hill.

Bayley, D. (1994). *Police for the Future.* New York: Oxford University Press.

Blumberg, M. (1997). Controlling police use of deadly force: Assessing two decades of progress. In R. G. Dunham and G. P. Alpert (eds.), *Critical Issues in Policing: Contemporary Readings,* 3rd ed. Prospect Heights, IL: Waveland Press, pp. 507–530.

Brand, D. C., and Scanlan, G. (1995). Strategic control through core competencies. *Long Range Planning* 28:102–114.

Brandl, S., and Frank, J. (1994). The relationship between evidence, detective effort, and the dispositions of burglary and robbery investigations. *American Journal of Police* 13(3):149–168.

Brazil, J., and Barry, S. (1992). Color of drivers is key to stops on I-95 videos. *Orlando Sentinel,* August 23, p. A-1.

Burpo, J. H., DeLord, R., and Shannon, M. (1997). *Police Association Power, Politics, and Confrontation.* Springfield, IL: Charles C Thomas.

Covey, S. (1990). *Principle-Centered Leadership.* New York: Summit Books.

Downs, A. (1967). *Inside Bureaucracy.* Boston: Little, Brown.

Edwards, M. R. (1983). Productivity improvement through innovations in performance appraisal. *Public Personnel Management* 12(1):13–24.

Fyfe, J. J. (1979). Administrative interventions on police shooting discretion: An empirical examination. *Journal of Criminal Justice* 7(4):309–323.

Geller, W. A., and Scott, M. (1992). *Deadly Force: What We Know.* Washington: Police Executive Research Forum.

Hatry, H. P. (1979). Wrestling with police crime control productivity measurement. In J. Wolfe and J. Heaphy (eds.), *Readings on Productivity in Policing*. Washington: Police Foundation.

Hersey, P., and Blanchard, K. H. (1982). *Management of Organizational Behavior: Utilizing Human Resources*, 4th ed. Englewood Cliffs, NJ: Prentice Hall.

Hirsch, G. B., and Riccio, L. J. (1974). Measuring and improving the productivity of police patrol. *Journal of Police Science and Administration* 2(2):169–184.

Holzer, M. (1973). Police productivity: A conceptual framework for measurement and improvement. *Journal of Police Science and Administration* 1(4):459–467.

Hyde, A. C. (1985). Productivity management for public sector organizations. *Public Personnel Management* 14(4):319–332.

Jones, G. R., George, J. M., and Hill, C. W. L. (1998). *Contemporary Management*. New York: McGraw-Hill.

Kelling, G., and Coles, C. (1996). *Fixing Broken Windows: Restoring Order and Reducing Crime in Our Communites*. New York: Touchstone.

Kuper, G. H. (1975). Productivity: A national concern. In J. Wolfe and J. Heaphy (eds.), *Readings on Productivity in Policing*. Washington: Police Foundation.

Lorange, P., Morton, M. F. S., and Ghoshal, S. (1986). *Strategic Control Systems*. St. Paul: West Publishing.

Meyer, M. W. (1980). Police shootings at minorities: The case of Los Angeles. *Annals of the American Academy of Political and Social Sciences* 452:89–110.

Morgan, J. P. (1975). Planning and implementing a productivity program. In J. Wolfe and J. Heaphy (eds.), *Readings on Productivity in Policing*. Washington: Police Foundation.

National Commission on Police Productivity (1973). *Opportunities for Improving Productivity in Police Services*. Washington: Government Printing Office.

Pate, T., Ferara, A., Bowers, R., Lorence, J. (1976). *Police Response Time: Its Determinants and Effects*, Washington: Police Foundation.

Schreyoff, G., and Steinmann, H. (1987). Strategic control: A new perspective. *Academy of Management Review* 12:91–103.

Sherman, L. W. (1983). Reducing police gun use: Critical events, administrative policy, and organizational change. In M. Punch (ed.), *Control in the Police Organization*. Cambridge, MA: MIT Press.

Simons, R. (1995). *Levels of Control: How Managers Use Innovative Control Systems to Drive Strategic Renewal*. Boston: Harvard Business School Press.

Spelman, W. (1988). *Beyond Bean Counting: New Approaches for Managing Crime Data*. Washington: Police Executive Research Forum.

Spelman, W., and Eck, J. (1987). Newport News tests problem-oriented policing. *NIJ Reports*. Washington: National Institute of Justice.

Thompson, J. D. (1967). *Organizations in Action*. New York: McGraw-Hill.

Trojanowicz, R., Kappeler, V., and Gaines, L. (2001). *Community Policing: A Contemporary Perspective*, 3rd ed. Cincinnati: Anderson Publishing.

Walsh, W. F. (1985). Patrol officer arrest rates: A study of the social organization of police work. *Justice Quarterly* 2(3):273–290.

Wasserman, M. P., Gardner, J., and Cohn, A. (1973). *Improving Police Community Relations.* Washington: NILECJ.

Weisburd, D., McElroy, J., and Hardyman, P. (1988). Challenges to supervision in community policing: Observations on a pilot project. *American Journal of Police* 7(2):29–50.

Wieland, G. F., and Ullrich, R. A. (1980). *Organizations: Behavior, Design, and Change.* Homewood, Il: Richard D. Irwin.

13

Planning Programming and Budgeting

Spencer Grant/Photo Researchers

Chapter Outline

Learning Objectives

After reading this chapter, you should be able to

1. Understand the nature of the planning process.
2. Describe several methods of planning.
3. Discuss the limitations associated with planning.
4. Plan for critical incidents.
5. Understand how to plan for terrorism.
6. Discuss the decision-making process and variables affecting the process.
7. Understand the importance and uses of crime analysis and mapping.
8. Appreciate the budgeting process, including types and functions of budgets.
9. Know the budget development and approval process.

The recent attacks on the World Trade Center and the Pentagon underscore the need for planning for future attacks. Law enforcement administrators have had to scramble to engage in a proactive role to prevent future outbreaks of terrorism. Some law enforcement agencies are spread so thin in attempting to stave off violence that they are hurting for resources. Budgets have been adversely impacted because of what happened on September 11, 2001, and programming for other priorities has, in many ways, taken a back seat in some organizations.

It is for these and other reasons that we focus on planning, programming, and budgeting in a single chapter. Planning leads to programming, which in turn requires a look at the budget. Failure to plan, however, can have significant and detrimental impacts on the entire process, as our nation's recent bout with terrorism seems to attest.

INTRODUCTION

Planning is a natural activity undertaken by individuals and organizations. Everyone plans, but some people and organizations plan more thoroughly and are more successful in meeting environmental challenges. Although planning does not guarantee success, it does minimize the losses sustained when exigent, countervailing problems arise. Simply stated, planning affords a degree of preparedness and increases the likelihood of accomplishing goals.

The degree of planning varies across individuals and organizations. For example, some police agencies use a formalized planning process, whereas others plan on an informal, ad hoc basis. Departments that do not use formal planning tend to react to problems; they do not anticipate and respond to issues before they become major problems; their operations tend to be lethargic. Departments that have formalized their planning and strategic actions tend to inspire public confidence through effective police operations. They anticipate major issues and respond by resolving the issues before they become uncontrollable.

Planning, roughly, is deciding what the police agency should be doing. It is the linking of current activities to future conditions. It is decision making regarding operational activities based on anticipated contingencies. Police executives monitor crime statistics, citizen requests for services, citizen complaints, and changes in the economy; attempt to determine trends; and plan to meet these changing needs. A police agency must have a data collection and analysis mechanism if it is to plan properly. Departments monitoring the crime trends are able to implement programs (operation identification, neighborhood watch programs, intensified patrols, or community policing initiatives) to counteract problems.

Programming translates planning into "action-oriented" strategies. Planning serves no purpose unless it is interpreted into actions or programs. Although a police agency may plan, it may fail to follow through and develop new programs. That is, it may fail to implement some strategy after identifying a need, or it may devise a strategy that cannot be implemented or implemented properly. Thus planning ultimately leads to action to resolve a problem or increase the ability of the department to respond to the community.

In planning the implementation of a potential program, three aspects must be considered. First, a program must be suitable. *Suitability* refers to whether a program addresses the problem. Too often programs address a problem only partially or focus on symptoms of the problem. When this occurs, the problem will not be solved. Second, a program must be *feasible.* The department must have the resources available to implement the program. If personnel are not available or cannot be made available, then there is no use in recommending a program of intensified patrol to solve a crime problem. Finally, a program must be *acceptable.* Political and social constraints within every community dictate what is acceptable and what is not acceptable. Police departments must operate within the bounds of these constraints. For example, police have faced acceptability problems in enforcing DUI programs. A number of police chiefs were severely criticized by citizens and the news media when officers used roadblocks or staked out bars to apprehend drivers who were under the influence of intoxicants. Such practices "shocked the conscience of the political community." Many citizens did not believe the means justified the end. Lack of citizen acceptance of programs often directly results from inadequate planning where administrators failed to comprehend community or political attitudes or failed to sell their programs prior to implementation.

Budgeting is another component of planning. Budgeting is the fiscal plan for resource acquisition and management. Budgeting is directly related to program feasibility. Administrators often fail to consider budgeting in their planning; however, it is a principal component in the planning process. Resources must be available for a program to be implemented. If the police chief decides to organize a new unit within the department, personnel must be available to staff the unit. Police executives frequently increase the size or develop new specialized units by taking personnel from existing units. In doing so they sometimes fail to consider the consequences of reassigning the personnel on the original units. Unless other adjustments are made, the original units still have the same level of work to perform.

In this context, budgeting refers to acquiring and managing resources. Resources include not only money provided to the department in its budgets but also personnel and equipment. All police agencies have limited resources, and these resources must be managed in a way that maximizes every dollar and every available person within the department. This philosophy necessitates the integration of planning and budgeting. Planning provides the executive with better justifications for the budget, and better budgeting leads to more effective programming and goal accomplishment. The management activities of planning, programming, and budgeting are intertwined, and one cannot be accomplished without considering the other two.

THE NATURE OF THE PLANNING PROCESS

Planning is a distinct discipline within the police organization. It is a discipline because it is continuous and establishes a framework for all activities within the department, and as a discipline, if planning is not utilized and followed properly, disaster usually ensues. Planning is an integral part of competent management. Cushman (1980) identified a number of positive organizational attributes resulting from good planning:

1. *Improved analysis of problems.* Planning produces the data and analyses police administrators need to improve their decision making.
2. *Improved cooperation and coordination.* Planning provides a mechanism for increasing cooperation and coordination among the various police units and between the police and other private, social, and governmental agencies.
3. *Clear goals, objectives, and priorities.* Planning permits precise articulation of purposes and links goals, objectives, tasks, and activities in meaningful ways.
4. *More effective allocation of resources.* Planning provides a framework for resource allocation decisions. It simplifies the setting of priorities for the use of resources to achieve police goals and objectives.
5. *Improved programs and services.* Planning sheds light on problems and needs, makes it easier to formulate goals and objectives, and provides a means to evaluate and compare alternative programs and procedures.
6. *Improved capacity and quality of personnel.* Planning focuses organizational effort and provides agency personnel with new knowledge and information about their jobs.

Planning entails a certain degree of risk. Many managers are content to follow a safer course and accept the status quo. Every decision to change a program or procedure offers a manager the possibility of making a wrong decision through lack of planning, use of inadequate of data in arriving at the decision, or changes in the environment or organization rendering the plan useless or less than acceptable. Many managers feel it is easier to defend problems resulting from old or traditional procedures than it is to defend problems arising from changes. Such managers are afraid to take risks and thus become stagnant in their approach to management (change is discussed in more detail in Chapter 15). Conversely, a manager who tends to take too many risks will create strain and instability within the department.

Lynch (1998) notes that police planning revolves around two concerns: concern for the system and risk. *Concern for the system* includes three key ingredients: purpose, stability, and entirety. *Purpose* refers to how well the planner attends to the goals and objectives of the department in the planning process. Plans must target essential goals and establish performance priorities to ensure the goals are accomplished. *Stability* refers to the sequential arrangement of departmental activities. This arranging applies not only to how activities are performed but also to how new problems are addressed. When new activities are assumed by the department, this change induces a degree of instability, even when the change focuses on valid departmental goals. Therefore, the manager must plan for change so that instability is reduced to the lowest possible level. Planning for contingencies and for implementation is the vehicle to attenuate

Figure 13–1
Management planning model.

Source: *Management Models—The Planning Process,* copyright 1968 by Educational Systems & Design, Inc., Westport, Conn.

this instability. Finally, *entirety* refers to the fact that planning must consider the department as a whole. When instituting changes, managers should be mindful of Isaac Newton: "To every action there is an equal and opposite reaction." In a managerial sense, this means a change at one level or area of the department may and usually does have ramifications in other areas of the department and may have external effects as well. Not only must the organization be considered; the internal human and social system within the department and the external environmental factors all should be considered.

Risk refers to the manager's attitude toward innovation and opportunity. When a manager takes advantage of new opportunities or attempts to depart from tradition, there is a degree of risk. The degree of risk hinges on the probability of success of the program or change. Risk is reduced when change is carefully planned, because planning reduces error and the probability of program failure. Managers must be willing to assume some risk, for if they are not willing to do so, they become status quo managers and the department suffers. Conversely, managers must not be overly zealous in their quest for change as such behavior leads to an overextension of the manager's and the department's ability to incorporate change into daily operations. There is a fine line separating too much and too little risk behavior. The manager must be able to make appropriate decisions relative to risk and change.

Lynch (1998) analyzed police planning in terms of concern for the system and risk and identified four types of planning approaches: purposeful, traditional, crisis, and entrepreneurial. Figure 13–1 shows these four planning approaches in relation to concern for the system and degree of risk.

When adapting the *purposeful approach*, managers are concerned with the system and want to take advantage of opportunities and thus are willing to take risks. Purposeful planners' primary concern is the department's direction, and they are willing to take risks for the improvement of the department's position in terms of goal achievement. *Traditional* planners' orientation is stability, tradition, and precedent. These managers do not want to rock the boat for fear of falling into the water. Creativity and innovation must come from a higher source for these managers to change. *Crisis* planners are managers who show little concern for the system and avoid risk. They manage and plan situationally. They make decisions spontaneously and then closely monitor the actions of subordinates to ensure they follow directions explicitly. This dictatorial type of manager has no concern for the past or the future, but considers only the present. Finally, *entrepreneurial* planners show little consideration for the system but embrace risk. Such managers tend to overextend themselves and their subordinates and spend a great deal of their resources and energies fighting organizational fires. Subordinates suffer from constant change and a lack of direction.

The police planner should use the purposeful planning approach for the most part since it entails a concern for system maintenance and a willingness to innovate. There are situations and times when the manager should utilize the other approaches on a temporary basis. However, the purposeful planning approach allows the manager to maximize goal achievement while ensuring the long-term stability and effectiveness of the department.

A POLICE SYSTEMWIDE PLANNING MODEL

Planning occurs at every level of the police agency. The chief's planning concerns may center on which community concerns or problems should receive the highest priority while a detective sergeant may be planning how to assign cases to subordinate detectives or how to reduce the unit's caseload by reassigning cases to patrol or to another unit. Hence everybody—administrators, commanders, and supervisors—plans, the differences lie in the type of planning taking place and how it fits the overall scheme within the department. Different types of planning are performed at the various levels within the police department, and each type of planning activity must be coordinated with the planning at the next higher and the next lower levels within the department.

Nanus (1974) outlined a hierarchy of planning which can be applied to police agencies. Figure 13–2 depicts a systemwide approach to planning.

There are four levels of planning that occur prior to the implementation and evaluation of programs: future studies planning, policy planning, strategic planning, and operational planning.

Future Studies Planning

Nanus's highest level of planning, *future studies*, refers to the research and analysis of societal trends and forecasting the future environmental picture as it relates to the police department. *Forecasting*, an integral part of future studies

Figure 13–2
A general model for a criminal justice planning process.

planning, is an effort to reduce uncertainty about the future by predicting environmental conditions so they can be addressed through departmental programming. There is not a high degree of specificity in forecasting, but the resultant generalized ideas of what the future holds allow police planners to prepare the department for future contingencies. Forecasting is an effort to maintain stability while reducing risk to the department.

Future studies planning is assigned to a planning unit where past and present data are collated and analyzed and future trends extrapolated. The planning unit amasses all types of data about the department, its activities, and social trends. Types of departmental and activity data collected include the frequency and types of crimes being committed; information about citizens' requests for services and complaints; and statistics regarding the department's ability to respond in terms of response times, arrest rates, services rendered, and crime clearance and citizen satisfaction with the police. These data yield information in two important areas: (1) how well the department currently responds to its environment, and, by examining the data over time, (2) what the projected activity pattern will look like. If the future activity pattern substantially differs from the current pattern, the manager must make decisions relative to personnel and organizational changes which will allow the department to respond better to these future contingencies.

Social trend data compose information about changes in society and the environment that affect demands for police services. A myriad of political, economic, and social data and information must be considered. Political changes

On the Job

SAN BERNARDINO POLICE DEPARTMENT

By Garrett Zimmon

Courtesy of Chief Zimmon

San Bernardino, California, is a community with a population of approximately 220,000. The San Bernardino Police Department has a force of approximately 300 officers serving the diverse, predominately blue-collar population. The city has a fairly high crime rate and number of citizen requests for service. This equates into a significant workload for the department. It also means that at any given time, the department must provide a broad range of services to its citizenry.

I am a new chief and have been with the department for only a few months. This results in my having a unique perspective on police planning. When a new chief takes control of a department, he or she must immediately develop an understanding of its priorities, programming, and needs. The chief must know where the department

stands in terms of services and community expectations. This is difficult for the new chief, who must not only assess the department's position, but at the same time set priorities for meeting numerous community leaders and groups who want to discuss their problems and perspectives about the department and community. The new chief is pulled in a variety of directions. Currently, a large part of my time is devoted to meeting with people. This substantially limits the amount of time I have to survey the department to develop a better perspective of where we are.

Once I have assessed the department and the community, I must make decisions about departmental priorities and programs. It should be noted that different segments of a community have varying ideas about what the police should be doing and the services they desire. It should also be remembered that these expectations are constantly changing. As such, I attempt to attend to as many of these requests and expectations as possible, while ensuring that more resources are devoted to the most critical problem areas. This, in some cases, equates to a realignment of departmental operations to reflect newly recognized community expectations. New programs must be developed, or old programs must be altered.

Community policing plays a key role in this planning process. Community policing means that we reorient the department so that service and

Continued

order maintenance receive more emphasis. However, at the same time, we cannot neglect our law enforcement obligations. A healthy balance between these perspectives must be maintained. Community policing means that we make our programs more community-based by attempting to work more closely with citizens and gain their cooperation and assistance with police efforts. In some cases, community policing is more time-consuming, and we must ensure that we have adequate resources to implement our programs correctly and effectively. A key to success here is supervision to ensure that any programs work as they should.

Budgeting is another important administrative function that plays into our planning and programming. Most police officers give little or no regard to budgeting, but a department cannot implement new programs unless there are adequate resources to fund them. At first glance, one might assume, based on the number of officers a department has, that a police department has ample resources or personnel to staff any desired program. However, most police chiefs have little play in how they can allocate personnel to new programs. Generally, when a new program is implemented, the resources must be taken from established programs, which have an established constituency. That is, they provide a distinct set of services that come to be expected by citizens or groups within the community. The chief is the one held accountable when making these types of decisions. Thus, as chief, I must give careful consideration to all programs, whether they are created, expanded, or reduced.

In summary, the police chief is ultimately responsible for a department's direction. This direction is established through proper planning. This is a comprehensive endeavor, and it cannot be taken lightly or neglected. Planning results in a variety of programs that require substantial attention to ensure that their operation matches expectations. Thus, planning begins with the chief and his or her staff, but directly affects everyone in the department.

in the jurisdiction's governing body may create new demands or directions for the police department. Long-term economic trends will affect the demands made on the police. An increase in unemployment could intensify crime problems and order maintenance activities. Budgetary shortfalls would affect all areas of the police department's budget, necessitating rapid decisions on which programs to cut or reduce. Conversely, economic growth would allow for new programs and new demands on the police. Social change usually is accompanied by changing public expectations of the police. In recent years, the public has demanded more effective police responses in such areas as community policing, driving under the influence (DUI) enforcement, domestic violence, missing and exploited children, and domestic terrorism. As societal concerns change and shift, so must a police department's efforts and direction. Table 13–1 lists some social changes and how they may affect a police department.

Table 13–1

Societal Changes and Their Effect on the Police

Social Change	Impact
Construction of a new shopping mall	Increase in traffic congestion, accidents, thefts from autos; a need for police traffic direction
Construction of a new high school	Increase in traffic violations and minor crime in immediate area and on routes to school
Increase in new housing construction in an area	Need for additional patrols; increase in traffic congestion, minor crimes, and calls for service
Closing several stores in downtown area	Increase in vagrancy, disorder, minor crimes
Construction of new bars or nightclubs	Increase in traffic problems and violations, disorder, and assaultive behaviors

In summary, future studies allow a department to narrow its range of priorities. They also provide lead time to develop and implement programs reducing organizational risk. Figure 13–3 presents the planning inputs and outputs for policy, strategy, and operational planning which are examined in the following sections.

Policy Planning

Policy planning is a product of future studies planning. Whereas future studies are the acquisition of data and information, policy studies are the first step in using the acquired information. Once the planning staff collects and collates information, the department's administrative staff attempts to determine its consequences on the department. *Policy planning* is the department's efforts to determine its future role, or what it should be doing based on future studies. Police managers examine the strengths and weaknesses of the department, forecasts of social data, and crime rates and trends.

The results of policy planning are policies prescribing direction for all members of the department. These policies are used to determine what types of program are implemented. For example, future studies may indicate that there is and will be a continued nationwide increase in terrorist acts. Policy planning is the evaluation of the possible targets, their probability of being targeted, and the likelihood of terrorists being in or moving into the jurisdiction. New York City, because of its banking, commerce, and population of foreign dignitaries, would have a higher probability of experiencing terrorism than Nashville, Tennessee. This is best evidenced by the World Trade Center bombing in 1993 and attack in 2001. New York City, in light of its perceived strategic problem, would give terrorism a higher policy priority than Nashville. Nashville, on the other hand, through its future studies and policy planning, would identify its own relevant policy issues.

Figure 13–3

Planning inputs and outputs.

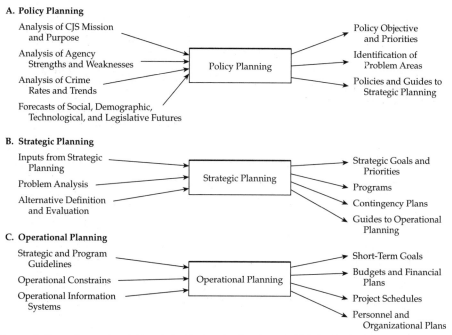

A. Policy Planning

Analysis of CJS Mission and Purpose

Analysis of Agency Strengths and Weaknesses

Policy Planning

Analysis of Crime Rates and Trends

Forecasts of Social, Demographic, Technological, and Legislative Futures

Policy Objective and Priorities

Identification of Problem Areas

Policies and Guides to Strategic Planning

B. Strategic Planning

Inputs from Strategic Planning

Problem Analysis

Strategic Planning

Alternative Definition and Evaluation

Strategic Goals and Priorities

Programs

Contingency Plans

Guides to Operational Planning

C. Operational Planning

Strategic and Program Guidelines

Operational Constrains

Operational Planning

Operational Information Systems

Short-Term Goals

Budgets and Financial Plans

Project Schedules

Personnel and Organizational Plans

Source: B. Nanus, A general model for criminal justice planning. *Journal of Criminal Justice* 2, no. 4 (1974), pp. 345–356.

The decision-making process in policy planning is collegial: Individuals within and outside the department contribute information and opinions on which issues they believe should be addressed by the department and their assessments regarding the priorities of these issues. These decisions are value judgments. The police administrator attempts to involve individuals who are knowledgeable about the department, the community, and the specific problem subject matter in the policy planning process. The resultant policies thus are the best estimates of what should be the department's specific goals and their associated priorities.

Strategic Planning

Strategic planning is programmatic and deals with determining how the department should achieve its policy goals and objectives. Strategic planning involves the department's administration, planning unit, and division commanders. They are provided goals and then asked to provide input on the best ways to achieve these goals. Strategic planning produces two types of plan: program plans and contingency plans. *Programs plans* are plans that the department implements on a continuous basis to achieve a policy goal. A *contingency plan* is a plan the department develops for implementation when a "critical incident" occurs such as flood, hurricane, tornado, bomb threat, or hostage taking. Both types of plan necessitate decisions regarding personnel allocation, organizational change, and duty assignments. However, the contingency plan is designed to allow implementation when the problem develops, whereas program plans are designed for immediate implementation.

Strategic planning usually follows a comprehensive strategic planning model based on a four-stage planning process: (1) problem identification, (2) identification of alternative strategies, (3) evaluation of alternative strategies, and (4) selection of the strategy to be implemented. These four steps are described in the following paragraphs.

Problem Identification.

A police department should be proactive and attempt to identify strategic problems before they become emergencies. The Scanning, Analysis, Response, Assessment (SARA) model of problem solving associated with community policing dictates that departments and officers scan the environment for problems. Problem identification is the first step in ensuring that a department is able to effectively serve a community.

Webster and Conners (1999) identified several methods police future studies and strategic planners should use in identifying problems. They include:

1. Officer observation and experience.
2. Citizen complaints.
3. Crime analysis.
4. Police reports.
5. Analysis of calls for service.
6. Crime mapping.
7. Information from community groups.
8. Citizen and community surveys.

Once a problem has been identified, Guyot (1977) noted three useful steps in developing a better understanding of the problem. First, identify and specify the problem (circle the problem) by consulting people and examining records and information relative to the planning issue. This provides a full understanding of the problem or planning issue. Second, write a clear statement about the problem or planning issue. This ensures that the problem is adequately defined and everyone involved in the planning has a complete understanding of the problem. Finally, seek out the various causes of the problem. It is important that all aspects of the problem, including its causes, be understood and considered. These three steps lead to a better understanding of the planning issue, and the department is in a better position to effectively proact to it.

Once the strategic planning problem is clearly defined, the next step is to identify and evaluate alternative strategies that counteract the problem. A number of alternative means or paths exist by which to accomplish a desired goal. Strategic planning involves identifying these alternatives, evaluating their relative efficacy, and deciding which one to implement. The key to this task is to ensure that many possible alternatives are identified and evaluated. The more alternatives one identifies, the more likely that an effective alternative will be selected for implementation.

Identification of Alternative Strategies.

Ideally, alternative strategies are identified through a series of planning meetings. Once the problem has been specified, the group sets out to identify and list the ways or alternatives that could be used to accomplish the desired goal. The meeting should have a free-form demeanor, whereby everyone throws out ideas on how to proceed. Hudzik and Cordner (1983) identified three levels of activity associated with generating alternatives: reviewing, searching, and designing. *Reviewing* refers to the examination of current and past organizational arrangements and activities to determine if any are appropriate for dealing with the problem at hand. It is much easier, administratively, to utilize current arrangements than to draft a new alternative strategy. However, if a current strategy does not appear to be capable of completely addressing the problem or issue, then a new strategy must be developed. If the department repertoire of programs does not contain an adequate strategy for addressing and solving the problem, then searching for new alternatives begins. *Searching* may go beyond the department; planners examine how other departments approach the problem, consult with other governmental departments, and review police research findings to generate plausible alternative actions. *Designing* is a last resort for generating alternatives. If an acceptable alternative has not been identified, the planning group attempts to design new alternatives. Brainstorming is a useful technique when designing alternatives.

Brainstorming is a process in which everyone in the planning group expresses his or her thoughts about the problem and possible solutions. This process of eliciting free-flowing ideas encourages the exploration of alternatives that otherwise might not be brought up by the participants. A vitally important element of brainstorming is that no positive or negative comment about the idea is allowed by any participant. Therefore, participants develop all alternatives before they discuss their relative merits. They may devise entirely new approaches, or they may be able to take pieces from several existing programs to construct a new one. The reviewing, searching, and designing process is quite a time-consuming endeavor, however, it is a critical part of the process to identify alternative strategies or programs.

Evaluation of Alternative Strategies

Once strategies are identified, they must be evaluated at two levels. First, a strategy's feasibility, suitability, and acceptability must be examined. In terms of *feasibility*, can the department implement the strategy? Does it have the resources and capabilities to implement the program? In terms of *acceptability*, will the strategy be accepted by the community and government? For example, in 2000, a number of departments experienced high-profile shootings where police officers killed members of the minority community. These shootings resulted in elevated tensions between the communities and the police. Prudent police administrators in these communities then began to emphasize community building rather than high levels of tactical law enforcement in an attempt to reduce tensions. Finally, a strategy must be *suitable*. Does it accomplish the desired goal?

The second level of strategy evaluation is an operational analysis of the strategy to determine or anticipate outcomes that may be produced if the strategy is implemented. The planners fully enumerate the strategy in implementation phases, and each phase is analyzed in terms of what will occur. Flowcharts are developed to show how the strategies are implemented and how various units and people are affected. Work activities and performance criteria are specified, probable outcomes are projected, and finally this information is compared with organizational goals, objectives, and needs. This process is a theoretical implementation of the strategy, and it provides police executives with information relative to the ultimate acceptability of the strategy.

Selection of the Strategy to Be Implemented

Once the strategies are evaluated and data relative to the performance of each strategy are developed, the manager, in consultation with departmental staff, will select the strategy to be implemented. Table 13–2 lists the strategic planning initiatives for the San Bernardino, California, Police Department and the operational programs used to achieve the planning goals. Notice that the operational programs include a wide variety of programs, which, taken together, represent a fairly comprehensive planning and operational guide.

Operational Planning

Operational planning is performed by midlevel managers and unit supervisors. The process is coordinated by the planning unit and midlevel managers. *Operational planning* is the specifying of unit work assignments. The planners at this level are provided all the program information generated at the strategic planning level, and this information serves as a guide for their activities. Essentially, the information provided acts as a "shell," or framework, for planning individual work assignments. The shell provides general direction and unit expectations. The operational planners then must complete the specifics of the program in terms of personnel assignments, work schedules, duty assignments, and equipment needs. Midlevel managers and supervisors are best suited for this task since they are most familiar with how changes or new programs will affect concurrent programs and activities within the unit. They also are more knowledgeable about the work ability of specific program elements.

Operational planners take the strategic plans and fill in the details to the point where all program activities are specified. They construct what Suchman (1967) terms a "hierarchy of objectives and assumptions" relative to the program.

Table 13–2

San Bernardino Police Department
Strategic Planning Goals and Operational Initiatives

Cooperative Problem-Solving Initiative

Implement distressed neighborhood program.
Implement area-specific crime prevention programs.
Develop collaborative partnership with drug court.
Develop collaborative partnership with private security vendors.
Enhance collaborative partnership with Parks and Recreation with an emphasis on youth mentoring.
Develop a bicycle safety program.
Refine crime-free rental housing program.

Violent Crime/Gangs/Narcotics Initiative

Increase violent crime clearance rate.
Participate in coalition against hate crimes.
Reduce number of Part I crimes.
Enhance domestic violence education and reduction programs.
Continue street-level drug suppression coordinated with detectives.
Enhance asset forfeitures.
Monitor, track, and reduce violent parolees.
Implement business robbery alert program with private sector.
Enhance enforcement in problem areas.

Information Management Initiative

Replace computer-aided dispatch and records management system.
Upgrade departmental computer networking capabilities.
Implement crime mapping.
Develop interface for unit computer needs and programs with the records management system.
Develop a bar code system to enhance property and evidence control.
Develop a better computerized link with the district attorney's office.
Develop a better computerized link with the Probation Department.
Implement computer traffic collision diagrams.
Pursue Internet college courses for the department.

This hierarchy of objectives details everything that must be accomplished from the lowest element to the highest. Each element is described in detail with regard to who, what, when, where, and how. Figure 13–4 is an example of a program shell that strategic planners may provide the operational planners. It outlines the scope of the problem and specific strategies to be employed by operational units.

The operational planners will consult with the crime analysis and records units to further clarify the scope of the problem in Step I. The information gained in this step is invaluable in determining on how to proceed—it specifies the scope of the problem. Step II is management's decision on how to approach the robbery problem—increased patrol and stakeout units. Specifying the problem enabled the planners to make precise recommendations in terms of strategies. For example, the crime analysis information probably showed a clustering of robberies,

Figure 13–4

Strategic planning shell to be used by the operational planner to implement a reduction in robberies.

Steps

I. Scope of Problem
   1. Jurisdiction experiencing a 23% increase in robberies over last year.
   2. Robberies concentrated in nine patrol areas.
   3. Although occurring every day of week, concentrated on Fridays, Saturdays, and Sundays.
   4. Majority occurring between 10:00 P.M. and 2:00 A.M.
II. Strategy to be developed
   1. Increase patrol concentration in key areas.
   2. Develop stake-out units for high potential victim businesses.

Operational Planning Activities

Steps

A. Determine manpower and equipment requirements.
B. Determined availability of equipment and funding for necessary equipment.
C. Determine manpower availability.
D. Make decisions relative to operational structure and relationship to other units.
E. Make personnel assignments.
F. Monitor program activities and performance.
G. Evaluate the needs for adjustments in program arrangements.

---

and a more precise examination of the clusters would reveal information relative to specific enforcement strategies—stakeouts, crime prevention, increased patrols, or portable alarms. Operational planners decide on the specifics of how the plans are implemented. Steps A, B, and C are activities relating to the needs for and potential regarding acquisition of personnel and equipment; if equipment is not available, then more personnel may be necessary. Step D is the determination of whether a separate unit will be formed or if new duties will be assigned to existing units. Step E is the implementation of the program, and Step F is the monitoring of program activities to ensure that it was implemented as planned. Step G is an evaluation of the program's effectiveness in abating the robbery problem. If the robbery problem is unabated, new strategies must be implmented.

Earlier in this chapter, programming was discussed as an essential part of planning. Strategic and operational planning are the vehicles for programming, or program development. Too often police managers fail to enumerate the specific details and expectations for programs. This usually leads to program failure as personnel and units are not given specific assignments and program elements are not adequately performed. For example, if any of the steps in Figure 13–4 are omitted or not fully accomplished, there is a high probability that maximum effectiveness in terms of robbery reduction would not be realized.

Operational planning enables administrators to assert some degree of operational control. Once a program is implemented, managers must not only make specific duty assignments, they must also ensure that they are carried out as specified. Only operational plans provide enough detail to operationally control specific assignments. Otherwise, officers and units would not clearly understand what is expected of them. Many police programs fail because there is a lack of program specificity or control activities. Police managers cannot assume that people are doing what they are supposed to do, they must follow up on activities.

In summary, police planning consists of four phases: future studies, policy planning, strategic planning, and operational planning. Each of these four phases must be completed if the police agency is to be maximally successful. It is not sufficient to accomplish one or a few of the phases; attention must be given to all phases of the planning process.

Limitations of the Comprehensive Planning Model

The preceding sections describe a comprehensive model of planning. Smith and Klosterman (1980) note that this comprehensive model of planning frequently is not effective, and managers must use a modified form of planning that would be appropriate at the strategic planning level. The comprehensive strategic planning model assumes that the police manager is able to gather all necessary data about the problem, the environment, and the organization. Smith and Klosterman argue that it is not always possible to gather all the data. Most planning decisions are based on partial data about the problem, environment, and organization. They recommend that a modified form of strategic planning be used.

Along these lines, Simon (1957) argued that most organizational decisions are "satisficing." They satisfy and suffice for the immediate problem. The decision maker searches for a workable and acceptable solution rather than formulating the best solution. The best solution frequently is not available due to a lack of information. Incremental adjustments must be made to ensure that the decision remains workable and acceptable. In this regard, Daft (1986) noted that decisions are "coalitional" when there is agreement among several managers as to the best decision. The coalition elements may change over time as new information surfaces and the problem definition changes. Thus decisions are dynamic, continuous processes rather than processes with identifiable beginning and ending points.

Modified Strategic Planning Model.

The modified form of strategic planning suggested by Smith and Klosterman (1980) consists of three elements: restricted analysis, concurrent analysis, and fragmented analysis. *Restricted analysis* requires the planner recognize the limitations of time, information, and resources in planning. When using restricted analysis, the planner gathers all available information relating to the problem and alternative strategies and makes a decision. *Concurrent analysis* refers to planning as a continuous process. Once an alternative has been identified and implemented, evaluation and planning continue. The assumption here is that the decision to implement a particular alternative strategy was based on limited information, so continuous monitoring will identify inadequacies with the strategy and allow for strategic adjustments. These adjustments will better ensure that program goals are achieved. *Fragmented analysis* entails planning to be performed throughout the department. All managers and supervisors who are involved in a program continuously plan relative to their specific roles and areas of concern. This incremental model of planning provides for an "adaptive organization." The department can take a proactive stance toward problems and changes. Although Smith and Klosterman's points are valid, the police manager's strategic planning should be as comprehensive as possible, and once the plan is implemented, concurrent and fragmented analyses should be performed.

CONTINGENCY OR CRITICAL INCIDENT PLANNING

An important aspect of operational planning is contingency or critical incident planning. Critical incidents are major problems such as riots; hostage situations; hazardous material exposures; airplane crashes; damage from severe weather such as tornadoes, flooding, or hurricanes; significant earthquakes; or fires that occur in large sections of a jurisdiction. A police department should have plans that can be activated when such a disaster occurs. Kemp (1989), in a study of cities and counties, found that even though they had emergency plans, many felt they were not adequately prepared to properly respond to an emergency. Thus planning is not enough; police executives must ensure that the plans enable the police to fully respond to the emergency.

Hess and Wrobleski (1993) advise that predisaster plans should address the following issues:

1. What emergencies to plan for.
2. What needs to be done in advance (equipment, training, and agency preparedness).
3. What functions are to be performed as a result of the emergency and who is responsible for performing them.
4. What actions will be needed to restore order in the aftermath of the critical incident.
5. How the response will be evaluated.

What critical incidents to plan for depends on the jurisdiction's location. For example, cities such as St. Louis or Louisville must prepare for flooding and tornadoes. Cities on the eastern seaboard must prepare for flooding and hurricanes. Most of the Midwest and South must have plans in the event of a tornado, and jurisdictions in California must prepare for earthquakes. Additionally, all agencies must prepare for explosions, hostage and crime situations, airplane disasters, fires, hazardous material disasters, and riots and civil strife.

Police departments must be prepared in the event of an emergency. This means that departments must have the proper training and equipment to react when a critical incident occurs. Police departments must ensure that they have

trained special weapons and tactics (SWAT) teams, riot squads, hostage negotiators, and hazardous materials (HAZMAT) response teams. Critical incidents
requiring such units occur very infrequently; consequently, some departments
tend to reduce these units' importance or allow them to deteriorate or slip into
a less effective mode. However, police executives must ensure that these units
remain adequately trained and ready to respond to an incident.

Potential critical incidents require that police departments possess or have
access to a variety of police equipment. A department should have a mobile
communications or command vehicle and transport vehicles that can safely
transport large numbers of officers to the scene of a critical incident. The
department's armory should have a variety of special weapons including rifles,
tear gas, bulletproof vests, and helmets. Some critical incidents require the
department to have specialized video surveillance equipment and unobtrusive
listening devices. Finally, a department should have traffic cones, tape, and barriers to cordon off any areas affected by the critical incident.

Critical incident planning should ensure that everyone involved in an operation knows his or her assignment. This is best accomplished by the formulation of critical incident procedures and training. Procedures should spell out
the responsibilities of each police unit when a critical incident occurs. Also,
when a large critical incident occurs, the police department will be coordinating its efforts with other agencies, including other police departments, fire
departments, hospitals, disaster relief agencies, National Guard units, streets
and road departments, and utility companies. It is critical that the role of each
agency be well defined in procedures, and that the agencies have the capacity
and training to fulfill that which is expected of them.

Restoring order in the aftermath of a critical incident requires just as much
planning as the emergency itself. In some cases, government must provide citizens with food, water, and shelter. The police generally are involved in coordinating these efforts. The police must protect areas that have been devastated
by riots or natural disasters to prevent looting or additional deaths or injuries.
In some cases, the police must work with utility companies to restore water or
power. This should be a coordinated and well-planned part of any critical incident response.

Finally, when a critical incident occurs, the department should evaluate its
response to determine if changes in training or procedures are needed. The
evaluation should focus on every aspect of the operation. Typically, most problems with critical incident responses occur in the areas of communication and
coordination, so they should be closely examined.

In summary, Adams (1998) identified the following steps in responding to
a critical incident:

1. Specify the nature and extent of the critical incident.
2. Communicate the existence of the critical incident to headquarters
   personnel and other agencies immediately.
3. Initiate rescue and first aid responses and activities.

4. Establish a command post.
5. Contain the area.
6. Maintain street access for emergency vehicles.
7. Evacuate survivors and other persons in the area.
8. Provide public information services.
9. Provide coordination with other agencies.
10. Arrange for access to the area by authorized personnel only.
11. Record the event.
12. Evaluate the department's response.

Planning for Terrorism

All law enforcement agencies must prepare for crisis situations, especially in light of the 2001 terrorist attacks on the World Trade Center and the Pentagon. If terrorist incidents take place, police administrators must be prepared to protect citizens, prevent further attacks, protect the crime scene, and apprehend wrongdoers. Coupled with these duties is the reality that several law enforcement agencies must work in tandem to prevent terrorist threats. The newly created Office of Homeland Security is one step toward coordinating the activities of multiple investigative and other law enforcement agencies for the purpose of preventing terrorism.

Dyson (2001) offers a number of suggestions designed to plan for responding to terrorist attacks. The first is to develop and maintain a *contingency plan*. This is the most basic form of crisis preparation, wherein the agency creates a plan that describes in detail the role of each employee in a crisis situation. Contingency plans should take into account individual employees' areas of expertise, assigning appropriately trained people to specific tasks. Plans should also be updated routinely, as many employees move about through the organization or leave. Dyson also suggests that one person be named "crisis coordinator." This person's job is to review contingency plans regularly and assume the role of monitoring the agency's level of preparedness, equipment inventory, and so on.

Another method of antiterrorism planning is what Dyson (2001) describes as a mutual aid agreement. Few local law enforcement agencies have the training and resources to cope with an international terrorist threat. They should therefore identify federal, state, and local law enforcement agencies that have jurisdiction over the problem. These agencies should then be contacted, and steps should be taken to ensure that all agencies having jurisdiction over the problem can work together in a crisis situation. As Dyson notes, "It may be prudent to establish a joint command center to direct the law enforcement and emergency response in a major crisis" (2001:374). What's more, a written agreement between the agencies should be pursued, much like an individual department's contingency plan. Such an agreement outlines each agency's responsibilities if a terrorist outbreak occurs.

Specific exercises can be undertaken to test the viability of an agency's contingency plan or an interagency agreement. For example, "table-top exercises" can be staged by a third-party evaluator. This means that an expert, such as a

World Trade Center destruction resulted in significant budget problems for the New York Police Department (NYPD).

Allan Tannenbaum/The Image Works

university professor, initiates a role play that puts the department's contingency plan into operation. The exercise is not a full-blown simulation of a terrorist attack but simply a "paper exercise" designed to assess the agency's level of preparedness. Police departments can also undertake "full-training exercises." These are simulations of actual crisis situations, complete with victims and perpetrators. Much attention has been given recently to the threat of a biological or chemical attack. Full-training exercises can give agencies the leg up in the face of a serious crisis situation.

No amount of planning or simulation can help a police agency prepare for crisis as much as effective leadership. As Dyson observes, "If a department is to perform well during a crisis, the leader must do his job and must insure that his subordinates do their jobs." Furthermore, "a few weak management personnel can greatly hamper, if not destroy, a department's investigation of a major crisis situation" (2001:381). This means that top administrative personnel need to ensure that all their subordinates are capable of and prepared to fulfill their duties in crisis situations. A lapse in one area may have harmful consequences for the agency's overall level of preparedness. Finally, the police administrator must make certain that lower-ranking management personnel are assigned where they are most likely to be needed. For example, it would make little sense to assign the chief of detectives to head up a crisis prevention team. It could prove useful, particularly for large police departments, to consult with or hire a "terrorism manager," someone who can assess the qualifications of the agency's personnel and make recommendations to the chief concerning who should be assigned to what specific terrorism-related function.

THE DECISION-MAKING PROCESS IN POLICE ORGANIZATIONS

A prerequisite to planning is the ability to make sound decisions. Decision making is a part of the planning process. The difference between decision making and planning is that planning is broader in scope. It is future-directed toward resolution of problems, potential problems, or improvement of the current status of the department. Decision making is present time. Decisions may be implemented in the future as they are in planning, but the choices must be made now.

Everyone routinely makes decisions. Almost everything each officer does, from the chief to the patrol officer, involves a decision. When we make decisions we apply knowledge from our past experiences and utilize our analytical skills. Each individual, when making a decision, follows a set pattern. Some people attempt to rationally evaluate all the information available before making a decision, whereas others are content to consider only what they perceive as the most important issues. How managers make decisions will ultimately influence the quality of their decisions.

Variables Affecting Decision Making

Nigro and Nigro (1980) identified several factors that exert influence on managers during the decision-making process: outside pressures, sunk costs, personality characteristics, influence from outside reference groups, and other past conditioning.

Outside Pressures

Outside pressures refers to laws, people, and conditions that impose boundaries on the decision maker. State laws often restrict the police manager's decisions in terms of working conditions, how to deal with police labor groups, and how appointments and promotions can be made within the department. Politicians and other government agency heads exert pressure relative to how the department should be managed or what officers should be doing. Social, political, and economic conditions frequently place constraints on the decision maker in terms of what is acceptable or feasible. These outside pressures must be dealt with on a continuous basis, and the successful police manager is able to mediate, bargain, and negotiate compromises in the best interests of the department and the community.

Sunk Costs

Sunk costs are the resources previously committed to a program that make it impossible for the department to enact changes in current procedures or operational policy. For example, if a department spent several thousand dollars on a crime prevention program, and upon evaluation found it to be unsuccessful, dismantling the program and formulating a new strategy would be an arduous task. The administrator is open to criticism for wasteful spending or incompetent planning and administration. Sunk costs, in essence, exert significant pressure on decision making.

Another type of sunk cost that can have the same restrictive pressures is commitment. If an administrator exerts a tremendous amount of pressure to promote a program, changing to another program or strategy becomes a forbidding task. Police managers can best avoid the sunk costs problem through comprehensive planning. However, there will be situations where programs must be changed, and the administrator must decide in the best interests of the department and community. Decisions to make changes should be made as soon as possible after implementation to minimize sunk costs and thus reduce the problems inherent to change.

Personality Characteristics

Personality characteristics refer to the decision maker's personality. Everyone has idiosyncrasies, biases, and strong feelings. It is important that these personality traits do not taint decisions. The police manager must be able to rationally analyze problems, situations, and people so as to make the decision that best resolves the problem or issue. Katz and Kahn (1966) identify several personality factors which potentially affect people's decision-making process: (1) their orientation toward either power or ideology, (2) their propensity toward either emotionalism or objectivity, (3) their emphasis on either innovativeness or common sense, and (4) their orientation toward either action or contemplation. Police managers must always make a conscious effort to be open-minded and consider all the facts when making decisions. This is a basic rule of good management, and when it is not followed, problems are often compounded rather than solved.

Influence of Outside Reference Groups

Many individuals and groups outside the department attempt to exert influence on police decisions. These groups exist within every community. They range from powerful, influential community leaders to collective groups such as the National Association for the Advancement of Colored People (NAACP) or the Chamber of Commerce. Each attempts to mold public policy to meet the individual's or group's needs. As the police department's constituency, these groups' perspectives must be seriously considered. To ignore them is to ignore reality. The police executive constantly must deal with these pressures, but while welcoming their input, he or she must keep the department on a path that best addresses the problems and concerns of the entire community.

The more varied and conflicting the reference groups are in terms of their desires for police action, the more difficult the police chief's position becomes. When there are varied perceptions as to what the role of the police should be in the community, the police manager is in a delicate position of choosing from among the competing role orientations. This is one of the most difficult issues facing the police manager.

Common Errors in Decision Making

Decision making is a routine, common managerial activity. Few people give any thought to the process they use in making decisions. They simply attempt to grasp the problem, identify and analyze plausible solutions, and make a decision. Differences in how people make decisions lie in the nature of how they analyze the problem; their ability to identify solutions; their analytical skills in terms of collecting and evaluating data; and the degree to which they consider all decision outcomes on the problem set, department, and environment. Although simply stated, the decision-making process actually is quite complicated, especially as problems become more difficult and serious.

Nigro and Nigro (1980) identified a number of common errors in decision making: cognitive nearsightedness, assumption that the future will repeat the past, oversimplification, overreliance on one's own experience, preconceived notions, unwillingness to experiment, and reluctance to decide. *Cognitive nearsightedness* refers to the decision maker's attempts to satisfy immediate needs without considering the long-term effects of the decision. Some managers are prone to be expedient rather than examining the big picture. *Assuming the future will repeat the past* pertains to the decision maker's basing decisions on past data, information, and events while neglecting to consider changes in the department and environment. Not everything is cyclical; new trends develop and changes occur. A failure to consider the possibility of change leads to decision-making errors. *Oversimplification* is a natural tendency among all decision makers and refers to the decision maker's attempting to reduce every problem to its lowest denominator. This process makes decision making easier, but when all the facts are not considered, decisions become less effective. *Overreliance on one's experience* is a decision-making failure to seek additional outside information. Many police managers equate rank or tenure with knowledge: the higher the rank or longer the tenure, the greater the knowledge. However, this is not always the case, and effective decision makers do not assume that their experiences are necessarily accurate representations of all experience. They seek information from all sources. *Preconceived notions* refer to subjective biases, which everyone has. One should remember that information that we often consider to be factual may in reality be half-truths or based on partial or old information that is no longer relevant. *Unwillingness to experiment* is the tendency to use past practices without considering the possibility of more appropriate strategies. Finally, many managers have a *general reluctance to make decisions*. They perceive an element of danger in making change, and decision making generally constitutes making change. Officers are given increased responsibility as they are promoted within the police department, and they must be willing to accept this increased responsibility. When a police manager does not make a decision, he or she is in fact making a decision to avoid change, and it usually is the wrong decision.

Group Decision-Making Model

Most people reason that decision making is best approached as a group activity, since multiple participation allows for more input and a wider range of input. This is central to Daft's (1986) coalition factor in decision making. For the most part, multiple input does contribute to better decisions. However, the dynamics of the group decision-making process should be controlled to ensure that the process operates correctly.

Nigro and Nigro (1980) examine the dysfunctional potential of group decision making known as "groupthink." In *groupthink*, group members concentrate on ensuring acceptance of their decision instead of realistically appraising alternatives of action. Groupthink has eight symptoms: (1) group invulnerability, where the group believes it must be right and must triumph over adversaries; (2) collective rationalization, which discounts warnings from outsiders who question the group's assumptions; (3) total faith in the group's morality to the point that the group is always right; (4) stereotyped views of outsiders as being weak, stupid enemies who are in disagreement with the group; (5) pressure on dissenters within the group, forcing them to be loyal to the group; (6) self-censorship, in which dissenting group members do not voice their doubts relative to the group consensus; (7) illusion of unanimity, where everyone is pressured into agreement; and (8) self-appointed "mind-guards," members who protect the group from adverse information that may affect complacent members' opinions. In essence, there is always the possibility of manipulation of group decisions and outcomes by stronger members of the group. Although group decision making makes the pretense of being participatory or even democratic, decisions may, in fact, be the result of veiled autocracy within the group.

Decision making is a complicated affair necessitating continuous involvement on the part of police managers. They must realize that decisions are dynamic, not static, and that the results of every decision must be continuously monitored to evaluate the efficacy of the decision. Moreover, they must be willing to consider all available information and make adjustments in their decisions when necessary. Police managers must avoid the "escalating commitment" phenomenon (sunk costs), in which managers lock themselves into a course of action which is costly but unproductive. Commitments to a faulty decision can undercut a manager's credibility and respect. Acknowledging mistakes in decision making by cutting losses and finding a better alternative is usually more acceptable in the long run.

STRATEGIC AND TACTICAL INFORMATION THROUGH CRIME MAPPING AND CRIME ANALYSIS

As noted in previous sections, planning and decision making evolve around information. The more information used in these processes, the more accurate the outcomes. Adequate information, however, is not always available: needed information sometimes is not collected, or the department may not take the necessary steps to ensure that information is collected and stored in a usable form. When information is not available, police managers can do little except constantly monitor the environment, department, and problem to gather information as it becomes available. Police managers must ensure that their records unit and crime analysis unit are collecting and storing needed information.

The number of departments using computerized records management systems (RMSs) to store, analyze, and retrieve data has increased substantially over the past decades. Two factors have led to this improvement: (1) police managers better understand the need for data and information and how computers can serve these needs, and (2) there has been an overall reduction in computer and software costs. RMSs allow for storage and rapid retrieval of large amounts of information. Manual data systems, consisting of original reports and index cards, require a significant amount of time to perform even the simplest information gathering task. Complex analyses using large quantities of data are virtually impossible with manual data systems. Today's desktop microcomputers are more powerful than many of the mainframe computers of 10 years ago. Only the largest police departments today require mainframe computers; all other departments are able to develop RMSs using the latest micro- and minicomputer systems. The following sections a discuss crime mapping and crime analysis and how they can assist the police manager in the planning process. *Crime mapping* provides a visual interpretation of crime so that its patterns can be better understood, and *crime analysis* is the analysis of crimes in an effort to discern whether similarities exist among a series of crimes.

Crime Mapping

Crime mapping is not a new technique. The New York City Police Department used crime maps as early as 1900 (Harries, 1999). Early maps, which were street maps with pins denoting the location of specific incidents or crimes, were static and could show the locations of crimes for only a short time. With the passage of time, a map would contain so many pins that it was virtually useless to the officers who were attempting to extract information from it. Since the mappers had to begin with clean maps periodically, it was impossible to follow crime trends over time. Pin maps, however, did provide officers with limited pictures of the crimes in their beats or patrol areas.

Today, many departments are able to map crime and other incidents using computer systems. When the police receive calls for service or reports of crime, the information is entered in the department's computer-aided dispatch (CAD) system. The CAD system represents the front end of the RMS, where records are stored. The CAD/RMS contains all the information related to each incident, including location, time, nature of police response, police response time, and criminal report numbers. Information from the CAD/RMS can then be loaded into a mapping program. The most frequently used mapping programs include ArcView from ESRI in Redlands, California, and MapInfo from the MapInfo Corporation in Troy, New York.

A map of crime and police call data is a flexible method that allows officers to "see" crime and calls for service. Vasiliev (1996) notes that computerized mapping allows the police to manipulate time and space when viewing activities. The police are able to view:

1. *Specific types of crime or calls across the jurisdiction or within a specific area for a given time period.* For example, investigators may want to visually examine all the rapes or robberies in an area to determine whether there is a geographical pattern. The crimes could be plotted for any given period, thus allowing the investigator to see whether a pattern emerges.

2. *Activities for a particular shift or watch.* Commanders might better deploy patrol personnel or redesign their patrol beats by examining activities during individual shifts. Since crime patterns change over time, the configuration of beats should probably change to remain abreast with the changes in police and crime activities.

3. *Activities for a particular beat or police district.* Commanders can visually examine what is occurring in a beat or district, which allows them to determine whether the area is properly staffed or to identify specific problems in the area which require additional attention by patrol or specialized units.

4. *Activities in and around a "hot spot," or concentration of crime and disorder.* Crime, disorder, and calls for service tend to concentrate in small geographical areas that may cut across beats and police districts. Mapping allows the police to identify hot spots and to examine activities in and around these geographic concentrations.

5. *Concentrations of activities in an area over time.* It is sometimes worthwhile to view areas over time, say, across six months, a year, or several years. This allows the administrator to see whether the concentrations are changing over time or to determine whether a problem-solving intervention has had an effect.

6. *Police activities in relation to social and ecological characteristics.* Crime and other activities can be mapped in conjunction with attributes in the environment that may contribute to crime. For example, La Vigne and Wartell (1998) discuss how mapping street robberies in relation to street lighting can provide insights into where robberies are more likely to occur in an area that is plagued with high robbery rates.

The Redlands, California, Police Department has been mapping crime in relation to measures of community disorder in order to better identify community interventions by community policing teams. Figure 13–5 is a map of the City of Redlands that provides a visual display of juvenile arrests. Although fairly well dispersed throughout a large area within the city, levels of juvenile crime are higher in some areas than others. Interlaced on the map with the juvenile arrests are areas with high levels of juvenile risk. The juvenile risk factor was determined through community surveys, socioeconomic data, and crime rates. Given this information, the Redlands Police Department is able to couple enforcement programs with crime prevention and community-building programs to alleviate the conditions that result in juvenile crime. The map also provides information on where the department should increase services to juveniles in the area of recreation and after-school activities.

Figure 13–5
Map of juvenile arrests in Redland, California.

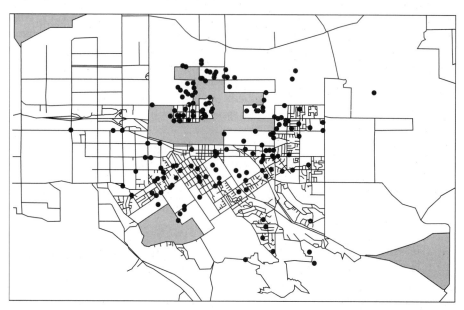

The biggest impediment to crime mapping has been the department's geocoding system. *Geocoding* refers to the storage and retrival of geographic points in the RMS. Mapping requires exact addresses so that they can be matched with a computerized map of the city. Many departments are losing large numbers of calls and crime data because of inaccurate addresses. This is particularly true when officers enter information directly into the system using mobile terminals or computers. Officers misspell or abbreviate street names in some cases, and in other cases they input landmarks such as shopping malls rather than the correct addresses. Some departments are losing as much as 40 percent of their data as a result of address problems. Departments must take action to ensure that address information is accurate.

Crime Analysis

Most police data analysis functions are housed in crime analysis units. These units generally are a part of or work in conjunction with the records unit. A vast amount of data and information is collected during daily police operations. Police officers make reports on every activity in which they are involved. These reports make up a database containing a wealth of raw information. Crime analysis is the act of analyzing the available raw data to provide crime pattern and trend information in a form that is easily usable for organizational planning and decision making. Figure 13–6 shows the crime analysis information flow network within a police agency.

Figure 13-6
Crime analysis information flow.

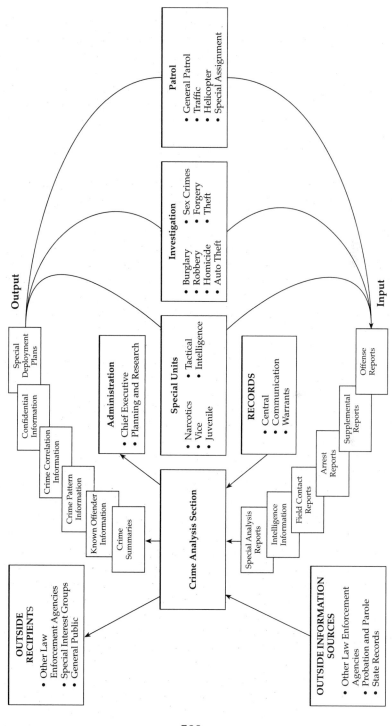

Source: G. A. Buck, *Police Crime Analysis Unit Handbook* (Prescriptive Package: Law Enforcement Assistance Administration and National Institute of Law Enforcement and Criminal Justice). Washington: Government Printing Office, 1973, p. 10.

509

Crime Analysis Process

All units in the police department produce reports containing potentially useful data and information. The offense, supplemental, arrest, field contact, intelligence, and special analysis reports are representative of all the activities performed by the department's officers and form a substantial portion of the crime analysis base. The remaining crime analysis information, as shown in Figure 13–6, comes from outside information sources. This includes reports from other police, criminal justice, governmental, and private agencies. For example, census data can provide socioeconomic background on police problems. Information from these sources is necessary for future studies planning.

Once the crime analysis unit receives the information, it produces reports that can be used by management and operational units. Examples of reports produced are crime summaries, known offender information, crime pattern information, crime correlation information, and special deployment plans. Figure 13–7 shows how some of this information can be utilized.

The crime analysis process consists of five steps:

Figure 13–7
The crime analysis mission.

THE CRIME ANALYSIS MISSION		
Support	**Activity**	**Method or Technique**
Detective	Case Investigation	Known Offender — MO / Associates / Status / Location
Detective	Case Investigation	Offense Correlation — Evidence / Location / Day, Week, Etc. / Property / Crime Specific / Victim, Witness
Detective	Special Operations	Locational Stake-Out Patterns
Patrol	Manpower Allocations	Crime Pattern Information Crime Prediction Profiles
Patrol	Tactical Assignments	Crime Location Patterns
Patrol	Suppression	I.D. Of Offenders Active in Area
Patrol	Patrol Effectiveness Improvement	Characteristics—Unique Crime Types
Planning	Strategy Development	Categorize Crime Problems Demographic Correlations Prediction of Future Problem Areas

Source: G. Buck, *Police Crime Analysis Unit Handbook* (Prescriptive Package: Law Enforcement Assistance Administration and National Institute of Law Enforcement and Clinical Justice). Washington: Government Printing Office, 1973, p. 1.

1. *Data collection.* Identification, receipt, and sorting of copies of all source documents in the department that contain information relevant to the crime analysis process. The primary source for this information is the operational units. The information is then entered into the department's CAD/RMS.
2. *Collation.* Examination and extraction of crime element information from all source documents and the arrangement of this information into a set format for subsequent retrieval and analysis. The crime analyst queries the RMS for reports that provide insights into crime patterns.
3. *Analysis.* Identification of crime patterns for the purpose of prevention and suppression of crime, identification of the criminal perpetrator, and early identification of the crime trends for the purposes of patrol and administrative planning.
4. *Dissemination.* Communication of target crime information to user groups, especially the patrol and investigative divisions. This may be in the form of crime maps or specific information about specific offenses or offenders.
5. *Feedback and evaluation.* Assessment of the crime analysis products and activities from user groups and self-evaluation of the unit's ability to satisfy ongoing user group needs. Crime analysts must ensure that they provide the kinds of data that are needed by operational units in the department.

Dissemination of Crime Analysis Information

In the past, police departments depended on pin maps and daily bulletins to provide officers and units with crime information. The pin map of the jurisdiction showed where criminal activity occurred, and the daily bulletin listed all criminal activity during a given period of time. This manual system of information dissemination presented problems, especially in large departments where daily crime activities are high. First, in many jurisdictions, the daily bulletin did not order crime information in a useful manner. The bulletin contained crime information about a particular part of the city or a listing of the various locations for a specific type of crime. It did not cross-reference specific information: victim type, time of day, geographical location, modus operandi, suspect information, and type of property stolen. It is difficult for officers to discern and thoroughly understand crime patterns without collating these crime variables. Today, computer mapping allows for a more useful display of crime data, and police CAD/RMSs allow crime analysts to provide more meaningful information.

At the heart of crime analysis is the accumulation of information in a useful manner. Computerization allows the analyst to identify crime patterns or crime clusters using assorted variables, but once this occurs, the analyst must manually examine crime reports for information that might link the various reports and crimes together. Although computerized expert systems will ultimately perform this task, currently all decisions in the analysis phase are judgmental and usually performed by the crime analyst.

Police official discusses police programs before city council.
Alan Carey/The Image Works

Identifying Crime Patterns and Trends

The factors that are useful in the crime analysis function include types of crime, times of occurrence, locations of occurrence, suspect information, victim information, modus operandi, and physical evidence. Analysis of this information is directed toward the identification of crime patterns and early identification of crime trends. There are two broad types of crime pattern, geographic-concentration pattern and similar-offense patterns.

Geographic-Concentration Pattern.   The geographic-concentration pattern shows a number of crimes or activities concentrated in a specific geographical area. Figure 13–8 displays the Part I or serious crimes for a three-month period in Redlands, California. Vast areas of the city are without crime. Other areas, however, have large amounts of Part I crimes. The map allows the police to concentrate their efforts on those areas that have the highest levels of crime.

Geographic concentrations with large numbers of police activities in a very small area are referred to as *hot spots*. Sherman (1995) defined a hot spot as a small place where the occurrence of crime is so frequent that it is highly predictable. He notes that crime tends to concentrate around places, not people. Roncek (1981) expands on this idea by focusing on "dangerous places." A dangerous place is a

Figure 13–8
Serious crimes for a three-month period in Redland, California.

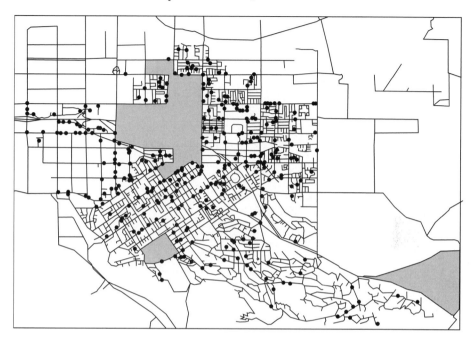

specific location where there is a concentration of crime activity, usually assaults and other street crimes. Dangerous places can include bars, street corners where drugs are being sold, schools, or other locations that tend to attract criminals. Dangerous places tend to cause or contribute to crime and have high levels of crime in and around them. Mapping programs can identify these hot spots or dangerous places and provide a visual account of exactly what is occurring. A visual display of the hot spot better enables the police to formulate a strategy to attack it.

When examining a hot spot, it is important that the analyst not only look for crimes but also scour the area for all sorts of related activities. Moreover, geographic concentrations should be examined for other types of call. For example, an area with a concentration of assaults may also have a high concentration of fight or disorder calls. A screening of all calls most likely will tell the analyst precisely where the problem lies. Once the problem is specified, a police intervention strategy can be developed.

Woodby and Johnson (2000) document an example of this procedure in Austin, Texas. In March 1999, a series of indecent exposures occurred near the University of Texas campus. Within a relatively short period, eight different offenses were recorded by the police. In each instance, the victims provided the police with similar descriptions of the perpetrator. Crime analysts mapped the

Figure 13–9
Map of serial sexual exposures, showing group home.

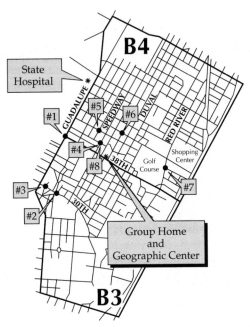

Source: K. Woodby and A. Johnson, Identifying a serial indecent exposure suspect. In N. LaVigne and J. Wartell (eds.), *Crime Mapping Case Studies: Successes in the Field*, vol. 2. Washington: Police Executive Research Forum.

crimes. They then examined the area for clues. There were a state hospital and a group home in the area, and the group home was located in the center of the pattern of offenses. Detectives then focused their investigative efforts on the residents in the group home and quickly identified the offender. Figure 13–9 is a map of the offenses and the group home.

Similar-Offense Pattern. Similar-offense patterns are developed much as the geographic-concentration patterns. Similar-offense patterns can be concentrated in an area, as was the example of the serial indecent exposures just discussed, or they may be spread over a large geographical area, as is the case of most serial rapists or serial armed robbers. The analyst studies suspect, victim, crime type, and modus operandi information, looking for similarities. If similarities exist, then an assumption is made that the crimes were committed by the same offenders.

For example, the analyst may search through all the rapes occurring in the jurisdiction, looking for unique characteristics. Figures 13–10a and 13–10b show the modus operandi from two rape cases. Based on the modi operandi, it appears the two crimes were committed by the same offender. If several such cases are identified, the analyst may be able to identify patterns in terms of

Figure 13–10a

Unique descriptors in rape case 1.

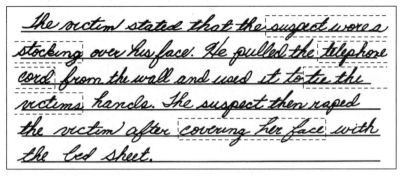

Source: R. Grassie, R. Waymire, J. Burrows, C. Anderson, and W. Wallace. *Crime Analysis Executive Manual.*
Washington: Law Enforcement Assistance Administration (LEAA), 1977, pp. 2–5.

Figure 13–10b

Unique descriptors in rape case 2.

Source: R. Grassie, R. Waymire, J. Burrows, C. Anderson, and W. Wallace. *Crime Analysis Executive Manual.*
Washington: Law Enforcement Assistance Administration (LEAA), 1977, pp. 2–5.

location, victim, time, or day of the week. In essence, the analyst is able to combine all the information from the various related reports. Each report in which the crime appears to be linked or related may contain pieces of information not contained in the other reports, and the combined total information provides investigators with more investigative leads. The information from the combined reports simplifies the investigation of all the cases and provides operations personnel with better information to develop crime prevention measures.

Crime analysis is critical to the operational function for every police agency and can be used both tactically and strategically. That is, crime analysis information is important for planning departmental strategies, and it is useful to individual officers and detectives in solving specific cases. It enhances the investigative and preventive patrol functions. For example, a recent study in

Boston showed that one out of eight police dispatches were to one of a few locations that had more than 100 dispatches in a single year. About half the police dispatches in Boston were to locations that had 10 or more calls per year (Pierce, Spaar, and Briggs, 1984). In a similar study in Minneapolis, Sherman (1987) found that 5 percent of the city's addresses were responsible for 64 percent of the police calls for service. If the police are able to implement strategies that have an impact on these hot spots, the overall crime and disorder problems for the department can be appreciably diminished.

Another important function of crime analysis is the production of management data. Through the crime analysis and record-keeping functions, crime and police activity information is stored so that the administrator can quickly examine a number of critical aspects of the department's operation. For example, if the department deploys a new strategy to combat a particular crime problem, crime analysis information is useful not only to develop the strategy but to evaluate the effectiveness of the strategy. Crime analysis can detect changes in the crime rates and patterns as a result of the strategy or the occurrence of a new problem. Crime analysis is an information generator for a number of levels of planning including future studies, strategic planning, and operational planning.

THE BUDGET PROCESS

The *budget* is the financial or fiscal plan for the department. Lee and Johnson describe a budget as "a document or set of documents that refers to the financial condition of an organization including information on revenues, expenditures, activities, and purposes or goals" (1998:14). The budget, in essence, describes what the organization does; it explains or provides a rationale for why activities are performed by the organization; and it establishes priorities by allocating resources to organizational areas and activities. The budget is a "decision document" since organizational priorities must be set with the submission of the budget.

The police consume a large part of any jurisdiction's budget. Since police departments must provide services to a jurisdiction 24 hours a day, 365 days a year, police departments are labor-intensive. This requires large numbers of personnel, which becomes relatively expensive in terms of a budget. For example, the total budget for the San Bernardino, California, Police Department is $35,311,700. Personnel accounted for $30,128,100, or 85 percent or the department's total budget. Figure 13–11 provides a breakdown of the budget of the City of San Bernardino by department. Note that the police department consumes almost half of the city's resources.

Budget Types and Functions

A budget serves a number of functions, and the type or kind of budget used by the organization is dependent on the function emphasized by the government. Schick (19882) noted that budgets are used to perform three basic functions in an organization: control, management, and planning.

Figure 13–11

City of San Bernardino, California, department expenditures.

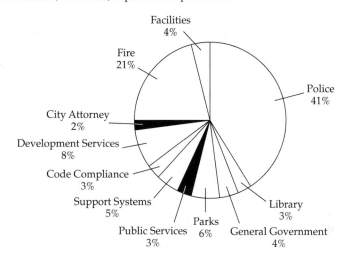

Table 13–3

San Bernardino Police Department Line-Item Budget Summary

Category	Expenditure Levels ($)
Personnel	$30,128,100
Maintenance and Operation	1,466,100
Contractual Services	1,060,500
Internal Service Charges	4,217,900
Capital Outlay	38,400
Debt Service	267,000
Credits	(1,866,300)
Total	$35,311,700

Control

Control is the basic function of a budget. Control refers to holding agencies and agency subunits accountable for how they expend resources. Control is exerted to ensure that money is spent for those activities and equipment for which it was intended when allocated by the legislative body. The line-item budget (see Table 13–3) is commonly used to exert control over departments within the general governmental structure. In the *line-item budget,* money is allocated to agencies by line areas (personnel, operating expenses such as fuel and office supplies, and capital outlay such as vehicles and equipment). The administrator generally cannot spend money from a line area for items that are not specified in that area without prior approval in the form of a budget modification. This procedure ensures executive control over administrators in terms of how resources are expended.

Table 13–4

San Bernardino Police Department Budget by Divisions

Division	Expenditure Levels ($)
Administration	$ 2,303,800
Station Command	886,600
Patrol	14,492,400
Mall Station	171,700
Vice and Narcotics	2,017,300
Multiple Enforcement Team	719,100
Traffic	1,145,500
Investigations	4,518,700
Identification and Property	750,000
Support Services	3,529,800
Dispatch	1,233,300
Records	1,452,500
Personnel and Training	1,028,800
Landlord Certification	77,200
COPS Universal Grant	92,300
City Jail	882,000
Distressed Neighborhoods	10,700
Total	$35,311,700

The line-item budget is also separated out by division or unit within the police department into a *departmental budget*. Departmental budgets are used in large police departments. In the departmental budget, the police executive provides division commanders with an allotment of resources, and they must operate their respective units within these budget parameters. The departmental budget delegates a substantial amount of fiscal discretion and accountability to the division or unit commanders. Table 13-4 provides a departmental budget for the San Bernardino Police Department.

Notice in Table 13–4 that patrol consumes the largest amount of resources. Approximately 75 percent of a police department's personnel are generally assigned to patrol. Also, the budget contains several unusual divisions: Distressed Neighborhoods, COPS Universal Grant, and Landlord Certification. The Distressed Neighborhoods and Landlord Certification categories represent special units that were created to attack special problems. They are funded by a state or federal grant. The COPS Universal Grant expenditures represent matching departmental funds for officers hired as a result of the federal COPS Universal Hiring Program.

Management

When the budget is used as a *management* tool, it is used to monitor the activities of the department and its various divisions. The primary purpose of the management budget is to evaluate the costs of activities. Here the budget is broken down into cost areas and expenditures are compared with productivity outcomes. The best-known management budget is the *program budget*. The program budget examines cost units as units of activity rather than units and subunits within the organization.

Criminal investigation is a cost area in most police departments. The outputs for investigation are (1) cases investigated, (2) cases cleared by arrest, and (3) recovery of stolen property. By dividing the budget for the activities by the units of output, the administrator can determine the relative cost for each unit of output or productivity. For example, if the budget for the investigations unit was $500,000 and the unit investigated 800 cases in a year, the average cost per investigation would be $625. If 300 of those cases were cleared by arrest, the average cost per cleared case would be $1,666. The program budget allows administrators to compare unit outcomes or productivity by reducing them to a dollar value. This often assists the administrator in making decisions in terms of increasing or decreasing a unit's budget or adding new programs.

Of course, the cost of criminal investigations entails more than just those costs incurred by the criminal investigation unit. There is the cost of patrol and other support units in the criminal investigation activity. The program budget is an extremely difficult form of budgeting to execute and administer because it requires tracking all personnel's time by activity as well as all support services and supplies. For this reason the program budget is rarely used in law enforcement and government. However, it can serve as a planning tool when various units are clambering for additional personnel or funding.

Another example of using the program budget to manage would be a case in which the commander of the criminal investigation unit requested an additional five detectives and the chief granted the request. The chief could later compare the relative costs of the unit with the additional five detectives to the previous unit structure when there were five fewer detectives. The chief can make managerial decisions relative to how productivity was affected by the additional five detectives. That is, if the relative cost of the unit per investigated case and cleared case went up appreciably, the need for additional detectives would be called into question. If this type of management planning were instituted throughout the department, better decisions could be made on the allocation of personnel and other resources. The police executive would be able to determine, at any given time, how productive a particular unit was relative to other units in the department. Thus program budgeting can be a primary tool for day-to-day operational planning.

Planning

The final use of a budget is policy *planning*. Two types of budget have evolved over the years which have been used to implement policy planning: (1) planning, programming, and budgeting systems (PPBSs) and (2) zero-base budgets (ZBBs). *PPBS* entails the combining of the planning process, program development, and budgeting process into one systematic product—the PPBS document.

The budget in this system specifies the cost for each program within each objective, within each goal. It may also be aligned by unit or department and by line item. Therefore, one can clearly identify the cost of any program. PPBS may be said to tie management by objectives (MBO) to a budget. The PPBS budget received substantial consideration and attention in the 1960s when Secretary of Defense Robert McNamara used it in making decisions relative to the selection of defense systems.

ZBB is very similar to PPBS. One difference between them is that the PPBS budget is based on previous expenditure requests: A request that has been explained and justified once need not be justified again. Each ZBB budget request is viewed as if it had never been requested previously: the budget is totally rejustified each year and funding for the upcoming year is not based on funding or expenditures from previous years. Another difference is that PPBS requires much more extensive analytical justification than the ZBB. The ZBB budget was used by Jimmy Carter when he was governor of Georgia, and he introduced it into the federal government when he became president.

The primary objective of these planning budgets is to link expenditures with organizational goals. Police departments have numerous goals, some with higher priority than others. Police administrators should earmark a larger percentage of their resources toward accomplishing higher-priority goals than toward lower-priority goals. The planning budget integrates the department's planning structure into the budget by organizing expenditures around goals and the programs or strategies used to achieve the goals.

The first step in the planning budget is the ranking of the department's goals—policy planning. Second, management studies are performed in an effort to determine the most efficient and effective way to accomplish the goals—strategic planning. At this point budgeting enters the process. All too often, the resources required to implement strategic plans are far greater than the anticipated resources for the department. The third step is a balancing act whereby various strategic plans and goals are weighed in an effort to bring the budget in line with the anticipated revenues. For example, a department will have numerous strategies by which the goals can be accomplished. Each strategy for a particular goal has a cost structure and an expected level of performance in terms of accomplishing the goal. Since the department may not have the resources to implement the best strategy, strategy decisions are based on costs relative to the importance of the goal and the degree of anticipated success (satisficing).

In many cases, the administrator may select strategies that will not produce the maximum results but that can be afforded. In essence, budgetary constraints are one of the factors that determine which strategies will be implemented. The administrator will be willing to implement more expensive strategies on higher-priority goals while implementing less expensive strategies for lower-level goals. The end result is maximizing the department's resources by expending a greater proportion of the resources for the most important goals.

Although PPBS and ZBB have received a great deal of attention over the years, they have not been widely accepted in management circles. This is because (1) most managers do not have the resources for their complicated operation, and (2) when they are used, they require voluminous amounts of data and preparation time. Most managers tend to use a departmental budget and incrementally link planning with the budget.

Integrating Planning in the Line-Item Budget

Today, most governments and police departments use the line-item budget for several reasons. First, its departmental breakdowns (departmental budget) make it fairly simple to administer. Also, elected officials find it easier to cut departments than to cut specific programs that may have a political constituency. Cuts in line-item budgets do not give the appearance of cutting programs. Second, the line-item budget allows mayors and other executive branch officials to exert maximum control over expenditures and agency heads. This is especially true when a jurisdiction experiences a shortfall in revenues and budgets must be cut.

The line-item budget, by its nature, does not incorporate organizational planning, and when this budget is used, organizational planning is a separate process. A potentially grave problem associated with this arrangement is what Schick (1969) referred to as "incremental budgeting," where emphasis is placed on budget outcomes rather than agency activities and outcomes. All too often, system politics dominate budgeting: Administrators are concerned with receiving their fair share of incremental increases in the budget. If one unit receives a 10 percent increase for the new operating year, then other agencies or unit heads insist on the same incremental increase regardless of whether the additional resources are needed or whether they could be better spent in other areas. This suboptimization of goals detracts from police agency effectiveness in that older, more established programs, regardless of their goal attainment effectiveness, receive higher priority over newer and possibly more effective programs.

Although a police agency uses a line-item budget, the police manager can avoid the problems inherent in the line-item budget by ensuring that planning is connected to the budget process. The chief should require all unit heads to link planning information to their budget requests. That is, unit heads should expound on what goals are to be achieved and how they will be achieved. There should be ongoing management and evaluation studies to determine whether performance objectives are being met. When unit managers do not achieve unit goals and objectives, the chief should hold them accountable. Accountability helps to avoid organizational stagnation in which unit heads are content to continue with old programs regardless of their effectiveness and neglect to search for better, more effective new programs. The chief is directly responsible for ensuring that this does not occur.

Budget Development and Approval

Within every unit of government, a specific office is responsible for coordinating the budget development process. The Bureau of the Budget, which reports directly to the president, has this responsibility at the federal level. The director of finance, city manager, or mayor has this responsibility at the local level. The responsibility of this office includes the timely preparation of the budget by coordinating the requests of the various departments within government. Once the budgets for all the departments are collected, the total budget package is submitted for legislative approval. Once the budget is approved, money is allocated to departments and their expenditures are monitored throughout the budget year. This process is referred to as the *budget cycle*. Essentially, the budget cycle has four phases: (1) preparation and submission, (2) approval, (3) execution, and (4) audit.

Budget Preparation and Submission

Government departments usually become involved in the budget process sometime between November and January, depending on the jurisdiction's timetable or fiscal year. Before and during the budget process the Finance Department develops revenue projections that serve as guidelines for the budget. These projections are estimates of how much money the jurisdiction will receive during the fiscal year. Table 13–5 provides a breakdown of the City of San Bernardino's revenue. As can be seen, cities are dependent on a variety of tax and income sources, and ensuring that revenue forecasts are met is a complicated matter.

The budget process is initiated with the issuance of the budget calendar, budget preparation manual, and a memorandum that outlines the department's budget constraints. The *budget calendar* notifies departments of the schedule of events for submitting their budgets. The *budget preparation manual* describes how the budget should be completed, explaining in great detail what information should be included and how calculations relative to requests should be made. In some cases, it requires departments to identify goals and objectives and relate proposed expenditures to the stated goals and objectives. It also includes copies of all forms to be used in the budget process. Budget targets are generally provided to department heads and are sometimes altered as

Table 13–5

Sources of Revenue for the City of San Bernardino

Source of Income	Amount of Income ($)
Property taxes	$ 6,993,600
Other taxes (sales, utility, franchise, etc.)	42,441,500
Licenses and permits (businesses, construction permits, fire code permits, and miscellaneous licenses)	5,427,600
Fines and penalties	612,000
Use of money and property (space rental, parking fees, interest, etc.)	1,298,500
Intergovernmental (reimbursement from state and federal governments)	13,054,100
Charges for services (EMS, weed abatement, false alarm fee, etc.)	3,099,700
Miscellaneous	3,266,700
Total	$76,211,700

the government fine-tunes its revenue and expenditure projections. Once the chief receives this information, the chief may request unit commanders to submit requests for their respective units. Table 13–6 is the budget calendar used by the San Bernardino Police Department.

The budget process is decentralized in that departmental unit heads are directly involved in budget preparation. The chief directs the unit heads to provide budget requests and justifications. In some cases, the chief may require justifications for any increases over the previous year. In other cases, the chief may require unit heads to justify part or all of their expenditure requests. The comprehensiveness of the justifications varies. For example, the chief may require unit heads to describe new programs or why ongoing programs require additional funding. A more comprehensive approach is for the chief to request unit heads to show that old and new programs or strategies effectively address a goal or objective. More effective strategic and operational planning is generated when the chief requires a comprehensive justification for all budget requests.

The administrative philosophy used to develop the budget varies across agencies and is linked to the philosophy of the government. Many chiefs view their job in the budget process as one of acquiring the largest amount of resources possible and view government's role as preventing the acquisition of resources. This philosophy politicizes the budget process. In many instances the chief will "pad" the budget by including items that are not necessary for the efficient operation of the department. Chiefs tend to use this ploy when the government body has a history of making across-the-board percentage cuts in department budgets as opposed to screening specific items when cuts are made. Another ploy is to solicit support for programs from political groups and elites such as council members, other government officials, or community leaders.

Table 13–6

San Bernardino Police Department Budget Calendar

Date	Activity
3/3	Distribute personnel/revenue projection information to service departments.
3/10	Chargebacks to individual departments are made. The chargebacks are based on services provided to departments by other or service-providing departments in city government.
	Distribute expenditure budget instructions to service departments.
3/17	Distribute personnel/revenue projection information to all departments.
3/23	Budget hearings with service departments.
3/24	Changes in departmental personnel and revenue requests are due to the Department of Finance.
3/31	Expenditure budget instructions are issued to all departments.
4/14	Departmental expenditure budgets are due back to the Department of Finance.
4/21–30	Budget hearings with departments.
5/17	Target date to distribute preliminary budget document.
6/30	Target date for mayor and council approval and adoption of new budget.

Stefanic (1985) suggests that successful police budgeting is linked to three management strategies: planning/strategy, minimizing cuts, and stretching dollars. *Planning/strategy* refers to the police department's planning, substantiating, and presenting the budget. Part of this planning strategy is to obtain a commitment from the governing body prior to budget approval. The chief should discuss with government officials their views on community problems, the plausibility of new programs, and how the department can better serve citizens. This, in effect, develops a degree of understanding if not commitment to the police budget on the part of the politicians. Most citizens and politicians do not understand policing and have a great deal of difficulty in understanding police budgetary needs. The chief and executive staff should make every effort to educate these people on what the police department is doing and its relative costs.

Minimizing cuts strategies are an extension of planning/strategies. Here the chief attempts to solicit support from community leaders and groups for both new and old programs submitted in the budget. The chief publicly presents funding proposals to various community forums and constituency groups and links them with efforts to solve community problems. For example, business leaders should be made aware of new programs such as foot patrols or bike patrols in business areas; residents in areas experiencing gang problems should be made aware of gang enforcement programs; or citizens with school-aged children should be made aware of drug enforcement and education programs.

Stretching dollars refers to efforts to develop outside and different funding sources. Today, departments throughout the country are receiving federal and state grant funding for a variety of programs. Table 13–7 provides a breakdown of the various external funds received by the San Bernardino Police Department in the 2000 fiscal year. Note the department received more than $1.3 million for the year. Chiefs should not neglect this potentially valuable funding source when the funding fits its strategic plan. One problem with these grants is that a department often seeks funding for programs that do not fit within its strategic plan, and the funding causes the department to splinter into too many directions, negating its primary focus. A number of departments have obtained funding from the community to fund such programs as Drug Abuse Resistance Education (DARE), neighborhood watches, and special police districts. The chief should always consider linking with community groups to raise additional resources.

Budget Approval

Once the budget is submitted, it must be approved by the legislative body. The approval process generally consists of a series of negotiations. The sum of the initial departmental budgets for a jurisdiction likely exceeds anticipated revenues for the city. At that point, the chief may be requested to make a blanket cut, or the legislative body may hold hearings to determine which programs are to be cut. Politics plays a key role in these negotiations in many jurisdictions, and the astute police executive must marshal community and political support for programs.

Table 13–7

Federal and State Grants to the San Bernardino Police Department

Source	Amount ($)
COPS (Community Oriented Policing Services) Universal Hiring Grant	$ 199,107
COPS More Clerical	63,300
Local Law Enforcement Block Grant	850,000
Graffiti Task Force Grant	147,095
Economic Development for Crime-Free Housing	87,000
Total	$1,346,502

Budget Execution

The execution or administration of the budget is vitally important. The adopted budget is a contract between the government and the police agency, and the police administrator is responsible for using the funds appropriately. If the department is using a departmental budget, funds are allocated to various unit budgets. The unit commanders are then charged with monitoring their budgets to ensure that money is expended appropriately and that expenditures remain within the budgeted limits

One person or unit within the police department should be assigned responsibility for fiscal management of the department. The roles, authority, and responsibilities of the fiscal functioning of the department should be clearly delineated in written directives. These written directives should include (1) the persons or positions authorized to accept or disburse funds; (2) the procedures for collecting, disbursing, and safeguarding cash; (3) procedures for the requisition and purchase of equipment and supplies; (4) procedures for requesting supplemental or emergency appropriations and fund transfers; and (5) the procedures for inventory control of agency property and equipment. The agency should have an accounting system that provides, on a monthly basis, the initial appropriation for each unit or program, balances at the beginning of the month, expenditures and encumbrances made during the month, and the unencumbered balance. These monthly statements should be carefully evaluated to determine the fiscal status of the organization.

Audit

The final phase in the budgeting process is the audit. Generally, a city's finance department or the city manager's office has responsibility for conducting the audit, although a police department should also periodically audit budgets to ensure that commanders are making proper expenditures. The audit is a process whereby auditors ensure that all money is spent appropriately. That is, a sum of money is apportioned to departments for specific items, and the departments should expend the funds accordingly. The audit ensures that this occurs.

SUMMARY

Planning, programming, and budgeting are critical elements in police administration. The police executive must be prepared to comprehensively plan for the department's future and be willing to seek or reallocate resources to execute the plans once they are developed. Planning occurs throughout the police department. The levels of planning include future studies, policy, strategic, and operational. Planning at each level of the police organization is tied to the planning outcomes at the other levels.

It is not enough to plan. The police administrator must make hard decisions ensuring that plans are followed. Police administrators must understand that decision making is a complicated activity and many pitfalls face decision makers. The best way to avoid making bad decisions is to plan properly and be decisive.

Effective planning, especially operational and strategic planning, requires that adequate data and information be available. Police departments as a natural part of daily operation collect immense amounts of data, which they were not able to adequately process before computerization. Police computerization has allowed police departments to use mapping and crime analysis to better understand what is happening in their respective communities.

Finally, the best plans are of little utility unless the department has the resources to implement them. This chapter provided an overview of the budget process that occurs in police departments. Budgeting, here, is seen as an integral part of the planning process.

Study Questions

1. Discuss the relationship among planning, programming, and budgeting. Why is it important that organizations be effective in performing these activities?

2. Why is risk taking a necessary evil in effective administration?

3. Discuss the levels of planning that occur in the police department. How do levels of planning match the administrative levels in the police department?

4. Discuss the variables that affect the decision-making process. What are their positive and negative implications for decision making? How might their impact be avoided or overcome?

5. Discuss the common errors in decision making. What impact can they have on organizational productivity and effectiveness?

6. What is crime mapping and how can it assist a police department?

7. Discuss the process and technique involved in crime analysis. Geographical-concentration patterns and similar-offense patterns are the two primary ways of examining police data. How do they operate?

8. Compare and contrast the line-item, departmental, program, and performance budgets. Evaluate each in terms of its utility for execution and administration of the budget.

9. Discuss the budget development and approval process. What are the most important factors administrators should consider when involved in this process?

Net Resources

http://nsi.org/terrorism.html The National Security Institute provides resources for preparing for terrortistic threats.

http://virlib.ncjrs.org/lawe.asp?category=48&subcategory=91 The National Criminal Justice Reference Service provides a number of documents on police planning.

http://www.lapdonline.org The LAPD website provides information relative to department programs.

http://www.usdoj.gov/cops/home.htm The COPS Office in the U.S. Department of Justice provides information for planning community policing.

References

Adams, T. F. (1998). *Police Field Operations,* 4th ed. Upper Saddle River, NJ: Prentice Hall.

Cushman, R. (1980). *Criminal Justice Planning for Local Governments.* Washington: National Institute of Law Enforcement and Criminal Justice.

Daft, R. L. (1986). *Organizational Theory and Design,* 2nd ed. St. Paul: West Publishing.

Dyson, W. (2001). *Terrorism: An Investigator's Handbook.* Cincinnati: Anderson.

Guyot, D. (1977). Planning begins with problem identification. *Journal of Police Science and Administration* 5(3):324–336.

Harries, K. (1999) *Crime Mapping: Principle and Practice.* Washington: National Institute of Justice.

Hess, K. M., and Wrobleski, H. M. (1993). *Police Operations.* St. Paul: West Publishing.

Hudzik, J., and Cordner, G. (1983). *Planning in Criminal Justice Organizations and Systems.* New York: Macmillan.

Katz, D., and Kahn, R. (1966). *The Social Psychology of Organizations.* New York: Wiley.

Kemp, R. T. (1989). Emergency management. In W. Bailey (ed.), *Encyclopedia of Police Science.* New York: Garland.

La Vigne, N., and Wartell, J. (1998). *Crime Mapping Case Studies: Successes in the Field.* Washington: Police Executive Research Forum.

Lee, R. D., and Johnson, R. W. (1998). *Public Budgeting Systems.* Gaithersburg, MD: Aspen Publishing.

Lynch, R. (1998). *The Police Manager,* 3rd ed. Cincinnati: Anderson Publishing.

Nanus, B. (1974). A general model for criminal justice planning. *Journal of Criminal Justice* 2:345–356.

Nigro, F., and Nigro, L. (1980). *Modern Public Administration,* 5th ed. New York: Harper & Row.

Pierce, G., Spaar, S., and Briggs, L. (1984). *The Character of Police Work: Implications for the Delivery of Police Services* (interim report to the National Institute of Justice). Boston: Northeastern University, Center for Applied Social Research.

Roncek, D. W. (1981). Dangerous places. *Social Forces* 60:74–96.

Schick, A. (1969). Systems politics and systems budgeting. *Public Administration Review* 29(2):137–151.

Schick, A. (1982). The road to PPB: The stages of budget reform. In F. Lyden and E. Miller (eds.), *Public Budgeting: Program Planning and Implementation,* 4th ed. Englewood Cliffs, NJ: Prentice Hall, pp. 46–68.

Sherman, L. (1987). *Repeat Calls to Police in Minneapolis.* Washington: Crime Control Institute.

Sherman, L. (1995). Hot spots of crime and criminal careers of places. In J. Eck and D. Weisburd (eds.), *Crime and Place.* Monsey, NY: Criminal Justice Press, pp. 35–52

Simon, H. A. (1957). *Administrative Behavior,* 2nd ed. New York: Macmillan.

Smith, R., and Klosterman, R. (1980). Criminal justice planning: An alternative model. *Criminology* 17(4):403–418.

Stefanic, M. D. (1985). Preparing a budget: Some tricks of the trade. *Police Chief* 52:51–55.

Suchman, E. A. (1967). *Evaluative Research.* New York: Russell Sage Foundation.

Visiliev, I. (1996). Design issues to be considered when mapping time. In C. Wood and C. Keller (eds.), *Cartographic Design: Theoretical and Practical Perspecitives.* Chichester, UK: Wiley.

Webster, B., and Conners, E. (1999). Police methods for identifying community problems. In R. Trojanowicz, V. Kappeler, L. Gaines, and B. Bucqueroux (eds.), *Community Policing: A Contemporary Perspective,* 2nd ed. Cincinnati: Anderson Publishing, pp. 183–204.

Woodby, K., and Johnson, A. (2000). Identifying a serial indecent exposure suspect. In N. LaVigne and J. Wartell (eds.), *Crime Mapping Case Studies: Successes in the Field,* vol. 2. Washington: Police Executive Research Forum.

14

Accountability

Bob Daemmrich/The Image Works

Chapter Outline

Introduction

Promoting Accountability from the Inside
Internal Affairs
Compstat and Its Progeny
Codes of Ethics

Promoting Accountability from the Outside
Civilian Review
Citizen Complaints
Civil Liability
Accreditation
Other Accountability Measures

Summary

Learning Objectives

After reading this chapter, you should be able to

1. Understand the importance of accountability.
2. Distinguish between internal and external accountability.
3. Understand procedures for ensuring accountability internally, including internal affairs, Compstat, and codes of ethics.
4. Develop procedures for ensuring accountability externally, including civilian review, citizen complaints, state tort and Section 1983 civil liability, accreditation, and criminal liability and the exclusionary rule.

On November 6, 1997, three suspects robbed a Los Angeles Bank of America. The investigation into the robbery led to arrest of Officer David Mack. He was assigned to the West Los Angeles area. On February 26, 1998, an incident involving the false imprisonment and beating of a handcuffed arrestee at the Rampart substation occurred. The officer responsible for the beating of the suspect was Brian Hewitt, an officer in the Rampart Community Resources Against Street Hoodlums (CRASH) Division, the elite street crime enforcement unit of the Los Angeles Police Department (LAPD). Two other CRASH officers admitted being involved in the beating. On March 2, 1998, six pounds of cocaine were checked out from a property room at LAPD headquarters, supposedly to be used as evidence in a trial. When the cocaine was not returned to the property room, police officials initiated an internal investigation on March 27 to ascertain the whereabouts of the cocaine. On August 25, Officer Rafael A. Perez (of the Rampart division) was arrested on suspicion of stealing the cocaine.

The investigations of all three incidents revealed that the suspect officers were associated with one another. They either worked as partners or were close friends, and all but one of them were assigned to the Rampart Division. Officer Mack, who was not

Officers make high-risk felony stop.
Evert Collection

assigned to the Rampart Division, had previously been assigned to Rampart, so a connection between the three officers was clear. Given these insights, Chief Bernard Parks
launched a special criminal Task Force in May 1998 to investigate the incidents further.

Ultimately, the CRASH unit officers involved in the beating at the Rampart substation were terminated. Mack was convicted in federal court of bank robbery. Perez
was prosecuted on drug charges, but his first trial resulted in a hung jury on December
23, 1998.

Nothing else of note occurred (or at least became publicized) until September 8,
1999. As the jury was being selected for Perez's second trial, he pled guilty to stealing
eight pounds of cocaine from LAPD storage facilities. He then entered into a confidential plea agreement according to which he was expected to receive a reduced sentence
on drug charges in exchange for identifying other police officers involved in illegal
activity in the Rampart Division. This agreement marked the beginning of the public
exposure of the Rampart scandal.

On September 15, 1999, the first public airing of the Rampart scandal, the chief of
the LAPD, Bernard Parks, called a press conference to announce that Perez had impli-
cated himself and another Rampart officer in the shooting of an unarmed man. Parks
went on to state that 12 officers had been either placed on leave or fired in connection

with the cover-up. On September 16, Javier Francisco Ovando, the unarmed man who had been shot and framed for assaulting the two officers, was freed from prison after serving three years of a lengthy term. At this point, the FBI began an investigation into civil rights violations in the LAPD.

On September 20, 1999, in a interview from jail, Perez called the corruption in the LAPD a cancer. On September 21, Chief Parks convened a Board of Inquiry (BOI) to investigate the scope of the Rampart scandal. All told, more than 300 people were involved in the Board of Inquiry investigation. Subcommittees were constructed to look into issues including personnel, work product, supervision and management, risk management, operations, corruption, integrity, and so on.

Next, on October 4, two LAPD officers linked to the Rampart corruption scandal were subpoenaed to testify before a grand jury focusing on two allegedly unjustified shootings by Rampart officers. In a flurry of ensuing court action, a judge overturned the convictions of four men and dismissed the case against the other. Since then, the scandal has ballooned out of control. As of May 18, 2000, eighty-four convictions have been vacated.

As of this writing, the U.S. Justice Department is contemplating forcing the LAPD to enter into a consent decree and agree to monitoring of its activities by a federal judge. The department has opposed this vigorously, but its management seems committed nonetheless to changing its ways. The consent decree would require the LAPD to implement significant reforms or face a lawsuit from the federal government. This is arguably not something the department wants to see, as the number of lawsuits being filed because of overturned convictions is growing. The costs of litigation tied to the Rampart incident will likely run into the hundreds of millions of dollars, a serious financial impact, even for a large city such as Los Angeles.

On February 29, 2000, the Board of Inquiry gave its 362-page report to Mayor Richard Riordan and members of the LAPD Police Commission (Parks's supervisors). According to the report, the scandal grew out of failures to check the backgrounds of new recruits, failure to monitor misconduct, failure to supervise officers in the field, and many other factors. In a letter accompanying the board's report, Chief Parks wrote that "we as an organization provided the opportunity" (Newton, Lait, and Glover, 2000). Similarly, as the board noted in the executive summary to its report, "Had the Department and the Rampart management team exercised more vigorous and coordinated oversight of area operations, and its CRASH unit in particular, the crimes and misconduct that occurred may have been prevented, discouraged, or discovered much earlier" (Board of Inquiry, 2000:4). Simply put, accountability and control were compromised in the LAPD. The scandal was made possible because supervision suffered and the department's internal accountability mechanisms proved ineffective.

The board presented 108 recommendations for improving the Los Angles Police Department, particularly for minimizing the potential for this type of scandal to resurface in the future. Its recommendations fell into nine categories: (1) testing and screening of police officer candidates; (2) personnel practices; (3) personnel investigations and management of risk; (4) corruption investigations; (5) operational controls; (6) anticorruption inspections and audits; (7) ethics and integrity training; (8) job-specific training;

and (9) continued Board of Inquiry work. A common theme running throughout all the recommendations is that the LAPD needs to improve on its ability to keep officers accountable. The Rampart scandal started to reveal two things. First, the scandal has shown that it is difficult to ensure accountability in large police departments, as evidenced by the extent of abuses that took place. Total supervision, for example, is difficult, if not impossible, in departments that are both large and spread across a substantial geographical area. At the same time, however, the scandal is a disturbing example of what can occur when control and accountability are not adequately achieved. What has been occurring in the Rampart Division deserves special attention, as it serves to reinforce the need for the accountability mechanisms introduced throughout this chapter as well as being a timely example of what can go wrong when those accountability mechanisms are either ignored or inadequate.

INTRODUCTION

The accomplishment of goals and objectives in police organizations hinges on accountability. Not only is it essential for police administrators to exercise a measure of control over their subordinates, but also it is important for them to hold their subordinates accountable for their actions. *Accountability* is the requirement that subordinates be able to provide satisfactory reasons for significant deviations from organizational goals and expectations. When mistakes and misconduct occur, performance falls below expectations, and outcomes differ from expectations, accountability is essential. Accountability is essential insofar as subordinates must be able to "account" for their actions (indeed, so too should administrators), otherwise control can be compromised.

Administrators themselves must also be accountable to their subordinates, their superiors, and the public. In many ways, accountability is a two-way street: Constituents as well as influential persons outside the police department are usually interested in seeing that police administrators, including the departments they are responsible for managing, operate within established guidelines.

Accountability is a complex, multifaceted administrative issue. This is particularly true for public organizations such as police departments. Accordingly, this chapter examines procedures to promote accountability arising from two sources: (1) within the police department and (2) outside the police department. Internal as well as external accountability mechanisms serve to keep administrators as well as subordinates "in check."

PROMOTING ACCOUNTABILITY FROM THE INSIDE

An important duty for administrators is promoting accountability of their subordinates. This is accomplished through any number of internal accountability mechanisms, namely, those mechanisms that are run and staffed by departmental employees, not anyone from outside the police department. Two internal accountability mechanisms that we examine in this section are internal affairs and Compstat, the latter being a relatively new approach to promoting accountability within law enforcement agencies.

Internal Affairs

Police managers of the 1950s created the internal investigations unit—a specialized staff unit with exclusive responsibility for policing the police. (Internal investigations is also known as internal affairs. The two terms are used interchangeably here.) This unique organizational invention for the internal processing of matters related to employee misbehavior seems to have no counterpart in other types of organizations. The police literature published prior to 1960 contains no mention of internal investigation units (see Leonard, 1951). The second edition of *Police Administration* by O. W. Wilson (1963) suggested that police departments should have staff units dedicated exclusively to the administration of accusations against police:

> In large departments it is necessary to have a division charged with the responsibility of recording, registering, supervising and controlling the investigation of complaints against officers and of ferreting out evidence of corruption within the force.

The first specialized internal affairs units resulted from a division of labor within police intelligence units. These intelligence units had previously been responsible for investigating organized crime, political corruption, and police officers suspected of corrupt behavior. This separation seems to have occurred originally in Los Angeles during the 1950s when the public pressure for establishment of an external civilian police review board was strong. The creation of a special internal investigation unit served to undercut support for civilian review by providing visible evidence of police management's ability and willingness to seek out and discipline misbehaving officers.

Pressure for the development of internal affairs units by police agencies increased throughout the nation in the 1960s as a result of civil rights demonstrations, antiwar demonstrations, and urban riots, which brought evidence of police misconduct into the family living rooms on nightly television news. The President's Commission on Law Enforcement and the Administration of Justice (1967) provided substantial evidence of police misconduct involving discourtesy and verbal abuse, physical brutality, racial discrimination, arrests for harassment, use of deadly force, and use of police dogs. The commission expressed grave concern over the failure of police agencies to control such deviant behavior by police officers, and *The Task Force Report* made it crystal clear that no police agency can be without specialized units for the handling of matters related to police misconduct. In an apparent effort to ensure that police agencies would take the importance of establishing internal investigation units seriously, the commission indicated that it was also necessary for political jurisdictions to create government-level agencies for review of citizen complaints.

On the Job

UNIVERSITY OF MISSOURI POLICE DEPARTMENT
Police Accountability in a University Setting

By Director Fred Otto

Courtesy of Director Otto

The University of Missouri at Columbia is a large urban university serving approximately 23,000 students. The department has about 40 sworn officers to provide police services to the campus. Campus policing and traditional municipal law enforcement have both similarities and dissimilarities. We are similar in that we are charged with preventing and investigating crime on campus. We are dissimilar from municipal law enforcement in that we are not accountable to a city commission or a city manager, but we basically report to a vice president who is responsible for a variety of service functions on campus. This vice president is concerned not only with crime, but with such innate problems as parking, treatment of students, and how well the department handles the many special functions that occur on campus.

The population of a typical campus is much different from the populations of cities or counties. The majority of people are young, predominantly between 18 and 22 years. The population is rather heterogeneous, with many races and ethnic groups represented. The university also has a number of foreign students. In many cases, students are experiencing the freedom of being away from home for the first time—thus they tend to engage in too much recreation, getting themselves in trouble on campus or in the city of Columbia. Also, there is the constant threat of people who are not members of the community entering the campus and committing crimes. This creates a different kind of law enforcement. It is an atmosphere where service rather than law enforcement is emphasized.

Given the nature of our population and the organizational setting, the campus police department is faced with a variety of accountability problems not experienced by local departments. First, although our mission is similar to that of other police agencies, we find many people, students and faculty, who are apathetic about law enforcement and crime prevention. Not only are they apathetic; they sometimes are hostile to the police and the need to

Continued

maintain a crime-free environment. Moreover, the commission of a serious crime, such as a campus rape, can have more ramifications on a college campus than in other jurisdictions.

Several years ago, the Clery Act was passed. This act requires all universities to collect crime information and make the information available to students, parents, and other interested parties. The Clery Act has resulted in much more accountability to the central administration because of the potential adverse problems that crime may cause.

The department has taken a number of actions to improve its performance and to make it more accountable. First, we have implemented community policing. We wanted to move away from the traditional law enforcement model with its emphasis on crime repression and confrontation to a style that encouraged better relations with the people we serve. Second, unlike a number of universities, we have an extensive training budget that allows our officers to receive training from a variety of training programs from across the country. Here, we constantly attempt to identify

training programs that are conducive to helping officers better understand the importance of community policing and developing community trust. This is a preventive measure in that it is designed to eliminate problems before they develop. Finally, the University of Missouri Police Department is one of the few campus law enforcement agencies receiving accreditation from the Commission on Accreditation for Law Enforcement Agencies (CALEA). This accreditation has been important. It sends a message to the administration that their department is a professional department. Too often, campus police are relegated to an inferior position, but accreditation shows that the department is capable of handling problems and is using the most up-to-date police methods.

Accountability is important. When police departments and individual officers are held accountable, they become more responsive to the citizens they serve. We strive to ensure that we provide the best possible services and constantly attempt to improve how we do business.

Internal Investigation Procedures

The purposes of internal investigation units have evolved to include

1. Receiving and recording complaints concerning police misconduct.
2. Investigating complaints and other indications of misconduct on the part of police.
3. Investigating incidents involving the police use of deadly force, homicide or serious injury, or possible breach of integrity or ethical standards by a member of the police agency.
4. Evaluating policies related to police ethics and behavior.
5. Providing administrative trial mechanisms for reviewing instances and accusations of police misconduct.

6. Prosecuting employees who are revealed by evidence to be responsible for serious misbehavior.
7. Providing commanders with intelligence on deviancy and misbehavior occurring within the agency.
8. Informing complainants and victims of police misconduct of actions on their behalf by the police agency.

The organizational design of police internal affairs units becomes more complex as the size of the police agency increases. Regardless of the size of the police agency, a chief executive should consider several important matters in designing internal affairs. Figure 14–1 depicts the disciplinary procedure from the initiation of a complaint to the final disposition in the city of Boston.

Obviously, the effectiveness of internal investigations of police misconduct depends on the accurate receipt and recording of all relevant information of improper personnel or organizational behavior, regardless of its source. Administrative efforts to minimize the potential for manipulating complaints have led to the designation of specifically identified persons or offices as the points for registering employee misconduct complaints. Internal investigation units receive complaints that are filed in various manners: orally or in writing, openly or anonymously, by civilian or sworn police officer, in person or by telephone, or by other means. Complaints must be investigated regardless of the manner of filing or the type of incident involved. The following three types of complaint are critical to effective managerial control and must be fully investigated: (1) a citizen complaining about the police department or one of its employees, (2) a police employee complaining about another police employee, and (3) a police employee complaining about the police agency or its practices (Angell, 1966).

It is important to assess the department's responsibility for the complaint as well as the officer's responsibility in cases of complaints of officer misconduct. Actions perceived by a citizen as officer misconduct may in reality be attributable to departmental policies. For example, a citizen may be incensed by a patrol officer who cuffs a pregnant woman's hands behind her back before placing her in the police car, when in actuality departmental policy left the officer no discretion on the matter.

Once recorded, complaints and reports must be managed in a fashion that ensures prompt, thorough, confidential investigation. Only the chief executive officer and police officials with a need to know are normally permitted access to information about the complainant, the complaint, or the investigation, at least during the initial investigative phase. Time limits for completion of various aspects of the investigation and reports to complainants are essential to the effective operation of internal affairs. The registration personnel normally have responsibility for ensuring adherence to investigative progress deadlines, and specific extensions for continuing investigations must be requested in writing by assigned investigators and approved by monitors at the registration unit. This arrangement of overlapping jurisdiction provides a measure of control over the performance of those investigators who have responsibility for independent monitoring of line operations and processes.

Figure 14–1
Boston's Internal Affairs Division (IAD) flowchart.

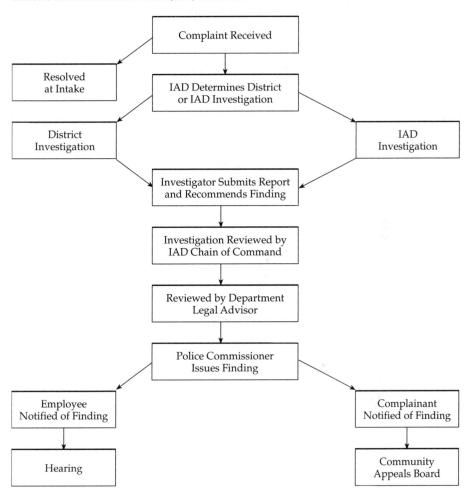

Another matter deserving careful consideration by the chief is the selection of staff investigators for internal affairs. Role conflicts are created when line police officers are assigned to investigate other line officers with whom they must work, or when investigative officers are shifted back and forth between the internal affairs unit and operation units that are subjected to investigations. In both of these cases investigators may be tempted to be lenient with or generous to those accused of misconduct.

Although agreement on this matter is not universal, internal investigations may be best served by police personnel whose careers will not allow them to be reassigned to work under officers who have been the subject of their investigations. To prevent this situation from occurring, small police agencies may want to make use of high-level staff commanders or investigators from other nearby police agencies or sheriffs' departments. Larger organizations usually have the option of developing separate career paths for those who specialize in the investigation of other police officers. Such separate career routes have the advantage of permitting the use of rewards for the vigorous, competent performance of objective investigations.

The Trial Board

Internal investigations are conducted only to determine the facts surrounding a question of employee misconduct. Internal affairs officers have no authority to initiate or carry out corrective actions against employees. Since internal affairs is an administrative tool of the chief, the unit has a responsibility for advising the chief on the general state of the organizational discipline and the adequacy of personnel control efforts of field commanders and supervisors. The internal affairs registration data and information from personnel investigations can be used as a basis for staff reports, which the chief and top commanders can rely on in management decision making. Even those cases that result in inconclusive or unfounded conclusions produce information that may be valuable in administering the police agency.

Where the information accumulated by internal investigations produces evidence of police conduct that is in violation of formal departmental standards and expectations, the evidence is subjected to further review and assessment by supervisors or a decision-making process called a "trial board." Trial boards assist line administrators, especially the chief executive, to ensure that administrative action is within the disciplinary authority of the agency and is appropriate for the control needs of the organization. Since several control devices (such as jurisdictionwide personnel units, civil service commissions, and courts) exist outside the police organization to check on the departmental personnel actions, the quality of these administrative personnel decisions will be tested.

The trial board is operated in conjunction with the internal investigation unit and is staffed on an ad hoc basis when thorough, impartial evaluation of alleged employee misconduct is needed. The trial board is modeled after the military court-martial arrangement. If the offense sustained by an internal affairs investigation merits it (i.e., it is serious enough to possibly lead to dismissal from the police agency), or if the accused officer requests it, a trial board is normally appointed by the chief. The board, consisting of three to five sworn officers, none below the rank of the accused officer, proceeds in a fashion parallel to a civil trial. The accused employee is tried on a specific formally drafted accusation; witnesses are called, examined, and cross-examined; evidence is introduced; and the board renders a decision based on a preponderance of evidence, as in civil proceedings. The board is responsible for rendering a judgment after hearing the case presented by internal affairs and including the findings and conclusions in an advisory report to the chief. Most police trial boards are expected to recommend one of five courses of action to the chief:

1. Further investigation with specific suggestions for how the reopened investigation should proceed.
2. Dismissal of the accusation.
3. Written reprimand.
4. Suspension.
5. Dismissal.

A trial board serves to protect the citizens, the police agency, and the accused by bringing the results of the police investigation before a deliberating body of experienced police personnel in a process that permits organized challenges and rational consideration of all available information. Careful selection of the board members serves to ensure sound, objective judgments. The final decision is made by the chief, who benefits by receiving a thorough exploration of the evidence and issues.

Police Officer Rights during Investigations

Vigorous personnel investigations create pressure to sometimes neglect employee rights to privacy and, perhaps more important, to neglect due process. Internal investigations officers may assume that accused officers are guilty until proven innocent. Given this fact, it should not be surprising that line police officers tend to be suspicious and fearful of police internal investigation personnel and units, and in many places refer to the internal investigation units in disparaging terms as the "God Squad" or the "Hatchet Detail." Administrative attention must always be given to ensuring that internal investigations are performed in a thorough but objective, impersonal fashion that will refute false accusations and suspicions of officer wrongdoing as readily as producing evidence of guilt.

A number of court cases have addressed the issue of police officer rights during the course of internal investigations. For example, in *Garrity v. New Jersey* (1967) the U.S. Supreme Court ruled that information gained from the interrogation of a police officer could not be used in a criminal trial because it was not voluntary. In this case, a state deputy attorney general was asking police officers about ticket fixing. The officers were read their rights and then told that if they failed to answer the questions, they would be dismissed. Subsequent criminal convictions based on admissions were deemed unconstitutional because the admissions were not voluntary. Similarly, in *Gardner v. Broderick* (1967) the Court ruled police officers could not be fired for invoking their constitutional rights against self-incrimination. In *Gardner,* a police officer refused to answer questions from a grand jury on the grounds that they might incriminate him. The department fired the officer. The Court held that the department could not fire the officer for invoking his constitutional rights.

Gardner and *Garrity* are often misinterpreted as granting unilateral privilege to police officers regarding the Fifth Amendment's protection against self-incrimination. However, if the purpose of an internal investigation is not criminal prosecution but, simply discipline, officers can be compelled to answer questions. The Supreme Court stated in *Gardner* and *Garrity* that officers can be required to answer questions (in essence, to waive their Fifth Amendment privilege), but the questions asked of the officers must be specifically, directly, and narrowly related to the officer's duties *and* the officers must be advised that the answers they provide will not be used in a criminal proceeding. The Court felt that it was fair to require that officers answer questions regarding their duties because of the need to protect the state and ensure that officers perform their duties faithfully. The Fifth Amendment, then, applies only when the responses to the questions are to be used in a criminal prosecution.

In 1998 the Supreme Court consolidated six internal investigations cases and rendered its decision in *LaChance v. Erickson* (1998). The issue in *LaChance* was whether police officers who gave untruthful statements during the course of an internal investigation could be dismissed. The lead case concerned an officer who allegedly made harassing telephone calls. The officer was asked about his involvement in the phone calls. He denied he was involved, despite evidence to the contrary from the investigation. The agency fired the officer for giving untruthful statements. A merit review board reduced the "punishment" to a 15-day suspension, and a federal circuit court basically agreed with the decision, stating that if officers were not allowed to make inaccurate statements, they might be coerced into admitting misconduct. The Supreme Court disagreed unanimously, holding that "willful falsehoods" made by an employee during the course of an internal investigation can be grounds for dismissal.

The disciplinary aspect of internal investigations also raises issues about the rights police officers enjoy. If, for example, an internal investigation results in a recommendation for suspension or dismissal, due process issues come into play. Two types of due process can be distinguished: procedural and substantive. Procedural due process, as the name suggests, applies to the legality of the *procedures* used for purposes of discipline. The essence of substantive due process is protection from arbitrary and unfair action. In the policing context, substantive due process issues have been raised with regard to unclear rules and regulations that serve as the basis for disciplinary action.

Procedural due process cases seem to be somewhat frequent in the area of public employment. For example, in *Cleveland Board of Education v. Loudermill,* the Supreme Court stated that public employees are "entitled to oral or written notice of the charges against [them], an explanation of the employer's evidence, and an opportunity to present [their] side of the story" (1985:546). In the recent case of *Gilbert v. Homar,* however, the Court interpreted *Loudermill* to mean that a public employee is entitled to only a "very limited hearing prior to his termination, to be followed by a more comprehensive post-termination hearing" (1997:929). The definitions of "very limited" and "more comprehensive" remain elusive.

A substantive due process case is *Bence v. Breier* (1974). In *Bence* the Seventh Circuit held that a Milwaukee Police Department rule that prohibited "conduct unbecoming a member and detrimental to the service" lacked "inherent, objective content from which ascertainable standards defining the proscribed conduct could be fashioned" (p. 1190). The court noted that the rule permitted "unfettered discretion" to those charged with enforcing it. This decision is important on an administrative level because it suggests departmental policies and regulations need to be clear and specific, leaving very little room for interpretation.

A Police Officer Bill of Rights?

To reduce the temptation for internal investigators to proceed against police employees in an insensitive fashion, some police agencies have formally adopted a statement of the rights of police officers who are accused of misconduct. Sometimes such conditions are contained in labor contracts; other times they are mandated by law. The most common conditions in such police "bill of rights" clauses in union contracts have been summarized by Krajack (1979:9-16):

1. A ban on the use of polygraphs and alcohol detection devices.
2. Defined hours when an interrogation of a suspected officer may be conducted by an investigator.
3. Advance notice to an officer who is being investigated, which includes the accusation and the name and address of any complainant.
4. Accusation and trial procedures that ensure an officer's right to counsel, cross-examination of accusers and witnesses, and established penalties.
5. A right of an accused officer to pick some members of any review panel or trial board which will sit in judgment of the officer upon completion of the investigation.

Although specific aspects of this summary can be debated, officers deserve reasonable protection from inappropriate investigative practices. Procedures for ensuring fair and appropriate treatment of officers at the hands of specialized internal affairs investigators and their supervisors should be observed in the investigative process. They should include the following:

1. The complaint to be investigated is assigned to an internal affairs investigator following registration with the central intake position.
2. The investigating officer reviews the details of the complaint, checking with the complainant to obtain an accurate understanding of the accusation or report if necessary.
3. The accused employee is presented with a summary of the accusation and given an opportunity to make a report concerning the reported matter. Unless exercising constitutional rights related to criminal prosecution, an accused can be expected to provide information about job-related actions and behavior. Further, in cases where serious criminal behavior is alleged, the investigator should proceed as one would in handling a criminal investigation. Policy should prevent accused employees from engaging in any actions that can be construed as intended to influence complainants or others regarding matters under investigation.
4. The internal affairs investigative process involves thorough, confidential activities carried out in the authority and on behalf of the chief.

5. Upon completion of an investigation, the investigator prepares a summary report of findings and recommendations. The alternative findings are labeled unfounded, inconclusive, or founded.
6. Investigations that produce unfounded or inconclusive findings should not result in notations or records in an employee's personnel file.
7. When misconduct is found, a recommendation for action is provided directly to the chief when serious misbehavior is found or to the appropriate lower-level supervisor when the less serious nature of the situation merits such a referral.
8. Employees should be afforded the opportunity for an appeal of supervisor action or, in serious matters, a departmental trial for complete hearing of a serious matter prior a decision by the chief executive.

Several states have adopted a police officer bill of rights (Chiuchiolo, 1981). Florida adopted one such statement as early as 1974. The Florida Law Enforcement Officer's Bill of Rights is reproduced in Figure 14–2. Supporters of such legislation argue that "the bill of rights merely ensures the officer under investigation knows the subject of the investigation and is afforded rights and protections against certain interrogation techniques subject to abuse" (Johnson, 1999:42). Critics of police officer bills of rights claim that "the basic premises of such legislation only confound an already complex area of public police without substantially improving police labor–management relations" (Scott, 1999:46).

Compstat and Its Progeny

It's just past seven on the third morning of the new year, and Lawrence, who runs the 10th Precinct in Midtown Manhattan, is standing on a podium in the command control center at police headquarters—the "war room." His face is bright red and a little clammy. His body is wired up tight. He is surrounded by sheaves of statistics, screens filled with computerized maps and charts and N.Y.P.D. bosses who, amazingly, seem to know as much about crime in his precinct as he does. "It's been 30 days since we've seen you, Tom," says Chief of Department Louis Anemone, a dark tone creeping into his voice. "And we're seeing an increase in robberies." "What's the pattern here, Cap?" asks Deputy Commissioner Jack Maple "What are you doing to take these guys out?" (Pooley and Rivera 1996:54)

This is what one reporter observed during an early NYPD Compstat meeting, one element of a relatively novel (and quickly growing) mechanism to ensure accountability in police agencies. Compstat represents the "cutting edge" in police accountability. It is not "reactive" in the sense that internal investigations are; rather, it is a proactive, preemptive attempt to hold high-level supervisors (captains, for example) responsible for problems in the areas for which they are responsible.

During the early years of his tenure as police commissioner of New York City, William Bratton called for weekly meetings with representatives from each of the NYPD's eight bureaus. Deputy Commissioner Jack Maple, in conjunction with other high-ranking officials, placed pressure on the bureaus to generate

FIGURE 14–2
Florida Law Enforcement Officers' Bill of Rights.

112.532 Law enforcement officers' and correctional officers' rights.—All law enforcement officers and correctional officers employed by or appointed to a law enforcement agency or a correctional agency shall have the following rights and privileges:

(1) RIGHTS OF LAW ENFORACEMENT OFFICERS AND CORRECTIONAL OFFICERS WHILE UNDER INVESTIGATION.—Whenever a law enforcement officer or correctional officer is under investigation and subject to interrogation by members of his or her agency for any reason which could lead to disciplinary action, demotion, or dismissal, such interrogation shall be conducted under the following conditions:

(a) The interrogation shall be conducted at a reasonable hour, preferably at a time when the law enforcement officer or correctional officer is on duty, unless the seriousness of the investigation is of such a degree that immediate action is required.

(b) The interrogation shall take place either at the office of the command of the investigating officer or at the office of the local precinct, police unit, or correctional unit in which the incident allegedly occurred, as designated by the investigating officer or agency.

(c) The law enforcement office or correctional officer under investigation shall be informed of the rank, name, and command of the officer in charge of the investigation, the interrogating officer, and all persons present during the interrogation. All questions directed to the officer under interrogation shall be asked by and through one interrogator at any one time.

(d) The law enforcement officer or correctional officer under investigation shall be informed of the nature of the investigation prior to any interrogation, and he or she shall be informed of the name of all complainants.

(e) Interrogating sessions shall be for reasonable periods and shall be timed to allow for such personal necessities and rest periods as are reasonably necessary.

(f) The law enforcement officer or correctional officer under interrogation shall not be subjected to offensive language or be threatened with transfer, dismissal, or disciplinary action. No promise or reward shall be made as an inducement to answer any questions.

(g) The formal interrogation of a law enforcement officer or correctional officer, including all recess periods, shall be recorded on audio tape, or otherwise preserved in such a manner as to allow a transcript to be prepared, and there shall be no unrecorded questions or statements. Upon the request of the interrogated officer, a copy of any such recording of the interrogation session must be made available to the interrogated officer no later than 72 hours, excluding holidays and weekends, following said interrogation.

(h) If the law enforcement officer or correctional officer under interrogation is under arrest, or is likely to be placed under arrest as a result of the interrogation, he or she shall be completely informed of all his or her rights prior to the commencement of the interrogation.

(i) At the request of any law enforcement officer or correctional officer under investigation, he or she shall have the right to be represented by counsel or any other representative of his or her choice, who shall be present at all times during such interrogation whenever the interrogation relates to the officer's continued fitness for law enforcement or correctional service.

(2) COMPLAINT REVIEW BOARDS.—A complaint review board shall be composed of three members: One member selected by the chief administrator of the agency or unit; one member selected by the aggrieved officer; and a third member to be selected by the other two members.

Continued

FIGURE 14–2

Florida Law Enforcement Officers' Bill of Rights. (*Concluded*)

Agencies or units having more than 100 law enforcement officers or correctional officers shall utilize a five-member board, with two members being selected by the administrator, two members being selected by the aggrieved officer, and the fifth member being selected by the other four members. The board members shall be law enforcement officers or correctional officers selected from any state, county, or municipal agency within the county. There shall be a board for law enforcement officers and a board for correctional officers whose members shall be from the same discipline as the aggrieved officer. The provisions of this subsection shall not apply to sheriffs or deputy sheriffs.

(3) CIVIL SUITS BROUGHT BY LAW ENFORCEMENT OFFICERS OR CORRECTIONAL OFFICERS.—Every law enforcement officer or correctional officer shall have the right to bring civil suit against any person, group of persons, or organization or corporation, or the head of such organization or corporation, for damages, either pecuniary or otherwise, suffered during the performance of the officer's official duties or for abridgment of the officer's civil rights arising out of the officer's performance of official duties.

(4) NOTICE OF DISCIPLINARY ACTION.—No dismissal, demotion, transfer, reassignment, or other personnel action which might result in loss of pay or benefits or which might otherwise be considered a punitive measure shall be taken against any law enforcement officer or correctional officer unless such law enforcement officer or correctional officer is notified of the action and the reason or reasons therefor prior to the effective date of such action.

(5) RETALIATION FOR EXERCISING RIGHTS.—No law enforcement officer or correctional officer shall be discharged; disciplined; demoted; denied promotion, transfer, or reassignment; or otherwise discriminated against in regard to his or her employment or appointment, or be threatened with any such treatment, by reason of his or her exercise of the rights granted by this part.

Source: Florida Statutes, 1999. Retrieved from http://www.leg.state.fl.us/citizen/documents/statutes/Statute Browser99/ind.../SEC532.HT.

crime statistics, which, surprisingly, were not kept up to date at the time. Precincts began to measure criminal activity more carefully; then the results were computerized and assembled into a document known as the "Compstat book" (Silverman, 1999). The crime figures reported in the Compstat book would eventually be used to hold precinct commanders responsible for the crime rates in their areas. NYPD leadership then began to hold meetings with precinct commanders, one of which is described in the quotation at the outset of this section.

Compstat is an acronym for computer statistics (in some locations, it is compare statistics). It has come to be widely imitated around the country, and several different designations can be identified. Table 14-1 includes other names for Compstat from around the country.

Generally speaking, Compstat emphasizes four important things: (1) accurate and timely intelligence, (2) rapid deployment, (3) effective tactics, and (4) relentless follow-up and assessment (Brady, 1997). The logic behind the intelligence aspect is that "Information describing how and where crimes are committed, as well as who criminals are, must be available to all levels of policing" (Harries, 1999:79). Rapid deployment is important because "the most effective

Table 14–1

Compstat around the Country

Jurisdiction	Term Used
New York	Compstat
Baltimore	Crimestac
San Antonio	MAP (Management Accountability Program)
Los Angeles	Fastrac
Minneapolis	Codefor
Los Angeles Sheriff's Office	CIF (Critical Issues Forum)
El Paso	SAC (Strategic Analysis of Crime)

plans require that personnel from several units and enforcement functions work together as a team" (Harries, 1999:79). "Tactics are designed to respond directly to facts discovered during the intelligence gathering process" (Harries, 1999:79), and relentless follow-up is necessary to ensure that desired outcomes occur.

New Orleans has had promising results with its version of Compstat (called Comstat). During 1996 the New Orleans Police Department undertook a major reorganization and philosophical change. All crime-fighting responsibilities were placed under the eight district commanders. New resources were also allocated to assist them in accomplishing their mission: reducing crime and violence in one of the most dangerous cities in the country. New Orleans's version of Compstat contained the four elements that were present in New York—intelligence, rapid deployment, effective tactics, and follow-up—but the means by which they were accomplished are particularly interesting. Table 14–2 depicts the elements of New Orleans's Comstat program.

The last step, relentless accountability, is extremely important and is usually accomplished most effectively in Compstat meetings. According to Jack Maple, former deputy commissioner of the NYPD, "the first step to crime reduction itself—the gathering and analyzing of accurate, timely intelligence—has to be quickened by the heat of accountability" (Maple, 1999:93). New Orleans's Compstat program maintains a similar philosophy: "Accountability is paramount in this procedure. Each District Commander is expected to be fully aware of the crimes that take place in his or her area of responsibility and is expected to not only react to these offense but to take proactive measures to reduce and deter them. In addition, each District Commander must prepare an extensive weekly report on the activity in his or her district" (New Orleans Police Department, 2000).

An important aspect of Compstat consists of crime mapping. Because crime data need to be portrayed clearly and in a timely fashion, computer technology is essential. According to Silverman, "A powerful software tool, MapInfo 94, became the NYPD's crime radar screen, with attention-grabbing colors and shapes. Red dots indicated drug complaints from the public, blue dots showed drug arrests, green triangles represented shooting incidents, and yellow dots indicated homicides" (1999:104). Computerized images generated by

Table 14–2

Elements of New Orleans's Compstat Model

Accurate and Timely Intelligence

Daily review of offense reports by District Investigative Unit
Cases with follow-up possibility assigned to investigator
Directed patrols ordered based on offense information

Rapid Deployment

Uniformed squads deployed in problem areas
Investigators shifted to coincide with crime patterns and trends

Effective Tactics

Detectives respond to all violent crimes
Canvass for witnesses conducted
All suspects arrested for UCR offenses debriefed by detectives

Relentless Follow-Up Assessment

Debriefing perpetrators arrested for felonies
Reinterview victims and witnesses of major crimes
Roll call training on crime fighting, evidence gathering, and reports
Weekly Comstat meetings involving District Commander and others

Source: New Orleans Police Department. Retrieved from http://www.acadiacom.net/nopd/comstat.htm.

MapInfo 94 brought together all the data in the Compstat books, where in the past crime statistics were not kept or presented in any single source. As Harries observed, "These visual presentations are a highly effective complement to the ComStat report, since they permit precinct commanders and executive staff members to instantly identify and explore trends, patterns, and possible solutions for crime and quality-of-life problems" (1999:80).

The most popular measure of success for precinct commanders is crime—specifically, the lack thereof. However, Garner and Hoover (2000) raise questions about the appropriateness of crime as a sole outcome measure. They cite quality-of-life issues as well as citizen complaints as barometers of police performance that agencies experimenting with Compstat may wish to consider. The appropriate success measure, they suggest, "communicates what issues are valued most in the department" (p. 11). Garner and Hoover also raise concerns about the NYPD version of Compstat, which is rather confrontational. Although NYPD's program has established greater accountability, increased awareness, improved problem-solving endeavors, and increased managerial control, they caution that weekly meetings may be too shortsighted, too aggressive an approach to reducing crime, possibly overemphasizing outcomes rather than underlying causes of problems. Indeed, Pedersen observes that "Compstat's approach ignores decades of expert research that has shown that crime levels are determined by vast social forces beyond police control—poverty, racism, [and] demographics" (1996:29).

Codes of Ethics

Another mechanism for promoting accountability from within the law enforcement agency consists of a code of ethics. A code of ethics is a useful document police officers can fall back on when faced with an ethical dilemma. According to Pollock, these codes consist of several standard elements, including "legality (enforcing and upholding the law), service (protecting and serving the public), honesty and integrity (telling the truth, being honest in action), loyalty (to other police officers), and the Golden Rule (treating people with respect or the way on would like to be treated)" (2001:366; see Pollock and Becker, 1996, for more information).

The development of a code of ethics for law enforcement can be traced to the movement to professionalize policing. During the 1930s the International Association of Chiefs of Police (IACP) created a committee to make recommendations designed to promote professionalism. The committee agreed that one of the criteria for accomplishing this goal was the creation of a code of ethics. Several years later in 1957 the Law Enforcement Code of Ethics was unanimously approved by delegates attending the 64th IACP conference in Honolulu, Hawaii. Then, in 1989, the IACP voted to replace the 1957 code with a newer version. The new code reflects concern over a wider range of issues than the 1957 version.

Among the issues covered in the 1989 IACP Code of Ethics are (1) responsibilities of police officers; (2) performance of police duties; (3) discretion; (4) use of force; (5) confidentiality; (6) integrity; (7) cooperation with other agencies; (8) personal and professional responsibilities; and (9) private life. For example, with respect to an officers private life, the code states: "Police officer will behave in a manner that does not bring discredit to their agencies or themselves." With respect to use of force, the code states: "A police officer will never employ unnecessary force or violence and will use only such force in the discharge of duty as is reasonable in all circumstances" (Gaines, Kappeler, and Vaughan, 1999:344–345).

PROMOTING ACCOUNTABILITY FROM THE OUTSIDE

Because police departments are public organizations, accountability is much more than an internal matter. That is, citizens and community groups, law and the courts, elected officials and members of the public, and many others are responsible for ensuring that police departments remain accountable to the people they serve, and that they take responsibility when expectations and goals are not satisfied.

The 1960s and 1970s witnessed numerous overt abuses of power and authority against citizens by the police, which ultimately led to external review of police behavior in many jurisdictions. Citizens came to distrust their police and feared that little action would be taken when officers overstepped their authority.

Kerstetter examined the various methods for reviewing police conduct and concluded that the department itself should have the *primary* authority to investigate and take action on complaints of police misconduct: "The departmental administrative structure has by far the greatest potential for efficient, effective action to prevent, to investigate, to adjudicate, or to punish police misconduct" (1985:178). Kerstetter recommended that a *secondary* level of authority be placed in *external* review. Meaningful external review serves to balance placing primary responsibility for misconduct investigations in the hands of the police. The external review of the internal review of misconduct allows outside scrutiny of the process and thereby lends credibility to internal review.

Conversely, Schwartz (1985), a former ACLU attorney, takes the position that external review should dominate the police review process. He argues that only when civilians have the primary responsibility for investigation of misconduct can true control occur:

> So long as the police themselves gather, assemble, present, interpret, and then judge the facts related to misconduct complaints, few serious complaints are likely to be sustained. As evidence gatherers and assemblers, the police will act as a fraternal brotherhood, protecting their own whenever possible against negative feedback. . . . Unfortunately, too few police departments have been capable of setting their own restraints and taking seriously the feedback that comes through the complaint process. Civilians then are called to the task as much by default as by constitutional imperative (1985:188, 191).

This section takes a position similar to Kerstetter's. The issue of police control must be examined as a partnership, a partnership between the chief (and those inside the organization) and the community. Accordingly, external accountability mechanisms are essential. History has shown that some are more effective than others, but each mechanism encourages to police to answer to issues, complaints, and criticisms voiced from *outside* the department. The external accountability mechanisms covered in this section are civilian review, citizen complaints, civil liability, and other procedures.

Civilian Review

West (1988) found that the vast majority of police departments use an internal process to handle disciplinary actions. In only 16.2 percent of the departments responding to his survey did some form of external treatment of disciplinary problems exist. For the most part, this external treatment consists of an appointed body reviewing the police department's actions and findings. Recently, however, an increasing number of cities have established external (citizen) complaint review procedures (Walker and Wright, 1995). Walker and Wright identified four reasons for the growth in civilian review:

> Citizen involvement in the complaint process will produce (1) more objective and more thorough investigations; (2) a higher rate of sustained complaints and more disciplinary actions against guilty officers; (3) greater deterrence of police misconduct (through both general and specific deterrence); and (4) higher levels of satisfaction on the part of both individual complainants and the general public (1997:322).

There is little consistency in the way external review is structured (Goldsmith, 1991). However, Kerstetter (1985) identified three models: civilian review, civilian input, and civilian monitor. The *civilian review model* is the strongest format; here a civilian body investigates, adjudicates, and recommends punishment. The civilian review has been tried in cities such as Washington, D.C., Philadelphia, Rochester, New York City, and Berkeley. The strongest argument against the civilian review model is that it vests responsibility and authority for police discipline in the hands of individuals who have no expertise in police work and who do not have the capacity for investigating and understanding the issues that normally surround a disciplinary problem (Americans for Effective Law Enforcement 1982; Wagner and Decker, 1997).

The *civilian input model* vests the receipt and investigation of complaints in the hands of civilians. All other functions remain the responsibility of the police department. Two examples of this model that Kerstetter (1985) identified are in Chicago and Kansas City. In Kansas City, the Office of Citizen Complaints (OCC) serves as the central clearinghouse for receiving complaints. The OCC reviews all complaints and assigns those requiring further action to the police department's internal affairs unit for investigation. Once the investigation is completed, the OCC reviews the results and makes recommendations to the chief. Police managers are then allowed to then respond to the recommendations. In Chicago, the Office of Professional Standards (OPS) is located in the police department and is staffed by nonsworn personnel. The OPS handles all citizen complaints involving excessive force, deadly force, and nondeadly force, while the department's internal affairs division is responsible for all other disciplinary issues.

Finally, the *civilian monitor model* is similar to an ombudsman approach. With the civilian monitor model, complaints are received by the police department and the process, from beginning to end, is monitored by the external unit. The monitoring consists of scrutinizing the internal process for inconsistencies or problems. For example, in San Jose, California, the ombudsman's office receives and investigates complaints. Next, it reviews those complaints received and investigated by the police department. A similar approach identified by Napper (1985) involves the Atlanta Police Department. The Atlanta Police Department adopted a review procedure whereby a pool of 25 appointed citizens and two cochairs form a rotating review board of five citizens. The board is able to select cases investigated by the department and review them for irregularities.

Walker and Bumphus (1991) developed a similar classification scheme. They identified four "classes" of civilian review. The first class of civilian review involves independent citizen review bodies, where nonsworn investigators conduct investigations and make recommendations to the police executive. Complaint procedures of this type are found, for example, in New Orleans and Cincinnati (Walker, 1995). The second class of systems involves initial investigations by sworn police officers, then review of the officers' reports by an individual or board that contains at least some nonsworn people. The individual or board then makes recommendations to the chief. Procedures of this type have been identified in Kansas City, Portland, and Albuquerque (Walker,

1995). Systems in the third class have internal affairs investigate complaints then make recommendations to the chief. Citizens who are not satisfied with the final disposition can appeal to a board containing at least some nonsworn individuals. The board reviews each complainant's case and may make different recommendations to the chief. This type of system can be found in Omaha (Walker, 1995). The final type of civilian review procedure has established auditors for citizen complaints. In both Seattle and San Jose, for example, and auditor does not investigate complaints, but rather reviews the department's complaint procedure and recommends changes as necessary. The auditor often contacts complainants to assess their satisfaction with the complaint process (Walker, 1995).

Finally, Walker (2001) distinguished between independent review of citizen complaints and civilian oversight. Independent review occurs when a civilian review body investigates complaints filed against law enforcement officers, then forwards its recommendation to the chief or sheriff. The monitoring role, by contrast, stresses community outreach, review of complaint policies by a civilian group, audits of complaint investigation procedures, information dissemination, and the like. Walker concludes that the monitoring role represents the best opportunity for success in civilian review.

In sum, civilian review represents an important step in promoting accountability. However, the effectiveness of civilian review in reducing or eliminating misconduct is unclear. This is because most civilian review mechanisms only provide for disciplinary *recommendations*. That is, most can only make advisory recommendations to the chief police executive (Perez, 1994). As Walker and Wright observed, "The powers of citizen review procedures are far more limited than those of judges in the criminal process." Nevertheless, certain cities vest citizens with the ability to make disciplinary decisions. As of this writing, the San Francisco Office of Citizen Complaints, the Milwaukee Fire and Police Commission, the Chicago Police Board, and the Detroit Police Commission all have ultimate authority to discipline police officers (Walker and Wright, 1997:333).

Citizen Complaints

Citizen complaints can be seen by administrators as "a barometer of police performance" (Wagner and Decker, 1997:310). Obviously, police officers act without constant supervision by management, so complaints serve as an indicator to supervisors of how well their subordinates are behaving on the street. The U.S. Commission on Civil Rights stated that complaints are "important indicators of public perception of the agency" (1981:50). According to this report, police agencies can use the information from complaints to improve performance, enhance their image, and strengthen relationships with citizens.

Many, perhaps most, police agencies have centralized citizen complaint reception points where all citizen complaints about police misbehavior or ill-treatment of citizens must be reported. Here complaints are confidentially

Police officer talks to citizen to foster better relations.
Robert Brenner/PhotoEdit

received and permanently logged in chronological order of receipt, complainant information is recorded, and experienced staff investigators are assigned to perform complete investigative follow-up.

Some departments go beyond simply attempting to prevent interference with the reporting and collection of complainants or information regarding employee misconduct; they publicize the existence and procedures of the police complaint system and actively seek out complaints. These police agencies have distributed citizen complaint forms to civic organizations and neighborhood groups. Some require any police employee who is approached by a citizen with a complaint about police to report the complaint to the internal investigation registration desk within a set time period after receiving the information.

In its model police misconduct policy, the Police Executive Research Forum listed three ways that the police could implement effective citizen complaint procedures: (1) "through the provision of meaningful and effective complaint procedures, citizen confidence in the integrity of police increases and this engenders community support and confidence in the police department; (2) through disciplinary procedures that permit police officials to monitor officers' compliance with departmental procedures; and (3) by clarifying rights and ensuring due process protection to citizens and officers alike" (1981:1).

Despite the apparent ease with which one could complain, a great deal of research suggests it is much more difficult to have a complaint sustained, that is, resolved in favor of the person filing the complaint. For example, Schwartz (1985) noted that in 1980 the San Francisco Police Department failed to sustain a single citizen complaint out of 301 received. The department did not seriously investigate complaints and discouraged citizens from filing them. In 1982, a voter initiative turned over the responsibility of investigating complaints to citizens and authority for adjudication over to the San Francisco Police Commission rather than the police chief as a result of the department's failure to discipline its personnel. San Francisco was just one of numerous departments that adopted external review for their police.

West (1988) surveyed 132 major American police departments to gauge the status of disciplinary procedures. He found that 83.9 percent of the departments used an internal mechanism to investigate citizen complaints, 9.7 percent used a system whereby the department rendered a disposition but was subject to external review in certain circumstances (Berkeley, California; Kansas City, Missouri; and Portland, Oregon are examples), and 6.5 percent of the departments used a bilateral system where the department and an external agency administered complaint investigations (for example, Washington, D.C.; Detroit; and San Francisco). While complaints emanate from outside the agency, the investigatory process, then, remains largely internal in nature.

In a more recent study, Griswold (1994) examined how the frequency of citizen complaints, the origin of complaints, and type of complaints affected their dispositions. He found that the frequency of complaints had no bearing on dispositions, but that complaints filed by police officers (as opposed to citizens) were more likely to be sustained. Moreover, complaints of excessive force were less likely to be sustained than other complaints, regardless of who filed the complaint. Both these conclusions suggest that citizens face an uphill battle when filing complaints *and* that the most serious complaints are the least likely to be resolved favorably for the complainer. Similar findings emerged in another study by Demers and his colleagues (1992), but they also looked at the race of the complainer. They found, somewhat disturbingly, that the "police were nearly twice as likely to sustain complaints filed against police officers by white citizens than by nonwhites." This finding is especially troubling because "nonwhite citizens, especially blacks, [are] more often the victims of police misconduct" (Wagner and Decker, 1997:306), and nonwhite citizens are responsible for the majority of complaints against the police in many jurisdictions (e.g., Minneapolis, 1996; Wagner, 1980).

More recently still, Lersch (1998) found that citizens in areas characterized by high unemployment were less likely to have their complaints substantiated. She also found that nonwhites were less likely to have their complaints resolved satisfactorily. Finally, she too found that complaints of excessive force were among the least likely to be resolved in favor of the complainant. In sum, the evidence suggests that a complaint's success (or lack thereof) ultimately hinges on who files it. Moreover, it would suggest that police agencies have a long way to go before citizen complaint procedures become an effective method of promoting accountability from outside the agency.

Civil Liability

As Glendon observed, the "heavy machinery of law is being wheeled out to deal with an expanding array of personal disputes" (1994:268). And as Pike reported, "Americans in all walks of life are being buried under an avalanche of lawsuits" (1978:50). Indeed, a former Supreme Court Justice lamented the litigious tendencies many people exhibit in this country:

> One reason our courts have become overburdened is that Americans are increasingly turning to the courts for relief from a range of personal distresses and anxieties. Remedies for personal wrongs that once were considered the responsibility of institutions other than the courts are now boldly asserted as legal "entitlements." The courts have been expected to fill the void created by the decline of church, family, and neighborhood unity. (Burger, 1982:275)

The police are caught right in the middle. Being one of the most visible branches of the executive arm of government, law enforcement officials occupy a precarious position with respect to liability. This is exacerbated by the nature of the policing occupation. Often, the police are required to use force, which frequently ignites heated debate, outcry, and disillusionment. This can come in the form of complaints and protest; all too often, however, it seems to come in the form of litigation.

The prospect of civil liability, being sued for misconduct, is an especially important issue for police administrators. Lawsuits are costly; they drive insurance premiums up, tarnish the department's image, and negatively affect morale, and they can even instill fear and paranoia in frontline police officers. Perhaps more important, administrators (even administrators' employers) can be held liable for the misconduct of their subordinates.

The two sections that follow consider two types of civil liability relevant to law enforcement officials, administrators in particular. The first is liability arising from Section 1983 of the U.S. Code. The second is state tort liability. Both causes of action have shaped and refined the law enforcement profession in many unmistakable ways. All told, lawsuits function to keep the police accountable to the public they serve. And even though commentators have lamented the evolution of civil liability, the prospect of suit nevertheless operates to keep police officers in compliance with the strictures of the law and the Constitution.

Section 1983

One of the most popular causes of action for aggrieved plaintiffs, or means for suing police officers, can be found in 42 U.S.C. Section 1983. Section 1983 allows plaintiffs to sue state officials in federal court (sometimes state court) for violations of federally protected rights. Among these federally protected rights are constitutional rights, violations of which are commonly alleged in Section 1983 lawsuits. Section 1983 provides:

> Every person who, under color of any statute, ordinance, regulation, custom, or usage, of any State or Territory, subjects or causes to be subjected, any citizen of the United States or other persons within the jurisdiction thereof to the deprivation of any rights, privileges, or immunities secured by the Constitution and laws, shall be liable to the person injured in an action of law, suit in equity, or other proper proceedings for redress.

The elements of a successful lawsuit under Section 1983 are thus twofold: (1) a constitutional violation (or violation of any other federally protected right) (2) under color of state law. That is, the plaintiff needs to demonstrate that his or her constitutional rights were violated by a law enforcement official acting under color of state law. "Color of law" is construed broadly to include actions of a law enforcement officer committed within the scope of his or her employment.

The Supreme Court recognized a similar cause of action in *Bivens v. Six Unknown Named Agents* (1971). The Court basically held that Section 1983 lawsuits against federal officials are permissible. The same standards apply for lawsuits against federal officials that apply for state officials. That is, plaintiffs must show that officials acted under color of law and the official deprived the plaintiff of his or her constitutional rights in some fashion. The *Bivens* case pertained to an alleged Fourth Amendment violation where federal officers, without a warrant, had manacled, searched, and arrested the plaintiff and ransacked his apartment. *Bivens* actions are not limited to Fourth Amendment claims, however.

Despite the apparent simplicity of Section 1983, determining whether a constitutional violation has occurred is actually very complex. For example, the courts have increasingly required a certain level of culpability in the commission of constitutional rights violations for a finding of liability. For example, if a plaintiff sues an individual police officer for a Fourth Amendment violation, he or she must show that the officer acted under color of state law and that the officer's actions were "unreasonable." The Supreme Court has sought to define what is and is not reasonable in terms of "objective reasonableness." As the Court remarked in *Graham v. Connor* "The question is whether the officers' actions are 'objectively reasonable' in light of the facts and circumstances confronting them, without regard to their underlying intent or motivation" (1989:397).

Another example points to the difficulties plaintiffs can face in proving a constitutional violation. If, for example, a plaintiff sues an individual officer under Section 1983 for a Fourteenth Amendment substantive due process violation (e.g., a third-party death during a high-speed pursuit), the plaintiff must show that the police action "shocks the conscience" (*County of Sacramento v. Lewis* 1998). In *County of Sacramento v. Lewis* (1998:2), the Supreme Court held: "In the circumstances of a high-speed chase aimed at apprehending a suspected offender, where unforeseen circumstances demand an instant judgment on the part of an officer who feels the pulls of competing obligations, only a purpose to cause harm unrelated to the legitimate object of arrest will satisfy the shocks the conscience test." In short, "Not every push or show is a constitutional violation" (*Graham v. Connor*, 1989:1), but a literal reading of 42 U.S.C. Section 1983 would seem to suggest otherwise.

The foregoing examples were limited to lawsuits against individual police officers, particularly those in nonadministrative positions. However, Section 1983 lawsuits can be filed against administrators as well. The requirements for a successful lawsuit are essentially the same (color of law and a constitutional violation), but here, too, what constitutes a constitutional violation has become a complex issue in recent years. Generally, police supervisors and administrators are confronted by Section 1983 liability on two fronts. The first is in their individual capacities. Individual supervisors, for example, can be sued for the unconstitutional activities of their subordinates. Second, administrators can face Section 1983 liability in their capacities as policymakers. They cannot be held individually liable for unconstitutional policies, but their role in promulgating policies that violate people's constitutional rights can lead to municipal (or county) liability.

Supervisors can be sued in their individual capacities if it can be determined that there was an "affirmative link" between the unconstitutional conduct of the subordinate and the supervisor (*Rizzo v. Goode*, 1976). Unfortunately, the courts have failed to adopt a uniform definition of what constitutes an affirmative link. Some courts have defined the affirmative link in terms of deliberate indifference, others in terms of knowledge, and still others in terms of negligence. For example, in *Starzenski v. City of Elkhart*, the Seventh Circuit held that an affirmative link should be defined in terms of supervisory conduct that "knowingly, willfully, or at least recklessly cause[d] the alleged deprivation" (1996:880). In *Hill v. Dekalb Regional Youth Detention Center*, the affirmative link was defined as "reckless or callous indifference" (1994:1192). In *Jojola v. Chavez*, the Tenth Circuit defined the affirmative link as conduct where supervisors "actually know of and acquiesced in [the subordinate's] behavior" (1995:490). And in *Black v. Coughlin*, the Second Circuit held that the affirmative link can be defined in terms of "gross negligence in managing subordinates" (1996). There are thus no clear answers as to what constitutes the affirmative link, but supervisors should nevertheless be aware that when they condone and/or turn a blind eye to the unconstitutional activities of their subordinates, they can be held liable.

Police administrators can also be responsible for Section 1983 liability in their positions as policymakers. That is, plaintiffs allege that an unconstitutional policy adopted or promulgated by a government unit was responsible for the constitutional deprivation they suffered. Governmental units usually include municipalities and counties, so police administrators are shielded individually from this type of liability. However, to the extent that they adopt or promulgate unconstitutional policies, the municipalities or counties for which they work can be held liable. For this reason, it is important for police administrators to understand that policies they adopt can be particularly costly. For a lawsuit to become a county or municipal liability case, the plaintiff need not necessarily sue only the county and/or the municipality. For example, if the plaintiff sues the agency, then the lawsuit effectively becomes a county/municipal case. Often, however, plaintiffs will name as many potential defendants as possible in their suits: individual officers, supervisors, the agency, and the municipality or county.

Perhaps the most significant case in this area was *Monell v. Department of Social Services* (1978). In this case, the Supreme Court ruled that municipalities could be held liable for constitutional violations sanctioned by official municipal policies or customs. *Monell* was not a policing case, but it began to establish the contours of municipal liability. *Monell* included, within its definition of "policy and custom," "custom [which] has not received formal approval through the body's official decision making channels." This suggests that unwritten, informal practice can form a basis for municipal liability. Indeed, that was exactly what occurred in the case of *Pembaur v. Cincinnati* (1986). In that case the Supreme Court held that a single incident was actionable under Section 1983 when police, acting under the county prosecutor's instructions to "go and get" the petitioner, chopped down the petitioner's door after he refused to grant them entry for lack of a warrant. The "policymaker" in *Pembaur* was the prosecutor, but other cases have considered the role of police administrators as policymakers (e.g., *Eversole v. Steele*, 1995; *Navarro v. Block*, 1996).

More recently, the courts have held that when certain forms of misconduct are alleged in lawsuits against municipalities and counties, a certain level of culpability is required. For example, in *City of Canton v. Harris* (1989), the Supreme Court observed that the *Monell* policy/custom requirement was not sufficient in certain situations. The plaintiff in that case alleged that the City of Canton failed to train one of its jailers, but the Court held that "only where a municipality's failure to train its employees in a relevant respect evidences a 'deliberate indifference' to the rights of its inhabitants can such a shortcoming be properly thought of as a city 'policy or custom' that is actionable under [Section] 1983" (*City of Canton v. Harris*, 1989:389). In a more recent case, this time at the county level, the Supreme Court had occasion to decide what culpability standard was required for a finding of county liability under Section 1983. In *Board of Commissioners of Bryan County v. Brown* (1997), the plaintiff, Brown, sued the sheriff (a county policymaker) for inadequate hiring because of injuries she suffered by a deputy sheriff whose two previous convictions for misdemeanor assault were overlooked in the hiring process. The Court held that "even assuming without deciding that proof of a single instance of inadequate screening could ever trigger municipal liability, [the sheriff's] failure to scrutinize [the deputy's] record cannot constitute 'deliberate indifference' to [the plaintiff's] federally protected right to be free from excessive force" (p. 5).

It should be pointed out that, like individual police officers, supervisors enjoy qualified immunity. Qualified immunity acts as an affirmative defense or provides immunity from suit, but it is available to supervisors and subordinate police officers only in their individual capacities. Qualified immunity is not available to government units, municipalities and counties alike.

Figure 14–3
Administrative liability under section 1983.

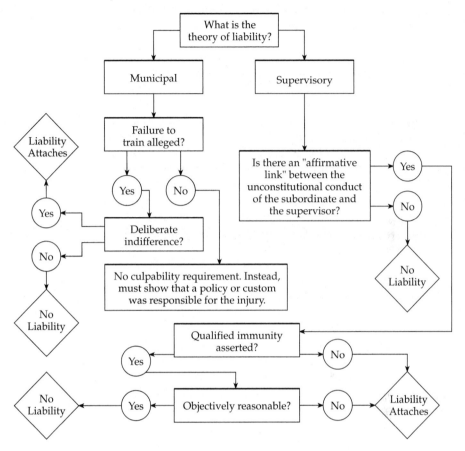

Qualified immunity basically protects certain police officers for reasonably mistaken beliefs. If the defendant is determined to have acted in an "objectively reasonable" fashion, qualified immunity can be granted. For example, a supervisor may know of her subordinates' tendency to use excessive force, but if she acted in an objectively reasonable fashion, she can be shielded from liability. For purposes of qualified immunity, a defendant is said to have acted in an objectively reasonable fashion if she does not violate clearly established rights that a reasonable person would have known of (*Harlow v. Fitzgerald*, 1982). In some Section 1983 cases, then, defendants have benefited from qualified immunity even for violating clearly established rights, provided that their mistaken beliefs were objectively reasonable (*Anderson v. Creighton*, 1987).

Figure 14–3 offers a simple visual depiction of the Section 1983 process as it pertains to police administrators. A number of questions are posed in the flowchart, beginning with the theory of liability. To theories of liability under Section

1983 can directly affect administrators, both supervisory and municipal. Directly under the municipal liability box another question is posed: Was failure to train alleged? If yes, the standard for liability is deliberate indifference (the same standard applies to inadequate hiring as in *Bryan County*). If no, there is no culpability requirement. Recall from *Monell* that no proof of culpability is required for municipal liability, provided the plaintiff alleges misconduct other than inadequate hiring or failure to train.

On the supervisory side of the flowchart, the question is whether there was an affirmative link between the unconstitutional conduct of the subordinate and the supervisor. If such a link exists, liability can attach. However, supervisors can assert qualified immunity (either as a defense or before going to trial). If their behavior was objectively reasonable, they can be immune from suit. Again, qualified immunity is not available to governmental entities, namely, counties and municipalities. Figure 14–3 leaves out the various forms of individual liability, that is, Section 1983 liability against individual police officers for unconstitutional conduct. It is important for administrators to take steps through policy and other procedures to guard against this form of liability, as it can become particularly costly in terms of damages and settlements, but we avoid going into detail on individual Section 1983 litigation because it affects police administrators only indirectly.

State Tort Liability

Law enforcement officers can be sued under state law for a variety of torts. A *tort* is a civil wrong for which a person can recover damages. Typically, to succeed with a tort lawsuit a plaintiff must show that the officer owed the plaintiff a legal duty, that the officer breached that duty, and that actual damage or injury resulted (*Estate v. Willis*, 1995). Plaintiffs usually pursue compensation for injuries suffered (damages) and/or they seek to punish the officer for the harms they suffered (punitive damages). The elements of state tort liability vary considerably by state, but varieties of two general categories of torts can be found in nearly every state: intentional torts and negligence torts.

Intentional torts are just that, civil wrongs that are intentional in nature. The plaintiff has to show that the officer's behavior was intended. Several varieties of intentional tort exist, but some common ones are wrongful death, assault and battery, and false arrest and imprisonment. If, for example, a plaintiff can show that an officer who kills a fleeing felon intended to kill the suspect, the officer may be held liable, provided he or she is unable to assert a successful defense. Generally speaking, police administrators are not sued for intentional torts. This is because they rarely engage in the types of police work which most commonly give rise to intentional tort litigation.

Lawsuits for negligence, on the other hand, can directly affect police administrators. They can also affect subordinates. A negligence tort does not require that the officer (or administrator) intend for harm to result. Rather, "it merely requires a citizen to show that a police officer owed the citizen a legal duty, that the officer acted unreasonably in discharging the duty, and that the breach of the duty resulted in damage to the citizen" (del Carmen and Smith, 1997:227). Seven general areas from which supervisory liability based on negligence may arise are in evidence: (1) negligent failure to train; (2) negligent hiring; (3) negligent assignment; (4) negligent failure to supervise; (5) negligent failure to direct; (6) negligent entrustment; and (7) negligent failure to investigate or discipline (del Carmen and Smith, 1997:234). The areas are not necessarily mutually exclusive. This is because a single lawsuit can allege negligence in two or more areas in the same lawsuit.

We have already seen two examples of negligence suits brought under the banner of Section 1983. Although they were not explicitly treated by the courts as negligence suits, the failure to train (*City of Canton*) and inadequate hiring (*Bryan County*) cases were basically Section 1983 counterparts of state tort negligence claims. Such suits remain relatively rare, however. Most negligence suits brought against police administrators and supervisors are filed at the state level.

An example a state tort failure to train case is *Meistinsky v. City of New York* (1955). In that case, a police officer interrupted a store robbery in progress and ended up shooting an innocent bystander. The court ruled that because of the state of extreme emergency during the robbery, there was no basis for holding the respondent liable for negligent failure to train. Part of the court's reasoning was that the officer involved had been on the force for nine years. An example of an state tort negligent hiring case is *Peters v. Bellinger* (1959). In that case an Illinois court held a city liable for the actions of a police officer who had a felony record. The city was held liable because it failed to conduct a background check of the officer prior to hiring.

Accreditation

The Commission on Accreditation for Law Enforcement Agencies (CALEA) was established in 1979 by the International Association of Chiefs of Police, the National Sheriffs' Association, the Police Executive Research Forum, and the National Organization of Black Law Enforcement Executives to evaluate and accredit police agencies meeting the commission's accreditation standards. The CALEA has developed standards designed to

1. increase law enforcement agency capabilities to prevent and control crime;
2. increase agency effectiveness and efficiency in the delivery of law enforcement services;
3. increase cooperation and coordination with other law enforcement agencies and with other agencies of the criminal justice system; and
4. increase citizen and employee confidence in goals, objectives, policies, and practices of the agency. (CALEA, 1999:xiii)

The standards set forth by the CALEA address nine major law enforcement subjects: (1) role, responsibilities, and relationships with other agencies; (2) organization, management, and administration; (3) personnel structure; (4) personnel process; (5) operations; (6) operational support; (7) traffic operations; (8) prisoner- and court-related activities; and (9) auxiliary and technical services (CALEA, 2000). These subjects are then broken into 38 content areas, resulting in (as of this writing) 439 standards (CALEA, 1999:xiv). This number is down from 1,012 standards during the early years of accreditation.

Departments must meet applicable standards, which include having adequate policies and procedures addressing the critical aspects of policing. An agency seeking accreditation must pass through five phases: (1) application, (2) self-assessment, (3) on-site assessment, (4) commission review and decision, and (5) maintaining compliance and reaccreditation. The accreditation process is a voluntary one, so only agencies interested in being accredited apply. Once eligibility has been confirmed, the agency and the commission sign an agreement which identifies what is expected of each party. Then the agency completes an Agency Profile Questionnaire. The responses to the questionnaire provide the accreditation manager with information that is important in facilitating interaction between the agency and the commission. Next, the agency conducts a self-assessment to determine whether it complies with standards set forth by the commission. "Proofs of compliance" are required. The on-site assessment is composed of a visit by commission officials to determine whether the agency is in compliance with commission standards. The assessors' final report is then forwarded to the commission for review. If the during the review period the commission is satisfied that the agency meets all relevant standards, accreditation is granted. Accredited agencies then submit annual reports to the commission attesting to their continued compliance with relevant standards.

External organizations such as CALEA can provide information concerning professional management standards and expectations which are valuable to a police executive. In addition, they help promote accountability because they require that agency performance be reviewed by outsiders. Additional benefits associated with accreditation may include reduced insurance premiums (Conser and Russell, 2000), better chances to qualify for grants for innovative police programs (Hill, 1999), and improved standardization of policies, procedures, and operations.

Despite the apparent benefits associated with national accreditation, there has been a great deal debate and controversy over the accreditation process (Eastman, 1985; Pearson 1985). Some state law enforcement associations have gone on the record in opposition to national accreditation standards, arguing that state-level accreditation is preferable. As early as 1976 the Washington Association of Sheriffs and Chiefs of Police (WASPC) was directed by the state legislature to develop accreditation standards. What emerged was the WASPC Law Enforcement Accreditation Program (Washington Association of Sheriffs and Police Chiefs, 1998). Table 14–3 outlines the benefits of state-level accreditation, according to the WASPC. Kentucky as well as several other states recently developed state-level accreditation programs (Bizzack and Delacruz, 1994).

Another area of controversy surrounding agency accreditation concerns its compatibility with community-oriented policing (Behan, 1992; Sykes, 1994). Much of the debate revolves around the apparently formal administrative,

Table 14–3

Benefits of State-Level Accreditation

Improved morale within the agency
Increased credibility with governing body
Increased pride in agency
Systemized self-assessment
Broadened perspectives
Intensified administrative and operational effectiveness
Confidence that recruitment, selection, and promotion processes are fair and equitable
Strengthened understanding of agency policies and procedures by all police personnel
Decreased susceptibility to litigation and costly civil court settlements
Potential reduction in premiums for liability insurance
Greater public confidence in the agency
State and local acknowledgment of professional competence

Source: Washington Associations of Sheriffs and Police Chiefs. Retrieved from http://www.waspc.org/accred.html.

bureaucratic characteristics of accreditation and the decentralized, flexible characteristics of community policing. However, Cordner and Williams (1999) report that accreditation and community policing are not incompatible, in part because accreditation standards do not necessarily encourage or require formal rules, centralization of authority, increased specialization, or more hierarchy. They also found that conflict between community policing and accreditation (if any) depends on the agency's view regarding the administrator's commitment to community policing, his or her organization and management philosophy, the manner in which accreditation and community policing are implemented, and on such variables as department size, labor–management relations, and other "idiosyncratic" factors. In their case studies they found "little evidence of conflict between accreditation and COP" (Cordner and Williams, 1999:374).

Other Accountability Measures

On something less than an administrative level, there are numerous other mechanisms available for ensuring accountability. Certain legal remedies, for example, are designed to deter misconduct and hold police officials to answer for inappropriate behavior. Two such mechanisms—the exclusionary rule and criminal liability—are discussed here. Because they affect administrators indirectly, however, the discussion is kept rather brief.

Exclusionary Rule

The landmark Supreme Court decision in *Mapp v. Ohio* (1961) applied the exclusionary rule to the states. The exclusionary rule requires that evidence obtained in violation of the Constitution cannot be admitted in a criminal trial to prove guilt. In *Elkins v. United States* (1960), Justice Clark provided eloquent reasoning for such a rule:

> The criminal goes free, if he must, but it is the law that sets him free. Nothing can destroy a government more quickly than its failure to observe its own law, or worse, its disregard of the charter of its own existence.

The so-called fruit of the poisonous tree doctrine has expanded the scope of the exclusionary rule. Suppose, for example, that the police illegally arrest someone. The fruit of the poisonous tree doctrine would not only require the exclusion of the evidence obtained in the search of the arrestee following that arrest, but potentially any other evidence (such as a confession) obtained after that initial illegal act. The doctrine is said to have originated in *Silverthorne Lumber Co. v. United States* (1920). The question of what is considered "fruit," however, has become complicated over the years. Courts look at the time elapsed between the illegal police misconduct and the receipt of derivative evidence (attenuation), the possibility that the evidence would have been discovered anyway (inevitable discovery), and other potential ways of obtaining the evidence that the exclusionary rule says should be excluded (independent source).

Despite the Supreme Court's noble intentions in calling for the exclusion of illegally obtained evidence, numerous court decisions in the wake of *Mapp* have chipped away at the exclusionary rule. Arguably, it does not serve the same deterrent effect today that it perhaps once did. In addition, its role in promoting police accountability has been somewhat discounted as the Supreme Court has become more conservative in its decisions. Exceptions to the rule such as good faith help to ensure that the criminal does not "go free" when reasonable mistakes are made. A deterrent effect is probably minimal, too, because the time elapsed between illegal police conduct and the decision to exclude evidence is usually rather lengthy (e.g., Wilkey, 1978).

There is evidence, however, that many police organizations, fearful of losing criminal cases on "technicalities," have instituted programs designed to teach trainees about constitutional guidelines. To that end, the exclusionary rule plays at least a minimal role in promoting accountability; when the police violate the constitution, criminals go free. When criminals go free, the public demands answers, so it is important for law enforcement officials to operate within established constitutional and legal boundaries.

Criminal Prosecution

At the state level most jurisdictions provide criminal sanctions for illegal police conduct. This includes false arrest and trespass, among other offenses. However, state prosecutions are relatively rare, and most states require criminal intent as an element of a crime, making good faith alone a defense to criminal liability. Accordingly, one tool for criminal prosecution of police officers is 18 U.S.C.A. Section 242, a federal statute. The statute reads:

> Whoever, under color of any law, statute, ordinance, regulation, or custom, willfully subjects any inhabitant of any State, Territory, or District to the deprivation of any rights, privileges, or immunities secured or protected by the Constitution or laws of the United States, or to different punishments, pains, or penalties, on

account of such inhabitant being an alien, or by reason of his color, or race, than are prescribed for the punishment of citizens, shall be fined not more than $1,000 or imprisoned not more than one year, or both; and if death results shall be subject to imprisonment for any term of years or for life.

This statute acts as a supplement to state criminal remedies. That is, police officers can also be convicted on criminal charges at the state level.

It is unlikely that Section 242 (or state statutes) is very effective in keeping the police accountable. This is because the statutes are (1) rarely invoked, (2) narrowly construed by the courts (e.g., *Screws v. United States*, 1945; *United States v. Lanier*, 1997), and (3) limited by the reach of the good-faith defense. Basically, criminal liability is reserved for the most outrageous kinds of police misconduct, usually involving brutality (e.g., *Miller v. United States*, 1968; *Williams v. United States*, 1951). With reference to federal statutes governing police misconduct, Whitebread and Slobogin stated that "few cases have applied these provisions, graphically underscoring the fact that these federal criminal statutes serve as little deterrent to police misconduct" (2000:62). The lack of a deterrent effect notwithstanding, however, state and federal statutes have been enacted in an effort to keep law enforcement officials accountable to the public they serve.

Summary

Accountability is an important consideration for police administrators, who will have trouble maintaining control without it. That is, if subordinates (even administrators) are not held to answer for their action, crime control and police services are compromised. Administrators can take any number of steps to promote accountability among their subordinates. Two of these—internal investigations and Compstat—were reviewed in this chapter.

It is also essential that accountability be ensured from outside the department. Since law enforcement agencies are public entities, numerous mechanisms have evolved aimed at holding the police accountable for their actions. Several such mechanisms were reviewed in this chapter, including civil liability, citizen complaints, and accreditation. Some have proved more effective than others in instituting reforms (e.g., civil liability rather than citizen complaints), but all are here to stay in one form or another. In all probability, the external accountability mechanisms will continue to evolve so as to ensure that police agencies are kept in check.

Study Questions

1. What are the methods for promoting accountability from the outside? What are their strengths and weaknesses?

2. What are the methods for promoting accountability from the inside? What are their strengths and weaknesses?

3. What rights do police officers enjoy during internal investigations?

4. What is a police bill of rights? What is it designed to accomplish?

5. What is Compstat? Why treat it as an accountability issue? What are some pitfalls and drawbacks of the Compstat model?

6. What are the various means by which civilian review is constructed? What are the criticisms of civilian review?

7. What does the research suggest about the citizen complaint process—in particular, the successfulness of complaints?

8. Distinguish between state tort liability and Section 1983 liability. With regard to Section 1983 liability, how can police administrators be held liable? What about under state tort law?

9. What is accreditation? What are the advantages of accreditation?

10. Explain how the exclusionary rule and criminal prosecution can promote accountability within police organizations.

Net Resources

http://commfaculty.fullerton.edu/lester/ethics/police.html Contains links to police ethics-related websites.

http://www.aclu.org/issues/policepractices/hmpolice.html ACLU's police practice website.

http://www.aele.org Website for Americans for Effective Law Enforcement, a useful resource for recent developments in police civil liability law and liability training.

http://www.calea.org/index1.htm Website for the Commission of Accreditation for Law Enforcement Agencies, Inc. Contains information on police agency accreditation.

http://www.hrw.org/reports98/police Provides information on police brutality and accountability in the United States.

References

Americans for Effective Law Enforcement (1982). *Police Civilian Review Boards.* AELE Defense Manual, Brief #82–3. San Francisco: AELE.

Anderson v. Creighton, 483 U.S. 635 (1987).

Angell, J. (1966). The adequacy of the internal processing of citizen complaints by police departments. Master's Thesis, Michigan State University, East Lansing, MI.

Behan, C. J. (1992). Allies, not adversaries: Accreditation and community policing. *Commission Update,* September 1, p. 1. Fairfax, VA: CALEA.

Bence v. Breier, 501 F.2d 1185 (1974).

Biehunik v. Felicetta, 441 F.2d 228 (1971).

Bivens v. Six Unknown Named Agents, 403 U.S. 388 (1971).

Bizzack, J. W., and Delacruz, V. (1994). Demystifying police accreditation. *Law Enforcement News* 20 (400):8, 11.

Black v. Coughlin, 76 F.3d 72 (2nd Cir. 1996).

Board of County Commissioners of Bryan County v. Brown, 117 S. Ct. 1382 (1997).

Board of Inquiry (2000). Executive summary. *Board of Inquiry Report into the Rampart Corruption Incident.* Los Angeles: Los Angeles Police Department.

Brady, E. (1997). Compstat: Mapping, accountability equal less crime. *USA Today,* December 1, p. 18A.

Burger, W. E. (1982). "Isn't there a better way?" *American Bar Association Journal* 68:274–277.

Chiuchiolo, M. (1981). The law enforcement officer's bill of rights: Panacea or problem? *Police Chief* 68(12):70–72.

City of Canton v. Harris, 489 U.S. 378 (1989).

Cleveland Board of Education v. Loudermill, 470 U.S. 532 (1985).

Commission on Accreditation for Law Enforcement Agencies (1999). *Standards for Law Enforcement Agencies,* 4th ed. Fairfax, VA: Commission on Accreditation for Law Enforcement Agencies.

Commission on Accreditation for Law Enforcement Agencies (2000). *Accreditation.* Retrieved from http://www.calea.org. Fairfax, VA: CALEA.

Conser, J. A., and Russell, G. D. (2000). *Law Enforcement in the United States.* Gaithersburg, MD: Aspen Publications.

Cordner, G. W., and Williams, G. L. (1999). Community policing and police agency accreditation. In L. K. Gaines and G. W. Cordner (eds.), *Policing Perspectives: An Anthology.* Los Angeles: Roxbury, pp. 372–379.

County of Sacramento v. Lewis, 118 S. Ct. 1708 (1998).

Del Carmen, R. V., and Smith, M. R. (1997). Police, civil liability, and the law. In R. G. Dunham and G. P. Alpert (eds.), *Critical Issues in Policing: Contemporary Readings,* 3rd ed. Prospect Heights, IL: Waveland Press, pp. 225-242.

Demers, D. P., Engebretson, M., Fitzsimmons, J., and Dennison, D. (1992). The color of justice. *Twin Cities Reader,* March 25–31, pp. 8–11.

Eastman, W. E. (1985). National accreditation: A costly, unneeded make-work scheme. In J. Fyfe (ed.), *Police Management Today.* Washington: International City Managers Association, pp. 49–54.

Elkins v. United States, 364 U.S. 206 (1960).

Estate v. Willis, 897 P.2d 78 (Alaska 1995).

Eversole v. Steele, 59 F.3d 710 (7th Cir. 1995).

Gaines, L. K., Kappeler, V. E., and Vaughn, J. B. (1999). *Policing in America,* 3rd ed. Cincinnati: Anderson Publishing.

Gardner v. Broderick, 392 U.S. 273 (1967).

Garner, R., and Hoover, L. (2000). The Compstat craze: Emphasizing accountability in policing. Paper presented at the Annual Meeting of the Academy of Criminal Justice Sciences, New Orleans, LA.

Garrity v. New Jersey, 385 U.S. 483 (1967).

Gilbert v. Homar, 520 U.S. 924 (1997).

Geller, W. A. (1985). *Police Leadership in America: Crisis and Opportunity*. Chicago: American Bar Association.

Glendon, M. A. (1994). *A Nation under Lawyers: How the Crisis in the Legal Profession Is Transforming American Society*. New York: Farrar, Straus, and Giroux.

Goldsmith, A. J. (1991). *Complaints against the Police: The Trend toward External Review*. Oxford: Clarendon Press.

Graham v. Connor, 490 U.S. 386 (1989).

Griswold, D. B. (1994). Complaints against the police: Predicting dispositions. *Journal of Criminal Justice* 22:215–221.

Harlow v. Fitzgerald, 457 U.S. 800 (1982).

Harries, K. (1999). *Mapping Crime: Principle and Practice*. Washington: National Institute of Justice.

Hill, S. J. (1999). The significance of police credentialing. *Police* 23(3):40–42.

Hill v. Dekalb Regional Youth Detention Center, 40 F.3d 1176 (11th Cir. 1994).

Johnson, H. (1999). A police officer's bill of rights: A needed protection for cops? In J. D. Sewell (ed.), *Controversial Issues in Policing*. Boston: Allyn and Bacon, pp. 36–43.

Jojola v. Chavez, 55 F.3d 4898 (10th Cir. 1995).

Kerstetter, W. A. (1985). Who disciplines the police? Who should? In W. Geller (ed.), *Police Leadership in America: Crisis and Opportunity*. Chicago: American Bar Association, pp. 149–182.

Krajack, K. (1979). Internal affairs. *Police Magazine*, pp. 9–16.

LaChance v. Erickson, 118 S. Ct. 753 (1998).

Leonard, V. A. (1951). *Police Organization and Management*. Brooklyn: Foundation Press.

Lersch, K. M. (1998). Police misconduct and malpractice: A critical analysis of citizens' complaints. *Policing: An International Journal of Police Strategies and Management* 21:80–96.

Maple, J. (1999). *The Crime Fighter*. New York: Doubleday.

Mapp v. Ohio, 367 U.S. 643 (1961).

Meistinsky v. City of New York, 140 N.Y.S. 2d 212 (1955).

Miller v. United States, 404 F.2d 611 (5th Cir. 1968).

Minneapolis. (1996). *Annual Report of the Civilian Police Review Board*. Minneapolis, MN: City of Minneapolis.

Monell v. Department of Social Services, 436 U.S. 658 (1978).

Napper, G. (1985). Who disciplines the police? I do! A response to Wayne Kerstetter. In W. Geller (ed.), *Police Leadership in America: Crisis and Opportunity*. Chicago: American Bar Association, pp. 193–195.

Navarro v. Block, 72 F.3d 712 (9th Cir. 1996).

New Orleans Police Department (2000). *Comstat.* Retrieved from http://www.acadiacom. net/nopd/comstat.htm.

Newton, J., Lait, M., and Glover, S. (2000). LAPD condemned by its own inquiry into Rampart scandal. *Los Angeles Times,* March 1, p. A1.

Pearson, J. (1985). National accreditation: A valuable management tool. In J. J. Fyfe (ed), *Police Management Today: Issues and Case Studies.* Washington: International City Management Association, pp. 45–48.

Pederson, D. (1996). Bullets in the big easy. *Newsweek* 128(26):29.

Pembaur v. City of Cincinnati, 475 U.S. 469 (1986).

Perez, D. W. (1994). *Common Sense about Police Review.* Philadelphia: Temple University Press.

Peters v. Bellinger, 159 N.E. 2d 528 (Ill. App. 1959).

Pike, D. F. (1978). Why is everybody suing everybody? *U.S. News and World Report,* December 4, pp. 50–54.

Police Executive Research Forum (1981). *Police Agency Handling of Officer Misconduct: A Model Policy Statement.* Washington: PERF.

Pollock, J., and Becker, R. (1996). Ethical dilemmas in police work. In M. Braswell, B. McCarthy, and B. McCarthy (eds.), *Justice, Crime and Ethics.* Cincinnati: Anderson Publishing, pp. 83–103.

Pollock, J. M. (2001). Ethics and law enforcement. In R. G. Dunham and G. P. Alpert (eds.), *Critical Issues in Policing: Contemporary Readings,* 4th ed. Prospect Heights, IL: Waveland Press, pp. 356–373.

Pooley, E., and Rivera, E. (1996). One good apple. *Time* 147(3):54.

President's Commission on Law Enforcement and the Administration of Justice (1967). *The Police.* Washington: Government Printing Office.

Rizzo v. Goode, 423 U.S. 362 (1976).

Scott, M. (1999). A police officer's bill of rights: A needed protection for cops? In J. D. Sewell (ed.), *Controversial Issues in Policing.* Boston: Allyn and Bacon, pp. 45–54.

Screws v. United States, 325 U.S. 91 (1945).

Silverman, E. B. (1999). *NYPD Battles Crime: Innovative Strategies in Policing.* Boston: Northeastern University Press.

Silverthorne Lumber Co. v. United States, 251 U.S. 385 (1920).

Starzenski v. City of Elkhart, 87 F.3d 872 (7th Cir. 1996).

Sykes, G. W. (1994). Accreditation and community policing: Passing fads or basic reforms? *Journal of Contemporary Criminal Justice* 10(1):1–16.

United States v. Lanier, 520 U.S. 259 (1997).

U.S. Commission on Civil Rights (1981). *Who Is Guarding the Guardians? A Report on Police Practices.* Washington: Government Printing Office.

Wagner, A. E. (1980). "Citizen complaints against the police: The complainant." *Journal of Police Science and Administration* 8:373–377.

Wagner, A. E., and Decker, S. H. (1997). Evaluating citizen complaints against the police. In R. G. Dunham and G. P. Alpert (eds.), *Critical Issues in Policing: Contemporary Readings,* 3rd ed. Prospect Heights, IL: Waveland Press, pp. 302–318.

Walker, S. (1995). *Citizen Review Resource Manual.* Washington: Police Executive Research Forum.

Walker, S. (2001). *Police Accountability: The Role of Citizen Oversight.* Belmont, CA: Wadsworth.

Walker, S., and Bumphus, V. W. (1991). *Civilian Review of the Police: A National Survey of the 50 Largest Cities.* Omaha: University of Nebraska at Omaha.

Walker, S., and Wright, B. (1995). *Citizen Review of the Police—1994: A National Survey.* Washington: Police Executive Research Forum.

Walker, S., and Wright, B. (1997). Varieties of citizen review: The relationship of mission, structure, and procedures to police accountability. In R. G. Dunham and G. P. Alpert (eds.), *Critical Issues in Policing: Contemporary Readings,* 3rd ed. Prospect Heights, IL: Waveland Press, pp. 319–336.

Washington Association of Sheriffs and Police Chiefs (1998). *Accreditation Program.* Olympia, WA: WASPC.

West, P. (1988). Investigation of complaints against the police: Summary report of a national survey. *American Journal of Police* 7(2):101–122.

Whitebread, C. H., and Slobogin, C. (2000). *Criminal Procedure: An Analysis of Cases and Concepts,* 4th ed. New York: Foundation Press.

Wilkey, M. (1978). Why suppress evidence? *Judicature* 62:214.

Williams v. United States, 341 U.S. 97 (1951).

Wilson, O. W. (1963). *Police Administration,* 2nd ed. New York: McGraw-Hill.

15

Change

Michael Newman/PhotoEdit

Chapter Outline

Introduction

Why Change Occurs

Goals of Police Organizational Change
Promotion of Participatory Organization Models
Resolution and Prevention of Problems
Adapting and Planning

Assessing the Need for Change
External Consultants
Internal Resources

Designing and Implementing Organizational Change
Identifying a Performance Gap
Recognition of a Need for Change
Creating a Proper Climate for Change
Diagnosing the Problem
Identifying Alternative Change Strategies
Selecting the Change Strategy
Determining and Operationalizing the Implementation Strategy
Evaluating and Modifying the Change Strategy

Organizational Development
Diagnosis
Intervention
Evaluation

Risks Associated with Change
Resistance to Change
Minimizing Resistance
Other Issues in Minimizing the Risks of Change

Approaches to Change
Individual Change
Organizational Structure and Systems Change
Organizational Climate and Interpersonal Style Change

Police Organizational Change
Participative Management
Flattening the Organization
Community Policing
Civilianization
Police–Community Collaboration
Interdepartmental Cooperation

Future Trends and Challenges

Summary

Learning Objectives

After reading this chapter, you should be able to

1. Understand goals of organizational change.
2. List the steps used to assess the need for change.
3. Understand the process of designing and implementing change.
4. Discuss the modern method of "organizational development."
5. Understand the potential risks of reform, including types of resistance and steps for overcoming them.
6. Outline the various approaches to change, including individual change, structural change, and climate change.
7. Understand specific types of change occurring in police organizations at the present time.

On February 1, 1999, New York City's comptroller announced that the New York Police Department (NYPD) could use "civilianization" to increase by 1,257 the number of police officers engaged in crime-fighting activities. Furthermore, the department could save $36.2 million per year by assigning civilians to positions vacated by retiring officers. Comptroller Alan Hevesi stated: "I am not suggesting that we cut the number of police officers fighting crime. But police officers get higher pay, as they should, because they perform a dangerous job. There is no reason to pay higher police wages for office clerks, secretaries, switchboard operators, custodians and bookkeepers." He further pointed out that increased hiring of civilian employees would allow the mayor to get more police officers on the street fighting crime.

Civilianization, such as that occurring in the NYPD, is one of many changes currently being pursued in law enforcement agencies across the country. Most people who want to change organizations (*change agents*) want to change the administrative structure or process of the organization. They are biased against bureaucratic norms and the rational model of human motivation (i.e., the classical model of organization and management) and they are biased toward democracy and participation in organizations. They believe that participatory models of organization and management—contingency models—provide opportunities for individuals to experience a wider scope of organizational satisfaction. They want to improve the human relations skills of managers, change organizational values to consider the attitudes and feelings of employees and the public, develop effective team management, reduce tension between and within organizational groups by improving their understandings of each other, and promote the notion that organizations are open systems (Fordyce and Weil, 1971).

INTRODUCTION

Skolnick and Bayley (1986) studied police change and identified four essential elements for successful police change. The first and most important is that the chief must have an abiding and energetic commitment to the values of the change. Second, the chief must be the institutional leader in the change by motivating and even manipulating the personnel into serving the change values. Third, the chief must defend the change once it is achieved. Last, change is not likely to happen unless there is public support for it. In short, change is difficult, especially in police organizations. Administrators need to be well attuned to the intricacies and nuances of change if they are be effective in their duties.

WHY CHANGE OCCURS

Some change is fairly predictable in law enforcement. That is, the conditions promoting change differ little from one agency to the next. Often, for example, a new police chief will be appointed from within or outside the police agency. This sometimes happens at the request of the mayor or city manager, someone who desires large-scale organizational change. Any number of events can give rise to these conditions, but typically one or more of the following events serves as the impetus for change:

1. The police department has been deemed deficient or inept by government officials or influential members of the community. For example, the chief has come under attack for lax enforcement of departmental policies and regulations governing the use of force.
2. Police–community relations have suffered because of misconduct, scandal, or other wrongdoing. Our discussion of the Rampart scandal in the previous chapter offers a classic example. The scandal caused the Los Angeles Police Department (LAPD) to consider a number of changes, especially the way officers are recruited, trained, and monitored.
3. Morale in the department is suffering. This can be manifested in high attrition rates, increases in citizen complaints and civil lawsuits, or union unrest.

Indeed, other conditions can prompt large-scale organizational change, but the point is that change is neither ad hoc nor pursued simply for its own sake. Usually, some larger problem exists that needs to be remedied. How these conditions are identified, then, is the focus of the remainder of this chapter. First, however, we consider the goals of organizational change in policing.

GOALS OF POLICE ORGANIZATIONAL CHANGE

Numerous goals of change exist. We consider three that are particularly relevant to law enforcement. The first goal is one of promoting participatory management models. The second goal is to resolve and prevent problems. The third is to adapt and plan. These goals can be pursued together or in isolation. One is no more important than the others. The particular goals to be pursued will depend on the nature of the conditions giving rise to the desire for change in the police agency of interest.

Promotion of Participatory Organization Models

Change agents in police organizations are no different from those in other organizations. They have the same motivations and the same desires for their organizations. One of the primary directions of change in police organizations has been from the traditional or classical model of organization to a more participative, contingency-oriented form of management and organization.

There are many reasons for proposing this direction for change in police organizations. First, police agencies are finding it necessary to adapt to *changing needs and aspirations of their organizational members* if they are to attract and retain high-quality personnel. Second, expansion and enrichment of the role of patrol officers is required to establish an environment in which individual officers can *maximize their potential* without marking time waiting for an opening in a specialized position in the police agency. Third, *continual change within the environment* of policing also affects the need for change in police organizations. Changes in the size of population served, the nature of services needed by the public, philosophy regarding the proper responsibility of police as a governmental agency, technology and knowledge, and the general rise in qualifications (education and training) of police personnel demonstrate the necessity of change and innovation.

Resolution and Prevention of Problems

A principle of change is: Do not make change merely for the sake of making change, but make change a means to address and solve problems as they occur and to prevent future problems. Change must significantly improve the organization if it is to be perceived as useful change. Toch, Grant, and Galvin (1975) emphasize the philosophy that change must be viewed as a means to further or progress toward more generalized change in the police organization. It is crucial that every problem be critically assessed because problems often manifest deeply rooted larger problems and conditions. The organization, individuals, group relationships, and community supports must be utilized as organizational vehicles to change. Those who produce problems must be at the center of problem solving because one must have experienced the problem to make the best use of it in corrective action or change.

Adapting and Planning

Law enforcement agencies are not static entities; they do not exist in a vacuum. Unplanned changes (e.g., technological advancements, demographic shifts) of all forms are constantly occurring in and outside the police agency. Accordingly, one particularly important goal of change is to adapt to changing conditions (open systems approach). For example, to the extent that technological developments create a new breed of criminal, police agencies need to adapt (through training, education, and resource allocation) to new forms of problems.

Another goal of change that is consistent with adaptation pertains to planning. It is important that law enforcement agencies "look ahead" and anticipate future problems and conditions warranting special attention (future studies, as discussed in Chapter 13). We consider the means by which police agencies can do this toward the end of the chapter.

ASSESSING THE NEED FOR CHANGE

There are two basic methods to assess the need for change in an organization: (1) the use of external consultants and (2) internal self-study. Each has its own particular strengths and weaknesses.

External Consultants

The external consultant is brought in and paid to identify problems and recommend solutions. The consultant tends not to be personally involved with the organization and thereby able to view the organization objectively. The consultant is generally familiar with the type of organization being studied and with organizational change issues. However, the external consultant frequently has to spend a good deal of time getting to know the specifics of the department so that problems can be identified and recommendations for successful change can be developed. Moreover, external consultants can be self-serving in that they know what the administration wants them to find and recommend and their report may merely reflect these preidentified administrative concerns.

On balance, external consultants should be utilized when internal efforts have failed to solve the problem. External consultants should be used only as the last resort. Also, when an external consultant is used, the administration should be careful not to reveal any predetermined or preferred solutions to try to ensure that the consultant does not become biased.

Internal Resources

The other means to evaluate the need for change is to use organizational members as a resource group to identify and recommend change. Toch and his colleagues (1975) suggest five principles that should be used when implementing an internal self-study designed to bring about change within the police organization. First, personnel must have participatory roles in the self-study. Second, those participating must have a degree of autonomy of action, decision, and choice. They must be able to control their part of the self-study. When provided with too many guidelines or restrictions, participants will feel that their suggestions are of no consequence or will have no impact on the organizational action. Third, the group culture must be built around a cause to which it can be committed. The self-study and its results must matter (be of consequence) to the group. Fourth, a meaningful future must be offered as the outcome of the self-study effort. Without meaning, there is no reason to expend the amount of energy required to do a meaningful self-study. Fifth, the organization must allow a natural leader to emerge within the group, that is, the leader must not be predetermined or forced on the group by the administration. Natural leadership is much more effective than forced leadership because it is more enthusiastic and honest, and it is perceived as such by those who willingly follow.

On the Job

CHARLOTTE-MECKLENBURG, NORTH CAROLINA, POLICE DEPARTMENT
Change Is Inevitable

By Darrel W. Stephens

Courtesy of Chief Stephens

Effectively leading and managing change is a fundamental requirement for today's successful police executive. Change is difficult for organizations. Change scares employees. Change is disruptive. Change is exciting. Change is inevitable.

In the 30-plus years that I have been involved in policing I have seen enormous change in almost every aspect of our work. Some of that change has been planned and implemented in a thoughtful manner. Some has been forced upon the police, and some change is the result of the police reacting to events in the world around them.

Like the rest of the world, technology has had the greatest impact on the police over the past 30 years. Technology has enabled the police to manage information and enhance its utility in ways never before imagined. Police officers have at their fingertips background information about locations they are responding to on a call. Computers have made it possible to search a single latent print against databases with millions of records. DNA is rapidly becoming a critical tool in both identifying and clearing criminal suspects. Millions of cellular telephones have given citizens immediate access to the police, and the police are working to resolve the huge volumes of calls coming into communication centers. Technology has required the police to change as they learn to use it in the most effective manner they can. The police have yet to make the adjustments needed to identify new forms of high-tech crime and keep up with the growing problem of cyber crime.

Police personnel have changed significantly as well. The police are much more diverse today. There are more African-Americans, Latinos, and Asian-Americans in policing. Women have become an integral part of today's police organizations. The police have made tremendous progress in the effort to reflect the makeup of the communities they serve but have significant challenges to close the gap even further. The change in personnel was forced on the police in the 1970s through civil rights legislation and enforcement through the EEOC.

Continued

Police personnel have much higher levels of education. Many departments require college credits for entry and promotion. These changes in police personnel have been good for policing—but they have also presented new challenges to supervision and management. Personnel policies and practices must take into account a work environment that includes a wide range of cultures and work relationships.

The police have also worked to change their methods. In the past 30 years research on what works in policing has exploded. It was virtually nonexistent prior to the President's Commission on Crime report in 1967. That research has brought into question long-held beliefs about patrol and investigative strategy. The result has been the implementation of community policing and problem-solving approaches to police work. After decades of moving away from the community, the police have begun to embrace and seek out problem-solving partnerships with members of the community and other agencies.

The progress the police have made in the past and the challenges they face in the future require thoughtful and deliberate strategies to manage change. Although change is difficult, the successful police executive understands that it is an essential part of creating and maintaining a safe community.

The Charlotte-Mecklenburg Police Department, in addition to experiencing all of the changes just described, consolidated the city and county police departments in 1994—blending two organizational cultures, command staffs, administrative systems, and officers into one. The success of this undertaking is attributable to the extensive planning the departments undertook before and during the change. A large number of employees from both organizations worked very hard to maintain open lines of communications to address the concerns of both employees and members of the community. The department continues to work to manage a fast pace of change as the community grows and new challenges emerge.

Change for the police is inevitable and it will always be difficult. It can, however, be managed in a way that minimizes any negative effects.

An internal self-study is an essential part of the accreditation process for law enforcement agencies. The accreditation guidelines also can be useful in guiding an internal self-study. Regardless of whether the agency is seeking accreditation, it will find this technique to be very valuable in assessing the need for change and the types of change that should be planned (see Chapter 14).

Thoughtful change requires that police administrators understand the change process and the climate for change in their department. With this understanding, the administrator may create effective change that will be accepted by the department and the community and that will meet the need for which it was designed. In the next section is a discussion of how to design and implement change.

Figure 15–1
The change process.

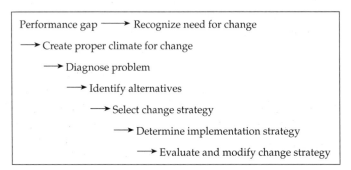

DESIGNING AND IMPLEMENTING ORGANIZATIONAL CHANGE

The change process in organizations involves eight steps (Johnson, 1978; Steers, 1977). The process begins with identifying a performance gap; then comes recognizing the need for change, creating the proper climate for change, diagnosing the problem, identifying alternative strategies, selecting a change strategy, implementing the strategy, and evaluating and/or modifying the strategy. See Figure 15–1 for an overview of the change process.

Identifying a Performance Gap

The first step of the organizational change process is identifying a *performance gap*, a gap between the organizational performance that is expected or needed and the actual performance. A performance gap exists whenever the police are not performing at the level the community or the organization wants or needs them to perform at or are not performing the functions that the community or the organization wants or needs them to perform. An example of a performance gap is failure of the police to arrest or cite drinking drivers who have been involved in a traffic accident when the community wants drinking and driving incidents to be minimized or reduced by active enforcement. A performance gap also exists when an agency has a high incidence of excessive use of force, while the public expects the police to protect the civil rights of all citizens. A third example occurs when the police agency emphasizes negotiation in hostage situations, while the special response team stresses the use of force to resolve hostage situations. From these examples, it is clear that performance gap is merely the difference between the expected behavior and the actual behavior.

Recognition of a Need for Change

The second step in the change process is the recognition of a *need for change*. In designing and implementing organizational change in police agencies, the most important consideration is to make a change only when the change will measurably improve the agency. The design of organizational change must be based on a thorough knowledge of the organization, its strengths and weaknesses, and how the agency fits into the society that it is responsible for policing. Such organizational knowledge should not be based on what the organization says it is doing or on what it says exists, but on what is actually happening (in existence or operationally) within the police agency. The following questions will provide direction to an evaluation of the need for change in a police agency: What are the goals of the police agency? What role or roles have been assumed by the police agency in society? What is the attitude or position of the agency toward members of society, other organizations or institutions, and employees of the police agency? How effective has the organization been in accomplishing its goal or goals? and Is the agency, as it is presently organized and managed, capable of meeting the present and future needs and expectations of the community? Armed with the answers to these questions, one is in a position to evaluate the magnitude of the need for change.

Generally speaking, the larger the performance gap and the more important the area of performance is to the agency or the community, the greater the need for change. In the use of force example mentioned earlier, the need for change is great because the actual behavior is far from the expected behavior and the behavior is in an area that is perceived to be very important. It should be assumed that all agencies need change of some sort, but the essential considerations are how much change is needed and whether change will measurably improve the agency.

Police administrators will realize the existence of the need for change either through a personal and continual assessment of the status of the department or by having the need for change brought to their attention by members of the department, government officials, the media, or the public. The temptation to ignore the performance gap exists even when others bring it to the administrator's attention. Some administrators will continue to ignore the performance gap, assuming that they are right and the "troublemakers" are wrong, and that therefore there is no gap. This situation may continue indefinitely; however, it will most likely result in some form of confrontation sooner or later. The smart administrator will be open to addressing performance gap issues and will be personally involved in uncovering the gap.

Creating a Proper Climate for Change

The third step in the change process is the creation of a proper *climate for change*. The climate for change in the department determines the ability to make change. Duncan (1976) examined the organizational climate for change in three police departments. His research noted the importance of the police personnel's perception of the climate for change in their department. Duncan's research examined the climate for change on the basis of four factors:

1. Perceived need for change.
2. Perceived openness of the organization to change.
3. Potential for change within the organization.
4. Perceived possibility of participation by the police officer in implementing change.

Duncan assessed the relationship between these four factors and found that when organizations were perceived by their members as open to change, having high potential for change, and having high possibility that police officers could participate in implementing change, the members of the organization perceived little need for change in the organization. The reverse was also true. If a great need for change was perceived by members of the organization, then the members also saw the organization as closed to change, having little potential for change, and having little possibility that police officers would be allowed to participate in implementing change. [This finding was supported by Dunning's research (1976).]

The external environment also influences the climate for change. Duncan (1976) found that as the environment became more turbulent and citizens and community opinion increasingly influenced the police agency, the police organization had a crisis reaction. The crisis reaction of police organizations was characterized by less participation in decision making, increased criticism between superiors and subordinates, reduced risk taking, and decreased general warmth and support in the interpersonal relationships in the department. A police agency experiencing this crisis reaction to a turbulent environment and political pressure would not have a good climate for change, but its members would probably see a need for changing the agency. The climate for change must be examined, and it must be positive toward change before the agency attempts significant change efforts. Attitudes toward change may need to be reversed before attempts are made to implement change. A crisis situation can be the catalyst that will start a department on its way to developing a proper climate for change.

Duncan's research indicates that the proper climate for change exists when the organization makes change a part of its routine business and encourages participation of all organizational members in suggesting and implementing change. Creating this climate is a gradual process of establishing the proper (open) attitude of all administrators and supervisory staff toward looking for, listening for, and acting on ideas that have potential to improve the functioning of the police organization. Only by beginning to implement change suggested by organizational members and crediting the members with these ideas will the membership perceive and believe a climate for change exists.

Diagnosing the Problem

The fourth step in the change process is *problem diagnosis*. This step involves identifying the specifics of the problem: What has caused the problem? How serious is the problem? What are the most serious symptoms? and How does the problem affect the organization?

The diagnosis phase is exemplified by the doctor presented with a patient who is experiencing a physical ailment. The doctor is interested in knowing the symptoms, how serious they are, and how they affect the patient's functioning. The doctor is also interested in determining the cause of these symptoms. The cause must be eliminated to remove the symptoms; otherwise the doctor will merely treat symptoms that will continue to exist in the body. Treatment of symptoms may reduce the effects of the problem, but it does not eliminate it. Eliminating the problem is the doctor's goal. It is not always possible because the problem is not always something that can be controlled by either the doctor or the patient. Nevertheless, the problem can never be removed without determining through proper diagnosis what the specific problem is.

Proper diagnosis in a department depends on a thorough knowledge of organizational behavior and theory, a thorough understanding of the history and current status of the department, and adequate questioning to find the source of the problem. For example, if a police organization has low morale, the administrator could misdiagnose the problem by solely relying on his or her own ideas concerning the source of the morale problem. Diagnosis will be better if the administrator considers the knowledge of the supervisors and other administrative staff. The best diagnosis will result if the administrator also asks police officers on the street what they consider to be the problem and what they want the organization to be. With these sources of input as well as a thorough knowledge about theory and research regarding organizational behavior and morale, the administrator will be in the *best* possible position to diagnose the problem.

Identifying Alternative Change Strategies

The fifth step is to search for appropriate *change strategies.* In this step the change agent identifies alternatives to resolve the problem that was diagnosed in the preceding step. The goal is to identify as many strategies as possible that might help to reduce the problem. If, for example, a police agency is suffering from high attrition and administrators desire to mitigate this problem, possible strategies include (1) increasing pay, (2) improving benefits, (3) improving possibilities for promotion, (4) minimizing mandatory overtime, and (5) refining the recruitment process.

Selecting the Change Strategy

The next step is the selection of a change strategy. Factors to consider in selecting the best change strategy are availability of resources (personnel and equipment), reaction of personnel and the community to the potential change, potential outcome of the change strategy (which will be the most effective), the amount of effort that will be needed to implement the change in comparison to the possible outcome (i.e., cost effectiveness). The strategy that will be selected depends on the goals of the change and the resources that can be committed to making the change.

Determining and Operationalizing the Implementation Strategy

After selecting the strategy to use in creating change, the change agents are ready to determine the implementation strategy and implement it. Whether a change strategy will be successful depends on the perceived characteristics of the desired change, the type of change decision, the communication channels used to implement the change, the nature of the social system of the organization, and the extent of the change agent's (or agents') promotional efforts and influence. People desiring to make change within police organizations must establish an organizational climate that is suitable for the desired change and that will influence organizational members to support the change.

The one indispensable ingredient to planned change is assertive commitment (leadership) on the part of the police chief. Change must move from the top down. The chief must secure the cooperation of those immediate subordinates who, along with the chief, must assume responsibility for implementation of the plan (Livingstone and Sylvia, 1979:16).

In times of change, the chief's charisma is of special significance, not only because of the uncertainty of obedience of subordinates, but also because reform of the department depends on the cooperation of the chief's immediate subordinates whose careers may depend on the chief's success. In such a situation, the chief's certainty becomes their hope (Bordua and Reiss, 1978).

The implementation strategy and the implementation itself must be designed and accomplished while minimizing the risks to the organization. Implementation and risk minimization require that administrators consider those factors that may limit the creation of organizational change. These risk factors will be presented in the following section.

Evaluating and Modifying the Change Strategy

The eighth step of the change cycle entails evaluating the change in terms of its effectiveness and modifying the change strategy when necessary. This evaluation and modification step should begin as soon as implementation is begun. If problems are caught early, they will be easier to resolve than if they are allowed to continue until the implementation process is completed. No amount of planning for change can eliminate all problems in implementation. If problems are allowed to build, they can effectively destroy the chances that the change will occur, because unresolved problems create hostility and resentment on the part of organizational members. Unresolved problems create an atmosphere in which members perceive that management has no concern with their interests and job satisfaction. Morale can be undermined in this instance.

In this step, the evaluator is concerned with comparing the outcome of the change to the desired outcome. The following questions should be asked: How effective is the change in resolving the problem for which it was designed? What problems is the change process facing? How well is the organization coping with the change? How is the community reacting to the change? and Is the change being internalized or is it merely a superficial change? After answering questions such as these, the change agent can determine the degree of success of the change, rated on a scale from miserable failure to glowing success. Usually some areas of difficulty will be discovered. These should be immediately assessed and a plan should be developed to modify the implementation so as to create a more effective change. On rare occasions, it will be necessary to abort the original implementation plan and start over. Usually modification will resolve the problems that exist in a plan for change if the change process has been thoughtfully developed.

ORGANIZATIONAL DEVELOPMENT

The change process, as we have illustrated, consists of many steps. Recently, however, researchers have advocated a holistic approach to organizational change known as *organizational development (OD)*. Organizational development is defined as "a systemwide application of behavioral science knowledge to the planned development and reinforcement of organizational strategies, structures, and processes for improving an organization's effectiveness" (Cummings and Worley, 1993:2).

Organizational development is significant because (1) it deals with whole organizations or divisions within organizations; (2) it uses behavioral science research to improve leadership, motivation, and other factors; (3) it is adaptive and flexible; and (4) it focuses on productivity and quality of life within the organization. As one researcher observed, "The main focus of organizational development is on improving the total system so that the organization, its subgroups, and its members have a greater ability to assess and solve their own problems. This process is based on behavioral-science knowledge and practices, and it involves the creating and management of change" (Ramirez, 1994:4).

According to Fagenson (1990), two basic strategies are used to achieve OD's objectives. The first is the "technostructural" strategy. This focuses on organizational structure, work flow, task accomplishment, and performance. The other strategy, the "human processual" approach, focuses on the needs of employees and is directed toward improving communication and other group processes within the organization. The human processual approach entails, among other things, team building, conflict interventions, and organizational diagnosis and feedback. Technostructural interventions, on the other hand, involve job design, enlargement, and refinement, job enrichment, and structural changes (e.g., cutting out middle management). Table 15–1 illustrates some activities OD practitioners engage in.

There is no one best way to pursue OD, but usually it is accomplished through the use of external consultants. Often these individuals are trained in the social sciences and are best able to apply scientific knowledge to the change process. Several consulting firms specializing in OD (e.g., the Organization Development Institute) can be found throughout the nation, and many universities offer advanced degrees in organizational development (e.g., American University).

The OD process is compatible with the change process discussed in the previous section. It consists of three steps, each of which is found in one form or another throughout the traditional change process. The three steps are (1) diagnosis, (2) intervention, and (3) evaluation.

Table 15–1

Activities Associated with Organizational Development

Career Development

Designing/redesigning performance and appraisal systems
Personnel planning
Integration of women and minorities into the organization
Job rotation
Designing/redesigning reward systems
Providing coaching and/or counseling
Job redesign

Strategy Development

Strategic planning
Strategic management
Establishing organizational goals
Long-range forecasting
Promoting structural changes

Management Style Enhancement

Developing managing styles that enhance efficiency
Developing managing styles that enhance productivity

Culture Change

Changing the corporate culture
Activities addressing organizational power and influence issues
Group values sharing and clarification of activities

Technology Integration

Integrating high technology into the workplace
Learning the technical work of the organization
Accommodating creativity and innovation in the organization

Source: E. A. Fagenson, (1990). Organization development practitioners' activities and interventions in organizations. *Journal of Applied Behavioral Science* 26, no. 3 (1990), p. 285.

Diagnosis

The first step, diagnosis, involves gathering data. This can be accomplished with interviews, questionnaires, observations of employee behavior, and examination of internal documents and reports. Bartol and Martin point out that this stage "often focuses particular attention on the shared beliefs, values, and norms of organization members that may be interfering with maximum effectiveness" (1998:363).

Intervention

Once the situation has been diagnosed, the next step is intervention. Numerous change strategies are available (as Table 15–1 attests), but OD specialists often use four major techniques:

Process consultation: the OD consultant observes the group and provides comments on organization dysfunction.

Team building: the OD consultant helps work groups become more
effective at tasks and communication.

Third-party intervention: the OD consultant serves as a mediator
between warring parties when problems become particularly severe.

Technostructural activities: the consultant makes recommendations for
improving work methods, task design, and organizational structure
(Huse and Cummings, 1985).

Evaluation

The third step is evaluation. It is important that any change effort be monitored
continually. The OD consultant's responsibility in this regard (as well as the
organization's) is to ensure that changes are producing desired results.

RISKS ASSOCIATED WITH CHANGE

Merton (1936) observed that unanticipated consequences are inevitable when
purposive action is undertaken. Similarly, Durkheim argued that "the pathological is an inextricable part of every social system because the conditions of
the normal are the preconditions of the pathological" ([1938] 1966:47-75 cited
in Vaughan 1999:4). Both of these scholars were prophetically attuned to the
problems and risks associated with change.

Fortunately, unanticipated consequences are not necessarily random,
chance occurrences. Instead, Vaughan pointed out quite correctly that organizational deviance (broadly defined in terms of unanticipated consequences) "is
a routine byproduct of the characteristics of the system itself . . . a predictable
and recurring product of all socially organized systems" (1999:4).

She identified three broad categories of factors that may contribute to unanticipated consequences: the environment, organizational characteristics, and
human cognition. In other words, change can be compromised by external
forces (e.g., political pressure), internal problems (e.g., lack of communication),
and human decisions (e.g., reluctance to pursue reforms enthusiastically).

Resistance to Change

One risk frequently associated with change comes in the form of resistance. People have a tendency to fear change, sometimes resisting even when the changes
will result in improved conditions for everyone. Nowhere is this more apparent
than in law enforcement. Guyot (1979) claims that changes in policing are akin
to "bending granite," that they are nearly impossible. Resistance can come in
one of two forms: (1) tokenism or (2) massive resistance (Bardach, 1977).

Tokenism

Tokenism is occurring when organizational participants who appear to be contributing to a program are actually making only a small (token) contribution. A
variation on tokenism is procrastination, in which participants "hold out" as long

as possible before adopting change imposed from above. In either case, people making token contributions to organizational change do "as little as it takes."

Massive Resistance

As the term suggests, organizational participants who pour all their energies into resisting change are exhibiting massive resistance. According to Bardach, it is "a means of evading the responsibility specified in the policy mandate to provide these elements by overwhelming the capacity of some administrative agency to enforce sanctions for noncompliance" (1977:108). Massive resistance is virtually nonexistent in policing, partly for fear of discipline for failing to follow superiors' orders. This form of resistance is usually manifested (at least in the policing profession) in the form of strikes, in which all employees refuse to do their jobs. Strikes are rare or even illegal, depending on the jurisdiction.

Regardless of its form, resistance is inevitably partnered with change. Why, then, do people resist change? There are many reasons, but several stand out (e.g., Kotter and Schlesinger, 1979). First, people resist out of *self-interest*. If someone perceives the consequences of change to affect them adversely, some effort will be made to resist the change. How much resistance is encountered of course depends on how much the individual perceives the change will affect him or her. Another reason for resistance to change is *misunderstanding:* people will resist change when they don't understand it. This can be compounded if the change to be pursued is not clearly articulated and/or there is a communication problem or problem of mistrust between administrators and subordinates. According to Bartol and Martin, resistance is also mounted because of "*differential assessments* of the virtues of the change" (1998:365), particularly if one group perceives a positive outcome while another group perceives a negative outcome. Finally, some people resist change simply because they have a *low tolerance for change.* They may be the people who fear that they will not be able to learn the new skills associated with the change program.

Minimizing Resistance

Fortunately, administrators can take several steps to minimize resistance to change. First and foremost, administrators need to be vigilant. Only then can they identify sources of resistance. Once resistance is encountered, at least eight different strategies are available to ensure that change progresses without a hitch, or at least with minimal delay and difficulty.

Unfreezing, Changing, and Refreezing

One well-known strategy for reducing resistance to change has been advocated by organizational researcher Kurt Lewin, who divides the change process into three steps (Lewin, 1947). The first step, *unfreezing,* calls for identifying the source of resistance. This is accomplished in much the same way the need for change is assessed—by being alert to potential problems. Reitz describes an example of unfreezing as follows:

A program designed to change a manager's leadership style could provide him with feedback that his current style is ineffective and inappropriate. It could involve changing his office location to make him more or less accessible to his employees. It could remove him from the situation and provide a "safe" climate in which he can experiment with alternative behaviors by sending him to a training program conducted away from the premises (1977:546–547).

The second step, *changing*, is the administrator's efforts to have subordinates learn the newly required behaviors. This can overcome resistance in the form of misunderstanding. The third step, *refreezing*, concerns reinforcing the new behaviors. This is usually accomplished through a system of rewards. Schein (1961) notes that when training subordinates about the change, efforts should be made to ensure that they accept and internalize the information associated with the change. For example, although many departments have adopted community policing, its effectiveness is questionable in some agencies because officers did not develop a commitment to the new philosophy.

Education and Communication

Education and communication can be used in situations where a lack of information or understanding is evident. An advantage of this strategy is that as people are educated and made aware, they become increasingly likely to assist in the implementation of change. A disadvantage associated with this strategy is that education and communication and be time-consuming and costly (Kotter and Schlesinger, 1979).

Participation and Involvement

If the instigators of change lack information and/or power to effectuate change, participation and involvement in the change process can be desirable. Participation and involvement form a two-way street; that is, when subordinates are allowed to participate and be involved in the change process, they may feel they are more a part of it. An advantage of participation and involvement by administration is that subordinates come to see that administration is truly committed to changing the old ways. This strategy, too, can be time-consuming. It can also result in a change that is different from what administrators expected.

Facilitation and Support

Administrators can also provide facilitation and support. This is particularly useful when subordinates resist out of fear and anxiety. Facilitation and support can be accomplished through education, training, and providing proper equipment and materials. This strategy is particularly well received (Bartol and Martin, 1998:366), but it can be expensive and time-consuming as well. For example, having beat officers in a patrol area participate in problem solving may result in effective solutions and a higher level of commitment by the officers.

Negotiation and Agreement

When one group perceives that it will be negatively affected by change, negotiation and agreement are useful strategies. If training and education fail, it may be necessary to negotiate in order to gain cooperation. Think of the relationship between unions and administration: unions often resist change, so administration's responsibility is to bring the union "to the table" to flesh out an agreement that is mutually beneficial.

Manipulation and Cooptation

A slightly more controversial strategy for minimizing resistance is manipulation and cooptation. According to Bartol and Martin, *manipulation,* "usually involves selectively providing information about a change so that it appears more attractive or necessary to potential resisters," whereas *cooptation* is where "a leader or an influential person among the potential resisters is given a seemingly desirable role in the change process in order to gain cooperation" (1998:367). Both strategies pose ethical problems because of the deception involved. This can lead to future problems if people find out they are being manipulated and deceived.

Explicit and Implicit Coercion

Yet another strategy for minimizing resistance is coercion, either explicit or implicit. This, like manipulation and cooptation, is another controversial strategy designed to ensure compliance; it is more authoritative than some of the aforementioned strategies. Basically, this strategy involves the use of power to pressure people into changing. Tactics employed can include threats of job loss, demotion, and suspension. A problem with coercion is that it can backfire. The recipients of the pressure may become resentful and escalate their resistance if the coercion is perceived as too serious. Unfortunately, research indicates that administrators rely on this strategy more often than they have to (Nutt, 1986).

Force-Field Analysis

According to Bartol and Martin, force-field analysis is "a method that involves analyzing the two types of forces, driving forces and restraining forces, that influence any proposed change and then assessing how best to overcome resistance" (1998:367). *Driving forces* are those forces that exert pressure for change. *Restraining forces,* as the term suggests, are those forces that pressure against change. At any point in time both forces are in operation. They push in opposite directions against one another and create an equilibrium, or status quo. The role of the administrator is to increase the driving forces and decrease restraining forces so change can be accomplished (Strebel, 1994). Developing and maintaining a driving force is best accomplished through participation and facilitation.

Other Issues in Minimizing the Risks of Change

Six generally accepted principles affect one's ability to minimize the difficulties and risks in attempting to change organizations (Taguiri and Litwin, 1968). Each of these six concepts is clearly related to the organizational climate. *Organizational climate* is basically another term for organizational culture, "the set of values, norms, standards of behavior, and common expectations that control the ways in which individuals and groups in an organization interact with each other and work to achieve organizational goals" (Jones, George, and Hill, 1998:285).

To minimize the risks and difficulties of innovating, the administrator must successfully account for each of these six forms of risk and difficulty. The administrator must identify the best types of change to initiate, then select the right circumstances and the proper time for initiating change. Success on the first attempt at change will make future changes much easier, so it is vital that first changes be successful.

Perpetuation of the Organizational Climate

The organizational climate (culture) is perpetuated from one generation of members to another through organizational socialization, unless the intraorganizational processes and structures are changed. The attitudes of organizational members toward change and work are part of the organizational climate. Processes and structures in the organization create the atmosphere within the work setting. The chapters dealing with organization, management, and leadership emphasized this notion. If the organizational structure and process is a classical one, we would expect the organizational climate to be opposed to change, and we would expect that opposition to change to be passed from one generation of members to another. However, if the organizational structure and process of that classical organization was influenced to change in the direction of a human relations or contingency model, the classical organization climate would no longer be passed to the next generation of employees in its original form. Over a period of time we would expect a new organizational climate to develop that would reflect the new process and structure of the agency. The new climate would then be perpetuated from one generation to another until or unless the intraorganizational processes and structures are changed again.

Maintenance of the Organizational Climate

Those inertial forces that maintain the organizational climate tend to increase as the size of the organization increases. Small organizations are much more easily changed than large police organizations. A good example of the difficulty in changing the organizational climate of a large police agency is the Chicago police department. O. W. Wilson's influence in the Chicago department brought about major changes while he was there to enforce these changes. Upon his exit from the department, the department reverted to the climate that had existed earlier. It is very difficult to create institutionalized change in the organizational climate of a very large agency because it is more difficult to identify and modify the forces that influence the maintenance of the climate. This is generally due to the mere numbers involved. Changing the organizational climate requires changes of individual perceptions and organizational rewards. Both necessitate contacting and influencing persons on an individual basis as well as in groups and a long-term commitment to change of the organizational climate. (Wilson tried to force change based on the strength of his personality alone. Change resulting from this method is not longlasting because it does not reach the depths of the organizational climate; it is only a skin-deep change.)

Members' Perceptions of the Climate

If members of the organization perceive the current organizational climate more favorably than they perceive the proposed (changed) organizational climate, there will be a lower rate of change because of reduced motivation to change. Conversely, if the climate of the proposed organization is perceived as more favorable than the climate of the current organization, there will be a higher rate of change. Change is much more natural if it complements the climate of the agency. The more drastic the attempted change to the climate the more the organizational members will resist the proposed change.

Consensus Regarding the Climate

Organizational climate is more susceptible to deliberate efforts to modify it when there is a low degree of consensus regarding the climate. One way to create change in the organizational climate is to undermine the consensus of the members about what the climate is. Consensus on the climate exists when all members have the same beliefs and attitudes about the goals of the organization and their role in the achievement of organizational goals. The more difference in these beliefs, the lower the degree of consensus in the climate of the organization.

Subunit Differences in Climate

There is a tendency for greater conflict concerning proposals for change and for differences in the rate of changes when subunits of an organization perceive the climate differently. When functional parts of the police agency (e.g., traffic, patrol, juvenile, homicide, vice) differ in organizational climate or the organizational climate differs between the geographic subdivisions (e.g., east/west, inner-city/suburbs), conflict is likely to occur over the type of change to be created, the method to achieve change, or the time schedule for making change. Generally, the more difference there is between these groups, the greater the conflict will be.

Organizational power struggles are an essential and important mechanism for consideration in organizational change (Blau and Scott, 1962). There seems to be a mutual dependence relationship between conflict and change in the formal organization; changes in the social structure often precipitate conflict, and conflicts generate change. Formal organizations slowly adjust their official structure to changing conditions. Changes that adapt operations to a new situation benefit the organization, but they are often developed and implemented informally, sometimes in violation of official procedures. Power struggles play a significant role in the process of adjustment to change in the organization. They provide managers with incentives for making informal changes, which help them cope with operating problems and extend the scope of their influence.

Technical versus Administrative Change

Technical changes generate faster changes in the organizational climate than administrative changes. This happens because technical changes are manifested in the products and services of the organization. Even extremely classical organizations have accepted technological advances in the areas of communications and equipment. Technology is perceived in such instances not as adversely affecting the individual's position in the organization, but as providing a means to make the work safer and easier to perform. In contrast, changes in management styles and organizational structure (e.g., community policing) have been the foci of much controversy within nearly every agency that has attempted to introduce these changes. Administrative changes often threaten the position of individuals. Resistance usually stems from protectionism of midmanagers in the police agency.

Technological changes are also more strongly supported by the external environment. The community is more aware of technical changes, and these changes have the potential to affect the police–community relationship. These changes usually have specific positive outcomes that can be identified by the public as being helpful in making their community more secure. However, the public is often not aware of administrative change because it has little direct impact on the services to which the citizens are exposed.

APPROACHES TO CHANGE

Whereas there is one basic process for making organizational change, there are several approaches that can be used in initiating change. Porter, Lawler, and Hackman (1975) provide an excellent description of the three most frequently used approaches to achieve organizational change—the individual approach, the organizational structure and systems approach, and the organizational climate and interpersonal style approach. Each approach evidences (1) its own assumptions about the major causes of behavior in organizations, (2) its own peculiar intervention techniques, and (3) specifically intended immediate outcomes. These three approaches to initiate organizational change are set forth in the next three sections.

Individual Change

The most typical approach to organizational change has been the *individual change* approach. The individual approach for initiating change within an organization utilizes education, training, socialization, and attitude change as intervention techniques. Katz and Kahn (1966) believe that the failure of the individual approach to create organizational change is due to the assumptions on which it is based. They indicate that the initial diagnosis—inappropriate organizational behavior caused by a lack of individual insight or another psychological shortcoming of the personnel in the organization—may be an incorrect diagnosis of the problem. Even if the diagnosis is correct, it rest on five very weak assumptions: (1) providing new insight and knowledge to individuals will produce significant alteration in their motivational patterns; (2) these new insights and motivations will be retained when an individual leaves the protected training situation and returns to the accustomed role in the organization; (3) the individual will be able to adapt the newly learned knowledge to the real-life situation of the workplace; (4) co-workers will be persuaded to accept the changes in the trainee's behavior; and (5) the trainee will also be able to convince the co-workers to make complementary changes in their own expectations and behavior. The problems of change are too complex for such a simplistic generalization. Organizational change requires more than an individualistic approach if it is to be effective and lasting in an organizational environment.

Organizational Structure and Systems Change

The second most frequent approach to implementing change is the *organizational structure and systems change* approach. The intervention techniques of this approach involve modifying actual organizational practices, procedures, and policies that affect what people do at work. The intended outcome is the creation of conditions that elicit and reward behavior that facilitates organizational goal achievement. Such an approach assumes that the behavior of people in organizations is largely determined by the characteristics of the organizational situation in which people work. (The neoclassical model approaches change in this manner.)

One relatively slow way to institute desired changes is to change the career path to top management positions. The career path dictates the kinds of experiences one must have to be eligible for promotion. If one is interested in changing the premises of decision making or the perspectives and values of management, this is a very valuable methodology. Changing the kinds of experiences of people who have access to top management positions was suggested by Perrow (1979). This concept is based on the premise that to change a person's behavior one must change the premises of his or her decision making. The premises of decision making are found in the structural aspects of the organization—the vocabulary of the organization, the structure of communication, the rules and regulations, the standard programs, and the selection criteria for entry and promotion. These structural aspects provide certain rewards and sanctions that determine whether one will be promoted to a position of prominence.

The career path for promotion provides certain experiences and reinforces certain orientations. For example, a department that has promoted primarily from patrol and criminal investigation units will probably have an enforcement orientation. The chief might promote more individuals from units such as community relations or crime prevention to mold more of a service orientation into the department's overall orientation. One's career path tends to shape the perspectives and values that one uses to make decisions. Perrow's position is that to shape managerial behavior, one has to shape the kinds of experiences the manager has prior to being placed in the managerial position.

Another structural and system type of change is the decentralization of authority and decision making. Weiland and Ullrich (1976) indicate that the most enduring change is the change program which moves authority and responsibility for decision making downward in the hierarchy through all levels of the organization. Other researchers (e.g., Mann, 1963) found that the greater the involvement of all organizational members through their organizational families—department heads, first-line supervisors, and employees—the greater the organizational change. Thus increasing the participation of employees is not only the most lasting form of change but it is necessary to achieve full cooperation to completely implement change.

Organizational structure and system style change generally has emphasized reorganization and decentralization while ignoring the need to make policy and reward systems changes. Therefore, in implementation, most change of this type has used only part of the total package. The ineffectiveness of many reorganization attempts can be traced to the failure to incorporate the corresponding policy and reward system changes.

Organizational Climate and Interpersonal Style Change

The typical intervention techniques of this approach are experimental techniques that are aimed at increasing members' awareness of the social determinants of their behavior and helping them to learn new ways of relating to and reacting to each other within the organizational context. The intended immediate outcome of *organizational climate and interpersonal style change* is the creation of a systemwide climate characterized by (1) high interpersonal trust, (2) openness, and (3) reduction of the dysfunctional consequences of excessive social conflict and competitiveness. Such an approach assumes that organizational behavior is largely determined by the emotional and social processes that characterize the relationships among organization members.

One such approach involves the management of the culture of the organization in an explicit and systematic manner. Of course, changing the distinctive culture of a large, old organization is extremely difficult and may take many years. Culture is hard to change because group processes limit deviation from group norms of behavior by imposing sanctions on individuals who deviate (Weiland and Ullrich, 1976). These sanctions range from mild sanctions (half-joking, half-critical comments) for slight deviations to severe sanctions (verbal rebuke or physical violence) for major deviations for the group norms.

Once a new culture is in place there must be continuous, ongoing activity utilizing a number of different tactics to maintain the desired culture. Role modeling is an effective technique that is used by successful managers to foster a desired culture. This technique consists of providing a model of behavior that is consistent with the desired norms and values. Some police departments are using this technique by selecting "model" officers as field training officers (FTOs). These FTOs show the new recruit what is expected and appropriate in the department. Thus the rookie models the police role acted out by the FTO. Other methods for developing culture are providing positive reinforcement, communicating or articulating the desired norms and values, and shaping the culture indirectly by influencing those factors that affect the culture (e.g., using recruitment, evaluation, promotion, transfer, and training to promote the desired organizational culture).

Organizational change is not a simple problem; it is a complex problem, which is not easily accomplished. There is no single process for creating change within organizations. It appears evident, however, that the goal of change and the assumptions and philosophical basis for the change must be made explicit if an appropriate method is to be selected for creating the desired organizational change. Even then, there is no guarantee that change will be accomplished successfully. A combination of these three approaches to change might provide the best results. Nevertheless, it is certain that the reward system and organizational policies must be consistent with the desired individual behavior and organizational culture if any change is to be effective.

Couper and Lobitz summed up organizational climate and interpersonal style change in policing:

> If we learn nothing else about police organizational change, let us remember that when change is implemented from the top of the organization, either by coercive force or without real employee input, it will surely fail. It is only by first changing the "inside" of our organizations that we will be able to implement effectively these new "outside" strategies of policing. (1988:84)

POLICE ORGANIZATIONAL CHANGE

Three broad changes in policing have occurred in the past three decades: (1) a breakdown in the rigidity of the police organization, (2) humanization of the police image, and (3) a reduction in the distance between police and citizens as well as between the administration and operations of police organizations (Sandler and Mintz, 1978). Many specific changes have brought about these three broad changes in policing (Murphy and Brown, 1973; Sandler and Mintz, 1979; Skolnick and Bayley, 1986). We consider six of them: (1) participative management, (2) flattening the organization, (3) community policing, (4) civilianization, (5) police–community collaboration, and (6) interdepartmental cooperation.

It is important to note that some of these changes are overlapping. For example, community policing can involve police–community collaboration. Similarly, civilianization provides for police–community collaboration. For the sake of illustration, however, we treat each of the six changes separately.

Participative Management

Police agencies have become more participative in the past decade or so. However, a study of police officers from throughout the United States who were attending the FBI National Academy in 1976 showed a significant change in police management styles as early as 1974–1976 (Shanahan, Hunger, and Wheelen, 1979). The officers indicated that for all areas examined, the management styles that they had been exposed to had changed from Likert's benevolent-authoritative in 1974 to a consultative style in 1976. This finding is significant even though it is based on the memory of these officers, who probably represent the best personnel of their agencies.

Skolnick and Bayley (1986) found a real decentralization of command in the six departments they examined. This structural and philosophical status of command creates "the possibility for more intensive police–community interaction and heightened identification by police officers with particular areas" (p. 214) by attaching police to geographical areas. This means that the police genuinely feel and communicate to the public that they see the community as a partner in the enterprise of policing. The police serve, learn from, and are accountable to the community. Together they are co-producers of crime prevention.

A think-tank approach within the department, bypassing the chain of command, is one method of participatory decision making. Another such approach is the neighborhood police team. The extension of team policing was not as rapid or as dominant as many would have liked. The difficulties arose from the failure to provide incentives (e.g., salary merit increases) for those working in the new teams. Difficulties of implementation also resulted from interference by middle managers who felt threatened by the loss of power and authority inherent in the team policing concept.

To an extent police administration still relies on submission to authority, but a different set of values and expectations has been established of late. Autocratic leadership of the past will not work today. As Withan observed, "The watchwords of the new leadership paradigm are coach, inspire, gain commitment, empower, affirm, flexibility, responsibility, self-management, shared power, autonomous teams, and entrepreneurial units" (1991:30).

Today's police officers have higher levels of education and are less likely to submit blindly to authority. They are more independent and less responsive to traditional, authoritative supervision. They also are more receptive to competing concerns, more supportive of peers and citizens, and more likely to adopt humanistic approaches to their jobs. They desire greater input into their jobs. As one author observed, "The field of law enforcement management is full of dinosaurs, and they are becoming extinct" (Story, 1992:7).

Flattening the Organization

Many police administrators are beginning to question whether the traditional, bureaucratic structure of most police departments will be effective in the twenty-first century. Robinette (1989) argued that the departmental organization chart of the future will no longer have a pyramid shape. Hierarchy will be pushed down and, instead, the sides of the organization will expand. Decision making will be less centralized, and middle management will be reduced, leaving the vertical differentiation in police departments less complex.

According to one study, there are two essential dimensions of organizational flattening: vertical differentiation and administrative density. *Vertical differentiation* refers to the "height" of the organization, "the distance from the bottom to the top of the organization, or the amount of social space between the lowest- and the highest-ranking employees" (Maguire, 1997:559). Those in favor of organizational flattening favor reductions in vertical differentiation through either (1) developing more informal managerial channels or (2) actually reducing the levels of command (Mastrofski, 1994). *Administrative density,* like vertical differentiation, refers to the size of the administrative component of the organization (Langworthy, 1985), including all supporting staff. Those in favor of organizational flattening desire reductions in the administrative component. They believe that the more people employed on the administrative side, the fewer the people who are available to perform the core work of the police organization, law enforcement and community service.

As researchers have observed, "Communication within the pyramid structure is often made difficult by many barriers and frustrated by the numerous levels of bureaucracy" (Glensor, Peak, and Gaines, 1999:348). A more horizontal structure lends itself to improved communication throughout the agency.

Unfortunately, it is unclear whether "flattening" of police organizations can occur to a significant extent. In his research concerning this very topic, Maguire (1997) found that structural changes—the kind that involve reworking the rank structure of police organizations—have been virtually nonexistent. He did find some evidence of reductions in vertical differentiation, but such changes have been offset by increased specialization. In his words, community policing "advocates may be discouraged by the increase in functional differentiation because they have pressed police departments to de-specialize as part of their overall reform prescriptions" (p. 572).

Community Policing

A recent survey found that 50 percent of police officials serving cities with populations in excess of 50,000 people were following the community policing model (Peak and Glensor, 1996). As researchers have observed, community policing "has become a mantra for police chiefs and mayors in cities big and small across the country" (Witkin and McGraw, 1993:28). Another source calls community policing the "new orthodoxy" in American policing (Eck and Rosenbaum, 1994).

We have already encountered community policing earlier in this text, but we consider it briefly here along with other large-scale changes currently being witnessed throughout the law enforcement profession. As was pointed out in Chapter 3, there are several dimensions to community policing. These dimensions—philosophical, strategic, and programmatic—illustrate the complexity of this new policing paradigm. They also translate into a number of guiding principles, including the following:

1. Community policing is both a philosophy and an organizational strategy that allows the police and community residents to work closely together in new ways to solve the problems of crime, fear of crime, physical and social disorder, and neighborhood conditions . . . ;
2. Community policing's organizational strategy demands that everyone in the department, including both civilian and sworn personnel, must investigate ways to translate the philosophy into practice . . . ;
3. To implement true community policing, police departments must also create and develop a new breed of line officer, the Community Policing Officer (CPO), who acts as the direct link between the police and people in the community . . . ;
4. The CPO's broad role demands continuous, sustained contact with the law-abiding people in the community, so that together they can explore creative new solutions to local concerns involving crime, fear of crime, disorder, and community conditions . . . ;
5. Community policing adds a vital proactive element to the traditional reactive role of the police, resulting in full-spectrum police service. (Trojanowicz et al. 1998:xi–xii)

As these principles suggest, community policing recognizes that the police need partners in the crime control mission. Law enforcement is one entity of many responsible for improving quality of life. Problem solving, police–community cooperation, improved coordination and communication, openness, and flexibility are all vital elements in this process. Police administrators need to be attuned to developments in community policing, which appears to be the policing paradigm that will survive well into the future.

Civilianization

Civilianization and lateral entry were relatively new police personnel policies in the early 1970s. *Civilianization* is the utilization of civilians instead of sworn police officers in positions not specifically requiring the authority of a sworn officer. The six departments examined by Skolnick and Bayley (1986) had innovated through civilianization. Civilianization allows police to concentrate on highly skilled police tasks while civilians perform the more routine tasks such as records, clerical, and communications tasks as well as other support areas, such as research and training, budgeting, forensic analysis, and equipment maintenance.

One particular strategy used by several police agencies to reduce the workload of sworn officers is the use of a *community service officer* (CSO). CSOs are nonsworn personnel in the field who respond to certain calls for service. According to one source, "A CSO may engage in traffic accident investigations, take vandalism reports, perform parking enforcement, conduct basic crime scene investigations and collect evidence, dust for fingerprints, and perform

Officer patrols public beach in Miami Beach, Florida, expanding services to the citizens.
Jeff Greenberg/PhotoEdit

other related duties" (Glensor, Peak, and Gaines, 1999:253). In other agencies, CSOs staff storefronts and handle telephone requests, eliminating the need to assign sworn personnel to these duties.

In the absence of programs providing for CSOs, many agencies still rely on citizen volunteers for duties that don't necessarily require a sworn officer. The removal of graffiti in Yucaipa, California, for example, is accomplished (in part) by citizens who can stop by the city office to pick up free cleaning chemicals for use in their neighborhoods.

Yet another means of reducing the need for sworn personnel is the use of citizen patrol. Many cities throughout the country rely on a corps of citizen volunteers (in marked citizen patrol vehicles) to help with proactive patrol. Since the citizens are not sworn officers, they rarely intervene, but rather call on officers when they are needed. For example, if citizen patrol witnesses a crime in progress, they will usually call for sworn personnel to intervene and apprehend the suspects.

Civilianization is a growing phenomenon in contemporary law enforcement. Police agencies are coming to realize that citizen volunteers compose a largely untapped resource. The police and citizens alike are coming to realize that crime control is necessarily a cooperative effort. With citizens beginning to perform duties that, in the past, would have been the responsibility of sworn personnel, the police are better able to accomplish their mission.

For civilianization to succeed, administrators must support the practice as well as sell it to the rest of the department. It has been noted that persuading sworn personnel to embrace civilianization poses a significant hurdle (Wilkerson, 1994). Administrators must also ensure that an appropriate balance between civilianization and traditional law enforcement is achieved. With attention and careful planning, much can be accomplished through civilianization. Unfortunately, however, civilianization (particularly the use of civilian volunteers) appears to take hold in smaller, rural agencies, or those agencies facing reductions in size (Crank, 1989).

Police–Community Collaboration

Collaborative models in which the police and community work together gained in acceptance and in numbers during the 1970s. Examples of such models are citizen advisory committees for guidance and assistance to the police agency, police representation on existing community and governmental agencies, neighborhood watch groups, and community action groups. Although these committees are sometimes created to focus on a single issue or area, they often mature to the point that they respond to an increasing number of issues or areas.

Skolnick and Bayley (1986) found that interplay between the police and the community significantly affects police change. One element of change in their study was police–community reciprocity. Skolnick and Bayley also discovered that their study cities had reoriented patrol to enlist the aid of the community in crime prevention efforts. Foot patrol, community policing, and problem solving are prime examples of patrol reorientation.

A relatively recent advancement in police–community collaboration comes in the form of citizen police academies (CPAs). Citizen police academies are designed to introduce average citizens to various aspects of the law enforcement profession (Cohn, 1996). Agencies usually choose a pool of applicants who attend a shortened/simplified version of a traditional police academy. According to Bumphus, Gaines, and Blakely, "The primary goals of a CPA are to educate the public, establish positive relations with citizen groups, and increase appreciation for police functions" (1999:69). Similarly, Hilson states, "The ultimate goal of the citizen police academy is the reduction of crime through a stronger citizen commitment to the police department and the community" (1994:1).

Researchers recently conducted a survey of municipal police departments and county sheriff's agencies to determine how many maintained citizen police academies (Bumphus, Gaines, and Blakely, 1999). They found that agencies serving larger populations are more likely to house a CPA. In addition, the average CPA participant, they found, was 42 years old and likely to be male (54 percent). They found that CPAs run for an average of 33 hours, over an 11-week period, with 24 students. Citizens have to fill out an application and pass a background check to be enrolled. The curricula in CPAs vary considerably, but several commonalities can be identified. Table 15–2 lists, in descending order of popularity, the types of topics covered in CPAs.

Table 15–2

Course Content of Citizen Police Academies

Patrol operations	Crimes against children
Use of force	Firearms at range
Community policing	DARE
Police ride-alongs	Officer survival
Community services	Police civil liability
Police training	Murder investigation
Crime prevention	Rape investigation
Narcotics enforcement	Trial court
Investigations	Victim assistance
Ethics/internal affairs	Jail/corrections
Criminal law	Elderly services
Police communications	Media relations
Narcotics and drug abuse	Building searches
Arrest procedures	Bomb unit
Juvenile crime problems	Defensive driving
Firearms in classrooms	Prostitution-related crime
SWAT	White-collar crime
Gang-related crime	Liquor laws
Homicide investigation	Gambling-related crime
K-9 operations	Organized crime
Police selection	First aid

Source: V. W. Bumphus, L. K. Gaines, and C. R. Blakely, Citizen police academies: Observing goals, objectives and recent trends. *American Journal of Criminal Justice* 24, no. 1 (1999), pp. 67–79.

Whether citizen police academies help with crime prevention or crime reduction is not clear. The biggest problem is that most CPA participants are already supportive of the police (Bumphus, Gaines, and Blakely, 1999). Younger citizens and minorities, the most vocal critics of police behavior, seem to be the citizens most likely to be excluded from these programs. "These individuals, due to higher levels of ambivalence towards the police, may be the most appropriate participants if the agency's goal is to foster more positive citizen–police relations" (p. 77). Nevertheless, CPAs seem to be in important step in the direction of police–community collaboration.

Interdepartmental Cooperation

Interdepartmental cooperation has also grown demonstrably. Coordination was established through active involvement of police and other criminal justice leaders in planning for their city, county, area, and state. The Law Enforcement Assistance Administration (LEAA) was the impetus for this involvement. Out of the efforts of these leaders came joint training projects, joint use of personnel and equipment, exchange of information and intelligence data, and cooperative development of criminal justice information systems. Some departments have ventured to share command officers through temporary exchange programs.

Even though LEAA is now defunct, it existed long enough to develop a network for communication to continue between agencies. (This network is now informal instead of formal in nature.) Of course the degree to which there is interdepartmental cooperation differs dramatically across the United States. The important thing is that police agencies are relying on information from each other to provide more effective enforcement and service than would be possible if each stood alone.

An example of current interdepartmental cooperation can be found in the form of multi-agency drug task forces. As part of the Anti-Drug Abuse Acts of 1986 and 1988, federal funds were made available to state and local units of government to expand drug enforcement efforts to create multijurisdictional drug enforcement task forces. Research indicates that there are several thousand such task forces in place around the United States. Schlegel and McGarrell (1991) note that single agencies, particularly those in low-to-moderate population areas, are not able to effectively cope with the drug problem. Small police agencies rarely have sufficient resources, personnel, expertise, equipment, or intelligence capabilities, especially when sophisticated drug networks are operating in their areas. Uncoordinated activity leads to the possible duplication of efforts and the potential endangerment of undercover personnel. Since drug distribution networks usually exist across several jurisdictions, cooperative arrangements are required.

The main goal of these task forces is to increase interagency communication and cooperation to reduce the supply and demand for illicit drugs (McGarrell and Schlegel, 1993). In particular, Sabath, Doyle, and Ransburg (1990) identified six interrelated goals of multijurisdictional drug task forces: (1) to disrupt drug trafficking in targeted communities; (2) to arrest drug traffickers, dealers, and users; (3) to develop intelligence systems; (4) to remove or severely limit drug availability; (5) to establish cooperative enforcement networks; and (6) to seize the assets of convicted drug offenders.

The departments taking part in an interdepartmental effort need not always be law enforcement agencies. For example, the Oakland, California, Specialized Multi-Agency Response Team (SMART) program is a problem-solving strategy that is characterized by coordinated enforcement of regulatory code violations (e.g., building and safety codes). The police use governmental agencies to enforce building and fire codes at structures where drug trafficking occurs. Code enforcement is sometimes more effective than enforcement in eliminating a drug hot spot (Green, 1996).

Still other agencies can get involved. Pratt and his colleagues (2000) note that local and federal prosecutors have been involved in such task forces. Whatever their form, task forces seek to pool their resources—be they personnel, money, or intelligence—to gain more complete understanding of drug problems and more effectively disrupt the illicit drug market with arrests, convictions, and asset seizures. Research suggests, however, that for task forces to be effective in their missions, careful attention needs to be paid to how success is measured and how interorganizational decision making occurs (Pratt et al., 2000).

FUTURE TRENDS AND CHALLENGES

The future of policing in America will be affected by several factors. For example, future recruiting efforts will be affected by continuing shifts in the nation's demographics. There will be more older workers, greater numbers of women and minorities, and an increase in immigration. Police agencies will have to tailor their search for qualified applicants in accordance with this change. They will also have to offer attractive wage and benefits packages, including day care, flexible schedules, maternity leave, and other perks in order to compete with private industry (McCord and Wicker, 1990). Moreover, police agencies of the future will need to encourage diversity in the ranks. The percentage of women in policing, for example, has risen about 10 percent in the last few years (U.S. Department of Justice, Bureau of Justice Statistics, 1996), so it will be important to increase the number of women (as well as other traditionally marginalized groups) in supervisory positions.

The nature of crime is also rapidly changing. There are approximately 43 million personal and property crime victimizations in the United States each year. Of these, about 14 million are serious offenses reported to the police (Maguire and Pastore, 1996). However, the advent of technology is rapidly changing the face of crime. And while high-tech crime may be less violent than traditional street crime, it poses new challenges for law enforcement officials. The police of the future will need to be well trained in new and cutting-edge investigative techniques, especially as they relate to computer crime. Police departments will also have to provide for the hiring of individuals with specialized, high-tech backgrounds to assist in the apprehension of the new generation of technologically savvy criminals (Glensor, Peak, and Gaines, 1999).

Indeed, countless other changes are beginning to occur. The future of policing will take an uncertain course; fortunately, there is much police administrators can do to anticipate changes. In particular, futures research has gained momentum as one tool for predicting coming changes in law enforcement.

Summary

Change is an important issue facing police administrators. The environment of policing is constantly changing, and police agencies must constantly stay abreast of these changes if they are to be effective in their mission. In particular, police administrators need to develop an awareness of the need for change and the change process. Administrators also need to be attuned to the many barriers to change as well as strategies to overcome them. And last but not least, administrators need to keep an eye toward the future.

We know that the administrator of tomorrow will deal with an increasingly decentralized, participatory, and diverse society. The strength of future police administrators will probably hinge on their ability to listen to others, their imagination, and their recognition of the limited nature of leadership in the new world. The new administrator must be prepared to share leadership that may prove more temporary, collegial, and consensual. As Toffler observed:

The responsibility of change, therefore, lies with us. We must begin with ourselves, teaching ourselves not to close our minds prematurely to the novel, the surprising, the seemingly radical. This means fighting off the idea-assassins who rush forward to kill any new suggestion on grounds of its impracticality, while defending whatever now exists as practical, no matter how absurd, oppressive, or workable it may be. It means fighting for freedom of expression—the right of people to voice their ideas, even if heretical. (1980:443)

If police administrators meet this challenge, they have the potential to be on the leading edge of the future, to establish better relationships with their communities, and to meet the needs of the society they serve. If they do not, policing will be incapable of serving the third-wave civilization.

Study Questions

1. Explain the goals of police organizational change.

2. How is the need for change assessed? Can you think of drawbacks posed by one method over the other?

3. How is organizational change implemented?

4. What is organizational development as it applies to the topic of organizational change?

5. Describe the risks associated with change.

6. How can police administrators minimize resistance to change?

7. Distinguish between three approaches to change.

8. How is change currently taking place in police organizations?

Net Resources

http://cor-ex.com/sites/bestchng/Sites/Change-Consultants.htm Links to charge consultants sites.

http://www.fbi.gov/publications/leb/2001/september2001/sept01p14.htm Information on organizational development in law enforcement.

http://www.usdoj.gov/cops/cp_resources/pubs_prod/s30.htm A list of publications and products related to community policing.

References

Bardach, E. (1977). *The Implementation Game: What Happens after a Bill Becomes a Law.* Cambridge, MA: MIT Press.

Bartol, K. M., and Martin, D. C. (1998). *Management,* 3rd ed. New York: McGraw-Hill.

Blau, P. M., and Scott, W. R. (1962). *Formal Organizations: A Comparative Approach*. San Francisco: Chandler.

Bumphus, V. W., Gaines, L. K., and Blakely, C. R. (1999). Citizen police academies: Observing goals, objectives, and recent trends. *American Journal of Criminal Justice* 24(1):67–79.

Campbell, J. H. (1990). Futures research: Here and abroad. *Police Chief* 57:30.

Cohn, E. (1996). The citizen police academy: A recipe for improving police–community relations. *Journal of Criminal Justice* 24:265–271.

Cole, G. F. (1989). *The American System of Justice*, 5th ed. Pacific Grove, CA: Brooks-Cole.

Couper, D. C., and Lobitz, S. H. (1988). Quality leadership: The first step towards quality policing. *Police Chief* 55(4):79–84.

Crank, J. P. (1989). Civilianization in small and medium police departments in Illinois, 1973–1986. *Journal of Criminal Justice* 17(3):167–177.

Cummings, T. G., and Worley, C. G. (1993). *Organizational Development and Change*, 5th ed. St. Paul: West Publishing.

Duncan, R. B. (1976). Organizational climate and climate for change in three police departments: Some preliminary findings. *Urban Affairs Quarterly* 8(2):205–245.

Dunning, C. M. (1972). Communication structure of three police organizations in relation to perceptions of the department as held by its members: An analysis. Doctoral dissertation, Michigan State University.

Eck, J. E., and Rosenbaum, D. P. (1994). The new police order: Effectiveness, equity, and efficiency in community policing. In D. P. Rosenbaum (ed.), *The Challenge of Community Policing*. Thousand Oaks, CA: Sage, pp. 3–26.

Fagenson, E. A. (1990). Organization development practitioners' activities and interventions in organizations. *Journal of Applied Behavioral Science* 26(3):285.

Fordyce, J. K., and Weil, R. (1971). *Managing with People: A Manager's Handbook of Organization Development Methods*. Reading, MA: Addison-Wesley.

Glensor, R. W., Peak, K. J., and Gaines, L. K. (1999). *Police Supervision*. New York: McGraw-Hill.

Green, L. (1996). *Policing Places with Drug Problems*. Thousand Oaks, CA: Sage.

Guyot, D. (1979). Bending granite: Attempts to change the rank structure of American police departments. *Journal of Police Science and Administration* 7:253–284.

Hilson, J. (1994). Citizen police academies. *TELEMASP Bulletin* 1(2):1–7.

Huse, E. F., and Cummings, T. G. (1985). *Organization Development and Change*, 3rd ed. St. Paul: West Publishing.

Johnson, T. A. (1978). The application of organizational theory to the problem of police resistance to police community relations. In L. Gaines and T. Ricks (eds.), *Managing the Police Organization*. St. Paul: West Publishing.

Jones, G. R., George, J. M., and Hill, C. W. L. (1998). *Contemporary Management*. New York: McGraw-Hill.

Katz, D., and Kahn, R. L. (1966). *The Social Psychology of Organizations*. New York: Wiley.

Kotter, J. P., and Schlesinger, L. A. (1979). Choosing strategies for change. *Harvard Business Review*, March–April, pp. 106–114.

Langworthy, R. H. (1985). Administrative overhead in municipal police departments. *American Journal of Police* 4:20–37.

Lewin, K. (1947). Frontiers in group dynamics: Concept, method, and reality in social science. *Human Relations* 1:5–41.

Livingstone, J., and Sylvia, R. (1979). Rethinking police organization. *Journal of Police Science and Administration* 7:12–17.

McCord, R., and Wicker, E. (1990). Tomorrow's America: Law enforcement's coming challenge. *FBI Law Enforcement Bulletin* 59 (January):31–33.

McGarrell, E. F., and Schlegel, K. (1993). The implementation of federally funded multijurisdictional drug task forces: Organizational structure and interagency relationships. *Journal of Criminal Justice* 21:231–244.

Maguire, E. R. (1997). Structural change in large municipal police organizations during the community policing era. *Justice Quarterly* 14:547–576.

Maguire, K., and Pastore, A. L. (eds.). (1996). *Sourcebook of Criminal Justice Statistics, 1995*. U.S. Department of Justice, Bureau of Justice Statistics. Washington: Government Printing Office.

Mann, F. C. (1963). Studying and creating change: A means to understand social organization. In R. A. Sutermeister (ed.), *People and Productivity*. New York: McGraw-Hill.

Mastrofski, S. D. (1994). Community policing and police organization structure. Presented at the Workshop on Evaluating Police Service Delivery, Centre for Comparative Criminology, University of Montreal.

Merton, R. K. (1936). The unanticipated consequences of purposive social action. *American Sociological Review* 1:894–904.

Murphy, P. V., and Brown, D. S. (1973). *Police Leader Looks at the Changing Nature of Police Organization*. Washington: Leadership Resources.

Naisbitt, J. (1984). *Megatrends: Ten New Directions Transforming Our Lives*. New York: Warner.

Nutt, P. C. (1986). Tactics of implementation. *Academy of Management Journal* 29:230–261.

Peak, K., and Glensor, R. (1996). *Community Policing and Problem Solving: Strategies and Practices*. Upper Saddle River, NJ: Prentice Hall.

Peak, K. J. (1997). *Policing America: Methods, Issues, Challenges*. Upper Saddle River, NJ: Prentice Hall.

Perrow, C. (1979). *Complex Organizations: A Critical Essay*. Glenview, IL: Scott, Foresman.

Porter, L. W., Lawler, E. E., and Hackman, J. R. (1975). *Behavior in Organizations*. New York: McGraw-Hill.

Pratt, T. P., Frank, J., Smith, B. W., and Novak, K. J. (2000). Conflict and consensus in multijurisdictional drug task forces: An organizational analysis of personnel attitudes. *Police Practice and Research: An International Journal*.

Ramirez, S. (1994). Organizational development: Planned change in an unplanned changing world. *Public Management* 76(10):4.

Reitz, H. J. (1977). *Behavior in Organizations*. Homewood, IL: Richard D. Irwin.

Robinette, H. (1989). Organizational streamlining. *Virginia Police Chief*, Spring, pp. 10–16.

Robinette, H. (1993). Supervising Tommorrow. *Virginia Police Chief*, Spring, pp. 10–16.

Sabath, M. J., Doyle, J. P., and Ransburg, J. W. (1990). *Multijurisdictional Drug Task Forces in Indiana: The First Two Years of Operation.* Indianapolis: Center for Criminal Justice Research and Information.

Sandler, G. B., and Mintz, E. (1978). Police organizations: Their changing internal and external relationships. In L. Gaines and T. Ricks (eds.), *Managing the Police Organization.* St. Paul: West Publishing.

Schein, E. H. (1961). Management development as a process of influence. *Industrial Management Review* 2:10.

Schlegel, K., and McGarrell, E. F. (1991). An examination of arrest practices in regions served by multijurisdictional drug task forces. *Crime and Delinquency* 37(3):408–426.

Shanahan, D. T., Hunger, J. D., and Wheelen, T. L. (1979). Organizational profile of police agencies in the United States. *Journal of Police Science and Administration* 7(3):354–360.

Skolnick, J. H., and Bayley, D. H. (1986). *The New Blue Line: Police Innovation in Six American Cities.* New York: Free Press.

Steers, R. M. (1977). *Organizational Effectiveness: A Behavioral View.* Santa Monica: Goodyear Publishing.

Story, D. (1992). What happens after all the dinosaurs are gone? The passing of the torch. *Law and Order,* October, pp. 47–48.

Strebel, P. (1994). Choosing the right change path. *California Management Review* 36:29–51.

Taguiri, R., and Litwin, G. (1968). *Organizational Climate: Explorations of a Concept.* Boston: Harvard University Press.

Toch, H., Grant, J. D., and Galvin, R. T. (1975). *Agents of Change: A Study in Police Reform.* New York: Wiley.

Toffler, A. (1980). *The Third Wave.* New York: Bantam Books.

Trojanowicz, R., Kappler, V. E., Gaines, L. K., and Bucqueroux, B. (1998). *Community policing: A contemporary perspective,* 2nd ed. Cincinnati, OH: Anderson.

U.S. Department of Justice, Bureau of Justice Statistics Bulletin. (1996). *Local Police Departments, 1993,* April, p. 4.

Vaughan, D. (1999). Forthcoming. The dark side of organizations: Mistake, misconduct, and disaster. *Annual Review of Sociology.*

Weiland, G. F., and Ullrich, R. A. (1976). *Organizations: Behavior, Design, and Change.* Homewood, IL: Richard D. Irwin.

Wilkerson, B. D. (1994). Civilian services. *FBI Law Enforcement Bulletin* 63(11):21–24.

Withan, D. C. (1991). Environmental scanning pays off. *Police Chief,* March, pp. 26–31.

Witkan, G., and McGraw, D. (1993). Beyond "Just the facts, ma'am." *U.S. News and World Report,* August 2, p. 28.

Index

400a